YEAR · BOOK · 1938

THE AMERICAN SOCIETY
OF
BOOKPLATE
COLLECTORS AND DESIGNERS
HURD
REVERE
ANDERSON
FRENCH
SPENCELEY
SMITH
EXITUS ACTA PROBAT
George Washington
WASHINGTON · D·C

BOOKPLATES

BOOKPLATES

A Selective Annotated Bibliography of the Periodical Literature

by Audrey Spencer Arellanes

Gale Research Company, Detroit, Michigan

Published by Gale Research Company,
Book Building, Detroit, Michigan 48226
Library of Congress number 71-123720
Designed by Richard Kinney

Note: The endpapers are reproductions of the covers of the American and English bookplate journals which endured the longest. It is seldom that individual copies of the Journal of the Ex Libris Society *are found and then the covers are usually badly damaged due to the brittle condition of the faded green paper. The copy of the* Journal *from which the reproduction was made originally belonged to Mrs. Mary E. Rath-Merrill, long active in bookplates and perhaps best known for her part in the Philippine Memorial Library, Ohio Alcove. Mrs. Clare Ryan Talbot kindly permitted the use of this copy of the* Journal, *now in her possession, for the endpapers.*

Dedicated
to the many authors, living and dead,
whose books have made my life exciting,
filled my mind with facts and fiction,
and created much pleasure and anguish
as do all good friends.
And especially to Edwin Wolf 2nd with John Fleming—
it was reading their biography of ROSENBACH
which aroused my interest in bookplates.

CONTENTS

PREFACE

THE BOOKPLATE ITSELF has a long history. Books about bookplates, however, are few. Not until 1874 did Paul Emmanuel Auguste Poulet-Malassis of Paris write the first one. Collectors of them *per se* were later still, starting with dear "Miss Jenkins of Bath." Slowly lists of a few books about bookplates began to appear in society yearbooks and in the consulted sources of books about books and bookplates. In 1951 my Hilprand Press published Dr. Samuel X. Radbill's *Bibliography of Medical Ex Libris Literature* wherein were mentioned a few medical periodicals. Carlyle S. Baer was keen enough to point out what had escaped both the author and the publisher: this was the largest specialty bibliography ever published in the bookplate field.

That great classic, *Bibliography of Bookplate Literature*, written by George W. Fuller and Verna B. Grimm in 1926, contained relatively few periodical entries.

Now appears a bibliographical tool in a field which is rarest of all: the periodicals devoted to bookplates and their mention. Bookplates are supposedly of limited appeal, yet we find their appearance in magazines which primarily feature fashion, outdoor life, juvenilia, technology, genealogy, theatre, science, medicine.

We who live in the collector's world of books, antiques, and history glorify the element of choice and the ability to take a stand. There is a high proportion of the literate world unable to do so. This quality is the steam which propels the world from private hobbies to discoveries, from personal and social trends to that first foot on the moon. This and the perseverance, calm judgment and poise of Audrey Arellanes have produced a distinguished addition to the books about bookplates, their art, their history, and their literature.

Periodicals in any subject are ephemeral in format. Their continuity depends on ample funds and dedicated editors, plus circulation. They are preserved by comparatively few sources, but no matter how slight, they may contain treasures which never appear later in book form. To have these now so conveniently assembled is the skill of this writer, herself a printer, a student of the graphic arts and its twin sister, the history of the book. In this she resembles the late Ruth Thomson Saunders whose place is unique in bookplate history. Praise is also due her for her annotations, which are made with judgment, wit and authority, bespeaking a wide background knowledge of the subject.

Clare Ryan Talbot
President and Founder
Society of Ex Libris Historians

Oakland, California
September 1969

INTRODUCTION

THIS IS A SELECTIVE bibliography of periodical literature pertaining to bookplates, restricted to articles in English, published primarily in the United States, Canada, Great Britain, Australia and New Zealand. A publication is considered a "periodical" if it appears in the *Readers' Guide to Periodical Literature* or similar indices, also publications appearing on a periodic basis from universities, colleges, professional associations, and industry, and yearbooks and society proceedings. Where recognized, newspapers have been excluded; the vast amount of bookplate literature in languages other than English has been excluded. The time covered is from 1822, the date of the earliest item, through August of 1969.

Full use has been made of the numerous bibliographies which have appeared previously, and they are listed separately following the Introduction. No attempt has been made to identify the source for each article as there is much overlapping. In addition to previous compilations, the various indices were consulted; they, too, are in a separate section. Another source for many items was the *Journal of the Ex Libris Society,* which during eighteen years of publication made reference to most of the current literature of the period both in book and journal form, foreign and domestic.

The only journals diligently searched through their entire span of publication were those devoted almost exclusively to bookplates, and in a few instances short-run journals which were at hand and because of their editor and/or contributors were strongly suspected of containing bookplate material. Numerous items were brought to the surface by these "fishing expeditions" and an occasional entry by browsing through the stacks. Even so unlikely a place as the modern "swap meet" was the source for several otherwise unknown articles (*Bellman* and *Mexican Life and Art*). Indeed, bookplates *are* where you find them, and often that is simply wherever you have the imagination to look. It is the old story of "up pops the devil" once you are on the alert, such as discovering two Marquis von Bayros bookplates used as illustration in *Eros in Art* by Jack Bacon (Elysium Inc., 1969).

The bibliography is presented alphabetically by journal and chronologically under each journal with the earliest date first. When known, both the title and author of the article are given, followed by the number of illustrations in parenthesis, volume and/or issue number, page numbers and date. In a few instances information was supplied from overseas which did not make for a complete bibliographical reference; however, sufficient data were available to properly identify the article and make it possible for others to find it, if they can locate the journal at all. On occasion an article could not be located as originally referenced and note is made of this with the original source; where it was felt the article undoubtedly did exist, it was assigned a number. Because of the ephemeral nature of the periodical, it has been impossible to locate the specific issues needed for some entries, and the entry is marked—[Unable to locate.]. A few entries are included (so their omission will not raise questions) because they appear in other bibliographies but are not assigned a number as they do not qualify for the present bibliography.

Articles are listed under the title the magazine had at the time the particular entry was published. When known, cross reference is made to other titles the same journal may have had which also contained bookplate material. A few journals merged so often that cross reference becomes burdensome beyond any benefit to be gained by the enumeration. The majority of journals can be located in one or more of the major libraries, but a few are elusive and seldom prove worth the time and effort required in the attempt to locate them.

The variant spellings of "bookplate" in titles and direct quotes are as the original author used the word. Elsewhere in the text the one word, bookplate, has been used consistently.

It is hoped that this bibliography will be a useful tool for bookplate enthusiasts and collectors, as well as those who might utilize this material for further study in literature, history, art, library science, genealogy, heraldry, science, or medicine. There are doubtless many bookplate references which have escaped the notice of the present bibliographer; a number of blank pages have been provided at the back of this book for your additional discoveries.

As in most specialty fields, there are divergent opinions among bookplate enthusiasts. There is more than one claim to the earliest bookplate in each country and occasionally new evidence is presented. There has been no attempt in this bibliography to editorialize. Rather than take sides in any of these disputes, each view is presented, using original quotations wherever possible. This gives the reader a glimpse of the prose of each original author, which not only reflects his own approach but in part that of the period in which he lived and wrote. Where possible, quotations have included some of the lighter touches on a subject alternately called pompous and dull by its detractors.

Other Bibliographies

American Book-Plates, Charles Dexter Allen. New York: Macmillan and Co., 1894. Includes bibliographies of literature by Eben Newell Hewins, W. H. Fincham and James Roberts Brown, and Walter Hamilton.

Bibliography of Book-plate Literature, Winward Prescott. Princeton: Princeton University Press for American Bookplate Society, 1914.

Bibliography of Bookplate Literature, George W. Fuller and Verna B. Grimm. Spokane: Spokane Public Library, 1926.

Bibliography of Bookplates Compiled from Various Sources, Philip C. Beddingham, 1962 (typescript for private use only).

"Bibliography of Ex Libris Literature Published in Australia," Camden Morrisby, published in *Australian Ex Libris Society Journal*, No. 1:18-25, 1930.

Bibliography of Medical Ex Libris Literature, Samuel X. Radbill. Los Angeles: Hilprand Press, 1951.

Book-Plate Literature, Winward Prescott. Kansas City: H. Alfred Fowler, 1914.

Checklist of Ex Libris Literature Published in Australia, H. B. Muir. Adelaide: Wakefield Press, 1942. (Draws on and adds to Morrisby.)

English Book-Plates, Egerton Castle. London: George Bell & Sons, 1894.

Rise of the Book-Plate, W. G. Bowdoin. New York: A. Wessels Co., 1901.

Some American College Bookplates, Harry Parker Ward. Columbus, Ohio: 1915. Includes "Check-List of Bookplate Literature," Winward Prescott.

Indices Consulted

A.L.A. Index To General Literature. Boston: American Library Association. To 1910.

Annual Literary Index. W. I. Fletcher and R. R. Bowker. New York: Office of *Publishers' Weekly*. 1892-1895.

Applied Science & Technology Index. New York: H. W. Wilson. 1958-June 1969.

Art Index. New York: H. W. Wilson. 1929 to 1969.

British Humanities Index. London: The Library Association. 1962-1969.

Business Periodicals Index. New York: H. W. Wilson. January 1958 to June 1969.

Canadian Index To Periodicals. Ottawa: Canadian Library Association and National Library of Canada. 1948-1959.

Cumulated Magazine Subject Index; 1907-1949. Boston: G. K. Hall & Co. 1964.

Education Index. New York: H. W. Wilson. 1929-June 1969.

Essay and General Literature Index. New York: H. W. Wilson. 1900-1939.

Industrial Arts Index. New York: H. W. Wilson. 1941-1957.

International Index. See *Social Sciences & Humanities Index*.

Library Literature, 1921-1932. Chicago: American Library Association. 1934.

Library Literature. 1933- . New York: H. W. Wilson. 1934-June 1969.

Poole's Index to Periodical Literature. William Frederick Poole. Boston: James R. Osgood and Co., 3rd ed. (1802-1881), 1882, and all supplements through the 5th and last (to 1907).

Readers' Guide To Periodical Literature. New York: H. W. Wilson. 1900-June 1969.

Social Sciences and Humanities Index. New York: H. W. Wilson. 1907-June 1969. (Volumes 1 through 52 entitled *International Index.*)

Subject Index To Periodicals. London: The Library Association. 1915-1961. Superseded by *British Humanities Index* and other publications covering other special subjects.

ACKNOWLEDGMENTS

IT IS IMPOSSIBLE to give proper recognition to the many individuals who have provided information necessary for the completion of this bibliography, as help in varying degrees has been offered by a great number of university, college and institutional libraries in the United States, Great Britain and Australia. My thanks to the legion of nameless librarians who not only furnished information as requested but volunteered facts and searched materials at hand in an attempt to find what I needed when my request was vague.

Individual note must be made of those who offered special help and continuing encouragement over the several years I have labored. I was particularly fortunate that the Henry E. Huntington Library in San Marino extended me the privileges of a Reader over a period of seven years of Saturdays. Not only were their holdings strong in the periodicals needed, but the staff, especially Miss Mary Isabel Fry and Miss Janet Hawkins, was ever helpful to a novice researcher. Dr. Edwin H. Carpenter, of the Huntington's Rare Book Room, shared his vast knowledge in answering my endless barrage of questions; his many kindnesses will be long remembered. Dr. James Thorpe, Director of the Huntington, happily mentioned two articles which otherwise might not have been included. Through Carey S. Bliss I acquired a number of fine bookplates from the Huntington's duplicates, together with human interest background on both artists and owners.

Through an exhibit of bookplates which I prepared for the Alhambra Public Library, I met Mrs. Rose Tisdel, who since then has been on the alert for bookplate items. Her keen eyes spotted both the

Bellman and *Mexican Life and Art* at swap-meets, a most unlikely source for bookplate material.

Carlyle S. Baer, who was the sustaining spirit of the American Society of Bookplate Collectors and Designers from its founding, until his death in 1969, made frequent and valuable suggestions concerning the bibliography, gave of his wealth of knowledge about bookplates, and made available source materials.

Mrs. Clare Ryan Talbot, who has had a long and distinguished career in the field of bookplates, has written a prodigious number of well-documented articles about ex libris as well as the magnificient book, *Historic California in Bookplates*. She has been most generous with encouragement as well as sharing treasured journals and rare bookplates.

I am indebted to Ruth Adomeit, well-known authority on and printer of miniature books, for the details and annotations possible on *Etcht Miniature Monthly Magazine*. She answered my call for help amid the confusion of moving; such a response is not based on personal friendship but on the bond of books which brings aid and delight into the lives of many who find each other through the printed word.

Various members of the American Society of Bookplate Collectors and Designers have corresponded with me, a beginning collector, offering their duplicates and much information gleaned from a lifetime interest in bookplates. A few I have been fortunate to meet as well as correspond with: Mrs. Mary Alice Ercolini, Miss Emma Van Allen Ford, Mrs. Geraldine Kelly Kirby. These bookplate friends have let me borrow precious back issues of the *Year Book* and ephemeral publications seldom found in any library but jealously hoarded by the confirmed bookplate enthusiast. Mrs. Ione K. Wiechel has been equally generous though I have not had the pleasure of meeting her. Other members have furnished much needed source materials, references to swell the list of annotations; as well as exchanged plates, which are the coin of the realm for the bookplate collector. Among these are: Louis Ginsberg, Dr. Samuel X. Radbill, Robert Hitchman, Rev. H. L. Hoover, Fridolf Johnson, Robert Metzdorf, Dr. Enrico C. S. Molnar, Rabbi Philip Goodman.

Artist members of the American Society of Bookplate Collectors and Designers have come to my aid with signed copies of their work and exciting bits of news; among them: Carl S. Junge, Sara B. Hill, Cleora Wheeler, Mildred Bryant Brooks, Dan Burne Jones.

With only a few exceptions where publications were available locally, all the material in Australian journals, mostly from the H. P.

Muir list, has been assembled by Noel Stockdale of Flinders University of South Australia. This entailed his finding the journals in several different Australian libraries, arranging to have the articles duplicated, and forwarding the material to me. I am grateful for his diligent assistance.

My thanks to Donald Duke of Golden West Publications for his thoughtful ferreting through catalogs for bookplate items and bringing to my attention the *Rocky Mountain Rail Report*.

Harold Tribolet and Justin G. Turner, both of the Manuscript Society, have shared their duplicates and furnished leads on articles.

I have been most fortunate to have James Ethridge as my editor at Gale Research, and to have the assistance of his staff members, in particular Leslie Shepard in London, Dorothy Dockterman in Washington, D.C., and Irwin Mayer in New York.

Lester Glenn Arellanes and Denetia Ynez Arellanes, my husband and daughter, have been patient and permissive in letting me spend Saturdays at the library, and have shared my delight in the flow of mail bringing bookplates of all descriptions, articles and correspondence.

Alhambra, California
October 31, 1969

Audrey Arellanes

LIST OF PERIODICALS INDEXED

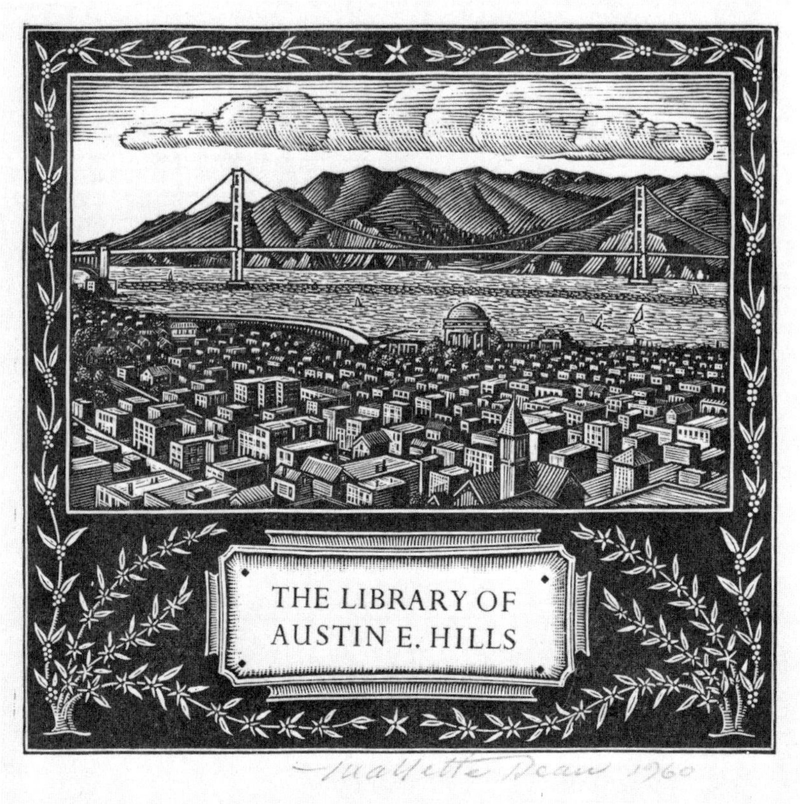

Mallette Dean's wood engraving reveals the view from Austin E. Hills' San Francisco apartment. Appropriately for the coffee heir, the border on the plate is from the coffee tree.

A James Webb plate showing "The Candle of God" is one of many used by Clare Ryan Talbot, author of *Historic California in Bookplates*.

Bookplate used by Clare Ryan Talbot for her extensive reference library on ex libris.

Carlyle S. Baer, secretary and editor of the American Society of Bookplate Collectors and Designers until his death in 1969, had numerous plates for his wide variety of collections. An Adrian Feint woodcut was converted to a bookplate for his Australian books, largely on art. Dan Burne Jones designed another of Baer's plates (below). (Plates reduced by one-third from originals.)

Louis Ginsberg, author and bookplate enthusiast, utilized a replica of the lion emblem used by the first Hebrew printer in his plate designed and printed in Holland.

Bookplate for Angela Crispin is by Australian artist Ella Dwyer.

Will Cheney blended type with a Bewick wood engraving, from *History of Quadrupeds*, in printing bookplate for Audrey Arellanes.

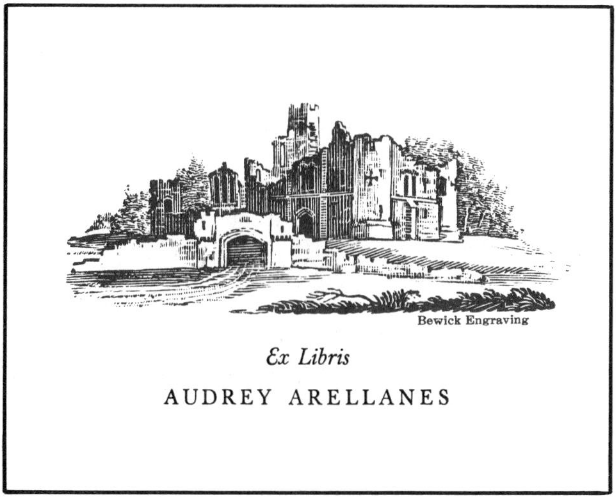

Bookplates of Members of American Society of Bookplate Collectors and Designers

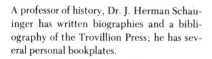

Rabbi Philip Goodman has written extensively on the various aspects of Jewish bookplates.

Carl S. Junge has made unusual use of his initials and name to form the owl's face.

A professor of history, Dr. J. Herman Schauinger has written biographies and a bibliography of the Trovillion Press; he has several personal bookplates.

Bookplates of Members of American Society of Bookplate Collectors and Designers

Mary Alice Ercolini both collects and writes about bookplates; she has a wide variety of personal plates, many of which show her love of cats as does this plate engraved in Denmark (above). Etching at left by Sara Blake Hill is from an old fourth grade reader and is used by Mary Alice Ercolini for garden books.

Plate for Glenn Wyatt Wolcott contains crest of a Signer of the Declaration of Independence who was his grandfather.

Bookplates of Members of American Society of Bookplate Collectors and Designers.

Bookplates of Members of American Society of Bookplate Collectors and Designers

Robert B. Turnbull has a self-designed plate with bull's head and early Scottish pitchfork taken from his family armorial bearing; motto translates "Fortune favors audacity."

Dr. Samuel Radbill, author of *Bibliography of Medical Ex Libris*, uses a plate designed by Dr. Theodore Vetter of Paris, which has a portrait of Dr. Michel Billard and the Hospital for Sick Children to represent Dr. Radbill's interest in the history of pediatrics. Dr. Vetter has written about medical and dental bookplates in a French journal.

Geraldine Kelly Kirby, many years with Dawson's Books, has written about bookplates as well as collected them. (Plate somewhat reduced.)

Bookplates of Members of American Society of Bookplate Collectors and Designers

One of several bookplates used by Dr. Robert F. Metzdorf, who compiled the Index for the ASBC&D

Typographic plate designed by George Harvey Petty for Ione Wiechel, avid collector.

Plate for Emma Van Allen Ford, a discerning collector for many years, who has a well-catalogued personal collection.

Bookplates of Members of American Society of Bookplate Collectors and Designers

Plate designed by Allan Jordan for John Gartner of the Hawthorne Press, Melbourne, Australia.

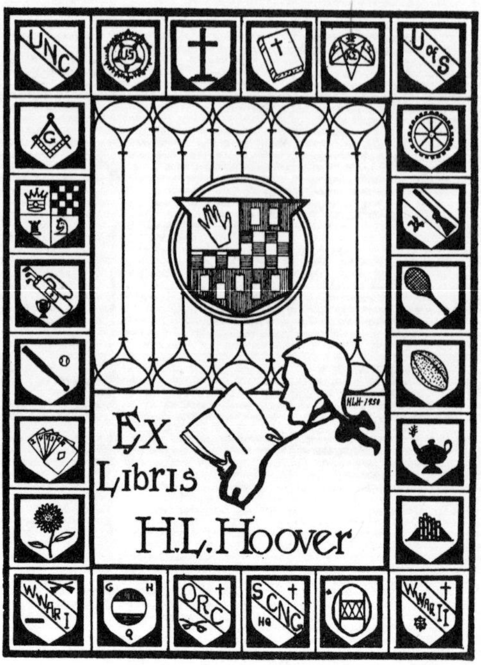

H. L. Hoover designed his own plate to reflect his many interests. (Reduced by one-tenth from the original.)

Robert Hitchman uses reproduction of Thomas Bewick wood engraving with lettering by Hewitt Jackson for his Place Names Collection.

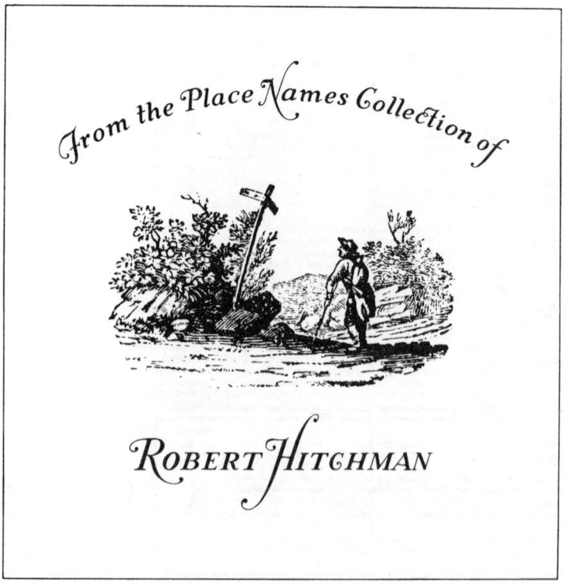

Artist Members of American Society of Bookplate Collectors and Designers

Rev. Canon Enrico C. S. Molnar, dean of Bloy House Theological School, designed this plate for F. Thomas Trotter of Claremont.

Among several plates used by artist Dan Burne Jones is one by wood engraver Lynd Ward.

Bank Gordon, an engraver of infinite skill, is still actively at work in the bookplate field though a septuagenarian.

Artist Members of American Society of Bookplate Collectors and Designers

Carl S. Junge has been an innovator with the use of color in bookplates, as shown in the Mary Day plate. He has also created several type faces. (Plate reduced by one-fourth from original.)

Plate for attorney Morris Earle was designed by Cleora Wheeler; it shows T'ai Shaw, sacred mountain of China.

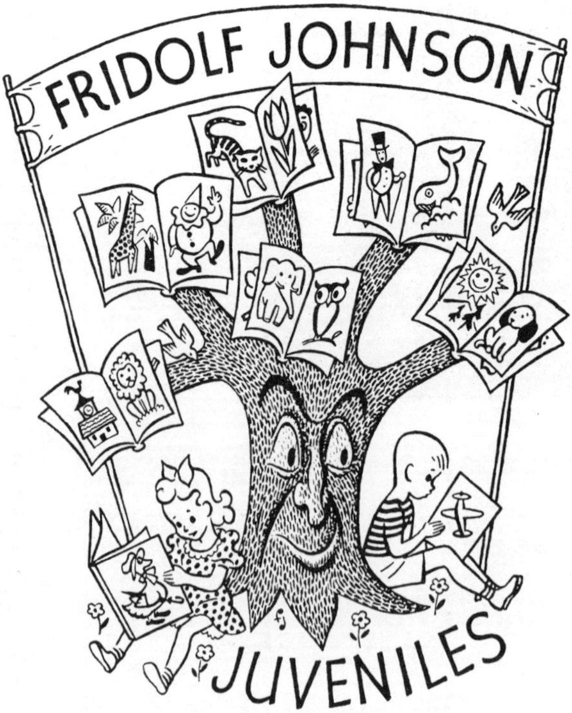

Fridolf Johnson, artist, printer, editor of *American Artist*, designed this plate for his juvenile collection.

Rev. Canon Enrico C. S. Molnar, of the Episcopal Bloy House Theological School, has designed more than forty ex libris since 1942. (Plate reduced by one-tenth.)

Toni Hofer created this plate for Franz and Leta Adler.

Mildred Bryant Brooks, artist and interior decorator, seems to let you look right through the open window and feel the sea breeze in her plate for Eleanor M. Homer.

Diana Bloomfield, a self-taught wood engraver, does free lance book illustration in addition to bookplate commissions such as the John Voysey plate.

Calligrapher James Hayes shows his incomparable skill in the Christine Penniman bookplate.

Louise Seymour Jones, author of *The Human Side of Bookplates*, had a delightful plate by Walo.

Louise Seymour Jones

The Sherman Foundation Library, specializing in historical research on the development of the Pacific Southwest, was formed by Moses Hazeltine Sherman, pioneer developer of Arizona and Southern California.

Thought-provoking plate designed by calligrapher James Hayes for C. A. Hurt.

Artist Norman Kent, frequent contributor of articles to *American Artist*, created a very masculine bookplate for Austin F. Dorhman, Jr.

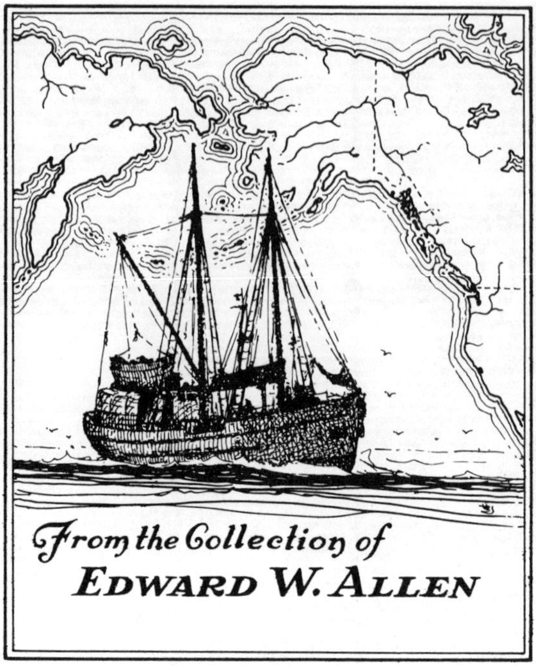

Seattle collector Edward W. Allen has plate designed by maritime illustrator Hewitt R. Jackson.

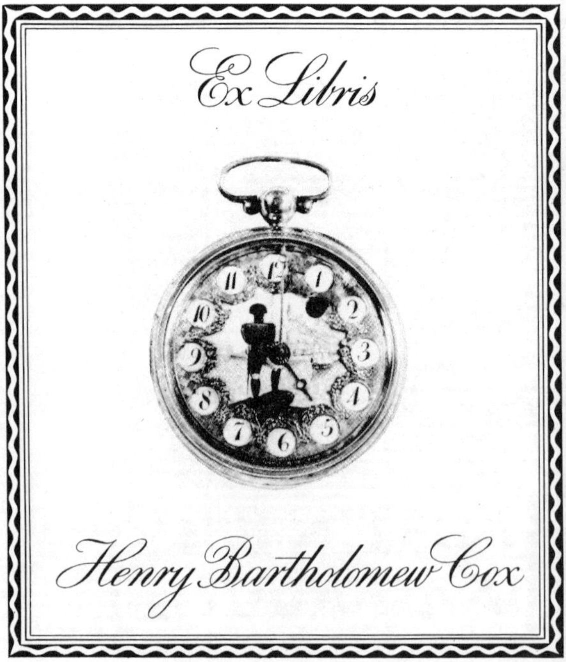

Manuscript Society member Henry Bartholomew Cox designed his own special collection bookplate using a watch with early 19th century French verge movement in a silver filigreed case with an enamelled scene showing a French military officer (possibly representing Napoleon).

Earl H. Gibson of Seattle has a bookplate by Rockwell Kent, perhaps the most generally known ex libris artist today.

Plate for Norman H. Strouse represents many of his interests, including the Silverado Press, Napa Valley, books, and manuscripts. It was engraved by Leo Wyatt, English artist of great skill and pictorial beauty.

Mathias J. Noheimer, professor of graphic arts, designed his own plate.

MATHIAS·NOHEIMER

R. Hunter Middleton has used one of his many original Bewick woodcuts for the Gail Leora Campbell plate.

Aesop's fable, The Mice In Council, teaches:
do not listen to the schemes of rash individuals who force them upon
the public without proving their usefulness.
Thomas Bewick engraved this block for the Fables of Aesop in 1818
Gail Leora Campbell

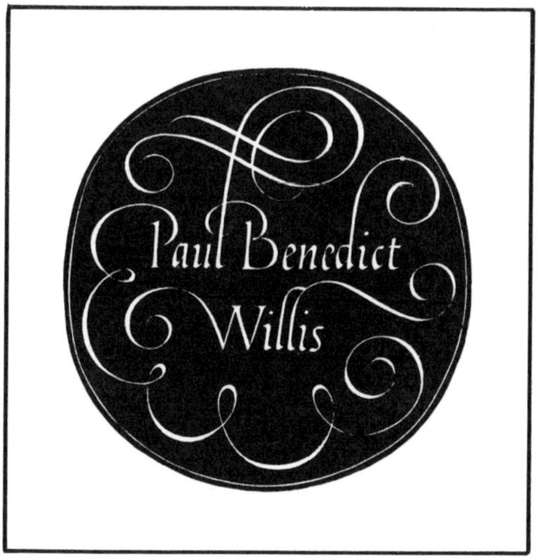

Reynolds Stone, English calligrapher, stone cutter, and typographer, is an artist of infinite beauty, as envinced in the plate for Paul Benedict Willis.

Mark F. Severin, author of *Making a Bookplate* as well as numerous ex libris articles in various languages, is also an artist of skill and imagination. Here is a fanciful plate for W. Winkworth.

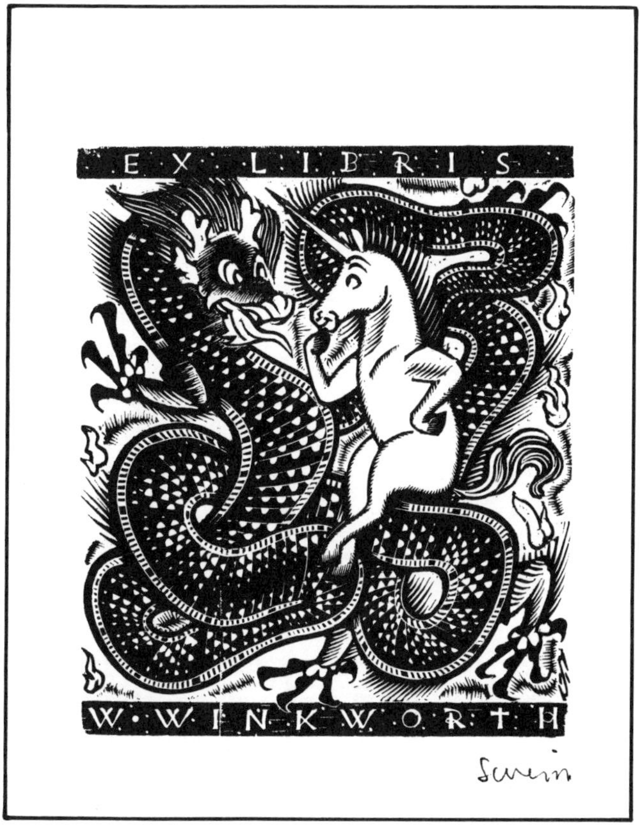

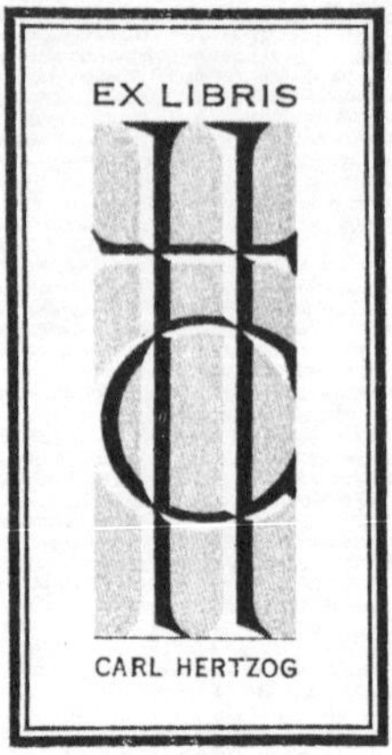

The distinctive design principles of Carl Hertzog are evident in his own two color plate.

Hellmut Lehmann-Haupt, author and bibliographer, has a small label printed on various colored paper stock which uses the walnut tree emblem, a family tradition.

Appropriately small plate for Julian Edison, editor of *Miniature Book News*.

Graphic artist Egdon Margo executed this plate for his friend George Harvey Petty.

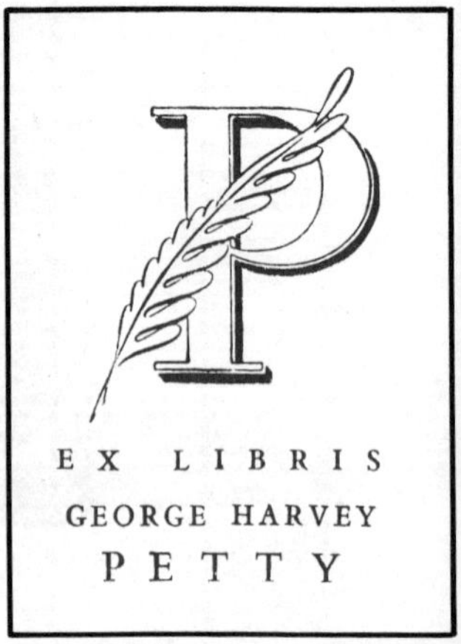

Stanley Marcus, famed retailer also active in community service, uses an ex libris minimis designed by Franco Ricci of Parma, Italy.

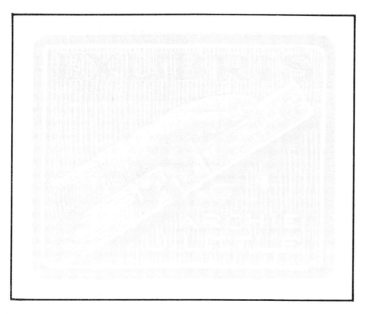

Archie J. Little, proprietor of a Seattle monotype firm, selected an appropriate design for his collection of books on printing.

Paul Gregg, staff artist of the *Denver Post*, designed Western flavored plate for Edward Shell, who enjoyed playing cowboy as a hobby.

David Kindersley, stone cutter and calligrapher in the tradition of his teacher Eric Gill, designed this simple plate for joint use with his wife Barbara.

Robert Armstrong Andrews gives a touch of humor to his plate for Eg Margo, who is himself a graphic artist.

William M. Cheney's talents as a printer are only exceeded by his flair for subtle humor. He says "Gen. Stonebone wrote a Pig Latin grammar, and Judge Jason Augustus Fleecestreet edited a revised version of this grammar."

MORRIS L. ERNST
Library
BANNED BOOKS

Plate designed for Collection of Banned Books given by attorney/author Morris L. Ernst to the University of California at Santa Barbara.

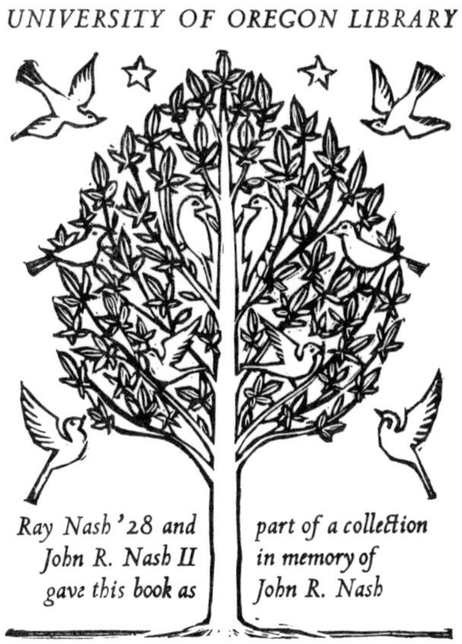
UNIVERSITY OF OREGON LIBRARY
Ray Nash '28 and
John R. Nash II
gave this book as
part of a collection
in memory of
John R. Nash

Professor of art Ray Nash designed memorial plate for use at the University of Oregon.

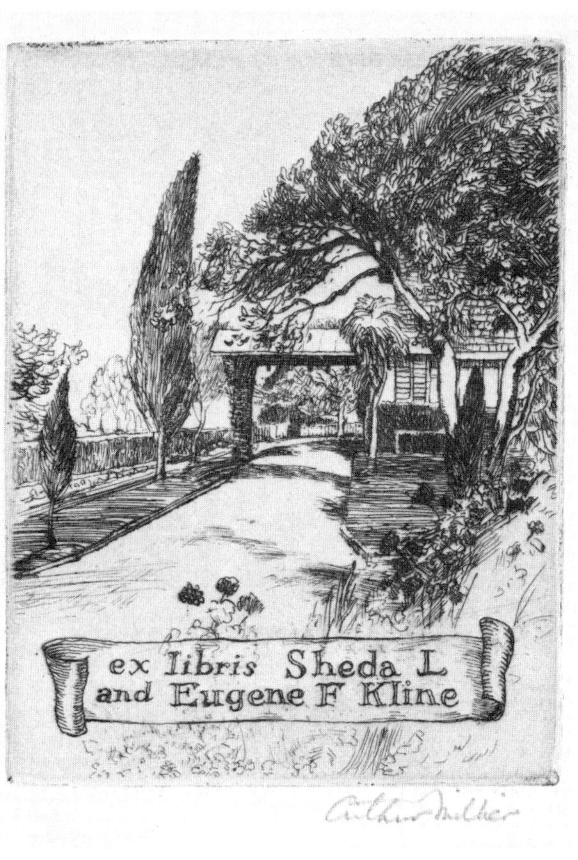
ex libris Sheda L
and Eugene F Kline

Arthur Millier, author and long-time art critic for the *Los Angeles Times*, is the artist for the Sheda L. and Eugene F. Kline plate.

Pall Bohne, printer, calligrapher, author of *Haiku with Birds* and *American Whaling* (both miniature books which he wrote, handset, printed and bound), uses a lobster buoy for one of his bookplates.

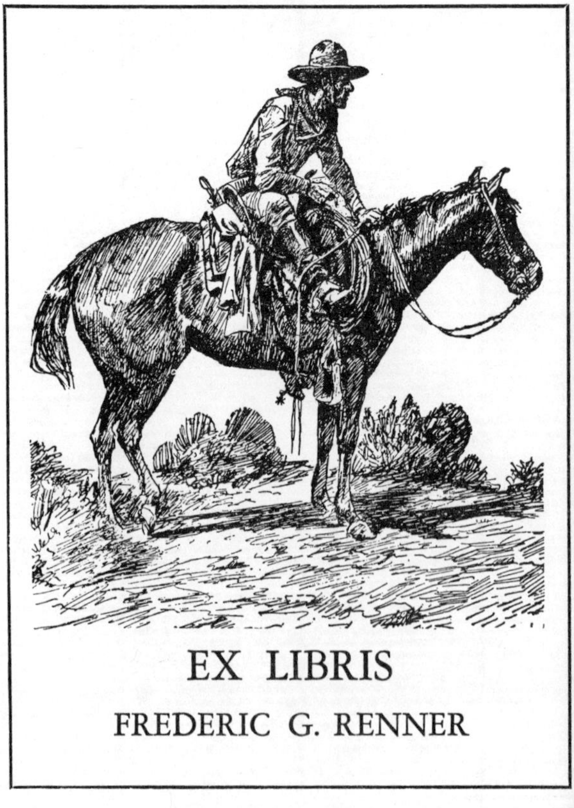

Frederic G. Renner was a range examiner with the U.S. Department of Agriculture before gaining wider fame for his descriptive catalog of the work of Charles M. Russell for the Amon Carter Museum of Western Art, and as co-author of a Russell bibliography. He has used Russell's "The Trail Boss" for his personal plate.

Calligrapher, printer, photographer, Theo Jung created this special collection plate for the San Francisco Public Library.

Delightful plate designed by famed illustrator of Milne's Pooh books, Ernest H. Shepard, for Hugh Sharp Collection at the National Library of Scotland, Edinburgh.

Henry Rusk designed plate used by John Haskell Kemble, author and historian.

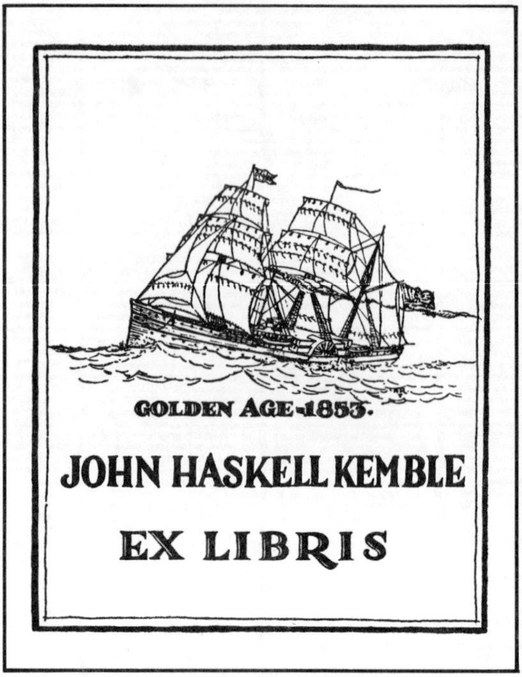

In 1927, artist Mabel Crotty created an appropriately Western atmosphere for the plate of historian Ray A. Billington, who shortly claimed the artist as his bride.

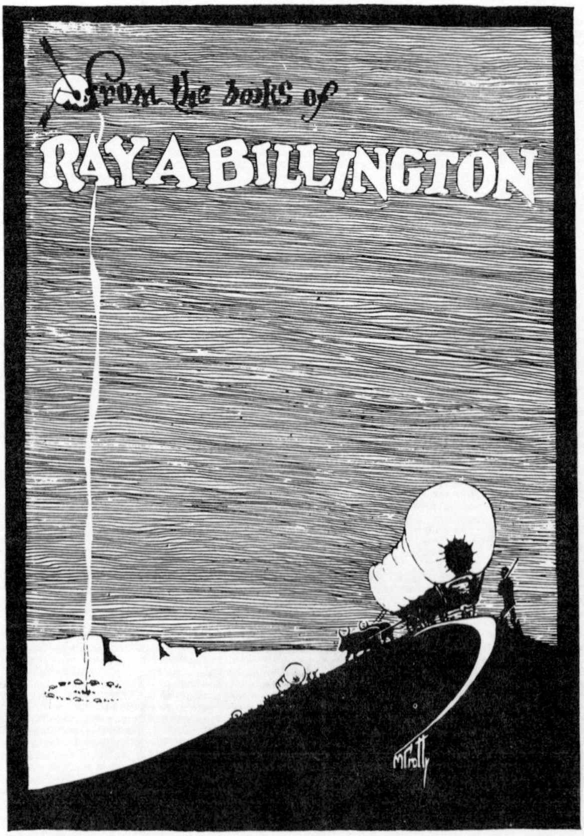

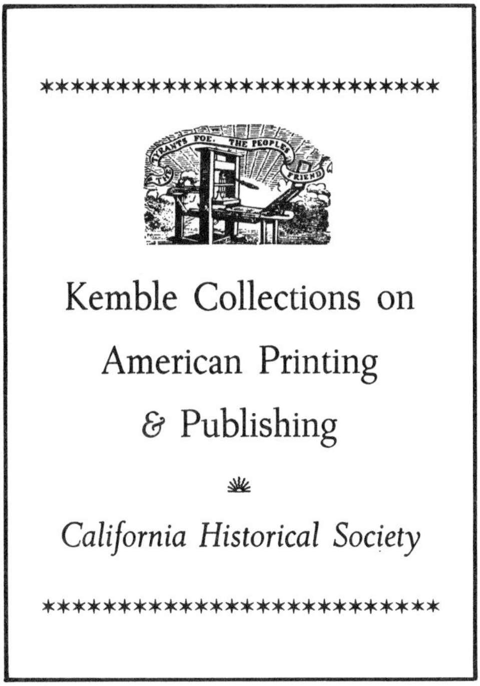

Roger Levenson of the Tamalpais Press designed the bookplate used by the California Historical Society for its collection on printing.

Dr. Henry P. deForest, a former resident of Fulton, was responsible for preserving the colorful history of the region on the Fulton Public Library bookplate. Included in the lunette is the painting by Darwin Styles and below it artist Robert Orr's visualization of a canoe trip over Oswego Falls by Natty Bumppo; also represented is a peace wampum belt and another showing the chief totems of the Six Nations.

One of many bookplates used by the Henry E. Huntington Library was designed by Ward Ritchie.

Herbert W. Simpson, who worked with and was influenced by Dwiggins, designed a plate of simple elegance for Egdon H. Margo, using Caslon Old Style with Dwiggins ornaments.

Edward H. Schickell, artist of *Bookplates for Libraries,* designed this gift plate for the San Francisco Public Library.

International folk singer and actor Theo Bikel has a simple plate with a musical motif.

Phil Dike was commissioned by friends of Bill Kimes to design a bookplate which would indicate his interest in mountains and books, and his background in school administration.

An interest in ships is shown in plate designed by artist Ann Noll for Watson B. Smith, who is active in the travel industry.

Francis Wilbur Allen is author of books about bookplate artists Charles R. Capon and William Fowler Hopson.

Commodore Lester G. Arellanes reveals in his bookplate a lifelong interest in railroads.

RAYMOND PERRY
In time the wheel became a cart; the cart a coach; the coach a railway train
LIBRARY OF
DONALD DUKE

Donald Duke, author, photographer and publisher of Golden West Books, specializes in volumes on the history and lore of railroads.

Rudolph Ruzicka designed this plate for Phillips Exeter Academy.

Henry H. Evans, noted for his botanical prints, designed his own plate for a collection of D. H. Lawrence books which now constitute the Evans Collection of the Burbank Public Library, California.

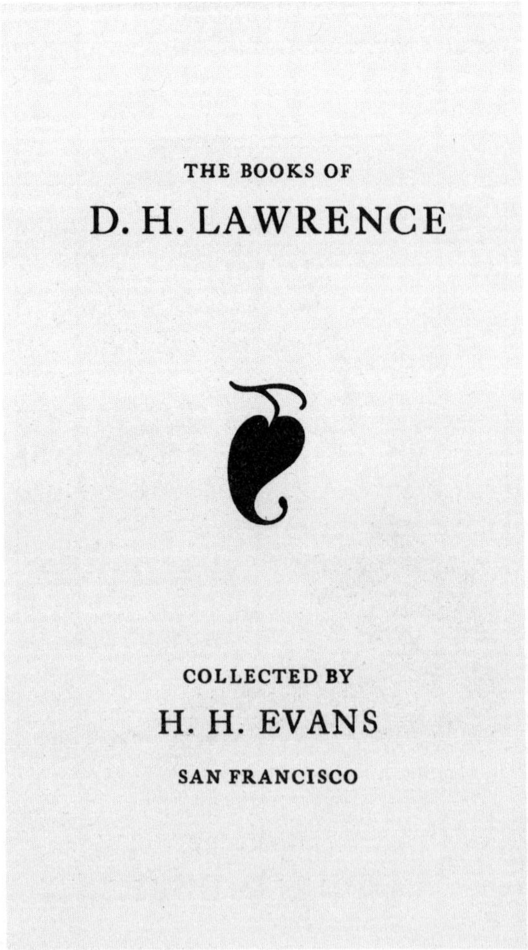

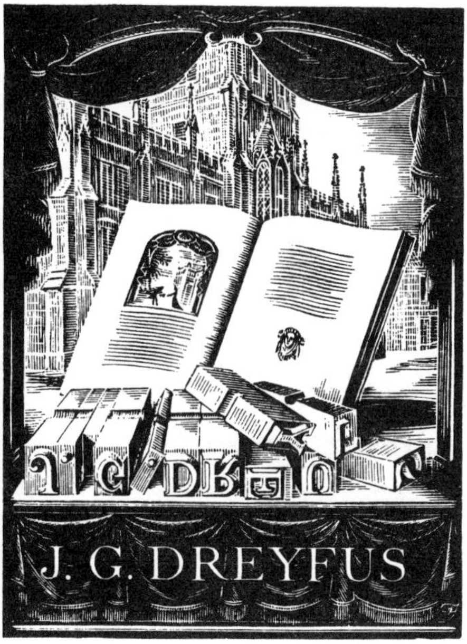

John Dreyfus, of the Cambridge University Press, is the happy owner of a plate by Joan Hassall; it shows Pitt Building erected for the Press in the 19th century.

Truly a master wood engraver, Mallette Dean shows an old Marin County landmark, the octagon house at the Marin Art and Garden Center in Ross, which houses the Jose Moya Del Pino memorial library; Moya was an artist noted for his portraits and murals.

A very striking plate has been created for the Navajo Historical Library at Window Rock, Arizona, by the use of two rubber stamps imprinted on a Dennison label. The symbol printed in red to match the plate's border is the Horned Moon, the registered trade mark for the Navajo Tribe.

BIBLIOGRAPHY

BOOKPLATES

A Selective Annotated Bibliography of the Periodical Literature

Numbers in parentheses preceding volume citations signify the number of bookplate illustrations in the article mentioned

ACADEMY

1 "Art Books." New Series 445: 353, November 13, 1880.

"The book *[A Guide To The Study of Book Plates]* would, perhaps, be all the better if he had resisted the temptation to waste descriptive paragraphs on the book-owners that he is brought across . . . but these, although they detract from the book's scientific value, are, perhaps, pardonable digressions in the midst of what, after all, is rather a dry and monotonous department of art history."

ACADIENSIS

2 "Book-Plates." David Russell Jack. (9) 1: Frontispiece, 90-103, April 1901.

"An heiress in the parlance of heraldry, be it understood, is not merely a lady of means, but one who, not having any surviving male relatives, who by right of precedence assumes the family arms, becomes herself entitled to wear them, and upon her marriage quarters them upon her husband's shield."

3 "Book-Plates." David Russell Jack. (4) 1: 115-20, July 1901.

Plates and owners described.

4 "Book-Plates." David Russell Jack. (5) 1:236-42, October 1901.

"A book-plate is often a partial index to the tastes and character of its owner, and is frequently the means of restoring a mislaid volume to its rightful possessor."

5 "Book-Plates." David Russell Jack. (5) 2: 37-43, January 1902.

"Among My Book-Plates—A Plea for Fads," by George May Elwood quoted: "Of all the fads which come of inoculation with the microbe of collecting, there is none which offers more attraction, is more satisfying, leads to more though[t]ful and profitable study, presents more varied and intrinsic beauties, brings one into more charming contact and correspondence with choice kindred spirits, than does a carefully selected and well arranged collection of book-plates."

6 "Book-Plates." David Russell Jack. (7) 2: 122-8, April 1902.

David McN. Stauffer, editor of *Engineering News*, designed bookplates for Jacob Miller Owen, Judge of Probate, and his wife, Isabella Anne.

7 "Book-Plates." E. M. Chadwick. 2: 129-30, April 1902.

Comment and criticism of prior articles and plates illustrated "of Georgian debased period of heraldry."

8 "Book-Plates." David Russell Jack. (5) 2: 189-98, July 1902.
More bookplate treasures noted.

9 "Book-Plates." David Russell Jack. (6) 2: 276-8, October 1902.
Plate of Very Rev. Dean Gilpin mounted on special heavy black sheet.

10 "Book-Plates." David Russell Jack. (2) 3:67, January 1903.
Three plates described.

11 "Book-Plates." David Russell Jack. (4) 3: 129-34, April 1903.
Tells of removing two plates from volume in St. John's Mechanics' Institute to reveal plate used by Institute about 1838.

12 "Book-Plates." David Russell Jack. (5) 3: 236-40, July 1903.
Unusual plate of George Edward Sears pictured but not explained.

13 "Book-Plates." David Russell Jack. (4) 3: 308-10, October 1903.
Comments of *Journal of Ex Libris Society* and *Book-Lover*.

14 "Book-Plates." David Russell Jack. (3) 4: 84-6, January 1904.
Plates of Nova Scotia notables.

15 "Book-Plates." David Russell Jack. (5) 6: 123-9, April 1906.
"Few book-plate collectors in the Maritime Provinces of Canada, and consequently but little opportunity for an interchange of information in this field."

16 "Col. Richard Hewlett, U. E. L. and Some of His Descendants." (1) 7: facing 62, January 1907.
Illustrations of Hewlett book-plate.

17 "General John Watts de Peyster." (2) 7: facing 287, July 1907.
Illustration of plates for John Watts de Peyster and Frederick de Peyster.

ALBUM

18 "Book-Plates, A Chat with Mr. Walter Hamilton." (4) 3: 180-1, November 25, 1895.
"The book-plate plays a most important part in reading the page of history. By it we are enabled to glean many interesting facts with regard to the biography of bygone celebrities which otherwise might have been lost to us."

ALL ABOUT BOOKS

19 "Relation of Ex Libris to Books." Camden Morrisby. (3) 211-2, June 18, 1929. [Volume number unavailable.]
"Is there any other hobby (apart from the collecting of books themselves) which offers such variety and charm" as collecting bookplates?

ALMA MATER

20 "Ex Libris." J. S. C. Elkington. (4) 5: 275-6, September 1900.
Well written comments on bookplates in general and artist Norman Lindsay in particular.

ALPHABET AND IMAGE

21 "The Engraved Letter-forms of Reynolds Stone." P. H. Muir. (16) 7: 3-12, May 1948.
Stone's use of white on black distinctive of his work; compared to Eric Gill.

AMATEUR BOOK COLLECTOR [See also **AMERICAN BOOK COLLECTOR**]

22 "A Richard LeGallienne Collection." H. Roy Mosnat. (1) 1: 2, April 1951.
Illustration is poem composed by LeGallienne and used as his ex libris.

23 "James Guthrie: Biographical Notes." Robin Guthrie. 4: 2, 6, October 1953.
Personal glimpse by one of artist-printer's sons; slight mention of bookplate work and publications.

24 "Ex Libris." Clare Ryan Bill. (2) 6: 17-8, October 1955.
Author exhorts collectors to be interested in the history of the plates they collect, not mere accumulation in quantity. "A bookplate collection becomes important only through the individual research of the owner."

25 "Ex Libris." Clare Ryan Bill. (2) 6: 8, November 1955
Plate of Frank H. MacDonald showing guns of ancient vintage and that for C. J. Phillips, noted London stamp dealer, suggest classification of plates by interests or hobbies: stamps, chess, firearms, coins, railroads, printing, etc.

AMATEUR PHOTOGRAPHER

26 "Book Plate by Photography." James G. Darling. (2) 29: 298, April 14, 1899.
Simple method for preparing a bookplate by photography.

27 "Book Plates—A Novel and Useful Application of Photography." Alfred P. Wire. (2) 33: 134, February 15, 1901.
Negative of Norman doorway of Colchester Castle (where Wire played as a boy) used for basis of bookplate; motto and name printed on slips of paper pasted in suitable places, block made, and then copies printed.

AMERICAN ANGLER

28 "Angling Book-Plates." Louis Rhead. (10) 2: 511-5, February 1918.
Among illustrations are plates for Charles E. Cameron, Frank Merton Buckland, Robert Hobart Davis, John Gerard Heckscher, Daniel B. Fearing, Henry A. Sherwin, Henry van Dyke, Dean Sage, and the author's own.

AMERICAN ANTIQUARIAN SOCIETY, PROCEEDINGS

29 "Libraries of the Presidents of the United States." Abraham S. W. Rosenbach. (25) 44: 337-64, October 1934.

A thorough, stimulating account of the libraries of various Presidents. Many Presidental bookplates are reproduced.

AMERICAN ARCHITECT

30 "Book Plates. Their Origin and Development with Notes as to Their Collecting." Henry Blackwell. (17) 95: 177-82, June 2, 1909.

"It may be truthfully said that a good fad, intelligently pursued, adds zest to life, and relieves the world of the monotony of one's daily occupation. Collecting book plates leads one along the line of good books and their makers, and opens up the possibility of mental recreation and improvement, bringing with it the satisfaction that always attaches to the acquirement of knowledge."

AMERICAN ARCHITECTS AND BUILDING NEWS

31 "James Gibbs' Bookplates." (1) 48: 29, April 20, 1895.

Gibbs, architect of St. Martin's-in-the-Fields and Radcliffe Library, Oxford, had a portrait plate engraved by Bernard Baron.

AMERICAN ARTIST

32 "*Dutch Book Plates* by D. Gilroy Veth." 15:57, April 1951.

Review of book featuring 80 bookplates of modern Dutch artists, mostly woodcuts and wood engravings.

33 "Art of the Bookplate." Fridolf Johnson. (34) 29: 48 *et seq.*, May 1965.

Profusely illustrated with a wide variety of designs and mediums of reproduction. "The best bookplates of the past [are] an important contribution to the miniature arts." Quotes Carlyle S. Baer, Secretary of the American Society of Bookplate Collectors and Designers, as saying that "traffic in bookplates rises to a peak every twenty-five years or so" and currently there are signs of such a revival.

34 "Genius of Rudolph Ruzicka." Ray Nash. (23) 31: 44-50, 71-3, December 1967.

Among examples illustrative of this great artist's work are seven memorial or personal bookplates.

35 "Bookplates of Vojtech Preissig." Norman Kent. (15) 32: 26-9, 60-1, February 1968.

Czech artist among those "responsible for the modern creative woodcut and wood engraving"; he also "brought and introduced the linoleum cut to America."

AMERICAN BIBLIOPOLIST

36 "A Curious Bookplate." 7: 60, February 1875.
Poem, "A Pleader to the Needer When a Reader."

37 "Steal Not This Book." 7: 253, December 1875.
Poem found in 17th century religious book.

AMERICAN BOOK COLLECTOR [See also **AMATEUR BOOK COLLECTOR**]

38 "Ex Libris." Clare Ryan Bill. (2) 6: 4, January 1956.
Sidelights on Jane Carlyle and Mrs. Brookfield as centers of social activity and describes their bookplates.

39 "Ex Libris." Clare Ryan Bill. (2) 6: 9, February 1956.
Plate designed by William Makepeace Thackeray for Edward Fitzgerald in 1842 illustrated.

40 "Ex Libris." Clare Ryan Bill. (2) 6: 24, March 1956.
Another informative article revealing extent of research devoted to owners and makers of bookplates. Indicates Pepys diary entry about "plate maker" does NOT refer to bookplates.

41 "Ex Libris." Clare Ryan Bill. (1) 6:11, Summer 1956.
Comments on bookplates of West Indies listed and annotated by Vere L. Oliver.

"Collecting Norman Lindsay." George Mackaness.
42 (2) 7: 15-20, September 1956.
43 7: 22-7, October 1956.
44 7: 17-20, November 1956.
Norman Lindsay wrote novels, essays, illustrated books, designed book jackets and covers, painted in oil, watercolors, as well as designing bookplates.

45 "Ex Libris." Clare Ryan Bill. (4) 8: 25-6, November 1957.
Plea for regrouping of old categories used by collectors, as well as new subjects with more imagination.

46 "Ex Libris." Clare Ryan Bill. 8: 19-20, January 1958.
Details of plate of Colonel Ethan Allen Hitchcock, one of Lincoln's generals.

47 "Ex Libris." Clare Ryan Bill. (1) 9: 30-1, June 1959.
Work of Bewick, Alexander Anderson, Timothy Cole, and William Fowler Hopson discussed.

48 "Great Bibliographer." Lawrence S. Thompson. (1) 10: 8-10, January 1961.
Illustration is bookplate used by University of Florida libraries for Medina Collection established by Maurey A. Bromsen in memory of his father, Herman Bromsen.

49 "James Guthrie and the Pear Tree Press." Robert P. Eckert, Jr. (3) 13: 13-33, Summer 1963.

Along with writing, illustrating and printing books, James Guthrie designed bookplates, and pleaded with collectors "to consider bookplate as a work of art."

50 "Descriptive Checklist of the Written and Illustrated Work of Rockwell Kent." Dan Burne Jones. 14: 21-4, Summer 1964.

Includes *Bookplates & Marks* (1929) and *Later Bookplates & Marks* (1939)

51 "Book Plates and Marks of Rockwell Kent." (11) 14:39, Summer 1964.

Plates for Katherine Brush, Leo Hart, and Kent's own "on earth Peace" symbol.

52 "Ex Libris." Lawrence S. Thompson. (5) 15: 6, December 1964.

James Lamar Weygand's Indiana Kid Press issued a *Packet of Sherlockian Bookplates* by Walter Klinefelter.

53 "Hippocampus Den." Warren P. MacFall. (°) (1) 15: 15, December 1964.

William Wallace Denslow illustrated many of the Oz books; bookplate has seahorse. (° Name corrected in subsequent issue to Russell P. MacFall.)

54 "Favores Celestiales and the Scriptorial Bookplate." Clare R. Talbot. (1) 17: 23-5, Summer 1967.

"The design [of a scriptorial bookplate] as originally wrought must include the actual handwriting or signature to qualify for this class."

55 "Antonio Palau Y Dulcet." Cayetano Casacuberta. (2) 17: 26-8, Summer 1967.

A noted Catalan book dealer and bibliographer for whom "from 1911 to 1913 the desire to collect 'ex libris' took on an extraordinary importance and he went after this material with great zest."

56 "Ex Libris." 19:6, January 1969.

Review of Edward H. Shickell and William R. Holman's *Bookplates for Libraries*. "Much useful information in this basic reference work."

AMERICAN BOOK COLLECTOR [Plainfield, New Jersey]

57 "Seventeenth Century American Book Labels." R.W. Vail. (27) 4: 164-76, September-October 1933.

Excellent article and check-list; says there are twenty-two book labels known to have been made in 17th century America.

AMERICAN BOOK-LORE

58 "Andrew Lang's Opinion of Bookplates." 1:118, July 1889.

"Plates also take up a good deal of room and modern plates are usually ugly, and exhibit the desperate efforts of unimaginative persons to display fancy."

59 "Book-Borrower in Verse." 1:25, June 1899.

Verses of admonition to book borrowers who fail to return volumes to rightful owners.

AMERICAN BOOKMAKER

60 "Book Plates." (2) 11:30-1, August 1890.

Illustrations of plates for Nicholas Bacon and Elizabeth Pindar "especially engraved" for *American Bookmaker*.

61 "Book-Plates." (1) 13: 83-4, September 1891.

"The anti-revolutionary Bostonian of fortune . . . regards any book of intrinsic merit as lacking what we may term its concomitant livery unless the possessor's coat of arms or other device was gummed inside."

AMERICAN COLLECTOR

62 "Famous American Bookseller, Charles Eliot Goodspeed." George H. Sargent. 3:150-5, January 1927.

Goodspeed collected bookplates, especially early American plates, until he found it was taking too much of his time. Collection given to American Antiquarian Society.

63 "Amos Doolittle, Engraver & Printer." Frank J. Metcalf. 4:53-6, May 1927.

Mentions he engraved bookplates for Yale, as well as diploma for 1807.

AMERICAN FORESTS AND FOREST LIFE

64 "Trees—Ex Libris." Eleanor Bradford Church. (5) 48:556-7, December 1942.

Bookplates featuring trees designed by James Webb for Clare Ryan Talbot, Helen Mooney Fentor, U.S.C., J. M. Sloan.

AMERICAN HEBREW

65 "An Hebraic Artist." [Ephraim Moses Lilien] Israel Zangwill. (1) 111:304, 320, August 11, 1922.

Only passing mention that Ephraim Lilien designed bookplates; illustration is portrait of artist.

66 "Artistic Jewish Bookplates." Harold S. Loeb. (5) 113:137, 146, June 29, 1923.

"The one outstanding artist who expresses Hebraic ideals with characteristic style, and who works in a thoroughly artistic manner, is Ephram Moses Lilien, of Austria, who has been designing book-plates of Jewish interest for many years."

AMERICAN HISTORICAL RECORD [POTTER'S AMERICAN HISTORICAL RECORD]

67 "Wood Engraving in America." (1) 1:152-3, April 1872.

Dr. Anderson, following in the tradition of excellence in wood engraving revived by Bewick, executed the numerous illustrations used in Noah Webster's best seller spelling book.

68 "American Pioneer Wood Engraver." (11) 2:201-5, May 1873.

While not mentioned specifically, Dr. Alexander Anderson engraved bookplates as did his inspiration, the "then peerless artist in that line, Thomas Bewick."

AMERICAN HOME

69 "Making Your Own Bookplate." Mabel Reagh Hutchins. (11) 5:215-6, December 1930.

Simple instructions for making plate from a linoleum block.

70 "Non-Priority Pursuits." Fanny Bull. (7) 29:54-5, April 1943.

Author's husband designed bookplate for library of Oradell, New York; using this plate for exchange, she assembled collection to present to library.

AMERICAN HOMES AND GARDENS

71 "Garden Book-Plates." Sheldon Cheney. (14) 11:259-61, August 1914.

"Gardening and book-collecting are, without doubt, the most refreshing and most wholesome of all the hobbies."

72 "Book-Plates." Gardner Teall. (18) 12:278-80, August 1915.

Quotes Gleeson White: "Wiser folk know that many 'etchings' are as valueless as the average engraving in a patent medicine pamphlet, and these care no more for a bad bookplate than they do for the chromo prints enclosed in packets of cheap cigarettes."

AMERICAN INSTITUTE OF ARCHITECTS [See JOURNAL OF AMERICAN INSTITUTE OF ARCHITECTS]

AMERICAN JEWISH HISTORICAL SOCIETY

73 "American Jewish Bookplates." Philip Goodman. (64) 45:129-216, March 1956.

Well documented book-length article.

AMERICAN JOURNAL OF NURSING

74 "Bookplate for Nursing Libraries." (1) 35:247-8, March 1935.

Bookplate designed by Arthur N. MacDonald for Teachers College Library, Adelaide Nutting Historical Nursing Collection, Columbia University.

75 "A Bookplate for a Nursing Library." Harriet H. Smith. (1) 36:692, July 1936.

Bookplate for library of Harborview Hall, University of Washington, shows Miss Nightingale at Scutari.

AMERICAN JUDAISM

76 "Some Book-Plates of Reform Interest." Julian N. Jablin. (10) 9:16-8, 1959.

Illustrated are plates of Irving Edison, Nathan Kraus, Justin G. Turner, Lee M. Friedman, Solomon B. Freehof, Bertram W. Korn, TV personality

Sam Levenson, Richard J. Hermann, Arthur J. Lelyveld, Leon J. Obermayer. Two (Turner and Kraus) have owner's signature incorporated in design.

AMERICAN MAGAZINE OF ART [See also **ART AND PROGRESS** and **MAGAZINE OF ART**]

77 "Contemporary Bookplates." Dorothy Sturgis Harding. (18) 25:219-28, October 1932.

High points of bookplate history along with suggestions for the selection of a bookplate. Quotes Howard Walher: "To keep it simple, and yet to express much, to make it detailed and not involved, to have it decoratively designed without its being mannered, is to achieve no mean accomplishment."

78 "Bookplate Competition, Portland, Oregon." 28:762, December 1935.

Reed College announcement of competition for bookplate design; winner to be awarded $50.

AMERICAN MONTHLY MAGAZINE [See also **DAUGHTERS OF AMERICAN REVOLUTION MAGAZINE**]

79 "Colonial Bookplates." Helen Frances Brockett. (7) 30:292-301, April 1907.

"The bookplates by Paul Revere are valuable to-day, not on account of their artistic workmanship, which is quite poor, but because every American loves the memory of the man."

AMERICAN PHOTOGRAPHER

80 "Making Photographic Bookplates." William Edwin Booth. (4) 31:44-6, January 1937.

Detailed information for the knowledgeable photographer; series of illustrations show bookplate from pencil sketch to finished plate.

AMERICAN PHOTOGRAPHY

81 "Art of the Bookplate." Warwick Borse Miller. 25:286-92, June 1931.

Various ideas for designing and producing bookplates by the use of photography.

AMERICAN PRINTER

82 "The Collecting of Book Plates." 25:209-10, December 1897.

Both Edmund Gosse and Andrew Lang quoted in disparagement of the "collecting mania."

83 "Some Bookplates and Their Advertising Lesson." (8) 33:108-9, October 1901.

Author suggests that "compression of wit and pictorial worth" displayed by bookplate artists could be put to good use by advertisers, book designers, and printers.

84 "More Bookplates and A Few Reflections." (4) 33:196-7, November 1901.
Illustrations include designs by William Edgar Fisher, J. W. Simpson, and Mrs. Annie B. Hooper.

85 "Snakes and Bones." Wilbur Macey Stone. (12) 51:448-9, December 1910.
Few women have bookplates employing these devices; an exception is Georgia M. Ovington whose plate features a black and yellow viper.

86 "Private Press Bookplates." Alfred Fowler. (12) 77:25-8, March 20, 1924.
Illustrations include plates used by Guthrie's Pear Tree Press, Dard Hunter, Steven Day, Bodoni, Cobden-Sanderson, and others.

AMONG FRIENDS

87 "Gifts from Individuals." Issue No. 1:9, Winter 1955.
John B. Larner Bookplate Collection (3,000 items) given to Detroit Public Library by William W. Wotherspoon.

88 "Gifts by the Friends, 1955-56." Mrs. Francis J. Brewer. Issue No. 3:7-8, Summer 1956.
John B. Larner had plate designed by E. D. French.

89 "Burton Historical Collection." Elleine H. Stones. (1) Issue No. 8:1-7, Fall 1957.
Bookplate for Clarence Monroe Burton collection, designed by Raymond Everett, includes three seals symbolizing occupation of Northwest by French, English and Americans, also drawing of Cadillac's village.

90 "Pro Libris." Issue No. 19:9, Summer 1960.
Additional "materials on bookplates and bookplate collecting" given by W. W. Wotherspoon.

91 "New Friends' Bookplate." (1) Issue No. 31:3, Summer 1963.
Special bookplate presented by the Friends of the Detroit Public Library in honor of Mabel L. Conat.

92 "From the Library of —" William Miles. Issue No. 50:1-4, Spring 1968.
Interesting details concerning the bookplate collection of the Detroit Public Library.

ANNALS OF MEDICAL HISTORY

93 "Edward Cutbush, M.D." F. L. Pleadwell. (1) 5:337-86, December 1923.
Lengthy biography of surgeon in U.S. Navy who lived from 1772-1843; last page has illustration of his plate.

ANSWERS

94 "The Collecting Fad." 8:47, December 12, 1891.
Comments on collecting bookplates, buttons, tickets placed in watch cases, signboards from old inns and taverns, and handbills.

ANTIOCHIAN

95 "Ten Years in the Bookplate Business." Ernest Morgan. Part 1 (2) and Part 2 (5), 4 pages, about May 1937. [Unable to locate original article; annotated from reprint.]

Son of President of Antioch College was associated with Antioch Bookplate Company, one of original college industries; relates hazards of small business during 30's.

ANTIQUARIAN

96 "Early Book-Plates." Karl Kup. (7) 12:34 *et seq.*, March 1929.

Early French and American Bookplates.

ANTIQUARIAN BOOKMAN

97 "Bookplates of Jewish Interest." Philip Goodman. (10) 9: cover, 1725, May 10, 1952.

A rationale for bookplate collecting.

98 "Library Notes." 38: 1609, October 24, 1966.

Selection from Mrs. Robert Sonnenschein's collection of 4,000 ex libris on exhibit at UCLA during September.

99 "Periodical Notes." 42:1070, September 30, 1968.

Article about bookplate collection of Detroit Public Library in *Among Friends*.

100 "UNESCO Bookplates." 42:1750, November 18-25, 1968.

Sale of bookplates in "new $100,000 drive to raise funds to combat world illiteracy."

101 "*Bookplates for Libraries*." 42:2259, December 23-30, 1968.

Review of Edward Shickell book containing designs for school, public, college and university libraries.

102 "Grabhorn Press Exhibit." 43:1207, March 31, 1969.

Exhibit at Wellesley College Library includes books, broadsides, trial sheets, bookplates, greeting cards, and all sorts of ephemera.

103 "Notes." 43:2108, June 2-9, 1969.

Houston Public Library had exhibit from Circle M Library of Major John E. T. Milsaps, who collected "almost everything from bookplates to Bibles."

104 "Exhibits." 44:414, August 18, 1969.

Bookplates from Roy Jansen collection exhibited at Pennsylvania State Library.

ANTIQUARIAN MAGAZINE & BIBLIOGRAPHER [WALFORD'S]

105 "Notes on English Book-Plates. No. 1. William John Hardy." (6) 1:173-77, April 1882.

Comments on scarcity of early dated and signed bookplates in England.

106 "Book-Plates." 2:48-9, July 1882.

Note by J. P. Edmond on early-dated bookplates he saw in collection of ex libris.

107 "Notes on English Book-Plates. No. II. John Harrop." (4) 2:53-5, August 1882.

Additional early dated plates, as well as several executed by Bewick.

108 "Book-Plates." 2:106, August 1882.

Emily Cole able to identify engraver and date on her copy of John Lloyd plate under the shell forming part of the ornament; referred to by Edmond in July issue.

109 "Book-Plates." 2:161-2, September 1882.

Notes from three individuals concerning previously reported bookplates.

110 "On Book Plates." F. J. Thairlwall. (4) 2:278-80, December 1882.

Suggested classification system based on Warren has nine categories plus miscellaneous. "For preservation and convenient reference" author mounts plates on right side of uniform-sized notepaper and on left side completely describes plate and any known facts about owner and his family history.

111 "Book-Plates." J. F. Meehan. 2:322, December 1882.

Author offers to exchange "some two or three hundred duplicate bookplates" and also specifically those of Sir Charles Style, "as I have an immense number of them."

112 "Book Plates, Part I." 3:2-7, January 1883.

Some 44 divisions for identifying style offered.

113 "Books Plates, Part II." (1) 3:53-6, February 1883.

And in conclusion "I quit with regret the endless details of a pursuit which is now perceived to be a study, and is recognized as having a distinguished place in the history of Art. The fact that it necessarily includes Genealogy and Heraldry gives it another value." The initials D.P. at the end of the article and numerous references to *Notes and Queries* suggest the author may be Daniel Parsons.

114 "Book-Plates." 3:104-5, February 1883.

Two notes, one a list of thirty-four 18th century dated bookplates.

115 "Book-Plates." 3:161-2, March 1883.

Interesting details concerning bequest by George I of John Moore's library to Cambridge.

116 "Book-Plates." 3:272-3, May 1883.

More details and additional list of early dated bookplates furnished by Robert Day.

117 "Inscriptions in Books." P. J. Mullin. 3:274, May 1883.

"A Pleader to the Needer when a Reader" is quoted. Lines "cannot be very old, as the allusion to the Ettick Shepard sufficiently shows . . . ." Editor's note: "Mr. Charles Clark was a well-known eccentric character in Essex, who had a private printing press at Totham. He has not been dead many years."

118 "A Book-Plate Wanted." 3:274, May 1883.

F. G. Lee offers "a dozen uncommon book-plates in exchange for a good impression of Phillips, of Ickford."

119 "Dated Book-Plates." Walter Hamilton. 4:110-1, August 1883.

Lengthy list of bookplates dated prior to 1800.

120 "Bibliography of Book-Plates." Walter Hamilton. 5:78-80, February 1884.

Earliest reference to 1837 article by Daniel Parsons in proceedings of Archaeological & Heraldic Society.

121 "Dated Book Plates: 1662-1713." J. F. Meehan. 5:106-7, February 1884.

Thirty-one plates listed.

122 "An Old Book-Plate." 5:107, February 1884.

W. V. asks help in identifying bookplate of a lady.

123 "An Old Book-Plate." 5:162, March 1884.

Identifies W. V.'s plate as "doubtless that of Bacon, the premier baronet of England."

124 "An Old Book-Plate." 5:217, April 1884.

Correspondent questions original description of plate.

125 "Francis Hoffman, 1711." Edward Solly. 9:6-13, January 1886.

Author of political pamphlets, "who served Swift and ridiculed Steele," was German wood engraver; for example of his bookplate work see *Journal of Ex Libris Society* 17:144, November 1907.

126 "Mottoes Inscribed in Books." W. Roberts. 12:128, August 1887.

"The majority [of mottoes] are . . . characterized more by perspicuity than for epigrammatical terseness."

"Whenever you borrow me
I hope you'll keep me clean;
For I'm not like a linen rag
That can be wash'd again."

ANTIQUARY

127 "Notes on Book-plates." 1:75-7, February 1880.

"What could be a more attractive arrangement than to collect autographs and book-plates together. A letter or a frank of some celebrated man, placed in one's album side by side with his book-plate and (where practical) his portrait, would form a combination full of interest and suggestion to any cultivated mind."

128 "Book Plates." Walter Hamilton. 1:117-8, March 1880.

"Old friends, old wine, old books! All are good. But old friends die; and wines, if kept beyond a certain period, lose their strength and bouquet;

old books, however, never die, never lose their charms, and are ever fresh to those who love them. So, in the words of old Pynson, written nearly four centuries ago, 'Styll am I besy bookes assemblyne; for to have plenty it is a pleasant Thynge.'"

129 "Book-Plates." 1:189, April 1880.
Correspondent comments on plate of grammarian, Thomas Ruddiman.

130 "Notes on Curious Book-Plates." 1:236-7, May 1880.
Brief note on plates of James Yates, William Fitzgerald and Adam Smith, author of *Wealth of Nations.*

131 "Another Chapter on Book-Plates." Alfred Wallis. 1:256-9, June 1880.
Interesting facts and poems including "A Pleader to the Needer when a Reader" used by Charles Clark of Totham, Essex, 1861.

132 "A Supplementary Chapter on Book-Plates." 2:6-10, July 1880.
Additional interesting facts and poems.

133 "An Essay on Book-Plates." E. P. Shirley. 2:115-8, September 1880.
Considerable list of and information about plates executed prior to 1750.

134 "Book-Plates." 2:133, September 1880.
Pedigree of Spearman (plate mentioned 1:236) to be found in Burke's *Landed Gentry.*

135 "Book-Plates." 2:272-3, December 1880.
Mentions Pepys diary reference to plates.

136 "Book-Plates." 3:77, February 1881.
Enlightening review of Warren's *A Guide to the Study of Book Plates.*

137 "Last Words on Book-Plates." 4:106-11, September 1881.
Curious bookplate created by cutting portrait from engraved framework and substituting your own.

138 "Correction." 5:85-6, February 1882.
Concerns bookplate described in issue of September 1881.

139 "Bookplate." 7:231, May 1883.
Bookplate mentioned in letter from artist David Loggan to Sir Thomas Isham (1675).

140 "Book-Plate." 13:231, May 1886.
Identity of arms on plate sought by E. W. B.

141 "Book-Plate." 13:278, June 1886.
E. W. B. referred to Elvin's "useful" *Handbook of Mottoes.*

142 "Book-Plates." 19:39, January 1889.
J. G. Bradford suggests magazine "dealing exclusively with book-plates."

143 "Notes of the Month." 23:142-3, April 1891.
New society to be formed for those interested in the "craze" of collecting bookplates; James Roberts Brown presided.

144 "Unique Book-Plate—Erasmus and Dr. Hector Pomer." H. W. Pereira. (1) 25:242-5, June 1892.

Plate for Dr. Pomer is dated 1525 and has initials of unknown artist R. A.

ANTIQUES

145 "Collecting Bookplates." Alfred Fowler. (10) 1:169-72, April 1922.

"A collection of bookplates is a collection of human documents which may be indicative not only of the trend of human thought but of the mind of the owner."

146 "Books—Old and Rare." George H. Sargent. (7) 7:85-7, February 1925.

Rare old bookplates occasionally uncovered beneath later ones in old volumes; those of Nicholas Bacon and Samuel Pepys illustrated.

147 "Check-list of William Hamlin's Engravings." 7:135-7, March 1925.

Numbers 38 and 42 are bookplates, one made for John H. Hamlin.

148 "Book Notes." George H. Sargent. (4) 9:320-1, May 1926.

Bookplate of Duke of Argyle found in Shakespeare "source book."

149 "Pennsylvania Bookplate." (1) 14:27, July 1928.

Bookplate for Maria Kolbin especially good example of *fractur* painting, "a curious German-American survival of the medieval art of illumination."

150 "Jacob Sargeant, Goldsmith and Clockmaker." Florence Thompson Howe. (6) 19:287-90, April 1931.

Jacob Sargeant's armorial bookplate was engraved by Richard Brunton, "early Connecticut engraver and counterfeiter."

151 "Thomas Coram, Engraver and Painter." Margaret Simons Middleton. (7) 29:242-4, June 1936.

Coram's bookplates illustrated, also $50 bill he engraved for state of South Carolina in 1799.

152 "What's In A Name Plate?" Edith A. Wright and J. Josephine McDevitt. (26) 36:182-3, October 1939.

Collection at Library of Congress of bound sheet music with dated hand-tooled leather name plates, dating back to 1792.

153 "Bookplates of Royal Society." (1) 61:454, May 1952.

Exhibition at Huntington Library of plates of members of Royal Society of London for Improving Natural Knowledge, oldest scientific society in Great Britain and one of oldest in Europe.

154 "Hearts and Flowers from Pennsylvania." Cornelius Weygandt. (6) 65:146-7, February 1954.

The flyleaves of early German Pennsylvania hymnals and other small books were often illuminated with hearts and flowers, included the owner's name and the date; some dated as early as 1798.

155 "Revere Bookplate at the Metropolitan." 68:68, July 1955.

Mention of article in *Museum of Art Bulletin* concerning Revere plate; motto: "I fight for my country."

156 "Franks Family Silver by Lamerie." Jessie McNab Dennis. (11) 93:636-41, May 1968.

Included among illustrations is bookplate of Sir William Cooper "with the arms of his wife Isabella Franks in an escutcheon of pretense."

APOLLO

157 "International Ex-Libris Exhibition in Brussels." (1) 9:400-1, June 1929.

Most European countries represented by own participation, but British only through collection of a Belgian woman.

158 "An Unknown Bookplate of Elias Ashmole." George H. Viner. (2) 21:98-9, February 1935.

Interesting detective work in unravelling questions posed by discovery of previously unknown heraldic plate of Ashmole, some of whose books are in Bodleian.

Also sleuthing on heraldic symbolism of Biddle Law Library, University of Pennsylvania, bookplate.

159 "Heraldry in Bookplates." F. Sydney Eden. (4) 31:168-70, June 1940.

Detailed descriptions of plates with sidelights on family history.

160 "A Modern Durer: Stephen Gooden, R. A." (1) 43:140, June 1946.

Illustration is bookplate Gooden designed for City of Liverpool Public Libraries.

"Armorial Bookbindings from the Clemments Collection." John P. Harthan.
161 (14) 72:179-83, December 1960.
162 (22) 74:186-91, June 1961.
163 (21) 75:165-71, December 1961.

Impressing heraldic marks of ownership on outer covers of book developed from the medieval custom of introducing coats of arms into the decoration of illuminated manuscripts.

ARCHAEOLOGIA CAMBRENSIS

164 "Two Welsh Bookplates." W. J. Hemp. (2) 95:252-3, December 1940.

Early 18th century plates for Arthur Meillionydd in which "draughtsmanship is very rude."

165 "Welsh Bookplates." W. J. Hemp. (2) 96:94-6, June 1941.

Plates for Thomas Edwards and Edward Wynne selected because "ownership of both is not obvious."

ARCHAEOLOGICAL JOURNAL

166 "*Journal of Ex Libris Society.*" 48:485-6, December 1891.

Reviewer feels *Journal* not only helping to establish collecting of bookplates "upon a scientific basis" but also it is forwarding study of heraldry and putting in print data on engravers "whose names might otherwise have passed into oblivion."

ARCHITECTS' JOURNAL

167 "Architects' Book-Plate." Grahame B. Tubbs. (13) 65:24-7, January 5, 1927.
Sidney Smirke, designer of the Reading Room of the British Museum, had an ex libris. Piranesi etched several bookplates.

ARCHITECTURAL FORUM

168 "Miniature Bookplates." April 1936. [Unable to locate in this issue.]
Source unknown.

ARCHITECTURAL RECORD

169 "The Book-plate and the Architect." Sheldon Cheney. (17) 32:141-51, August 1912.
Some architects turned bookplate designers are Howard Sill, Frank Chouteau Brown, Claude Bragdon, Bertram G. Goodhue.

ARGUS

170 "Lino-Cut Bookplates Work of George D. Perrottet." (1) 1 page, April 21, 1934. [Volume and page number unavailable.]
Australian artist featured in *Year Book* of American Society of Bookplate Collectors and Designers; he has produced forty-two plates.

ARMORIAL

171 "Heraldic Art—Armorial Bookplate or Ex Libris." (2) 1:41-2, November 1959.
Subscribers requested to send copies of bookplates in triplicate for inclusion in this section in future issues.

172 "Editorial." 1:58, February 1960.
Space allowed bookplates increased due to fact *Bookplate Collectors News* ceased publication.

173 "Heraldic Art—Armorial Bookplate or Ex Libris." (4) 1:96-8, February 1960.
Each plate illustrated and fully detailed including name of artist.

174 "*Bookplate Collectors News*." 1:105, February 1960.
Reviews last two issues of this journal.

175 "*Nordish Ex Libris Tidsskrift*." 1:111-2, February 1960.
Journal of Danish Society with English summaries.

176 "Heraldic Art—Armorial Bookplate or Ex Libris." (4) 1:156-8, May 1960.
One from New Zealand; Canadian plate multicolor.

177 "*Ex Libris*." 1:165, May 1960.
Trieste publication.

178 "*Scots Heraldry.*" (1) 1:168-9, May 1960.
Review and multicolor plate illustrated.

179 "Heraldic Art—Armorial Bookplate or Ex Libris." (4) 1:218-21, August 1960.
Details include matriculation, granted date, arms, crest, motto, mantling, etc.

180 "Heraldic Art—Armorial Bookplate or Ex Libris." (3) 2:49-50, November 1960.
Another multi-colored plate; also one from Italy.

181 "Heraldic Art—Armorial Bookplate or Ex Libris." (7) 2:107-10, February 1961.
Interesting plate of Scot transplanted to Australia featuring kangaroo, printed in yellow and black.

182 "Heraldic Art—Armorial Bookplates or Ex Libris." 2:180-1, August 1961.
"As the purpose of this section is not that of a heraldic register, but heraldic art, arms of doubtful or of *bürgerlich* origin may from time to time be shown as examples of armorial design."

183 "Books Received." 2:184, August 1961.
Danish ex libris journal included.

184 "*A Artes Do Ex Libris.*" 2:186, August 1961.
Issue of Portuguese journal reviewed.

185 "Heraldic Art—Armorial Bookplates or Ex Libris." (3) 2:245-6, November 1961.
One from Sweden.

186 "Contents of Other Journals." 2:251, November 1961.
Journals from Trieste and Portugal.

187 "Heraldic Art—Armorial Bookplates or Ex Libris." (1) 3:56, February 1962.
Plate of Anders Gustaf Ahlin of Sweden.

188 "Heraldic Art—Armorial Bookplates or Ex Libris." (2) 3:115, May 1962.
Plates of Bo Tennberg, Finland, and that of Swedish army officer.

189 "Insignia of Stait Lazarus in Book Stamps." W. S. Scott. 4:27-9, February 1963.
"The external embossed stamp as a means of branding books antedates the internal bookplate by at least a century."

190 "Hogarth, Heraldry and Healing." Julian Franklyn. (4) 4:57-63, May 1963.
Well written article; two bookplates illustrated.

191 "Bookplates of George Taylor Friend." P. C. Beddingham. (8) 4:118-24, August 1963.
Engraving since age 14, this English artist produced over 400 bookplates.

192 "Books Reviewed." 5:48, February 1965.
Includes journal *A Artes Do Ex Libris.*

ART AMATEUR

193 "Ex Libris Notes." (12) 30:92-3, February 1894.
Review of Castle's *English Book-Plates*, notes on Colonial bookplates.

194 "Ex Libris." (12) 30:121, March 1894.
Letter on misuse of coats of arms.

195 "Ex Libris." (19) 30:148-9, April 1894.
Henry Blackwell gives notes on removing, cleaning and repairing bookplates.

196 "Ex Libris" (17) 30:170-1, May 1894.
Additional Colonial plates, notes on Sherborn exhibit.

197 "Checklist of American Bookplates." 30:171-2, May 1894.
A and B of checklist made by Henry Blackwell.

198 "Ex Libris." (3) 31:18, June 1894.
Illustrated are plates for Walter D. Marks, Robert Jackson, and R.S. Philpott.

199 "Ex Libris." (9) 31:19, June 1894.
Some items reprinted from *Journal of Ex Libris Society*.

200 "Checklist of American Bookplates." 30:19, June 1894.
Continuation through B and C.

201 "Ex Libris." (12) 31:41, July 1894.
Checklist continued through D and E.

202 "Ex Libris." (9) 31:63, August 1894.
F through I on checklist.

203 "Ex Libris." (11) 31:82-3, September 1894.
Letters, plates for identification.

204 "Checklist of American Bookplates." 31:83, September 1894.
J through L.

205 "Ex Libris." (8) 31:109, October 1894.
Checklist continues through O.

206 "Ex Libris." (13) 31:138-9, November 1894.
Grolier Club exhibit and colonial bookplates.

207 "Checklist of American Bookplates." 31:141, November 1894.
Continued O through R.

208 "Ex Libris." (10) 32:36-7, December 1894.
Two new plates for Henry Blackwell.

209 "Checklist of American Bookplates." 32:37, December 1894.
R to S.

210 "Ex Libris." (6) 32:70, January 1895.
Review of Charles Dexter Allen's *American Book-Plates*.

211 "Ex Libris." (9) 32:98-9, February 1895.
Blackwell checklist continued T to W.

212 "Ex Libris." (13) 32:128-9, March 1895.
Review of Allen's book by Henry Blackwell.

213 "Checklist of American Bookplates." 32:129, March 1895.
Conclusion of list.

214 "Ex Libris." (8) 32:152-3, April 1895.
List of plates exhibited at Brentano's.

215 "Ex Libris." (6) 32:170-1, May 1895.
J. R. Brown letter to *Ex Libris Journal* re Blackwell's criticism of Allen's book printed together with Henry Blackwell's rebuttal.

216 "Ex-Libris." (12) 33:18-9, June 1895.
More plates for identification, various Bossuet arms pictured and more on American coats of arms.

217 "Ex-Libris." (8) 33:38-9, July 1895.
Quotes writer in London *Daily News:* "Why of all things collect bookplates? Are there not door-knockers which a man may collect, or visiting cards of all ages, or muffin balls, or political walking sticks, or pocket-handkerchiefs of the anti-slavery period?"

218 "Bookplates." (6) 33:60-1, August 1895.
Plates shown for Gleeson White, Frank House Baer, Richard B. Contant, Nanni Smith, and Francis E. Murray.

219 "Ex-Libris." (2) 33:81, September 1895.
Mortimer Delano notes distinctions in heraldry of different countries.

220 "Elements of Heraldry." Mortimer Delano. (27) 33:106-7, October 1895.
Notes on the armorial shield and its Partition Lines.

221 "Elements of Heraldry." Mortimer Delano. (27) 33:132, November 1895.
Notes on Ordinaries.

222 "Book-Plates Identified." 33:132, November 1895.
Numbers 27, 48, 62 and 66 identified.

223 "Gossip About Book-Plates." 33:132, November 1895.
William Penn "does not show impalement of the arms of Hannah Callowhill, to whom he was married in 1695"; bookplate artist Henry Dawkins was convicted of counterfeiting; Lichtenstein tells collector how to recognize George Washington forgery.

224 "Early American Book-Plates." (4) 33:133, November 1895.
Pictured are plates for Maturin Livington, John Quincy Adams, Florence Bell and William Smith, L.L.D.

225 "Elements of Heraldry." (22) 34:28, December 1895.
Various crosses and lions shown.

226 "E. N. Hewins Collection." 34:28, December 1895.

Three albums containing 3,000 bookplates to be auctioned at Libbie's in Boston.

227 "Book-Plate Notes." (2) 34:27-8, December 1895.
Stamp hinges recommended as bookplate mounts.

228 "Elements of Heraldry." (28) 34:52, January 1896,
"Differences" or marks of "cadency" which distinguish different members or branches of a family noted.

229 "Mr. Hewin's Book-Plates Sold." (5) 34:52-3, January 1896.
Entire lot of 3,229 purchased by W. E. Baillie of Bridgeport, Conn; no price mentioned.

230 "Elements of Heraldry." 34:76, February 1896.
Five kinds of coronets described.

231 "Book-Plates Designed by Mr. Claude F. Brangdon." (3) 34:77, February 1896.
Two armorial plates and one modern treatment for Post Express Printing Company, Rochester, New York.

232 "Bookplates." (4) 34:98-9, March 1896.
No text; plates for Colonial Dames of America, Mrs. Nellie Heaton, a German convent, and a "device suitable for a lady's book-plate."

233 "Hint for Ex-Libris Collectors." 34:123-4, April 1896.
". . . no system [of arrangement] is perfect which does not admit of a collection being arranged according to one plan to-day and another to-morrow, i.e., no arrangement is satisfactory which is necessarily permanent."

234 "Bookplate." (1) 34:143, May 1896.
Illustration only of circular plate for Marie S. Petersen.

235 "Ex Libris." (2) 38:124, April 1898.
Illustration of plates for Marie S. Petersen and E. Fitz-Gerald.

ART & ARCHAEOLOGY

236 "Presidential Book-Plates." Alfred Fowler. (8) 10:142-5, October 1920.
Illustrations include those of: George Washington, John and John Quincy Adams, Theodore Roosevelt, William Howard Taft, and Woodrow Wilson.

237 "Some Literary Bookplates." Alfred Fowler. (9) 11:239-43, June 1921.
Illustrations include plates for A. Edward Newton, Swinburne, Victor Hugo, Yeats, Keats-Shelley Memorial, one designed by Howard Pyle.

ART AND ARCHITECTURE

238 "Some Australian Book Plates." John Lane Mullins. (9) 2:125-30, May-June 1905.
Plates falling in six categories described: labels, armorials, literary, historical, pictorial, and plates of particular engravers and designers.

239 "Some Early Australian Book-Plates." John Lane Mullins. (2) 5:16-7, January-February 1908.

Biographical details and descriptions of plates for Judge Barron Field and Dr. William Bland.

240 "Modern Bookplate Designers—William Phillips Barrett." P. Neville Barnett. (4) 6:134-6, September-October 1909.

Born in Christchurch, New Zealand, Barrett early left for the "old Country" where he received art training.

241 "Bookplate." (1) 7:84, May-June 1910.

Illustration only of D. H. Souter's plate for Alexis Grant Souter.

242 "Modern Bookplate Designers. No. 2. Charles William Sherborn. 'The Little Master.'" (6) 7:111-4 July-August 1910.

"Happier still the man who retains until old age a keen interest in some department of life, however small, whose treasures he may collect and study. . . . he finds in them a consolation in time of trouble, a hold on life when all else may fail." Such a hobby is bookplates.

243 "Phil May and Bookplates." P. Neville Barnett. 1910. (Unable to locate journal.)

As annotated by H. B. Muir: A short appreciation of Phil May's work generally, with illustrations from C. K. Shorter's plate (the only one, it is believed, this artist designed) and that drawn for him by W. P. Nicholson.

244 "Royal Bookplates from the Designs of W. P. Barrett." (9) 9:422-7, January-February 1912.

Bookplate designer holds "important position with Messrs J. and E. Bumpus, Ltd., the great London booksellers."

ART AND PROGRESS [See also **MAGAZINE OF ART** and **AMERICAN MAGAZINE OF ART**]

245 "Book-Plates, Notes on an Exhibition Held in Detroit." Helen Plumb. (9) 2:189-94, May 1911.

"Indeed, next to an umbrella, there is no loan of personal property concerning the appropriation of which such lax ideas of morality are current as a book; and so to engrave on one's *Ex libris* some fulmination against the borrower is a virtuous proceeding revealing, withal, often an intimate glimpse of the owner's personality."

ART DIGEST

246 " 'Up and Downs' of Aviation Subject of Newark Museum Exhibit." (2) 7:21, December 1, 1932.

Prints, many from Bella C. Landauer Collection, of men flying on exhibit; illustrated is bookplate E. B. Bird designed for Charles A. Lindberg.

247 "Bookplate International." 7:18, January 15, 1933.

Ninth annual competition and exhibition of Bookplate Association International of Los Angeles.

248 "Museum Gets 1600 Bookplates." 7:18, June 1933.
Brooklyn Museum acquired collection of Lady Anne Bowring.

249 "Bookplate Annual." 8:16, July 1, 1934.
Entries from 17 foreign countries at tenth International Bookplate Competition, Los Angeles.

250 "Bookplates by Kent." (1) 11:31, May 15, 1937.
Review of *Later Bookplates and Marks* by Rockwell Kent, published by Pynson Printers.

251 "Ex Libris." 18:20, January 1, 1944.
Dr. Herman T. Radin's collection of 3,000 bookplates given to New York Public Library.

ART IN AMERICA

"Richard Brunton—Itinerant Craftsman." William L. Warren.
252 (1) 39:91-94, February 1951.
253 (1) 41:69-78, Spring 1951
254 (1) 42:221, October 1954.
Early engraver; one illustration is bookplate for Daniel & Elijah Boardman (1790).

ART IN AUSTRALIA

255 "Charm of the Bookplate." William Moore. (58) 3rd S., Issue No. 5, 18 unnumbered pages, August 1, 1923.
"What is more diverse than the art of the bookplates," writes the French George Lambert. "It escapes from all theories by its diversity; it adopts every form and adapts itself to all conceptions."

256 "Lionel Lindsay." J. S. MacDonald. March 1928.
"Lionel Lindsay Prints." Harold Wright. March 1928.
[Reference incomplete and unable to locate journal again.]
No specific reference to artist's bookplate work.

257 "Woodcut by Adrian Feint." 3rd S:26, October-November 1930.
Design awarded First Prize by Australian Ex Libris Society in 1930 competition; bookplate is for Enid De Chair.

258 "An Interview with Norman Lindsay." Kenneth Slessor. (41) 3rd S:8-64, December 1930.
Interesting interview but no definite reference to bookplates; recurring reference to *Redheap*, apparently a censored novel turned into a movie; illustrations verge on erotic.

ART INSTRUCTION

259 "Rockwell Kent Again!" (7) 1:29, June 1937.
Bookplates illustrated from *Later Bookplates & Marks*, edition of 1250 published by Pynson Printers and signed by artist.

260 "Bookplates and Marks." Norman Kent. (9) 3:26, May 1939.
Illustrations only.

ART JOURNAL

261 "Alexander Anderson, M.D." J. B. Lossing. (2) 10:271-2, 1858.
Pioneer engraver on wood in United States.

262 "Notes on Book-Plates." M. A. Tooke. (7) 28:267-70, 1876.
"Bundles of old ones [bookplates] are to be had at the bookstalls and second-hand bookshops 'where each one has been saved, like a single spar, from the wreck of an old book.' " Poulet-Malassis quoted: "Who can tell but some day our daughters may receive dowries of book-plates, and she who possesses the finest collection will be sought after as the best match."(!)

263 "Some Art Books of the Year." (2) 47:373-6, 1895.
Among other art books is mentioned *Ladies' Book Plates.*

264 "Passing Events." (1) 53:320, October 1901.
Bookplate designed and engraved by J. B. Hadlow for Hove Public Library using arms and crest of the borough.

265 "William Monk—Painter-Etcher." E. G. Halton. (12) 55:321-6, November 1903.
In addition to larger works illustrated is a copy of the artist's own bookplate.

ART NEWS

266 "Book Plate Show at Smithsonian." 29:8, January 3, 1931.
Collection of Mrs. William S. Corby including those she acquired from Sir George Armytage.

ARTIST

267 "A Young Illustrator—Celia Levetus." Unable to locate.
Source: *Journal Ex Libris Society*, 7:108, August 1897, indicates article "appeared some time ago."

268 "A Young Artist—James J. Guthrie." (8) 22:238-41, August 1898.
Among the illustrations are bookplates for Margaret O'Hara and Joshua Buchanan Guthrie.

269 "*The Elf* and Some Book-Plates by James G. Guthrie." (7) 25:125-7, August 1899.
Cover design and bookplates from *The Elf.*

270 "A Tree-Lover's Book-Plate." (1) 25:216, September 1899.
Plate designed by W. T. Horton.

271 "A Book-Plate Designed by J. J. Guthrie." (1) 25:222, September 1899.
Illustration only.

272 "Book-Plates by May Fisher." (4) 26:115, November 1899.

Four illustrations only, include plate for a child and three for young girls.

273 "*German Bookplates.*" (1) 31:169-70, August 1901.

"It is impossible to examine this volume without feeling that the author has some justification in his boast that a well-arranged collection 'will provide a fund of interest and instruction, not only to the specialist, but to anyone who is interested in art, history, genealogy, heraldry, engraving or decorative design—subjects of which few educated people nowadays can afford to be wholly ignorant.' "

274 "Designer from the Birmingham School." (3) 31:171-2, August 1901.

One illustration is bookplate for Frederick Hollyer.

ARTISTIC BOOK PLATES

275 "American Designers of Book-Plates: Wm. Edgar Fisher." W. G. Bowdoin. (15) 1:3-8, Autumn 1901.

"The general eastern notion in regard to (Fargo) North Dakota is that nothing artistic can come out of the state, but the work done there by Mr. Fisher quickly dispels such an idea."

276 "Nineteen Examples of Decorative Book-Plates by Modern British Designers (From *London Studio*)." (19) 1:9-18, Autumn 1901.

Illustrations only including plates by R. Anning Bell, J. W. Simpson, Gordon Craig, Harold Nelson.

277 "The Artistic Book-Plate." Temple Scott. (1) 1:19-22, Autumn 1901.

"It should be like no other book-plate in the sense that it possesses some *flavor* that is private and personal."

278 "Thirty-two Examples of Book-Plates from Private Collections and Other Sources." (32) 1:23-32, Autumn 1901.

Among those reproduced are E. D. French plate for Worcester Art Museum, George Wharton Edwards' for the Authors Club Library, steel engravings by William Phillips Barrett, designs by Thomas M. Cleland.

279 "Book-Plates and the Nude." Wilbur Macey Stone. (8) 1:33-38, Autumn 1901.

"Judging by the examples we have been able to cite, and they are representative, it would seem that the best advice we can give those tempted to use the undraped beautiful in their book-plates is—don't."

280 "American Designers of Book-Plates. I—Frank Chouteau Brown." Stuart Bartlett. (14) N.S. 1:1-9, June 1903.

Boston architect who designed bookplates and music covers.

281 "American Designers of Book-Plates. II—Haydon Jones." Randolph Cooper Lewis. (7) N.S. 1:10-16, June 1903.

Illustrator of Western and Oriental subjects, artist for New York daily, became bookplate designer by chance when Wilbur Macey Stone saw his drawing of a schoolmaster keeping a boy after school and bought it as a bookplate design for his son.

ARTS & DECORATION

282 "'From the Books of—,' Book-plates by Elisha Brown Bird." Matlack Price. (5) 14:382, March 1921.

"Booklover's real reason for wanting a book-plate is two-fold . . . wishes to mark his ownership . . cannot bear the idea of writing his name on one of its front pages and must therefore make his mark of ownership artistic."

ARTWORK

283 "A Bookplate." (1) 1:20, 1924

Plate by Sidney Hunt illustrated.

284 "A Master Craftsman: Frank Brangwyn, R. A." Amelia Defries. 1:54-60, 1924.

A bookplate designer as well as an artist in other fields.

285 "Linocut Bookplate." (1) 1:180, February-April 1925.

Illustration of J. Guthrie's plate for Agnes Thomson.

ASSOCIATION OF HOSPITAL AND INDUSTRIAL LIBRARIES QUARTERLY

286 "Bookplates Bring Books Back." (2) 2:14, Winter 1962.

Reprint of *Library Journal* article concerning use of bookplate which in many hospitals is also in Spanish to assure return of books borrowed by patients.

ATHENAEUM

287 "Book-Plates." Issue No. 2502:469, October 9, 1875.

Review of *Les Ex-Libris Francais* by Poulet-Malassis. "To *dilettanti* anxious not to follow trodden paths a new field of research is open in the vast realms of curiosity. It is no question of morbid fancy like, for instance, the collecting of pipes or of patterns of buttons. The collecting of book-plates goes hand in hand with the love of fine books and of masterpieces of the best engravers."

288 "Literary Gossip." Issue No. 2795:689, May 21, 1881.

"Mr. Thoms has devised a new kind of bookplate—a photograph of the possessor, and below it his coat of arms and his name." [Entire entry.]

289 "Mr. Thoms's Book-Plate." Issue No. 2796:719, May 28, 1881.

Detailed "development" of photographic plate using portrait of William J. Thoms in the style of Houbraken's engravings.

290 "Literary Gossip." Issue No. 3363:471, April 9, 1892.

Kegan Paul & Co. to publish a volume on bookplates in their Books About Books series, while Bell & Sons plan two volumes on English and French bookplates.

291 "Laws of Book-Borrowing." G. H. Powell. Issue No. 3452:883, December 23, 1893.

Fifteen rules in Latin used by Cavalier Francesco Vargas Macciucca.

292 "Abuse of the Book-Plate." Edmund Gosse. Issue No. 3509:118, January 26, 1895.

"But book-plates are nowadays treated as if they were a sort of Christmas card or valentine. They are sent around to the owner's friends, and people make scrap-albums of them; the last use to which they seem now to be put is the original one . . . . I would as soon 'swap' pocket-handkerchiefs with a man as book plates . . . . collectors, who tired of postage stamps and cigar-ends, are now turning their attention to *ex libris*."

293 "Book of Public Arms." Issue No. 3511:189-90, February 9, 1895.

Sharp review of book by A. C. Fox-Davies and M. E. B. Crookes whom reviewer felt indulged in "sarcastic remarks at the expense of the London County Council, manufacturers of perambulators, hansom cab proprietors, and others."

294 "Book-Plates." Issue No. 3570:409-10, March 28, 1896.

Reviews *Ladies' Book-Plates* (Labouchere); *American Book-Plates* (Allen); and *Dated Book-Plates* (Hamilton). "The craze for collecting book-plates shows no signs of weakening. . . . Nowadays [bookplates] are not used for putting in books but merely for bartering for other plates to be ultimately arranged in albums."

295 "Literary Gossip." Issue No. 3682:664, May 21, 1898.

Blunder in issue of Chaucer's Head Book circular when describing the bookplate Sir John Millais designed for Sir Christopher Sykes; catalog says allegory bears on owner's Christian name and "illustrates the legend of St. Christopher ferrying Christ through the waters."

296 "Ashur-bani-pal's Bookplate." Issue No. 3793:29, July 7, 1900.

Ex Libris Members told that equivalent to modern bookplate to mark possession placed on tablets in Royal Library of Ninevah, per "Guide to Babylonia & Assyrian Antiquities," British Museum.

297 "*German Book-Plates: A Handbook for Collectors.*" Issue No. 3851:218, August 17, 1901.

Review of Karl Emich's book, translated by G. R. Dennis, which is said to have numerous excellent illustrations.

298 "English Heraldic Book-Stamps." Issue No. 4267:160, August 7, 1909.

Bookstamps followed by armorial bookplates.

299 "Books and Book-Plates." Issue No. 4414:618, June 1, 1912.

C. W. Sherborn collection sold at Sotheby's.

300 "Books, Manuscripts and Book-Plates." Issue No. 4444:783, December 28, 1912.

Bookplate collection of Hon. Gerald Ponsonby totaling 8,700 sold at Sotheby's.

ATLANTIC MONTHLY

301 "Book Plates." 97:431-2, March 1906.

Essay protesting use of bookplates in lieu of owner writing his name. "Finally the defacer of books is cruel, for he strikes a mortal blow at one of the most innocent sources of pride in the lives of bibliophiles. No more will books command a high price because some great man had written his name there."

AUCTION

302 "A Late Victorian Craze." David Lasswell. (5) 1:cover, 2-3, March 1968.

Brief article as prelude to spring auction of William R. H. Hayes' collection of 35,000 plates and correspondence with Van Bayros, "eminent among the German erotic designers," on assembling the collection and on commissions to the artist.

AUSTRALASIAN

303 "Bookplates. Some Australian Examples." R. H. Croll. (5) 1 page, April 24, 1926. [Volume and page number unavailable.]

"There is so much charm in a plate at once artistic and expressing a personal preference that a booklover without one deprives himself of much innocent satisfaction."

304 [Review, anonymous.] March 23, 1929. [Unable to locate journal.]

As annotated by H. B. Muir: Review of the 1928 brochure, with illustrations from designs by George Collingridge, Adrian Feint and Cyril Dillon.

305 "Ex Libris." (3) 1 page, April 23, 1929. [Volume and page number unavailable.]

Australian Ex Libris Society has ninety members in Sydney and seven in Victoria.

AUSTRALIA, NATIONAL JOURNAL

306 "Adrian Feint Bookplates." (7) 2:42-3, January 1, 1941.

In addition to designing more than 200 bookplates, this artist is "noted for his book illustrations and decorative pen work"; also he paints in oil.

AUSTRALIAN EX LIBRIS SOCIETY

307 "Rachael Cecily Forster." (1) Frontispiece, 1926.

Etching by Adrian Feint.

308 "Report of the Australian Ex Libris Society." P. Neville Barnett. (8) 9-21, 1926.

Third annual report. "Most notable event of year under review was an exhibition of bookplates."

309 "Presidential Address." John Lane Mullins. (4) 22-31, 1926.

Mentions artists Norman and Lionel Lindsay and Adrian Feint.

310 "Members." 32-4, 1926.
Over 80 members listed including Mrs. W. H. Burnham and Winward Prescott of the U.S.

311 "Meetings." 35, 1926.
Quarterly meetings scheduled.

312 "His Royal Higness the Duke of York." (1) Frontispiece, 1927.
Etching by Adrian Feint.

313 "Report of Australian Ex Libris Society." P. Neville Barnett. (9) 8-23, 1927.
Outstanding event presentation of personal bookplates to Duke and Duchess of York on occasion of opening Canberra as seat of government.

314 "Presidential Address." John Lane Mullins. (5) 23-33, 1927.
Summarizes work of Australian bookplate artists during previous year.

315 "Members." (1) 34-7, 1927.
Increased membership.

316 "Dame Nellie Melba." (1) Frontispiece, 1928.
Etched by Cyril Dillon.

317 "Report of Australian Ex Libris Society." (7) 8-19, 1928.
Australia well represented in the Annual Exhibition of the Bookplate Association International at Los Angeles.

318 "Presidential Address," John Lane Mullins. (8) 20-34, 1928.
Outstanding event publication of book by Adrian Feint.

319 "Members." (1) 35-8, 1928.
Gradual increase in membership.

320 "D. & H. Thomas." (1) Frontispiece, 1929.
Woodcut by Adrian Feint.

321 "Report of Australian Ex Libris Society." (8) 9-26, 1929.
Membership now totals 173; sent fifty-six plates to Los Angeles for exhibit; New Zealand to form own society.

322 "Presidential Address." John Lane Mullins. (3) 29-38, 1929.
Quotes E. Gordon Craig, "Somehow a large bookplate is an absurdity."

323 "Members." 39-45, 1929.
Now five members from the United States.

324 "Enid De Chair." (1) Frontispiece, 1930.
Woodcut by Adrian Feint.

325 "Seventh Annual Report of the Australian Ex Libris Society." 6-19, 1930.
Again represented in Los Angeles exhibit; *Year Book* of American Society features Australian bookplates.

326 "Presidential Address." (8) 20-41, 1930.
Annual *Journal* launched.

327 "Members." 42-6, 1930.
Membership now about 180 with majority located in Sydney.

328 "Eighth Annual Report." P. Neville Barnett. 6-23, 1930-31.
Seattle Professor Frederick Starr delivered lecture on Australian bookplates at Oregon University. *Year Book* of American Society included article on Adrian Feint.

329 "Presidential Address." John Lane Mullins. (6) 24-37, 1930-31
Neville Barnett published *Pictorial Bookplates*.

330 "Membership." (2) 39-44, 1930-31.
Membership slightly reduced because of formation of New Zealand Society.

331 "Douglas Miller." (1) Frontispiece, 1933.
Plate by Adrian Feint.

332 "Presidential Address." John Lane Mullins. (12) 8-30, 1933.
Devoted mostly to comments on creations of Australian bookplate artists.

333 "Armorial Book-plates of Some Early Victorians." Charles Sutton. (5) 31-8, 1933.
"Armorial book-plates possess a significance and have a certain dignity of their own, and those belonging to citizens who have played an important part in our public life naturally have also a very distinct historic interest."

334 "Members." 39-43, 1933.
Membership remains steady.

335 "Lord Huntingfield." (1) Frontispiece, 1934.
By P. Roach Pierson.

336 "Presidential Address." John Lane Mullins. (12) 6-27, 1934.
Adrian Feint designed plate for Prince of Wales (Edward VIII).

337 "South Australian Book-Plates," F. Millward Grey. (8) 29-37. 1934.
Exhibition during year given good publicity.

338 "Australian Ex Libris Society." 38-42, 1934.
P. Neville Barnett made honorary life member.

AUSTRALIAN GENEALOGIST

339 "Concerning Bookplates and Their Heraldic Interest." Camden Morrisby. (1) 1:27-33, April 1933.
"It [the bookplate] is simply an artistic device of a personal flavour which those of us who care for books and their decorative accessories, i.e., such things as type, illustrations, binding—it is a distinctive personal device which we add to our books to beautify them, as well as make it known they are ours."

AUSTRALIAN MAGAZINE

340 "On Bookplates." P. Neville Barnett. (6) 641, April 1, 1908. [Volume number unavailable.]

Illustrated are plates of Robert Harley, Sir Harry Rawson, Sir Alfred S. Scott-Gatty, Lord Rothchild, Lord Roberts and that of artist D. H. Souter with "our old friend again, the Souter Cat, so familiar to us per the medium of a much-read Sidney weekly."

AUSTRALIAN WOMAN'S MIRROR

341 "Bookplates in Australia." P. Neville Barnett. (7) 11, 54, October 1927. [Volume number unavailable.]

Numerous women artists in the bookplate field in Australia named including Eirene Mort, Ethel Stephens, Ada Parsons, Margaret Arnott, Ethel Spowers, Pixie O'Harris, Nora Riceman, Ethel Lewis, Hilda Wiseman. Among illustrations is plate for Charmian London.

342 "Bookplates by Photography." R. R. Lens. June 6, 1933. [Unable to locate journal.]

As annotated by H. B. Muir: Describes an unusual medium for bookplates, one illustration.

B

BAKER STREET JOURNAL

343 "Henriksen Bookplate." (1) 11:45, March 1961.

A. D. Henriksen is a "connoisseur of bookplates" and author of *Lidt Om Exlibris* (A Wee Bit on Bookplates), published in Denmark.

344 "E. W. Smith Bookplate." (1) 11:115, June 1961.

Bookplate for Edgar Wadsworth Smith.

345 "Bookplate." (1) 12:125, June 1962.

Pictured is plate of Marquis of Donegall who held the title from 1791 to 1799.

346 "Some Family Facts." Adrian M. Conan Doyle. (1) 12:139-41, September 1962.

Son details family arms; states his "father's ancestors were granted Estates in County Wexford in the year 1333 by Edward III."

347 "Bookplate." (1) 13:66, March 1963.

W. S. Hall has made a bookplate of the "solution to the crossword puzzle used as the admission test for the first dinner of the Baker Street Irregulars."

348 "Sherlockian Book-Plate." (1) 13:191, September 1963.
Plate by Henry Lauritzen for Page Pedersen.

349 "Bell Bookplate." (1) 13:254, December 1963.
Canting plate for Charles Bell.

350 "Bookplates." (2) 15:191, September 1965.
One is armorial which was engraved in 1732 by J. Skinner for Musgrave mentioned in *The White Company;* the second designed by Roy Hunt of Denver for Luther Norris.

BASF DIGEST [See **DIE BASF**]

BAZAAR, EXCHANGE AND MART

351 "Royal Book-Plate." 53:620, September 13, 1895.
Inquiries to be directed to John Leighton concerning "impression of Royal book-plate of the reign of George IV."

352 "Bookplates." E. J. Moore. 55:1345-6, December 28, 1896.
Correspondent feels bookplate belongs under the heading of "Library" and not "Bric-a-Brac."

353 "The Library. Book-Plates." (7) 60:38-9, January 6, 1899.
Various styles illustrated.

BELLMAN

354 "Master of Decoration." Arthur Adams. (12) 17:783-7, December 19, 1914.
Ludvig Sandoe Ipsen, born in Copenhagen, studied originally to be an architect and drifted into decorative designing which included title pages, headpieces, and bookplates, several of which are illustrated.

BIBLIO

355 "American Book-Plate Society." 1:11-5, March 1913.
Constitution and list of 18 charter members.

356 "*A List of Book-Plates by Sidney L. Smith.*" Winward Prescott. 1:15-6, March 1913.
Edition limited to 15 copies.

357 "Book-Plate of a Jester." Frank E. Marshall. (1) 1:16-7, March 1913.
"A showman born in New York City in 1832."

358 "Book-plates by J. Smither." Frederic Cattle and Frank E. Marshall. (3) 1:22-7, March 1913.
Questions statements made by Allen and Fincham concerning this early engraver.

359 "Notes." 1:34-7, March 1913.
Statement made that American Book-Plate Society needs membership of 200.

360 "Bookplates." (4) 1:38-41, March 1913.
Plates designed by Howard Pyle and engraved by E. D. French, plus two title pages for bookplate publications.

361 "Report of May Meeting." 1:47-52, June 1913.
Includes membership list.

362 "Book-Plate Collecting." William F. Hopson. 1:52-6, June 1913.
For those who collect there is "the keen excitement of the hunt, the pride of possession and the joys of contemplation."

363 "Book-Plate of a Colonial Poet." Frank E. Marshall. (1) 1:60-2, June 1913.
Plate for David French, born 1700.

364 "Story of a Re-Union." Wellington Reid Townley. (2) 1:64-9, June 1913.
A book dealer aroused author's interest in book-plates; he acquired plates of John Townley and later a memorandum book of this same early ancestor.

365 "Bookplates." (3) 1:75-7, June 1913.
Plates by C. W. Sherborn and S. L. Smith.

366 "Some Early American Book Collectors." Moses Primrose. (2) 1:77-84, September 1913.
James Logan (1674-1751) gave his library to Philadelphia; Thomas Prince's (1687-1758) collection became part of Boston Public Library; William Byrd's (1674-1744) library at Library Company of Philadelphia.

367 "Book-Plate Literature." Winward Prescott. 1:84-93, September 1913.
Excellent summary of periodicals and books representing many of the European countries.

368 "Exhibition of the Engravings of William Faithorne." Frank Weitenkampf. 1:93-4, September 1913.
Faithorne (1616-1691) engraved an occasional bookplate as well as portraits, title pages, and illustrations.

369 "Notes." 1:95-6, September 1913.
Pre-notice of two publications by American Bookplate Society secretary Carver.

370 "Mitchell Memorial Library." (1) 1:97, September 1913.
Article on Spenceley plate in *New Haven Saturday Chronicle* for July 12.

371 "Book-Plate Collecting." William F. Hopson. 1:98-103, September 1913.
A knowledge of the various methods of making and printing bookplates will add to the collector's enjoyment.

372 "Lettering on Book-Plates." Arthur Howard Noll. (2) 1: 106-8, September 1913.
Lettering not only helps establish ownership of a bookplate but if properly selected should be decorative as well.

373 "Bookplates." (4) 1:109-12, September 1913.
Plates by Graham Johnston and Franz Von Bayros.

374 "Book-Plate Miscellany." Frank E. Marshall. 1:113-6, December 1913.
Mention of several versions of a bookplate used by different members of same family.

375 "Book-Plate Literature." Winward Prescott. (3) 1:117-26, December 1913.
Additional names of publications in English and various European languages.

376 "*The Book-Plate Work of the Marquis Von Bayros.*" 1:126-7, December 1913.
Limited to twenty-five numbered copies; seven Americans have plates by this European designer.

377 "Notes." 1:127-31, December 1913.
The Biblio to close with this issue.

378 "Bannerman Sales." 1:131-4, December 1913.
Bookplates "sandwiched between 285 other lots consisting of books of all denominations" in sale at Sotheby's.

379 "Bookplates." (2) 1:136-7, December 1913.
Both etched by Sidney L. Smith, one designed by Howard Pyle for Edith Kermit Roosevelt.

BIBLIOGRAPHER

380 "Library Book-Plates." 2:183, November 1882.
Request for public and semi-public library bookplates.

381 "Book-plates." 3:48, January 1883.
Notice of first two of a series of illustrated articles on curiosities of bookplates in the November and December issues of *Printing Times & Lithographer.*

BIBLIOGRAPHICA

382 "Book-Plates by J. Skinner of Bath." W. J. Hardy. (6) 2:422-37, 1896.
Little known about this engraver who worked in Bath from 1739 to 1753; good sleuthing on part of author tracing various signatures and styles of "Skinner Sculp."

BIBLIOGRAPHICAL SOCIETY OF AMERICA [Papers of]

383 "Concerning Book Plates." Theodore W. Koch. (11) 9:3-20, 1915.
"A bookplate has been described as a name plate decorated, not a decoration defaced by a name plate." Background information, collectors, etc.

BIBLIOGRAPHICAL SOCIETY OF LONDON. NEWS SHEET

384 "Notes and News." No. 9:35-6, January 1895.
Grolier Club bookplate designed by E. D. French executed first idea similar to that proposed for Bibliographical Society device.

BIBLIONOTES

385 "Ex Libris."

386 "Bookplates of Samuel Pepys."

387 "C. W. Sherborn."

1953 [Unable to obtain.]
Source: *Bibliography of Bookplates Compiled from Various Sources* by P. C. Beddingham, 1962: "Three essays contained by *Biblionotes*, a typescript journal circulated among members of the book trade, London, 1953."

BIBLIOPHILE

388 "W. E. Henley, Poet." G. K. Chesterton. (1) 1:5, March 1908.
Picture of Henley's bookplate.

389 "History in Book-Plates." Dr. George C. Peachey. (3) 1:29-32, March 1908.
Comments on plates of Igler, Cardinal Wolsey, and T. Bradford, M.D.

390 "Robins Bookplate." (1) 1:79, April 1908.
Picture only of portrait bookplate of actress Gertrude Robins by Charles E. Dawson.

391 "History in Book-Plates." Dr. George C. Peachey. (3) 1:153-5, May 1908.
Discusses plates of William Henry Fitton, M.D., Sylvester, Lord Glenbervie, and Benjamin Bates, M.D.

392 "Bookplate of John H. Vincent Lane." (1) 1:190, June 1908.
Plate designed by Messrs. John and Edward Bumpus, who also created plates for members of English royal family and Queen of Norway.

393 "Bookplate from Ex Libris Catalogue of Herr Rosenthal." (1) 1:335, August 1908.
Woodcut dating to 1440.

394 "Book-Plates of Celebrities." Harold F. B. Wheeler. (10) 2:8-17, September 1908.
17th Exhibit of Ex Libris Society held in London "proved that bookplate has lost none of its popularity, notwithstanding the all-conquering motor car" which is pictured on plate of Hon. C. S. Rolls. Plate of Henry Rider Haggard has hieroglyphics rather in keeping with his novels.

395 "Bookplate for a Garden Lover." (1) 2:159, November 1908.
Picture only of plate by G. H. McCale which was awarded prize of a guinea.

396 "Ex Libris of Clement Shorter." (1) 2:199, December 1908.
Picture only of plate designed by Percy Home for books concerning Napoleon.

"Book-Plates of Some American Authors." Sheldon Cheney.
397 (4) 3:170-3, June 1909.

398 (9) 3:223-7, July 1909.
Very interesting articles.

399 "Bookplate by Leslie Brooke." (1) 3:194, June 1909.
Picture only.

400 "Bookplate of W. B. Slater." (1) 3:237, July 1909.
Picture only.

THE BLACK ART

401 "Engravings of Leo Wyatt." Ellis Howe. (15) 2:46-8, September 1963.
Taught pictorial engraving (bookplates, heraldic work) by George Taylor Friend; engraves on wood. His work is commercial as well as creative.

BOEKCIER [Tijdschrift van de Stichting Nederlandsche Exlibris-Kring, Wassenaar]

"Jewish Bookplates of Dutch Interest." Philip Goodman. (5) Issue No. 2, 21-6, April 1954.
Well detailed account of Jewish artists and owners from 17th century, through years when Jews sought and found refuge from the Nazis in Holland.

BOOK BUYER

"American Bookplates." Laurence Hutton.
402 (5) 3:7-9, February 1886.
403 (7) 3:63-5, March 1886.
404 (7) 3:112-4, April 1886.
405 (5) 3:159-61, May 1886.
History of bookplates as background to American examples, early colonial plates; major engravers including Nathaniel Hurd, Henry Dawkins, Paul Revere, Alexander Anderson (American Bewick).

406 "Book-Plate Collectors." 3:166, May 1886.
Names and addresses of collectors.

407 "American Book-Plates." 3:179, May 1886.
Ad expressing desire to purchase or exchange.

408 "Book-plate Collectors." 3:198, June 1886.
Names of additional collectors.

409 "The Original and the Imitation." (2) 3:234, July 1886.
Original George Washington plate from collection of C. Moreau and forgery courtesy of Dr. Swan M. Burnett, believed made by Washington, D.C., second-hand book dealer.

410 "News & Notes." 3:269, August 1886.
Note of receipt of reprint of Lichtenstein's article "New England and New York Heraldic Book-Plates" from *Historical and Genealogical Register*.

411 "Practical Suggestions for Book-Plates." (4) 3:377, November 1886.

Design by George R. Halm for bookplate which could be used on fine arts, drama, de luxe editions of a public library.

412 "Some English Book-Plates." (8) 10:19-20, February 1893.
Review of Egerton Castle's *English Book-Plates*. Austin Dobson's plate designed by Alfred Parsons "At the Sign of the Lyre," originally used as a tailpiece in volume of verses with same title.

413 "Some French Book-Plates." (6) 10:65-7, March 1893.
Review of Walter Hamilton's *French-Book-Plates*. Heraldic bookplates on wane after Revolution.

414 "American Book-Plates at Grolier Club." (8) 11:476-9, November 1894.
States collecting bookplates of comparatively recent origin and almost youngest of collecting manias. First U.S. exhibit, 1,200 plates, on October 4-20, 1894.

415 "Book-Plate Collections." Henry Blackwell. (4) 12:146-8, April 1895.
Excellent summation of publication activity in last 50 years, establishment of societies of collectors.

416 "Sewall Collection of Book-Plates." Henry Blackwell. (3) 12:231-2, May 1895.
H. F. Sewall of New York is oldest living collector. "Mr. Sewall has no bookplate of his own and does not exchange."

417 "Dodge Collection of Book-Plates." Henry Blackwell. (5) 12:288-90, June 1895.
Pickering Dodge of Washington, D.C., had small collection of 2,000. Washington and Baltimore at that time were "ungleaned fields and pastures new. To find a dozen plates of a kind was not uncommon." Another collector who had no plate of his own.

418 "Hewins Collection of Book Plates." Henry Blackwell. (4) 12:340-2, July 1895.
Eben H. Hewins of Boston began collecting in 1881, has 3,000 plates but none of his own.

419 "Clark Collection of Book Plates." Henry Blackwell. (6) 12:396-9, August 1895.
Dr. Charles E. Clark, Lynn, Mass., accumulated collection of 3,500 in 10 years. Suggestions for arrangement of collection given. Dr. Clark had two personal plates, both designed by E. D. French, and willing to exchange with "those owning good specimens."

420 "Libbie Collection of Book Plates." Henry Blackwell. (4) 12:444-7, September 1895.
Fred J. Libbie, Boston, had collection of 5,000 including complete Revere set; some used for Grolier Exhibit.

421 "Rowe Collection of Book Plates." Henry Blackwell. (4) 12:823-5, January 1896.
Henry S. Rowe, Boston, possessed second largest collection including those acquired from H. W. Bryant, E. H. Bierstadt, and Charles Dexter Allen. Possessed three personal plates, one designed by E. D. French.

422 "Charm of Collecting Book Plates." F. E. Marshall. (3) 13:79-81, March 1896.

Two great delights enjoyed by bookplate collector: surprise of discovering unknown specimens, and second, state of delight achieved when they are handiwork of early American engravers or plates of early patriots.

423 "Book-Plate of David Turnure." (1) 23:535-6, January 1902.

Bookplate for 2 year old boy by Louis Rhead.

424 [Bowdoin's *Rise of the Bookplate.*] 1902.

[Unable to locate.]

Source: *Journal of Ex Libris Society* 12:16-7, February 1902. "The literature of the book-plate is rapidly increasing, as is evidenced by the bibliography (helpful, though not always lucid in detail) in Mr. Bowdoin's book."

425 "Literary News in England." J. M. Bullock. 24:388-91, June 1902.

Last paragraph in the article concerns King Edward's private bookplate which was a plate originally done by George W. Eve in 1897 and 1898 for Queen Victoria and later altered to suit the King.

BOOK CLUB OF CALIFORNIA [See **QUARTERLY NEWS-LETTER**]

BOOK COLLECTOR

426 "Early Book Labels." 3:227, Autumn 1954.

A. N. L. Mumby seeks knowledge of early book labels other than those of John Bickner and Robert Hedrington, both of mid-16th century.

427 "Early Book Labels." 4:172, Summer 1955.

Identity of James Miller, whose book label "suggests the sixteenth century," is sought.

428 "Earliest Dated Woodcut Bookplate." Albert Ehrman. (1) 8:426-7, Winter 1959.

Plate of Telamonius Limberger, reproduced in actual size; Swiss bookplates described in Wegmann's *Schweizer Ex Libris* (Zurich 1933-7) No. 288.

429 "Earliest Dated Woodcut Bookplate." Albert Ehrman. 9:326, Autumn 1960.

Ex Libris woodcut subsequently used for broadside printed in 1498.

430 "Earliest Extant French Armorial Ex-Libris." Arthur Rau. (1) 10:331-2, Autumn 1961.

Jacques Thiboust's woodcut armorial stamp (1520).

431 "Earliest Extant French Armorial Ex-Libris." 11:212-3, Summer 1962.

Further details on placing date of Thiboust plate.

432 "Admonition to Borrowers." 13:211, Summer 1964.

Bookbinder John Shipp's admonition quoted.

433 "John Ruskin's Bookplates." James S. Dearden. (4) 13:335-9, Autumn 1964.

While no particular question that volumes actually belong to Ruskin, only one of the plates was probably used by John Ruskin himself as indicated by author's detective work.

434 "Book-Stamps of the Tollemache Family of Helmingham and Ham." Edward Wilson. (6) 16:178-85, Summer 1967.
One of the stamps used by the fourth Earl of Dysart is nearly identical in design and size with the Dysart bookplate in the Franks collection.

435 "John Ruskin's Bookplates." James S. Dearden. (1) 18:88-9, Spring 1969.
Book label thought to have been used by W. G. Collingwood in books givens to him by Ruskin.

BOOK COLLECTOR'S PACKET

436 "Book Plates." (5) Issue No. 10:49-51, January 1933.
Difficulties for the artist in presenting in an artistic manner the customer's interests.

437 "Ephemera of Printing." William A. Kitteredge. (11) 2:13-4, May 1938.
Bookplates included among "ephemera" are those of Bruce Rogers; John Updike and Rudolph Ruzicka mentioned.

438 "Ex Libris: Ephemerida Bookplate Prints." Dan Burne Jones. (1) 3:13-4, September 1938.
Essay on bookplates as works of art.

439 "Ex Librians: Book Plate Prints." Dan Burne Jones. (1) 3:13-4, April 1939.
Another essay illustrated by William Saroyan's plate which was designed by the author-artist.

440 "Bookplate Design." Dan Burne Jones. (1) 4:24, October 1945.
Illustration only.

441 "Lynd Ward the Magnificent." L. O. Cheever. (2) 4:4-8, March 1946.
As well as book illustrator, Ward is top bookplate artist, outstanding in woodcut medium.

BOOK-COLLECTOR'S QUARTERLY

"Check List of English Armorial Book-Stamps." H. F. B. Clements.
442 Part I 14:64-72, April-June 1934.
443 Part II 15:68-78, July-Sept. 1934
444 Part III 16:64-72, Oct.-Dec. 1934.
445 Part IV 17:36-46, April-June 1935
Alphabetical list of personal book-stamps, excluding schools and other corporate bodies.

BOOK CRAFTSMAN

446 "The Hand Printer and His Work." James Guthrie. Issue No. 1:1-17, October 1934.
Mentions *The Elf* and *Itaglio Book-Plates* among Guthrie's work.

447 "Design for a Bookplate." (1) Issue No. 2:28, Spring 1935.
Illustration only of plate "To William Blake."

448 "A Bookplate." (1) Issue No. 4:66, Winter 1935.
Illustration of plate for Geare and Daphne Vaughn.

449 "Bookplates." (1) Issue No. 4:77-9, Winter 1935.
"A bookplate, to be correct, should belong to the category of decoration."

BOOK DIAL

450 "Bookplates by J. J. Lankes." Midsummer issue, 1929. [Unable to locate; does not appear to be DIAL.]
Source: Irving Lew, 109 Broad Street, New York, "A Catalogue of Books and Pamphlets Relating to Bookplates," item #187, "wrapper 12 mo., fine, $1.50." No date on catalog but 1948 appears to be latest date of any published item in it.

BOOK EXCHANGE

451 "*Bookplates for Libraries*." Issue No. 248:25, November 1968.
"Printed in four colours, and limited to 400 copies, this fine book combines the highest standards of typography, graphic art, and production."

BOOKFELLOW

452 "[Norman Lindsay.]" A. G. Stephens. November 1912.
[Unable to locate.]
Source unknown; not in Muir.

453 "Book Plates." (2) 8:77, January 1925.
"Bookplate-collectors are less numerous than stamp-collectors, but they claim to be more artful and quite as honest." Muir indicates this article by A. G. Stephens.

BOOK HANDBOOK

454 "Samuel Rogers, His Illustrators, J. M. W. Turner and Thomas Stothard, and Other Friends." Harry Rycroft. 1:200, 1947.
Author had two volumes of Roger's *Poem* each bearing bookplate of Blair Adam Library with crest and name of William Patrick Adam, grandson of man to whom Rogers gave volumes (about 1834).

455 "Australian Book-Plates, Some Makers and Owners." R. H. Croll. (6) 1:381 *et seq*., 1948.
Brief historical review by Vice President of Australian Ex Libris Society. (See *Wilson Library Bulletin* 23:53-5, September 1948.)

BOOK-LOVER

456 "Warnings in Rhyme to Book Borrowers." 2:174-5, Winter 1899-1900.
More verses quoted from *Notes and Queries*.

457 "For the Bookplate of a Married Couple." Ford M. Hueffer. 2:34, September-November 1900.
Two stanza poem of no great distinction.

458 "King's Book-Plate." 3:135, May-June 1902.
Royal plate etched by G. W. Eve several years ago used by King Edward with small alterations.

459 "Motto for a Bookplate." 3:179, May-June 1902.
If to my friend,/My friend I lend,
My friend and friend/Have gained a friend.
If back my friend/My friend doth send
I shall retain both/Friend and friend.

460 "Book Plates. Address by Sir James Balfour Paul." (47) 3:396-404, November-December 1902.
Address given to Ex Libris Society; illustrations are the best part.

461 "*Book-Plates of Today.*" 3:565-6, January-February 1903.
Book edited and reviewed by Wilbur Macey Stone. Gives chatty review including mention of a few typographical errors.

462 "Book Plates." (35) 4:15-9, March-April 1903.
Great variety of styles; no text.

463 "Book-Plates." Malcolm Chandler. (3) 4:321, September-October 1903.
Reprinted from *Western Camera Notes*.

464 "Book-Plates." (13) 4:322-5, September-October 1903.
Illustrations only.

465 "Books Once Owned by Napoleon." 4:341-2, September-October 1903.
Three volumes in secondhand book store identified by "red circular stamp."

466 "Franks Collection of Armorial Book-Stamps." Alfred W. Pollard. (13) 4: 418, 422-9, November 1903.
Armorial book-stamps used to mark ownership, which "book-plates first rivalled and then, alas, almost entirely superseded."

467 "Bookseller's Plate." Emma Carleton. (21) 4:528-9, December 1903.
"The bookseller's label or plate is coeval with the earliest book-owner's plate."

468 "Book Plates." (24) 5:321-6, March 1904.
No text. Includes plates for George Ade, John Drew, Henry Irving.

BOOK LOVER

469 "Book Plates." (1) 1:13, December 1888.
Plate by Louis J. Rhead introduces series on bookplates.

470 "Design for a Book Plate." (1) 1:23, January 1889.
Another original Louis J. Rhead design. *Book Lover* readers may purchase it, have own initials inserted. Design copyrighted and cannot be used without permission.

471 "An American Book Plate." (1) 1:35, February 1889.

George Wharton Edwards designed plate for *Book Lover*, especially appropriate for collector of Washingtoniana or Americana.

472 "Washington's Library and Its Restoration." (1) 1:40-1, February 1889.

Mentions imitation plate of 1865; also attempt to restore some of original volumes to Mount Vernon library.

473 "Book Plate by Rhead." (1) 1:53, March 1889.

Another in special series available for use of *Book Lover* readers.

474 "A Classical Book Plate." (1) 1:60, April 1889.

Rhead design.

475 "Centennial Book Plate by A. B. Bogart." (1) 1:69, May 1889.

Another copyrighted plate, American flag in shape of shield.

476 "An Artistic Book Plate." (1) 1:79, September 1889.

Louis Rhead design.

477 "*Book Lover* Series of Book Plates." (1) 1:91, October 1889.

This series perhaps loses something because the plates are not designed with a particular person or library in mind; some seem much too large.

478 "Book Plate for Cultured Collector." (1) 1:115, December 1889.

Rhead design which, it is suggested, could be used for a leather stamped label with design in gilt by keeping circular portion of design and omitting the flaming lamp at the bottom.

BOOK-LOVER'S ALMANAC

479 "Carroll Book-Plate." Charles Dexter Allen. (1) 2:2 unnumbered pages, 1894.

Charles Carroll was last surviving (1832) signer of the Declaration of Indepdendence.

480 "Art of the Book-Plate." Henri P. du Bois. (7) 2:12 unnumbered pages, 1894.

Author unhappy generally with state of bookplate art in England and America.

481 "Recent Ex Libris." (2) 3:52-3, 1895.

Plates by Edwin D. French and S. Vigneron.

482 "Dedication Border: Eight Ex-Libris." (8) 5: opposite 4, 1897.

Almanac for 1897 dedicated to book-lovers whose bookplates are illustrated.

BOOK-LOVER'S MAGAZINE [See also **BOOKS AND BOOK-PLATES** and **BOOK OF BOOK-PLATES.**]

483 "Asselineau's Book-Plate, Drawn by Bracquemont." (1) 6:23, 1905.

Charles Asselineau, literary historian, had bookplate with a stork standing on a turtle.

484 "Book-Plates by David H. Becket." (2) 6:31-2, 1905.
Illustrations are plates for "Katie" and artist's own.

485 "Coloured Book-Plate by M. L. A. Girardot." (1) 6:33, 1905.
Bookplate for Archibald Younger.

486 "Book-Plate by A. de Riquer." (1) 6:34, 1905.
Illustration only.

487 "Book-Plates." J. Vinycomb. (3) 6:49, 60, 94, 1906.
Illustrations only.

488 "Book-Plate by J. B. Pirie." (1) 6:55, 1906.
Plate with motto: "Read—Mark—Learn—Digest."

489 "*American Book-Plates.*" 6:74, 1906.
Review of Charles Dexter Allen's book, "a veritable mine of reliable information."

490 "*Ex-Libris.* Monografie Willi Geiger." (1) 6:83, 1906.
Warning review of Leipzig publication.

491 "Sporting Book-Plates." Mrs. F. Nevill Jackson. (15) 6:116-9, 1906.
Among early artists to design sporting plates were Joseph Barber, Thomas Bewick, J. Scott.

492 "*Fifty Book-Plates.*" (1) 6:166, 1906.
Review of publication of plates designed by J. Vinycomb.

493 "Book-Plates by Bruno Hiroux." (2) 6:186, 208, 1906.
One is artist's own plate.

494 "*David Becket: His Book of Book-Plates of Twenty-four Original Designs.*" 6:204, 1906.
Review states, "The most characteristic of the plates in this book are probably the masks."

495 "Book-Plate by Alfred Jones." (1) 6:223, 1907.
Plate for Gilbert R. Redgrave.

496 "Book-Plate by G. E. Kruger." (1) 6:228, 1907.
Charles Spackman plate.

497 "Book-Plates of Some Actors." Mrs. E. Nevill Jackson. (3) 6:229-31, 1907.
Plates shown are for David Garrick, James Murden, William Charles Macready; other actors having plates were Sir Henry Irving and Edwin Booth.

498 "Book-Plate by Harold Nelson." (1) 6:237, 1907.
Plate for William Cumming Craig.

499 "The Late Mr. E. D. French." Frank Weitenkampf. 6:243, 1907.
Originally an engraver on silver, French later devoted talent to book-plates; also illustrated for Andre's Journal, Society of Iconophiles, Bibliophile Society. His hobby was universal language including Volapuk Society, Esperanto and Idiom Neutral.

500 "Book-Plate by Charles E. Dawson." (1) 6:243, 1907.
Alethea Broome plate.

501 "College Book-Plate." (1) 7:12, 1907.
Plate for Library of Trinity College, Dublin.

502 "Book-Plate by J. Vinycomb." (1) 7:36, 1907
Queen's College, Belfast, plate.

503 "Book-Plate by Otto Ubbelohde." (1) 7:42, 1907.
Plate for Dr. K. Schaefer.

504 "Book-Plate by A. D. Macbeth." (1) 7:44, 1907.
Interesting shell design for Natural History Society.

505 "Historic American Book-Plates, Concerning Their Engravers and Original Owners." Anne C. Justice. (11) 7:69-75, 1907.
"The book-plate collector finds that book-plates not only link individuals, countries, and governments together, but forcibly bring to mind the dead wits, buried monarchs, and faded beauties of the past."

506 "Book-Plate by David Becket." (1) 7:103, 1907.
Plate for J. Denholm.

507 "Book-Plate by James C. Paterson." (1) 7:119, 1907.
Quentin Campbell Ferguson's plate.

508 "Book-Plate by T. Sturge Moore." (1) 7:152, 1907.
Plate for George Harry Milsted.

509 "Book-Plate by J. Vinycomb." (1) 7:165, 1907.
J. N. N. Swiney's plate.

510 "Reviews of Some Recent Books." (1) 7:172-4, 1907.
Reviews of books by James Guthrie and Charles E. Dawson concerning bookplates.

511 "Book-Plate by David Becket." (1) 7:178, 1907.
Plate for J. M. Grant.

512 "Miss Jessie M. King." E. A. Taylor. (3) 7:196-201, 1907.
In addition to bookplates, this artist illustrated poems by Shelley, Spenser, Chaucer.

513 "Book-Plate by David Becket." (1) 7:208, 1907.
Bookplate for Natalie.

514 "Book-Plate by Pickford Waller." (1) 7:214, 1907.
Plate for Maud Waller.

515 "Book-Plate by Graham Johnson." (1) 7:247, 1907.
Attractive plate for Arthur Charles Fox-Davies.

516 "Illustrative Work by Robert Anning Bell." G. R. Dennis. (21) 7:248-63, 1907.
Mention is made of bookplate designs but none are included in illustrations.

517 "Book-Plate by Pickford Waller." (1) 7:280, 1907.
Plate for Natalie Mexia Capron.

518 "Dun Emer Press." Adeline Hill Tichell. (11) 8:6-14, 1908.
Elizabeth Yeats with assistance of Emery Walker set up this hand press in 1902; eight of the illustrations are bookplates.

519 "Book-Plate by Pickford Waller." (1) 8:39, 1908.
Plate for Edith Marzetti.

520 "Book-Plate by Pickford Waller." (1) 8:64, 1908.
John Brierley's plate.

521 "Book-Plate by Emil Sarkadi." (1) 8:104, 1908.
Dr. Reigh Milton Scar's plate.

522 "Book-Plate by James Guthrie." (1) 8:131, 1908.
Plate for Thomas Francis Richardson.

523 "Book-Plate by Pickford Waller." 8:142, 1908.
Plate for Sybil Waller.

524 "Book-Plate." (1) 8:170, 1909.
Ralph Straus plate.

525 "Book-Plate by Austin Osman Spare." (1) 8:173, 1909.
Plate for Pickford Waller.

526 "Book-Plate by James Guthrie." (1) 8:191, 1909.
Charles Hubbard Wells' plate.

527 "Book-Plate by Austin O. Spare." (1) 8:230, 1909.
Plate for M. Robert Boss.

BOOKMAN [London]

528 "A Bookman's Rambles. Mr. Gladstone As a Bookbuyer." Claudius Clear. (1) 2:51-2, May 1892.
Interesting comments on tactics used by the Prime Minister in attempting to claim bookdealer's discount.

529 "William Cowper's Copy of Robert Burns's Poems: 1787." Alexander B. Grosart. (1) 4:174-6, September 1893.
Illustration is bookplate which William Cowper "had engraved on his appointment as clerk of the Journals of the House of Lords."

530 "William Cowper's Copy of Robert Burns's Poems: 1787." Alexander B. Grosart and W. Craibe Angus. 5:16-7, October 1893.
Angus maintains bookplate was that of the poet's uncle; also questions qualities of one edition over another. Grosart concedes bookplate actually was uncle's but poet used it as his own as witness its appearance in books published subsequent to uncle's death.

BOOKMAN [New York]

531 "Ex Libris Exhibition at the Caxton Club, Chicago." W. Irving Way. 3:43-6, March 1896.

Books of double interest when bearing a bookplate as well as being inscribed by the author or owner in case of well-known individuals.

532 "Book-Plate of S.S. *Oceanic*." (1) 10:199, November 1899. [Not October as in Bowdoin]

Plate designed by Linley Sambourne, *Punch* artist, for use on White Star Liner; printed in photogravure, it shows launching of liner.

533 "German Ex-Librists." Gardner Teall. (16) 31:578-82, August 1910.

Joseph Sattler suggested as "Germany's greatest designer of book-plates" and "Howard Pyle seems to have a conservative sympathy with Sattler's creations."

534 "Some Government Bookplates." Marcus Benjamin. (6) 39:652-7, August 1914.

Description of plates used by Library of Congress, Smithsonian Institute, and various government departments; the Library of the Patent office is one of the oldest.

535 "Curiosities of a Book-Plate Collection." Sargent Romer. (15) 43:398-403, June 1916.

Bookplate with address but no name; French collector pictured man on gibbet; Willie Geiger's shows man with top of head cut off; Alice Babbitt Bennet used thumb print; "Hazel Mills Prescott—Her Husband's Book."

536 "*Bookplate Booklet*." 52:283, November 1920.

Marquis de Bayros feels bookplates reveal the character of their owners. Bookplate designers should draw out the book-owner "just as a doctor tries to form a picture of his patient's health and mind by conversing with him . . . art and psychology are combined."

537 "New Tradition in Book Plates." Babette Deutsch. (2) 58:271-4, November 1923.

Illustrations are work of Ralph M. Pearson (Taos) and Aaron Levy, who printed wood blocks on his own proof press.

538 "In the Bookman's Mail." 58:598, January 1924.

Calls attention to misidentification in Deutsch article of Edwin Davis French and J. Winfred Spenceley.

539 "A Hundred Years Old." (1) 75:197, December 1928.

Review of book in the *Spectator*, 100-year old newspaper; wood engraving of early editor, R. H. Hulton, looks like a portrait bookplate.

BOOKMAN'S JOURNAL & PRINT COLLECTOR

540 "Books on Bookplates." F. C. P. 1:301, February 6, 1920.

Periodicals as well as books by Walter Hamilton, J. H. Slater, W. H. K. Wright, John Vinycomb.

541 "Books on Bookplates." F. C. P. 1:321, February 13, 1920.

Notes on Irish bookplates and special Winter 1898-1899 issue of *Studio*.

542 "L' Ex-Libris." 1:321, February 13, 1920.
Belgian journal first appeared in November, 1913; last published in May, 1914.

543 "Books on Bookplates." F. C. P. 1:337, February 20, 1920.
Two French journals discussed.

544 "Books on Bookplates." F. C. P. 1:351, February 27, 1920.
More on French journals, especially one edited by L. Joly on imaginary bookplates.

545 "Books on Bookplates, Aubrey Beardsley." F. C. P. (1) 1:381, March 12, 1920.
Several articles on Beardsley mentioned; plate for Rainforth Armitage Waller illustrated.

546 "Books on Bookplates." F. C. P. 1:404, March 19, 1920.
Discussion of bookplate literature in Spain.

547 "Books on Bookplates." F. C. P. 1:422, March 26, 1920.
Comment on Pickford Waller book and James Guthrie periodical.

548 "Books on Bookplates." F. C. P. 1:437, April 2, 1920.
Review of reference volumes published by George Bell and Sons on English, French, American, German and ladies' bookplates.

549 "Books on Bookplates." F. C. P. 1:470, April 16, 1920.
Several Belgian publications discussed.

550 "Books on Bookplates." F. C. P. 2:123, June 18, 1920.
Good review of magazines and books currently being published.

551 "Confessions of a Bookplate Artist." 2:179, July 16, 1920.
Notice of Ralph Pearson letter.

552 "Bookplate Artist's Confessions." 2:182, July 16, 1920.
Letter reprinted from Alfred Fowler's *Bookplate Chronicle* written by artist Ralph Pearson, currently pig ranching in Taos, New Mexico. Interesting comments on relationship of public and artist.

553 "Books on Bookplates." F. C. P. 2:214, July 30, 1920.
Miscellany and *A Purple Book of Bookplates* discussed.

554 "Charm of the Bookplate." 2:384, October 8, 1920.
Comments on *Bookplate Magazine* issued by Morland Press.

555 "Ideas and Detail in Bookplates." 3:32-3, November 5, 1920.
Comments on *The Bookplate* and *Bookplate Magazine*.

556 "Bookplate Items." 3:47, November 12, 1920.
Hamilton's *Dated Bookplates* brought 9s at Sotheby's.

557 "Bookplates of the Marquis von Bayros." 3:50, November 12, 1920.
Quotes from article appearing in *Bookplate Booklet*.

558 "Where Can I Get A Bookplate?" 3:197, January 14, 1921.
Review of Alfred Fowler's *Directory of Bookplate Artists*.

559 "Taste in Bookplates." 3:207, January 21, 1921.
Book collector can have his own individuality expressed in bookplate design.

560 "Some American Bookplates." Alfred Fowler. (6) 3:392-3, March 25, 1921.
Sixth Annual Exhibition of Contemporary Bookplates currently in New York.

561 "Book-Plates in Book History." 3:415, April 1, 1921.
Quote from address of George H. Sargent, bibliographer of *Boston Transcript*, to annual meeting of American Bookplate Society. "The more one knows of the *provenance* of a previous volume, the more it is treasured. The bookplate is of especial association value, and forms a part of the life-history of a book."

562 "Bookplate Riddle." 5:135, January 1922.
Existence of two copper-plates for David Garrick bookplate prompts question of whether first plate was thought lost.

563 "The Bookplate of Samuel Pepys." (1) 5:168, February 1922.
Portrait ex libris reproduced from Alfred Fowler's *Bookplates for Beginners*.

564 "Bookplates and Their Makers." 6:22, April 1922.
Comment from *Ex Libris* on the publication edited by James Guthrie for English Bookplate Society.

565 "The Personal Motif in Book-Plates." 10:219-20, September 1924.
Affinity needed between bookman for whom plate designed and his books.

566 "A Bookplate by R. James Williams, A.R.C.A." (1) 11:227, February 1927.
Illustration only of plate for Cuthbert H. Cook.

BOOKMARK

567 "Raleigh Bookplate by Clare Leighton." (1) Issue No. 1, April 1944.
Tipped in copy of bookplate designed by English wood engraver, Clare Leighton, for University of North Carolina's collection of Sir Walter Raleigh material.

568 "Bryan Collection." (1) Issue No. 2, June 1944.
Family collection of local material marked by bookplate using photograph of Bryan memorial window in Christ Church at New Bern.

569 "W. R. Davie Bookplate." (1) Issue No. 4, February 1945.
Plate illustrated is that of early governor.

570 "By the Name of Bryan." Issue No. 26, October 1956.
Mention of Bryan collection and bookplate; new plate patterned after original designed for additional material.

BOOK-MART [Pittsburgh]

571 [Flyleaf Inscriptions.] 111:27, 1885.
Original stanzas for insertion on flyleaves of lent books.

BOOK NEWS MONTHLY

572 "*Little Books on Art.*" (1) 27:286-7, December 1908.
Review of Edward Almack's booklet on bookplates.

573 "Gordon Craig—Ex Librist." Gardner Teall. (15) 27:427-9, February 1909.
"All of Gordon Craig's designs for book-plates were drawn on wood and engraved by his own hand—even printed by him."

574 "Precious Riley Books." D. Laurence Chambers. (1) 29:246-9, December 1910.
Bookplate of Riley collector, Frank G. Darlington of Indianapolis, pictured central figure of skelton and the frame was a cobra.

575 "Origin and Object of Book Plates." Harry M. Basford. (3) 32:153-4, November 1913.
Brief general review of bookplates; in 18th Century "habit of using visiting cards as book plates was initiated."

BOOK NOTES [Rhode Island]

576 "Rhode Island Bookplate." (1) 10:208, September 9, 1893.
A lady's plate featuring an Indian arrowhead, flowers, music, art and book.

577 "Another Rhode Island Lady's Book Plate." (1) 10:219, September 23, 1893.
A plate "designed according to the laws of heraldry for a lady of the family."

BOOK NOTES [See **BOOK NOTES ILLUSTRATED**]

BOOK NOTES ILLUSTRATED

578 "Samuel Pepys Plate." (1) 1: Cover, Spring 1922.
Bookplate used as cover illustration.

579 "Recent Bookplates." Alfred Fowler. (5) 1:68-9, February-March 1923.
"The use of impressionistic bookplates will probably never become very popular because a book is usually something which leads us to deep thinking and deep thinking is not usually consistent with impressionism."

580 "A Russian Bookplate." (1) 2:111, April-May 1924.
Illustration only; name in Russian.

581 "Bookplate of Samuel Pepys." (1) 2:144, April-May 1924.
Illustration only.

582 "Bookplate of George MacDonald." (1) 3:5, October-November 1924.
Illustration only.

BOOK OF BOOK-PLATES [See also **Book-Lovers Magazine** and **Books and Book Plates**]

583 "Maisie Phillips, Her Book." (1) 1:Frontispiece, April 1900.
Illustration only.

584 "James Guthrie's Designs for Book-Plates." Joseph W. Simpson. (6) 1:11-23, April 1900.
These six designs "seem . . . to possess all that is essential in the ideal book-plate . . . art, beauty, and utility." Gives complete list (23) of plates designed by this artist.

585 "On Choosing a Book-Plate." Richard Stewart. 1:25, April 1900.
"The function of a book-plate is merely to state in an ornamental way the ownership of the volume to which it is affixed. . . . A book-plate is affected by three personalities, that of the artist, the owner, and lastly, that of the book in which it is placed."

586 "By the Way." (8) 1:28-43, April 1900.
An appreciation to artists for permission to reproduce their plates.

587 "Samuel Tinsley, His Book." (1) 1:Frontispiece, June 1900.
Illustration only.

588 "By the Way." Joseph W. Simpson. 1:53-6, June 1900.
Comments on articles and reviews in various other journals mostly devoted to bookplates.

589 "The Collector." Richard Stewart. 1:57-60, June 1900.
Author expresses unfavorable view of collectors generally, their lack of "culture" and emphasis on dollar (or in this case pound sterling) values.

590 "Six Book-Plates Designed and Engraved by Edward Gordon Craig." (6) 1: 61-71, June 1900.
Illustrations only.

591 "Gordon Craig, His Book-Plates." John Dore. 1:73-4, June 1900.
Complete list (52) of plates designed by Craig.

592 "Eight Book-Plates." (8) 1:75-89, June 1900.
Various artists.

593 "John Binning." (1) 1: Frontispiece, October 1900.
Plate designed by Joseph W. Simpson.

594 "The Book-Plate Society." 1:101-4, October 1900.
New Society for "lovers of book-plate art" as opposed to bookplate collectors of Ex Libris Society.

595 "By the Way." Joseph W. Simpson. 1:105-6, October 1900.
Comments and poems.

596 "Six Book-Plates by Celia Levetus." (6) 1:107-16, October 1900.
Illustrations only.

597 "Book-Plate Designs of Miss Celia Levetus." Richard Stewart. 1:117-8, October 1900.
Comments and complete list of plates designed by this artist.

598 "Among My Book-Plates." George May Elwood. (1) 1:119-21, October 1900.
"Of all the fads which come of innoculation with the microbe of collecting, there is none which offers more . . . , brings one into more charming contact and correspondence with choice kindred spirits, than does a . . . well arranged collection of book-plates."

599 "Book-Plates." (10) 1:121-35, October 1900.
Includes plates by Guthrie, Bell, Stone, Craig.

600 "T. H. Foulis." (1) 1:Frontispiece, March 1901.
Plate designed by Joseph W. Simpson.

601 "On Book-Plates." James J. Guthrie. 1:149-51, March 1901.
Descriptions of styles and requirements for making a plate.

602 "Hand Coloured." Oliver Bath. (1) 1:152-3, March 1901.
Before paint-by-number or the *Executive Coloring Book* there were bookplates to color by hand.

603 "Reviews." (1) 1:154-5, March 1901.
Volumes by James Guthrie and the "Triptych," a three-man design group composed of Wilbur Macey Stone, Jordan, and J. J. Chambers, reviewed favorably.

604 "By The Way." 1:156, March 1901.
American edition of *Book of Book Plates* to be published. Minutes of Book-Plate Society.

605 "Five Book-Plates by D. Y. Cameron." (5) 1:157-67, March 1901.
Illustrations only.

606 "Etched Book-Plates of D. Y. Cameron." Joseph W. Simpson. 1: 169-70, March 1901.
Complete list of his plates given.

607 "Book-Plates." (7) 1:171-83, March 1901.
Work of various artists.

608 "By the Way." (1) 2:5-6, June 1901.
Again emphasizes that Book-Plate Society deals with the "study of *art* in book-plates."

609 "Book-Plate Designs of Edmund H. New." Richard Stewart. (9) 2:7-27, June 1901.
Very pleasing work of illustrator of Issac Walton who did numerous "architectural" bookplates.

610 "Lettering of Book-Plates." Arthur Howard Noll. (1) 2:29-30, June 1901.
History of lettering enables artistic use in designing bookplates.

611 "The Society's First Exhibit." Lucius. 2:31-2, June 1901.
Etched plates by D. Y. Cameron favorite, along with J. W. Simpson and Wilbur Macey Stone, Louis Rhead, and many more equally well-known.

612 "Book-Plates." (6) 2:33-43, June 1901.
Illustrations only.

613 "Concerning Collectors of Book-Plates." George Cruikshank. (2) 2:52-4, November 1901.
". . . average collector does not collect beauty . . . ."

614 "Book-Plate Designs of Charles M. Gere." Richard Stewart. (7) 2:55-71, November 1901.
"A pleasing feature of the book plate designs of Mr. Chas. M. Gere is the quiet good taste which pervades them."

615 "William Phillips Barrett." Joseph W. Simpson. 2:73-4, November 1901.
Article reads like a clever "put on."

616 "By the Way." Joseph W. Simpson. 2:75-6, November 1901.
Review of *German Book-Plates*.

617 "Book-Plates." (8) 2:77-89, November 1901.
Includes admonition plate by Guthrie.

618 "Book-Plate Designs of E. B. Ricketts." (8) 2:103-22, April 1902.
Richetts credited with designing 200 plates within 4 years, shows influence of William Morris.
" 'The New Art in black and white work' in general, and book-plates in particular . . . import into their work the rule of golf—to win the game in as few strokes as possible!"

619 "Reviews." 2:123-6, April 1902.
Comments on foreign ex libris publications, C. D. Allen article, and Wilbur Macey Stone book on children's plates.

620 "Bookplates." (9) 2:127-43, April 1902.
Illustrations only.

621 "On Coloured Book-Plates." (1) 2:147, August 1902.
Gilding and color add richness when placed in handsomely bound volumes.

622 "Ex Libris." Richard Stewart. 2:148-9, August 1902.
With use of this Latin phrase, owner's name should be similarly Latinized in the case required by grammatical rule.

623 "Book-Plate." (1) 2:151, August 1902.
Designed by Douglas Strachan for George and Mary Cooper.

624 "By the Way." Lucius. 2:153-7, August 1902.
Lengthy quotation of article from recent *Inland Printer*.

625 "Notes." 2:158-9, August 1902.
Comments on collectors and designers.

626 "Plate by James Guthrie." (1) 3:facing 5, October 1902.
Color plate for Florence Gould.

627 "English Book-Plates." Stewart Dick. 3:5-8, October 1902.
Mention of work of current artists, many previously illustrated in this journal.

628 "By the Way." 3:9-12, October 1902
Includes poem "Index Expurgatorius" from *Munsey's Magazine*.

629 "Book-Plate." (1) 3:facing 13, October 1902.
Designed by Jessie M. King for Richard Rosendorff.

630 "Five Book-Plates by Harold Nelson." (5) 3:13-23, October 1902.
Charging knight in Evelyn Parton plate attractive.

631 "Book-Plates of Harold Nelson." 3:25-6, October 1902.
"One of few modern designers whose heraldic work is worthy."

632 "Book-Plate Society Notes." 3:27-9, October 1902.
Reminder of dues; note from Sussex.

633 "Book-Plates." (8) 3:31-45, October 1902.
Plates designed by Simpson, Craig and others.

634 "Book-plate by Georg Barlösius." (1) 3:facing 53, January 1903.
Illustration only.

635 "German Book-Plates." Stewart Dick. 3:53-6, January 1903.
Comparison of English and German bookplate art, as well as modern German artists such as Max Klinger.

636 "Some Remarks on the Work of Miss Rosie M. M. Pitman." 3:57-8, January 1903.
Praise for this artist's work.

637 "Three Book-Plates by Rosie M. M. Pitman." (3) 3:59-63, January 1903.
Especially like fine detail of Maisie Key Clarke plate.

638 "By the Way." 3:65-8, January 1903.
Comments on articles and books recently published concerning book-plates.

639 "Book-Plate by Mathieu Molitor." (1) 3: facing 68, January 1903.
Illustration only.

640 "Book-Plate Society News." 3:69-70, January 1903.
Notice of Second Exhibition in London and comment on exhibit in Norway.

641 "Eleven Book-Plates by German Artists." (11) 3:73-93, January 1903.
Andrews Needra plate by Richards Sarrin noteworthy.

642 "A Book-Plate by Richards Sarrin." (1) 3:102, April 1903.
Artist's own plate.

643 "French, Belgian, and Other Continental Book-Plates." Stewart Dick. 3:103-4, April 1903.

French designers disappointing; Belgians do good work though output small; also good designers in Spain, Norway and Latvia.

644 "By the Way." 3:105-8, April 1903.
Mentions articles in several other journals; verses quoted.

645 "Book-Plate by A. De Riquer." (1) 3:facing 109, April 1903.
White on dark background.

646 "Book-Plates of Leslie Brooke." 3:109-10, April 1903.
Artist has designed six bookplates all of country scenes.

647 "Four Book-Plates by Leslie Brooke." (4) 3:111-19, April 1903.
Illustrations only.

648 "Book-Plate Society Notes." 3:121, April 1903.
Exhibit included sixty plates by Edward Gordon Craig, as well as those of J. J. Guthrie and other well known artists. Mentions Guthrie's *The Elf*.

649 "Book-Plates." (10) 3:123-41, April 1903.
Some reprinted from *Studio;* one grim death symbol.

650 "Book-Plate by Arthur Robertson." (1) 3:facing 149, July 1903.
Illustration only.

651 "California Designer of Book-Plates." 3:149-50, July 1903.
Work of Mrs. Albertine Randall Wheelan displays "fine thoughtfulness."

652 "Four Book-Plates by Mrs. Albertine Randall Wheelan, San Francisco, Cal." (4) 3:151-7, July 1903.
Sketch Club plate depicts woman with Japanese hair style sitting astride a dragon and sketching.

653 "American Book-Plates." Stewart Dick. 3:159-61, July 1903.
Comments on artists William Edgar Fisher, Claude F. Bragdon, Howard Pyle and nearly a dozen women designers.

654 "Book-Plates of Arthur Robertson." 3:112, July 1903.
Versatile designer excels in armorial plates.

655 "Three Book-Plates by Arthur Robertson." (3) 3:163-7, July 1903.
Illustrations only.

656 "By the Way." 3:169-72, July 1903.
Elbert Hubbard did plate for William M. Elliott. Comment on articles from other journals.

657 "Ten Book-Plates by American Artists." (10) 3:173-189, July 1903.
Plates by Wilbur Macey Stone, William Edgar Fisher, Claude F. Bragdon.

THE BOOKPLATE [Stuart Guthrie, editor. English Bookplate Society]

658 "Line Engraving on Copper." Herbert Wauthier. (7) N.S. 1:3-12, July 1924.
Brief description of process.

659 "Observations and Comments." (2) N.S. 1:13-9, July 1924.
"A good bookplate is lineal in character, like type, decorative, as the compositor's art is decorative, a comely thing in that it is well-planned to fit its place among other law-abiding elements."

660 "In the Library." Z.Z. (6) N.S. 2:22-30, no date.
"What strikes me most about the modern critic, and it is probably true of critics as a whole, is that they do not arrive at conclusions, but at problems."

661 "Eight Bookplates." William J. Ibbett. (2) N.S. 2:31-4, no date.
Mostly four-liners to Keats, Shelley, Herrick and Yeats.

662 "Frivolous and Real Values." James Guthrie. N.S. 2:35-6, no date.
Judging on the basis of whether "drawn with the pen or cut with the graver" is "equivalent to judging artists by their beautiful blue eyes or the cut of their waistcoats."

663 "Observations & Comments." (1) N.S. 2:37-43, no date.
Includes untranslated excerpts from Belgian ex libris publication.

664 "Plate Printing." James Guthrie. (6) N.S. 3:46-55, July 1925.
Artist/author expresses personal approach to plate printing.

665 "About Hand Presses." (1) N.S. 3:56-9, July 1925.
Important alterations to wooden press made by William Jansen Blaew.

666 "Observations & Comments." (1) N.S. 3:60-3, July 1925.
Subjects include "small editions"; no printer as judge at recent Paris printing exhibition; handprinter believed unfairly taxed by having to "deliver five free copies of every book to the Museum and University Libraries."

THE BOOKPLATE [Sydney Hunt, London]

667 "Observations and Comments." (2) N.S. 1:1-3, 1926.
Deplores lack of "freshness, even youthful crudity" in work reproduced in year book of Australian Ex Libris Society.

668 "Jack B. Yeats, Artist." Sydney Hunt. (2) N.S. 1:4-6, 1926.
"His work is beautiful and direct, the outcome of genuine feeling."

669 "Bookplate." (1) N.S. 1:6, 1926.
Plate by Laurence Bradshaw.

670 "Advice on Choosing a Bookplate." Grace Rogers. N.S. 1:7-9, 1926.
Imaginary dialogue which says in short—leave it to the artist.

671 "Bookplate of an Undertaker." (1) N.S. 1:12, 1926.
Artist anonymous, as indeed he should be, for this plate, which is solid black, is box shaped.

672 "Bookplate." (1) N.S. 1:13, 1926.
Plate by Sidney Hunt dated 1924.

673 "Recent Bookplate Publications." Herbert Wauthier. (3) N.S. 1:14-7, 1926.
Comments on publications from Japan, United States, Germany, and Czechoslovakia.

674 "P. Copeli." (1) N.S. 1:18-9, 1926.
Artist of the "weird and wonderful."

675 "Forthcoming Publications." (4) N.S. 1:20-3, 1926.
Authors include Winward Prescott, Celia Fiennes and Agnes Swaine.

BOOKPLATE ANNUAL [Alfred Fowler, editor]

676 "Stanley Harrod." (1) 1:Frontispiece, 1921.
Artist's own plate.

677 "Bookplates of Frank Brangwyn, R.A." Haldane Macfall. (7) 1:11-21, 1921.
"Brangwyn makes a bookplate with such a musical sense of black and white within the narrow confines of his label that one feels convinced he would bring distinction even to a postage stamp."

678 "A Bookplate Problem." (1) 1:23-4, 1921.
Plate for "Steven Day, January 11, 1642" would appear to be for the early printer Daye.

679 "Sixth Annual Exhibition of Contemporary Plates." (4) 1:25-9, 1921.
American Bookplate Society exhibited at Grolier Club 130 designs by 53 artists; list by artist of plates shown.

680 "Bookplate Treasure Trove." Gilbert S. Perez. (1) 1:32-3, 1921.
Bookplate of assassinated (1897) Spanish Premier Don A. Canovas del Castillo found in volume in small Filipino village on east coast of Luzon.

681 "American Bookplate Society." 1:37-41, 1921.
Founded February 1, 1913, by 1921 had 170 members.

682 "List of Members of the American Bookplate Society, 15 April 1921." 1:45-51, 1921.
A. Edward Newton and many artists among membership.

683 "Bookplates." (13) 1:various, 1921.
Illustrations spread throughout the publication.

684 "Ex Libris Campbell Dodgson." (1) 2: Frontispiece, 1922.
Plate by T. Sturge Moore.

685 "Chiaroscuro Bookplates of Allen Lewis." Gardner Teall. (4) 2:11-19, 1922.
Chiaro (bright) oscuro (dark) woodcut plates printed in color; Allen also etcher of note.

686 "Sturge Moore's Bookplates." Alexander J. Finberg. (8) 2:20-9, 1922.
In Moore's work the emphasis appears to be on the areas of black.

687 "Seventh Annual Exhibition of Contemporary Bookplates." (5) 2:30-8, 1922.
Current exhibit has 222 designs by 75 artists; judges were Frederick W. Goudy, Charles B. Falls, and William Edgar Fisher.

688 "Notes on the Bookplates." (8) 2:39-49, 1922.
Notes on plates for Albert Einstein, William Beebe, Charles Osborn, etc.

689 "A Bookplate Exchange List." (1) 2:50-4, 1922.
Among those interested in exchange are Carlyle S. Baer, George W. Fuller, Alfred Fowler, Winward Prescott.

690 "Frederick Starr." (1) 1:Frontispiece, 1923.
Plate by J. W. Spenceley.

691 "Mexican Bookplates." Frederick Starr. (15) 3:8-14, 1923.
Particularly like few plates using Aztec and Mayan designs.

692 "Bookplates of Harold Nelson." James Guthrie. (6) 3:16-23, 1923.
Artist has unusual skill in manipulating not only black on white and white on black, but "grey passages."

693 "Bookplates of Horace Walpole and His Contemporaries." W. R. Townley. (8) 3:24-31, 1923.
Walpole himself had four plates.

694 "Eighth Annual Exhibition of Contemporary Bookplates." (4) 3:33-8, 1923.
Plates numbering 167 by 61 artists displayed; judges were Charles B. Falls, Wilbur Macey Stone, and George A. Licht.

695 "Directory of Bookplate Artists." 3:39-47, 1923.
List includes address, media, price, and how long making bookplates.

696 "Bookplates." (6) 3:47-52, 1923.
Illustrations only.

697 "Henry Pelham Archibald Douglas." (1) 4: Frontispiece, 1924.
Plate for 7th Duke of Newcastle by W. P. Barrett.

698 "Art of Sidney L. Smith." Gardner Teall. (3) 4:10-8, 1924.
Smith completed unfinished work left by J. Winfred Spenceley, did a memorial portrait of Charles William Sherborn; plate for District of Columbia Public Library is "most successful of Smith's figure designs."

699 "Check-List of Bookplates by Sidney L. Smith." 4:19-20, 1924.
Chronological list of 183 plates.

700 "Bookplates As Works of Art." Ralph M. Pearson. (9) 4:21-8, 1924.
Bookplates "may be *thought about* as bookplates . . . or they may be *looked* at as works of art."

701 "Sidney Hunt's Bookplates." James Guthrie. (8) 4:29-34, 1924.
"We should be able to see in Sidney Hunt's designs for bookplates the evidence of right principles and of taste which is willing to forego the impedimenta of affected bookishness."

702 "Bookplates." (4) 4:34-8, 1924.
Brief captions for plates by Cleora Wheeler, Charles B. Cochran, J. J. Lankes, and E. H. Tielemans.

703 "Directory of Bookplate Artists." (1) 4:39-48, 1924.
Artists listed alphabetically with address, media in which they work, approximate cost (from $10 to $350).

704 "Bookplate Exchange List." (1) 4:49-52, 1924.
Name, address, and type of plates exchanged.

705 "Ninth Annual Exhibition of Contemporary Bookplates." (4) 4:53-8, 1924.
Two hundred and forty-eight plates by sixty-eight artists judged by Wilbur Macey Stone and O. W. Jaquish.

706 "Bookplates of Dugald Stewart Walker." Gardner Teall. (2) 5:10-13, 1925.
Some of the fairyland delight of the artist's illustrations for children's books is carried over to his bookplate designs.

707 "Bookplates of D. Y. Cameron." Haldane Macfall. (1) 5:14-7, 1925.
Chronological checklist includes thirty-seven plates. "D. Y. Cameron's bookplates will always be eagerly scrambled for at auction; their high position as etchings will make them a part of the treasure of the times."

708 "Bookplates Designed by Robert Anning Bell, A.R.A." Walter Shaw Sparrow. (2) 5:18-25, 1925.
Chronological checklist includes eighty-five though artist created additional plates of which copies for identification are not available.

709 "George Washington Bookplate Myth." Charles O. Cornelius. (3) 5:26-8, 1925.
Original copper-plate in Metropolitan Museum of Art.

710 "Portfolio of Contemporary Bookplates." (12) 5:29-42, 1925.
Plates by several artists, including fanciful circular bookplate by George W. Fuller lettered "Ex Libris Arcanorum."

711 "Bookplate Exchange List." 5:43-6, 1925.
Names, addresses and desired exchanges.

712 "Tenth Annual Exhibition of Contemporary Bookplates." (4) 5:47-53, 1925.
Catalog of the exhibit by artist.

BOOK-PLATE ANNUAL & ARMORIAL YEAR BOOK

713 "George and Mary Gift Plate." Arthur J. Jewers. (1) 1:4-5, 1894.
Bookplate designed and presented by John Leighton to the Duke of York and his bride on the occasion of their marriage in July, 1893.

714 "Albert Durer." (1) 1:6, 1894.
Portrait of the "Great Master of Symbolism and Heraldry."

715 "Royal Standard." (3) 1:7-9, 1894.
Wales claims a quarter of the Standard of the United Kingdom.

716 "Imaginary Ex Libris." (1) 1:9, 1894.
For the Constitutional Club.

717 "The Library: Books and Binding." (4) 1:9-18, 1894.
"Book-plates in old volumes, I am sorry to say, are not always to be trusted as evidences of ownership, booksellers sometimes . . ." inserting them in other volumes to deceive customers.

718 "How to Keep Ex Libris." (2) 1:19-20, 1894.
Suggestions for mounting and housing a collection.

719 "Ex Libris Society of London." 1:20, 1894.
Brief description of Society.

720 "Bookplates." (4) 1:21, 1894.
Some designed by Leighton.

721 "Ex Libris Imaginaires." (3) 1:22, 1894.
Suggested plates for a pessimist poet and an optimist historian.

722 "Taxes Upon Vanity." (5) 1:23-5, 1894.
Among unusual taxes is one on armorial bearings which could include ex libris.

723 "Suggestion for Societies." (5) 1:26, 1894.
Plate illustrated for Ex Libris Society of London.

724 "Find of the Year." (2) 1:32-4, 1894.
Plate in question is that of Virginia Council of Colonial days.

725 "Hints for Ex Libris." John Leighton. (7) 1:35, 1894.
Illustrations include suggestions for Little Sisters of the Poor, Topographical Society, etc.

726 "Our Public Libraries—No. 1. Bibliotheca Leightoniana at Dunblane." (3) 2:6-13, 1895.
Library of Archbishop Leighton willed to the Cathedral of Dunblane in Scotland.

727 "Had Shakspere A Library?" (1) 2:14-7, 1895.
Doubtful if he had library or bookplate; Garrick Club utilized Stratford monument in bookplate.

728 "Did Handel Possess an Ex Libris?" (2) 2:21-3, 1895.
Probably not, but his family had a coat of arms and two plates are illustrated, one a portrait circled with music.

729 "Notes on Books and Bindings." John Leighton. 2:24-5, 1895.
Rule #7 includes "never . . . cast away the bookplates of a former owner, for they become matters of history, often in themselves extremely curious."

730 "Find of the Year: Book-Plate of the Chevalier D'Eon." (3) 2:26-39, 1895.
An exciting life spent in the service of Louis XV, often in female attire.

731 "A Plea for Styles of Design in Book-Plates." (1) 2:40-1, 1895.
"Chippendale is but a bastard renaissance."

732 "Ex Libris Suggestifs." (2) 2:41, 1895.
Illustrations only.

733 "An Englishman's View of the Works of Oliver Wendell Holmes." (2) 2:42-5, 1895.
"Each page is full of golden thoughts, pregnant with information."

734 "American Book-Plates." (1) 2:45, 1895.
W. E. Baille's plate engraved by E. D. French.

735 "On Signatures and Scribbling in Books." 2:46-9, 1895.
"The autograph depends entirely upon whose it is; the book-plate, even of a mediocrity, possesses some interest."

736 "Ex Libris Imaginaire." (1) 2:49, 1895.
For Edward Lightmaker.

737 "Book of the Year: Sattler's *Art in Book-Plates*." 2:50-1, 1895.
It contains 42 "original and suggestive Ex Libris" with an introduction by Friedrich Warnecke.

738 "In Piam Memoriam." 2:51, 1895.
Brief tribute to Friedrich Warnecke, dead at 58.

739 "Book Plate for the Holy Bible." (1) 3:6-7, 1896.
Pictures Adam and Eve, the Tree of Life surrounded by Zodiacal Signs, stars celestial and flames terrestrial.

740 "Dispersion of the Treasures Collected by Horace Walpole at Strawberry Hill." (6) 3:10-22, 1895.
Walpole spoke of his library as "his shop."

741 "Ex Libris of the Ladies." (7) 3:23-5, 1896.
Review of Miss Labouchere's book.

742 "Ex Libris for the Burns Centenary." (4) 3:26-7, 1896.
"I have invented arms for myself, and by the courtesy of Scotland will likewise be entitled to supporters."

743 "Worship of Heroes and Houses—The Carlyle Memorial Trust." (2) 3:28-9, 1896.
Carlyle was a bookmaker rather than a book-buyer.

744 "Ex Libris for the Philosopher of Fleet Street—Mr. Punch." (1) 3:30-1, 1896.
Letter to the publisher and design by John Leighton.

745 "Book-Plate for an Actor." (1) 3:32-3, 1896.
Proposed plate for Sir Henry Irving, though he has one.

746 "In Piam Memoriam." (2) 3:36, 1896.
Brief tribute to Lord de Tabley and Rev. Carson, who died within a day of each other.

747 "Leighton and Millais." (9) 4:4-13, 1897.
Frederich Leighton and John Everett Millais, who each held the post of President of Royal Academy of Arts, died within months of each other.

748 "In Piam Memoriam: George Du Maurier." (5) 4:14-8, 1897.
Artist-author perhaps most frequently remembered as satirist in pages of *Punch*.

749 "Jewish Coats of Arms." (7) 4:19-24, 1897.
"European heraldry only became systematised in the thirteenth century; but long prior to that date the Jews had used family and tribal emblems."

750 "Archiepiscopic and Episcopic Heraldry." (2) 4:24-6, 1897.
Details correctness of use of "mitre issuing from a ducal coronet."

751 "Ex Libris Suggestifs." (2) 4:27, 1897.
Two designs by John Leighton.

752 "Ex Libris Imaginaire." (1) 4:238-42, 1897.
Clever sketch of "Susan Grundy, *nee* Prejudice."

753 "Victorian Celebration." (2) 4:32-3, 1897.
Royal Standard and coin pictured "as they ought to be" including St. David for Wales.

754 "Book-Plates of Tower of London and the Bastille, Paris." (6) 4:33-6, 1897.
Tower plate used in the "Record Office when the Fortress was partially occupied as a despository for deeds."

BOOK-PLATE BOOKLET [Sheldon Cheney, editor]

755 "Editorial." (3) 1:3-5, November 1906.
First issue entirely work of editor, Sheldon Cheney.

756 "California Book-Plates—A Survey." (5) 1:6-14, November 1906.
Earliest California plate for William D. Olds, dated 1849.

757 "Notes." 1:15, November 1906.
Announcement of forthcoming Charles Dexter Allen book.

758 "Exchange List." (1) 1:16, November 1906.
Seven listed, including editor.

759 "Orville Dwight Baldwin." (1) 1:Frontispiece, February 1907.
Artist G. H. Gibon.

760 "Arthur Howard Noll." Juan Lapiz. (5) 1:19-24,27, February 1907.
Prior to entering the ministry in 1897, Rev. Noll practiced law from 1876 to 1888; his earliest bookplate dates back to 1871.

761 "Exchange List." 1:23, February 1907.
Five additional names.

762 "Editorial Comment." 1:25-7, February 1907.
Edwin Davis French, "greatest of American book-plate engravers," dead.

763 "Recent Work of William Edgar Fisher." (4) 1:28-32, February 1907.
Fourth portfolio of signed proofs recently issued (Baker's dozen) at $2.50 the set.

764 "Plates of C. Valentine Kirby." (6) 1:35-44, May 1907.
List of fifty-four plates by this artist.

765 "Editorial." 1:45, May 1907.
Bookplate Booklet will adopt the forms "book-plate" and "ex libris," hopefully avoiding the various forms appearing as in the January issue of *Ex Libris Journal*.

766 "California Book-Plate Society." (1) 1:46-9, May 1907.
Seven charter members, including editor, Sheldon Cheney, tentatively adopted constitution.

767 "Notes." 1:50, May 1907.
Winfred Porter Truesdell has published bookplate designs of Louis Rhead and Herbert Gregson.

768 "Designs of Mr. Claude Bragdon." Claude Bragdon. (2) 1:53-7, August 1907.
Check list of forty-two plates.

769 "University of California Plates." (1) 1:57 & 66, August 1907.
Commends use of bookplates for special bequest collections.

770 "Designs of Emma J. Totten." (2) 1:58-9, August 1907.
Amateur designer lists eleven plates created between 1898 and 1905.

771 "Designs of Mary E. Curran." 1:60, August 1907.
Designer from Los Angeles firm, A. E. Little.

772 "California Book-Plate Society." 1:61, August 1907.
First meeting held June 22, 1907 in Berkeley.

773 "San Francisco Public Library." (1) 1:62, August 1907.
Plate designed by Albertine Randall Wheelan.

774 "Editorial." (1) 1:63-5, August 1907.
Two San Francisco designers, Arthur F. Mathews and Albertine Randall Wheelan, have caught spirit of city's rebuilding after fire of 1906, as represented in plates illustrated for the San Francisco Public Library and Mechanic's Mercantile Library.

775 "University of California Plate." (1) 1:66, August 1907.
James K. Moffitt Fund plate designed by A. R. Wheelan.

776 "Notes." 1:67-8, August, 1907.
Mention of additional bookplate volumes from press of W. Porter Truesdell.

777 "Exchange List." 1:68, August 1907.
Four names including one each from France and Germany.

778 "A Visit to Mr. Spenceley's Summer Studio." (1) 1:70-3, November 1907.
New Hampshire village in view of Mt. Chocorua offers subject matter for landscape bookplates which were J. W. Spenceley's favorites.

779 "Plates Etched and Engraved by Mr. Spenceley from June, 1904 to January, 1906." 1:73-4, November 1907.
Previous list accounted for 135 plates; current list through 172.

780 "Editorial." 1:75, November 1907.
Booklet celebrates year of publication.

781 "Old California Plates of Interest." (1) 1:76-7, November 1907.
Design for plate of General Ralph Wilson Kirkham represents agriculture, mining, and commerce as well as two vignettes suggesting San Francisco Bay scenes.

782 "Designs of Arthur Wellington Clark." A. P. Steven. (2) 1:78-82, November 1907.
Dr. Clark's "style is chiefly in masses of black and white rather than line."

783 "List of Plates by A. W. Clark." (1) 1:83-5, November 1907.
Fifty plates listed.

784 "Notes." 1:86, November 1907.
California Book-plate Society contemplates winter exhibit in San Francisco.

785 "Theodore Roosevelt." (1) 2:Frontispiece, February 1908.
Plate only.

786 "Designs of William Edgar Fisher." (3) 2:3-9, February 1908.
Western designer in pen and ink who "drifted to New York City." Chronological list of 125 plates.

787 "Editorial." 2:10, February 1908.
Philadelphia book publisher has issued brochure of bookplate designs requiring only the addition of the individual's name. However, at least fifteen are poor copies from well known plates such as those of Brander Matthews and John Herbert Corning.

788 "Guild of Book Workers." C[harles] D. A[llen]. 2:11, February 1908.
There are 135 members, among them T. J. Cobden-Sanderson.

789 "Designs of E. J. Cross." Sheldon Cheney. (2) 2:12-5, February 1908.
Best known plate doubtless one for Jack London using wolf's head and crossed snowshoes. Cross studied under Howard Pyle.

790 "California Book-Plate Society." 2:15, February 1908.
At second semi-annual meeting Charles Dexter Allen made honorary life member.

791 "Book-plate Publication." 2:16-7, February 1908.
Mostly foreign journals.

792 "Notes and Exchanges." (1) 2:18, February 1908.
Harold G. Rugg of Dartmouth on exchange list.

793 "Henry Rowland Memorial Library." (1) 2:Frontispiece, May 1908.
Plate designed by Edwin Davis French.

794 "A World in Memory." Charles Dexter Allen. 2:20-5, May 1908.
"In the long history of book-plate art the finished work of no one man

has meant more, or contributed more to the raising of the art,—unless it were Albert Durer." The artist in question was Edwin Davis French.

795 "Rowland Memorial Plate." 2:25, May 1908.
Plate "achieved both simplicity of design and dignity, and added that decorative richness which characterizes the great majority of his engravings."

796 "Editorial." 2:26-7, May 1908.
Morris Co. criticized in previous issue states local artist Hammond represented challenged "copies" as original work."

797 "Book-Plate Curiosity." (1) 2:27, May 1908.
Two small circles (one-quarter inch across); one with owner's name, Jacobi Manzoni, the other with a small crown and an animal.

798 "Work of Albertine R. Wheelan." Sheldon Cheney. (4) 2:28-32, May 1908.
In addition to bookplates, Mrs. Wheelan designed costumes for David Belasco's productions in New York.

799 "Book-Plate Publications." 2:33-5, May 1908.
Chiefly foreign publications, as well as comments on the memorial volume on Edwin D. French printed by the DeVinne Press.

800 "Notes and Exchanges." 2:36, May 1908.
Four additional names on exchange list, including men from Scotland and France.

801 "Queen's University." (1) 2:Frontispiece, August 1908.
Edwin Davis French design.

802 "Designs of Margaret E. Webb." Wilbur Macey Stone. (2) 2:39-43, August 1908.
"MEW" signature appeared on pleasing illustration in *St. Nicholas* and other children's magazines as well as on bookplates.

803 "Exchanges." 2:43, August 1908.
Spain and Germany represented.

804 "Queen's University Plate." 2:44, August 1908.
Kingston, Canada, library of 45,000 volumes uses this E. D. French plate.

805 "Book-Plate Publications." 2:44-5, August 1908.
More foreign publications and suggestions that American and English collectors might benefit by the example of European activity.

806 "Editorial." 2:48, August 1908.
New York Public Library is forming collection of bookplates.

807 "Francis Tolles Chamberlain and His Book-Plates." Charles Dexter Allen. (1) 2:49-53, August 1908.
Letter to Sheldon Cheney extolling virtues of Chamberlain as individual and as bookplate artist.

808 "Chronological List of Book-Plates Designed and Etched by Francis Tolles Chamberlain." (1) 2:53-5, August 1908.

Seven plates including New Rochelle Public Library (Knowledge is Power).

809 "Notes." 2:55, August 1908.
Three American journal articles mentioned.

810 "Edwin Davis French Sale." 2:56-8, August 1908.
Top prices ($16) for plates designed for Henry Renwick Sedgwick proof; a few went for 25¢; total $290.90.

811 "Grace Elizabeth Lawson." (1) 2:Frontispiece, November 1908.
English artist's plate for her sister.

812 "A Tribute." Georgia M. Preston. 2:61-3, November 1908.
J. Winfred Spenceley died young "not yet forty-three." His strong belief was the Brotherhood of Man.

813 "Plates of Mary C. Lawson." Sheldon Cheney. 2:64, November 1908.
Young artist shows promise of attaining "ultimate place on a par with Sherborn and Eve."

814 "List of Members of California Book-Plate Society." 2:69, November 1908.
Twelve regular members, one honorary (Charles Dexter Allen), and two associates.

815 "Masonic Book-Plates." (1) 2:70-1, November 1908.
Comments from A. Winthrop Pope's monograph which originally appeared in three installments in a Masonic publication.

816 "Book-Plate Publications." 2:72-3, November 1908.
Foreign journals and American books mentioned.

817 "Notes." (1) 2:74-5, November 1908.
Comment on completion of second year of publication.

818 "Public Library Book-Plate." Sheldon Cheney. (4) 3:2-10, February 1909.
"Two fundamental requisites of a satisfactory personal book-plate are beauty and individuality. The public library plate should have the added quality of dignity of design."

819 "California Book-Plate Society." 3:10, February 1909.
Membership to be limited to "bona fide collectors and designers" and "commercial element to be rigidly excluded."

820 "In Memoria. J. W. S." 3:11, February 1909.
Three stanza poem.
"Treasure his noble work so nobly done;
Nature has only taken back her own."

821 "News and Comments." 3:12-3, February 1909.
Exhibitions, catalogues, lectures.

822 "Foster Book-Plate." 3:14-5, February 1909.
Further attempts to identify #281 from Allen's list of early American bookplates.

823 "Exchanges." 3:15, February 1909.
Three listed.

824 "Editorial." 3:16, February 1909.
Rumored end to publication of *Ex Libris Journal* lamented.

825 "Thomas Bewick." E. J. Crose. 3:17, February 1909.
In his work we "observe the strong, vibrating fullness of mother nature."

826 "Book-Plate Publications." 3:17-8, February 1909.
Books and journals in England, Italy and France.

827 "Work of Frederick Spenceley." (1) 3:21-4, May 1909.
Brother of late J. W. Spenceley also bookplate designer; chronological list of fifty plates executed from 1899 to 1909, including one for William Howard Taft.

828 "Plate of Meredith Nicholson." (1) 3:24, May 1909.
A prolific writer of romance, his best sellers "are too well known to need mention here, and his work as a poet is no less meritorious than his novels." (!) Plate designed by Franklin Booth.

829 "In Memorian, The Ex Libris Society." Sheldon Cheney. 3:25, May 1909.
English Society, oldest of bookplate organizations, disbanded after eighteen years.

830 "Engravings of J. H. Fincken." (1) 3:26-8, May 1909.
Chronological list from 1900 to 1909 indicates twenty-two plates including one for Geographical Society of Philadelphia.

831 "Plate by Cornelius Tiebout." (1) 3:29, May 1909.
Plate "not in Allen"; owner unknown but artist prolific engraver of portraits, landscapes and subject pictures whose work dates back to 1789.

832 "California Book-Plate Society." 3:31, May 1909.
Meeting in honor of Mr. and Mrs. William Fowler Hopson.

833 "Book-Plate Publications." (1) 3:32-3, May 1909.
Article on bookplates in Esperanto.

834 "Notes and Comment." 3:34-5, May 1909.
Bookplate collection under gavel at Sotheby's; American collection went for "ridiculously low" $622.40.

835 "Willi Geiger." (2) 3:32, 35-6, May 1909.
Controversial German artist some of whose plates "we cannot publish on account of our desire to use the United States mails."

836 "Book-plates of Mr. Hopson." Charles Dexter Allen. (1) 3:38-41, May 1910.
In 17 years Hopson created 100 bookplates. "Color, not perhaps considered by many as possible in the engraved book-plate, is in truth a very present and distinguishing mark of his work."

837 "List of Mr. Hopson's Book-Plates." (2) 3:42-9, May 1910.
Chronological list giving style of plate and method for years 1892 to 1909.

838 "Notes." 3:49, May 1910.
Frank Weitenkampf, print department of New York Public Library, directing bookplate display in Lenox Building.

839 "Note on the Wood-Engraving of George Wolfe Plank." Olive Percival. (3) 3:50-3, 70, May 1910.
"Mr. Plank in his wood-engravings is constantly romancing for us in a new, an individual way and about a number of things—past, present, and to come."

840 "Notes." 3:54, May 1910.
Lament for *The Butterfly:* "The good and the beautiful ever die young."

841 "Charles William Sherborn, R.C., an Appreciation by W. F. Hopson." (2) 3: 56-63, November 1910.
Sherborn possessed "supreme quality of beauty of line, sweet line, atmospheric line . . . it is the highest quality of all engraving."

842 "Notes." 3:63, November 1910.
Pamphlet published by Dr. Roland G. Curtin of Philadelphia on "The Book-plates of Physicians, with Remarks on the Physician's Leisure Hour Hobbies."

843 "To Charles William Sherborn." Sheldon Cheney. 3:64, November 1910.
Poem.

844 "California Book-Plate Society." 3:65, November 1910.
Sixth semi-annual meeting held at Hotel Stewart, San Francisco. Hopson designed Society's letterhead.

845 "Book-Plate of President Taft." (1) 3:66, November 1910.
Designed by Frederick Spenceley.

846 "Spenceley Memorial Book." 3:67, November 1910.
Printed by Torch Press on handmade Fabriano paper. Regrets no portrait or prints from original coppers.

847 "Newman Club Plate." (1) 3:68-9, November 1910.
Plate for Catholic student club designed by Adele Barnes of California School of Arts and Crafts.

848 "Notes." 3:69, November 1910.
Exhibit of Arthur N. Macdonald plates at Newark Public Library.

849 "Farewell." 3:71-2, November 1910.
After four years of irregular publication "as a financial venture it has not been a success. . . . Nor has the magazine been eminently successful as a periodical publication. . . . The friendships I have made are the greatest pleasures I have had in the Booklet."

BOOK-PLATE BOOKLET [Alfred Fowler, editor]

850 "Art of William Edgar Fisher." Sheldon Cheney. (1) 4:2-5, March 1911.
Fifth Portfolio of Bookplates issued by W. E. Fisher.

851 "Humor in Book-plates." (2) 4:6-7, March 1911.
Plate by Dr. Noll for minister shows plant silhouette of Jack-in-the-Pulpit.

852 "Venturesome Spirit." 4:8-9, March 1911.
Booklet originally edited by Sheldon Cheney reactivated by Alfred Fowler in Kansas City.

853 "*Indiana Book-Plates.*" (1) 4:10-1, March 1911.
New book has over 90 full-page illustrations.

854 "Book-plate of Maxim Gorky." (1) 4:12-3, March 1911.
Designed by Ephraim Mose Lilien.

855 "Charles Edward Clark." 4:13, March 1911.
Dr. Clark, enthusiastic pioneer collector, died.

856 "Columbia College Bookplate." Clara Therese Hill. (1) 4:14-5, March 1911.
Plate was first designed by Alexander Anderson in 1795; had also made anatomical plates and commencement plate of previous year.

857 "Notes." 4:16, March 1911.
Two periodicals mentioned.

858 "Exchanges." 4:16, March 1911.
Most exchanges specify plates by master etchers or engravers.

859 "Dickens Testimonial Stamp." (2) 4:18-20, May 1911.
Testimonial Stamps offered to public "to create a small income for the heirs of Charles Dickens, who are in less than moderate circumstances, although they might well be otherwise had the author's works been properly copyrighted and the just royalties received."

860 "Book-plate Collecting." 4:21-2, May 1911.
"A collection of bookplates is at once a luxury and a necessity, a pleasure and an education."

861 "Early Book-plates." 4:23, May 1911.
Bookplate verses.

862 "Book-plates by F. B. Siegrist." (1) 4:24-5, May 1911.
Young artist has had much experience in copperplate engraving.

863 "An Additional Check-list." 4:25, May 1911.
No. 126 through 137 of plates designed by William Edgar Fisher.

864 "Comment." 4:26-7, May 1911.
Exhibits by Rowfant Club (Cleveland), Society of Arts and Crafts (Detroit), Friday Morning Breakfast Club (Los Angeles).

865 "Book-plate of Daniel Dulany." Frederich Castle. (1) 4:28-9, 1911.
Opposed the Stamp Act of 1765 but otherwise took Loyalist side; plate printed in red.

866 "*Some Book-Plates.*" 4:29, May 1911.
Essays most of which originally appeared as press notices dealing with the Detroit exhibit.

867 "*Book-plates of Well-known Americans.*" (1) 4:30-1, May 1911.
Princeton University Press produced limited edition of 250 copies of well illustrated volume by Clifford N. Carver.

868 "Notes." 4:32, May 1911.
Exhibit in Glasgow to feature plates of British monarchs and family members.

869 "Book-plates by Miss Bertha Gorst." (1) 4:34-7, September 1911.
English etcher known for her views of historical places near Chester.

870 "Notice." 4:37, September 1911.
Exhibit of Water Craft Bookplates at Peabody Museum, Salem, Mass.

871 "Book-plates by Beulah Mitchell Clute." (3) 4:38-41, September 1911.
Prefers zinc etching process; some hand colored.

872 "California Book-plate Society." 4:41, September 1911.
Sheldon Cheney elected new president; Society to have bookplate exhibit at Panama-Pacific Exposition.

873 "[Editorial]" 4:42-3, September 1911.
Probes possibility of national bookplate society.

874 "A Well Known Book-plate." (1) 4:44-5, September 1911.
Plate of Anna Damer of Strawberry Hill fame and sculptress of George III and Nelson, designed by Agnes Berry, also a friend of Horace Walpole.

875 "New England Notes." 4:46-7, September 1911.
Several items concerning J. Winfred Spenceley.

876 "Notes." 4:48, September 1911.
Periodicals featuring bookplates mentioned.

877 "Aylward Plate." William F. Hopson. (3) 4:50-7, December 1911.
Plate executed by Hopson borrowed "without leave" by a Buffalo engraver to use as specimen.

878 "Triumvirate of Boston Designers." Winward Prescott. (3) 4:58-61, December 1911.
Checklists for Adrian J. Iorio, William A. Dwiggins, and Brainard L. Bates.

879 "[Editorial]" 4:62-3, December 1911.
Farewell again to *Book-Plate Booklet*. To be followed by *Ex. Librian*.

880 "Thaxter Early American Book-Plate." A. Winthrop Pope. (1) 4:64-5, December 1911.
Studied law under (President) John Adams and taught his son, John Quincy Adams.

881 "In Memoriam." 4:67, December 1911.
Minnie C. Holbrook, friend of J. Winfred Spenceley who designed her bookplate, died in August.

882 "Book-plates by George Moore." (1) 4:66-7, December 1911.
Boston designer who engraved plate of pioneer American collector, R. C. Lichtenstein.

883 "Notes." 4:58, December 1911.
Exchange list and comment on article for children's plates in *Delineator*.

BOOKPLATE BOOKLET [Alfred Fowler, editor]

884 "Second Annual Exhibition of Contemporary Bookplates." (4) N.S. 1:3-6, 10, January 1917.
Exhibit at Avery Library, Columbia University.

885 "Catalogue of Bookplates." N.S. 1:7, January 1917.
Work by forty different artists.

886 "Notice." N.S. 1:9, January 1917.
Winward Prescott announced publication of Society of Bookplate Bibliophiles.

887 "Minutes of Fifth Annual Meeting." N.S. 1:11-2, January 1917.
W. F. Hopson re-elected president; Alfred Fowler re-elected Secretary-Treasurer.

888 "Report of Secretary-Treasurer." N.S. 1:13-23, January 1917.
"The Society has no indebtedness."

889 "*Bookplate Booklet*." N.S. 1:24-5, January 1917.
Notes concerning revival of new series.

890 "Bookplate Affairs in France." N.S. 1:25-6, January 1917.
Announcement of new periodical and bookplate competition for soldiers.

891 "Notes." N.S. 1:26, January 1917.
Second Annual Exhibition scheduled for Cleveland Museum of Art.

892 "List of Officers and Constitution." N.S. 1:27-9, January 1917.
"The objects and purposes of this Society shall be to promote good-fellowship among the collectors of bookplates." Annual dues three dollars.

893 "Bookplate Exchange List." N.S. 1:30-2, January 1917.
Most exchangers seek plates by "masters."

894 "Charles Harvey Bentley." (Third Series) 1:Frontispiece, May 1919.
Bookplate only.

895 "Cuala Press and Its Bookplate." W. G. Blaikie-Murdock. (5) (Third Series) 1:8-20, May 1919.
Originally called Dun Emer Press, under supervision of W. B. Yeats' sister, publisher of *Broadsheet* and *Broadside*. Jack Yeats gifted bookplate artist.

896 "Bookplate Fantasy." (Third Series) 1:21-3, May 1919.
Written in olde English.

897 "Notes." (Third Series) 1:24, May 1919.
Comment on end of "grim-visaged war" and future bookplate contributions.

898 "Enrico Caruso." (Third Series) 1: Frontispiece, October 1919.
Bookplate engraved by A. N. Macdonald.

899 "Of Bookplates." James Guthrie. (Third Series) 1:27-31, October 1919.
"Beautiful prints delicately wrought by hand represent not only pleasure but value."

900 "Bookplates of Aubrey Beardsley." Georges Derry. (4) (Third Series) 1:32-42, October 1919.
"Unconventional but . . . decorative to the last degree." Chronological list from 1893 to 1898 includes twelve bookplates, all for individuals.

901 "Notes." (Third Series) 1:43-4, October 1919.
Request for information for a Beardsley bibliography.

902 "Bookplates by Henry J. Stock, R. I." James Guthrie. (9) (Third Series) 1:48-62, 64, March 1920.
Checklist of twelve bookplates all titled.

903 "Eugene Field on Bookplates." (Third Series) 1:63-5, March 1920.
"Whenever I see a book that bears its owner's plate I feel myself obligated to treat that book with special consideration."

904 "[Notes]" (Third Series) 1:66, March 1920.
Forthcoming issues to have "competent criticism of the modern bookplate."

905 "My Bookplates." Marquis von Bayros. (1) (Third Series) 1:68-75, September 1920.
Artist explains how he entwines owner's personality subtly into bookplate design.

906 "Lost Word Restored by a Bookplate." George H. Viner. (Third Series) 1:76-9, September 1920.
Biddle Law Library plate showed double-brackets; a biddle is an obsolete term for a double-bracket.

907 "[Notes]" (Third Series) 1:80, September 1920.
First year of new series completed.

908 "Iahannis Plate." (1) (Third Series) 2:Frontispiece, 20, September 1921.
J. M. Andreini loaned C. W. Sherborn copperplate for this illustration.

909 "Bookplates of Ludwig Sandöe Ipsen." S. Van B. Nichols. (5) (Third Series) 2:6-15, September 1921.
Greatest contribution to bookplate design was "perfection of detail."

910 "Bookplates of David Garrick." (Third Series) 2:16-9, September 1921.
A second copperplate appears to have been made with slight difference in design; reason for second plate unknown.

BOOKPLATE BULLETIN

911 "January Meeting." 1:1, January 1919.
Seventh Annual meeting of American Bookplate Society held in Avery Library at Columbia University.

912 "*Bookplate Chronicle.*" 1:1, January 1919.
Notes on forthcoming publications.

913 "List of Officers and Constitution." 1:2, January 1919.
Approximately 75 members.

914 "*Bookplate Magazine.*" 1:3, February 1919.
English publication edited by James Guthrie.

915 "California Bookplate Society." 1:3, February 1919.
Twenty-fourth semi-annual meeting will be in May.

916 "New English Bookplate Society." 1:3, February 1919.
Publication will be *Bookplate Magazine.*

917 "Bookplate Exchange List." 1:3-4, February 1919.
Name, address, and desired exchanges.

918 "Correspondence." 1:4, February 1919.
Letter from James Guthrie.

919 "*Bookplate Chronicle.*" 1:4, February 1919.
Notes on *Directory of Bookplate Artists* and checklist of bookplates engraved on copper by Arthur N. Macdonald, edited by Clifford N. Carver.

920 "Fourth Annual Exhibition." (1) 1:5, March 1919.
Catalog of American Bookplate Society exhibit.

921 "Fifth Annual Exhibition of Contemporary Bookplates." 1:6, March 1919.
Bookplates designed during 1919 to be exhibited in New York during January of 1920.

922 "*Directory of Bookplate Artists.*" 1:6, March 1919.
Information sought as to media used, design style, cost, how long in bookplate field.

923 "May Meeting." 1:7, June 1919.
Report of F. R. Fraprie, secretary *pro tem.*

924 "Report of Secretary-Treasurer." 1:7-8, June 1919.
One hundred three members in good standing.

925 "Kenyon Cos—1856-1919." 1:8, June 1919.
Artist, Society member, died March 17, 1919.

926 "Exchange List Additions." 1:8, June 1919.
Three added.

927 "Debt of Gratitude." 1:9, October 1919.
Thanks extended to George H. Sargent for his article on American Bookplate Society in *Boston Transcript.*

928 "A Dream Come True." William A. Beardsley. 1:9, October 1919.
Bookplate collection acquired from granddaughter of original collector at time of move.

BOOKPLATE CHRONICLE

929 "*Bookplate Chronicle.*" 1:1, January 1920.
New publication succeeds *Bookplate Bulletin* issued by American Bookplate Society.

930 "Fifth Annual Exhibition of Contemporary Bookplates." 1:1, January 1920
Grolier Club exhibit of plates designed during 1919.

931 "Century Bookplate Brotherhood." 1:2, January 1920.
Dr. MacDowel Cosgrave (Dublin) seeks one hundred bookplate owners to join, send 100 prints of their plates; packets of 100 different plates will be made and returned to the members.

932 "*Bookplate Chronicle.*" 1:2, January 1920.
Notes of future publications and acquisition of Marshall collection by American Antiquarian Society.

933 "Correspondence." 1:2, January 1920.
Mrs. Winthrop Girling reminds collectors of custom of sending two of one's own plate when asking exchange.

934 "Canadian Bookplates." 1:3, January 1920.
New Winward Prescott book limited to 250 copies at five dollars.

935 "Notes & Queries." 1:3, January 1920.
Queries by Alfred Fowler and J. T. Armstrong for help in identifying plates.

936 "At the Bookplate Exhibition." 1:3, January 1920.
Unlikely remarks overheard.

937 "Constitution of the American Bookplate Society." 1:3-4, January 1920.
Membership limited to 200, 190 regular and 10 honorary.

938 "Advertising Section." 1:4, January 1920.
Listing of various bookplate publications.

939 "Minutes of the Eighth Annual Meeting." 1:5, March 1920.
Meeting held at Grolier Club.

940 "Eighth Annual Report of the Secretary-Treasurer." Alfred Fowler. 1:5-6, March 1920.
December 31st showed 130 members in good standing, and more sought.

941 "Fifth Annual Exhibition." 1:6-7, March 1920.
Announcement of design awards.

942 "Sixth Annual Exhibition." 1:6-7, March 1920.
Suggests that artists submit designs during year to avoid being late.

943 "Bookplate Exchange List." 1:7-8, March 1920.
Name, address, and exchanges desired for sixty-four members.

944 "Advertising Section." 1:8 March 1920.
Bookplate printer Henry I. Jenkins only advertiser. Publications for Alfred Fowler.

945 "Memorial to George Clulon." 1:9-11, April 1920.
Honorary English member.

946 "Fifth Annual Exhibition." 1:9-11, April 1920.
Catalog of bookplates exhibited.

947 "*Second Year Book.*" 1:11, April 1920.
Limited to 250 copies at $2.50 to members, $3.00 to others.

948 "*Bookplate Chronicle.*" 1:11, April 1920.
Notes on membership and progress of Century Bookplate Brotherhood.

949 "Belgian Bookplate Society." 1:11, April 1920.
Announcement as originally presented in Belgian.

950 "Correspondence." 1:11-2, April 1920.
Elisha B. Bird seeks to interest bookplate artists in joining American Bookplate Society.

951 "Exchange List Additions." 1:12, April 1920.
Notice of George W. Eve book.

952 "Bookplate Screen." Harold S. Loeb (1) 1:13-4, June 1920.
Utility and beauty combined to display collection under glass.

953 "Minutes of the May Meeting." 1:14-5, June 1920.
Studio of Sara B. Hill site of meeting.

954 "Bookplate Collections in American Institutions." 1:15, June 1920.
Louis J. Bailey asks help in compiling Descriptive Check List.

955 "Advertising Section." 1:15-6, June 1920.
United Arts and Crafts handling new bookplates portfolio priced at sixteen dollars.

956 "Correspondence." 1:16, June 1920.
Ralph M. Pearson writes from Taos where he is a pig-rancher.

957 "Sixth Annual Exhibition." 1:17, October 1920.
Bookplates designed during 1920 sought for exhibit in February, 1921.

958 "Exhibition of Colonial Bookplates." 1:17, October 1920.
Exhibit in connection with Tercentenary of International Celebration of the Meeting of the First American Legislature.

959 "*Bookplate Booklet.*" 1:18, October 1920.
Comment on current issue and future articles.

960 "English Bookplate Society." 1:18-9, October 1920.
Journal, *The Bookplate*, to be edited by James Guthrie and hand printed. Copies sold non-menbers will not contain special plates.

961 "*Bookplate Magazine*." 1:19, October.
Some questions as to official connection of the publication with English Bookplate Society.

962 "Bohemian Ex-Libris." 1:19, October 1920.
Society of Ex-Libris Collectors and Friends in Prague formed in November 1918.

963 "Portfolio of Bookplates." 1:19, October 1920.
Comments on portfolio of Continental bookplates published, Wilbur Macey Stone preface.

964 "*Bookplate Chronicle*." 1:19-20, October 1920.
Fifth Annual Exhibit circulated to Avery Library, New York; Print Club of Philadelphia; Detroit Society of Arts and Crafts; Carnegie Library in Pittsburgh; Los Angeles Public Library; and Toledo Art Museum.

965 "Correspondence." 1:20, October 1920.
Query in French concerning plates dated before 1750 forwarded by Winward Prescott.

966 "Exchange List Additions." 1:20, October 1920.
Five.

967 "Advertising Section." 1:20, October 1920.
Collection of rare bookplates advertised by Denver man.

968 "Ninth Annual Meeting." 1:21, January 1921.
Proposal to be made to raise membership limits.

969 "Sixth Annual Exhibition." 1:21, January 1921.
To be held at Grolier Club in February.

970 "Exhibition of Colonial Bookplates." 1:21, January 1921.
Held at National Arts Club, bulk of items lent by American Antiquarian Society.

971 "New Exchange List." 1:22, January 1921.
Readers requested to send in their names and wants.

972 "A Fine Gift." 1:22, January 1921.
Baille Collection of approximately 25,000 items presented to Metropolitan Museum of Art.

973 "Woodbury Collection." 1:22, January 1921.
Collection including Edwin D. French presentation proofs given to American Antiquarian Society.

974 "Italian Bookplate Society." 1:22, January 1921.
Italian society just formed.

975 "Samuel Putnam Avery." 1:22, January 1921.
Society member since 1915, he died September 24, 1920.

976 "*Bookplate Chronicle*." 1:22-3, January 1921.
Notes on publications, exhibits, and other societies.

977 "Exchange List Additions." 1:23, January 1921.
Dr. Potter among those added.

978 "Advertising Section." 1:24, January 1921.
Notice that *Directory of Bookplate Artists* may be obtained from Alfred Fowler for $1.

979 "*Second Year Book*." (1) 1:24, January 1921
Plate of Florence O'Neill illustrated.

980 "Minutes of Ninth Annual Meeting." 1:25, March 1921.
Membership limit raised to 300.

981 "Address by Mr. George H. Sargent Before the Ninth Annual Meeting." 1: 25, March 1921.
Address printed in full as given by bibliographer of *Boston Transcript*.

982 "Bookplates by Sydney L. Smith." 1:25, March 1921.
Checklist with appreciative essay by Gardner Teall.

983 "*Print Connoisseur*." 1:26-7, March 1921.
New publication by Winfred Porter Truesdell.

984 "*Bookplate Chronicle*." 1:27, March 1921.
Print-Collector's Quarterly to be revived.

985 "Ninth Annual Report of Secretary-Treasurer." 1:27, March 1921.
Partial report, to be continued in next issue.

986 "Advertising Section." (1) 1:28, March 1921.
Ads for Ralph M. Pearson portfolio and Teall book on Sydney L. Smith.

987 "Minutes of Semi-Annual Meeting." 1:29, June 1921.
Article concerning dues amended.

988 "*Bookplate Chronicle*." 1:29-30, June 1921.
Notes on numerous publications.

989 "*Bookplate Annual* for 1921." 1:30, June 1921.
Limited to 500 copies.

990 "*Print Collector's Quarterly*." 1:30-1, June 1921.
Welcome extended to reappearance of this journal.

991 "Exchange List Additions." 1:31, June 1921.
Several additions.

992 "Ninth Annual Report of Secretary-Treasurer." 1:31, June 1921.
Ads of the Society's publications appearing in *Atlantic Monthly* "were particularly valuable."

993 "Advertising Section." (1) 1:32, June 1921.
Includes announcement of J. J. Lankes volume.

994 "Seventh Annual Exhibition of Contemporary Bookplates." 1:33, October 1921.

Bookplates submitted for the competition must have been designed during 1921.

995 "Claud Lovat Fraser." Haldane MacFall. (1) 1:33-4, October 1921.
Eulogy by friend who writes in vibrant phrases of this promising artist, dead at 31.

996 "Bookplate Exchange List." 1:34-5, October 1921.
List to be included in *Bookplate Annual* for 1922; subscription price five dollars.

997 "*Bookplate Chronicle.*" 1:35, October 1921.
American Art Sales furnishes valuable information concerning artists as well as object of art sold.

998 "Bookplates by Frank Brangwyn, R. A." 1:36, October 1921.
Reprint from *Art & Archaeology* concerning new Brangwyn book.

999 "Advertising Section." 1:36, October 1921,
Includes press comments on *Bookplate Annual* for 1921.

1000 "Seventh Annual Exhibition of Contemporary Bookplates." (3) 1:37-9, March 1922.
Full details of exhibit including list of artists and names of those for whom they designed plates.

1001 "Advertising Section." 1:40, March 1922.
Edition limited to 500 copies at $5 each of Alfred Fowler's *Bookplates for Beginners*.

1002 "Minutes of the May Meeting." J. M. Andreini. 1:41, June 1922.
Routine business.

1003 "New Bookplate Idea." 1:41, June 1922.
"Frank Hartley Anderson conceived the idea of having a bookplate to mark his bookplate collection."

1004 "*Antiques*." 1:41, June 1922.
Address given in Boston for those who want full particulars on this publication.

1005 "Catalog of the Seventh Annual Exhibition." (2) 1:42-3, June 1922.
List of artists who exhibited continued.

1006 "Advertising Section." (1) 1:44, June 1922.
Contents of *Bookplate Annual* for 1922 listed.

1007 "Eighth Annual Exhibition of Contemporary Bookplates." 1:45, October 1922.
Announcement of exhibit to be held in January, 1923.

1008 "*Bookplate Chronicle*." 1:45, October 1922.
This number completes first volume.

1009 "Recent Bookplate Sale." 1:46-7, October 1922.
Sotheby's handled J. C. Getting sale of 954 items. Details of interest to collector.

1010 "Society of Bookplate Bibliophiles." 1:47, October 1922.
Publishing society headed by Winward Prescott.

1011 "*Bookplate Chronicle.*" (1) 1:47, October 1922.
German bookplate designer Prof. Otto Ubbelohde died in May.

1012 "Advertising Section." 1:48, October 1922.
Continental bookplates for sale by private collector.

1013 "Eleventh Annual Meeting." 2:1, December 1922.
January 6th set as date in Little Gallery of National Arts Club.

1014 "Eighth Annual Exhibition." 2:1, December 1922.
Exhibit planned at National Arts Club during January.

1015 "Bookplates for Children." (1) 2:1-2, December 1922.
John Martin's Bookplate Book attractively printed and profusely illustrated.

1016 "Horace Walpole and His Contemporaries." (1) 2:2-3, December 1922.
Article by W. R. Townley to appear in *Bookplate Annual* for 1923.

1017 "Mexican Bookplates." (1) 2:3, December 1922.
Frederick Starr to have article in forthcoming *Annual*.

1018 "Exchange List Additions." 2:3, December 1922.
Three names added.

1019 "*Bookplate Chronicle.*" 2:3, December 1922.
Lankes, His Woodcut Bookplates by Wilbur Macey Stone will be reviewed in next number.

1020 "Advertising Section." 2:4, December 1922.
Includes order form for 1923 *Bookplate Annual*.

1021 "Eighth Annual Exhibition of Contemporary Bookplates." (4) 2:5-7, May 1923.
Listing of artists and plates they submitted for exhibit.

1022 "Advertising Section." 2:8, May 1923.
Malcolm Pava of Crescent Tool Co. advertising 500 American plates for sale.

1023 "Ninth Annual Exhibition of Contemporary Bookplates." 2:9-10, September 1923.
Request for plates designed during 1923 for exhibit.

1024 "Woodcut Bookplates." 2:10, September 1923.
Review of Wilbur Macey Stone book on J. J. Lankes.

1025 "What Art Means to Me." C. Valentine Kirby. 2:10, September 1923.
Prose-poem.

1026 "*Bookplate Chronicle.*" 2:10-11, September 1923.
Australian Ex-Libris Society formed in Sydney.

1027 "The Complete Booklover." Keith Preston. 2:11, September 1923.
Poem from *The Periscope*.

1028 "Advertising Section." 2:12, September 1923.
Publications about Dickens, T. J. Cobden-Sanderson, George W. Eve mentioned.

1029 "Australian Ex-Libris Society." 2:13, October 1923.
John Lane Mullins president of recently formed society.

1030 "Bookplates of Carl S. Junge." 2:13, October 1923.
Artist also designs type faces, ornaments and book illustrations.

1031 "66 Etchings." 2:13-4, October 1923.
Publications of Print Society valuable to beginner.

1032 "A New *Year Book*." 2:14, October 1923.
Publication of ASBC&D limited to 150 copies.

1033 "To All Bookplate Artists." 2:14, October 1923.
Requests designs for Ninth Annual Exhibit.

1034 "*Bookplate Chronicle*." (2) 2:14-5, October 1923.
Notes on *Bookplate Calendar* for 1924 and *Annual*.

1035 "Mount Fuji Exhibition." 2:15-6, October 1923.
Assembled by Frederick Starr and shown in 1922 at Chicago.

1036 "Advertising." 2:16, October 1923.
Alfred Fowler publications.

1037 "Minutes of Twelfth Annual Meeting of the American Bookplate Society." 2:17, February 1924.
Less than dozen members seem to have attended.

1038 "Twelfth Annual Report of Secretary-Treasurer." (1) 2:17-9, February 1924.
Membership at 147 and a "small credit balance in the bank."

1039 "Bookplate Values." 2:19-20, February 1924.
Furman collection sold in two parts at Walpole Galleries. Allen's "ordinary edition" of *American Bookplates* sold for $10, limited for $35 (75 copies de luxe edition), Fincham's *Artists and Engravers* for $2.50.

1040 "Ninth Annual Exhibition of Contemporary Bookplates." (3) 2:21-4, April 1924.
Award winners listed and alphabetical list by artist of plates exhibited A to Noll.

1041 "Report of Secretary-Treasurer of American Bookplate Society, Before Regular Semi-Annual Meeting, May Third, 1924." 2:25, June 1924.
Membership at 120.

1042 "New Art Monograph." 2:26, June 1924.
Art of Hesketh Hubbard by Major Haldane Macfall features bookplate designed by this artist printed within the front cover.

1043 "Catalogue of Ninth Annual Exhibition." (1) 2:26, June 1924.
List concluded.

1044 "Bookplate Values." 2:27-8, June 1924.

Low prices at Furman sale attributed to inadequate advertising with consequent small attendance and little competition.

1045 "New Bookplate Exchange List." 2:29, September 1924.
New list will appear in 1925 *Annual* at five dollars a copy.

1046 "Tenth Annual Exhibition." 2:29, September 1924.
Request for bookplates designed during 1924.

1047 "Franz Von Bayros." 2:29, September 1924.
Artist died during April in Vienna.

1048 "English Bookplate Society." 2:29, September 1924.
New Series of *The Bookplate* is official journal.

1049 "*American Graphic Art.*" 2:30, September 1924.
New, enlarged edition of Frank Weitenkampf's text.

1050 "Print Society." E. Hesketh Hubbard. 2:30-1, September 1924.
English society sponsors public exhibitions, circulating portfolios and publications.

1051 "Don'ts for Bookplate Beginners." Harold W. Kearney. 2:31, September 1924.
Directed at the beginning designer.

1052 "Advertising Section." 2:32, September 1924.
New Fowler publication, *Golden Galleon*, notice; request by Charles Dexter Allen for Allen bookplates.

1053 "Tenth Annual Exhibition." 2:33, November 1924.
Exhibit scheduled for January in New York.

1054 "*Bookplate Chronicle*." 2:33-4, November 1924.
Gordon Craig's *Nothing Or The Bookplate* to be published by Curwen Press.

1055 "Bookplate Gift." (1) 2:34-5, November 1924.
Dudley C. Meyers presented bookplate designed by Carl S. Junge for use of the Oak Park Public Library.

1056 "Don'ts for Bookplate Beginners." Harold W. Kearney. 2:34-5, November 1924.
Simple suggestions for the beginning engraver.

1057 "Modern American Bookplates." 2:35, November 1924.
Excerpts from bookplate chapter in Weitenkampf's *American Graphic Art*.

1058 "Minutes of Thirteenth Annual Meeting." J. M. Andreini. 2:37, April 1925.
Apparently four members present; bookplate exhibit postponed due to president's illness.

1059 "Thirteenth Annual Report of Secretary-Treasurer." Alfred Fowler. 2:37-8, April 1925.
Society had small ad in *Atlantic Monthly* for December 1924.

1060 "Tenth Annual Exhibition of Contemporary Bookplates." (4) 2:38-41, April 1925.

Alphabetical list by artist.

1061 "American Bookplate Society." (1) 2:41-3, April 1925.

Society formed in December 1911. Constitution consisting of seven brief articles printed.

BOOKPLATE COLLECTORS CLUB

[Unable to locate.]

Source: Dr. S. X. Radbill who noted Annual for 1946.

BOOK-PLATE COLLECTOR'S MISCELLANY [Supplement of **WESTERN ANTIQUARY**]

1062 "Bibliography of Book-Plates." J. Roberts Brown and H. W. Fincham. 9:2-4, 1890.

Books and articles including Rev. Parson's article of 1837 and illustration of bookplate from Dibdin book of 1838.

1063 "Book Plate Collector's Miscellany." 9:5, 1890.

Notice of new supplement to *Western Antiquary*.

1064 "Book-Plate Bibliography." Rev. Carson. 9:5, 1890.

Eight additional items.

1065 "To the Editor." 9:5, 1890.

J. R. Brown thanks Rev. Carson for transcript of Rev. Parson's article which he had never seen because it wasn't in the National Library.

1066 "On Book-Plates." Rev. Daniel Parson. 9:6-7, 1890.

Article which appeared originally in *Third Annual Report of Proceedings of Oxford University Archaeological and Heraldic Society*, 1837.

1067 "Quaint and Humorous Mottoes on Book-Plates." Walter Hamilton. 9:7-8, 1890.

Includes "Book-Plate's Petition."

1068 "Quaint and Humorous Mottoes on Book-Plates." Walter Hamilton. 10:9-10, 1890 (July).

Again "A Pleader to the Needer When a Reader."

1069 "Book Plate Notes & Queries." (2) 10:10-2, 1890 (July).

Illustrations are William Robinson plate by Sherborn and one for Sir Thomas Tresame with date 1585.

1070 "Quaint and Humorous Mottoes on Book-Plates." Walter Hamilton. 10:13-6, 1890 (August).

Variety of shorter verses in several languages.

1071 "Editorial." W. H. K. Wright. (4) 10:16, 1890 (August).

Andrew W. Tuer submitted "very quaint" plates by his "humourous artist-friend, W. H. Hooper."

1072 "A Few Additional Mottoes on Book-Plates." Gerald Ponsonby. 10:17, 1890.
Mottoes with sources.

1073 "Library Interior. Literary and Book-Pile Book-Plates." 10:18, 1890.
Arthur Vicars' letter soliciting help in compiling list for catalogue he hopes to print.

1074 "Moules—Ex Libris. Book-Plate Notes." 10:18, 1890.
Note from James R. Brown.

1075 "Additional Bibliographical Notes." H. W. Fincham. 10:18, 1890.
English and foreign language entries.

1076 "Query—Unnamed Book-Plate." 10:18-9, 1890.
James W. Lloyd describes plate of 1687.

1077 "Tresham Book-Plates." 10:19, 1890.
Correction of motto translation and description of quartering.

1078 "Book Plates of Elias Ashmole." 10:19, 1890.
"Plate exists in only 14 out of more than 1500 volumes of Ashmole's library; . . . apparently only found in the M.S. volumes."

1079 "Dictionary of English Book-Collectors." 10:19-20, 1890.
Details of publication given by Bernard Quaritch.

1080 "Book-Plate Notes." 10:20, 1890.
Mention of December 1890 article edited by J. G. Howard.

1081 "Early Book-Plate Reference." 10:20, 1890.
Dublin article dated 1720.

1082 "List of Book-Plate Collectors." 10:20, 1890.
Almost eighty listed.

1083 "Supplemental Notes on Book-Plate Mottoes, and Inscriptions." Walter Hamilton. 10:21-3, 1891 (?)
Small is the wren,/Black is the rook,
Great is the sinner,/That steals this book.

1084 "Book-Plates Stanzas." H. W. Fincham. 10:23-4, 1891.
In part: Shun, oh, shun the devil's hook
Baited with this borrow'd book!

1085 "Book-Plate Illustrations." (2) 10:24, 1891.
Plates for Sir Charles Frederick and Martha Bartlett.

1086 "Modern Dated Book-Plates." Walter Hamilton. 10:25-6, 1891.
Listed by date, name, style and motto.

1087 "Joseph Barber." James Roberts Brown. 10:27-9, 1891.
Bookseller and copperplate printer, Barber had bookplate "done for him by his friend Bewick" as well as two business plates.

1088 "Miscellaneous Notes." 10:29-32, 1891.
Items concerning plates of Martha Bartlett, Thomas Cook, Wilmer, Tresham, and the Ex Libris Society.

1089 "Modern Dated Book-Plates." Walter Hamilton. 10:33-4, 1891.
Continuation from 1807 to 1819.

1090 "Book Plates." 10:35-6, 1891
Article from the *Daily Chronicle*, April 1, 1891.

1091 "Some West Country Book-Plates." Alfred Wallis. 10:36-8, 1891.
Collector describes some of his "hundred or two of ex libris."

1092 "Curious Book-Plate." 10:38, 1891.
Item from *Notes and Queries*, February *1791*!

1093 "Ex Libris Society." W. H. K. Wright. 10:38, 1891.
Two hundred members sought, next meeting planned for May.

1094 "Modern Dated Book-Plates." Walter Hamilton. 10:39-41, 1891.
List continued from 1820 to 1840.

1095 "List of Subscribers to Joseph Barber's Copper-Plate Engraving of a Statue of James II." James Roberts Brown. 10:42-3, 1891.
About 150 names.

1096 "Modern Dated Book-Plates." 10:43, 1891.
Additional information on William Beauchamp Lygon plate to place plate at earlier date.

1097 "Adam Book-Plates." 10:43, 1891.
Two plates pasted one over the other with exact same name but different arms.

1098 "Book-Plate of Samuel Knight, Esq." (1) 10:43, 1891.
Interesting plate for architect, with hawk.

1099 "Book-Plate of H. Stacy Marks, Esq." (1) 10:43, 1891.
Designed about 1864-5 by Marks, plate features a jester "moralising on a skull."

1100 "Additions to Book-Plate Bibliography." James Roberts Brown, H. W. Fincham, R. C. Lichtenstein, *et al.* 10:44, 1891.
Books, magazines and newspaper items.

1101 "Ex Libris Society." 10:44, 1891.
Society established and journal to be published; next Supplement will be last.

1102 "Council of Ex Libris Society." 10:44, 1891.
Fifteen elected including Leighton, J. R. Brown, R. Day, Fincham, Hamilton, Jewers, Lichtenstein, Sherborn and Vicars.

1103 "Modern Dated Book-Plates." Walter Hamilton. 10:45-6, 1891.
List completed through 1850.

1104 "Index to *Book Plate Collector's Miscellany*." 10:46, 1891.
Brief index (half page).

1105 "Ex Libris Society." 10:47-8, 1891.
"The following Gentlemen, and Institutions are identified with the

newly-formed" Society; however, of 137 members there are four maiden ladies and one matron.

1106 "Public Library Notice." W. H. K. Wright. 10:48, 1891.
Request for bookplates for exhibit at forthcoming annual meeting of Library Association.

BOOKPLATE COLLECTORS NEWS

1107 "Letter from the Editor." Issue No. 1:1, October 1956.
A. B. Keeves outlines scope of publication he will issue from London.

1108 "Forthcoming Bookplate Exhibition." Issue No. 1:1-2, October 1956.
French bookplates of 16th and 17th century to be shown at Keeves' home Sunday through Friday, November 4-9.

1109 "Sale List." Issue No. 1:2-5, October 1956.
Priced list of sale items includes English and foreign bookplates as well as books and catalogues.

1110 "Editorial." Issue No. 2:6-8, January 1957.
Exhibition well received; overwhelmed with exchange requests; limited number of serious collectors will not permit BCN to be more than "duplicate brochure" with subscription rate of ten shillings.

1111 "Random Notes and News." Issue No. 2:8-10, January 1957.
Philip Goodman sent copy of recent publication "American Jewish Bookplates"; Philip Beddingham promises article on bookplate designers.

1112 "Name for Bookplate Collectors." Issue No. 2:10-11, January 1957.
"Phil E Brist," meaning "lover of bookplates" suggested.

1113 "Sale List." Issue No. 2:11-4, January 1957.
Also includes wanted items at three pence per word.

1114 "Editorial." Issue No. 3:15-9, April 1957.
Those who are missing pages nineteen onwards of the current issue are thus reminded that payment for their subscription has not been received.

1115 "Subscribers to the B.C.N." Issue No. 2:19, April 1957.
Names of twenty-five subscribers from England, Sweden, Holland, Portugal, Spain, Poland, U.S.A., Dutch West Indies, Belgium, Italy, Denmark, Norway, Germany.

1116 "Recent Publications Reviewed." Issue No. 3:19-21, April 1957.
Publications from Poland, South Africa, etc.

1117 "Joan Hassall R. E." Issue No. 3:21-2, April 1957.
Brief biographical sketch and chronological checklist of sixteen bookplates executed by this fine artist.

1118 "Random Notes and News." Issue No. 3:22-3, April 1957.
Fifth European Ex Libris Congress scheduled July 25-28 in Amsterdam.

1119 "How Many Different Bookplates Are There?" Issue No. 3:24-6, April 1957.
In addition to narrative, a table is given in fifty year increments from 1450 to 1956 for England, France, Germany and "other countries."

1120 "Advertisements." Issue No. 3:26, April 1957.
Four individuals list wants or exchanges.

1121 "Editorial." Issue No. 4:27-8, July 1957.
Comments on difficulties and requirements for continued publication.

1122 "Subscribers to the B.C.N." Issue No. 4:28-9, July 1957.
Membership list continued through fifty.

1123 "Stephen Gooden (1892-1955)." P. Beddingham. Issue No. 4:29-31, July 1957.
Biographical sketch and chronological list of plates executed.

1124 "Value of Bookplates—Part 1." Issue No. 4:31-3, July 1957.
Another chart presented affixing price in excess of one pound to 5,500 bookplates, 216,000 worth less than one shilling; editor feels values compared with those for coins and stamps.

1125 "How I Became An Ex Libris Artist." Sara Eugenia Blake. Issue No. 4:33-5, July 1957.
Confession presented informally as if in conversation.

1126 "The Mantero-Catasus Plan." Issue No. 4:35-7, July 1957.
Sponsors of the Plan from Italy and Spain for a world federation of bookplate collectors.

1127 "Third List of Bookplates and Books About Them." Issue No. 4:37, July 1957.
Items offered for sale or exchange; specific wants solicited.

1128 "Editorial." Issue No. 5:38-9, October 1957.
BCN will continue another year but printing and illustrations are still out of the question.

1129 "Subscribers to the B.C.N." Issue No. 5:39, October 1957.
List continued through #67.

1130 "International Ex Libris Bureau." Issue No. 5:39-43, October 1957.
Minutes of meeting in Amsterdam and delegates attending, A. B. Keeves secretary of the organization.

1131 "Recent Publication Reviewed." Issue No. 5:43-4, October 1957.
Includes *Year Book* of ASBC&D, and three European journals.

1132 "Alan Reynolds Stone, C.B.E., R.D.I., R.E." P. Beddingham. Issue No. 5: 44-6, October 1957.
Artist given award of Royal Designer in Industry for his contribution in lettering; alphabetical checklist of fifty-four bookplates.

1133 "Advertisements." Issue No. 5:46, October 1957.
Want and exchange lists include royal plates, Jewish, well known artists, and erotic.

1134 "The Value of Bookplates, Part II." Issue No. 5:46-8, October 1957.
Four chief factors which give value to a plate are: 1—The plate belonged to an owner who rose above the common level in life. 2—The plate was made by a celebrated artist. 3—The plate bears a printed date. 4—The plate is over 250 years old.

1135 "Amsterdam Congress." Issue No. 5:48-50, October 1957.
Over 160 attended from fourteen different countries.

1136 "Random Notes and News." Issue No. 5:50-1, October 1957.
Names of several English bookplate artists given.

1137 "Fourth List of Items for Sale or Exchange." Issue No. 5:51-2, October 1957.
English and foreign plates; also books.

1138 "Index to Date." Issue No. 6:53, January 1958.
Index to first six numbers given.

1139 "Editorial." Issue No. 6:53-6, January 1958.
No. 1 of B.C.N. long since exhausted; those who lack it ask that another fifty be printed—"idea . . . postponed."

1140 "Alan Reynolds Stone." Issue No. 6:56, January 1958.
Additions to checklist bring total to sixty-seven.

1141 "Modern & Contemporary Bookplates & Modern Art—Part 1." Issue No. 6: 56-8, January 1958.
Modern is within last 100 years; contemporary within last dozen; comments very outspoken.

1142 "Advertisements." Issue No. 6:58-9, January 1958.
Charge reduced to two pence per word.

1143 "Johannesburg Story." Michael Coetzer. Issue No. 6:59-62, January 1958.
Story told by a collector who drove 200 miles to buy a bookplate and was bitten by a Tsetse fly on the way home!

1144 "Random Notes & News." Issue No. 6:62-4, January 1958.
Suggests a competition to discover "the most desirable bookplate in the world."

1145 "Subscribers to the B.C.N." Issue No. 6:64-5, January 1958.
Additional names through #94 including ten whose full names are not given as they do not wish to correspond.

1146 "Poetry—Ancient & Modern." Issue No. 6:65, January 1958.
Modern poem salutes Sputnik!

1147 "Deutsche Inhaltsangabe." Issue No. 6:65-6, January 1958.
Summary in German.

1148 "Eric Gill & His Bookplates—Part 1." Issue No. 6:66, January 1958.
Brief biographical sketch.

1149 "Editorial." Issue No. 7:67-9, May 1958.
No. 1 of B.C.N. will be reprinted and marked "Reissue."

1150 "*Ex Libris* by Arvid Berghman—A Review." Issue No. 7:69-70, May 1958.
Swedish volume well illustrated and with even a reference to B.C.N.

1151 "Modern & Contemporary Bookplates & Modern Art—Part II." Issue No. 7:70-3, May 1958.
"The great faults of this century seem to be the two extremes of over-elaboration and over-simplicity."

1152 "C. W. Sherborn." Issue No. 7:73-4, May 1958.
Ten notes added to "The Life & Work of Charles William Sherborn" now that both C. D. Sherborn and G. H. Viner, the compilers, are dead.

1153 "Erotic Bookplates—Part 1." Issue No. 7:74-6, May 1958.
"The only books that are difficult to obtain, that are the most expensive to buy, and which are most likely to be stolen, are those of an erotic nature. Hence the emergence of the erotic ex libris."

1154 "A 'New' Medical Bookplate." Issue No. 7:76, May 1958.
Plate of French chemist dated 1693; perhaps oldest known dated French medical bookplate.

1155 "Random Notes & News." Issue No. 7:77, May 1958.
Sixth Ex Libris Congress will be held in Barcelona from July 3rd to 6th.

1156 "Fifth List of Items for Sale or Exchange." Issue No. 7:78-9, May 1958.
Wide assortment offered.

1157 "Eric Gill & His Bookplates—Part II." Issue No. 7:79-80, May 1958.
Chronological checklist of 49 plates, wood engravings except four which were copperplates.

1158 "Editorial." Issue No. 8:81-2, September 1958.
Costs for duplicating the publication and postage far exceed receipts from subscriptions.

1159 "Programme for 1959." Issue No. 8:82-3, September 1958.
Twenty-two subjects suggested including corrections to "Sir J. Warren's 'Guide,'" identification of 641 unidentified plates in the *Ex Libris Journal*, 1895-1909.

1160 "Letter from a Bookplate." Issue No. 8:83-4, September 1958.
A Dutch bookplate, 493 years old, requests "a windowmount to protect my edges."

1161 "Short History of the Ex Libris Art in Japan." Taro Shimo. Issue No. 8:84-5, September 1958.
European style bookplates were first printed in Japan about 1900.

1162 "Sixth Barcelona Congress." Issue No. 8:85-8, September 1958.
Rather intricate methods suggested for evaluating plates to be exchanged.

1163 "Your Questions Answered." Issue No. 8:88, September 1958.
Answer offered to "How many Bookplate Collectors are there in the world & what is the size of their collections?"

1164 "Recent Publications Reviewed." Issue No. 8:88-9, September 1958.
Includes publications from Rotterdam, Stockholm and Norway.

1165 "Random Notes and News." Issue No. 8:89-90, September 1958.
"Ex Libris Wereld" new review from Holland.

1166 "From the Editor's Postbag." Issue No. 8:91-2, September 1958.
One correspondence quoted: "I like your forthright, almost brazen approach—so refreshing after the so dull articles and lists one sees in all the other Ex Libris Journals."

1167 "Editorial." Issue No. 9:93, January 1959.
Only three issues will appear at "convenient" intervals.

1168 "Chat on Choosing Your Own Plate." Issue No. 9:94-6, January 1959.
Quotes Edmund Gosse: "To have a bookplate gives a collector great serenity and self-confidence."

1169 "Subscribers to the B.C.N.—Fifth List." Issue No. 9:96-7, January 1959.
List has now grown to 114.

1170 "Your Questions Answered." Issue No. 9:97-8, January 1959.
Hints given on approach to be used in seeking the plates of prominent personalities.

1171 "Random Notes and News." Issue No. 9:98-9, January 1959.
The next International Heraldic Congress will be in Stockholm during 1960.

1172 "From the Editor's Postbag." Issue No. 9:99-101, January 1959.
Anonymous excerpts from letters sent to the editor "printed in a spirit of goodwill" though individual correspondents may feel otherwise.

1173 "Checklist of French Dated Bookplates of the Seventeenth Century—Part 1." Issue No. 9:101-2, January 1959.
Editor's first research effort.

1174 "Editorial." Issue No. 10:103, April 1959.
Dr. S. X. Radbill will be visiting Europe during July and August.

1175 "Exhibition of Austrian Bookplates." Issue No. 10:103-4, April 1959.
Plates by twenty-two artists created during the last thirty years.

1176 "Random Notes and News." Issue No. 10:104-5, April 1959.
Interesting notes on those who have a great number of different personal plates.

1177 "More About Japan." Issue No. 10:106, April 1959.
Mark Severin gives date of 900 A.D. for earliest Japanese bookplate; 1470 according to T. Shimo.

1178 "Treasure Trove—An American (?) Find." Issue No. 10:106-7, April 1959.
Tells of finding four different plates, one on top of the other, for various Dukes of Bedford; dated 1703, 1736, and 1873.

1179 "An Appreciation." Jimmy McCarroll. Issue No. 10:107, April 1959.
Poem written by the office boy which spells out ***Bookplate Collectors News*** with the initial letter of each line.

1180 "A Harry Soane Problem." Issue No. 10:108-9, April 1959.
To quote the introduction: "Here is a truly uninteresting article packed with technical data. . . . It is intended for my antiquarian friends who are always moaning that the magazine is not dull enough."

1181 "From the Editor's Postbag." Issue No. 10:109-10, April 1959.
"Your instructions for writing to bookplate owners prove to me you are a super snob."

1182 "Your Questions Answered." Issue No. 10:110-2, April 1959.
Gives names of six bookplate journals editor recommends from Denmark, Portugal (two), Holland, France and Italy.

1183 "Recent Publications Reviewed." Issue No. 10:112-3, April 1959.
One on "Estonian Artistic Bookplates."

1184 "Checklist of French Dated Bookplates of the 17th Century. Part II." Issue No. 10:113-4, April 1959.
List continued.

1185 "Editorial." Issue No. 11:115, October 1959.
Souvenir Album has returned from U.S.A. and is now on tour in Europe.

1186 "Checklist of French Dated Bookplates of the 17th Century. Third & Last Part." Issue No. 11:115-7, October 1959.
Seventy plates in completed list.

1187 "Sixth List of Items for Sale or Exchange." Issue No. 11:117-9, October 1959.
English and foreign plates, and three volumes of *Ex Libris Journal*.

1188 "Notes on Some Rare or Interesting Bookplates You Can Inspect If You Come and Visit Me." Issue No. 11:119-25, October 1959.
Editor's collection divided into twenty-seven sections by geographical areas, English engravers, and erotics.

1189 "Bibliographical Notes." Issue No. 11:125-6, October 1959.
Books commented upon from Poland, Italy, Belgium, Portugal, France, and Norway.

1190 "Editorial." Issue No. 12:127-9, January 1960.
This will be the last issue of BCN; probably not more than 150 complete sets exist. Going to form the British Bookplate Club.

1191 "Random Notes and News." Issue No. 12:129-31, January 1960.
The 7th International Ex Libris Congress will be held in Vienna from July 8th to 10th.

1192 "Viner Bookplates." Issue No. 12:131-3, January 1960.
Details various states of Viner bookplates.

1193 "From the Editor's Postbag." Issue No. 12:133, January 1960.
One correspondent says the "magazine is an extraordinary mixture of T. S. Eliot, Alice in Wonderland and G. B. Shaw."

1194 "British Museum." Issue No. 12:133-7, January 1960.
Some very straightforward comments about the actual housing of the famed Franks Collection, also Viner and general collection.

1195 "Your Questions Answered." Issue No. 12:137-8, January 1960.
You cease to be a beginner collector when you have more than 1,000 different plates.

1196 "Epitaph on the Bookplate Collectors News." Issue No. 12:138, January 1960.
Short was thy life,/Yet livest thou ever;
Death hath his due,/Yet dyest thou never.

BOOKPLATE MAGAZINE [James Guthrie, London]

1197 "Bookplate." (1) 1:2, July 1919.
For W. Bradley by Frank Brangwyn.

1198 "Concerning the English Pictorial Bookplate. Part I: Historical Reflections." 1:5-8, July 1919.
"It [pictorial bookplate] owes a great deal to the invention of the cheap line process by which designs made with the pen could be printed without the expense or delay incident to copperplate engraving."

1199 "Three Bookplates by Harold Nelson." (3) 1:9-11, July 1919.
Plates for Joan Phillips, Charles Alfieri, Elizabeth Radcliffe.

1200 "First Principles for Collectors." 1:12-5, July 1919.
"For the collector it may be said at once that the artistic value of his possessions should come first in his estimation."

1201 "Bookplate." (1) 1:16, July 1919.
Designed by Frank Brangwyn, R.A.

1202 "Four Bookplates by James Guthrie." (4) 1:17-20, July 1919.
One is a two-color print.

1203 "Bookplate by T. Erat Harrison." (1) 1:21, July 1919.
For John Ballinger.

1204 "English Society." (1) 1:22-3, July 1919.
Comments on formation of English Bookplate Society.

1205 "Bookplates." (4) 1:24-7, July 1919.
Plates by H. J. Stack, J. Paul Cooper, Pickford Waller and Bernard Sleigh.

1206 "Notes and Reviews." (1) 1:28-30, July 1919.
Bookplate activity in Europe and United States noted.

1207 "The Bare Idea." James Guthrie. (3) 1:32-7, October 1919.
It is difficult to find "a single nude figure that is thoroughly well-judged and adequately disposed and welded into the sort of design which we who care for bookplates recognize as entirely good and suitable."

1208 "The Collection of Bookplates." (1) 1:38-40, October 1919.
"The true wise man seeks rather for beauty and variety in his choice, always busily eliminating the poor and adding to the fine examples."

1209 "Two Designs by E. Bengough." (2) 1:41-2, October 1919.
Both plates for Beatrice Gregan.

1210 "Concerning the English Pictorial Bookplate. Historical Reflections (continued)." (1) 1:43-6, October 1919.
Comments on Joseph Simpson's *The Book of Bookplates*.

1211 "Two Bookplates by F. Brangwyn, R. A." (2) 1:47-8, October 1919.
Plates for Charles Holme and E. Esser.

1212 "Note on Wood Engraving." Bernard Sleigh. (1) 1:49-51, October 1919.
"The golden age of the engraver on wood may be past; yet the germ of this ancient and honourable craft flourishes strongly, and will continually put forth shoots and tendrils of beauty."

1213 "Bookplates." (3) 1:52-4, October 1919.
Plates by James and Robin Guthrie and D. C. L. Dewar.

1214 "Notes and Reviews." 1:55-9, October 1919.
Mention of Boston enthusiast issuing occasional pamphlet under imprint of Society of Bookplate Bibliophiles.

1215 "Herald at the Breakfast Table." F. Gordon Roe. (1) 1:62-8, January 1920.
The old designers were instructed to "cover your field."

1216 "Bookplate." (1) 1:69, January 1920.
G. M. Ellwood's design for Bronson Gossop.

1217 "Two Bookplates by L. Syrett." (2) 1:70-1, January 1920.
Plates for Sarah A. Chapman and Gertie I. Holton.

1218 "Bookplate." (1) 1:72, January 1920.
Plate by Philip Hapgreen.

1219 "Care of Bookplates." Simon Sneyd. (1) 1:73-9, January 1920.
"In many respects, a collector is a rescuer."

1220 "Bookplates."(3) 1:80-2, January 1920.
Plates by Ludovic Rodo, Emile H. Tielemans, and Jean Thizeloup.

1221 "Three Bookplates by Robert Gibbings." (3) 1:83-5, January 1920.
William Pennefather plate shows head-on silhouette of ships of varying size.

1222 "Bookplates." (2) 1:86-7, January 1920.
Plates for Hugh Stokes and Hilda Griffin.

1223 "Notes and Reviews." 1:88-91, January 1920.
Notes about Frank Brangwyn and Timothy Cole.

1224 "Thomas Sturge Moore, Poet." F. Gordon Roe. (1) 1:94-8, April 1920.
"Moore should have been an ancient pagan mystic."

1225 "Two Bookplates by T. Sturge Moore." (2) 1:99-100, April 1920.
Plates for George Yeats and one featuring Leda and the Swan.

1226 "Three Bookplates by Lucien Pissarro." (3) 1:101-3, April 1920.
Plates for J. L. and S. L. Bensusan and Esther and Lucien Pissarro.

1227 "Bookplate." (1) 1:104, April 1920.
Plate by Austin O. Spare for Pickford Waller.

1228 "Bookplates of Major Haldane Macfall." W. G. Blaikie Murdock. (1) 1:105-7, April 1920.
Novelist, painter-historian, biographer of Irving as well as bookplate artist.

1229 "Five Bookplates by Haldane Macfall." (5) 1:108-12, April 1920.
Variety of designs.

1230 "Pickford Waller." (1) 1:113, April 1920.
Plate for Margaret H. Seymour.

1231 "Two Bookplates by Fred Roe, R. I." (2) 1:114-5, April 1920.
Initials indicate plates for family members.

1232 "Bookplate." (1) 1:116, April 1920.
Plate for Katherine Mower.

1233 "Four Bookplates (American)." (4) 1:117-20, April 1920.
Plates for George Washington, William Howard Taft, Woodrow Wilson, and George Bancroft.

1234 "Notes and Reviews." (1) 1:121-5, April 1920.
Colour features article on Frank Brangwyn.

1235 "Old Danish Bookplates." (3) 1:128-33, November 1920.
Admonishment in Greek translates:
"Ye Robbers, go ye to the Houses of the Rich!
Poverty is the Guardian of my House."

1236 "Four Bookplates by H. C. Barenholdt." (4) 1:134-5, November 1920.
Three feature animals; fourth Adam and Eve.

1237 "Four Bookplates by Dr. Phil. Viggo Von Holstein-Rathlon" (4) 1:136-8, November 1920.
One is elaborate stained glass religious scene.

1238 "Modern Danish Bookplates." (2) 1:139-41, November 1920.
Plates are "almost always sincere, very rarely extravagant, and hardly ever in bad taste."

1239 "Three Bookplates by Prof. Hans Tegner." (3) 1:142, November 1920.
Much detail in small area.

1240 "Two Bookplates by Th. Bindesball." (2) 1:143, November 1920.
Both feature initials.

1241 "Two Bookplates by Gudmund Hentze." (2) 1:144-5, November 1920.
One detailed waterfront scene.

1242 "Three Bookplates by Kristian Kongstad." (3) 1:146, November 1920.
Two very detailed interiors.

1243 "Bookplate by P. A. Schou." (1) 1:147, November 1920.
Plate for Palsgaard.

1244 "Bookplate by Viggo Bang." (1) 1:148, November 1920.
Old ship under full sail.

1245 "Bookplate and Illustrations." Jens Lund. (4) 1:149-50, November 1920.
Artist also author of *The Book of the Dreamer*.

1246 "*Dyrehaven*." Sigvart Werner. 1:153-4, November 1920.
Book of photographs, eighty pages, took six months to print 160 copies.

1247 "Title Page." Axel Hau. (1) 1:155, November 1920.
Reprint of book eighty years old with type of the period and vignette.

1248 "Unique Bookplate." F. Gordon Roe. (1) 1:156-8, November 1920.
Only bookplate designed by promising artist, Ken Kemp, dead at 23.

1249 "Notes and Reviews." (1) 1:159-62, November 1920.
Those interested in augmenting collection of British Museum should contact Department of Prints and Drawings.

1250 "Bookplate." (1) 2:170, March 1921.
Plate by R. Anning Bell.

1251 "Bookplates of Gordon Craig." Haldane Macfall. (1) 2:171-4, March 1921.
"Craig is never commonplace—far less is he ever guilty of the mechanical—still less does he strain after the antique."

1252 "Six Bookplates by Gordon Craig." (6) 2:175-8, March 1921.
One features cat and owner's initials, KD; dated 1900.

1253 "Bookplates of Garth Jones." Hayter Preston. 2:179-80, March 1921.
Work "akin to Dürer."

1254 "Five Bookplates by Garth Jones." (5) 2:181-5, March 1921.
A feeling of yesteryear and fairy tales suggested by plates.

1255 "Bookplates of R. Anning Bell, A.R.A." G. M. Ellwood. (1) 2:186-8, March 1921.
Designer of stained glass and painter as well as bookplate artist.

1256 "Four Bookplates by R. Anning Bell." (4) 2:189-92, March 1921.
Plates for Walter Lloyd, Joshua Sing, Charles and Hilda Keane, and Edward P. Warren.

1257 "Bookplates." (2) 2:193-4, March 1921.
Plates by Lucien Pissaro and John R. Sutherland.

1258 "Notes and Reviews." (1) 2:195-202, March 1921.
Forthcoming publications in France, Spain and America, and sales notice.

1259 "Armand Rossenfosse." (3) 2:204-9, June 1921.
Checklist includes plates from 1890 to 1921.

1260 "Art of Armand Rels." M. Roberts. (1) 2:210-3, June 1921.
Belgian artist feels bookplates should be "marks of possession."

1261 "Bookplate by Armand Rels." (1) 2:214, June 1921.
Plate for Barbanson.

1262 "Some Reflections." Louis Titz. (1) 2:215-18, June 1921.
Checklist of fifty-five plates by Brussels artist.

1263 "Notes on Five Swiss Bookplates." E. W. Netter. (5) 2:219-26, June 1921.
Artists are Emil Anner, Alfred Soder, Paul Flury, Fritz Pauli, and Fritz Gilsi.

1264 "Notes and Reviews." (1) 2:227-34, June 1921.
Illustration is Lucien Pissarro plate for Harry Alfred Fowler. News from Belgium, France, America, and Spain.

1265 "Bookplates of Claud Lovat Fraser." Haldane Macfall. (8) 2:236-46, September 1921.
Dead at thirty-one, Lovat Fraser was active in theatre design as well as bookplate artist; made plate for Herbert Beerbohm Tree.

1266 "Bookplate in Belgium." Em.-H. Tielemans. (11) 2:247-61, September 1921.
Comments on activity before the war and gradual reactivation since.

1267 "Two Bohemian Bookplate Artists." Bed. Beněs, Buchlovan. (2) 2:262-5, September 1921.
Work of Stanislav Kulhanek and Josef Hodek discussed.

1268 "Three Bookplates by Thomas P. Elmes." (3) 2:266-8, September 1921.
Plates for Hayter Preston, Crossley Davies, and W. Bradley.

1269 "Modern French Bookplates." 2:269-70, September 1921.
Havermans has published book of thirty bookplates, mostly from original wood blocks.

1270 "Badges and Bookplates." F. Gordon Roe. (1) 2:271-6, September 1921.
"There never were any hard and fast rules relating to badges." Therefore, "employment of a badge on a bookplate possesses undeniable advantages over a dubious coat-of-arms."

1271 "Three American Bookplates." (3) 2:277-9, September 1921.
All for Cleveland Public Library.

1272 "Notes and Reviews." 2:280-2, September 1921.
Farewell issue of *Bookplate Magazine*.

BOOKPLATE QUARTERLY [American Bookplate Society]

1273 "Masonic Book-Plates." Winward Prescott. (11) 1:3-21, December 1917.
Interesting background on Masonic Order plus list of over 170 Masonic bookplates including those from Robert Day and A. W. Pope articles.

1274 "Fred Thompson's Bookplates." (3) 1:22-4, December 1917.
Brief comment and chronological list of about twenty bookplates.

1275 "An Indiana Collector." Esther Griffin White. (3) 1:25-9, December 1917.
Off-hand humorous style doesn't quite succeed.

1276 "Ex Libris Ana." 1:31-51, December 1917.
"Free translation" of some notes from monthly Paris journal first appearing in fall of 1893.

1277 "Concerning Borrowers." 1:37-8, December 1917.
More admonitions including—"Each of you is a wife, who may allow herself to be seen without blame, but who ought never to be loaned."

1278 "*Bookplate Quarterly*." 1:39-40, December 1917.
Editorial comment and announcement of articles for future issues.

1279 "To the Members of the American Book-Plate Society." W. F. Hopson. 1: 41, December 1917.
Letter commending Miss Hovey for assuming the editorship since Alfred Fowler became a lieutenant in the Army; name change of journal since Fowler wants to resume publication of "The Booklet" on his return.

1280 "Exhibition of Contemporary Bookplates." Ralph E. Lord. 1:42-3, December 1917.
Plates designed during 1917 eligible for exhibit from January 5 to 19, 1918.

1281 "Book-Plate Affairs in France." 1:44, December 1917.
Dictionary of designers and engravers of French bookplates begun in 1897 finally near completion after deaths of two editors.

1282 "Interesting Exhibition by New Orleans Collectors." 1:45, December 1917.
Mrs. Arthur Griswold Palfrey and Miss Jane Grey Rogers exhibited about 2,000 plates.

1283 "Publications of Society of Bookplate Bibliophiles." 1:45, December 1917.
Second publication is *Norwegian Ex Libris* by Gerhard Gade, Norwegian Consulate in Chicago.

1284 "Exchange List." 1:47-8, December 1917.
Names, addresses and exchanges available and desired.

1285 "Columbia Bookplate Collection." Clara Therese Evans. (2) 1:3-18, April 1918.
Laurence Hutton once observed that 927 out of 1,000 book owners

don't know what a bookplate is "though all of them know about fashion-plates, boiler-plates, armor-plates, soup-plates. . . ."

1286 "Collection of the American Antiquarian Society." Herbert Edwin Lombard. (6) 1:19-25, April 1918.

"Some seventy-five plates by E. D. French, J. W. Spenceley, and S. L. Smith are owned or controlled, at least partially, by members of the American Antiquarian Society."

1287 "Third Annual Exhibition of Contemporary Bookplates." 1:27, April 1918.

About one hundred plates by thirty-six American artists shown.

1288 "Statement by President Hopson." 1:28-9, April 1918.

Mrs. Clare Therese Evans has "consented to assume gratuitously" duties of editorship.

1289 "Editorial." 1:30-2, April 1918.

New editor asks for membership cooperation and support (only $70 in treasury after paying bills for last *Quarterly*). $10,000 paid for Frank E. Marshall collection at auction.

1290 "William Fowler Hopson and His Bookplates." William A. Breadsley. (3) 1:3-12, July 1918.

"There is no end of pleasure, if one collects with intelligence, discrimination and moderation."

1291 "How I Became A Collector." Georgia Medora Preston. 1:12-6, July 1918.

Chance acquaintance in 1902 at summer hotel with booklover who was also bookplate enthusiast was starting point; received a registered packet of seventy-five prints and message: "If you have any duplicates I can use them. If not, you're quite welcome to these."!

1292 "Some Observations of An Amateur." Charles Colebrook Sherman. (2) 1:17-25, July 1918.

Interesting comments on books and plates by a bookman not primarily a bookplate collector.

1293 "Contemporary Bookplates." (2) 1:26-7, July 1918.

Plate of Herbert D. Mandelbaum, by W. W. Aikman, incorporates library/desk interior, skull and entwined snakes, winged torch of learning, steamship and steam train, and banner motto "System and thoroughness."

1294 "Daniel B. Fearing. 1859-1918." 1:28-9, July 1918.

Fearing, ex-mayor of Newport, R.I., famed for his angling and watercraft collection which he gave to his alma mater, Harvard, dropped dead on a Sunday afternoon while directing final arrangements for a Red Cross singing benefit.

1295 "The Offending Hyphen." 1:29-31, July 1918.

"Even conservative old Oxford had adapted the modern form 'bookplate.'"

1296 "Bookplate Society." 1:31-2, July 1918.

"After dropping all delinquents, the Society has ninety-nine active and five honorary members."

1297 "Hawaiian Bookplates." Helen J. Stearns. (4) 1:3, October 1918.
Since there was no printed language prior to the missionaries in 1820, there are few early plates but many recent ones reflecting the natural beauty of the Islands.

1298 "Horatio Nelson Poole and His Bookplates." Clara Therese Evans. 1:13-6, October 1918.
"Along with the lure of the Orient he brings to us the charm of the vast Pacific."

1299 "Allen Lewis: His Woodcut Bookplates." Wilbur Macey Stone. (4) 1:17-26, October 1918.
Artist often used two-block designs "obtaining light and shade effects quite beyond any to be attained with one printing."

1300 "Peace." Agnes Lee. 1:27, October 1918.
Poem.

1301 "Editorial Comment." 1:28-31, October 1918.
With the "status of affairs in Europe . . . now so favorable" it is anticipated Captain Fowler will soon return to edit the official publication of the American Bookplate Society.

1302 "News and Notes." 1:31-2, October 1918.
Members requested to return any extra copies of the December 1917 *Quarterly* since, through oversight, no copies "were preserved for the archives of the Society."

BOOK-PLATES

1303 "About Book-Plates." 1:4, February 1902.
Brief paragraphs from *Studio* article.

1304 "Book-Plate in Chicago." 1:5-7, February 1902.
Many good ex libris designers in area to accommodate needs of book-lovers.

1305 "For Book Borrowers." 1:8, February 1902.
Poem quoted from *Notes and Queries*.

1306 "Illustrations." (19) 1:9-29, February 1902.
Includes plates designed by W. A. Dwiggins, F. W. Goudy and plate for Queen Victoria.

1307 "Early Printed Type Labels." (2) 1:31-2, February 1902.
Plates illustrated are for Elizabeth Obee and Charles Dickens.

BOOK-PLATES OF TODAY [See **ARTISTIC BOOK-PLATES**]

BOOK REVIEWS

1308 "American Book-Plates." Charles Dexter Allen. 2:5-8, May 1894.
Background on early plates: heraldic, Jacobean, Chippendale. Early Southern plates often work of English engravers.

BOOK WORLD

1309 "Review." (1) 1:410-11, December 1898.

Bookplates: Old and New by John A. Gade (90¢), a volume for collectors of ex libris; Henry Irving's plate illustrated.

1310 "Book-Plate Mottoes." Wilbur Macey Stone. (4) 2:27-30, January 1899.

"Anyone may borrow/but a gentleman returns."

1311 "Book Plates: Their Origin, History and Value." John De Morgan. (6) 7:839-45, August 1901.

General background.

BOOKS AND BOOK-PLATES [See also **Book of Book-Plates** and **Book-Lover's Magazine**]

1312 "About Book-Plates and the Society." James Guthrie. 4:45-7, 1903-4.

Editorial concerning exaggeration of the bookplate as an art form. "Let the book-plate stand in its own little corner, serenely if you will, but humbly."

Announcement of Bookplate Society for designers, not collectors.

1313 "Book-Plates." (6) 4:48-50, 1903-4.

Plates designed by A. D. Carse, C. Richardson, R. P. Gossop, and J. J. Guthrie.

1314 "The Modern Book-Plate." 4:102, 1903-4.

A "blast" at bookplate designers and collectors.

1315 "Book-Plates." (6) 4:105-9, 1903-4.

Plates designed by Pickford Waller, C. E. Dawson, and E. Pope.

1316 "Book or Book-Plate?" Edith Roberts. 4:110, 1903-4.

Warning against abuses practiced by the bookplate collector.

1317 "Book-Plate and the Public Library." 4:150-2, 1903-4.

"Bare utility cannot be allowed to stand. . . ." A plea for beauty as well as utility in public library bookplates.

1318 "Book-Plates." (5) 4:158-62, 1903-4.

Plates by R. Anning Bell, F. Y. Cary, D. H. Becket, and Pickford Waller.

1319 "Books and Book-Plates at the Harting Guild." 4:163-4, 1903-4.

Harting Guild of Handicraft included bookplates in its third exhibition of "choicely printed books of strictly limited edition."

1320 "Book-Plate Notes." 4:171-5, 1903-4.

Makes reference to articles or items about bookplates in half a dozen or more other current magazines.

1321 "Correspondence, The Other Side." 4:176, 1903-4.

Writer enthusiastic only about heraldic plates and questions value of most pictorial plates.

1322 "By the Way." 4:195-203, 1903-4.
Comments on Edward Almack's bookplate volume, sale prices of various plates, cataloging of Franks Collection, "A Pleader to the Needer When a Reader" printed in full, Budapest exhibition, Ex Libris Society exhibit, William Edgar Fisher, David H. Becket.

1323 "Ten Book-Plates." Wilbur Macey Stone. (10) 4:222-6, 1903-4.
Illustrations only.

1324 "Concerning the Book-Plate Designs of Wilbur Macey Stone." Wilbur Macey Stone. 4:227-32, 1903-4.
"Somewhere among the unwritten but mouldy laws of art and letters is a section forbidding an artist or author to review his own work. For the life of me I can't see the sense of it."
Mechanical engineer by trade.

1325 "Two Book-Plates by James Guthrie." (2) 4:233, 1903-4.
Initial plates for MP and AJR.

1326 "A Book-Plate." (1) 4:235, 1903-4.
Ex libris for Marion.

1327 "Four Book-Plates by D. H. Becket." (4) 4:236-7, 1903-4.
Illustrations only.

1328 "Book-Plate by E. Bengongh Ricketts." (1) 4:237, 1903-4.
Illustration only.

1329 "On Book-Plates." Harold E. H. Nelson. (7) 5:58-72, 1904-5.
A bookplate should "bear the stamp of decorative unity" and never be a "hotch-potch of unrelated odds and ends."

1330 "Seven Book-Plates by William Edgar Fisher." (7) 5:102-15, 1904-5.
No text.

1331 "Book-Plate by Wilson Eyre." (1) 5:117, 1904-5.
Plate for Edwin Fetterolf.

1332 "Joseph Sattler." M. Smyth. (20) 5:119-50, 1904-5.
German artist's distinctive style sharply shown in several bookplates, one with Death carrying many books piled high.

1333 "Book-Plates." (8) 5:206-19, 1904-5.
Designs by Wilbur Macey Stone, A. de Riquer, G. C. Michelet, J. W. Simpson and Harold Nelson.

1334 "Concerning the Book-Plates of Thomas Bewick." Basil Anderton. (7) 5:220-43, 1904-5.
Brief biographical sketch and chronological list of his major works in addition to descriptive alphabetical list of bookplates (eighty or ninety).

1335 "Coloured Book-Plates." Stewart Dick. (1) 5:244-9, 1904-5.
Plate illustrated was designed by French artist, L. A. Girardot, for Arch. Younger to be used for a music library. Joseph Sattler deemed best color plate designer.

1336 "Swiss Book-Plates." G. R. Dennis. (6) 5:263-9, 1904-5.
Review of volume published in Basel authored by Von Emanuel Stickelberger, whom reviewer says has "love of the sentimental—the great failing of German critics."

1337 "Durer Book-Plates in the British Museum." Stewart Dick. (9) 5:299-316, 1904-5.
Durer "was entitled by his social and intellectual qualities, no less than by his artistic genius, to a place in the most exclusive circles. His book-plates, only some half-dozen in all, appear generally not to have been artistic commissions, but gifts to his literary friends."

BOOKSELLER

1338 "*A Guide to the Study of Book-Plates.*" Issue No. 275:920, October 6, 1880.
Review of Warren's book. "Collecting such plates is a passion, kindred to that for first edition of books."

BOOKSELLER AND COLLECTOR

1339 "Book-Plates for Sale." 2:8, October 13, 1927.
Foreign subscriber offers 35,000 to 40,000 plates to be sold as a collection.

BOOKSELLER AND NEWSMAN

1340 "The Collecting of Book Plates." W. G. Bowdoin. 14:10, December 1897.
"One interested in book plates . . . is brought into contact with the great ones of earth, diplomats, poets, dramatists, those who stand out prominently in the ages to which they belong: for the more ordinary men and women do not often come into ownership of book plates any more than scrubwomen appear as figures in historic salons."

1341 "Joseph Sattler, Book-Plate Designer." W. G. Bowdoin. (1) 16:5, March 1899.
"He may safely be given a high artistic rank."

BOOKWORM

1342 "Book-plates and Their Mottoes." 2:205-6, 1899.
Several mottoes quoted. Comment that currently new owners of books tend to place their own plates to one side of the original, on the fly-leaf or back cover rather than tear out or paste over the plates of previous possessors.

1343 "Some Book Plates." (2) 4:57-60, 1891.
General historical review.

1344 "Bookplates." (2) 4:97-9, 1891.
Quotes from book by Bouchet, who "scorns the utility of the book-plate: he glories in the fact that the greatest of French and Italian booklovers

never used a book-plate, and he contends that the proper course to be taken is to follow their plan of stamping arms and mottoes in gold on our bindings. The British Museum follows this practice."

1345 "The 'Ex Libris' Society." 4:301-2, 1891.
Review of the Society and its journal.

1346 "A Hunt for Book-plates in Paris." Walter Hamilton. 5:171-3, 1892.
Chatty essay on seeking bookplates in Paris shops.

1347 "Avery Library Bookplate." 5:202, 1892.
Avery Architectural Library at Columbia established in memory of Henry Ogden Avery.

1348 "Ex-Libris at the Royal Academy." 5:312, 1892.
Exhibition list of bookplates including those by C. W. Sherborn, H. Stacy Marks, T. Erat Harrison, George W. Eve, and L. Leslie Brooke.

1349 "French and English Bookplates." (6) 6:105-8, 1893.
Bookplate collecting as a hobby given impetus and direction by Ex-Libris Society. First editions of books by Castle and Hamilton exhausted within a few weeks of publication.

1350 "Book-Plate Society." 6:137-44, 1893.
Address delivered by James Roberts Brown, February 24, 1893, quotes Edmund Gosse: "the outward and visible marks of the citizenship of the booklover" known as ex-libris or bookplates.

1351 "Irish Bookplates." 6:240, 1893.
Notice of collection of early Irish bookplates to be published for a limited (150) number of subscribers.

1352 "Bookplates." 6:354, 1893.
Mention of earliest known bookplate, that of Jean Knabensperg or Igler, appearing in Incunabula catalog.

1353 "A Remarkable Bookplate." G. H. Powell. 7:49-50, 1894.
Bookplate of Marquis of Macciucca (1699-1785) with fifteen rules printed in Latin expounding the principles upon which he lent his books.

1354 "Dated Bookplates." (3) 7:337-40, 1894.
Walter Hamilton preparing classification for bookplates and annotated list of dated bookplates for all countries during last four centuries.

BOOK WORM [Rockport, Maine. See also **HOBBY TIMES AND BOOKWORM**]

1355 "Bookplates." (3) 1:5, June 1968.
Plates of Raymond A. Smith, Doray Press, New Hampshire, designed by his daughter.

BRADLEY, HIS BOOK

1356 "Book Plate by Claude F. Bragdon." (1) 1:unnumbered, May 1896.
Illustration only, featuring a chicken.

1357 "William S. Hadaway." (4) 2:90-2, January 1897.
Only one illustration is a bookplate. Artist's drawings are "original only in their arrangement, the detail being suggested by, or copied from, early missals."

BRISTOL MEDICO-CHIRURGICAL JOURNAL

1358 "Presentation to Mr. L. M. Griffiths." (1) 18:97-103, June 1900.
Among other presentations upon retirement from post of Assistant-Editor of the *Journal* was a bookplate designed by W. V. Collette.

1359 "Presentation to Mr. L. M. Griffiths." (1) 18:282-3, September 1900.
Detailed description of the various symbols introduced in the bookplate for Mr. Griffiths.

BRITISH AND COLONIAL PRINTER AND STATIONER

1360 "Ex Libris Society." 28:10, July 16, 1891.
Quotes from the first number of the *Journal of the Ex Libris Society* concerning origin and development of the Society.

1361 "Book-Plates Ancient and Modern." (4) 28:7, August 6, 1891.
"The following interesting article by John Leighton, F.S.A., is quoted by the *Journal of the Ex Libris Society* from the *Gentleman's Magazine*."

1362 "Book Plates." 28:5, October 15, 1891.
Article from *American Bookmaker* quoted "*in extenso*."

BRITISH BOOKMAKER

1363 "Book Notes." (9) 4:5-6, May 1891.
Review of two books by Henri Bouchat, *Les Ex-Libris* and *Des Livres Modernes*.

1364 "Ex Libris." (4) 4:4, June 1891.
"The collection of book-plates now needs no apology—it is recognized as a legitimate pursuit."

1365 "Book-Plates." 5:8, July 1891.
Reprint of *Daily Chronicle* article. "The collecting of book-plates is so far an evil that their labels are often taken out of books where they are of more interest than when collected with others in a scrap book."

BRITISH MUSEUM QUARTERLY

1366 "Rosenheim Ex-Libris." (1) 7:8, June 1932.
G. H. Viner examined Rosenheim's collection of foreign plates to select those to be accepted by Museum.

BRITISH PRINTER

1367 "Bookplate Design by R. Anning Bell." (1) 9:between 30 and 31, Jan-Feb. 1896.

Mander Brothers' Inks have bookplate stating: "This book is the property of Mander Brothers and forms part of their Workpeople's Library. The workpeople employed in our various factories are at liberty to take out books, only one book can be withdrawn at once and may be kept a reasonable time, but must be returned in any case, immediately on request of the librarian." Lettering and design by R. Anning Bell.

BROOKLYN JEWISH CENTER REVIEW

1368 "Biblical Bookplates." Philip Goodman. (7) 37:12-3, October 1955.

Interesting details about contemporary plates by Jewish artists or for Jewish owners.

THE BUILDER

1369 "Book-Plates." 69:269-70, October 19, 1895.

"The collecting of book-plates is a harmless if not a very intellectual hobby; it is something higher than the collecting of postage stamps, but altogether behind the amassing of prints, etchings or old china."

"We have no wish . . . to throw cold water on the study and collection of book-plates, for the more hobbies there are the greater are the sources of human happiness."

BULLETIN OF THE AMERICAN COLLEGE OF SURGEONS

1370 "Library and Department of Literary Research. Magic Mirrors." 22:106-7, January 1937.

"Among the magic mirrors at the College headquarters is the small but growing collection of bookplates. . . . Whether your bookplate possesses the virtue of simplicity or reflects your diversified interests, your cooperation in forwarding duplicate copies will be appreciated."

BULLETIN OF THE CINCINNATI ART MUSEUM

1371 "New Bookplate for the Museum Library." (1) 2:109, October 1931.

Cover of *Bulletin* pictures bookplates designed for Museum by William E. Hentschel, instructor in design at Cincinnati Art Academy.

BULLETIN OF THE HISTORY OF MEDICINE

1372 "Influence of Benjamin Rush on Practice of Bleeding." Joseph Ioor Waring. (1) 35:230-7, May-June 1961.

Illustrated is bookplate by Thomas Smith Denny, M.D., of the late 18th century.

BULLETIN OF THE MEDICAL LIBRARY ASSOCIATION

1373 "Book-Plates." Edna M. Poole. 24:145-8, February 1936.

Interesting details concerning medical bookplates.

1374 "Ex-Libris In a Medical Library." Ethel A. Washburn. (6) 27:230-6, June 1939.

Symbols frequently seen on medical bookplates are: microscope, scale, skull, Roentgen ray apparatus, death, the serpent, and wand of Aesculapius.

BULLETIN OF MEDICAL WOMEN'S CLUB OF CHICAGO

1375 "Medical Women's Library of the American Medical Women's Association." (1) 4 pages, 1950. [Unable to locate.]

Source: *Bibliography of Medical Ex Libris Literature* by Samuel X. Radbill, M.D. "A four-page reprint outlining the history, purposes and goal of this library."

BULLETIN OF METROPOLITAN MUSEUM OF ART

1376 "Baillie Collection of Bookplates." William M. Ivins, Jr. (4) 15:246-8, November 1920.

"Would one really know a man, consult not Dunn or Bradstreet, but find his plate."

1377 "Notes. Sherborn Prints." William M. Ivins, Jr. 16:63, March 1921.

Son of C. W. Sherborn gave Museum 261 prints and proofs of his father's work including bookplates.

1378 "Five Years in the Department of Prints." William M. Ivins, Jr. 16:258-62, December 1921.

Comment on Baillie bookplate collection: "the most important general one in the country and in the particularly interesting early American field second only to that in the possession of the Antiquarian Society of Worcester."

BULLETIN OF THE MINNEAPOLIS INSTITUTE OF ARTS

1379 "Bookplates." (2) 25:169-71, December 12, 1936.

Details about exhibition from collection of Oscar T. Blackburn, Minneapolis bookplate designer, engraver, and hobbyist.

BULLETIN OF NEW YORK PUBLIC LIBRARY

1380 "Bookplate Exhibit." 13:5, January 1909.

Astor Branch featuring exhibit of eighty bookplates by late J. W. Spenceley.

1381 "List of Works in the New York Public Library Relating to Prints and Their Production." Frank Weitenkampf. 19:959-1002, December 1915.

Pages 968-72 specifically list bookplates and there are additional artist entries throughout the report.

1382 "Book Plates." 21:609, September 1917.

A supplement. "Prints and Their Production," by Dr. Frank Weitenkampf includes reference to books by F. J. Fontency, Herman T. Radin, Arthur Sjogren and Harry P. Ward.

1383 "A Modern 'Little Master'—Charles William Sherborn and the Bookplate." 29:861, December 1925.

"Father of modern engraved bookplate" has work on exhibit in library; praised for fine sense of light and shade; "produced veritable works of art in the smallest space."

1384 "Book Plates." 31:227-8, March 1927.

List of books on this subject added to library in last five years.

1385 "Jay Chambers, Artist." Wilbur Macey Stone. (2) 34:9-10, January 1930.

Versatile artist created more than 100 bookplates.

1386 "Book Plates in the Print Room, Recent Gifts." 35:700, October 1931.

Gift from Dr. Radin of foreign plates (600).

1387 "Bookplates for Various Tastes; the Bookplate Owner and the Artist." 36: 744, November 1932.

Exhibit during December and January of modern European bookplates presented by Dr. Herman T. Radin.

1388 "Gift Bookplates." 38:276, April 1934.

P. Neville Barnett, of Sydney, Australia, gave forty-three of his plates and copy of annual report of Australian Ex Libris Society to the library.

1389 "Gift Bookplates." 42:642, August 1938.

P. Neville Barnett gave 180 additional bookplates.

1390 "An Exhibition of Bookplates." Dr. Herman T. Radin. 47:863-6, December 1943.

Only since about 1860 has "bookplate designing and engraving achieved a status as a fairly important branch of the graphic arts." About 3,000 European, British and American plates exhibited.

BULLETIN OF ORANGE COUNTY MEDICAL ASSOCIATION

1391 "Bookplates and Biography." Samuel X. Radbill. (3) 30:21-3, October 1961.

Interesting comments on numerous medical bookplates. Dr. Radbill uses term "philibrist" to denote one who collects or is interested in bookplates/ex libris.

BULLETIN OF THE SOCIETY OF MEDICAL HISTORY OF CHICAGO

1392 "Medical Bookplates." Morris Fishbein. (20) 2:302-20, March 1922.

General "bookplate art" background, details on each illustration, warning poems to borrowers, symbolism, early American plates starting with Alexander Anderson who was physician turned engraver, and a list of medical plates exhibited. "Your plate is as personal a matter as your Sunday hat and should fit you as well."

BUTTERFLY

1393 "Jeanne de Novarre." (1) 1:316, September 1893.

By Edgar Wilson; it certainly appears to be a bookplate.

1394 "N S" (1) 2:56, November 1893.
Another by Edgar Wilson with initials only.

C

CALIFORNIA ARTS & ARCHITECTURE

1395 "The Art of Ben Kutcher." Clare Talbot. (1) 52:1 *et seq.*, October 1937.
Russian born artist who won laurels in illustrating books, designing bookplates, advertising, and theatre work.

1396 "*Historic California in Bookplates.*" Reviewed by Edwin Turnbladh. 52:13, October 1937.
To quote reviewer of Clare Ryan Talbot's book: "Whether your curiosity runs to history, art or human beings (this book) is apt to contribute well to your enjoyment of life."

CALIFORNIA BOOKPLATES [See **BOOK-PLATE BOOKLET**, Sheldon Cheney, editor]

CALIFORNIA LIBRARIAN

"Ex Libris California."
Bookplates from the extensive collection of the California Historical Society and booksellers' labels from Professor Hugh S. Baker's collection; many interesting highlights of California history revealed through owners of bookplates.

1397 (5) 24: cover, insert 176-7, July 1963.
Plates for Adam A. McAlister, Santa Fe *California Limited*, Thomas Wayne Norris, and Riverside Public Library illustrated and described.

1398 (5) 24: cover, insert 240-1, October 1963.
Plates for Lassen County Free Library, Unity Sunday School of Santa Cruz, John Henry Nash, and Walter Schilling, M.D., illustrated and described.

1399 (5) 25: cover and insert 32-3, January 1964.
Plates for Philip Baldwin Bekeart, Marysville City Library, Franklin Eugene Perham and Mechanics' Institute illustrated and described.

1400 (5) 25: cover, insert 96-7, April 1964.
Plates illustrated and described for Joseph Noland, Alice Eastwood, Trinity Church, and James D. Phelan.

1401 (5) 25: cover, insert 160-1, July 1964.
Plates for Yosemite Ranger's Club Library, Caroline Constance Elliott Ver Huell collection of Oakland Public Library, St. John's Church, and Dr. Charles C. Park illustrated and described.

1402 (5) 25: cover, insert 236-7, October 1964.
Described and illustrated are plates for Aubrey Dury, Negro literature belonging to Nathan Van Patten, Henry H. Haight and Society of California Pioneers.

1403 (5) 26: cover, insert 32-3, January 1965.
Booksellers' labels for Burgress, Gilbert & Still, Marvie & Hitchcock, Lecount & Strong, and Henry Payat.

1404 (6) 26: cover, insert 96-7, April 1965.
Plates for Epes Ellery, Loewy Bros. & Birgham, Roman's Bookstore and New Emporium, Allen and Spier.

1405 (5) 26: cover, insert 160-1, July 1965.
Described and illustrated are plates for Abe Ruef, San Francisco political boss who served term in San Quentin Prison; Frances Schirmer Otto; Laurence Klauber; and Children of Mary Library.

1406 (5) 26:cover, insert 228-9, October 1965.
Described and illustrated are plates for Olivia Rolfe, Ernest Dawson, Mary Louise Phelan, and The Bend, Victorian mansion built by Charles S. Wheeler and later purchased by Hearst family.

1407 (5) 27: cover, insert 32-3, January 1966.
Plates for William H. Parks, Jr., Arthur R. Anderson, Sutro Library and Maude Lee Flood's which shows Linden Towers in Menlo Park.

1408 (5) 27: cover, insert 96-7, April 1966.
Plates for Robert Ernest Cowan, Jewel Fund plate for Stanford, Mechanics' Institute, and Albertine Stone Memorial.

CANADIAN BOOKMAN

1409 "Canadian Bookplates." R. H. Hathaway. (1) 2:28-9, December 1920.
Review of "*A List of Canadian Bookplates, with a Review of the History of Ex Libris in the Dominion*," compiled by Stanley Harrod and Morley J. Ayearst and published by Society of Bookplate Bibliophiles of Boston and Toronto.

CARLISLE PATRIOT

1410 "Mr. Claud Lonsdale on Book Plates." 41[Issue No. 4512]:3, February 17, 1899.
Lecture with slides given under the auspices of the Cumberland and Westmoreland Society of Arts and Crafts.

CARRIBEANA

1411 "West Indian Bookplates." Vere Langford Oliver. Supplement to 3:1-100, 1914.
Descriptive list of 752 plates giving arms, crest, motto and brief biographical data as available. Information drawn from collections of Sir Franks,

W. E. Baille, Frederic Cattle, Frank Evans Marshall, Julian Marshall. Twleve page index.

CENTURY

1412 "The Grolier Club." Brander Matthews. (1) 39:87-97, November 1889. (N.S.17)

Illustration of club bookplate included in lengthy article; club named for Treasurer-General of France noted for his books which were bound especially to his requirements.

1413 "Colonel William Byrd of Westover, Virginia." Constance Cary Harrison. (10) 42:163-78, June 1891. (N.S.20)

Chatty history of this early book collector; one illustration is of coat of arms used on bookplate.

1414 "Appeal of the Book-Plate, Antiquarian and Artistic." Charles Dexter Allen. (11) 63:238-47, December 1901. (N.S.41)

Excellent summarization of bookplate artists and historical background.

1415 "Master of Make-Believe." Christian Brinton. (15) 84:340-52, July 1912. (N.S. 62)

All illustrations by Maxfield Parrish; though only one a bookplate, many would make delightful plates for young people or the young-in-heart.

CHAMBERS'S JOURNAL

1416 "Royal Standard of England." John Leighton. 14:321-2, May 22, 1897.

Article mentioned in *Journal of Ex Libris Society* about adding "an extra device to include Wales" along with England, Scotland and Ireland on the Royal Standard.

1417 "Borrowers, Beware!" Marie W. Stuart. (9th Ser.) 2:659-62, December 1948.

Various inscriptions denoting ownership and warning borrowers.

CHAP BOOK

1418 "Design for a Book-Plate." Will H.Bradley. (1) 2:233, January 15, 1895.

Illustration only of plate for Owen W. Brewer.

1419 "On a Bookplate." Charles F. Lummis. 4:314, February 15, 1896.

By Books may Learning, perhaps befall;
But Wisdom, never by Books at all—
Yet Thought should shiver at least the less
With them to cover her nakedness.

1420 "Reviews." 7:327-8, September 1897.

"To learn that Paul Revere made a bookplate for Epes Sargent, and Thackeray one for Edward Fitzgerald—is enough to interest almost any one in book-plates."

CHEMIST AND DRUGGIST

1421 "Book-Plates." (1) 62:670, April 25, 1903.
Illustration of plate used by Pharmaceutical Society of Switzerland.

1422 "Pharmaceutical Book-Plates." (1) 62:902, June 6, 1903.
Plate for library of Pharmaceutic Institute of University of Bern shows an alchemist and a glimpse of the Swiss town.

1423 "Pharmaceutical Book-Plates." (1) 62:982, June 20, 1903.
Plate of Dr. Maurice Greshoff, Director of the Chemical Laboratory, Colonial Museum, Haarlem; original "is in crimson ink."

1424 "Some Old Book-Plates." (8) 65:216-7, July 30, 1904.
"Book-plate collecting . . . is not merely a harmless pursuit, but one bringing with it a good deal of insight into the social life of past generations."

1425 "French Pharmaceutical Ex Libris." 71:292, August 17, 1907.
Brief mention of bookplates of Assistant-Professor of the Paris Superior School of Pharmacy, the editor of *Chronique Medicale* and a professor of Parasitology at Paris.

1426 "Pharmaceutical Book-Plates." (2) 71:349, August 24, 1907.
Two plates for William Oliver (1695-1746) who is "best remembered by most people as the inventor of the 'Bath Oliver' biscuits."

1427 "Pharmaceutical Book-Plates." (1) 71:390, August 31, 1907.
Illustration only of plate for Johannes Kinnard.

1428 "Pharmaceutical Book-Plates." (1) 71:404, September 7, 1907.
Plate, probably engraved by George Virtue, for John Maud, who is described on his book-plate as "Philochymist at the sign of the Golden Key in the street commonly called Aldersgate Street, London."

CHICAGO CLINIC AND PURE WATER JOURNAL

1429 "Book-plates of American Physicians." 21:216, August 1908.
"We believe we have undertaken no single feature which has created more favorable comment."

1430 "The Doctor & His Book-Plate." George Thomas Palmer. (8) 21:219-24, August 1908.
Wide variety of designs and interesting comments on individual physicans.

1431 "The Doctor & His Book-Plate." George Thomas Palmer. (13) 21:253-8, September 1908.
Wealth of information on physicans.

1432 "The Doctor & His Book-Plate." George Thomas Palmer. (6) 21:287-91, October 1908.
Plates of European doctors as well as American.

1433 "The Doctor & His Book-Plate." George Thomas Palmer. 21:324-6, November 1908.

Describes processes of reproducing bookplates and approximate prices, specifically for a half-tone engraving.

CHICAGO JEWISH FORUM

1434 "Books." (1) 16:124-6, Winter 1957-58.

Philip Goodman's *American Jewish Bookplates* reviewed by Leah Yablonsky Mishkin. To Rabbi Goodman "these artistic labels constitute a miniature world for study and research."

THE CHURCHMAN

1435 "A Few Words on Book-Plates or Ex-Libris." Louis J. Rhead. (4) 71:577-9, April 20, 1895.

Author-artist's own bookplate among those illustrated; quotes from Edmund Gosse's article in *The Anthenaeum* against bookplate collecting.

CINCINNATI ART MUSEUM BULLETIN [See **BULLETIN OF CINCINNATI ART MUSEUM**]

CLASSICAL JOURNAL

1436 "An Early Ex Libris." Dorothy M. Schullian. 39:290-3, February 1944.

More warnings in verse, some in Latin; one found in volume printed in 1575.

COAT OF ARMS

"Heraldic Book Plates." B. C. Trappes-Lomas.

1437 (7) 3:No. 21:184-6, 1954-55.
1438 (7) 3:No. 22:229-31, 1954-55.
1439 (12) 3:No. 23:263-7, 1954-55.
1440 (5) 3:No. 24:308-10, 1954-55.

Various aspects of heraldry are detailed through armorial bookplates. Plate for Edward Bullock has blank space for arms of his wife.

COLBY LIBRARY QUARTERLY

1441 "Bookplates at Colby." Edward F. Stevens. Series 1, 165-8, March 1945.

Mrs. Frank Cowdery bestowed collection of 1,000 ex libris to Colby (Waterville, Maine); includes plates by Bewick (twelve), William Blake, Alexander Anderson, as well as many other distinguished bookplate designers.

COLLECTOR [Alfred Trumble, editor]

1442 "Notes and Novelties." 4:199, May 1, 1893.

Quotes scathing article by London *Daily News* on bookplates and Mr. Hardy.

1443 "Notes and Novelties." 4:216, May 15, 1893.
Notes publication in France by L. Jolly concerning imaginery bookplates.

1444 "About Bookplates." 4:221, May 15, 1893.
In spite of "truculent disapproval of the London *Daily News*" author feels "collection of bookplates is by no means puerile and merely a waste of time."

1445 "Notes and Novelties." 4:303-4, October 1, 1893.
Artist Edwin A. Abbey designed plates for Brander Matthews and Edmund Gosse; editor of *Collector* has plate by Joseph Lauber, artist with Tiffany Glass Company, which he is willing to exchange with subscribers.

1446 "Notes and Novelties." 4:312-3, October 15, 1893.
Macmillan & Co. announces forthcoming book by Charles Dexter Allen; one of largest collections of bookplates in America is that of Frederic J. Libbie.

1447 "Brander Matthews' Bookplate." 5:8, November 1, 1893.
Description of plate designed by Edwin A. Abbey for Matthews, "an enthusiastic student and admirer of Molière."

1448 "Notes and Novelties." 5:123, February 15, 1894.
Charles Dexter Allen sent editor artist's proof of bookplate designed for him by W. H. W. Bicknell and etched by Edmund H. Garrett.

1449 "Notes and Novelties." 5:137, March 1, 1894.
W. F. Hopson sent proof of bookplate for himself bearing inscription "Old Books to read; Old prints to scan; To carve old wood; Old friends to greet."

COLLECTOR [Walter Benjamin, editor]

1450 "Some Historic Book-Plates, I." 5:151-3, June 1892.
Details on early ecclesiastical plates.

1451 "Some Historic Book-Plates, II." 5:164-5, July 1892.
Plate of Francis Frampton (1633) mentioned as oldest English specimen, though some possibly date as early as 1571.

1452 "Some Historic Book-Plates, III." 5:176-7, August 1892.
American plates of various historic periods discussed.

1453 "German Book-Plates of Pennsylvania." (1) 6:3-5, September 1892.
Arms of Rev. Michael Schlotter illustrated.

1454 "Book-Plate of Jacob Sargeant." (1) 6:26, November 1892.
Designed and engraved by the owner in a semi-heraldic form which seemed to indicate disapproval of heraldry for Americans.

1455 "Collection of Book-Plates." 6:29-30, November 1892.
Item from *London Post* on renewed interest in collecting bookplates. Part of Pirckheimer's library acquired by Earl of Arundel who afterwards bestowed volumes upon Royal Society which in turn parted with duplicates, some of which contained the Durer plate.

1456 "Book Plates." 8:95-6, May 1895.
List of plates for sale and prices; editor says plates "sent on approval to persons known to me."

1457 "Book Plates." 8:97, June 1895.
With this issue magazine sub-titled "A Historical-Magazine for Autograph and Book Plate Collectors." Contributions "will be welcomed and paid for."

1458 "Book Plates." 8:107, June 1895.
Plates offered for sale, listed by name and dimensions, at fifty cents each.

1459 "Some Noted Book-Plates." R. S. Holland. 8:112, July 1895.
Plates of Matthew Prior, Lawrence, Sterne, David Garrick, Horace Walpole, and Victor Hugo mentioned among others.

1460 "Book Plates for Sale." 8:119-20, July 1895.
Facsimile of George Washington's offered for $1; others at 25¢ to $3.50.

1461 "Allen's Book." 8:121-2, August 1895.
Review of *American Book Plates* with comment in particular on Rhode Island plates which the reviewer feels inadequately covered by Charles Dexter Allen.

1462 "Book Plates." 8:131-2, August 1895.
Further sale list.

1463 "Speaking of Book-Plates." Charlotte Charles Herr. 8:135-6, September 1895.
In order of value to collecter, first are early signed and dated plates, then those of noted engravers, those of eminent people, and last those of special beauty or oddity of design.

1464 "Book Plates." 8:143-4, September 1895.
A Thomas Bewick for $1.25; Victor Hugo's at 75¢.

1465 "Ex-Libris Department. Introductory." Walter R. Benjamin. 9:6, October 1895.
New department begun in order that collectors may freely communicate.

1466 "The Lynch Plate." Walter R. Benjamin. (2) 9:7, October 1895.
Plates of father and son illustrated; Thomas Lynch Jr. was a signer of the Declaration of Independence.

1467 "Ex-Libris in Germany." 9:8, October 1895.

Increased interest in bookplate collecting puts amateur at a disadvantage because of scarcity and cost of desired quality plates.

1468 "Book Plates." 9:14-5, October 1895.
Sale list.

1469 "Commercial Book-Plates." (1) 9:21-2, November 1895.
Usually small plates used by booksellers to identify shop from which book purchased.

1470 "Lancaster Book-Plates." (1) 9:22, November 1895.
List of individuals and institutions in Lancaster owning bookplates.

1471 "Ex Libris Journal." 9:24, November 1895.
Comments on journal established five years previously.

1472 "Notice." 9:24, November 1895.
Publication of third part of Walter Hamilton's *Dated Book-Plates*.

1473 "Inquiry." 9:24, November 1895.
Location of "Bernardston" requested and who is "Bill Bismarck."

1474 "Book Plates." 9:31, November 1895.
Hildebrand Brandenburger plate in three colors for sale at twenty dollars and others listed for much less.

1475 "Study of American Book-Plates." 9:37, December 1895.
Suggests being a "general collector" as early American plates "not generally of high artistic excellence." Study of biography helpful; also heraldry, engravers.

1476 "Lancaster Book-Plates." (1) 9:38-9, December 1895.
Conclusion of November listing.

1477 "Inquiry Answer." 9:39, December 1895.
Answer to location question about Bernardston and additional information on Lynch plate.

1478 "Hewins Sale." 9:39-40, December 1895.
Sale in Boston of collection of 3,229 plates assembled in 4 volumes, purchased for $1,250 by W. E. Baille of Bridgeport, Conn.

1479 "Inquiry." 9:40, December 1895.
Question concerning Tower of Alloa.

1480 "Plate Illustrated." (1) 9:40, December 1895.
Ex libris of Col. Huizinga Messchert, which dates from 1850, illustrated.

1481 "Book Plates." 9:47, December 1895.
List of plates for sale, some by Hopson, fifty cents each.

1482 "Humorous Book-Plates." 9:53-4, January 1896.
Plate of Benedictine monastery exclaims: "Ho, there! Take me back to my master."

1483 "In Memoriam." 9:54, January 1896.

Deaths of Lord de Tabley and Rev. Thomas William Carson of Dublin noted.

1484 "Plates Illustrated." (2) 9:55, January 1896.

Plates of Michael Schlotter and Manuel Welles.

1485 "Plate Identified." 9:55, January 1896.

Plate illustrated in November issue was incomplete and should have scroll inscription above arms to identify it as that of "Christophorus Adamus Rinder, I.V. Dr." of Nuremberg, a canting plate. Rinder signified horned cattle, and three bullocks' heads are on escutcheon.

1486 "Nack Plate." 9:56, January 1896.

Incorrectly identified as "commercial" in a prior article.

1487 "Old American Book-Plates." 9:45, January 1896.

List from collection of Rev. T. W. Carson.

1488 "Matter of Arrangement." 9:69-70, February 1896.

Large collection divided into periods: Colonial (1725-77), First National (1776-1820), Second National (1820-61), Third National (1861 to present) or Old and New with Civil War as dividing point. No set rule for mounting, but should allow for free removal of plates.

1489 "Enoch Pratt Free Library Collection of Ex-Libris." 9:70, February 1896.

This Baltimore library has 900 bookplates.

1490 "Dubbs Plate." (1) 9:71, February 1896.

Joseph Henry Dubbs, D.D., was editor of Ex Libris Department of *Collector*. Dubbs of Bohemian origin; means "Oak"; thus plate has oak and Bohemian crest of plumes; designed by D. McN. Stauffer in 1880.

1491 "Some Interesting Labels." 9:71-2, February 1896.

Seven printed labels described.

1492 "Plate of Simon P. Eby—Correction on Messchert Plate." (1) 9:72, February 1896.

Eby plate designed by Stauffer, dated 1891. Plate engraved for Col. Messchert in 1826 when he was eighteen.

1493 "Shall Americans Assume Badges?" 9:85-6, March 1896.

Badges used before coats of arms. Since most Americans not properly entitled to heraldic devices, perhaps badges or emblems would be the answer.

1494 "Lancaster Book-Plates." 9:86, March 1896.

Addenda to previous list.

1495 "Isaiah Thomas." (1) 9:87, March 1896.

Next to Franklin, Thomas most eminent American printer during Revolution. Founded Antiquarian Society of Worcester in 1812.

1496 "Cleansing Book-Plates." 9:87-8, March 1896.

Answer: DON'T.

1497 "Rev. Carson Collection." 9:88, March 1896.
Collection of 32,000 sold for 1,150 pounds.

1498 "Rudolph Benkard." (1) 9:88, March 1896.
German bookplate illustrated.

1499 "Hobbies." 9:101-2, April 1896.
Bookplate collecting mentioned.

1500 "Matter of Exchanges." 9:102-3, April 1896.
When there were only a very few collectors they exchanged among themselves; often large numbers of plates available from a printer when a library rebound its books. Now necessary to purchase rarities.

1501 "Book-Plates." 9:103, April 1896.
Three miscellaneous items.

1502 "Franklin & Marshall College." (1) 9:103, April 1896.
Bookplate designed by alumnus D. McN. Stauffer illustrated.

1503 "Book-Plates." (1) 9:104, April 1896.
Plate of German historian Dr. John Gustave Droysen illustrated; that of James Ward described; work of D. McN. Stauffer mentioned.

1504 "Book-Plates of Signers of the Declaration." 9:117-8, May 1896.
At least eleven signers had bookplates and each is commented upon.

1505 "Jenison-Walworth Book-Plate." 9:118-9, May 1896.
First count was Englishman; family moved to Bavaria, later America.

1506 "Elias Hicks Plate." 9:119 1896.
Maverick designed plate misidentified by Allen according to correspondent.

1507 "Book-Plate Auction." 9:119, May 1896.
Books on auction contain bookplate of man who never parted with any books bearing his bookplate.

1508 "Marks Plates." 9:120, May 1896.
Plates by H. Stacy Marks in collection of Dr. Dubbs listed.

1509 "Robertus Shippen." (1) 9:119, May 1896.
Illustration only.

1510 "William Penn's Bookplate." (1) 9:120, May 1896.
Illustration only.

1511 "James Monroe and Upton Reade." 9:120, May 1896.
Brief comment.

1512 "Shall We Collect Book-Plates?" W. G. Bowdoin. 9:131-2, June 1896.
When a person knows about bookplates "you find as a rule a person of refinement and culture, an agreeable person to meet."

1513 "Book-Plate of Sophia Penn." 9:132, June 1896.
Attempt to identify Sophia Penn as descendant of William Penn; plate bears initials of English engraver R. Mountaine.

1514 "Book-Plates." 9:133, June 1896.
Asked which ex libris would be accorded place of honor, editor chose portrait plate engraved by Durer for Bilibaldus Pirckheimer, dated 1524.

1515 "Virginia Council Chamber Plate." (1) 9:133, June 1896.
Illustration only.

1516 "Ex Libris Typothetae Diaboli." 9:133, June 1896.
F. S. King, artist and engraver, issued bookplate of Printer's Devil, 8 3/4 x 11 1/2; 250 impressions published by Max Williams Co., 390 W. 5th Ave., N.Y.

1517 "Thaddeus Stevens." 9:134, June 1896.
Stevens probably didn't have a bookplate but merely signed his name on the engraved bookplate already in books he acquired from previous owner.

1518 "James Morris." (1) 9:134, June 1896.
Illustration of plate of New York family of colonial and revolutionary period.

1519 "Miscellaneous." 9:134, June 1896.
Three brief bookplate items.

1520 "Ecclesiastical Book-Plates." 9:143-4, July 1896.
Explanations concerning Latin inscriptions; how to identify "episcopal hat (number of tassels and color indicate whether cardinal, archbishop, bishop, or abbot's mitred hat).

1521 "Book-Plates." (1) 9:144, July 1896.
Brothers of Unity of Yale (literary society) bookplate shown; brief comment on Igler plate; "book-plate collecting is a sentiment."

1522 "Book-Plates." 9:145, July 1896.
Miscellaneous brief comments.

1523 "Bookworm on Book-Plates." 9:145-6, July 1896.
Sir Walter Scott: "although most of my friends are bad arithmeticians, they all appear to be good book keepers."

1524 "Book-Plates." 9:146, July 1896.
American collectors tend to undervalue ex libris of other countries and other brief comments.

1525 "Ex Libris Societies." 9:156, August 1896.
Society formed in Washington.

1526 "English Engravers of Book-Plates." Walter Hamilton. 9:156-8, August 1896.
Mentions that none known to have been done by George Cruikshank.

1527 "Book-Plates." (2) 9:158, August 1896.
Plates of Philip Judwell and Ralph Wormley illustrated; miscellaneous comments.

1528 "Fringes of History." 9:3-4, October 1896.
Collectors usually student of these minor sciences: numismatics, palaeography, as well as engraving which would include bookplates.

1529 "Book-Plates and Printers Marks." 9:4-5, October 1896.
Item from *Printing Times and Lithographer*, November 15, 1882.

1530 "Bookplates." 10:25, December 1896.
Sentence each on bookplates of historian George Grate and George Fitz Clarence, Earl of Munster.

1531 "Some English Inscriptions on Book-Plates." W. G. Bowdoin, 10:26-7, December 1896.
"Be true to your work and your work will be true to you," Pratt Institute, Brooklyn.

1532 "Book-Plate Zoology." W. G. Bowdoin. 10:39-40, January 1897.
Gryphon (body and tail of lion, head of cock, wings and sharp claws), wyvern (two legged dragon), chimera (lion's head, goat's body, dragon's tail, vomiting flames); among others the unicorn, centaur, scollog, phoenix.

1533 "Ladies' Book-Plates." W. G. Bowdoin. 10:52-3, February 1897.
When lady did have a separate plate, copper first cut with lady's name, then same plate altered to husband's name and retained for his use.

1534 "Book-Plate Hunting in Europe." 10:61-2, March 1897.
Quality and variety at reasonable prices make it a rewarding search.

1535 "Identification of Book-Plates." W. G. Bowdoin, 10:63-4, March 1897.
Inexperienced collectors will find identity of nameless plates serious problem; experience will help to place period, school, style; knowledge of heraldry helpful; a good reference library and help from other knowledgeable collectors also useful.

1536 "Book-Plate Hunting." W. G. Bowdoin. 10:73-4, April 1897.
"Vacations can be utilized incidentally by hunting in distant domestic or foreign points; . . . no school for book-plate hunters."

1537 "Book-Plate Notes." 10:84, May 1897.
Revision of Allen's book unlikely; frequently commands premium price.

1538 "Sale of Book Plates." 10:109-10, July 1897.
Auction in Boston on May 21 by C. F. Libbie & Co. at which George Washington restrike brought thirteen dollars.

1539 "Some Contintental Notes on Book-Plates." William G. Bowdoin. 10:118-20, September 1897.
Noblemen who had plates engraved during Revolutionary epoch replaced crested coronet with liberty cap.

1540 "French Book-Plates." W. G. Bowdoin. 11:2-4, October 1897.
"One must be very guarded in buying, however, as the French custom of reproducing rare plates is very prevalent."

1541 "Notes." 11:25, December 1897.
"Some book-plate collectors illustrate their collections by autographs of the original owners of the plates."

1542 "A Plea for Bookplates." W. G. Bowdoin. 11:25-6, December 1897.
"The world has a place for the bookplate hobby in the hours of leisure and relaxation, and the celestial fire once kindled should be carefully guarded and kept burning on the sacred altar."

1543 "Bookplates." 11:44-5, January 1898.
List of priced plates for sale by editor, Walter Benjamin, 15¢, to $1.00.

1544 "American Bookplates." 11:57, February 1898.
Priced list, 30¢ to a top of $5 for Paul Revere restrike of D. Greene plate and Oliver Wendell Holmes' Nautilus.

1545 "Brooklyn Bookplate." W. G. Bowdoin. (1) 11:60, March 1898.
Plate used by twenty physicians for Medical Society of the County of Kings library.

1546 "On Book Plates." 11:60-1, March 1898.
Biting attack on bookplate collectors in general and on Fincham's book in particular.

1547 "American Bookplates." 11:70-1, March 1898.
Many priced at 25¢, a few as high as $1, top $2.50.

1548 "Hostility to Book-Plate Collecting." W. G. Bowdoin. 11:89-90, May 1898.
"Book-plate collection pleases the eye and cultivates the mind." However, there are those who brand bookplate collectors as "VANDALS."

1549 "Book-Plates." 11:98-9, May 1898.
"Old German plate on vellum. Not in any list . . . $10."

1550 "Notes." 11:122, September 1898.
"Beginning with the next number—No. 1 of Vol. 12—the *Collector* will cease to trouble itself about bookplates. . . . It will probably publish book-plate articles from time to time, but book-plates hereafter will be treated as they deserve—as a very small unimportant side-issue to autographs. After an experience of two years, I can truthfully state it is the meanest business that any dealer ever got into. It is a good thing to let alone."
"Some book-plates have a certain minor and languid interest, but the great majority are utter trash, and to collect them is far below the dignity even of a stamp collector. It is a silly fad which has pretty nearly exhausted itself."

1551 "Book-Plate Collecting As A Hobby." W. G. Bowdoin. 12:24-5, December 1899.
A low-keyed but firm defense.

1552 "Book-Plate Art of Joseph Sattler." W. G. Bowdoin. (1) 12:36, January 1899.
German artist whose work "stands for high excellence and bold design."

1553 "Inscription on Book-Plate." George Wightwick. 12:50, February 1899.
Poetic admonishment to return borrowed book.

1554 "Book-Plates—Old and New." 12:67, March 1899.
Review of John A. Gade's book, priced at $1.25.

1555 "Note." 12:78, April 1899.
Paul Lemperly announces publication of Edwin D. French checklist.

1556 "Modern Tendency in Book-Plate Designing." W. G. Bowdoin. 12:81, April 1899.
"The fantastic and the grotesque that found original expression in the poster have entered into and found a too prominent place in the book-plate world."

1557 "Book-Plate Work of Homer W. Colby." W. G. Bowdoin. (2) 14:144-5, October 1901.
One illustration shows a monastery library.

1558 "Book-Plates of Hugh M. and Margaret Fernie Eaton." W. G. Bowdoin. (2) 16:40, February 1903.
Valhall Studio in Brooklyn used by Eatons.

1559 "Some Book-Plates Designed by Gardner C. Teall." W. G. Bowdoin. (3) 16:64, April 1903.
Teall, Art Editor of *Good Housekeeping,* designed twenty bookplates.

1560 "Margaret Laing Crowell: Book-Plate Designer." W. G. Bowdoin. (3) 18:39-40, February 1905.
One plate illustrated is for botanist, featuring the aster.

1561 "Book-Plates." (2) 19:77, May 1906.
Work of Canadian artists Anthony H. Euwer and Arthur W. Crisp illustrated.

COLLECTORS' ILLUSTRATED CIRCULAR

1562 "Book-plates and Books." Edward Almack. (2) Issue No. 34:5-6, July 9, 1904.
One illustration is plate of Owen Wynne, which has a shield displaying twenty quarterings.

1563 "Book-plates and Books." Edward Almack. (3) Issue No. 37:70-1, August 20, 1904.
"The writer makes bold to confess that for him to enjoy looking at a book-plate, that book-plate must be resting in the book to which it properly belongs."

1564 "Books and Book-plates." Edward Almack. (3) Issue No. 44:215-6, November 26, 1904.
"With *ex libris,* more essentially than with other objects of the collector's hunger, a monotonous sameness is to be shunned."

1565 "Books and Book-plates." Edward Almack. (4) Issue No. 46:243-5, December 24, 1904.

Plates illustrated for Sir Jonathan Lovett, Elijah Impey, Forbes of Shellater and James Forbes.

COLLECTOR'S JOURNAL

1566 "A Plea for the Bookplate." Carlyle S. Baer. 3:346-7, January-February-March 1933.

Collecting bookplates will "bring in its wake a knowledge of graphic art medium, paper stock, reproduction processes, heraldry, family history, intimate biography. . . ."

1567 "Bookplates' Speculative Future." Geraldine D. Kelly. 3:347-8, January-February-March 1933.

Those of particular value may be plates which are signed, dated, and/or those of well-known individuals.

COLOPHON

1568 "Curious Book Labels." (2) 2:134, Autumn 1936.

One illustration for the Library Association of the Diligent Hose Company.

1569 "George Brinley's Book Label." (1) 2:135, Autumn 1936.

Simply name within a double ruled oblong. Letter quoted showing interest in having "a classic design and elaborate finish without ostentation" but apparently plate was never completed.

1570 "Pennsylvania German Bookplates." Henry S. Borneman. (4) 2:432-42, Summer 1937.

Bookplates illustrated are "invariably the size of the page of the book"; colors used as in medieval art of illumination.

1571 "Ex-Libris Van der Kuylen." W. Van der Kuylen. (14) 3:411-26, Summer 1938.

Extensive details about current European engravers of bookplates; work of fourteen designers shown.

COLOUR

1572 "Brangwyn: His Place in Art." "Tis." (4) 5:2,4,6,7,9, August 1916.

No illustration or mention of bookplates for which this artist received considerable acclaim.

COMMON SENSE [Dublin]

1573 "Half Hours Among My Book-Plates." June 1899. [Unable to locate.]

Source: *Journal Ex Libris Society*, 9:122, September 1899: "The subject of mottoes, of canting arms, and the symbolism of heraldry, is well treated."

CONNECTICUT MAGAZINE

1574 "Ex Libris." (13) 10:15-8, January-March 1906.
Bookplates designed by three-man design group, "The Triptych," loaned for exhibition by Kendall Banning. One punning plate for George F. Bear features a polar bear.

CONNOISSEUR

1575 "Mr. Julian Marshall's Bookplates." (9) 3:87-91, June 1902.
Marshall collection second only to Frank's in British Museum.

1576 "Notes." 5:59, January 1903.
Comments on forged bookplates for Gore and Washington.

1577 "Collecting of Bookplates." (Mrs.) L. Nevill Jackson. (14) 14:15-20, January 1906.
"A bookplate of whatever date may be valuable for different reasons:
1. dated; 2. artistic merit; 3. skill in production; 4. ingenuity of design; 5. fame of artist; 6. ownership of bookplate; 7. error in design."

1578 "Cult of Book-Plates." George C. Peachey. (9) 15:183-6, July 1906.
When Marshall collection sold, auctioneer's catalog comprised 242 pages.

1579 "Book-Plates of Oxford Colleges." (4) 22:52-5, September 1908.
Plate by M. Burghers was used in book presented to the college in 1710 by Christopher Codrington.

1580 "Cambridge College Bookplates." Fred W. Burgess. (4) 25:172-3, November 1909.
One plate dated as early as 1715, although not engraved until 1737.

1581 "Landscape Book-Plates." P. Miller. (7) 29:235-7, April 1911.
Illustrated and described are several plates by Thomas Bewick, as well as lesser known artists.

1582 "Some American Bookplates." Clifford N. Carver. (10) 44:137-40, March 1916.
Interesting illustrations include bookplates of William Howard Taft, Woodrow Wilson, George Bancroft, Theodore Roosevelt, Andrew Carnegie, Dr. Henry van Dyke.

1583 "Two Copley Book-plates." Latham Burton. (2) 78:102-3, June 1927.
Bookplates for John Singleton Copley, Lord Chancellor, later Chief Baron of the Exchequer, and his first wife.

1584 "Book-Plates at Cartier's." 78:252, August 1927.
Description of plates exhibited at Cartier's including Cumberland bookplate by William Blake (1827), Pepys, Dr. Peachey's medical collection, and some by Cartier.

1585 "Ex-Libris at Brussels." 83:378, June 1929.
Tenth anniversary of Belgian Association. Great Britain among few

governments which gave no official support to exhibition. German work center of attraction.

1586 "George Washington Book-Plate." Helen Comstock. (4) 94:54-55, July 1934.
Excellent article on original and counterfeit of George Washington's plate; also similar plates of Richard Washington by George Bickham (about 1750) and Bushrod Washington. Original metal plate of George Washington's in Metropolitan Museum of Art.

1587 "Book-Plate in Duten's *Journal* 1782." (1) 96:115, August 1935.
Plate of Cornelius O'Callaghan (1775-1857).

1588 "Book-Plate of Armorer Donkin." (1) 96:352, Christmas 1935.
Friend of Bewick, an attorney of NewCastle-on-Tyne "had not right of the achievement which Bewick included in the cut which he made for his book-plate."

1589 "*Making a Bookplate* by Mark F. Severin." 125:60, March 1950.
Review of Severin's book on designing bookplates.

1590 "Connoisseur's Diary." 136:53, September 1955.
One of few remaining bookplate engravers "can now accept a limited number of commissions."

1591 "Bookplates of Rex Whistler." Laurence Whistler. (17) 144:86-90, November 1959.
Details relating how each plate happened to be created. Artist did not attach much importance to bookplates and often drew them on fly-leaf of book when making a present of it.

CONNOISSEUR YEAR BOOK

1592 "Some Book-Plates of Schools, Colleges and Universities." Mark Severin. (27) 61-8, 1962.
Discusses plates for Eaton, one of which, by Reynolds Stone, "is elegant, simple and striking." Sherborn did plates for Winchester College and Magdalen College; Will Carter also designed a plate for Winchester.

CONTINENT [Philadelphia]

1593 "Right to Bear Arms." Frank Willing Leach. (39) 3:513-23, April 25, 1883.
"Most of the illustrations given are *facsimiles* or reproduced copies of book-plates—that is, engravings of family arms placed upon the inside front cover of the books comprising a library."

CORNHILL BOOKLET

1594 "Recent American Ex Libris." Wilbur Macey Stone. (20) 2:43-62, September 1901.
All plates shown are printed from original blocks.

1595 "Selections from *The Page* Concerning Bookplates." (1) 2:105-6, December 1901.

"A Bookplate is to a Book what a Collar is to a Dog." quoted from Gordon Craig publication.

1596 "Notes." (1) 3:17-22, Autumn 1902.

Wilbur Macey Stone volume on Jay Chambers to be published by "Triptych," three-man design team to which both belong. Comment on Gordon Craig—he is "a decadent in the best sense of the word. He goes back to the pre-railroad era."

1597 "Some German Book-Plates." Winfred Porter Truesdell. (8) 3:77-88, December 1903.

Artists represented have created many plates for Imperial Family.

CORNHILL MAGAZINE [London]

1598 "Humours of Heraldry." N.S.23:375-82, October 1894.

"The very existence of such an institution as the College of Arms at the end of the nineteenth century must be regarded as an anomaly, an anachronism, or a prehistoric survival." Very entertaining article.

1599 "Collecting of Bookplates." G. H. Viner. 160:677-85, November 1939.

Comments on individual plates, artists, and the hazards and pleasures of collecting.

COROS CHRONICLE

1600 "Bookplates and Philately." Rev. Canon Enrico S. Molnar. (4) 17:72-3, August 1965.

"Since there are philatelists who collect books as well as stamps, there must inevitably be philatelic bookplates."

COUNTRY LIFE

1601 "Book-Plates." (6) 14:9-10, July 4, 1903

"The finest edition new issued from the printing house has not a fourth of the interest of the old thumbed volume held precious by some dead man of genius whose property the book-plate declares it to have been."

1602 "Chippendale Book-Plates." W. H. K. Wright. (6) 14:200-2, August 8, 1903.

The style "follows closely that of the much-prized furniture of Thomas Chippendale . . . reproducing all of its salient characteristics."

1603 "Two More Chippendale Book-Plates." W. H. K. Wright. (3) 14:288, August 22, 1903.

Plates for Robert Dalzell, Henry Emmett, and Will Horton.

1604 "Landscape Bookplates." (11) 14:886-8, December 19, 1903.

Very attractive plates with personalized landscapes rather than the general scenes by the Bewicks.

1605 "Book Plates of Country Dwellers." Stephen Allard. (12) 31:50-1, November 1916.

Author exhorts individual to "go not to stationer or commercial artist, but to one of those few designers who have made the book plate field peculiarly their own." Plates illustrated feature out-of-door scenes, angling, riding.

1606 "Bookplates for Confirmed Bibliophiles; Designed by E. B. Bird." (6) 59:42, December 1930.

Article states no book is complete without its bookplate, that symbol of intimate possession.

CRAFTSMAN

1607 "*Some Indiana Bookplates.*" Esther Griffin White. (22) 4:93-100, May 1903.

Artists and owners of bookplates from author's native state.

1608 "Plea for the Decorative Book-Plate." Frank Chonteau Brown. (20) 5:552-62, March 1904.

Artist gives problems and pleasures of designing bookplates.

1609 "Book-Plate Idea." C. Valentine Kirby. (16) 6:54-61, April 1904.

"The book-plate idea is appreciated by some, regarded as a mania by others, and misunderstood by the majority."

1610 "Work of Anthony H. Euwer—An Appreciation by Will Larrymore Smedley." (21) 6:561-69, September 1904.

All but three illustrations are bookplates. Artist authored volume of nonsense verse titled *Rickety Rimes and Rigmaro.*

CREATIVE ART

1611 "Concerning Stanislaw Ostoja-Chrostowski." Pauline A. Pickney. (10) 9:235-37, September 1931.

Polish artist who did primarily wood engravings.

CRITIC

1612 "(London Letter)." E. B. Wolford. 22 (n.s.19):80, February 11, 1893.

Plugs for two volumes on bookplates: *English Bookplates* by Warren, and Castle's book of the same title.

1613 "Book-Plates of Some English Authors." (6) 22 (n.s.19):82-3, February 11, 1893.

Comments on Castle's book, published only a few weeks and already out-of-print.

1614 "Book Plates." (1) 22 (n.s.19):326, May 20, 1893.

Reviewer claims Hardy's volume more solidly written than Castle's; historical study especially good on Colonial period.

1615 "Some American Book-Plates." (5) 23(n.s.20):88-9, August 5, 1893.

Recommends *Handbook of American Book-Plates* by Allen.

1616 "(Notes)." 25(n.s.22):99, August 11, 1894.
Notice of Grolier Club exhibition of American bookplates.

1617 "Book-plates at the Grolier Club." (1) 25(n.s.22):263, October 20, 1894.
Review of exhibit and illustration of photoetched card of invitation issued by the Grolier Club.

1618 "*American Book-Plates.*" (2) 26 (n.s.23):81-2, February 2, 1895.
Review of Charles Dexter Allen's book; also *Processes for Production of Ex Libris* by John Vinycomb.

1619 "Sale of Foote Collection of English Literature." (1) 26(n.s.23):101-7, February 9, 1895.
Sale by Bangs & Co. of well-known banker's collection; bookplate illustrated with quote from *Ship of Fools* [1509].

1620 "Edmund Gosse's Letter on Bookplates." 26(n.s.23):131, February 16, 1895.
Mention of amusing letter in current *Athenaeum* on bookplate collecting. Gosse, when receiving requests for his bookplate, reminds "his correspondents, with good show of reason, that the bookplate is a personal possession with which outsiders can have positively no concern."

1621 "Mr. Blackwell's Book-Plates." (3) 26(n.s.23):226 March 23, 1895.
Exhibit of 4,000 bookplates from collection of Henry Blackwell at Brentano's on March 14-19, 1895.

1622 "Ladies Book-Plates." 28(n.s. 25):290-1, April 25, 1896.
Review of Norna Labouchere's monograph issued by Macmillan; 17th century barren of ladies' bookplates, but 18th abundant.

1623 "Frederick Locker's Bookplate." (2) 28 (n.s.25):293-5 April 1896.
Illustration of Frederick Locker's bookplate in an article on his death and review of his published autobiography.

1624 "A Book-Plate for the Authors Club." 28(n.s.25): 300, April 25, 1896.
Mead prize given to design featuring mediaeval author writing.

1625 "Bookplate Inquiry." 28(n.s.25):344, May 9, 1896.
Charles Dexter Allen answers inquiry; advertisement quoted: "WANTED. Will the person who borrowed the second volume of my set of Roosevelt's *Winning the West* kindly return the same at once, or call at my house and get the first volume, that one of us may have the complete set?" Desired results achieved.

1626 "Book-Plate Design for the Authors Club." (1) 28 (n.s.25):391, May 30, 1896.
George Wharton Edwards drew winning design ($100 award); bookplate protected by copyright.

1627 "Julia Marlowe Taber's Book-Plate." (1) 34:27, January 1899.
Bookplate illustrated and identified as designed by Ida Waughof of Philadelphia for the popular actress.

1628 "Some New York Book-Plates." William Henry Shelton. (8) 34:342-7, April 1899.

Interesting descriptions of libraries and plates of New York Society Library, Grolier Club, The Players, University Club, Lambs Club, Columbia College, Apprentices' Library, New York Public Library, etc.

CROOKES DIGEST

1629 "Ex-Libris Medicorum." 11:6-10, May-August 1948.

". . . book-plates have been divided into various 'styles,' the most commonly accepted designations being Early Armorial (1500-1700), Jacobean (1700-1775), Wreath, Ribbon or Festoon (1775-1800), Modern Armorial (1800-1905), and Modern Pictorial and Allegorical."

1630 "Ars Ex Libris Medicorum." (8) 11:4 unnumbered pages, May-August 1948.

Plates illustrated for Carl Sternberg, Silas Weir Michell, Oliver Wendell Holmes, Jerome Collot, Benjamin Rush, Edmund Symes Thompson, Georg Abelsdorf.

CURIO

"American Book-Plates and Their Engravers." Richard C. Lichtenstein.

1631 (17) 1:11-7, September 1887.

1632 (12) 1:61-6, October 1887.

1633 (8) 1:110-4, November 1887.

Thorough description, including arms, of various early American plates; qualities making bookplate of special value: engraver's name signed to it, dated and bearing owner's name and address.

1634 "Periodicals of the Month." 1:48, September 1887.

Among articles listed is one on bookplates in *New England Historical and Genealogical Register*.

1635 "Washington's Library." Richard C. Lichtenstein. (2) 1:246-52, January-February 1888.

Washington's bookplate illustrated; details of disposal of library including fact offered to British Museum which raised great "hue and cry."

CURRENT LIST OF MEDICAL LITERATURE

"Bookplates." Harold Wellington Jones. 2:120. [Unable to locate. CURRENT LIST OF MEDICAL LITERATURE is an index and not a journal; volume 2 is for 1941-42.]

Source: Personal correspondence from Dr. Samuel X. Radbill, June 25, 1966.

CURRENT LITERATURE

1636 "Book Plates and Collectors." 32:357-8, March 1902.

Digest of article by Charles Dexter Allen in *Century*.

CURRENT MEDICAL DIGEST [CMD]

1637 "Medical Bookplates." Samuel X. Radbill, M.D. (20) 29:51-60, November 1962.

Well written, thoroughly researched article condensed from *Journal of Albert Einstein Medical Center.*

D

D. C. LIBRARIES

1638 "Bookplate of the D. C. Public Library."(1) 36:62 Fall 1965.

Plate designed by Sidney L. Smith between March and July 1899.

1639 "Bookplate of the National Cathedral School." (1) 37:2, Winter 1966.

Competition sponsored by the school for bookplate design, won by Kathleen Kilgore in 1963.

1640 "Bookplate and Seal of the Alexandria Library." (2) 37:14, Spring 1966.

Originally established in 1794 as a subscription library, it became a city-supported library in 1937 and the new building is represented in the plate designed by Frederick Taylor.

1641 "Bookplate of the Foundry Methodist Church Library." (1) 37:34, Summer 1966.

Laws Memorial Library started in 1920's; plate by John Bryans designed in 1962.

1642 "Seal and Bookplate of the U.S. Department of the Interior." (1) 37:50, Fall 1966.

Originally known as the "Department of the West," the seal picturing a buffalo was adopted as the library's bookplate in 1949.

1643 "Bookplate of the Folger Shakespeare Library." (1) 38:2, Winter 1967.

Plate features the arms and crest of Shakespeare.

1644 "Bookplate and Marker of the Reading-Is-Fundamental Committee." (2) 38: 22, Spring 1967.

"Designed by Mrs. Robert J. Nash, the bookplate is intended to give the children a sense of pride in their personal ownership" of books.

1645 "Bookplate of the American Institute of Architects." (1) 38:42, Summer 1967.

Library established in 1857; plate illustrated designed by Paul Cret, noted Philadelphia architect, in 1932.

1646 "Bookplate of the Riggs Memorial Library, Georgetown University." (1) 38: 62, Fall 1967.

Various bookplates have been used; the current one is simple and features the university seal.

1647 "Bookplate of the Catholic University of America Libraries." (1) 39:2, Winter 1968.

Only bookplate used is for gift books and was designed by John Aleksandravicius, restorer in the Bindery Division of the library.

1648 "Seal and Bookplate of the George Washington University Library." (1) 39:22, Spring 1968.

Founded in 1921 and originally known as The Columbian College, the University has used various plates. The current plate features the Gilbert Stuart portrait, an open bible and the motto "Deus nobis fiducia."

1649 "Bookplate of the American Psychiatric Museum Association." (1) 39:46, Summer 1968.

Plate features portrait of Benjamin Rush, "Father of American Psychiatry."

1650 "Bookplates of Gallaudet College Library." (1) 39:66, Fall 1968.

Bookplate of 100 year old college offering "liberal higher education specifically for the deaf."

1651 "Bookplate of American Pharmaceutical Association." (1) 40:2, Winter 1969.

Organization founded in 1852; simple bookplate, using the APhA device, was designed in 1961.

1652 "Seal and Bookplate of National Gallery of Art." (1) 40:22, Spring 1969.

Bookplate adopted from Seal; National Gallery of Art was opened in 1941.

DARTMOUTH MAGAZINE

1653 "Mellen Chamberlain Book-Plate." Frank Gardner Moore. 16:301-7, June 1902.

Chamberlain, Class of 1844, left 2,000 books to the Dartmouth Library plus funds to provide "a book-plate, and to cover the cost of binding and repairs, further, a residuary legacy of perhaps five thousand dollars for the library."

DAUGHTERS OF AMERICAN REVOLUTION MAGAZINE [See also AMERICAN MONTHLY MAGAZINE]

1654 "Book-Plates of Colonial Gentry." Florence Seville Berryman. (12) 59:15-24, January 1925.

Interesting details on twelve plates illustrated and their owners.

1655 "Book Plates in Memorial Continental Hall." Florence Seville Berryman. (10) 62:201-7, April 1928.

DAR collection akin to those of the Metropolitan Museum of Art and the American Antiquarian Society of Worcester.

1656 "Book-Plates in the DAR Library." Florence Seville Berryman. (12) 64:19-26, January 1930.

Illustrations include bookplates for various state DAR organizations.

DELINEATOR

1657 "Scissors Pictures." Eleanor Colby. (11) 78:392, November 1911.

Eleven bookplates for a child to cut out, print his name upon, and paste in a book; some with verses—

"Rain or shine/This book is mine———"

DENTAL RESEARCH AND GRADUATE STUDY QUARTERLY

1658 "Our New Library Bookplate." (1) 41:2-4, Winter 1941.

Design by artist Dr. W. H. von Bernstorff includes much appropriate detail.

DESIDERATA

1659 "Bookplates." William Moore. Issue No. 5, 19-20, August 1930.

Mention of various Australian ex libris publications.

1660 "A Johnson Bookplate." Camden Morrisby. (1) Issue No. 5, 20-1, August 1930.

Interesting details concerning Johnson and bookseller Thomas Osborne shown in wood engraved bookplate which Lionel Lindsay did for Camden Morrisby.

DESIGN [See also KERAMIC STUDIO]

1661 "Make Your Own Book Plates." William S. Rice. 42:19, March 1941.

Brief procedure for making bookplates by the blue print process.

1662 "Spatter Cards and Book Plates." William S. Rice. (2) 55:66 *et seq.*, November-December 1953.

Simple instructions for home made bookplates.

DIAL

1663 "Private Book-Marks." 26:88, February 1, 1894.

"It is a harmless mania, this collecting of book-tickets—at least so long as it does not mean the destruction of books."

DICKENSIAN

1664 "A Pickwick Bookplate." (1) 3:223, August 1907.

Plate of E. S. Williamson, Toronto.

1665 "A Dickens Book-Plate from New Zealand." (1) 5:191-2, July 1909.

Letter and bookplate from Charles Wilson, Chief Librarian, Wellington, New Zealand.

1666 "A Dickens Book-Plate." (1) 6:185, July 1910.
Plate of actor Frank Staff, designed by Phillippe A. Mairet, pictured him in role of Sim Tappertit.

1667 "A Dickens Book-Plate." (1) 9:101, April 1913.
Plate of Edward Joseph Timings picturing Charles Dickens.

1668 "Dickens and His 'Heraldic Crest.' " T. P. Cooper. (2) 18:194-6, October 1922.
Dickens used crest on his bookplate and silverplate, which was originally granted by College of Arms to William Dickens in 1625, to which he had no hereditary or lawful claim.

DIE BASF

"Ex Libris." Hans Laut. (8) 103-6, 1966.
"Just as the poem maintains its place beside the novel and the drama, the little ex libris can include all the forms of expression characteristic of a real work of art."

DOLPHIN

1669 "Work of W. A. Dwiggins." Philip Hofer. (1) Issue No. 2:220-55, 1935.
Biographical sketch, checklist of work, and many illustrations of sample work including a bookplate for William and Mabel Dwiggins.

1670 "Mexican Book Labels." (10) Issue No. 4, Part I:88-90, Fall 1940.
Felipe Teixider published *Ex Libris y Bibliotecos de Mexico* in 1931.

1671 "The Libraries Men Live By. II Library at Centaurs." Paul Standard. (11) Issue No. 4, Part II:166-72, Winter 1941.
Banker and book collector Alfred E. Hamill had bookplate designed by T. M. Cleland.

THE DOME

1672 "Reviews and Notices." (1) 2:167-70, February 1899.
Comments on Edward Gordon Craig's *The Page* though with no specific reference to bookplates.

1673 "Elinor Monsell, A Book-Plate." (1) 7:185-7, July 1900.
Circular plate; no text.

1674 "Louise M. Glazier." (1) 7:89 and 95, July 1900.
Two children on a village street pictured on bookplate; no text.

DOWNSIDE REVIEW

1675 "Book-Plate of St. Gregory's." (1) 22(n.s.3):66-8, Easter 1903.
Plate designed by C. W. Sherborn for St. Gregory's Abbey.

DUBLIN JOURNAL OF MEDICAL SCIENCE

1676 "Book-Plates of Irish Medical Men." MacDowel Cosgrave 146:274-83, December 1918.

Of 131 plates in author's collection, majority (111) are armorial; in a list of 206 by Dr. Curtin, a third were "medical" and only one-quarter armorial.

E

EAST ANGLIAN

1677 "Pretyman of St. Edmund's Bury." J. C. Ford. N. S.1: 246, 1885-1886.

Correspondent has bookplate of Mr. Baron Pretyman and Geo. Pretyman who was an Alderman in 1787.

THE ELF

1678 "Minnie Churchill." (1) Issue No. 2: Winter 1899.

"This plate is included in the first 100 copies of *The Elf*, No. 2, and is sold to Annual Subscribers only."

1679 "A Book plate." (1) Issue No. 2: Winter 1899.

Plate for T. F. G.

1680 "Margaret O'Hara." (1) [Issue No. 3]: Spring, April 1900.

Another special for Annual Subscribers.

1681 "Ophelia Fowler Duhme." (1) [Issue No. 3]: Spring, April 1900.

Bookplate by J. J. Guthrie.

1682 "A Book plate." (1) Issue No. 4, Summer 1900.

Monogram MSC and motto: *amor omnia vincit.*

ELITE

1683 "Book Plates." (13) 13:10, 13-4, April 1895.

Henry Blackwell's collection to be exhibited at Brentano's book shop.

ENGLISH ILLUSTRATED MAGAZINE

1684 "How the Other Half Lives." J. D. Symon. (3) 12:59-63, October 1894.

At the bottom of the ladder of bookdealers is the "book-barrow man." One in London was "keen" on bookplates, and said "The demand is not what it was, but I've 'ad some foine plates through my 'ands in my toime."

1685 "Some New Book-Plates, Illustrated with Designs by Charles E. Dawson." (9) 37:238-40, June 1907.

The bookplate "is a patent of nobility conferred upon his volumes; it is a password recognized by the whole craft of genuine readers. But with its translation into democratic uses its character is changing. It is no longer a mediaeval trademark but a personal declaration; it no longer belongs to a family but to an individual; it may even be a badge of personal idiosyncrasy, and to whatever extent it does this it is significant of character."

ETCHED MONTHLY [See also **WALL'S ETCHED MONTHLY**]

1686 "A Connecticut Bookplate Maker." Bernhardt Wall. (1) 1:one unnumbered page and Plate 14, November 1928.

William Fowler Hopson, "one of the foremost engravers on wood," accidentally found the Etcherie of Bernhardt Wall off the beaten path in Warren, Connecticut. Illustration is bookplate by Hopson dated 1910.

1687 "Bookplate." (1) 1:Plate 14, March 1929.

W. F. Hopson's own plate for books on the graphic arts.

1688 "Bookplate." Bernhardt Wall. (1) 1:unnumbered plate, April 1929.

Plate for Marjorie Meeker by Bernhardt Wall.

ETCHED QUARTERLY [See **WALL'S ETCHED QUARTERLY**]

ETCHT MINIATURE MONTHLY MAGAZINE

1689 "Washington's Bookplate." (1) one unnumbered page, February 1948.

Copy of Washington's own plate.

1690 "Bookplates." Charles Dexter Allen. (1) two unnumbered pages, March 1948.

Allen quote appeared in 1921 issue of *Wall's Etched Monthly:* "To the observant, the personal bookplate carries unmistakable, though unconscious, revealment of character." Illustration is plate etched by Bernhardt Wall for Carl W. Schaefer.

1691 "Markham." Bernhardt Wall. (2) 4 unnumbered pages, May 1948.

One illustration is bookplate etched by Bernhardt Wall for Edwin Markham, famed poet, author of "The Man with the Hoe."

EVERYBODY'S MAGAZINE

1692 "The Art of the Bookplate." Alys Myers. September 1943. [Unable to locate.]

Source: *A Bibliography of Bookplates Compiled from Various Sources* by P. C. Beddingham, 1962. Illustrated.

EX LIBRAN

1693 "Edwin Davis French." (3) 1: Issue No. 1:5-11, 1912.

Checklist of 22 plates designed by French but usually engraved by another artist.

1694 "Impressionistic Book-plates." Mary E. Curran. (1) 1: Issue No. 1:12-3, 1912.

In addition to copper plate engravings, "the more impressionistic qualities of the other processes, . . . have also their particular beauties and fascinations."

1695 "*The Ex Libran.*" 1: Issue No. 1:14-5, 1912.

"An occasional magazine" edited by Alfred Fowler.

1696 "Book-plate of Isaac Hunt." Frank E. Marshall. (1) 1: Issue No. 1:16-7, 1912.

Enticing details briefly sketched in words of Isaac's son Leigh Hunt.

1697 "William Strickland, Architect." Frank E. Marshall. (1) 1: Issue No. 1:18-20, 1912.

Philadelphia architect also a "painter and engraver in acquatint, in which latter art a specimen of his work may be seen in his bookplate."

1698 "Archbishop's House, Boston." 1: Issue No. 1:20, 1912.

J. Winfred Spenceley engraved an ecclesiastical coat of arms used by Reverend Archbishop O'Connell.

1699 "Charles William Sherborn." (1) 1: Issue No. 2:22-4, 1912.

Tribute to this fine artist who died February 10, 1912.

1700 "An Afternoon with Mr. Sherborn." Winward Prescott, 1: Issue No. 2,25-7, 1912.

Artist at that time working on bookplate for Alfred Fowler.

1701 "Notes upon a Collection of Book-plates by Charles William Sherborn, R.E." 1: Issue No. 2:27-34, 1912.

Executed plates for English Royal Family, Mrs. Grover Cleveland, Rothschild family and many other "celebrities."

1702 "*The Ex Librian.*" (1) 1:Issue No. 2, 35-6, 1912.

Sherborn's home illustrated and comment made on forthcoming book by his son.

1703 "Notes on Book-plates of Esther and Lucien Pissarro; and on Their Eragny Press." J. M. Andreini. (3) 1: Issue No. 3:38-43, 1912.

Artists and printers, this couple have created about six bookplates.

1704 "A Memorial Book-plate." (1) 1: Issue No. 3:44-5, 1912.

Engraved Hopson plate for the Ohio Alcove in the American Library of Manila.

1705 "Book-plate of Marie Antoinette." Frank E. Marshall. (1) 1: Issue No. 3, 46-9, 1912.

"Some critics, without apparent warrant, have asserted that the engraving is not a book-plate but is a frontispiece to the catalogue of the illustrious owner's first library."

1706 "Book-plate of the Earl of Moray." (1) 1:Issue No. 3:49-50, 1912.

Wood block designed and executed by Graham Johnston, "His Majesty's Heraldic Artist at the Court of the Lord Lyon, Edinburgh."

1707 "*The Ex Libran.*" 1:Issue No. 3:51-2, 1912.
Mentions bookplate articles in current publications and that a Boston bank "recently advertised their safe deposit vaults for the storage of bookplates among other valuables."

1708 "Book-plates by Arthur N. Macdonald." (2) 1: Issue No. 4, 54-8, 1912.
"He is possibly unique in that his exquisite work is done wholly with the burin, or engraver, without etching, and entirely without mechanical ruling."

1709 "The Life & Work of C. W. Sherborn." 1: Issue No. 4:58, 1912
Charles Davis Sherborn and George Heath Viner have issued Sherborn Memorial book which is excellent reference work though typography and paper are disappointing.

1710 "Evolution of a Book-plate." George Clulow. 1: Issue No. 4, 59-61, 1912.
Full story of deception played upon H. W. Fincham with skillful assistance of Sherborn.

1711 "An American Book-plate Society." Clifford N. Carver. 1: Issue No. 4:62-3, 1912.
New society to be formed in January partly at suggestion of Sheldon Cheney, leader of the California Society.

1712 "*The Ex Libran.*" 1:Issue No. 4:63-6, 1912.
The Biblio to succeed current publication in which the editor set type, sewed covers and pasted the inserts!

1713 "Index." 1:Issue No. 4:67-8, 1912.
Index of titles and separate one of illustrations.

EX LIBRIS [Pickering Dodge, editor. Washington Ex Libris Society]

1714 "Authors Club Library." (1) 1:Frontispiece, July 1896.
Designed by George Wharton Edwards.

1715 "Salutatory." Pickering Dodge. 1:1-3, July 1896.
"In collecting bookplates it is always the unexpected which happens."

1716 "Paulding Bookplates." R. B. Coutant. (1) 1:3-6, July 1896.
Design of the plate from the Captor's Medal given to captors of Major Andre; right to use it questioned.

1717 "General Washington Johnston." John T. Loomis. (1) 1:6-9, July 1896.
Plate includes devices indicating his Masonic activities; General was given name, not military title.

1718 "Samuel Chase." Howard Sill. (2) 1:10-6, July 1896.
Signer of Declaration of Independence, Maryland Judge Chase had plate in Chippendale style.

1719 "Branford Library." 1:16, July 1896.
Paragraph on Blackstone Library for which W. F. Hopson designed plate.

1720 "Plea for Small Collections." Charles Dexter Allen. 1:17-9, July 1896.
Plea for quality rather than quantity.

1721 "Yale Plate." 1:19, July 1896.
Memorial plate designed by Edwin Davis French.

1722 "John Leach." Frederick J. Libbie. (1) 1:20-7, July 1896.
Plate designed and signed by Callender for John Leach who "kept a school of navigation in Boston previous to the Revolution."

1723 "Ex Libris Revered." W. H. Shir-Cliff. 1:28, July 1896.
Poem about bookplate.

1724 "Butterfield Collection of Bookplates." Henry Blackwell. 1:29-33, July 1896.
Boston man started collecting after reading Castle's *English Book Plates*.

1725 "Notes." 1:33-5, July 1896.
Comments on Printer's Devil bookplate, competition sponsored by *Modern Art*.

1726 "Check List of American Bookplates." Henry Blackwell. 1:36-8, July 1896.
Present list covers nearly 400 plates by owner with signature of engraver, date, state, and style.

1727 "McLaughlin Memorial Bookplate." George Dudley Seymour. (1) 1:39-40, October 1896.
Memorial plate designed by E. D. French to be used in books awarded for excellence in English at Yale.

1728 "Chevalier De Tonsard." Frank E. Marshall. (2) 1:41-5, October 1896.
Bookplate of French officer who served as aide-de-camp to Lafayette during American Revolution includes mention of membership in Society of the Cincinnati.

1729 "Gabriel Duvall." Howard Sill. (2) 1:46-54, October 1896.
Simple bookplate whose border was engraved by Thomas Sparrow; considerable family history.

1730 "Moses Lippitt." Francis J. Lippitt. (1) 1:54-7, October 1896.
Family history; simple printed plate with typographical border.

1731 "Ogle-Tayloe." Pickering Dodge. (2) 1:58-65, October 1896.
Plates of two early American families.

1732 "James McBride." Theodore L. Cole. (1) 1:66-8, October 1896.
Bookplate of Ohio historian who also advocated "Symmes theory of concentric spheres, demonstrating that the earth is hollow, inhabitable within, and widely open about the poles."

1733 "Check List of American Bookplates." Henry Blackwell. 1:69-72, October 1896.
Continued from July.

1734 "Nathaniel Hurd." (1) 1:73-7, January 1897.
Article from *New England Magazine* quoted at length.

1735 "Jarvis-Grainger-Pace." John T. Loomis. (2) 1:78-83, January 1897.
Three previously little-known plates by Nathaniel Hurd reproduced and discussed.

1736 "Ralph Wormeley of Rosegill." Elizabeth Wormeley Latimer. (1) 1:84-92, January 1897.
Family name may be "found on the roll of the Knights who came over to England in 1066 with William the Conqueror."

1737 "Henry Caswall." W. E. Baillie. (2) 1:93-4, January 1897.
Plate by R. Mountaine used by two family members with slight change in design.

1738 "Ex Libris—Essays of a Collector." Pickering Dodge. 1:95-6, January 1897.
Review of Charles Dexter Allen's book calling attention to various errors as well as commending the illustration on vellum from original coppers and the fine printing.

1739 "Notes." 1:97-100, January 1897.
Revere plates discovered by Lichtenstein, review of second edition of Hamilton's *French Book Plates*, comments on James Terry bookplate leaflets.

1740 "Check List of American Bookplates." Henry Blackwell. 1:101-4, January 1897.
Continuation.

1741 "American Bookplate Society." 1:105-8, January 1897.
Constitution and membership list.

1742 "Something of Rhead." W. H. Shir-Cliff, (1) 1:109-13, April 1897.
Louis Rhead was designer of posters and bookplates, member of Grolier Club.

1743 "Exhibition of Club of Odd Volumes." Frederic J. Libbie. 1:114-6, April 1897.
Ex libris displayed for first time in Boston.

1744 "Mary L. Prindiville." Charles L. Dering. (3) 1:117-9, April 1897.
Bookplates designed by young Chicago art student.

1745 "Psychology of Collecting." Elbert Hubbard. 1:120-4, April 1897.
"The psychic basis of collecting is human sympathy, and not a mere lust for possession. . . . You exchange plates and at the same time you exchange courtesy, kindliness, and mutual goodwill."

1746 "Frank Chouteau Brown." Samuel Davis. (2) 1:125-7, April 1897.
Young artist has designed six plates.

1747 "Alexander Anderson." Frederic M. Burr. (1) 1:128-33, April 1897.
Doctor, engraver credited with seven known bookplates; good biographical sketch.

1748 "Herring Plate." (1) 1:134, April 1897.
Designed by Howard Sill.

1749 "Announcement." 1:134, April 1897.
Lack of collectors' support forces discontinuance of *Ex Libris*.

1750 "Check List of American Bookplates." Henry Blackwell. 1:135-6, April 1897.
Continued into letter "D."

EX LIBRIS LEAFLETS

1751 "Rose Family of Suffield, Connecticut." James Terry. (1) 1:1-2, November 1896.
Plate originally had only the family name of Rose, leaving space for successive members to add their given name.

1752 "Rev. John Tyler of Norwich, Connecticut." James Terry. 2:1-2, November 1896.
Rev. Tyler appointed to Norwich Mission by the Society for the Propagation of the Gospel in Foreign Parts.

1753 "Abraham Pettibone of Burlington, Connecticut." James Terry. (1) 3:1-2, November 1896.
Volumes from Pettibone library in Connecticut Historical Society.

1754 "Allyn Hyde of Ellington, Connecticut." James Terry. 4:1-17, July 1906.
Allyn Hyde (1774-1856) received honorary M.D. degree from Yale in 1824.
Also includes review of *An Early American Engraver and His Work*, in which Terry presents material to disprove Richard Brunton, "a degenerate convict" of Newgate Prison, as the engraver of various bookplates.

THE EXPERT

1755 "Book Plate Collecting." "An Old Collector." (4) 1:34-5, May 25, 1907.
"Now, however, the collection of *ex libris* is an established craze, and systems of arranging the treasures snapped from the fate which awaits worn out and valueless books have been devised."

F

FLEURON

1756 "Claud Loval Fraser: Illustrator." Holbrook Jackson. (2) 1:49-5, 1923.
While not mentioned, artist also created bookplates.

1757 "Bookplate Annual." 2:112, 1924.
Review of Fowler yearbooks for 1922 and 1923.

1758 "D. B. Updike and the Merrymount Press." W. A. Dwiggins. (13) 3:1-8, 1924.

Several bookplates among material illustrated.

1759 "*Nothing or the Bookplate*." 4:162, 1925.

Review of book by E. Gordon Craig.

FOLIO MAGAZINE

1760 "Book-plates." Paul March. (3) 8:6-9, Autumn 1954.

About the middle of the eighteenth century "ordinary mortals began to have book-plates as well as mighty lords."

1761 "Ex Libris." Susan Coward. 8:9, Autumn 1954.

Eight line poem about "Jane Searle, her book."

FORERUNNER

1762 "A Note On Book Plates." Edward Morgan. (1) 4-5, October 1933. [Volume number not available.]

"Its [bookplate's] purpose [to show ownership] comes first; its decoration second. This is a point which some designers are inclined to lose sight of."

FOREST AND STREAM

1763 "Angling Ex-Libris." Louis Rhead. (10) 68:139-41, January 26, 1907.

Among the angling plates illustrated are those for Henry Van Dyke, Charles E. Cameron, Daniel B. Fearing, John Gerard Heckscher, and the author's own plate.

FORUM

1764 "Reviews." 1:37, October 1921.

After two years *Bookplate Magazine* ceases publication.

1765 "Woodcut." 1:62, November & December 1921.

Bookplate for W. Bradley by Frank Brangwyn.

1766 "Bookplates." 1:74, November & December 1921.

Volume featuring sixty-nine examples by Frank Brangwyn published by Morland Press.

1767 "Woodcut." (1) 1:105, January 1922.

Bookplate for Phyllis by Ludovic Rodo.

FRANKLIN LECTURES

1768 "English Literature as Reflected in Bookplate Design." Lewis M. Stark. 1:3-104, August 1935.

Master of Arts thesis from University of New Hampshire using literary quotations chronologically by author and the various individuals who have adapted them to their bookplates. Quotations from Chaucer to Joyce Kilmer; author portrait plates and bookplates of authors.

FRANKLIN NEWS [Franklin Society Federal Savings and Loan Association, New York]

1769 "A Member of Our Society." (2) 6:3, August 1929.

Portrait of bookplate artist Elisha Brown Bird and illustration of his plate designed for Barron G. Collier.

FULLER LIBRARY BULLETIN

1770 "Bookplate of Marco Birnholz." Philip Goodman. (1) Issue No. 19:2, July-September 1953.

Note on this famous bookplate collector.

FULTON PATRIOT

1771 "Two Fulton Bookplates: Colorful Fulton History Preserved by Bookplates." (Dr.) Henry P. DeForest. (1) 94:1, May 7, 1930.

Details of bookplate for the Fulton High School.

1772 "Bookplate of the Fulton Public Library: Historical Beauty of Oswego River Inspires Public Library Bookplate." (Dr.) Henry P. DeForest. (1) 94:1, May 14, 1930.

Details of research required in varied elements of Public Library bookplate.

G

GAZETTE [Grolier Club]

1773 "Dedication Copies." N.S. 1:8-21, June 1966.

Exhibition of dedication copies "with the printed arms of the dedicatee, bound for the dedicatee, with special dedication leaves, with dedicatee's bookplate, with his signature." Fourteen of the items are bookplates.

GEBRAUCHSGRAPHIK [International Advertising Art, Berlin]

"Tribute to German Writers in the Goethe Year 1932." (10) 9:62-4, March 1932.

Pictorial souvenirs of Goethe year issued in form of Ex Libris; ten German artists made ten drawings and woodcuts for bookplates; portfolio of ten on sale at bookstores.

"The Meaning of Ex-Libris." Dr. Eberhard Holscher. (35) 13:48-53, August 1936.

Author feels ex librists have caused serious harm in their favorite sphere owing to excessive and unsystematic passion for collecting.

"An Ex Libris Competition." (15) 15:37-40, April 1938.

Competition to design ex libris for books of Libraries of the Chambers contained in Reich Cultural Chamber.

"Popular Art in Pennsylvania German Bookplates." Christa Pieske. (11) 31: 36-41, July 1960.

Handpainted bookplates drawn and painted directly on flyleaves of few books, mostly religious, brought to America by German emigrants in 18th and 19th century.

GENEALOGICAL MAGAZINE

1774 "Heraldic Bookplates and Their Value." W. H. K. Wright. 1:100-6, June 1897.

Gone are the days when collectors could take "wasted covers" containing bookplates away by the sackful.

1775 "Ex Libris Sixth Annual Exhibition." 1:224-6, August 1897.

"Many were well worthy of exhibition as works of art, as rarities, as curiosities and as examples of engraving."

1776 "Nicolas Fouquet: The Man in the Iron Mask." (1) 1:Frontispiece, 581-2, February 1898.

Bookplate, featuring two squirrels, of Lord High Treasurer of France under Louis XIV.

1777 "Ex Libris Exhibition." 2:122, July 1898.

Illustrated catalog "is well worth the modest shilling for which it is sold."

1778 "Notes on the Walpoles with Some Account of a Junior Branch." H. S. Vade-Walpole. (8) 3:Frontispiece, 1-13, May 1899.

Details on various members and plates reproduced.

1779 "Washington Family." Mortimer Delano de Lannoy. (2) 3:384-94, January 1900.

Bookplate illustrated.

1780 "Miss C. Helard, A Book-Plate Designer." (1) 5:380,394-5, January 1902.

Young artist familiar with armory and its laws; thus none of her plates are "disfigured by glaring heraldic errors."

1781 "Queries and Correspondence." 5:517, March 1902.

Correspondent says tendency to "lengthen out the torse or wreath" is a mistake giving it "the appearance of taking a flying leap."

1782 "Editorial Notice." 5:564, April 1902.

Notice concerning presentation plates.

1783 "Bookplate Presented by the *Genealogical Magazine* to Mr. Luke G. Dillon." (1) 6:41-2, May 1902.

A new feature each month will be a presentation bookplate. Send application with year's subscription or front covers of last 12 issues; 100 prints of plate will be included. Artists will be Graham and Miss Helard.

1784 "Armorial Families." (4) 6:78-80, June 1902.
Bookplates for W. Bruce Bannerman, Alexander Sinclair, Glazebroad, and Richardson.

1785 "Bookplates." (1) 6:83,87, June 1902.
Miss Helard designed this month's presentation plate.

1786 "Bookplate." (1) 6:129, 131-2, July 1902.
Another designed by Miss Helard.

1787 "Bookplate." (1) 6:178-9, August 1902.
Miss Helard designed plate.

1788 "Bookplate." (1) 6:218-9, September 1902.
Plate for Henry Clement by Helard.

1789 "Bookplate." (1) 6:271-3, October 1902.
Graham Johnston design.

1790 "Bookplate." 6:324-5, November 1902.
Block too late to be included.

1791 "Bookplate." (2)6:332, 336, December 1902.
Two by Miss Helard.

1792 "Bookplate." (1) 6:380, January 1903.
Plate for Rev. Dickinson by Miss Helard.

1793 "Bookplate." (1) 6:428, February 1903.
Plate for Sir Maurice Boileau.

1794 "Bookplate of Marquis D'Oyley." (1) 7:Frontispiece, May 1903.
Illustration only.

1795 "Bookplate." (1) 7:228, September 1903.
Reproduction of plate of Cheltenham College.

GENEALOGIST

1796 "Book-Plate of Anthony Stewart." (1) 2:Frontispiece, 192, 1878.
W. F. Marsh Jackson sent bookplate of Anthony Stewart, Annapolis, Maryland, for further identification.

1797 "Notices of Books." (1) 5:74-7, 1881.
"Mr. Warren has not laboured in vain, his book [*Guide to Study of Book Plates*] is instructive as well as entertaining, and demonstrates that the study of book plates is not so wearisome or unprofitable as might be supposed."

1798 "Grant of Arms to John Leyland." (1) 5:184-5, 1881.
Grant made 19th December 1863.

GENERAL MAGAZINE AND HISTORICAL CHRONICLE

1799 "A Forgotten Pioneer Biologist of Philadelphia and a Problem Ex-Libris." Frederick Haven Pratt. (2) 36:502-10, 1934.

Concerns Joseph J. Allison. "Beyond the bare entries in academic registers, the manuscript of the essay, the two published papers, and the death notice, this interesting and so far as known unique example of ex-libris is the sole witness to the name it carries."

GENTLEMAN'S MAGAZINE

1800 "Historical Anecdotes of the Family of Gibbons." 58:698-700, August 1788.

Early description of arms with f's for s's in typesetting. (*Journal Ex Libris Society*, 9:66-7, May 1899 refers to this article.)

1801 "*Bibliotheca Heraldica Magnae Britanniae*." Thomas Maule. 92:part 2:537-40, and Supplement, 613-4, December 1822.

Included in review is discourse on a 1743 advertisement placed by Joseph Barber, bookseller of Newcastle, offering 100 prints of gentlemen's coats of arms to be used as bookplates on a "fine paper at the price of 2S. 6d"; the same ad gives notice of a cockfight.

1802 "Letter to Editor (Sylvanus Urban)." 93:198-9, March 1823.

Comments on previous article disputing date of earliest use of bookplates.

1803 "Book-Plates, Ancient and Modern, with Examples." John Leighton. (7) 220:798-804, June 1866.

" 'Preserve and protect' should be the book-owner's text . . . . Depend upon it, he is no friend of art or history who disregards the past."

1804 "Bookplate of Carolus Agricola Hammonius, J.U.D." Job J. Bardwell. 221: 72, July 1866.

Further identification of bookplate illustrated and described in Leighton article.

1805 "Heraldic Charlatanerie." Lancelot Bayard. (1) 225:555-6, September 1868.

Correspondent berates "heraldic studio" and feels heraldic devices should be protected by law as are merchant's marks and prize awards (Exhibition Metals Art).

GENTLEMAN'S MAGAZINE LIBRARY

1806 "Bookplates." 82-6, 325, 1888.

Recapitulation of articles appearing in *Gentleman's Magazine* during 1822, 1823 and 1866. A footnote says: "The subject of bookplates came much to the front a few years ago."

GENTLEWOMAN

1807 "Cosy Corner Chat." 18:495, April 15, 1899.

Gossipy dislogue includes several admonitions against stealing which appear on bookplates in verse.

1808 "Ladies' Book-Plates." (7) 22:499-500, April 13, 1901.
"The real collector must know something of heraldry; and to decipher the mottoes it is necessary to learn a smattering at least of Latin, German, French, and Italian."

1809 "The King's Private Book-Plates." (3) 24:527, April 19, 1902.
Three plates have been altered for King Edward from those originally designed and etched by George W. Eve for Queen Victoria; fifty sets of proofs are to be sold to raise funds for the King's Hospital Fund.

GIRL'S OWN PAPER

1810 "Book-Plates." (8) 17:627-9, August 1896.
Good, though brief, summary of bookplates for the novice.

GLIM [*G*ray's Inn, *L*incoln's Inn, *I*nner Temple, and *M*iddle Temple student publication]

1811 "Legal Bookplates." Philip C. Beddingham. (5) 29th Issue: 3, 5-7, Trinity and Michaelmus, 1960.
"After this date [1860] the 'fade away' in bookplate art is very noticeable. In place of the expert draughtsmanship of the inspired artist there appeared in large numbers the stationer's end product, very efficiently engraved, extremely dull, and completely without interest except for their genealogical associations."

GLOBE

1812 "Ex Libris." 1-2, January 22, 1897.
"Many interesting discoveries in the byways of history and literature are his, as he prosecutes his search for those interesting little examples of the graver's art which are used to denote the ownership of books."

GLOUCESTERSHIRE NOTES AND QUERIES

1813 "Book Notices." 6:91-9, December 1894.
Includes review of *Tyde What May* (partial motto of Scottish family, Haigs of Bermerside), a privately printed magazine of family histories limited to 130 copies; bookplate articles included.

GOLFER AND SPORTSMAN

1814 "Ex Libris." Florence G. Keenan. (31) 18:32-3, 52-3, February 1936.
Plates illustrated were designed by Cleora Wheeler; many of the plates discussed are for Minnesota residents.

GOLDEN GALLEON

1815 "A Way to Immortality." A. Edward Newton. (1) 2:68-72, Summer 1925.

The use of a bookplate "is a way to a certain sort of immortality—the only sort of immortality within the reach of most of us." Article concerns Robert B. Adams of Buffalo, who was a Johnson and Boswell collector; he used a leather label with Johnson portrait from Bartolozzi's engraving which is Josiah Wedgewood medallion with wig added.

"The selection of a bookplate is a more difficult matter than the selection of a wife."

GRADE TEACHER

1816 "Collection of Book Plate Designs." F. Shoemaker. 52:42-3, October 1934.

Suggestions for student project.

1817 "Book Plates for Book Week." Frances Pattersen. (4) 53:33, 77, November 1935.

Four simple designs with directions for children to follow to make them.

1818 "Book Plates or Decorations." Hazel F. Showalter. (4) 56:33, 79, November 1938.

Directions and samples for student project.

1819 "Book Plates." Eldah Burk. (2) 58:35, 78, November 1940.

"Jolly bookplate ideas for use in connection with Book Week activities."

1820 "Book Plates." Olive and Grace Barnett. (4) 61:37, 76, November 1943.

"Bookplates are among the most popular seatwork occupations for Book Week."

1821 "Book Plates." Grace Barnett. (4) 65:63, September 1947.

Four simple designs, no text.

1822 "Bookplates." Grace T. Barnett. (4) 66:53, 84, October 1948.

Sample page of bookplates may be hectographed so each child may color plates individually.

1823 "Book Plates." Grace T. Barnett. (4) 69:23, 116, November 1951.

Simple bookplates to be made by school children as Book Week project or Christmas gifts.

1824 "Book Plates." Eldah Burk. (4) 69:45, 116, November 1951.

More simple plates for school children.

1825 "Bookmarks and Bookplates." Hazel F. Showalter and Julia Schaefer. (11) 69:22-3, 78, 80, December 1951.

Simple "how to" ideas for grade school children.

1826 "Book Plates." Grace T. Barnett. (4) 71:33, November 1953.

Simple designs for children.

GRAPHIC

1827 "The Reader." 22:382, October 16, 1880.
Reviewer of Warren's *A Guide to the Study of Book-Plates* says John Pine "was the favourite Georgian book-plate maker, and that which he engraved for the books given by the King to Cambridge University is a masterpiece of ugliness."

1828 "The Bystander." J. Ashby-Sterry. 43:700, June 20, 1891.
Poem to help remember tinctures quoted from *Heraldry Made Easy*.

1829 "The Bystander." J. Ashby-Sterry. 45:367, March 19, 1892.
Question raised by Walter Hamilton if author of poem quoted from *Heraldry Made Easy* had ever seen French book with similar poem printed in 1691!

1830 "Book-Plate Presented by the Ex Libris Society." (1) 48:88, July 15, 1893.
Illustration only of plate designed by John Leighton for Duke and Duchess of York (George & Mary); see *Journal of Ex Libris Society* entry disputing presentation.

GRAPHIC ARTS

1831 "A Collection of Bookplates and Commercial Designs Made by William Edgar Fisher." Oliver Herford. (21) 5:25-32, July 1913.
Fisher was in charge of Typographic Art Department of American Lithographic Company; versatile in art of bookplate designing.

GRAPHIS [Zurich, Switzerland]

"English Bookplates To-day." Mark F. Severin. (9) 3:308 *et seq.*, 1947.
Briefly mentions work of such artists as Eric Gill, Reynolds Stone, Joan Hassall, Rex Whistler; also Exchange Club.

H

HANDICRAFT

1832 "With the Societies—Detroit." (3) 4:34-8, April 1911.
Exhibit of several thousand bookplates; special thanks to Sheldon Cheney for his assistance.

HARNESS HORSE

1833 "Urge for Another Bookplate." Carlyle S. Baer. (1) [Unable to locate.]
Illustration is Alexander Pope painting of Major Delmar, champion

trotter; amplification of this item appeared in YEAR BOOK of American Society of Bookplate Collectors and Designers, 27:30-3, 1956.

HARPER'S MONTHLY MAGAZINE

1834 "Ex Libris." Mary Tracy Earle. 105:66-74, June 1902.

A short story concerning Stella who is left in the library to "regain her temper" and passed the time writing personal inscriptions in top shelf volumes which her grandmother said should be burned.

HARVARD ALUMNI BULLETIN

1835 "Fearing Collection of Bookplates." (5) 21:131-3, November 7, 1918.

Plates of angling, fishes and watercraft numbering at least 3,000 given to Harvard.

HARVARD GRADUATE MAGAZINE

1836 "Harvard Book-plates." Winward Prescott. (8) 21:58-65, Summer 1912.

Description and comments on bookplates used for various memorial collections in Harvard Library and clubs such as Hasty Pudding Society.

1837 "Boston Harvard Club Bookplate." (1) 23:554-6, March 1915.

Plate designed by architect Alexander E. Hoyle, engraved by Frederick Spenceley; explanation of its significance given by designer.

HEARTH AND HOME

1838 "Collector's Note Book." John Hodgkin. (4) 28:165, November 24, 1904.

In mounting bookplates "if paste be the adhesive employed, see that it is not lumpy, boil it till the starch granules are all burst; if gum be employed, use the finest dextrine."

HERALD AND GENEALOGIST

1839 "Earliest Known Bookplate." 1:132, 1863.

Manuscript has engraved plate "bearing the name of Andreas Imhoff, 1555."

1840 "Anglo-American Coat Armour." (3) 5:25-32, 1870.

Plate for elder brother of Benjamin Franklin, John, illustrated; comment on bookplate of Philip Ludwell.

1841 "Notes and Queries." 5:95, 1870.

Correspondent describes plate of James Temple Bowdoin.

1842 "Notes and Queries." 6:95, 1871.

Samuel Herbert and Samuel Beilby bookplates, one on top of the other in a single volume, have same motto; question of relationship or even same person.

HERALDIC JOURNAL

1843 "Herald Painters. No. 1 Thomas Johnson." 1:6-7, January 1865.

Engraver and artist (1708-1767) who probably engraved portrait of Increase Mather, copy of which is in Massachusetts Historical Society library.

1844 "Herald Painters. No. 2 Nathaniel Hurd." 1:19-21, February 1865.

Hurd (1729-1777) engraved a Tracy coat of arms as a bookplate. "He owned and used a copy of Guillim's Heraldry; and it would therefore be unwise to accept a book-plate engraved by him as sufficient proof in itself. Still we must be guided by the circumstances under which he worked. A book-plate, rarely seen, is not so public a mode of claiming arms as a seal or an engraving on silver. I am not prepared to concede that in Hurd's time any man would have dared to make a public claim to arms falsely, whilst I would reserve the more private use in his library for further investigation."

1845 "Herald Painters. No. 3 John Coles." 1:95-6, June 1865.

Another engraver "who furnished arms in the same well-known manner as the modern herald painters."

1846 "Herald Painters. No. 3 John Coles." 1:108-9, July 1865.

Any arms "not in use prior to 1750 or 1760, should be summarily dismissed, as a rule. . . . He (Coles) was in the habit of giving arms to applicants, whenever he found them assigned in that book to the family name of his employer, without much if any genealogical research or inquiry."

1847 "Heraldic Notes and Queries." 2:94, April 1866.

James Turner (1752) engraved a series of psalm music and a Franklin coat of arms on a bookplate.

1848 "Book-Plates." 3:21-4, January 1867.

Collection of bookplates made by Harvard librarian, Thaddeus William Harris, and his grandfather, includes work done by Hurd, Johnson, and Callender.

1849 "Heraldic Notes and Queries." 3:190, October 1867.

Dr. John Appleton of Boston has a volume containing a bookplate engraved by Nathaniel Hurd for Thomas Child.

1850 "Heraldic Notes and Queries." 4:45, January 1868.

Nathanial Hurd engraved a bookplate for Alden Spooner (1757-1827), a noted printer, using arms for Sponer of Wickwantford, Co. Worcester, 1589, mentioned by Burke.

1851 "The Atkinson Family." 4:119-21, July 1868.

William King Atkinson had his bookplate engraved by Callender.

1852 "Herald Painters." 4:192, October 1868.

Additional artists noted briefly.

HISTORIC SOCIETY OF LANCASHIRE AND CHESHIRE

1853 "Description of a Warrington Book-Plate." James Kendrick. (1) 6:134-5, June 8, 1854.

Seven medallions of Warrington buildings and a view of Warrington in 1783 at the bottom of this bookplate.

1854 "Notes on Book-Plates and a Proposed Nomenclature for the Shapes of Shields." John Paul Rylands. (12) 40(N.S.4): 1-54 [read October 18], 1888.

Much interesting information including a chart of thirty-eight differently shaped shields plus descriptions of top and bottom variations.

1855 "List of Lancashire & Cheshire Book-Plates." 40(N.S.4):55-76 [read October 18], 1888.

List includes collegiate, early armorial, Jacobean, Chippendale, festoon, allegoric, book-pile, landscape, late armorial, mantles of estate, etc.

1856 "Armorial Bearings of the City of Liverpool." J. Paul Rylands. (2) 42(N.S. 6): 1-14 [read November 2], 1890.

Only incidental mention of bookplates.

1857 "Athenaeum Book-Plate." Fred G. Blair. (4) 77(N.S. 41): 17-25 [read February 12], 1925

First reference to Athenaeum bookplate, dated August 11, 1817, mentions design of "Mr. Clements for a wood engraving." Later plate engraved by Edwin Smith.

HISTORY OF MEDICINE BULLETIN [See **BULLETIN OF HISTORY OF MEDICINE**]

HOBBIES

1858 "How to Collect Bookplate Prints." Don [sic] Burne Jones. (3) 46:106-7, December 1941.

"Those who form a collection of these little worthwhile prints which are fastly coming to the top on the merit of their artistic character and esthetic quality have a real hobby."

"Heraldry for Collectors: Armorial Book-Plates." Mabel Louise Keech.

1859 (6) 46:96-7, January 1942.

1860 (7) 46:96-7, February 1942.

Gradually, after the 15th century, bookplates replaced chains to proclaim and maintain possession of books.

1861 "Perine Coat-of-Arms." Mabel Louise Keech. (1) 46:115-6, February 1942.

Thorough description of coat of arms and family history; bookplate of Fred Agens Perine shown.

1862 "Bookplates." Isobel Gordon. (2) 53:134-5, June 1948.

Plates of Vincent Astor for his yacht *Nourmahl* and A. Edward Newton; poem "Book-Plates' Petition" reprinted. Quotes from Eugene Field.

1863 "Naphin (Nevins) Coat-of-Arms." Mabel Louise Keech. (1) 53:153-4, June 1948.

Mostly heraldry, but ex libris pictured which incorporates it in design.

1864 "More Thoughts on Book-Plate Collecting." Ula Milner Gregory. 53:153-4, November 1948.

Inexpensive, delightful hobby with many opportunities for friendships through exchange of correspondence and bookplates.

1865 "Tiny Bookplates." P. Bons. 61:121, August 1956.

Miniature plate by Wilbur Macey Stone, 1898.

HOBBY TIMES AND BOOKWORM [See also **BOOKWORM** (Rockport, Maine)]

1866 "Bookplates." H. L. Hoover. (1) 1:22-3, January 1969.

General interest article.

HOME CHAT

1867 "A Chat with Mr. Walter Hamilton." (4) 8:94-6, March 27, 1897.

Hamilton quoted: "They [bookplates] are delightful from so many points of view. We can read in them genealogy and heraldry, whilst many of them are beautiful as works of art; the quaintest anecdotes, phases of personal character, are crystallised in some, and the private history of many noble families is enshrined in others. As aids in the compilation of county history, they are invaluable."

HOME COUNTIES MAGAZINE

1868 "Three Early London Bookplates." Alfred A. Bethune-Baker. (3) 5:6-8, January 1903.

"The local collector could add many interesting 'items' to his collection if he devoted a little more attention to the bookplates of his chosen district."

1869 "Essex Bookplates." Alfred A. Bethune-Baker. (3) 5:175-9, May 1903.

"It is noteworthy that few of the great nobles of England are extensive landowners in the places from which they derive their chief title."

1870 "Middlesex Bookplates." Alfred A. Bethune-Baker. (3) 5:153-6, April 1903.

Middlesex, containing the City of London, includes Law Courts, Parliament, Government offices, learned societies; so comprehensive is the area that subdivisions are needed for useful collecting.

1871 "Herts Bookplates." Alfred A. Bethune-Baker. (4) 5:300-6, 1903.

Sir Francis Bacon listed as well as Cowper family.

1872 "Bucks Bookplates." Alfred A. Bethune-Baker. (3) 6:85-9, 1904.

"First [bookplate] that comes instantly to one's mind" is that of Sir John Aubrey; wealth of local detail.

1873 "Reviews." 6:247-8, 1904.

Little Books on Art-Bookplates by Edward Almack given a generally favorable review.

HOME MAGAZINE

1874 "Something About Book-Plates." W. B. Bowdoin. (5) 12:169-72, February 1899.

"Book-plates are a pretty conceit. They mark the owner's book more elegantly than with written signature and denote ownership more or less artistically according to the ability and skill of the designer and engraver."

HOMES AND GARDENS [Adelaide, Australia]

1875 "The Bookplate: Its Relation to Australia." John Preece. (4) June 1933. [Unable to locate.]

Source: *A Checklist of Ex Libris Literature Published in Australia* by H. B. Muir: "A general article with four illustrations."

THE HONEY JAR

1876 "George Washington's Bookplate." (1) 1:37, January 15, 1899.
Motto: "The end shows the deed."

1877 "Columbia College Bookplate." (1) 1:52, January 15, 1899.
Illustration only.

1878 "Oliver Wendell Holmes' Bookplate." (1) 1:53, February 15, 1899.
Indexed as Holmes, but actually repeat of the Washington plate.

1879 "An Inscription for a Bookplate." 1:59, February 15, 1899.
Hee hoe dothe thys boke borowe,
An yte doeth ne' brynge backs:
Certys, shal hee hav sorowe,
An comforte shal hee lacks.

1880 "Harvard College Bookplate." (1) 1:72, February 15, 1899.
Indexed as Harvard; actually repeat of Columbia plate.

1881 "Bookplate of Ellen Terry." (1) 1:73, March 15, 1899.
Designed by Gordon Craig.

1882 "Evolution of a Bookplate." (5) 1:86-8, March 15, 1899.
Shows progress from name plate, inscription, coat of arms, symbol, and rebus.

1883 "Bookplate of Francis Wilson." (1) 1:86, March 15, 1899.
Plate and autograph shown.

1884 "Bookplate of Eugene Field." (1) 1:89, April 15, 1899.
From collection of Horace W. Whayman.

1885 "Bookplate of S. P. G. and William Ewart Gladstone." (2) 2:105, May 15, 1899.
Plate for Society for Propagation of Gospel.

1886 "Bookplates." (3) 2:120, May 15, 1899.
Plates for A. M. Steinfeld, Richard Wynkoop, and "A Pleader to the Needer When a Reader" printed within border as book label.

1887 "Bookplates." (2) 2:121, June 15, 1899.
Plates for Clement K. Shorter and John Adams.

1888 "Bookplate Designing." 2:131-2, June 15, 1899.
"A book plate is a name-label decorated, not a decoration defaced by a name-label."

1889 "Bookplates." (2) 2:138, June 15, 1899.
Plates for Henry M. Rubel and Charles Denroche.

1890 "Bookplates." (4) 2:137, July 15, 1899.
Plates for John Boyle O'Reilly, Jean Baptiste Moliere, E. Fitz-Gerald, and Mary E. Rath-Merrill.

1891 "Bookplate." (1) 2:145, July 15, 1899.
Plate of Roukens found in Elzevirs publication.

1892 "Bookplates." (4) 2:152, July 15, 1899.
Plates for Thomas Bailey Aldrich, William G. Pengelly, Henry D. Gilpin, Joseph Edgar Boehm.

1893 "Bookplates." (2) 2:153, August 15, 1899.
Plates for Princeton and Library of New York Society.

1894 "Bookplates." (2) 2:168, August 15, 1899.
Yale's Linonian Library and Harvard's Hasty Pudding Library.

1895 "Bookplates." (4) 2:169, September 15, 1899.
One motto: "Read, mark, learn, and inwardly digest."

1896 "Bookplates." (4) 2:189, September 15, 1899.
Includes plate for collector Horace W. Whayman.

1897 "Bookplates." (3) 2:185, October 15, 1899.
Plate for N.E. Heisser indicates Egyptian interest.

1898 "Bookplates." (4) 2:200, October 15, 1899.
Plates for Nina M. Cohen, William C. Semple, William S. Mack, Charles B. Elliott.

1899 "Bookplates." (2) 3:1, November 15, 1899.
Interesting plate for Thomas B. Mosher, publisher.

1900 "Early Bookplates." 3:14-5, November 15, 1899.
In Thebes and Chaldees bookplate-type identifications were made of the same materials as the written works.

1901 "Bookplate Comments." (2) 3:15-6, November 15, 1899.
Brief comments on plates illustrated.

1902 "Bookplate." (1) 3:17, December 15, 1899.
Plate for George Rowland Agate.

1903 "Bookplate Comments." (2) 3:32, December 15, 1899.
Bookplates illustrated further described.

1904 "Bookplate." (1) 3:33, January 15, 1900.
Plate for George Fox.

1905 "Bookplate Comments." (2) 3:48, January 15, 1900.
Further description of plates illustrated.

1906 "Curious Bookplate Mottoes." 3:48, January 15, 1900.
"This book was bought and paid for by D. C. Colesworthy. Borrowing members are recommended to supply themselves in the same manner. Price seventy five cents."

1907 "Bookplate." (1) 3:49, February 15, 1900.
Plate for Thomas Hedges.

1908 "Bookplate Comments." (2) 3:634, February 15, 1900.
Plates for George W. Childs and John Fiott.

1909 "Bookplate." (1) 3:65, March 15, 1900.
Plate for Henry Andre.

1910 "Bookplate Comments." (2) 3:79-80, March 15, 1900.
Interesting plate for Maine Historical Society.

1911 "Bookplate." (1) 3:81, April 15, 1900
Unusual plate in memory of Ginery Twitchell for American Antiquarian Society.

1912 "Fly-Leaf Inscriptions." (2) 4:1-8, May 15, 1900.
In addition to admonitions to borrowers on bookplates there are many inscriptions handwritten on flyleaves.

1913 "Bookplate Comments." (2) 4:15-6, May 15, 1900.
James Murray, whose plate is shown, is willing to exchange personal plates.

1914 "Bookplate." (1). 4:17, June 15, 1900.
Illustration only.

1915 "Bookplate Comment." (2) 4:31-2, June 15, 1900.
Plate by H. T. Sears for Henry Blackwell shown.

1916 "Bookplate." (1) 4:33, July 15, 1900.
Plate for Herman D. Jenkins.

1917 "Bookplate Comment." (2) 4:47-8, July 15, 1900.
Plate for W. F. Hopson's own graphic arts collection.

1918 "Book Plate Comments." (2) 4:64, July 15, 1900.
Plates for George Dashwood and Thomas R. Gage.

1919 "Bookplates." (3) 4:65, September 15, 1900.
Plates for Daniel Webster, May Braghon, and William D. Washburn.

1920 "Bookplates." (2) 4:80, September 15, 1900.
Plates each for Agnes and George Harrison.

1921 "Bookplates." (5) 4:81, October 15, 1900.
Includes plates for Walter Hamilton and James Smith (in verse).

1922 "Bookplates." (4) 4:104, October 15, 1900.
Plate of W. W. Wright is portrait with signature.

HORN BOOK

1923 "Sidney Smith and the Bookshop's Colophon." (2) 9:91-3, May 1933.
Bookshop for Boys and Girls used drawing designed by "Little Master"; *Horn Book* grew "out of all the Bookshop's roots."

1924 "Creating a Bookplate." Anne Carroll Moore. 17:163-7, May-June 1941.
Child's bookplate designed by illustrator Leslie Brooke and engraved by Sir Emery Walker.

HOUSE & GARDEN

1925A "Bookplates of Booklovers." (21) 33: 18 *et seq.*, February 1918.
"Without books," said Bartholin, "God is silent, justice dormant, natural science at a stand, philosophy lame, letters dumb, and all things involved in Cimmerian darkness," and other general comments.

1925B "Book-plates." Mark F. Severin. (8) 11:60-1, 105, June 1956.
"Book-plates can be fascinating and instructive in that they teach history and heraldry, make one acquainted with the work of many artists of the past and of today, and often provide a chance of collecting very charming lesser-known original works by artists whose other productions might prove unobtainable. They create bonds of friendship between collectors and artists from different countries and, of all collections, they take little room, are easiest of upkeep, fit in with all tastes, are cheap to acquire, and can be limited or unlimited."

HOUSE BEAUTIFUL

1926 "A Few Chicago Bookplates." Richard Shaw. (9) 1:138-41, April 15, 1897.
"There is considerable argument concerning bookplates, as to their seriousness as an art, and whether the collecting of them is to be regarded as a mania of doubtful dignity."

1927 "Some Western Book-Plates." Charlotte Whitcomb. (13) 11:111-3, January 1902.
Plates of "westerners" in Minneapolis, St. Paul, Omaha, Kansas City and Lawrence.

1928 "Child's Book-Plate." Gardner C. Teall. (11) 12:231-3, September 1902.
Among illustrations are E. D. French's "exquisite" plate for Ruth Adams, and Gordon Craig's design for his daughter, Rosemary Craig.

1929 "Outdoor Book-Plates." Sheldon Cheney. (10) 24:23-4, June 1908.
Outdoor plates include those of fishermen Stewart Edward White, Louis Rhead; hunter Andrew Strong White; woman's angling plate for Caroline Rees; yachting plate by E. D. French for the New York Yacht Club, and various landscape and nature scenes.

1930 "Some Los Angeles Bookplates." Olive Percival. (10) 36:92-3, August 1914.
"[The] worst possible examples seem to be owned by the public libraries (such as would be scorned by the trustees of a New England village) and our many large clubs have no bookplates at all."

1931 "Collection of Rare Bookplates." Photographed by Baldwin Coolidge. (9) 39:22-3, December 1915.

Henry R. Rowe, Boston, had one of the largest collections (20,000) in U.S. Photographs include plates dating back to 1730.

1932 "Some Contemporary Bookplates." Clara Therese Evans. (6) 42:30, June 1917.

Two hundred bookplates designed by fifty artists during 1916 exhibited by American Bookplate Society at Avery Library, Columbia University.

HYGEIA

1933 "The Aesculapian." E. O. Laughlin. (2) 5:288, June 1927.

Illustrated are bookplates by Max Brodel for Osler Fund books and John M. T. Finney Fund books, both at the Library of Medical and Chirurgical Faculty of State of Maryland; text is poem.

I

ILLUSTRATED AMERICAN

1934 "Bookplates of America and England." S. T. Willis. (5) 17:502-3, April 20, 1895.

Description of some of Henry Blackwell's collection.

IMPRIMATUR

1935 "Bookplates." James Guthrie. 1:8-9, January 1947.

"In modern times the so-called 'pictorial bookplate,' . . . was too often a picture with a name attached to it, a bookplate by courtesy rather than deliberation."

1936 "Book Plate by Dan Burne Jones." (1) 1:44, April-July 1947.

Plate printed in blue for Alice M. Hitchcock.

INDEPENDENT

1937 "Book-Plates: The Bookman's Hobby." Charles Dexter Allen. 49:2-3, December 9, 1897.

Quotes Edmund Gosse: "There are many good bibliophiles who abide in the trenches, and never proclaim their loyalty by a book-plate."

1938 "Book-Plates and the Collecting of Them." W. G. Bowdoin. (11) 53:2931-6, December 12, 1901.

Touches briefly on past history, trends in design, collectors, and methods of arranging collection.

1939 "Bookplates and Their Vanities." Vincent Starrett. 119:603 *et seq.*, December 17, 1927.

Some historical background and general comments on selecting a design for a bookplate. "The soul of man may express itself in several ways. It may be reflected in his socks, his neckties, or his bookplate. Formerly, it was perhaps best expressed in his waistcoat."

INDUSTRIAL ARTS & VOCATIONAL EDUCATION

1940 "Bookplates." Mary Lillian Lampe. (12) 30:327-30, October 1941.

Historical survey; also suggestions on designing your own plate. Six of the plates illustrated were executed by the author.

1941 "What Factors Make a Good Bookplate." Burl N. Osburn. (9) 34:414, November 1945.

Correct details, such as heraldry. Dignity in institutional plates. Uniqueness of design. Typographic materials used by themselves. Good lettering, in an enduring style. Autographic methods of production. Obvious symbolism. Treatment suitable to medium employed. Each of the bookplates reproduced illustrates one of these factors.

INK

1942 "The Friendly Bookplate." Vera G. Dwyer. (4) 59-60, 1932. [Volume number unavailable.]

Illustrations are etched bookplates by Ella Dwyer.

INLAND PRINTER

1943 "The Book-Plate, Its Literature, etc." W. Irving Way. (6) 12:460-1, March 1894.

Examples include work by G. W. Eve, Paul Avril, R. Anning Bell, Walter Crane's plate for Clement K. Shorter, and one in hieroglyphics for Rider Haggard.

1944 "Book-Plates and Their Production." W. Irving Way. (4) 14:527-9, March 1895.

"Persons of good taste, yet modest and unostentatious in all ways, believe that a book-plate of artistic and decorative design printed from copper adds distinction to a bit of decorative binding."

1945 "Chicago & Alton Railroad." (1) 24:600, January 1900.

Bookplate for use in "Alton Limited" between Chicago and St. Louis, designed by F. W. Goudy.

1946 "Notes on the Pictorial Book-Plate." Thomas Wood Stevens. (20) 29:41-4, April 1902.

Among many interesting designs is that by Harry Everett Townsend for the Santa Fe Railroad's "California Limited."

IN LANTERN-LAND

1947 "Ex Libris." (1) 1:26, January 7, 1899.
Words of praise for Gleeson White who recently died. Bookplate for Gilbert North on page-size loose insert.

1948 "Book-Plates." (1) 1:62-3, April 1, 1899.
Notice of publications, sale, Gleeson White Memorial Fund. Supplement is plate designed by Louis Rhead for Frank J. Pool of Cleveland's Rowfant Club.

1949 "On Book-Plate Designs." 1:74-5, May 6, 1899.
Quotes from article in *Journal of Ex Libris Society*. Supplement is bookplate by J. Bryant.

INSTRUCTOR

1950 "Posters or Bookplates." Eldah Burk. (4) 59:41 November 1949.
Simple "how to" project for middle and upper grade school children during Book Week.

1951 "Book Plates." Opal Hoagland. (10) 61:54, November 1951.
Book Week project using among other suggested materials rolls of brown gummed paper on which to design bookplates.

THE INTERIOR

1952 "Hobbies and How to Ride Them." Rev. J. H. Dubbs. 22:6, June 11, 1891, and 22:6, June 18, 1891.
Bookplates are not specifically mentioned; related hobbies are, such as book collecting, study of heraldry, collecting of prints and engravings. Eben Newell Hewins made similar distinction in his bibliography included in Charles Dexter Allen's *American Book-Plates*.

INTERNATIONAL CLINICS

1953 "Book-Plates of Physicians, with Remarks on the Physician's Leisure-Hour 'Hobbies.'" Roland G. Curtin. (24) 20th Series, 2:222-53, 1910.
A wealth of detail—Dr. Samuel Pritchard rode with Paul Revere to rouse the countryside; quotes Dr. Gatling on why he invented the gun named for him; guillotine invented by French physician of that name.

INTERNATIONAL PRINTER

1954 "Ex Libris: Book-Plates and Their Makers." John V. Sears. (6) 22:97-103, February 1902.
A survey of bookplates since the days of the rubrishers to Will Denslow and Maxfield Parrish.

INTERNATIONAL STUDIO

1955 "Some Recent Book-Plates, Mostly Pictorial." Gleeson White. (18) 1:110-8, April 1897.

The bookplate is a "name-label decorated, and not decoration with a name-label defacing it."

1956 "Work of Mr. Byam Shaw." Gleeson White. (12) 1:209-21, June 1897.

One bookplate illustrated.

1957 "Reviews of Recent Publications." 1:141, April 1897.

Essays by C. D. Allen reviewed.

1958 "Reviews of Recent Publications." 2:67, July 1897.

Monograph on musical bookplates listing more than 300 mottoes published in Amsterdam by Frederick Müller and Co.

1959 "Studio-Talk." 2:119, August 1897.

Annual Ex Libris Society exhibit "was once again more impressive by reason of its wasted opportunities than for any noticeable improvement in its standard for modern designs."

1960 "Some Glasgow Designers and Their Work." Gleeson White. (19) 2:86-100, August 1897.

One bookplate by Margaret MacDonald among illustrations.

1961 "Some Glasgow Designers and Their Work." Gleeson White. (19) 2:227-36, October 1897.

Three bookplates by J. Herbert McNair among illustrations.

1962 "Reviews." 4:59, March 1898.

G. W. Eve's *Decorative Heraldry*, "new volume of Ex Libris series," favorably reviewed.

1963 "Some Artists at Liege." Fernand Khnopff. (10) 4:178-85, May 1898.

One bookplate by A. Rossenfosse shown.

1964 "Future of Wood-Engraving." A. L. Baldry. (5) 5:10-6, July 1898.

One illustration appears to be a bookplate showing a man hanging, crows on the cross beam, and wording "who goes a-borrowing of the goods of E. E. M. Creak goes a-sorrowing."

1965 "Reviews." 5:70, July 1898.

Importance of collecting *ex libris* "amply proven by the production of this portly tome" [*Artists and Engravers of British and American Bookplates* by H. W. Fincham].

1966 "Design for a Pictorial Book-Plate." 5:216-7, September 1898.

Winners listed.

1967 "Book-Plate." (1) 6:276, February 1899.

Illustration of plate for Michael Adler by Miss Sandheim.

1968 "Book-Plates." (11) 10:268-71, 276, June 1900.

Plates designed by Harold Nelson, Alexander Fisher, and Maurice De Lambert.

1969 "Awards." (16) 11:61, 64-7, July 1900.
Design awards for pictorial bookplates.

1970 "Awards." (16) 13:61, 64-7, March 1901.
Ethel Larcombe and W. B. Pearson won first and second prizes.

1971 "American Studio Talk: Notes on Art in New York." (1) 13:73,75, June 1901.
Bookplates included in Architectural League exhibit.

1972 "Recent Etching and Engraving." Frederick Wedmore. (8) 14:14-20, July 1901.
One bookplate shown by "Little Master" C. W. Sherborn whose work consists of "provision of bookplates . . . for . . . the least impecunious of the learned."

1973 "Some Thoughts on the Art of Gordon Craig, with Particular Reference to Stage Craft." Haldane Macfall. (14) 14:246-56, October 1901.
Four bookplates among illustrations.

1974 "Bookplate." (1) 15:276-281, February 1902.
Plate for Howard Wilford Bell by J. Walter West.

1975 "King Edward's Bookplates." (3) 17:53-4, July 1902.
Three plates designed by George W. Eve.

1976 "Design for a Bookplate." 18:71, November 1902.
Awards will be made known at an "early date."

1977 "Designs for Book-Plates. Some Remarks Upon the Results of Competition." Aymer Vallance. (35) 18:120-9, December 1902.
Quantity and high quality of work submitted for awards "seemed to call for exceptional notice."

1978 "Bookplates of Hans Przibram." (3) 18:22-3, January 1903.
"A touch of quaint humor renders his small [animal] book-plates very charming."

1979 "Life and Genius of the Late Phil May." (7) 20:280-7, October 1903.
Though not mentioned in article, artist designed bookplates.

1980 "Design for a Book-Plate." (15) 21:272-5, January 1904.
First and second prizes to Elisabeth Weinberger and Clifford J. Beese.

1981 "Reviews." 23:271, September 1904.
Bookplates by Edward Almack reviewed briefly.

1982 "Book Review." (3) 24:LI, December 1904.
A Portfolio of Book Plates by William Fisher issued in limited edition of 135, contains a dozen signed proofs.

1983 "Four Book Plates by Messrs. Euwer and Crisp." (4) 24:LXX-LXXI, January 1905.
Two former members of Art Students' League have Fifth Avenue shop featuring bookplates.

1984 "Bookplate." (1) 25:30, March 1905.
Designed by artist H. Volkert for himself.

1985 "Bookplates." (2) 25:138-9, April 1905.
Plates by Italian draughtsman Alfredo Baruffi.

1986 "Reviews." 25:179, April 1905.
Ex Libris by Spanish artist A. de Riquer.

1987 "Studio-Talk." (1) 25:349, June 1905.
Blank bookplate designed by D. Waterson.

1988 "Current Art Events." (3) 25:XIX, n.d. (follows June 1905).
Winners in December competition announced.

1989 "Studio-Talk." (2) 26:74, 78, July 1905.
Bookplates designed by W. Mellor.

1990 "Studio-Talk." (3) 26:327-330, October 1905.
Three bookplates designed by Winifred Stamp.

1991 "From Edward Penfield's Studio." (1) 26:LVI, n.d.
Artist's own bookplate.

1992 "Design for a Book Label." (7) 27:89-90,93, November 1905.
H. Brockhurst won first prize.

1993 "Minnesota State Art Exhibition." (1) 28:CXV, n.d.
Among illustrations is Mary Moneton Cheney's design for Harvey Earl Partridge's bookplate.

1994 "Imperial Arts and Crafts Schools, Vienna." (2) 30:328, February 1907.
Bookplates by Oswald Dittrich and U. Zovetti.

1995 "Studio-Talk." (4) 30:348,351, February 1907.
Bookplates designed by Harold Nelson.

1996 "Arts-Crafts Society of Denver." Alice M. Best. (1) 30:CXIV-VI, n.d.
One bookplate by C. Valentine Kirby.

1997 "Recent Work of Mr. J. Walter West, R.W.S." A. L. Baldry. (3) 31:87-100, April 1907.
Three bookplates by this artist included.

1998 "Reviews." 33:84, November 1907.
Edinburgh publication reviewed, *Charles E. Dawson: His Book of Book-Plates*.

1999 "Studio-Talk." (2) 33:316-7, February 1908.
Bookplates of Lewthwaite Dewar.

2000 "Reviews." 33:337, February 1908.
G. W. Eve's *Heraldry in Art* reviewed.

2001 "Studio-Talk." (2) 37:147-8, April 1909.
Both bookplates by Jessie M. King.

2002 "Reviews." 37:336, June 1909.
Bookplate artist and Herald-Painter of the Lyon Court, Graham Johnston enhanced *Complete Guide to Heraldry* by A. C. Fox-Davies with "coloured plates and multitudinous designs."

2003 "Monograms, Marks and Ex Libris by George Auriol." (39) 38:227, September 1909.
Only one specifically a bookplate.

2004 "Etched Book-Plates." Frank Newbolt. (11) 39:216-23, January 1910.
Bookplates are "inexpensive, useful and a graceful addition to the most modest library. They may be printed from any kind of block or plate, and each kind has some special quality to recommend it, but etched book-plates appeal to the taste of many as the most interesting."

2005 "Book Plate Design." (4) XLIV, April 1910.
Two plates each, by Frederick Spenceley and A. A. Stoughton.

2006 "National Competition of Schools of Art, 1910." (1) 41:302, October 1910.
Bookplate by Dorothy M. Payne.

2007 "Bookplate." (1) 42:74, November 1910.
Woodcut bookplate from four blocks by Marie Stiefel.

2008 "Studio-Talk." (3) 43:227-8, May 1911.
Designs by R. Anning Bell.

2009 "Studio-Talk." 44:330-4, October 1911.
Brief mention of Bruno Hiroux's bookplates at Leipzig Exhibition.

2010 "*A Portfolio of Bookplates*." (3) 47:17-8, September 1912.
Review of William Edgar Fisher's privately printed signed copper-plates.

2011 "School Notes." (1) 47:9, October 1912.
Bookplate for Robert McNaughton Barker designed by Syracuse student.

2012 "*The Ex Libran*." (2) 48:16, 19, December 1912.
New publication "commended for the strong individualism of its typography."

2013 "Outdoor Book Plate." (1) 48:15, January 1913.
A German plate by Hirzel (1899) for F. Kessler with rustic scene amid trees, slopes and hollyhocks.

2014 "Studio-Talk." 49:137-8, April 1913.
Bookplates by G. W. Eve included in exhibit of Royal Society of Painter-Etchers and Engravers.

2015 "Some Designs for Ex-Libris." (29) 52:53-9, March 1914.
Designs by George Auriol, J. Walter West, D. Y. Cameron, Edmund H. New, James Guthrie, Jessie M. King, Charles Pace, F. Pickford Marriott, Ernst Aufseeser, Marquis Franz von Bayros, and Heinrich Wieynk.

2016 "National Competition of Schools of Art, 1914." (2) 53:286, October 1914.
Two bookplates by William Liley from wood blocks.

2017 "Fairy Folk of Dugald Stewart Walker." Jessie Lemont. (8) 53:LXXIII-IX, October 1914.
"The book-plates of Stewart Walker are designed with the same

fecund fancy . . . into these book-plates also is wrought the magic of the out-of-doors."

2018 "Studio-Talk." (2) 54:148, December 1914.
Designs by Harold Nelson for Advocates Library and Arthur Webb.

2019 "Studio-Talk." (6) 55:50-1, March 1915.
Six bookplates designed by architect Charles F. A. Voysey.

2020 "Reviews." 56:289, October 1915.
Ex Libris Engraved on Wood published in Turin.

2021 "Bookplates." (2) 57:29,38, November 1915.
Two bookplates designed and engraved by T. Sturge Moore which look more like book illustrations.

2022 "Studio-Talk." (2) 62:38, July 1917.
Bookplates by F. Stanley Harrod, one for the government of Ontario.

2023 "Studio-Talk." (4) 64:67-8, April 1918.
Bookplates designed by Harold Nelson.

2024 "Heraldic Bookplates." (13) 66:83-6, January 1919.
Illustrations of plates by Major Nevile R. Wilkinson, J. F. Badeley, Alf J. Downey, Colonel Hugh R. Wallace, Graham Johnston and Robert Gibbings.

2025 "Woodcuts and Colour Prints of Captain Robert Gibbings." Malcolm C. Salaman. (8) 67:3-9, March 1919.
One illustration of bookplate for William Pennefeather showing naval vessels with smoke in silhoutte.

2026 "Reviews." (2) 69:412, November 1919.
Ex Libris by E. H. Tielmans published in Brussels.

2027 "Studio Talk." 71:188, August 1920.
R. Anning Bell is President of recently formed English Book-Plate Society.

2028 "Reviews." (1) 72:163-4, December 1920.
Bookplates by Frank Brangwyn published by Morland Press, London.

2029 "Studio Talk." (1) 73:117, April 1921.
Bookplate for Hilda Griffin by Molly Powers.

2030 "The Many-Sided Waugh." Henry Rankin Poore. (12) 74:CXXV-CXXXV, December 1921.
Seascapes, fairies and goblins, portraits and two eerie bookplates are illustrated.

2031 "McCall, of Books and Bookplates." William B. M'Cormick. (10) 76:245-8, December 1922.
Librarian G. H. McCall designed and engraved 300 bookplates in England, France, and U.S.

2032 "Etchings as Works of Art." Ralph M. Pearson. (11) 81:159-69, June 1925.
Three unusual etchings by Gregor Rabinovich are labeled ex libris.

2033 "Revival of Interest in the Book-Plate." Gardner Teall. (12) 86:71-6, January 1927.

"Like the tulip craze, it [bookplate collecting] was, for a time, gone into madly, and equally like the tulip craze, came a slump in public interest."

". . . it is not too much to speak of the return of the book-plate, for although it has never left us, there are indications on every side of an awakening interest of a better sort in the subject, both as to its art and as to its offering a delightful field to the collector."

J

JAPAN

2034 "Ex-Libris in Japan." Frederick Starr. (23) 12:12-14, June 1923.

Book seals, stamped in red ink, are used for Japanese style books and bookplates are used in foreign made books. Mention also of *nosatsu* or little placards bearing a worshipper's name which were pasted up at temples; these too were collected in much the same way as ex libris.

JEWISH BOOK ANNUAL

2035 "Love of Books as Revealed in Jewish Bookplates." Philip Goodman. (11) 12:77-90, 1954.

Study of bookplates reveals Jewish attitude toward lending and stealing books, pride of possession and book production.

JEWISH HERITAGE

2036 "Love of Learning as Reflected in Bookplates." Philip Goodman. (6) 2:17-9, Fall 1959.

Brief article with illustrations fully annotated.

JEWISH MUSIC NOTES

2037 "Musical Motifs in Jewish Bookplates." Philip Goodman. (3) 3:April 1953.

Musical theme used on ex libris of David Friedlander which was engraved by Samuel N. Chadowiecki in 1774.

JOURNAL OF THE ALBERT EINSTEIN MEDICAL CENTER

2038 "Symbolism of the Staff of Aesculapius as Illustrated by Medical Bookplates." Samuel X. Radbill. (24) 10:108-19, July 1962.

The staff is discussed in detail as a walking stick, the tree of life, a hero symbol, phallic symbol, magic wand, and a cross.

JOURNAL OF AMERICAN HISTORY

2039 "Ex Libris." (2) 1:304, April-May-June 1907.
Plates for Paul Revere and William Penn pictured.

2040 "Book Plate of Reverend Thomas Ruggles Pynchon." (1) 1:516, July-August-September 1907.
Plate for President of Trinity College pictured.

2041 "Governor Lewis Morris." (1) 2:120, January-February-March 1908.
Illustrated is plate of New Jersey governor about 1743.

JOURNAL OF AMERICAN INSTITUTE OF ARCHITECTS

2042 "Library Notes. Bookplates Again." 30:56, April 1959.
Mrs. Rudolph Stanley-Brown presented copy of *Year Books* of ASBC &D for 1957 which featured article on her architect husband.

JOURNAL OF THE ARCHAEOLOGICAL SOCIETY OF THE COUNTY OF KILDARE AND SURROUNDING DISTRICTS

2043 "Some Old Kildare Book-Plates." William Chamney. (2) 7:280-7, January 1914.
Catalog of plates identified, where possible, by name, inscription and style; many more than 100 years old.

2044 "County Kildare Book-Plates." William Chamney. (2) 9:90-1, Supplement 1918.
Three additional plates.

JOURNAL OF AUSTRALIAN EX LIBRIS SOCIETY

2045 "Bookplate Work of Norman Lindsay." Hugh McCrae. (8) 1:4-17, 1930.
Quoting from a Lindsay letter: "They are perplexing to design; and, moreover, nearly every man, who thinks he needs a bookplate, requires the assistance of a mysterious symbolism which shall define the substance of his age in its most occult manifestation. . . . A man, who reads much, and loves books, can't help feeling that his personality really exists as an extract of books; which, of course, it does; and he wishes his bookplate to say so in explicit terms. I know that I have never satisfied a man with a bookplate yet."

2046 "Bibliography of Ex Libris Literature Published in Australia." 1:18-23, 1930.
Annotated entries for books, newspapers, and periodicals.

2047 "Notes on Bibliography." Camden Morrisby. 1:24-5, 1930.
Requests for additional entries to include in subsequent bibliographies.

2048 "An Old Album: Ruminations." P. Neville Barnett. (8) 1:26-41, 1930.
Chatty comments on owners and artists.

2049 "Member's Exchange List." 1:42-4, 1930.
Perference of exchange expressed and plates available.

2050 "Society's Exchange List." 1:45, 1930.
Request for additional members to join exchange list.

2051 "Editorial Notes." 1:46-7, 1930.
Members requested to send copies of their plates for general collection of Society.

JOURNAL OF BIRMINGHAM CENTRAL LITERARY ASSOCIATION

2052 "Ex Libris." [Robert Day.] 131-8, 1885. [Volume number unavailable.]
Chatty details about numerous bookplates and several verses of admonition against borrowing books and not returning them.

JOURNAL OF CHEMICAL EDUCATION

2053 "Priestley's Life in Northumberland and Discussion of the Priestley Relics on Exhibition in the Museum." C. A. Browne. (6) 4:159-71, February 1927.
Article contains mention of "famous book plate" of Joseph Priestley who discovered carbon monoxide in 1799.

JOURNAL OF CORK HISTORICAL AND ARCHAEOLOGICAL SOCIETY

2054 "Bookplate of Very Rev. Rowland Davies. (1) July 1892. [Unable to find illustration in this issue.]
Source: *Journal of Ex Libris Society* 2:80, August 1892: "The *Journal of Cork Historical and Archaeological Society* for July 1892 contains an illustration of the 'Book-plate of Very Rev. Rowland Davies, LL.D.' Dean of Cork, under the heading, 'Historical Notes [of Cork] from the Croker and Caufield Manuscripts.' Our readers will remember that we were enabled to give this interesting plate, with some notes, in our May number, through the kindness of Mr. Robert Day, of Cork."

2055 "Carden Terry." (1) Second Series 8:123-5, April-June 1902.
Bookplate illustrated is for Carden Terry, a Cork silversmith who died in 1821 at age seventy-nine.

JOURNAL OF EGYPTIAN ARCHAEOLOGY.

2056 "Egyptian Royal Bookplate: The Ex Libris of Amenophis III and Teie." H. R. Hall. (2) 12:30-3, 1926.
A label or plaque for an ancient manuscript, the title of which seems to be in dispute between Hall and Dr. Opitz. Hieroglyphics and translation/interpretation are offered.

JOURNAL OF THE EX LIBRIS SOCIETY

2057 "Book-Plates, Ancient & Modern, with Examples." John Leighton. (4) 1:1-6, July 1891.
Reprint of the June, 1866 article from *Gentleman's Magazine*.

2058 "The Complete Ex Libris Collector: or, Another Recreation for Contemplative Men." Piscator Junior [Walter Hamilton]. 1:7-9, July 1891.
"The ideal collector is one who has money, taste, and leisure—he then has all the world before him."

2059 "Book-Plates." (3) 1:10-12, July 1891.
General background article.

2060 "Book-Plate Mottoes." R. C. Lichtenstein. 1:13, July 1891.
"This book was bought at the sign of the Shakespear Head. Borrowing neighbors are recommended to supply themselves in the same manner."

2061 "Book Notices." 1:14-5, July 1891.
Review of Swedish and German publications.

2062 "Letters." 1:16, July 1891.
Word of warning from Heraldic Assistant Editor.

2063 "Notes." 1:17, July 1891.
Advance notice of Brown-Fincham bibliography.

2064 "Ex Libris Society." 1:18-9, July 1891.
Among resolutions adopted: "That no known dealer in second-hand Book-Plates be eligible for election as a member of the Ex Libris Society."

2065 "Names of Members and Subscribers." 1:20, July 1891.
About 95 members.

2066 "Library Interior Book-Plates." Arthur Vicars. (2) 1:21-4, August 1891.
Identified by owner, country, engraver and collector's name.

2067 "Book-Plates Engraved by Cork Artists." Robert Day. (2) 1:25-30, August 1891.
Forty-eight plates listed as engraved by Green of Cork; many other local artists named.

2068 "The Oldest Ex Libris." John Leighton. 1:30, August 1891.
Details concerning Carolus Agricola Hammonivsivris plate.

2069 "Book Notices." (1) 1:31-3, August 1891.
Review of Bouchot's book.

2070 "Notes." (1) 1:33-5, August 1891.
Reprint from *Notes and Queries* of a punning bookplate, and other brief articles.

2071 "Editorial Notes." 1:36, August 1891.
Subscribers in the metropolitan London area may obtain their copies of the *Journal* directly from the publisher and avoid possible damage from its being sent through the mail.

2072 "American Book-Plates and Their Engravers." Richard C. Lichtenstein. (19) 1:37-46, September 1891.
Interesting, well-detailed article.

2073 "Library Interior Book-Plates." Arthur Vicars. 1:47-9, September 1891.
Continuation of list.

2074 "Book Notices." 1:50-1, September 1891.
Review of Leicester Warren book and one privately printed by Griggs.

2075 "Miscellanea." 1:51-3, September 1891.
Mostly inquiries.

2076 "Editorial Notes." 1:54, September 1891.
Request for public library bookplates for exhibit at annual meeting of Library Association of the United Kingdom.

2077 "Remarques sur Quelques Ex Libris Contemporains." Octave Uzanne. (11) 1:55-62, October 1891.
Article reprinted from *Le Livre Moderne* in French; if text matches illustrations should be excellent article.

2078 "Library Interior Book-Plates." Arthur Vicars. 1:63-5, October 1891.
Lists H through M, with special notes on five of them.

2079 "Some Anomalies in Armorial Ex Libris." Arthur J. Jewers. 1:66-8, October 1891.
"Making fancy devices assume semi-heraldic form . . . is very bad taste, though not deserving of such unmitigated condemnation as the assumption of other persons' armorial bearings."

2080 "Is This a Book-Plate?" 1:68, October 1891.
Description of engraving "designed and engraved by George Cruikshank in September 1871."

2081 "Heraldic Charlatanerie." (1) 1:69-70, October 1891.
Reprint of letter by Lancelot Bayard from *Gentleman's Magazine*, September 1868.

2082 "Miscellanea." 1:70-2, October 1891.
Queries and answers.

2083 "Editorial Notes." 1:72, October 1891.
Original articles requested for *Journal* and new members sought.

2084 "Ship Ex Libris." John Leighton. (7) 73-7, November 1891.
Woodcut plate of John Scott Russell, naval architect who constructed the *Leviathan*, afterwards called the *Great Eastern;* illustrated.

2085 "Book-Plate of James Riddell of Kinglass, dated 1639." R. Garraway Rice. (1) 1:77-9, November 1891.
Not mentioned in Franks' list covering 1574-1800.

2086 "American Book-Plates and Their Engravers." R. C. Lichtenstein. (9) 1:79-84, November 1891.
This second article deals with the Livingston family; the author as well as the Heraldic Editor point out errors—"not strictly correct in some of the genealogical and heraldic details."

2087 "Use of Armorial Bearings." 1:84, November 1891.
Man wearing ring with armorial bearings required to take out a license; hauled into court and fined because he had not done so.

2088 "Library Interior Book-Plates." Arthur Vicars. 1:85-6, November 1891.
Continuation of list to letter R.

2089 "List of Modern Dated Book-Plates." Walter Hamilton. 1:87-8, November 1891.
Extension of Franks' list and Hamilton's own previous list to 1850; listed chronologically through 1860.

2090 "Letters." 1:89-90, November 1891.
More inquiries and spirited replies.

2091 "Bibliography of Book-Plates." H. W. Fincham and James Roberts Brown. (1) 1:91-4, December 1891.
First seventy-one items listed.

2092 "What Is A Library?" C. M. Carlander. 1:95, December 1891.
A library is a *planned* collection of books says this Stockholm correspondent.

2093 "Tinctures in Heraldry." Walter Hamilton. 1:96, December 1891.
Seeks information on early source books which offer system of representing heraldic metals and colors.

2094 "Library Interior Book-Plates." Arthur Vicars. (4) 1:97-9, December 1891.
To letter W.

2095 "List of Modern Dated Book-Plates." Walter Hamilton. 1:100-1, December 1891.
To the year 1872.

2096 "Book Notices." 1:102, December 1891.
Review of Hulme book on heraldry.

2097 "Ex Libris Society of Berlin." 1:102-3, December 1891.
Friedrich Warnecke president of new society.

2098 "Letters and Miscellanea." 1:103-5, December 1891.
Further information sought concerning a bookplate belonging to the Sober Society.

2099 "Editorial Notes." 1:106, December 1891.
It is suggested that the Ex Libris Society be represented at the Chicago World's Fair, 1892.

2100 "Book-Plates Engraved by Cork Artists." Robert Day. (4) 1:107-12, January 1892.
Some of this material appeared elsewhere as early as 1885 and is here updated.

2101 "Gladstone Book-Plate." (1) 1:112, January 1892.
Plate designed by T. Erat Harrison was gift of Lord Northbourne in 1889 on occasion of the Gladstones' golden wedding anniversary.

2102 "List of Modern Dated Book-Plates." Walter Hamilton. 1:113-4, January 1892.
To the year 1880.

2103 "An Ancient Library Interior." W. H. K. Wright. (1) 1:115, January 1892.
Quote from Dibdin and speculation that illustration may have been used as bookplate.

2104 "Bibliography of Book-Plates." H. W. Fincham and J. R. Roberts. 1:116-7, January 1892.
Items 72 through 113.

2105 "Library Interior Book-Plates." Arthur Vicars. 1:118-9, January 1892.
Conclusion of list.

2106 "Grevis Family, of Moseley Hall, Worcestershire." W. Salt Brassington. 1: 119-20, January 1892.
Questions concerning the arms presented in the bookplate illustrated on page 63.

2107 "Letters and Miscellanea." 1:120-1, January 1892.
Suggested means of restoring soiled and discolored bookplates.

2108 "Editorial Notes." 1:122, January 1892.
Plans underway for Annual Meeting in February, as well as representation in Chicago Fair in 1893.

2109 "Humour in Heraldry." Walter Hamilton. (1) 1:123-5, February 1892.
Numerous amusing examples of incorrect and improper use of heraldry in bookplates.

2110 "A Book-Lover's Epitaph." 1:125, February 1892.
One reads: "To live in hearts we leave behind, Is not to Die."

2111 "Bibliography of Book-Plates." H. W. Fincham and J. R. Brown. 1:126-9, February 1892.
Conclusion including alphabetical index.

2112 "Letters." (2) 1:129-30, February 1892.
Walter Hamilton among others offers to exchange bookplates with other members.

2113 "List of Modern Dated Book-Plates." Walter Hamilton. 1:131-2, February 1892.
List continues to 1884.

2114 "Miscellanea." 1:133-4, February 1892.
More on the Grevis Arms.

2115 "Editorial Notes." 1:134-5, February 1892.
Members requested to send copies of their bookplates for exhibit at annual meeting.

2116 "Complete List of Members and Subscribers." 1:136-8, February 1892.
Alphabetical list including address and whether a member of the Council or an Officer.

2117 "Address Delivered before Members of Ex Libris Society." John Leighton. (2) 1:139-43, March 1892.

A speech in generalities presented at the annual meeting, February 16, 1892.

2118 "Humor in Heraldry—II." Walter Hamilton. 1:144-5, March 1892.
Verses to assist in remembering the English equilvalents of the Norman-French tinctures.

2119 "The 'Bouton' Plate (p. 68)." 1:145, March 1892.
The original was a watercolor used as the title page of a second-hand book catalog, said to be an etching by Cruikshank.

2120 "List of Modern Dated Book-Plates." Walter Hamilton. 1:146-8, March 1892.
From 1885 to 1890.

2121 "Letters and Miscellanea." 1:149-50, March 1892.
Quaint motto submitted by James Roberts Brown:
"Neither blemish this Book; nor the leaves double down,
nor lend it to each idle friend in the town;
Return it when read—or if lost please supply
another as good to the mind and the eye.
With right and with reason you need but be friends
and each Book in my study your pleasure attends."

2122 "Annual General Meeting." 1:151-6, March 1892.
Treasurer's report shows after expenses a "balance in Treasurer's hands 18 pounds, 1s 7d."

2123 "Editorial Notes." 1:156, March 1892.
New members sought.

2124 "Notes on the Ex Libris Exhibition." (3) 2:1-6, April 1892.
Seven collectors exhibited, including artists who design bookplates.

2125 "List of Modern Dated Book-Plates." Walter Hamilton. 2:7, April 1892.
Conclusion of list.

2126 "Illustrations." (3) 2:8-9, April 1892.
Three bookplates for Dr. Glynn Clobery.

2127 "Curious Printed Book-Plate." 2:9, April 1892.
Plate for John Willme who died in 1767 at age seventy.

2128 "Humour in Heraldry—III." Walter Hamilton. 2:10-11, April 1892.
Tinctures differ for "gentility, nobility, and royalty."

2129 "Book Notice." 2:11-3, April 1892.
Review of John Vinycomb's book on the Belfast Arms.

2130 "Miscellanea." (3) 2:13-5, April 1892.
Bewick cut of Fenwich plate. Poem "The Book-Plate's Petition Rewrit," updates Austin Dobson.

2131 "Letters." 2:16, April 1892.
More exchanges sought.

2132 "Anachronisms in Book-Plates." William Bolton. (2) 2:17-20, May 1892.
Specific cases where date and style don't agree or facts about the owner don't agree with the date.

2133 "Bewick Book-Plates." 2:21-3, May 1892.
List compiled from Hugo's *Bewick Collector*.

2134 "Humour in Heraldry—IV." Walter Hamilton. (3) 2:24-7, May 1892.
Comments on the English "leopard," heraldry's Christian origin, and rules relating to arms born by Ladies; very interesting and informative.

2135 "Book-Plate of Lord Byron." 2:27, May 1892.
Byron letter appears to refer to his bookplate.

2136 "Book-Plate of Dean Davies." Robert Day. 2:28, May 1892.
Born in 1649 near Cork.

2137 "Illustrations and Letters." (1) 2:29-31, May 1892.
William Stirling bookplate presented by John Leighton.

2138 "Miscellanea." 2:31-2, May 1892.
When books could be obtained in sheets, the ex libris could be "affixed" (printed) on the reverse of title pages.

2139 "Modern Book-Plate Designers. No. 1—Mr. H. Stacy Marks." (1) 2:33-7, June 1892.
Designed first plate in 1864; complete checklist includes forty; artist probably has only complete set; of many he has only a solitary specimen.

2140 "Heraldic Charlatanerie." Heraldic Editor. 2:37, June 1892.
Pedigree of ancient family attached to modern family; at point of joining wedding date is listed four months prior to birth date of known ancestor!

2141 "Humour in Heraldry—V." Walter Hamilton. 2:38, June 1892.
Satirical coats of arms and one invented by Hogarth.

2142 "St. John and Knight Book-Plates." 2:39-40, June 1892.
Discussion of four bookplates discovered one on top of the other, three owners being related.

2143 "A Bookseller's Label." 2:40, June 1892.
Plate engraved by Coffin of Exeter for Pope.

2144 "Ex Libris." (1) 2:40, June 1892.
Illustration of bookplate of Wright, Hon. Sec. of Ex Libris Society, which he will be pleased to exchange with members.

2145 "Scottish Book-Plate Engravers." J. Orr. 2:41, June 1892.
Name of engraver and owner, style of plate.

2146 "Some American Book-Plates." Laurence Hutton. 2:42-3, June 1892.
Reprinted from February-March 1886 issues of *Book Buyer* (New York).

2147 "Some American Book-Plates." (1) 2:44, June 1892.
Charles Dexter Allen sent notes and illustration of Jacob Sargeant bookplate.

2148 "Daniel Ravenel Book-Plate." 2:44, June 1892.
Description and suggestion exchange would be welcome.

2149 "Book-Plate of Dr. Dubbs." 2:44-5, June 1892.
Brief family history given from 1446.

2150 "Book Notice and Illustrations." 2:45, June 1892.
Discussion of Alexander Petau and Treshame plates.

2151 "Letters and Miscellanea." 2:46-8, June 1892.
Correspondent writes that his experience is that "ordinary home-made flour paste . . . turns sour and breeds worms and destruction."

2152 "On Some French Ecclesiastical Ex Libris." Walter Hamilton. (7) 2:49-51, July 1892.
Information apparently from privately printed French pamphlet by French priest, Rev. Father Ingold.

2153 "Some American Book-Plates." Laurence Hutton. 2:52-6, July 1892.
Continuation of *Book Buyer* reprint.

2154 "Illustrations." (2) 2:56-7, July 1892.
Plates of Chevalier De Fleurier and Nichols.

2155 "Miscellanea." 2:57, July 1892.
Suggested method of exchange to be handled by Society with small fee for postage.

2156 "Supplementary List of Modern Dated Book-Plates (English)." J. Carlton Stitt. 2:58-9, July 1892.
List in answer to Walter Hamilton's request.

2157 "Miscellanea." 2:59, July 1892.
New plate designed by and for W. E. Bools.

2158 "Unique Book-Plate—Erasmus and Dr. Hector Pomer." (1) 2:60-1, July 1892.
Rev. Pereira's article from *Antiquary* extracted.

2159 "Letters." 2:61-3, July 1892.
Lengthy quote from *Morning Post* of June 14, 1892.

2160 "Editorial Notes." 2:63-4, July 1892.
Collectors warned against high prices charged by dealers.

2161 "Fust Book-Plates." James Roberts Brown. (2) 2:64-8, August 1892.
Large plate is nearly 7" x 4" and contains no less than forty "coats."

2162 "Book-Plates at the Royal Academy, 1892." 2:68, August 1892.
Eleven bookplates listed from the Official Catalogue as being in the Black and White Room.

2163 "Some American Book-Plates." Laurence Hutton. 2:69-70, August 1892.
Conclusion of reprint.

2164 "Plate of Hildebrand Brandenburg, of Bibrach." Walter Hamilton. (1) 2:71, August 1892.

Identifies colors usually found on this rudely colored bookplate dating from about 1480.

2165 "Modern Book-Plate Designers. No. 2—Mr. Thomas Erat Harrison." (2) 2: 72-5, August 1892.
Among fourteen plates described is one designed for William E. Gladstone.

2166 "Illustrations." (2) 2:75, August 1892.
Plates for Comtesse de Du Barry and Mons. J. B. Michaud.

2167 "Letters." 2:75-6, August 1892.
Correspondence concerning exchange list, mottoes, and new bookplates.

2168 "Literary Book-Plates. Series II." Arthur Vicars. 2:77-8, August 1892.
Definition: "all plates not strictly interiors . . . but [those] in which books form the *prominent* feature of the design."

2169 "Book Notice—Editorial Notes." 2:79-80, August 1892.
Book on heraldry reviewed; note on Bernard Quaritch publication including bookplates.

2170 "On the Removal From or Retention of Book-Plates in Books." 2:81-4, September 1892.
Sensible reasons *pro* and *con* given.

2171 "Illustrations." (1) 2:84, September 1892.
Plate for Andre Felibien, Historiographer to French king, dated 1650.

2172 "Book-Plate of Robert Dinwiddie." (1) 2:84-6, September 1892.
Dinwiddie was Lieutenant-Governor of Virginia, 1751-58.

2173 "Query." 2:86, September 1892.
Requests explanation of inscription and whether R. Sherwood plate engraved by Bewick.

2174 "Literary Ex Libris." Arthur Vicars. (2) 2:87-91, September 1892.
Series II, partial list.

2175 "Book-Plate of George Washington." 2:92-3, September 1892.
Quotes at length Lichtenstein's article from an 1888 issue of *Curio*.

2176 "Book Notice." (1) 2:93, September 1892.
Book by A. D. Weld French of interest to armorial bookplate collectors.

2177 "Letters." (1) 2:94, September 1892.
Additional Fust plate revealed.

2178 "Miscellanea." 2:95, September 1892.
Quotes from Edmund Gosse's *Gossip in a Library*.

2179 "Editorial Notes." 2:96, September 1892.
Request for early submission of copy for next issue as editor will be on vacation.

2180 "Our Ex Libris Album." 2:97-100, October 1892.
List includes 117 private members and 17 libraries; plates were exhibited at annual meeting.

2181 "Collectors in the United States." Walter Hamilton. 2:101, October 1892.
"The cult is new."

2182 "*The Queen—The Collector.*" 2:101, October 1892.
Brief quotes from these publications.

2183 "Literary Ex Libris." Arthur Vicars. (3) 2:102-6, October 1892.
Continuation of list.

2184 "Heraldic Notes." 2:107-8, October 1892.
Heraldic Editor takes to task authors of previous articles.

2185 "Letters." 2:108-110, October 1892.
More of Fust bookplates.

2186 "Miscellanea—Illustrations." (2) 2:110-1, October 1892.
Additional facts on Andre Felibien.

2187 "Editorial Notes." 2:112, October 1892.
Collectors warned against extortionate prices charged by some dealers.

2188 "Ex Libris in Paris." 2:113-6, November 1892.
Survey made by John Leighton listed.

2189 "Some Historical Book-Plates." 2:118-20, November 1892.
Reprinted from *Collector*, June, 1892.

2190 "Berlin Ex Libris Society." 2:120, November 1892.
"Sustained excellence" of German publication lauded.

2191 "The *Morning Post* on Book-Plate Collecting." 2:121, November 1892.
A collector should never add a plate "that is not interesting in itself as a work of art, or for curious information afforded by it, or interesting from associations with some historical character. A book-plate is of no more value as a book-plate than a picture as a picture."

2192 "Portrait Ex Libris." 2:121, November 1892.
Contributions requested by Arthur Vicars for contemplated list.

2193 "Literary Ex Libris." Arthur Vicars. (2) 2:117, 122-4, November 1892.
H through M.

2194 "Letters." 2:125-7, November 1892.
Letters from James Roberts Brown, Mary Dinwiddie, Walter Hamilton, John Vinycomb—lively reading.

2195 "Illustrations—Queries." (3) 2:128-9, November 1892.
Question and answer reprinted from *Notes and Queries.*

2196 "Editorial Notes." 2:130, November 1892.
Subscriptions for current year should be paid.

2197 "The Beaver in Book-Plates: (Heraldry & Zoology)." John Leighton. (1) 2: 131-2, December 1892.
Three examples described.

2198 "Tax on Armorial Bearings." Heraldic Editor. 2:133, December 1892.
Tax scheme should afford protection to those who rightfully are entitled to armorial bearings.

2199 "Literary Ex Libris." Arthur Vicars. (7) 2:134-43, December 1892.
Conclusion.

2200 "Collection of Armorial Book-Plates." 2:143, December 1892.
About 250 plates from collection of C. Williams discovered in Exeter shop and subsequently bought by American.

2201 "Letters—Illustrations." (1) 2:144-6, December 1892.
More lively exchange with the Heraldic Editor.

2202 "Editorial Notes." 2:146, December 1892.
Membership up to 288.

2203 "William Hogarth As a Book-Plate Designer." (6) 3:1-6, January 1893.
Evidence to indicate he designed and executed four bookplates.

2204 "Yorkshire Bookplates." John H. Ashworth. 3:7-9, January 1893.
Alphabetical list giving dates when known.

2205 "Kerrich Book-Plate." 3:10-2, January 1893.
Letter from engraver sending 800 prints dated 1754.

2206 "Book-Plate of General Francis Columbine." (1) 3:12-3, January 1893.
In 1738 he was appointed Governor of Gibraltar.

2207 "Hogarth Book-Plates." John Leighton. 3:13, January 1893.
Question asked here which was answered by editor in lead article of this issue.

2208 "The Beaver in Heraldry." Heraldic Editor. 3:14, January 1893.
Heraldic Editor questions whether one properly knowledgeable in zoology could be equally well informed on heraldry!

2209 "Letters—Miscellanea." 3:15, January 1893.
Second request for information on Sober Society.

2210 "Editorial Notes." 3:16, January 1893.
Annual meeting scheduled for February.

2211 "American Notes on Book-Plate Collecting." 3:17-8, February 1893.
"We have only about forty known collectors at work."

2212 "Modern Book-Plate Designers. No. 3 - John Vinycomb." (5) 3:19-24, February 1893.
List of 67 bookplates included.

2213 "Book Notices." (7) 3:25-8, February 1893.
Reviews of books by Egerton Castle and Walter Hamilton.

2214 "Letters." 3:29-31, February 1893.
More on the beaver.

2215 "Editorial Notes." 3:32, February 1893.
In attending the annual meeting "members may introduce a lady friend."

2216 "Chairman's Address." James Roberts Brown. (1) 3:33-9, March 1893.
Knowledge of heraldry is invaluable "to the lover of book-plates; it is essential, in fact, if he would be anything more than a mere collector."

2217 "An Annotated List of Early American Book-Plates." Charles Dexter Allen. (5) 3:40-2, 45, March 1893.
Alphabetical list to be continued.

2218 "Letters—Miscellanea." 3:43-4, 46, March 1893.
Notes on Berlin Society and P. Sparrow, sculpt.

2219 "Annual Meeting." 3:47-52, March 1893.
Reports from the Secretary and the Treasurer.

2220 "Hints on Designing Heraldic Ex Libris." Heraldic Editor. 3:53-6, April 1893.
Essentials are arms and crest with supporters; non-essentials include ornamental surroundings, helmet, mantling, and shape of shield.

2221 "Letters." (1) 3:56, April 1893.
Illustration of Sober Society plate.

2222 "An Annotated List of Early American Book-Plates." Charles Dexter Allen. 3:57-9, April 1893.
Letters A and B.

2223 "Exhibition at St. Martin's Hall, London." (4) 3:60-4, April 1893.
Comments on exhibit in connection with annual meeting; details of plates shown by members to be continued in next issue.

2224 "American Notes on Book-Plates." 3:65, April 1893.
Collection of James Eddy Mauran, approximately 3,500 plates, appraised at $300. Plates mounted on assorted paper stock; ladies' plates mounted on bits of silk, satin, damask, brocade.

2225 "Michael Begon and the Chapius Arms." (1) 3:66, April 1893.
Query concerning relation of 1702 plate and present family of Shoppee.

2226 "Letters, Miscellanea, Illustrations." 3:67, April 1893.
F. J. Thairlwall wants journal to print "going prices" for bookplates, furnish classification and nomenclature information, and publish facsimile reproductions of unusual "newly acquired treasures."

2227 "Editorial Notes." 3:68, April 1893.
Some members have submitted material for exhibit at Columbian World's Fair in Chicago.

2228 "Book-Pile Ex Libris. Series III." Arthur Vicars. (1) 3:69-72, May 1893.
Check list continued.

2229 "Burden of Book-Plates." Walter Hamilton. 3:73-4, May 1893.
"Presumptuous and flippant critic" berated bookplates in *Daily News* (April 7, 1893) saying "We (cannot) conceive a topic less worthy of attention from an adult and unimpaired intellect."

2230 "Ex Libris of H. G. Seaman by Randolph Caldecott." James Roberts Brown. (1) 3:74-5, May 1893.
Design originally drawn by artist on back of post-card.

2231 "Humorous Fly-Leaf Inscription." 3:75, May 1893.
Two inscriptions dated about 1628.

2232 "Singular Ex Libris of the Knapp Family." 3:75, May 1893.
Plate and inscription occupy flyleaf.

2233 "Book Notice." (2) 3:76-78, May 1893.
Review of Hardy's *Book-Plates* expressing some disappointment that nearly half of thirty-seven illustrations have been previously reproduced.

2234 "Book-Plate of a Famous Librarian." H. W. Fincham. (1) 3:78, May 1893.
Antonio Magliabechi, born 1633, was librarian to two Cardinals of Tuscany.

2235 "Exhibition at St. Martin's Hall, London." (1) 3:79-82, May 1893.
Continuation of list of plates exhibited by members.

2236 "Letters." 3:83, May 1893.
Egerton Castle "glad to exchange a set of his own pictorial plates" for plates with the name Castle or Castell.

2237 "Editorial Notes." 3:83-4, May 1893.
Non-member suggests Society run popularity contest by having each member submit three favorite bookplates and three he would most like to possess.

2238 "Heraldry and Book-Plates of Some British Poets, I. Sir Walter Scott, Earl of Dorset, Robert Bloomfield, Robert Burns." William Bolton. (2) 3:85-8, June 1893.
Scott introduced "false heraldry" in both poem and novel (Ivanhoe).

2239 "Book-Pile Ex Libris." Arthur Vicars. (2) 3:89-91, June 1893.
Continued G through P.

2240 "Gore Book-Plates." (2) 3:92, June 1893.
Three plates attributed to Thomas Gore, earliest dated about 1656.

2241 "Illustrations." (1) 3:93-4, June 1893.
John Vennitzer's is "one of finest portrait ex libris."

2242 "An Annotated List of Early American Book-Plates." Charles Dexter Allen. 3:95-7, June 1893.
Continuation B through C.

2243 "Letters." 3:98-100, June 1893.

"I say confidently that those who are wise will not despise the collecting of *anything*,—even 'muffin bells,' 'old boots,' or 'warming pans.' " (F.J.T.)

2244 "Editorial Notes." 3:100, June 1893.

Receipt of exhibit bookplates for World's Columbian Exposition at Chicago acknowledged by Melvil Dewey.

2245 "Heraldry and Book-Plates of Some British Poets, II. William Cowper, John Kookham Frere, Christopher Anstey." William Bolton. (2) 3:101-3, July 1893.

Interesting comments about the poets as well as their bookplates.

2246 "Letters." 3:104-5, July 1893.

More correspondence generated by "Burden of Book-Plates" article.

2247 "Book-Pile Ex Libris." Arthur Vicars. 3:106-8, July 1893.

Conclusion of list and addenda.

2248 "Library Interior Ex Libris." Arthur Vicars. 3:109-12, July 1893.

Conclusion of list.

2249 "Literary Ex Libris." Arthur Vicars. 3:113, July 1893.

Conclusion.

2250 "Heraldic Editorship." 3:114, July 1893.

Resignation of Arthur J. Jewers accepted as "they feel it is not the function of the Society to assume the duties of the authorities of Heralds' College, nor to head a crusade against any persons who may think proper to assume arms to which they are not legally entitled."

2251 "Illustrations." (1) 3:114, July 1893.

Bookplate of Count Maximilian Louis Breiner.

2252 "Editorial Notes." 3:115-6, July 1893.

Notice of articles in other publications.

2253 "Mistakes in Heraldry on Book-Plates." F. J. Thairlwall. 3:117-9, August 1893.

Article considers bookplate incorrect "as an heraldic composition" usually from "mere ignorance or carelessness."

2254 "Notes on Some Swedish Ex Libris." C. M. Carlander. (6) 3:120-3, August 1893.

Baroness Hedvig Ulrika De Geer had a large library in contrast to her mother-in-law who sold mouldering manuscripts to grocer's shop!

2255 "Book Notices." 3:123, August 1893.

Reviews Charles Norton Elvin's *Handbook of the Orders of Chivalry, War Medals and Crosses.*

2256 "Annotated List of Early American Book-Plates." Charles Dexter Allen. 3: 124-6, August 1893.

List includes names of owner and engraver, date, description, notes and present owner.

2257 "Letters." 3:127-9, August 1893.
Lengthy one on Burn's seal.

2258 "Illustrations." (2) 3:130-1, August 1893.
Several communications on bookplates of John Boswell.

2259 "Editorial Notes." 3:132, August 1893.
Mention of several bookplate items from other journals.

2260 "Book-Plate of Captain Cook." (2) 3:133-5, September 1893.
Posthumous grant of arms to Cook's family used in bookplate.

2261 "Heraldry and Book-Plates of Some British Poets, III. Henry J. Pye, Robert Southey, Reginald Heber, H. F. Lyte." William Bolton. (2) 3:136-9, September 1893.
Discussion of two British Poet Laureates and two hymn writers.

2262 "Book Notices." 3:139, September 1893.
Review of Bethune-Baker volume.

2263 "Illustrations." (3) 3:139-40, September 1893.
New York Society Library plate; H. Stacy Marks plate designed for Robert Jackson.

2264 "Letters." 3:141, September 1893.
Three correspondents.

2265 "Annotated List of Early American Book-Plates." Charles Dexter Allen. 3:142-3, September 1893.
To be continued.

2266 "Dated Book-Plates." Walter Hamilton. 3:144-6, September 1893.
Advantages of dating to identify.

2267 "Ex Libris Imaginaires et Supposes de Personages Celebres Anciens et Modernes." 3:146-7, September 1893.
Imaginary bookplates "pourtraying in some manner the peculiarities or idiosyncrasies of the personages whom they pretend to represent."

2268 "F. V. Hadlow, SC. Brighton." (1) 3:147-8, September 1893.
Large plate for Charles Leeson Prince, 1882, used as frontispiece and described.

2269 "Editorial Notes." 3:148, September 1893.
John Leighton to send disclaimer to *Graphic* concerning presentation of plate to Duke and Duchess of York.

2270 "The Processes for the Production of Ex Libris." John Vinycomb. (1) 3:149-51, October 1893.
Originally only methods were by woodblocks or engraved copper plates; now numerous methods of reproduction.

2271 "Scope of Book-Plate Collecting." Walter Hamilton. 3:151, October 1893.

Translation of letter by Frenchman questioning whether "there really (are) as many collectors as some folks would have us believe."

2272 "Prince Library and Book-Plates, Compiled by the Editor." (2) 3:152-4, October 1893.
Considerable detail concerning "Father of American Bibliography."

2273 "Oliver Cromwell's Book-Plate." 3:155, October 1893.
Purported plate of Cromwell received from Rev. Ellis.

2274 "Illustrations." (2) 3:156, October 1893.
Interesting plate for Public Libraries for Saint George, Hanover Square, London.

2275 "Book-Plate of Samuel Provoost, First Bishop of New York." W. H. K. Wright. (1) 3:157, October 1893.
Early American bibliophile had plate engraved by Maverick.

2276 "Book-Plate of L. Sterne." Walter Hamilton. 3:157, October 1893.
Print of Laurence Sterne's plate inserted in early edition of *Sentimental Journey*.

2277 "Book-Plates or Seals." 3:157, October 1893.
Philip Connor seeks plates of Powell.

2278 "Annotated List of Early American Book-Plates." Charles Dexter Allen. 3:158-9, October 1893.
Listing for E and F.

2279 "Letters." 3:160-3, October 1893.
Queries on Perceval family, Cowper, Col. Grant, and partial translation from *El Curioso Americano*.

2280 "Editorial Notes." 3:163-4, October 1893.
Members requested to send plates for Ex Libris Album.

2281 "Book-Plates of Samuel Pepys." (4) 3:165-9, November 1893.
While there are five Pepys plates "only the portrait and official plates appear in books in the Pepysian Library, Magdalene College, Cambridge."

2282 "Processes for the Production of Ex Libris." John Vinycomb. (7) 3:170-4, November 1893.
History and process of wood engraving detailed.

2283 "*World* on Ex Libris". 3:174, November 1893.
Review "in complimentary terms" of Hardy book.

2284 "American Notes." 3:176, November 1893.
Quotes article by Bruce Edwards in *Hartford Post*.

2285 "Book-Plate of New College, Oxford." 3:176, November 1893.
Member submitted photograph.

2286 "Letters—Illustration." (1) 3:175, 177-9, November 1893.
H. W. Fincham gives an inscription of cryptogramic bookplate.

2287 "Arms of Virginia Company." 3:179, November 1893.
Quote from *Richmond Dispatch.*

2288 "Editorial Notes." 3:179-80, November 1893.
Opinions and experience of members requested "on how to preserve and arrange Ex Libris."

2289 "A Plea for Book-Plates." H. S. Ashbee. 3:181-2, December 1893.
"Savage and civilised men alike hoard, the difference being . . . a bead or a book, a scalp or a banner."

2290 "German Book-Plates." Walter Hamilton. (2) 3:183-5, December 1893.
Certain distinctive features are helpful in identifying German plates.

2291 "Monastic Plates." 3:183, December 1893.
One is designed, etched and signed by M. Paul Avril.

2292 "American Notes." Charles Dexter Allen. (2) 3:186-9, December 1893.
Plate finally identified as that of Virginia Council Chamber of Colonial days.

2293 "Armorial Book-Plate of Captain Cook." 3:189, December 1893.
Additional details to enlighten article in a previous *Journal.*

2294 "The Clerk of the Parliaments." William Bolton. 3:191-2, December 1893.
Court intrigue and family quarrels among the Cowpers.

2295 "Book-Plate of Mr. H. Berkeley Score." (1) 3:193-4, December 1893.
Frontispiece of 1820 edition of La Fontaine's *Fables* used as frame for bookplate.

2296 "Book-Plate of Thomas Carlyle." (1) 3:194, December 1893.
Quotes letter from Carlyle to artist who designed his plate.

2297 "Letters—Book Notices." (2) 3:190, 194-8, December 1893.
Variety of queries and replies.

2298 "Editorial Notes." (1) 3:199-200, December 1893.
Illustration is official monogram or device of the Society designed by C. W. Sherborn.

2299 "Royal Book-Plate of the Cambridge University Library." Octavius Johnson. 4:1-2, January 1894.
J. Pine engraved bookplate for use with library of George I which was given to Cambridge.

2300 "American Notes." Charles Dexter Allen. (2) 4:3-6, January 1894.
Edwin Davis French designed bookplate with inscription in Volapuk (universal language).

2301 "How to Arrange Book-Plates." R. Garraway Rice. 4:7-8, January 1894.
Mounts nine bookplates on sheet of drawing paper 15"x11"; index by surname of plate owner, mottoes, places, engravers, dates.

2302 "Illustrations." (5) 4:9-11, January 1894.
Includes plates for Nuremberg family of Kress of Kressenstein, Duke of Kent, Francis Gwyn, and Columbia College.

2303 "Letters." 4:12-5, January 1894.
More on Sir Walter Scott.

2304 "Editorial Notes." 4:15-6, January 1894.
Annual meeting scheduled for February 14th

2305 "On the Processes for the Production of Ex Libris." John Vinycomb. (12) 4: 17-24, February 1894.
Examples and descriptions of various processes.

2306 "Horn-Book in Ex Libris." (1) 4:25, February 1894.
Andrew Tuer, writing illustrated monograph on subject, requests references.

2307 "Queries and Replies." 4:25, February 1894.
Additional information on Ruddiman.

2308 "La Societe Francaise Des Collectionneurs D'Ex-Libris." Walter Hamilton. 4:26-7, February, 1894.
Comments on newly formed French society and its journal; warns against risk of using hydrochloric acid to clean bookplates.

2309 "New Book-plates and Exchanges." 4:27, February 1894.
Names of several willing to exchange.

2310 "American Book-plates." 4:27, February 1894.
Announcement of Charles Dexter Allen's book.

2311 "Additional Bibliography of Book-Plates." H. W. Fincham. 4:28-9, February 1894.
Forty-one items and more to come.

2312 "Book-Plates of the Duke of Kent." Albert Hartshorne. 4:30, February 1894.
Considerable family history.

2313 "Letters." 4:30, February 1894.
List of duplicates available for exchange.

2314 "Editorial Notes." 4:31-2, February 1894.
More controversy stirred by *Daily News* item.

2315 "Our Third Annual Meeting." (1) 4:33-41, March 1894.
Detailed report.

2316 "Illustrations." (1) 4:42, March 1894.
Plate shows punning arms for William Jackson (a jack and a sun).

2317 "On the Processes for the Production of Ex Libris." John Vinycomb. (9) 4: 43-6, March 1894.
Mostly on lithographic process.

2318 "Report of the Hon. Treasurer of the Ex Libris Society." Walter Hamilton. 4:46-8, March 1894.
Among expenditures was an item for straw boards to protect the *Journal* in the mails.

2319 "Additional Bibliography of Book-Plates." H. W. Fincham. 4:49, March 1894.

Another twenty-odd items.

2320 "Castle's *English Book-Plates.*" 4:50-1, March 1894.

Critical review by John Heanley giving page and quotation with which he differs.

2321 "Letters." 4:51, March 1894.

Walter Hamilton supplies corrections with page references to Hardy's book.

2322 "Editorial Notes." 4:52, March 1894.

Notes on foreign publications and *Studio.*

2323 "Notes on the Annual Exhibition." (3) 4:53-6, April 1894.

Detailed account with list of exhibitors and their addresses, and then a list by exhibitor of actual plates on display.

2324 "On the Processes for the Production of Ex Libris." John Vinycomb. (4) 4:57-61, April 1894.

Process blocks—line work.

2325 "Letters." 4:61, April 1894.

Inquiry and poem.

2326 "Littleton Book-Plate." (2) 4:62-4, April 1894.

Heraldic notes and family tree.

2327 "Some Stray Notes on Eccentric Heraldry." W. Bolton. 4:64-5, April 1894.

Enlightening and well expressed.

2328 "A Wee Protest." 4:65, April 1894.

Member who offered to exchange his plate justly complains that correspondents fail to send copy of their own plate or a stamped return envelope.

2329 "Armorial Bearings." 4:66, April 1894.

Reprint from *Notes and Queries* concerning statement in *Chamber's Encyclopedia.*

2330 "Letters." 4:67, April 1894.

Correspondent feels price of Bewick plates too high for quantity available.

2331 "Editorial Notes." 4:67-8, April 1894.

Numerous notices of periodical articles.

2332 "American Notes." Charles Dexter Allen. 4:69-71, May 1894.

Prefers the "good old way of making exchanges, that is by letter."

2333 "The Late Mr. J. M. Gray." J. Balfour Paul. 4:71, May 1894.

Death of Curator of Scottish National Portrait Gallery noted.

2334 "An Index." 4:72-5, May 1894.

F. J. Thairlwall has furnished index to Leicester's *A Guide to the Study of Book-Plates;* A to G.

2335 "Illustrations." (3) 4:76, May 1894.
Plate of Charles Bonaventure dated 1723.

2336 "A Critic on Heraldry." 4:77, May 1894.
The *Daily News* taken to task for its jocular tone in reviewing Dr. Woodward's book on heraldry.

2337 "Lord Carmichael's Book-Plate." 4:77, May 1894.
Questions proper title.

2338 "Notes on the Annual Exhibition." 4:78-81, May 1894.
Concludes list of plates and by whom exhibited.

2339 "Monastic Plate of St. Ulrick and Afra, Augsburg, Germany." 4:82, May 1894.
Disputes previously published comments.

2340 "Dobyns-Yate Book-Plate." 4:82-3, May 1894.
Brief family history and description of plate.

2341 "Editorial and Passing Notes." 4:83-4, May 1894.
Designs to be solicited for a Certificate of Membership or Diploma.

2342 "Hungerford Book-Plate." J. Whitmarsh. (3) 4:84-7, June 1894.
Plates for different family members and history.

2343 "Exchanges and Book-Plate Identification." (12) 4:87, 92-3, 96, June 1894.
Five indicate exchanges available and desired; J. R. Brown and H. W. Fincham to handle identification department.

2344 "Original Book-Rhyme." 4:87, June 1894.
Four stanza poem in old English with moral by J.V.: "Never buy a boke iff thatte ye can cozen one from a friend, and then be sure to stikke your boke-plate on,—on top off hys!"

2345 "Index to Warren's Guide." 4:88-91, June 1894.
H to P.

2346 "On the Processes for the Reproduction of Ex Libris." John Vinycomb. (1) 4: 89, 92, June 1894.
Example of soft-ground etching shown.

2347 "Did the Poet Byron Use a Book-Plate?" 4:94, June 1894.
Still a question though various sources quoted.

2348 "New Book-Plate of the Plymouth Public Library." 4:95, June 1894.
Designed and executed by W. H. Foster.

2349 "Book-Plate of Portsmouth Free Library." 4:95, June 1894.
Description submitted by T. D. A. Jewers.

2350 "Illustrations." (2) 4:97, June 1894.
William Taylor one of few signed by Bewick.

2351 "Dobyns-Yate Book-Plate." 4:97, June 1894.
Two correspondents submitted additional facts.

2352 "Letters, Query." 4:98-9, June 1894.
Surcharge on postal cards from U.S., use of "aristocratic hyphens" in compound names.

2353 "Editorial and Passing Notes." 4:99-102, June 1894.
Some members still haven't paid their dues.

2354 "Book-Plates of Celebrities." H. S. Ashbee. (1) 4:103-5, July 1894.
Carlyle, Garrick, Gladstone, Holmes, Trollope, Schopenhauer among celebrities whose plates are described.

2355 "Samuel Pepy's Bookplates." 4:105, July 1894.
Additional details by Henry B. Wheatley.

2356 "Index to Warren's Guide." 4:106-9, July 1894.
Conclusion of index.

2357 "Letters, Query." 4:109, July 1894.
Bookdealer Meehan mentions finding Byron plate and inscription in same volume which "ought to clearly identify the poet with the plate described."

2358 "Book-Plate Identification." (11) 4:110-11, July 1894.
Another eleven for identification.

2359 "Notes on Illustrations." 4:111, July 1894.
Various states of Bewick plate of William Taylor.

2360 "Heraldic Exhibition at Burlington House." Walter Hamilton. (2) 4:112-6, July 1894.
Sir A. Wollaston Franks created a K.C.B.

2361 "The Book to Its Mistress." 4:116, July 1894.
Translation of poem in French from prior *Journal*.

2362 "Illustrations." (1) 4:116, July 1894.
Plate for Sir Charles Frederick dated 1752.

2363 "Recent Book-Plates." (1) 4:116-7, July 1894.
Henry Blackwell's Welsh plate illustrated.

2364 "Book Notices." 4:118, July 1894.
Volume on heraldry, French book by Jadart, and Warnecke's *Rare Book-Plates* (15th and 16th century).

2365 "Book-Plate for Father Adam." 4:118, July 1894.
Hopson, in the manner of Joly, created plate which might have been used by Adam "had such artistic trifles been in fashion."

2366 "Editorial and Passing Notes." 4:119-22, July 1894.
Notes from French Society, forthcoming articles, and articles in other journals.

2367 "Modern Book-Plate Designers. No. 4 - John Forbes Nixon." (6) 4:123-6, August 1894.
"Nixon's abilities stretch over almost every field in which heraldry

. . . can appear" including stained glass windows, book covers, monumental brasses, and bookplates.

2368 "Book-Plate Identification." (9) 4:127, August 1894.
H. W. Fincham and J. R. Brown in charge of Identification Department; nine pictured for identification.

2369 "Book-Plates of the Humes of Polwarth, Co. Berwick." 4:127, August 1894.
Description of four plates.

2370 "Some Early Entries Referring to Book Ownership." William Bolton. 4:128-30, August 1894.
Early manuscript entries marking ownership described.

2371 "Book Notices." (3) 4:130-4, August 1894.
Thirty-eight shapes of shields illustrated from *Dated Book Plates.*

2372 "American Notes." Charles Dexter Allen. 4:135, August 1894.
Comments on the bookplate exhibit scheduled for the Grolier Club in October.

2373 "Query." 4:136, August 1894.
Questions the arms of Christopher Columbus.

2374 "Recent Book-Plates." 4:136-7, August 1894.
Several members send descriptions of their plates.

2375 "Editorial and Passing Notes." 4:137-8, August 1894.
Notes from Switzerland and France as well as mention of articles in American and English periodicals.

2376 "German Book-Plates of Pennsylvania." Joseph Henry Dubbs. (1) 4:139-43, September 1894.
Many German families entitled to heraldic honors which appear on their plates.

2377 "Queries." 4:143, September 1894.
Quote from *Notes and Queries* and question on crest of Henry VIII.

2378 "Book-Plate Identification." (10) 4:144-5, September 1894.
Currently forty-one plates for identification.

2379 "Dated Book-Plates." Walter Hamilton. (2) 4:145-7, September 1894.
Hamilton asks help of brother collectors in furnishing additional facts on certain plates dated between 1700-95 for forthcoming publication.

2380 "Tinctures in Heraldry." W. G. Brown. (3) 4:148-50, September 1894.
Detailed comments on three plates.

2381 "Bewick Book-Plate." (1) 4:150, September 1894.
Reproduction of variant of John Anderson plate.

2382 "Letters." 4:150-1, September 1894.
Questions concerning plate for Cowper and one possibly designed by Blake.

2383 "Recent Book-Plates." 4:151, September 1894.
Three more members describe their plates.

2384 "Future Arrangements of the Society." Walter Hamilton 4:152-3, September 1894.
More meetings which would facilitate exchange of plates including duplicates, encourage study of heraldry and furnish more material for the *Journal*.

2385 "Carolus Agricola Hammonius." 4:153, September 1894.
Date questioned due to method of representing tinctures but John Leighton gives explanation which should have been printed in original item.

2386 "Arms of Christopher Columbus." 4:153, September 1894.
Additional details.

2387 "Editorial and Passing Notes." 4:153-4, September 1894.
Album with plates and portraits of some members on way to America for exhibit at Grolier Club.

2388 "A Few Words on Ex Libris and Marks of Ownership in Books." 4:155-8, October 1894.
Condensed form of speech by John Vinycomb.

2389 "Queries." 4:158, October 1894.
Requests arms of St. Bernard Monastery and identification of P. Simms, engraver.

2390 "An American Book-Plate Designer." 4:159, October 1894.
Reprint from *Art Amateur* of list of plates designed by D. McN. Stauffer.

2391 "Book-Plate of 'The Deemster Christian.'" 4:159, October 1894.
Item from *Literary World* on unusual coincidence during theatre rehearsal.

2392 "Book-Plate Identification." (12) 4:160-1, October 1894.
Indicates plates identified and offers forty-two through fifty-three for identification.

2393 "Forthcoming Work on *American Book-Plates*." 4:161, October 1894.
Favorable comments on proof sheets; publication expected in November.

2394 "Exchanges." 4:161, October 1894.
Member requests addresses of two who sent her plates but failed to include name or address.

2395 "Illustrations." (2) 4:162-3, October 1894.
Question as to whether Bartolozzi plate for George III is actually a bookplate.

2396 "Chevalier D'Eon's Book-Plate." 4:163, October 1894.
Another exchange reprinted from *Notes and Queries*.

2397 "Late Daniel Ravenel." 4:165, October 1894.
Obituary notice reprinted from *News and Courier*.

2398 "Electoral Library of the Dukes of Bavaria." (1) 4:164-5, October 1894.
Full-page plate dated 1618.

2399 "Recent Book-Plates." (1) 4:166-7, October 1894.
Interesting plate for Francis Joseph Bigger designed by J. Vinycomb.

2400 "Letters." 4:167, October 1894.
A "thank you" from Walter Hamilton for help given him.

2401 "Editorial and Passing Notes." 4:168-70, October 1894.
Comment on articles in other journals and newspapers, including a return thrust at the *Daily News*.

2402 "Heraldry & Book-Plates of Some British Poets." William Bolton. (3) 4:171-5, November 1894.
Lord Halifax, Samuel Rogers and Lord Byron discussed.

2403 "Book-Plate Identification." (9) 4:175-6, October 1894.
A few more identified and nine more added.

2404 "Book-Labels." Albert Hartshorne. 4:177, November 1894.
Discusses labels and the volumes in which they were pasted.

2405 "Arms of Christopher Columbus." Walter Hamilton. 4:177, November 1894.
Quotes extract in French dated 1705.

2406 "Letters." 4:177, November 1894.
Edward Heron-Allen seeks plates with violins.

2407 "Two Hamburg Book-Plates." A. Forbes Steveking. (3) 4:178-80, November 1894.
One dated 1766, the second current and very "modern"; both for same family show lime tree and mower with scythe.

2408 "A True Ballad of Book-Plate Hunting." 4:180, November 1894.
Then as now, the hunt leads to the book stalls in "a dark, unsavoury lane." Twelve stanza poem.

2409 "Curious Dated Book-Label." 4:180, November 1894.
Label dated 1639.

2410 "Humor in Heraldry." 4:181-2, November 1894.
Extensive quotes from *Cornhill* article whose author must have "re-searched" a 1878 imprint titled *Ye Comic History of Heraldry*.

2411 "Query." 4:182, November 1894.
Seeks to identify plate for William Pitt, whether for statesman or another of same name.

2412 "Illustrations." (3) 4:183, November 1894.
F. C. Tilney designed plate for ship owner, A. Bilbrough, which includes shipping items and marine monsters.

2413 "Recent Book-Plates." 4:183-4, November 1894.
Society's Vice President, Robert Day, has new plate designed by R. Thomson.

2414 "Book-Plates and Their Early Engravers." 4:184, November 1894.
Quotes 1888 article from *City Mission Record*, Hartford, Conn.

2415 "Editorial and Passing Notes." 4:185-6, November 1894.
Notices of articles in other periodicals, books, and a plea that members pay their dues.

2416 "American Notes." Charles Dexter Allen. (2) 4:185-91, December 1894.
Account of the exhibition at the Grolier Club.

2417 "Book Notices." 4:191, December 1894.
Examples of Irish Book-Plates, one hundred copies privately printed.

2418 "Heraldry & Book-Plates of Some British Poets." William Bolton. (3) 4:192-5, December 1894.
Discussion of Surrey, Tennyson and Kingsley.

2419 "Lecture on Book-Plates at Plymouth." 4:198, December 1894.
Paper read by W. H. K. Wright with list of fifty-eight book-plate slides exhibited.

2420 "Modern Book-Plate Design. No. 5 C. E. Tute. (5)" 4:196-7, 199, December 1894.
In addition to bookplates, artist designed stained glass.

2421 "Book-Plate Identification." (6) 4:200-1, December 1894.
Some previous plates identified and six added.

2422 "Book-Plate of James Gibbs, Architect, 1736." (1) 4:202, December 1894.
Architect of St. Martin's-in-the-Fields.

2423 "An Early Warning to Book-Borrowers." 4:202, December 1894.
"This book is oon, the curse of crist ys a nother, He that steleth thoon shall have the othir."

2424 "Book Notices." 4:203, December 1894.
Review of John Vinycomb's book and one printed in Stockholm by C. M. Carlander III.

2425 "Letters." 4:203-4, December 1894.
James Roberts Brown names book in which Bartolozzi engraving appears on title page, raising doubt that it was ever *used* as a bookplate despite *intention*.

2426 "Editorial and Passing Notes." 4:204-6, December 1894.
Lantern slides used to illustrate talk by Wright.

2427 "Gray Bequest to the Lyon Office." J. Balfour Paul. (2) 5:1-5, January 1895.
Nearly one hundred volumes given to Lyon Office and special book-plate designed to be used in them.

2428 "Curious Book-Rhyme." 5:5, January 1895.
One stanza dated March 7th, 1741.

2429 "Book-Plate of Robert Vyner." James Roberts Brown. (1) 5:5-6, January 1895.
It is thought bookplate executed shortly after 1665.

2430 "The Late Frederick Warnecke." 5:7, January 1895.
Gives list of publications (in German); born April 21, 1837 and died November 25, 1894 from influenza.

2431 "Book-Plate Identification." (5) 5:8, January 1895.
Five additional plates and previous one identified.

2432 "Supplementary American Notes." Charles Dexter Allen. 5:9-10, January 1895.
Grolier Club monograph on bookplate exhibit issued from De Vinne Press.

2433 "Exchanges." 5:10, January 1895.
Two members offer exchange.

2434 "Japanese Book-Plates." (4) 5:11-2, January 1895.
Two combine English and Japanese inscriptions.

2435 "Recent Book-Plates." (1) 5:12, January 1895.
Pictured is plate designed by F. C. Tilney for Thomas James Wise, "well-known literary man."

2436 "Mr. H. Stacy Marks, R. A., on Book-Plates." 5:13, January 1895.
Brief quote from artist's autobiography.

2437 "Ex Libris Album." 5:13, January 1895.
Contributions solicited for exhibit at annual meeting.

2438 "Book-Plate of the Rev. Dr. Trusler." 5:14, January 1895.
While not signed, plate appears to be by "one of the brothers Bewick."

2439 "Heraldry, From an American Point of View." 5:14, January 1895.
John P. Woodbury of Boston interested in information relating to his family in England.

2440 "Tennyson Book-Plate." 5:14, 1895.
Belated note that plate printed by permission of George Bell & Sons.

2441 "John Leighton's Book-Plate Annual." 5:15, January 1895.
Reviewer feels volume of "interest to bibliophiles" but that it is "difficult to understand its exact place in the literature of Ex Libris."

2442 "Sattler's *Ex Libris*." 5:15, January 1895.
Only one hundred copies printed.

2443 "*American Book-Plates*." 5:16, January 1895.
Favorable review, but suggests bibliography might better have been chronological than divided by origin (French, German, etc.).

2444 "For Identification." (1) 5:16, January 1895.
No. 74 pictured; no text.

2445 "Queries." 5:17-8, January 1895.
Walter Hamilton seeking identity of Mrs. Margaret Combridge.

2446 "Notes of the Month." 5:18-20, January 1895.
Owners of E. D. French plates asked to send impressions to be described in forthcoming article.

2447 "Modern Book-Plate Designers. No. 6—Joseph Sattler." (6) 5:21-6, February 1895.
Art in Bookplates contains forty-two original bookplates by Sattler and an introduction by Warnecke; comments on each plate by number.

2448 "Letters." 5:26, February 1895.
From John Leighton on the Chevalier D'Eon.

2449 "Book-Plate Identification." (4) 5:27-8, February 1895.
Plates #69 through #74 have been identified.

2450 "Book-Plate Competition." 5:27, February 1895.
"A prize of £3 3s. is offered for the best design for a Book-plate (Ex Libris) for the Bournemouth Public Library."

2451 "Lambert as an Engraver of Book-Plates." John Vinycomb. 5:29-33, February 1895.
A pupil of Bewick, Lambert followed "prosaic lines of copperplate and silver engraving."

2452 "The Late Mr. W. Lane Joynt." 5:33, February 1895.
Native of Limerick, one-time Lord Mayor of Dublin, and recent member of Ex Libris Society.

2453 "Irish Book-Plates." 5:33, February 1895.
Supplementary volume containing thirty plates but no text; only thirty copies printed.

2454 "Some Ex Libris Notes." Colonel Acton C. Havelock. (1) 5:34-5, February 1895.
Sir John Ligonier's plate discussed.

2455 "Shields in the Middle Temple." W. H. [Walter Hamilton] 5:35-6, February 1895.
"For many decades the habit has prevailed for the Readers of the Middle Temple to blazon their coats-of-arms on the old oak panelling of the dining-hall."

2456 "*Ex Libris Zeitschrift.*" 5:37, February 1895.
Death of Herr F. Warnecke, president of Berlin Ex Libris Verein, has not curtailed publication of the Society's journal.

2457 "Letters." 5:37-8, February 1895.
In 1834 Major Edward Moar had written: "I had been some time thinking of having a conceit, heraldic perhaps or allegorical, engraved as a distinguishing mark of the volumes on my bookshelves."

2458 "Notes of the Month." 5:38-40, February 1895.
Various publications noted.

2459 "Chairman's Address at the Fourth Annual Meeting." 5:41-5, March 1895.
Review of progress during last four years.

2460 "Recent Book-Plates." 5:45, March 1895.
F. E. Murray and Alexander Geoffroy offer exchange of their plates.

2461 "Lambert as an Engraver of Book-Plates." John Vinycomb. (10) 5:46, March 1895.
Beginning list of 124 engraved plates by this Newcastle artist whose work reflects Bewick influence.

2462 "American Notes." C.D.A. [Charles Dexter Allen] 5:47-8, March 1895.
"We are in the midst of a most engrossing 'craze.' . . . prices for good things are tending skyward, the hunt for the rarities grows hot, and the newest collectors are the very ones to advance prices."

2463 "Book-Plate of Robert Vyner of Swakeley." 5:48, March 1895.
Additional family history communicated by James Roberts Brown.

2464 "Book-Plate Identification." 5:49, March 1895.
Four identified and one more submitted.

2465 "Recent Book-Plates." 5:49, March 1895.
Plates of eight members briefly described; most willing to exchange.

2466 "Fourth Annual Meeting." (3) 5:50-9, March 1895.
Financial report, exhibits, publications, etc.

2467 "Book-Plates of Similar Design." 5:59, March 1895.
Two in question for Rev. Rowland Hill and Benjamin Way; believes engravers had "some common source of design."

2468 "Letters." 5:60-2, March 1895.
Edmund Gosse letter reprinted from *Athenaeum;* complaints and comments on exchanging plates.

2469 "Notes of the Month." 5:62-4, March 1895.
Publications and activities of various societies.

2470 "Modern Book-Plate Designers. No. 7—Edwin Davis French." (5) 5:65-9, April 1895.
In short span of two years French designed and executed thirty-five plates which are listed.

2471 "Our Annual Exhibition." 5:70, April 1895.
Alphabetical list of exhibitors.

2472 "Recent Book-Plates." 5:70, April 1895.
Three more willing to exchange.

2473 "Lambert as an Engraver of Book-Plates." John Vinycomb. 5:71-2, April 1895.
Conclusion of list totaling 124.

2474 "Ex Libris Collection of Ducal Library at Wolfenbuttel." 5:72-3, April 1895.
Review favorable; only 100 copies printed.

2475 "Queries." (1) 5:74, April 1895.
Identification of G. Fage sought.

2476 "Recent Book-plates." 5:74, April 1895.
Joseph Knight has new plate "*not for exchange except among friends.*"

2477 "Book-Plates for Identification." (6) 5:75, 77-8, April 1895.
Five more offered for identification.

2478 "Hamilton's *Dated Book-Plates.* Part II—18th Century." (2) 5:76-77, April 1895.
Favorable review.

2479 "Letters." (1) 5:78-80, April 1895.
About exchanges, Gilpin plate, Blackwell review of Allen book.

2480 "Recent Book-Plates." 5:80-1, April 1895.
Three plates described.

2481 "Notes of the Month." 5:81-4, April 1895.
Publications, meetings and exhibits.

2482 "On 'Stock Patterns' in Book-Plates." F. J. Thairlwall. (5) 5:85-9, 91, May 1895.
"Some bookplate engravers have repeated their own or others' designs exactly . . . except the armorial bearings." Numerous examples especially among Jacobean and Chippendale styles.

2483 "To Our Members." 5:90-1, May 1895.
Society not an exchange club. "Primarily its object was Old Ex Libris, their collection, their history, and their art; the study of modern bookplates only came secondarily."

2484 "Letters." 5:91, May 1895.
Walter Hamilton explains pagination of *Dated Book-Plates* as issued in parts.

2485 "Book-Plate Identification." (5) 5:92-3, May 1895.
Four identified and five more added.

2486 "Our Illustrations." (1) 5:92, May 1895.
Frontispiece is large plate of Ambrosius Count of Virmont, whose family became extinct in 1722.

2487 "Inscription from the Library of Don Juan Arbol of Mexico." 5:92, May 1895.
An admonition against lending from the Spanish.

2488 "Note." 5:92, May 1895.
James H. Aitken gives notice he "cannot distribute any more copies of his book-plate amongst his fellow members."

2489 "American Notes." Charles Dexter Allen. (5) 5:94-6, May 1895.
Unusual triangular plate designed by M. H. Hapgood.

2490 "Haig Book-Plates." (3) 5:97-8, May 1895.
Article by Mrs. Alexander Stuart originally privately printed in *Tyde What May*.

2491 "Recent Book-Plates." (2) 5:98-100, May 1895.
Miniature plates used by James Orrock and J. Potter Briscoe, also John Hall.

2492 "Letters." 5:100-1, May 1895.
Corrections offered to prior articles.

2493 "Book Notices." 5:101, May 1895.
Three publications by M. L. Joly reviewed.

2494 "For Identification." (5) 5:93, 101, May 1895.
Five offered for identification.

2495 "Notes of the Month." 5:102-4, May 1895.
Reference to several magazine and newspaper articles.

2496 "Modern Book-Plate Designers. No. 8—W. R. Weyer." (6) 5:105-9, June 1895.
Artist received silver medal at local art exhibit for five bookplates in November, 1894.

2497 "Book-Plate Identification." (5) 5:109, 113, June 1895.
About twenty plates from previous issues still unidentified.

2498 "Recent Book-Plates." 5:109, June 1895.
Among new plates one by Hopson and two by E. D. French.

2499 "Fourth Annual Exhibition of the Ex Libris Society." 5:110-2, 134-5, June 1895.
Detailed list of plates by each exhibitor.

2500 "American Notes." Charles Dexter Allen. (2) 5:114-6, June 1895.
Facts about W. F. Hopson, sale of Revere plate to Dodd, Mead and Co. for $75, and comments from newspapers.

2501 "Book Notices." (2) 5:116-8, June 1895.
Armorial volume by Arthur Charles Fox-Davies, incunabula catalog of Besancon library.

2502 "An Imaginary Conversation re Ex. Libris." (1) 5:119-20, June 1895.
Goldsmith, Boswell and Johnson discuss David Garrick's bookplate and others.

2503 "Our Illustrations." (1) 5:121, June 1895.
Plate for Sir William Brownlow dated 1698.

2504 "Letters." 5:121-2, June 1895.
U.S. Consul from Weimar, Germany warns of counterfeit Washington plate.

2505 "Notes of the Month." 5:122-4, June 1895.
News of the French society.

2506 "Horace Walpole and His Book-Plates." H. B. Wheatley. (3) 5:125-9, July 1895.
Walpole also as letter writer, collector, and private press proprietor; good article.

2507 "Book-Plate Identification." (7) 5:130-1, 136, July 1895.
One plate quite large with sailing ship and horse.

2508 "Recent Book-Plates." 5:131, July 1895.
Variety of styles and methods of reproduction.

2509 "Our Illustrations." (3) 5:132-3, July 1895.
Two plates by John Leighton.

2510 "Letters." 5:133, July 1895.
More on "stock patterns."

2511 "Fourth Annual Exhibition of the Ex Libris Society." 5:134-5, July 1895.
Continuation of list.

2512 "Book Notices." 5:137-8, July 1895.
A more critical review of Fox-Davies armorial volume.

2513 "Notes of the Month." 5:138-40, July 1895.
H. W. Fincham seeks assistance in compiling his list of *Artists and Engravers of British and American Book-Plates*.

2514 "Modern Book-Plate Designers. No. 9—R. Anning Bell." Gleeson White. (5) 5:141-8, August 1895.
Bell switched careers from architecture to painting; has designed thirty-two bookplates which are listed.

2515 "Book-Plate of Charles Hoare." (1) 5:149-50, August 1895.
Member asked for identity of plate owner which is promised for subsequent issue.

2516 "Book-Plate Identification." (6) 5:150-1, August 1895.
Five plates identified.

2517 "Query." 5:150, August 1895.
Question concerning several plates for Mackenzie family.

2518 "Fourth Annual Exhibition of the Ex Libris Society." 5:152-3, August 1895.
Conclusion of list.

2519 "Letters." 5:153-4, August 1895.
Member suggests cutting the leaves of the *Journal* so it could be rolled to save postage but the editor notes objection to both suggestions!

2520 "Book Notices." 5:154-5, August 1895.
French publication and London issue on armorials.

2521 "Notes of the Month." 5:156, August 1895.
Two hundred invitations issued for Mrs. Walter Hamilton's "At Home" and garden party.

2522 "American Notes." Charles Dexter Allen. (4) 5:157-60, September 1895.
W. R. Benjamin's *Collector* will have bookplate department commencing in October.

2523 "Art of the Book-Plate." Henri Pene du Bois. (3) 5:161-4, September 1895.
Effusive reprint from *Book-Lover's Magazine* criticized in editorial footnote.

2524 "Exchanges." 5:164, September 1895.
George W. Eve gives notice he cannot exchange plates he designs as they are all commissioned.

2525 "Notes of the Month." (1) 5:165, September 1895.
Concerning German ex libris article.

2526 "Book-Plate Identification." (7) 5:166-7, September 1895.
Several more plates identified.

2527 "Letters." 5:168-70, September 1895.
Letter from C. D. Allen on Peter Osborne plate.

2528 "Recent Bookplates." 5:170, September 1895.
Pickering Dodge plate received.

2529 "Notes of the Month." (2) 5:171-2, September 1895.
Plates of Randolph Churchill and Jennie Spencer Churchill shown.

2530 "A Plea for the Old-Fashioned Book-Plate." William Bolton. (2) 5:173-6, October 1895.
"Many new Bookplates need their symbolism to be explained" and furnish printed information "to make apparent what otherwise would be inexplicable."

2531 "Bookplate Identification." (4) 5:177-8, October 1895.
Six identified and four more offered.

2532 "Cronstern Book-Plate." (1) 5:177, October 1895.
Plate and description from Hamilton's *Dated Book-Plates*.

2533 "Modern Book-Plate Designers. No. 10 John Henry Metcalfe." (3) 5:179-82, October 1895.
"He has . . . made armorial stained glass, heraldic carving, and armorial designs generally . . . book-plates . . . his *spécialité*."

2534 "Book-Plate of Peter Osborne." 5:182, October 1895.
Identification of plate in September issue.

2535 "Recent Book-Plates." (2) 5:183-4, October 1895.
Illustrated are plates of James Ward and Eugene Monteuuis.

2536 "Letters." (1) 5:184-5, October 1895.
Walter Hamilton asks for further samples of burlesque heraldry.

2537 "Exchanges." 5:186, October 1895.
One from Holland; also a royal bookplate advertised in *Bazaar, Exchange, and Mart.*

2538 "Notes of the Month." 5:186-8, October 1895.
Mention of books and articles currently published; also that "packets" of bookplates from the USA are being received with postage due.

2539 "American Notes." Charles Dexter Allen. (1) 5:189-92, November 1895.
Evidence given which seems to support that there was a Strawberry Hill bookplate.

2540 "Book Notices." 5:193, November 1895.
Brochure contains twenty plates by German artist, Shulte vom Brühl.

2541 "Book-Plate Identification." (6) 5:194-5, November 1895.
Two more identified.

2542 "Book-Plate of Thos. Phillips." (1) 5:194, 204, November 1895.
"Unusual shape for a book-plate, being oblong."

2543 "An Astronomer's Book-Plate." (1) 5:194, November 1895.
Portrait plate of discoverer of Neptune.

2544 "*Dated Book-Plates.*" (2) 5:196-9, November 1895.
Favorable review including special commendation of the Index.

2545 "Cronstern Book-Plate." 5:199, November 1895.
Additional family history.

2546 "Letters." (4) 5:200-3, November 1895.
Numerous letters from "regulars."

2547 "Notes of the Month." 5:203-4, November 1895.
Members cautioned against Thos. Palmer of Bromley, Kent plate being "hawked" by a London dealer.

2548 "Modern Book-Plate Designers. No. 11 G. W. Eve." Gleeson White. (8) 5: 205-12, December 1895.
Eve is a "master of heraldry taking his place as a designer."

2549 "Book Notice." 5:212, December 1895.
Review of W. Roberts' *Book-Hunter in London.*

2550 "Recent Book-Plates." 5:213, December 1895.
Among them one designed by E. D. French for A. C. Bernheim, signed and dated.

2551 "Book-Plate of Ralph Sheldon." James Roberts Brown. (2) 5:214-6, December 1895.
"If the writer followed his predilections, he would make the *Journal* a high-class monthly, devoted in the main to Heraldic Book-plates."

2552 "Book-Plate Identification." (6) 5:217-8, December 1895.
Eight plates identified.

2553 "Burlesque Heraldry on Book-Plates." 5:218, December 1895.
Previous entry actually arms and crest of Worshipful Company of Brown-Bakers of the City of London.

2554 "Letters." (2) 5:219-22, December 1895.

Lively exchange between experts; also notes on Hogarth's plate for John Holland.

2555 "Notes of the Month." 5:233-4, December 1895.
Two pioneers among book collectors dead—Rev. T. W. Carson and Lord de Tabley, once mentioned as likely successor to the late Poet-Laureate.

2556 "Wood-Cut Ex Libris of Balthasar Beniwalt (or Brennwald) De Walestat, 1502." (1) 6:1, January 1896.
An ecclesiastical plate which is one of the largest and oldest.

2557 "American Notes." Charles Dexter Allen. 6:2, January 1896.
E. N. Hewins' collection sold *en bloc* at auction to W. E. Baillie for $1,250, about 3,200 plates.

2558 "Book Notices." (1) 6:3-4, January 1896.
Review of Labouchere's book.

2559 "Fraudulent Book-Plates." 6:4, January 1896.
Re-strike of Washington plate, imitation of "Society for the Propagation of the Gospell 1704," and many other early dated plates.

2560 "Palmer Label." 6:4, January 1896.
"The block was made for the headings of hotel bills."

2561 "Gracilla Boddington Book-Plate." 6:4, January 1896.
Naval emblem on account of "her brother being in the Royal Navy."

2562 "Bookplate of the Earl of Gainsborough." (1) 6:5, January 1896.
Copy of plate and description sent by George H. Viner.

2563 "Alava Plate." 6:5, January 1896.
Explanation offered of decorations on plate.

2564 "Canting Heraldry." 6:5, January 1896.
Quotation from Walpole's letters.

2565 "Book-Rhymes and Inscriptions." 6:5, January 1896.
"This boke is oon the curse of crist ys a nothir/He that steleth thoon shall have the othir."

2566 "Book-Plates for Identification." (6) 6:6, 9, January 1896.
Six identified; equal number added.

2567 "Recent Book-Plates." (2) 6:7-8, January 1896.
J. P. Emslie completed plate for Folk-Lore Society.

2568 "Letters." 6:9-10, January 1896.
"Literary Ghoul" discovers a charming Chippendale beneath a common, damaged book label.

2569 "Punning Heraldry on Book-Plates." 6:11, January 1896.
Fincham submitted list "all of genuine heraldry, containing punning allusions to the owners' names."

2570 "Wants and Exchanges." 6:11-2, January 1896.
Specific plates listed for exchange or purchase.

2571 "Notes of the Month." 6:12, January 1896.
It is suggested that "our friends in the United States should study at least the rudiments of French and British heradry" for proper identification of plates.

2572 "Early Scotch Book-Plate Designer: Archibald Burden." John Orr. (3) 6:13-5, February 1896.
Fourteen plates listed as signed by Burden.

2573 "Late Rev. T. W. Carson." 6:15, February 1896.
Bookplate collection of 32,000 purchased by London dealer for 1150 pounds.

2574 " 'Baker' Book-Plates." Alfred A. Bethune-Baker. (2) 6:16-8, February 1896.
Assistance sought in identifying two plates; considerable Baker family history given.

2575 "Book-Plate Identification." (11) 6:18-21, February 1896.
Five plates identified.

2576 "Artists of the Hoarding." 6:19, February 1896.
Reprint from London *Daily News* about artistic street placards.

2577 "Letters." 6:22-3, February 1896.
Bookshop owner noticed "an eccentric elderly man going round my book-shelves and looking only at the inside covers of the books." A bookplate collector, naturally!

2578 "Bournemouth Public Library Book-Plate." (1) 6:24, February 1896.
Design award won by J. Stewart Pearce, architect.

2579 "Folk-Lore Society." (1) 6:24-5, February 1896.
Plate designed by J. P. Emslie.

2580 "Recent Bookplates." 6:25, February 1896.
Two designed by E. D. French.

2581 "Exchanges." 6:25-6, February 1896.
Suggestions for exchange notices in *Journal*.

2582 "Book-plate Queries." 6:26, February 1896.
Further identification sought on two plates.

2583 "Book Rhyme." 6:27, February 1896.
French verse dated 1775.

2584 "Notes of the Month." 6:27-8, February 1896.
News on journals in France and America.

2585 "Sir Francis Blake Delaval." John Robinson. (2) 6:29-33, March 1896.
Considerable family history.

2586 "Sweeting Book-Plates." Rev. W. D. Sweeting. (1) 6:33-4, March 1896.
Plate features violins transposed and dogs which "look more like talbots than greyhounds."

2587 "Punning Heraldry." (1) 6:34, March 1896.
Plate engraved by Bowley, about whom little is known.

2588 "Book-Plate of Madame De Stael." C. M. Carlander. (1) 6:35-6, March 1896.
From inscription on plate, "it may be concluded that her library was brought together in her father's castle, *Coppet*, at the Lake of Geneva in Switzerland."

2589 "Sale of Book-Plates." 6:36, March 1896.
Collection of about 3,000 bookplates and heraldic prints brought thirty-nine pounds at auction.

2590 "Book Rhyme." 6:36, March 1896.
"When greedy worms my body eat,/Here you shall see my name Compleat:/When I am dead and in my grave,/This Book always my name shall have." Dated 1830.

2591 "Book-Plate of Lord Glenbervie." (1) 6:36-7, March 1896.
A student of medicine who turned to law; was Chief Secretary of Ireland, 1794-5.

2592 "De Trafford Family." 6:37-8, March 1896.
Lavishly illustrated and printed family history limited to twenty-five copies.

2593 "Book-Plate Identification." (6) 6:38-9, March 1896.
Nine identified.

2594 "On Exchanges." 6:40, March 1896.
". . . those who wish to get good things must be prepared to send good things in exchange."

2595 "Book-Plates of J. Skinner, of Bath." 6:41, March 1896.
Quotes from W. J. Hardy's article in *Bibliographica*.

2596 "Hamilton's *Dated Book-Plates*." 6:41, March 1896.
Quotes from E. D. French letter concerning "incorrect tinctures" of Grolier Club plate.

2597 "Recent Book-Plates." 6:42, March 1896.
Entomologist's plate by Maclauchlan depicts various species of beetles.

2598 "Leighton's Annual for 1896." 6:42, March 1896.
Review of third *Bookplate Annual and Armorial Year Book*.

2599 "Book Rhyme." 6:43, March 1896.
". . . that larning is better than welth & lands."

2600 "Note to Our Members." 6:43, March 1896.
Statement of accounts shows small cash reserve.

2601 "Letter." 6:44, March 1896.
"Will Whimble," the sharp bookseller who bought a collection of books and bookplates for five pounds and sold half of them for ninety

pounds, whose letter was published in previous issue has roused considerable annoyance among Society's membership.

2602 "Notes of the Month." 6:44, March 1896.

John Leighton called to task for calling the Society the "Ex Libris Society of London."

2603 "Book-Plate of Dr. Christoph Jacob Trew." (1) 6:45-6, April 1896.

Plate engraved about 1760 exceedingly large to judge by quarter size reproduction measuring 4x5."

2604 "Leighton's Annual." 6:46, April 1896.

Count Leiningen-Westerburg points out misidentification of book-plates of two royal ladies.

2605 "Stock Patterns in Book-Plates: The Jacobean." W. Bolton. (4) 6:46-50, April 1896.

"Of one pattern he mentions no less than six different plates, all alike except the arms."

2606 "A Liverpool Book-Plate." 6:50, April 1896.

Anning Bell designed plate for Liverpool Royal Institution at Tate Library.

2607 "Book-Plate of William Musgrave, M.D., of the City of Exeter." James Roberts Brown. (1) 6:50-1, April 1896.

Plate dated 1700; another family member had plate signed "J. Skinner Sculp 1732."

2608 "Rev. T. W. Carson Sale." 6:51, April 1896.

Collection of 32,500 plates sold for 1,150 pounds to James Dorman.

2609 "Earliest French Armorial Book-Plate." Walter Hamilton. 6:52, April 1896.

L. Joly claims this distinction for the plate of Francois de la Rochefoucauld Randan with a date prior to 1585.

2610 "Book-Plates of Lord Glenbervie." 6:52, April 1896.

Three different, additional plates used prior to being created a Baron in 1800.

2611 "Book-Plates of Mr. Clement K. Shorter." (2) 6:53-4, April 1896.

Editor of *Illustrated London News* and *Sketch* had seven different plates designed by Walter Crane, Phil May, Linley Sambourne, Dudley Hardy, Herbert Railton (two), and C. Forestier.

2612 "New Heraldic Work." 6:54, April 1896.

The Notebook of Tristram Risdon should be a valuable genealogical and heraldic publication.

2613 "Book-Plates for Identification." (6) 6:55-6, April 1896.

Four plates identified.

2614 "Recent Book-Plates." 6:56-7, April 1896.

Entomologist G. C. Bignell has plate "representing him as prosecuting his researches in the woods and fields."

2615 "Letters." 6:57, April 1896.
Thairlwall comments on "Will Whimble" letter.

2616 "Notes of the Month." 6:58-60, April 1896.
Articles in current *Studio, Book Buyer, Art Amateur*. Book catalog by Frank Hollings contains long list of ex libris works.

2617 "Coffin Book-Plates." (1) 6:61-4, May 1896.
Plate illustrated is for Pine Coffin, dated about 1797.

2618 "Book Rhymes." 6:64, May 1896.
Two doleful verses.

2619 "Stock Patterns in Book-Plates. The Chippendale." W. Bolton. (3) 6:65-9, May 1896.
This "beautiful style . . . die[d] a natural death from inanition after a life of only twenty years."

2620 "Spottiswoode Book-Plate." (1) 6:69, May 1896.
A "half-date" (1778 with the last two figures written in) not included in Hamilton.

2621 "Book-Plate Identification." (8) 6:69-71, May 1896.
Six identified.

2622 "*Ex Libris Zeitschrift*." 6:72, May 1896.
Berlin publication in sixth year.

2623 "Peg Woffington's Library." 6:72, May 1896.
"Miss Woffington, her book, God give her grace therein to look."

2624 "Humours of Heraldry." 6:73, May 1896.
"Two horn spoons *or*, a porridge pot gules, with supporters of two nude Highland savages, each holding a spoon aloft. Motto: Meal mak's men. The gentleman boasting these armorial bearings might have added that his ancestry went back to one Adam, a gardener, who lost his situation for stealing his Master's fruit."

2625 "Book-Plate of Robert Sorsbie." (1) 6:73, May 1896.
Believed to be the work of Sherwin.

2626 "Letters." 6:74-6, May 1896.
Last letter from Charles D. Allen as Secretary of the Ex Libris Society.

2627 "Book-Plate of Bradford Free Public Library." (1) 6:76, May 1896.
Designed by R. Paton Brown and engraved by H. Milword.

2628 "Recent Book-Plates." 6:76-7, May 1896.
Sherborn and French both well represented.

2629 "Book-Plate of Daniel Shirley." (1) 6:77, May 1896.
Information solicited concerning plates dated 1560-1775.

2630 "Dated Episcopal Plate." (1) 6:78, May 1896.
Information requested concerning plate "unknown to the late Rev. T. W. Carson."

2631 "Notes of the Month." 6:78-80, May 1896.
Articles noted in a variety of publications.

2632 "Chairman's Address at the Fifth Annual Meeting." Walter Hamilton. 6:82-7, June 1896.
Notes passing of both the Rev. Carson and Leicester Warren. Also, "the exchange of one's duplicates by post is a weariness to the flesh and a trial to the temper."

2633 "Stock Patterns in Book-Plates. The Later Styles." W. Bolton. (2) 6:88-91, June 1896.
Jacobean described as "monumental and severe," Chippendale "floral and free" and third style "wreath and ribbon."

2634 "Query." 6:91, June 1896.
Question regarding Thomas Gaisford.

2635 "Autographic Ex Libris." C. M. Carlander. (1) 6:81, 92, June 1896.
Long inscription in French translated.

2636 "Book-Plate Identification." (5) 6:92-3, June 1896.
Identification keeps almost current with new submissions except for most elusive plates.

2637 "Fifth Annual Meeting." 6:94-8, June 1896.
New members elected bring total to 540.

2638 "Recent Book-Plates." (1) 6:98, June 1896.
Pictured is plate for F. Mitchell by W. H. Foster.

2639 "Letter." 6:99, June 1896.
Arthur Vicars thanks members for honor of being elected president.

2640 "Laonensis-Killaloe." 6:99, June 1896.
Hamilton explains 1661 entry in *Dated Book-Plates*. Latin name derived from Irish form.

2641 "Book Notice." 6:99, June 1896.
History of Horn Book reviewed.

2642 "Notes of the Month." 6:100, June 1896.
Royal Academy Exhibit includes several bookplates.

2643 "List of Ladies' Armorial Book-Plates." J. Carlton Stitt. (8) 6:101-4, July 1896.
Alphabetical list includes engraver, style, and relationship (spinster, wife, widow).

2644 "Fifth Annual Exhibition." (1) 6:105-8, July 1896.
First installment of list includes name and address of exhibitor plus items displayed.

2645 "Book-Plates for Identification." (5) 6:109-11, July 1896.
Ten plates identified.

2646 "Reply." 6:111, July 1896.
Details concerning Thomas Gaisford.

2647 "Letters." (1) 6:111-2, July 1896.
Wm. Bolton passes along Rev. Carson's identification of the Laonensis-Killaloe plate as the frontispiece (copy of a seal) of Dwyer's *History of the Diocese* (1878).

2648 "Recent Book-Plates." (3) 6:113-4, July 1896.
Interesting plate by H. Stacy Marks features birds.

2649 "Notes of the Month." 6:115-6, July 1896.
Publications in France, Germany, U.S. and England.

2650 "Notes of the Month." 6:117-8, August 1896.
Eight additional members elected since Annual Meeting.

2651 "List of English Ladies' Armorial Book-Plates." J. Carlton Stitt. (5) 6:118-21, August 1896.
B's continued.

2652 "Fifth Annual Exhibition." 6:122-3, August 1896.
Exhibit list concluded.

2653 "A Word or Two More on the Sheldon Book-Plates." 6:124, August 1896.
Assistance asked in identifying watermark and thus establishing date of plate.

2654 "Book-Plate Identification." (5) 6:123-5, August 1896.
Five also identified.

2655 "Book-Plate of King Oscar II, of Sweden." (1) 6:126, August 1896.
Simple plate with motto: "Beyond the depths, towards the height."

2656 "Letters." 6:126, August 1896.
Sorsbie and Sowerby identified by Brown as two different people from Newcastle.

2657 "Recent Bookplates." (2) 6:127-8, August 1896.
One is large plate used in musical library.

2658 "Notes of the Month." 6:129-31, September 1896.
Newly elected president of Society has been knighted, now Sir Arthur Vicars.

2659 "List of Ladies' Armorial Book-Plates." J. Carlton Stitt. (3) 6:131-3, September 1896.
Conclusion of B and beginning of C.

2660 "Book-Plate of Viscount Keith." (1) 6:134, September 1896.
Commander of fleet in 1795 when Cape of Good Hope captured; his second wife was eldest daughter of Thrale.

2661 "Musical Ex Libris." (1) 6:134, September 1896.
Frankfort Public Library has copies in two sizes of unusual Offenbach plate.

2662 "Further Note on Stock Patterns." (2) 6:135-6, September 1896.
One shows shield leaning against tree; another is ribbon and wreath.

2663 "Queries." 6:136, September 1896.
Identity of French family Dufour sought.

2664 "Book-Plate Identification." (4) 6:136-7, September 1896.
Also four identified.

2665 "Illustrations." (2) 6:136, 139, September 1896.
E. D. French's plate for Club of Odd Volumes pictured.

2666 "Recent Book-Plates." (1) 6:138-9, September 1896.
Illustrated is plate for Ulster Club, Belfast.

2667 "Sales of Book-Plates." 6:140, September 1896.
Twenty-two items, priced and annotated.

2668 "Notes of the Month." 6:141-3, October 1896.
Review of advance copy of Fincham's *Artists and Engravers of British and American Book-Plates*.

2669 "List of English Ladies' Armorial Book-Plates." J. Carlton Stitt. (3) 6:143-6, October 1896.
Through letters C and D.

2670 "Book-Plates for Identification." (5) 6:147, 149, October 1896.
Four identified.

2671 "Pine-Coffin Family." 6:148-9, October 1896.
Details of manuscript holdings of this family.

2672 "Book-Plate of John Waugh." (1) 6:150, October 1896.
Heraldic engraver, Thomas Moring, has added owner's name in small white area on engraving of many-columned building.

2673 "Ex Libris H. Card de York." (1) 6:150-1, October 1896.
Suspicion as to whether actually a bookplate as simple design not in keeping with owner's "exalted position both by birth and in the Chruch."

2674 "Queries." (2) 6:151-2, October 1896.
South Australian gentleman sends two plates for further identification.

2675 "Important." 6:152, October 1896.
Notice on complimentary dinner for President, Sir Arthur Vicars, on the occasion of his knighthood; "evening dress" is indicated.

2676 "Notes of the Month." (2) 6:153-5, November 1896.
Recounts details of dinner for Sir Arthur Vicars.

2677 "List of English Ladies' Armorial Book-Plates." (1) 6:155-8, November 1896.
D through G.

2678 "Modern Book-Plate Designers. No. 12—W. F. Hopson." (2) 6:159-62, November 1896.
At fourteen he was put to work in a button factory and at eighteen began study of wood engraving.

2679 "Book-Plate Identification." (4) 6:162-3, November 1896.
A total of 203 plates have been submitted for identification.

2680 "Book-Plate of the Bastille." Walter Hamilton. 6:164-5, November 1896.
Requested information from those who believe they possess a genuine copy, as very scarce.

2681 "Book-Plates Engraved by William Henshaw." (5) 6:165-7, November 1896.
Abstract of remarks by Fincham on identity of artist who used several signature forms.

2682 "Letter." 6:167, November 1896.
Comments on Cardinal York plate.

2683 "Dinner to Sir Arthur Vicars." 6:167-8, November 1896.
"The man without a hobby is a poor, hum-drum nonentity. Even the hobby of pocket-picking has something in its favor."

2684 "Notes of the Month." 6:169-71, December 1896.
Leaflets published by James Terry mentioned, as well as German and French publications.

2685 "Book-Plate of Messrs. Sharp." (1) 6:172-4, December 1896.
Three brothers shared plate used primarily for music books.

2686 "Mrs. Delariviere Manley." 6:174, December 1896.
Inquiry seeks to determine if "notorious Mrs. Manley" is daughter of Thomas Discipline because of same given name.

2687 "Book-Plate Identification." (5) 6:174-5, December 1896.
Identification keeps almost current with new entries.

2688 "List of English Ladies' Armorial Book-Plates." J. Carlton Stitt. (4) 6:176-80, December 1896.
G through K.

2689 "Recent Bookplates." (4) 6:181-3, December 1896.
Several attractive designs illustrated.

2690 "Book Notice." 6:183-4, December 1896.
Review of Walter Hamilton's *French Book-Plates*.

2691 "Book-Label of Mrs. Trimmer." 6:184, December 1896.
Authoress born in 1741.

2692 "Notes of the Month." (1) 7:1-3, January 1897.
Charles Dexter Allen will renew "his official connection with the Society with the New Year."

2693 "Book-Plate Identification." (5) 7:3-4, January 1897.
Plates submitted for identification must not be mounted and must be accompanied by stamped addressed envelope.

2694 "Solace of the Book-Plate." W. Bolton. 7:5-8, January 1897.
Much used motto of "old books, old wine, old friends" traced back to

Goldsmith, Walter Scott and King Alphonso of Castile who may have quoted from an even earlier source.

2695 "Book-Plate of Sir Mountstuart Grant-Duff." (1) 7:8-9, January 1897.
"First Anglo-Indian book-plate" executed in Madras in 1886.

2696 "Notes on Some Rawdon Book-Plates." (4) 7:9-10, January 1897.
Noble family received "title-deed of the estate granted by William the Conqueror."

2697 "List of English Ladies' Armorial Book-Plates." J. Carlton Stitt. 7:11-2, January 1897.
K through M.

2698 "Notes of the Month." 7:13-4, February 1897.
Articles mentioned in *Bazaar, Daily Chronicle, Globe, Northern Echo, Ludgate*.

2699 "Book-Plate Identification." (4) 7:14-5, February 1897.
Two identified and four added.

2700 "Portrait Book-Plate of Thomas Barritt." (1) 7:16, February 1897.
Etched bookplate probably Barritt's own work.

2701 "Letter." 7:16, February 1897.
Proprietor of Snare's Circulating Library "nearly ruined by controversy and litigation concerning painting believed to be by Velasquez."

2702 "Book-Plate of Cardinal York." (1) 7:17, February 1897.
Simple plate upon which members are invited to comment.

2703 "American Book-Plate: Vassall." 7:17, February 1897.
Believes plate designed by Doolittle, not Hurd.

2704 "Gosden Book-Plate." (1) 7:17-8, February 1897.
Sporting plate somewhat similar to Bewick and Lambert.

2705 "Letters." (1) 7:18, February 1897.
Further identity sought of Thomas Moore, Oscar Turge.

2706 "List of English Ladies' Armorial Book-Plates." J. Carlton Stitt. 7:19-20, February 1897.
M's continued.

2707 "Notes of the Month." 7:21-3, February 1897.
New members listed; several publications reviewed.

2708 "Dutch Bibliography of Book-Plates." J. F. Verster. 7:24, March 1897.
Journal's name in Dutch and English, date and sentence descriptive of subject matter.

2709 "Book-Plates for Identification." (5) 7:25, 27, February 1897.
Illustrations only.

2710 "Notes on Some Percival Book-Plates." (4) 7:26-7, March 1897.
Sir John's first plate engraved in 1702; two of this family name assassinated.

2711 "Exchanges." 7:27, March 1897.
One member lists several plates he would like to obtain through exchange or purchase.

2712 "Edwin Davis French and Ex Libris in America." James T. Armstrong. 7:27-9, March 1897.
Artist has "fitted up a special arrangement of incandescent lighting" to permit night work.

2713 "Book Notice." 7:29-30, March 1897.
Allen shows bookplate collector "in his true light . . . as an intelligent being embued with some sense of the value of things, and a deep reverence for books and their interesting associations."

2714 "Book-Plate Identification." 7:30, March 1897.
Four identified.

2715 "Book-Plate of Ildephonsus Kennedy." (1) 7:30-1, March 1897.
Plate of Scottish gentleman who migrated to Germany in 18th century and became an ecclesiastic.

2716 "Letters." (2) 7:31-2, March 1897.
More on the brothers Sharp.

2717 "List of English Ladies' Armorial Book-Plates." J. Carlton Stitt. (2) 7:32-6, March 1897.
M through R.

2718 "Additional Dated Book-Plates." Walter Hamilton. March 1897.
Pages 5-7 numbered separately to complete "dated list."

2719 "Sixth Annual Meeting." 7:37, April 1897.
Meeting set for June 10th at Westminster Palace Hotel.

2720 "Notes of the Month." 7:37-8, April 1897.
Book-Plates and Their Value authored by editor of *Book Prices Current.*

2721 "Book-Plate of Philip D'Auvergne." Alfred A. Bethune-Baker. (1) 7:39-41, April 1897.
Detailed family history.

2722 "American Notes." Charles Dexter Allen. 7:42, April 1897.
Close examination makes Allen doubt Vassall plate by Doolittle; prices at recent auction given.

2723 "Book-Plate of Marie De Bourbon." Ross O'Connell. (1) 7:43, April 1897.
Brief family history given.

2724 "'Sharp' Book-Plates." 7:43, April 1897.
Author of original articles happy with existence of additional Sharp-family plates.

2725 "Book-Plate Identification." (2) 7:44, 48, April 1897.
Three identified.

2726 "Book-Plate of 'John Cowper, A.M.' " (1) 7:44-5, April 1897.
Despite inconsistencies believes plate that of father of poet.

2727 "Letters." (2) 7:45-6, April 1897.
John Leighton disagrees with "severe" criticism of his latest *Annual* while editor still feels comment was "mild."

2728 "Book Notices." 7:46-7, April 1897.
Books published in Holland and Leipzig reviewed.

2729 "List of English Ladies' Armorial Book-Plates." J. Carlton Stitt. 7:49-52, April 1897.
List continued.

2730 "Notes of the Month." 7:53-5, May 1897.
Annual banquet on June 10th—"Ladies are invited."

2731 "Book-Plate Identification." (5) 7:56, May 1897.
Detailed descriptions identifying two plates.

2732 "Notes on Some Boyle Book-Plates." (3) 7:57-8, May 1897.
Plate of Earl of Orrery and his Countess, Elizabeth, believed earliest "connubial" or "joint" plate; executed prior to 1708.

2733 "Walter Hamilton's List of 'Dated Book-Plates.' " 7:58, May 1897.
From time to time additions will be printed.

2734 "Recent Book-Plates and Exchanges." (3) 7:58-60, May 1897.
Plate of Phillis Innocent Alt is from a design in stencil.

2735 "Letters." (2) 7:60-3, May 1897.
Two more writers feel Cowper plate that of poet's father.

2736 "List of English Ladies' Armorial Book Plates." J. Carlton Stitt. (7) 7:63-8, May 1897.
Conclusion of list plus correction.

2737 "Notes of the Month." 7:69-73, 84, June 1897.
Prices from latest auction, caution against imitation plates, a Duke who is a barber, Society's statement of accounts for 1896.

2738 "Book-Plate Identification." (8) 7:74, 79-80, June 1897.
Three more identified.

2739 "Book-Plates of Members of the Inns of Court." 7:74, June 1897.
R. C. Lichtenstein submits list of Americans who attended and marks with asterisk those he knows had a plate.

2740 "Modern Book-Plate Designers. No. 13—Samuel Hollyer." (5) 7:75-8, June 1897.
Noted for his portraits; called "The Doctor" because of his skill in restoring and retouching old plates.

2741 "American Notes." Charles Dexter Allen. (1) 7:81-2, June 1897.
Bookplates by Bostonians featured at Arts Crafts Exhibition.

2742 "Military or Trophy Book-Plates." (1) 7:83, June 1897.
List of such plates requested for future publication.

2743 "Child's Book-Plate." (1) 7:82-3, June 1897.
Artist Harvey Ellis includes Palmer Cox's Brownies in plate for six-year old.

2744 "Notes of the Month." 7:85-7, July 1897.
New members bring total to 607.

2745 "Letters." 7:87, July 1897.
German author writing in "journal for book-lovers" takes critic to task; members warned against dealer in Turin.

2746 "Book-Plates for Identification." (5) 7:88, 103-4, July 1897.
To date 242 offered for identification.

2747 "Annual Meeting and Exhibition." (1) 7:89-95, July 1897.
Menu printed; actual membership after deaths, resignations and non-payment of dues totals 460.

2748 "Book Rhymes." 7:95, July 1897.
One from a Book of Common Prayer dated 1781.

2749 "President's Address." Arthur Vicars. (4) 7:96-8, July 1897.
Laments passing of Sir Wollaston Franks; comments on membership among "fair sex" for whom the bookplate "is a study eminently lending itself to their attention."

2750 "Rashleigh Book-Plates." Arthur J. Jewers. (4) 7:99-101, July 1897.
Earliest plate for Jonathan Rashleigh who died in 1675.

2751 "Early Library Book-Plates of Philadelphia." 7:101, July 1897.
A simple label used by Union Library Company (1746).

2752 "Recent Book-Plates and Exchanges." (1) 7:102-3, July 1897.
Plate for Bedford College illustrated.

2753 "American Notes." Charles Dexter Allen. 7:104, July 1897.
Notes prices for individual plates at American sale; $24 top for William Smith by Gallaudet, "a Jacobean of indifferent design."

2754 "Notes of the Month." (1) 7:105-7, August 1897.
Catalog of 1897 exhibit available at one shilling for an ordinary edition and five shillings for large paper edition.

2755 "Trophy Plates." (3) 7:107, August 1897.
List will appear in September issue.

2756 "Modern Book-Plate Designers. No. 14—Miss Celia Levetus." (8) 7:108-13, August 1897.
Work lauded by Gleeson White and Walter Crane.

2757 "Recent Book-Plates and Exchanges." 7:113, August 1897.
Three new plates by E. D. French.

2758 "Book-Plates for Identification." (6) 7:114, 116, August 1897.
Identification continues to keep pace with submissions.

2759 "Some Nonconforming Church Libraries and Their Book-Plates." Rev. George Eyre Evans. (3) 7:115, August 1897.
Some of the simple plates look like "an apothecary's bottle-label."

2760 "Letters." 7:116, August 1897.
Another victim of Turin dealer sought aid of Vice-Consul.

2761 "Ex Libris Society, Constitution and Rules." (4 unnumbered pages)
Officers and council listed; twenty-rules; two by-laws increasing dues and provision to drop member nine-months in arrears on dues.

2762 "Notes of the Month." 7:117-8, September 1897.
Complaint on unfavorable American postal rate for bookplate packets containing catalog notations, thus requiring letter rate.

2763 "Trophy or Military Book-Plates." (8) 7:119-22, September 1897.
Text plus alphabetical listing without details.

2764 "Book-Plate Identification." (7) 7:122, 125-7, September 1897.
At long last #103 identified; latest submitted is #255.

2765 "Note on Poulet-Malassis." Col. W. F. Prideaux. 7:123-5, September 1897.
In addition to his pioneer work on ex libris, he was friend and "literary guide to Gautier, Baudelaire."

2766 "Some Nonconforming Church Libraries and Their Book-Plates." Rev. George Eyre Evans. (3) 7:128, September 1897.
One label dates from 1817-20.

2767 "American Letter." Charles Dexter Allen. (1) 7:129-30, September 1897.
Reviews book about Samuel Sewall, *The Puritan Pepys.*

2768 "Notes on the Sale of Part of Col. Havelock's Collection." 7:130, September 1897.
Lot arrangements seemed to favor dealers.

2769 "Letters." (1) 7:131-2, September 1897.
Prices from American sale in Columbus; top of $7.50.

2770 "Notes of the Month." 7:133-5, October 1897.
Quotes *New York Tribune* review of Hardy's *Book-Plates:* "Book deals with an amusing subject, but it deserves an especially cordial greeting for the reason that the author takes an unusually sane view of the theme. The book-plate, like the poster, hath become a fetish and a lunacy in the land."

2771 "Guernsey Book-Plates." Edith Carey. (5) 7:136-9, October 1897.
All plates are of the Tupper family.

2772 "Our Frontispiece." (1) 7:139, October 1897.
Plate for Rev. John Wilkinson Crake designed and engraved by Will Foster.

2773 "Rhymes." 7:139, October 1897.
One in Welsh with free translation.

2774 "Catalogue of English Trophy Plates." W. H. K. Wright. (4) 7:140-4, October 1897.
Alphabetical, annotated list, A through H.

2775 "Book-Plates for Identification." (4) 7:145, 148, October 1897.
Four also identified.

2776 "American Letter." Charles Dexter Allen. 7:146-7, October 1897.
Comment on current work of French, Bird and Spenceley.

2777 "Book Notice." 7:147, October 1897.
Review of *Courtenay Family A'rmorial.*

2778 "Book-Plate of Mr. Robert Bagster." (1) 7:148, October 1897.
Plate of London publisher.

2779 "Notes of the Month." 7:149-52, November 1897.
Several articles in related fields mentioned.

2780 "Book-Plate Identification." (6) 7:152, 161, November 1897.
Four more identified.

2781 "Guernsey Book-Plates." Edith Carey. (6) 7:153-7, November 1897.
Le Mesurier family, who have been "Guernsey folk" for several hundred years, featured.

2782 "Recent Book-Plates." 7:157, November 1897.
R. Anning Bell made copper engraving for William H. Booth.

2783 "Catalogue of English Trophy Plates." W. H. K. Wright. (5) 7:158-61, November 1897.
J through S.

2784 "Some Nonconforming Church Libraries and Their Book-Plates." Rev. George Eyre Evans. (2) 7:162, November 1897.
Wall plaque in memory of Charles Darwin in church he had attended.

2785 "Book Notices." 7:163, November 1897.
Review of volume II of *Miscellanea Genealogica et Heraldic* and Eve's *Decorative Heraldry.*

2786 "Letters." 7:163-4, November 1897.
Further evidence concerning Messrs. Sharp bookplate.

2787 "Notes of the Month." (1) 7:165-8, December 1897.
Prices noted on sale in Holland.

2788 "Letters." 7:168, December 1897.
Thairlwall furnishes information on Currer, Bennet and Gage bookplates.

2789 "Book-Plates of Some British Poets." William Bolton. (4) 7:169-72, December 1897.
Matthew Prior, William Mason, Robert Merry, and Oliver Wendell Holmes—biographical details reveal first three to be interesting if not admirable people.

2790 "Recent Book-Plates." 7:172, December 1897.
Designs submitted by Henri Andre and Celia Levetus.

2791 "Catalogue of English Trophy Plates." W. H. K. Wright. (6) 7:173-4, December 1897.
Conclusion of list of about 150; additional plates sought.

2792 "Book-Plate Identification." (4) 7:175, 177, December 1897.
Seven identified.

2793 "Book Notices." 7:175-6, December 1897.
"At last!" Review of *Artists and Engravers of British and American Book-Plates* by Henry W. Fincham.

2794 "Letter." 7:176, December 1897.
Arthur Vicars requests information to compile "notice on book-plates of Heralds."

2795 "American Letter." Charles Dexter Allen. 7:178-9, December 1897.
Exhibits anticipated at Club of Odd Volumes; prize for designing plate offered by Society of Mayflower Descendants.

2796 "Messrs. Puttick & Simpson's Fifth Sale of Book-Plates." 7:179, December 1897.
During two days 530 lots knocked down.

2797 "Cecil T. Davis Plate." (1) 7:180, December 1897.
Collector of insurance plates and merchants' marks, "his book-plate is of the latter style."

2798 "Notes of the Month." 8:1-4, January 1898.
Numerous publications mentioned.

2799 "Notes on Swiss Book-Plates." Jean Grellet. (6) 8:5-9, January 1898.
Earliest Swiss plate stated as being for Hospital of the Holy Ghost at Berne.

2800 "Frontispiece." (1) 8:9, January 1898.
Will Foster designed plate for Mrs. Rath-Merrill who played important part in restoring "embroidery to its former high position."

2801 "Guernsey Book-Plates." Edith Carey. (6) 8:10-3, January 1898.
Plates for the Bonamy family.

2802 "Book-Plate of Washington Sewallis, Earl Ferrers." Alfred A. Bethune-Baker. (1) 8:13-5, January 1898.
Owner of this plate born in 1822.

2803 "Book-Plate Identification." (1) 8:15, January 1898.
Two identified.

2804 "Letters." 8:15, January 1898.
Member suggests reprinting plates for identification and selling them, so they could be kept separate from the *Journal* for ready reference.

2805 "American Letter." Charles Dexter Allen. (1) 8:16, January 1898.
Illustrated is Wilbur Macey Stone plate for YMCA in Hartford, Conn.

2806 "Notes of the Month." 8:17-8, February 1898.
Comments on passing of H. Stacy Marks, "one of our earliest and most distinguished members."

2807 "Modern Book-Plate Designers. No. 15—J. Winfred Spenceley." (5) 8:19-24, February 1898.
Includes descriptive list of about forty plates which this artist etched or engraved.

2808 "Book-Plate Identification." (4) 8:24, February 1898.
Two identified.

2809 " 'Odd Volumes' and Their Book-Plates." (4) 8:25-8, February 1898.
London club in existence about twenty years; membership limited to twenty-one—number of volumes in Variorum Shakespeare of 1821.

2810 "Exchanges." 8:28, February 1898.
"Equitable exchanges" sought and "on no account will process or lithographed plates be accepted in exchange."

2811 "Recent Book-Plates." (1) 8:29, February 1898.
Illustrated is plate Henry Andre designed for Madame Gabrielle Moynel.

2812 " 'Duplicated' Book-Plates." 8:30-1, February 1898.
These are plates which are alike except for some omission or addition (such as "detail in armorial bearings or the heraldic or decorative accessories") which appears in the second plate.

2813 "Letters." (1) 8:31-2, February 1898.
Large plate for David Duncan, dated 1720, pictured.

2814 "Notes of the Month." 8:33-6, March 1898.
Rebuttal to attack on bookplate collectors in *New York Times* book section.

2815 "Book-Plates of Eminent Lawyers." F. J. Thairlwall. (2) 8:37-40, March 1898.
"Earliest dated English book-plate at present known is that of an eminent lawyer, Sr. Nicholas Bacon."

2816 "British Trophy Book-Plates." W. H. K. Wright. (4) 8:41-4, March 1898.
Nearly 100 additional plates brought to editor's attention since publication of list.

2817 "Book-Plates for Identification." (6) 8:1 unnumbered, 46, 48, March 1898.
Four illustrations only.

2818 "American Letter." Charles Dexter Allen. (1) 8:45-6, March 1898.
More on the *Times* exchange, auction prices, reviews.

2819 "Query." (2) 8:46, March 1898.
Identity of odd looking plate sought, which may have been bookplate but carries no name.

2820 "Letters." (2) 8:47-8, March 1898.
Writer believes "bookplate" cut from title page of book dedicated to Cardinal York.

2821 "Notes of the Month." 8:49-51, April 1898.
Annual meeting scheduled for early June at Westminister Palace Hotel.

2822 "Queries." 8:51, April 1898.
Identity of plate described in detail sought.

2823 "Guernsey Book-Plates." Edith Carey. (7) 8:52-6, April 1898.
". . . arms were confirmed to them by grant dated the 25th April, 1726. . . ."

2824 "Book-Plates of Eminent Lawyers." F. J. Thairlwall. (4) 8:57-60, April 1898.
Among those illustrated is that of Sir William Blackstone, author of "Commentaries on the laws of England."

2825 "Book-Plate Identification." (6) 8:60, 67-8, April 1898.
Nine identified.

2826 " 'Odd Volumes' and Their Book-Plates." (3) 8:61-3, April 1898.
Limitation to twenty-one members ignored and almost immediately doubled.

2827 "Buchanan of that Ilk." (1) 8:63, April 1898.
A Burden engraving whose authenticity as a bookplate questioned.

2828 "Letters." 8:64, April 1898.
Caution against bookseller who cut illustrations on plate edge-line and sold them as bookplates at sixpence each.

2829 "American Letter." Charles Dexter Allen. (1) 8:64-7, April 1898.
Auction, reviews, new plates.

2830 "Notes of the Month." 8:69-71, May 1898.
Articles in several journals both English and foreign mentioned.

2831 "Book-Plates for Identification." (4) 8:72, 83-4, May 1898.
Six identified.

2832 "British Trophy Book-Plates." W. H. K. Wright. (5) 8:73-8, May 1898.
Listing continued.

2833 "Gift Inscriptions." 8:78, May 1898.
From theological libraries.

2834 " 'Odd Volumes' and Their Book-Plates." (3) 8:79-81, May 1898.
Member James Roberts Brown, indefatigable bookplate collector, has plate designed by Henry Stacy Marks.

2835 "Recent Book-Plates." (1) 8:81-2, May 1898.
Several described including one by John Vinycomb.

2836 "Letters." 8:83, May 1898.
Suggests distinctive mark be placed by names of members who "are

willing to exchange their plate, or to answer letters or even to return Ex Libris submitted to them for exchange."

2837 "Mottoes on Musical Book-Plates." 8:84, May 1898.
Additional 76 mottoes since book containing 343 published.

2838 "Notes of the Month." 8:85-7, June 1898.
Another sale of "over three hundred lots" at Messrs. Puttick & Simpson's.

2839 "Book-Plate Identification." (11) 8:87, 92, between 96-7, June 1898.
Thus far 296 plates submitted.

2840 "Rhyming Warning to Book-Borrowers." 8:87, June 1898.
Two poems quoted from *Notes and Queries*, one earlier from *London Journal* for 1834.

2841 "Seventeenth Century Perthshire Public Library and Its Book-Plate." J. Paul Rylands. (2) 8:88-91, June 1898.
Founder, Lord Madderty, was born in 1612.

2842 " 'Odd Volumes' and Their Book-Plates." (3) 8:93-7, June 1898.
Member A. T. Hollingsworth had monogram bookplate with circles inside circular border which the author feels "must have been originally suggested by some feeling of graditude towards the proprietor of Carter's Little Liver Pills."

2843 "Exhibition of Book-Plates at Boston, U.S.A." 8:98-100, June 1898.
Exhibit mostly work of Club of Odd Volumes and catalog fills nearly 200 pages.

2844 "Recent Book-Plates." 8:100, June 1898.
Unusual plate for library of botanical works.

2845 "Letters." 8:100, June 1898.
Plate in Latin submitted for its "quaintness of wording."

2846 "Knox Book-Plates." (1) 8:100, June 1898.
Plate used as frontispiece.

2847 "Presidential Address." 8:101-3,105, July 1898.
"Popularity of book-plate collecting and its study is still rising, and the membership . . . is rapidly increasing."

2848 "Book-Plates for Identification." (6) 8:104, 112-3, July 1898.
One, with three bells, looks like a slot machine winner!

2849 "Letter." 8:105, July 1898.
Older plate found beneath Pennington plate (Allen No. 658) and identification sought.

2850 "Seventh Annual Meeting." (2) 8:105-112, July 1898.
Includes financial statement showing small profit, menu in French, list of officers, publications containing notice of exhibit, list of artists and exhibitors and new members.

2851 "John Collet's Book-Label." 8:112, July 1898.
Family details.

2852 "Corrections." 8:113, July 1898.
Author of article reprinted from *Boston Globe* was A. J. Philpot; E. D. French *not* too ill to execute commissions.

2853 "Notes of the Month." 8:114-6, July 1898.
Several European publications listed.

2854 "Notes of the Month." 8:117-8, August 1898.
"In America the war with Spain is putting all ideas about such trifling matters as book-plates out of the minds of our members."

2855 "Book-Plate Identification." (9) 8:118, 121-2, 125, August 1898.
Four identified.

2856 " 'Odd Volumes' and Their Book-Plates." (2) 8:119-21, August 1898.
Quotes criticism of his articles from another journal.

2857 "British Trophy Book-Plates." W. H. K. Wright. (2) 8:123-4, August 1898.
Conclusion of list.

2858 "Book-Rhyme." 8:124, August 1898.
Numerous short lines all admonishing borrower not to soil book.

2859 "Book-Plates at the Shrewsbury Exhibition of Antiquities." 8:125, August 1898.
Collection of 125 plates before 1840 included.

2860 "Book-Plates in Stowe Mss." Arthur J. Jewers. (1) 8:126, August 1898.
More like "pen-and-ink trickings of arms."

2861 "Letter." (2) 8:127-8, August 1898.
List of Governors of New York from 1664 to 1754; plates of Ellen Terry and John Dumont.

2862 "Notes of the Month." 8:129-31, September 1898.
Article from French Society says "scarcely anyone seems to think it worth while [to assume a title], except perhaps an occasional *Chevalier d' Industrie* of the very lowest type of the common or garden swindler."

2863 "Book-Plates for Identification." (5) 8:132, 137, September 1898.
Record of thirteen identified; total submitted now 323.

2864 " 'Odd Volumes' and Their Book-Plates." (4) 8:133-5, September 1898.
Each member of the "brotherly" organization assumes a title upon entry, such as "Knyghte Errant."

2865 "Dated Book-Plates." 8:135-6, September 1898.
Correspondents have submitted twenty additions for Walter Hamilton's list.

2866 "Lord Nelson's Book-Plate." (1) 8:136, September 1898.
Plate illustrated features *San Josef*, vessel Admiral captured, but question arises as to whether Nelson actually had or used a bookplate.

2867 "Caryll Book-Plate." Arthur J. Jewers. 8:138, September 1898.
Detailed correction of identification of plate in prior issue.

2868 "Ex Libris Collector." 8:139-40, September 1898.
"The miser loves the gold for its own sake, the collector loves a book-plate for what it suggests." "The psychic basis of collecting is human sympathy, and not a mere lust for possession." "You exchange plates, and at the same time you exchange courtesy, kindliness, and mutual good-will."

2869 "Book-Plate of William Ayres." (1) 8:139-40, September 1898.
Illustration of scarce plate.

2870 "Frontispiece." (1) 8:140, September 1898.
"Bookseller's label of last century" for which further identification is sought.

2871 "Notes of the Month." (11) 8:141-2, 146, 148, 151, October 1898.
Circular issued by member indicating full information on both owner and artist which he seeks on all exchanges; plates for identification.

2872 "Book Notice." 8:142, October 1898.
Titled *Pages and Pictures from Forgotten Children's Books.*

2873 " 'Odd Volumes' and Their Book-Plates." (3) 8:143-5, October 1898.
Plate illustrated for Walter Hamilton, Keeper of the Archives.

2874 "Good Taste in Book-Plates." James J. Guthrie. 8:147-8, October 1898.
"It is well to guard against the danger of making our plate an advertisement of our virtues, our pedigree, or a catalogue of our most beloved books. It is really astonishing to see how, in some instances, the book-plate rivals the poster."

2875 "Book-Plate of Major-General Robert Hunter." A. A. Hunter. 8:149-50, October 1898.
The Major-General was a former Royal Governor of New York.

2876 "William Milton, A Book-Plate Designer." (1) 8:150, October 1898.
Reprints item seeking further details on this artist who "practised in London . . . died in 1790."

2877 "Book-Plate of Mrs. Duhme." (1) 8:152, October 1898.
Plate created by Paris artist and engraver, Devambez.

2878 "A Whimsical Book-Plate." 8:152, October 1898.
Punning coat of arms for Mr. Cudahy of Chicago includes: "Crest: a setting ham on a gold brick upon four links of sausage. Supporters: Two shorn lambs. Motto: 'Root hog or die.' "

2879 "Letters." (1) 8:152-4, October 1898.
Restrained comment on *Collector* notice that with next issue it will "cease to trouble itself about book-plates."

2880 "Dated Book-Plates." 8:155-6, October 1898.
Additions from French correspondent.

2881 "Price of Book-Plates." 8:156, October 1898.
Plate by Hogarth listed at top price of four pounds 4 shillings.

2882 "Notes of the Month." (1) 8:157-8, November 1898.
Gleeson White died of typhoid fever contracted while on holiday in Italy.

2883 "Degradation of the Book-Plate." 8:158, November 1898.
London publisher "utilized a design by a celebrated black-and-white artist now dead" as a bookplate, printed 175 copies, and is hawking them at half-a-guinea or more according to condition.

2884 "Book-Plate Identification." 8:158, 172, November 1898.
Six identified; none for identification due to lack to space.

2885 "Guernsey Book-Plates." Edith Carey. (6) 8:159-64, November 1898.
Plates for various members of the Le Marchant family detailed.

2886 "Book-Plate of Major-General Robert Hunter." 8:164, November 1898.
Pedigree appeared in *Genealogist* (1879).

2887 "Another Perceval Book-Plate." 8:164, November 1898.
Plate slightly different from 1702 version, probably engraved about 1698.

2888 " 'Odd Volumes' and Their Book-Plates." (2) 8:165-8, November 1898.
Each member has distinctive badge designed by Charles Holme "corresponding to his title in the Sette"; they are the size of a postage stamp.

2889 "Letters." 8:168, November 1898.
Member has bookplate with Horatio Nelson autograph and added motto.

2890 "Note on Some Philipse Book-Plates." Oswald Carnegy Johnson. (5) 8:168-70, November 1898.
Family group of plates with Anglo-American interest.

2891 "General Catalogue of Book-Plates." 8:171, November 1898.
James Dorman, purchaser of Rev. Carson's collection, has issued first part of annotated catalog.

2892 "American Letter." Charles Dexter Allen. 8:171-2, November 1898.
Bookplate 3/8" x 4/8" engraved by Mr. Smith for Mr. Chase of Boston to fit tiny dictionary.

2893 "Notes of the Month." 8:173-5, December 1898.
Special Winter number of *Studio* devoted to bookplates.

2894 "Book-Plate Identification." (5) 8:176, December 1898.
Information on four given.

2895 "Perceval Book-Plates." 8:176, December 1898.
Alfred Bethune-Baker questions evidence for setting date 1698 for plate Mr. Ellis mentioned.

2896 "Parker Book-Plates." A. J. Jewers. (6) 8:177-80, December 1898.
Plates for several different Parker families.

2897 "Mr. Lawson's Book-Plate." 8:180, December 1898.
Corrects misstatement that Robertson Lawson spent boyhood at Huntly Castle.

2898 "Miss Edith Carey's Article on the Le Marchant Book-Plates." 8:180, December 1898.
Missing words supplied for Eleazar Le Marchant plate.

2899 " 'The Smiths' Arms.' " W. Bolton. (1) 8:181-2, December 1898.
"I regret . . . the Smiths never had any Arms and have invariably sealed their letters with their thumbs."

2900 "Wales and the Royal Standard." 8:182, December 1898.
"Whilst we may all well be proud to be Britons, natives of Wales, of Scotland, and of Ireland do not always care to be classed as Englishmen."

2901 "Seventeenth-Century Booksellers Trade-Label or Book-Plate." (1) 8:183-4, December 1898.
Interesting details on tradesman William Thorpp.

2902 "Beckwith Book-Plate." (1) 8:185, December 1898.
" . . . a comparatively early mantle of estate."

2903 "Lord Nelson's Arms." (1) 8:185, December 1898.
Plate illustrated gives appearance of being patched together.

2904 "American Letter." 8:185-6, December 1898.
Warning that a number of "quaint old book-plates" were stolen from the Village Library of Farmington, Connecticut, in event they would be offered for sale.

2905 "Trophy Plates." (2) 8:186, December 1898.
Information sought on plates of J. Cleoburey and MacDuff.

2906 "Letters." 8:187-8, December 1898.
Warning against plate advertised as that of Queen Caroline.

2907 "Notes of the Month." (1) 9:1-2, January 1899.
Revealed that Walter Hamilton authored Odd Volumes articles.

2908 "Beauty versus Utility." Walter Hamilton. (8) 9:3-8, January 1899.
Hamilton takes critical look at bookplates as presented by Gleeson White in the *Studio*.

2909 "Book-Rhyme." 9:8, January 1899.
Rhyme used by architect George Wightwick.

2910 "Book-Plate Identification." (6) 9:8, 16, January 1899.
Two identified.

2911 "Parker Book-Plates." Arthur J. Jewers. (6) 9:9-13, January 1899.
Four additional Parker families detailed.

2912 "Book-Plate Auctions of 1898." 9:13-4, January 1899.
Lack of rare plates appears to account for falling prices during last four sales.

2913 "Misuse of Arms." (2) 9:15, January 1899.
Descendants of Dr. Philip Tenison, who died in 1661, appear to have lost sight of his grant of arms and assumed an entirely different one.

2914 "Notes of the Month." (1) 9:17-8, February 1899.
Partial reprint of eulogy to Gleeson White by Charles Dexter Allen from *In Lantern Land.*

2915 "Book-Plates of All Souls' College, Oxford." J. Henderson Smith. (5) 9:19-23, February 1899.
Fourteen plates described including variations in size, design and inscriptions.

2916 "Parker Book-Plates." Arthur J. Jewers. (3) 9:24-6, February 1899.
Additional Parker families.

2917 "Gerster's *Die Schweizerischen Bibliothekzeichen.*" (4) 9:26-7, February 1899.
Written in German about Swiss bookplates; however, exchange list and many illustrations of interest to English reader.

2918 "Book-Plate Identification." (6) 9:27-8, February 1899.
Total of 351 plates have been submitted.

2919 "Notes of the Month." 9:29-30, March 1899.
"An *edition de luxe*" consisting of twelve copies (ten for sale) of Gordon Craig's *The Page* will be offered for ten guineas; each includes one original wood block from which bookplate was printed.

2920 "English Armorial Stamps on Bindings." W. Y. Fletcher. 9:31-4, March 1899.
Practice of stamping arms on bindings not as common in England as in France and Italy.

2921 "Book-Plates for Identification." (4) 9:35, 42, March 1899.
Three identified.

2922 "Parker Book-Plates." Arthur J. Jewers. (5) 9:36-9, March 1899.
More descendants of the North Molton family.

2923 "Late Walter Hamilton." James Roberts Brown. (1) 9:39-40, March 1899.
Heart disease claimed him at fifty-five.

2924 "Letters." 9:40, March 1899.
Hazlitt, compiler of *Dictionary of English Book-Collectors*, includes comments on bookplates.

2925 "Dated Book-Plates: A Protest." 9:41, March 1899.
Dated and signed plates useful tools as points of reference in identifying plates which do not bear owner's name.

2926 "Recent Book-Plates." (3) 9:41-2, March 1899.
Sherborn did plate for George H. Viner.

2927 "Two Latest Book-Plate Auctions." 9:43-4, March 1899.
Prices at Puttick & Simpson's continued low, those at Sotheby rather high.

2928 "Notes of the Month." 9:45-6, April 1899.
W. E. Henley to have "Ex Libris" column in *Pall Mall Magazine* but believe it will be book chats.

2929 "Book-Plates for Identification." (4) 9:47, 56, April 1899.
No. 119 belatedly identified.

2930 "English Armorial Stamps on Bindings." W. Y. Fletcher. 9:48-52, April 1899.
Editor regrets "that circumstances have not been favorable to the illustration of this article by reproduction of arms, as originally intended."

2931 " 'Dogs' Dates.' " 9:52, April 1899.
Suggests this is copyist's error for some plant such as dog daisies.

2932 "Altered Plates: Chippendales and a Few Others." Frederic Cattle. (5) 9:53-5, April 1899.
Two main categories: plates altered by same owner and by a later owner.

2933 "New Variety of Robert Bloomfield's Book-Plate." (1) 9:55, 59, April 1899.
Undated, unsigned and part of design altered.

2934 "Letter." 9:56, April 1899.
J. R. Brown replies to correspondent on Hazlitt; imposters have been "run to earth as impudent fabrications."

2935 "Recent Book-Plates." (2) 9:57-8, April 1899.
Frontispiece is plate designed by Henry Andre for M. Volaire.

2936 "Mr. Claud Lonsdale on Book-Plates." 9:58, April 1899.
Reprint from *Carlisle Patroit* concerning lecture at Art Gallery of Tullie House.

2937 "Exhibition of the Royal Society of Painter-Etchers and Engravers for 1899." (1) 9:59-60, April 1899.
Author feels sharp contrast between excellent work exhibited and that of "newer movement" which was illustrated in recent *Studio* issue.

2938 "Notes of the Month." 9:61-3, May 1899.
Numerous articles mentioned, exhibit and sale.

2939 "Book-Plate Identification." (6) 9:63, 74, May 1899.
Four identified.

2940 "Frontispiece." (1) 9:63, May 1899.
New member, William Chamney, submitted copper from which frontispiece pulled; rather large and probably not originally intended as book-plate.

2941 "Gibbon Arms." W. Bolton. (1) 9:64-7, May 1899.
Interesting sidelights on the historian's eagerness to assume ancestors with worthy, old pedigree.

2942 "Letter." 9:67, May 1899.
Further discussion as how to best handle exchange listing.

2943 "Book-Plates of K. E. Graf Zu Leiningen-Westerburg." (4) 9:68-71, May 1899.

Four distinctly different plates used by this collector of more than 15,000 bookplates.

2944 "Book-Plate of Count De Pertingue." (1) 9:69,75, May 1899.

Plate for French Count engraved by London engraver of "middle of last century."

2945 "Last Sale of Book-Plates." 9:69-71, May 1899.

Collectors vying with each other drove prices up in many cases.

2946 "*Composite Book-Plates.*" (4) 9:71-2, May 1899.

Book of process-block designs by Major E. Bengough Ricketts.

2947 "Query." 9:72, May 1899.

Letter from *Notes and Queries* requesting identity of bookplate.

2948 "An Eighteenth-Century Criticism on Some Artists Who Engraved Book-Plates." 9:73, May 1899.

"Essay on Prints" printed 1768 gives interesting assessment of Hogarth, Vertue, Piranesi, S. Gribelin, R. White—all artists who engraved bookplates.

2949 "Parker Book-Plates." Arthur J. Jewers. 9:75-6, May 1899.

Abstract from will with interesting family relationships.

2950 "Notes of the Month." 9:77-8, June 1899.

Amusing anecdote involving Walter Hamilton and his collection of "Parodies of the Works of English and American Poets." (Offered Milton's *Paradise Lost* and *Paradise Regained!*)

2951 "Notes on Festoon Plates." J. F. Verster. (9) 9:79-82, June 1899.

"A festoon is in most instances a garland of flowers, leaves, beads, etc., and suspended on wall-pins or hanging through rings above the shield." Also called ribbon and wreath.

2952 "A Painter-Etcher." 9:83-4, June 1899.

Title represents "the *doyen* of book-plate engravers" C. W. Sherborn in his workroom.

2953 "Letters." 9:84, 88, June 1899.

More on exchange lists, and the Gibbon arms.

2954 "Book-Plate Identification." (6) 9:84-5, June 1899.

Three identified.

2955 "Modern Book-Plate Designers. No. 16—Miss C. Helard." W. H. K. Wright. 9:86, June 1899.

Checklist of over thirty; at time of Fincham's list ten plates under this young woman's name.

2956 "Sir Robert Naunton" Gilbert I. Ellis. (1) 9:87, June 1899.

Sir Naunton (1563-1635) held various offices under James I.

2957 "Book Notice." 9:88, June 1899.
Metcalfe's book on the Earldom of Wiltes includes illustration of large bookplate dated 1698.

2958 "Annual Meeting. 1899." (14) 9:89-100, July 1899.
Sir Vicars re-elected president; banquet, exhibition, and balance sheet all covered.

2959 "*Oceanic* Book-Plate by Linley Sambourne." (1) 9:100-1, July 1899.
Interesting plate for new White Star steamer.

2960 "Latest Auction of Book-Plates." 9:101, 103, July 1899.
Catalog annotations raise questions, especially that John Sturt was a bookplate artist.

2961 "Book-Plate Identification." (6) 9:102-3, July 1899.
Thirteenth plate submitted identified; now up to #377.

2962 "Notes of the Month." 9:104, July 1899.
"The ideal design for a lady's plate should be graceful, dainty, and sweetly serious, a thing of beauty, neither flippant nor yet ultra-ambitious or grandiloquent."

2963 "Notes of the Month." 9:105-6, August 1899.
E. D. French catalog is work of Paul Lemperley, Cleveland book collector.

2964 "Notes on Wreath-and-Ribbon Plates." J. F. Verster. (4) 9:107-10, August 1899.
John Quincy Adams specimen "of a perfect Wreath-and-Ribbon plate."

2965 "Ferrar Book-Plates." (3) 9:110, 119-20, August 1899.
Request plates showing any variations in spelling of this family name to assist in preparation of article.

2966 "Modern Book-Plate Designers. No. 17—Charles William Sherborn." K. E. Graf zu Leiningen-Westerburg. (1) 9:111-14, August 1899.
Article translated from German ex libris journal.

2967 "Coltman Book-Plate." (1) 9:114, August 1899.
Original copper kindly lent to *Journal*.

2968 "Parker Book-Plates." Arthur J. Jewers. (5) 9:115-6, August 1899.
Three of the plates engraved about 1820-50.

2969 "Letters." 9:116-7, August 1899.
Help sought in finding plate of Dr. Anthony Scattergood.

2970 "Book-Plates for Identification." (4) 9: between 116-117, August 1899.
No text.

2971 "Gibbon Arms." (1) 9:117, August 1899.
Plate for Samuel Egerton Brydges with thirty-two quarterings; editor's note indicates probably never intended nor used as a bookplate.

2972 "Few Words on Behalf of 'Process' Work." John Vinycomb. (2) 9:118-9, August 1899.

"The fact is, *the merit of the original conception and the quality of the drawing* are the chief elements in a good bookplate; the mode of reproduction is of less account."

2973 "Process-Block v. Engraved Book-Plates." 9:119-20, August 1899.

This correspondent also stresses that "if the design is good, it follows mechanically that the book-plate will be good."

2974 "Notes of the Month." 9:121-2, September 1899.

In Lantern-Land succumbs after six months; Charles Dexter Allen an editor.

2975 "Homes and Humes." W. Bolton. (3) 9:123-6, September 1899.

"The Homes have been conspicuous in Scottish history and ballad . . . though they cannot be charged with much tenderness to their foes or chivalry to their friends."

2976 "Our Illustrations." (4) 9:126-9, 135, September 1899.

Plates designed by May Sandheim, Joseph Simpson, and Samuel Hollyer.

2977 "Urn Book-Plates." 9:127-31, September 1899.

Also called funeral plates, described by Walter Hamilton as a "dismal device."

2978 "Book-Plate Identification." (6) 9:131, 134, September 1899.

Seven identified.

2979 "Book-Plates of Mr. W. Bruce Bannerman." (3) 9:132, September 1899.

Plates by Graham Johnston and Fred A. Sly.

2980 "Book Notice." 9:133-4, September 1899.

Review of *Right to Bear Arms* by "X." Much historical background plus caution to those who wish to use arms.

2981 "Notes on W. R. Weyer of Norwich." 9:134, September 1899.

Quotes article from *Eastern Daily Press* on artist doing stained glass windows and heraldic bookplates.

2982 "Book-Plate Exchange Club." 9:134-5, September 1899.

Thirteen rules for Exchange Club printed.

2983 "Notes of the Month." 9:137-8, October 1899.

Quaritch's *Dictionary of English Book-Collectors,* part XIII, contains bookplate of Maurice Johnson.

2984 "Homes and Humes." W. Bolton. (2) 9:139-41, October 1899.

"David Hume, the rival of Gibbon, is one historian of England whose *complete* history has kept its place and is not yet superseded."

2985 "Urn Plates." (8) 9:141-8, October 1899.

Annotated list.

2986 "Our Illustrations." (4) 9:136, 149-51, October 1899.
John Morgan's designed by Charles Ricketts.

2987 "Book-Plate Exchange Club." 9:151, October 1899.
"Absence from home" of several members delayed distribution.

2988 "Letter." 9:151, October 1899.
Ann Stuart plate originally an illustration and only later believed to have been used as a bookplate.

2989 "Book-Plate Identification." (2) 9:152, October 1899.
Three identified.

2990 "Notes of the Month." 9:153-5, November 1899.
Mentions new publication, *The Elf*, edited by James Guthrie.

2991 "Book-Plates for Identification." (4) 9:156, 165, November 1899.
Three identified.

2992 "Men of Many Book-Plates." F. J. Thairlwall. (7) 9:157-61, November 1899.
Fincham identified no less than twenty varieties for Sir Philip Sydenham, divided into five classes: large and small armorial, book pile, Gribelin, and Jacobean.

2993 "Urn Book-Plates." (11) 9:Frontispiece, 162-3, November 1899.
Illustrations only; list deferred until December.

2994 "Mr. Daniel Parsons, the Pioneer Book-Plate Collector." John W. Singer. 9:164-5, November 1899.
Parsons, "an Anglican clergyman until he seceded to Rome," left his collection of about 1,100 plates to Downside Abbey, a Benedictine Monastery.

2995 "Heraldic Query." 9:165, November 1899.
Armorial bearings given for identification.

2996 "To Subscribers." 9:165, November 1899.
Some members still delinquent in dues payment for current year. For shame!

2997 "Stock-Pattern Plates." Carnegy Johnson. 9:166-7, November 1899.
Lists additional owners of stock patterns previously mentioned by Thairlwall. and Bolton.

2998 "Book-Plate of the 'Amicable Society Galway.' " (1) 9:168, November 1899.
Founded in 1891, its purpose was "acquiring and disseminating useful information on agriculture, science, etc."

2999 "Letter." 9:168, November 1899.
James Roberts Brown furnished correction to Bolton's article on Homes and Humes.

3000 "Book-Plates." (4) 9:Frontispiece, December 1899.
Designed by Major E. Bengough Ricketts.

3001 "To the Members of the Ex Libris Society." 9:169, December 1899.
Additional members (and dues) needed to support *Journal*.

3002 "Notes of the Month." 9:170-1, December 1899.
Over 100 subscriptions still due and some members are two years in arrears; funds needed for current bills.

3003 "Book-Plate Identification." (3) 9:171, between 172-3, December 1899.
Identification and submissions continue to keep about equal.

3004 "Humes of Polworth." W. Bolton. (4) 9:172-6, December 1899.
Sir Patrick had seventeen children.

3005 "Letters." 9:176, December 1899.
Member sends list of institution plates he seeks to "fill up some gaps."

3006 "On Some Ferrar Book-Plates." M. L. Ferrar. (3) 9:177-81, December 1899.
Request in August issue for additional Ferrar plates proves fruitful.

3007 "Book-Plate of Edward Stibbs, Esq. Chester Herald" (1) 9:181, December, 1899.
Chester Herald suspected of having bookplate which "bore unauthorised arms."

3008 "Bannerman." (1) 9:181, December 1899.
Miniature plate ommitted in prior article.

3009 "Notes on an Old Book-Plate of the Trevelyans." E. Bengough Ricketts. (1) 9:182-3, December 1899.
Sixteen quarterings described.

3010 "Answers to Heraldic Query." 9:183, December 1899.
One correspondent identified as Simmons, a second as Simeon.

3011 "Letter." 9:184, December 1899.
Correspondent notes similarity between a Bateman plate and #386 offered for identification.

3012 "To Our Subscribers and Readers." W. H. K. Wright. 10:1-2, January 1900.
Beginning tenth year of publication.

3013 "Notes of the Month." 10:2-4, January 1900.
Numerous articles both foreign and English.

3014 "Book-Plates Designed by Miss May Fisher." (3) 10:5, 15, January 1900.
Three of seven plates designed by this Manchester School of Art student illustrated.

3015 "Altered Chippendales." Frederick Cattle. (3) 10:6-8, January 1900.
Most indicate a portion of plate re-engraved; a few are completely new plates with design altered.

3016 "Letter." 10:8, January 1900.
James Robert Brown warns of spurious plate for Sir Thomas Littleton.

3017 "Stock Patterns: 'Cupid Chip.' Types." Carnegy Johnson. (4) 10:8-11, January 1900.
Thomas Baker pattern stated to be most prolific.

3018 "Arms on Book-Plate." 10:11, January 1900.

Paragraph reprinted from *Notes & Queries* questions whether plate in Dr. G. R. Mather's book is actually that of famous surgeon John Hunter.

3019 "Book-Plates for Identification." (6) 10:12, 14, January 1900.
Five identified.

3020 "Urn Plates." 10:13-4, January 1900.
Supplementary list started.

3021 "Notes to Illustrations." (4) 10:Frontispiece, 3, 14-6, January 1900.
Bookplate design competition at Municipal Science, Art and Technical Schools in Plymouth.

3022 "Letters." 10:16, January 1900.
Two correspondents bought William Penn plates from sale of Bishop of Limerick's library and question whether first impression or not.

3023 "Notes of the Month." 10:17, February 1900.
During last year six members died, twenty resigned.

3024 "Fenwick." W. Bolton. (3) 10:18-22, February 1900.
Plate of John Fenwick gives his date and place of birth plus date and place of his marriage.

3025 "Urn Plates." 10:22-4, February 1900.
List concluded.

3026 "Book-Plates by F. Carruthers Gould." (2) 10:24-5, February 1900.
Very modern plates including artist's own.

3027 "Book-Plate of Charles Townley, Esq., York Herald." (1) 10:26-7, February 1900.
Post of York Herald purchased for 400 pounds though considerable time required before King would "pass his patent of appointment."

3028 "French Book-Plates." 10:27, February 1900.
Supposition regarding identity of plate in Hamilton's *French Book-Plates*.

3029 "Book-Plate Identification." (2) 10:27-8, February 1900.
Five identified; total of 404 submitted.

3030 "Letters." 10:27-8, February 1900.
Additional details on plate #397 previously identified and more on William Penn plate.

3031 "Notes of the Month." 10:29-30, March 1900.
Prospectus from Joseph W. Simpson on new serial *The Book of Book-Plates*.

3032 "Ex Libris in Sweden." (17) 10:31-5, 41, March 1900.
Carl Carlander in 1889 published "a stately volume on *Swedish Book-Plates*."

3033 "Urn Book-Plates." (6) 10:36, March 1900.
Illustrations for article in February issue.

3034 "Further Notes on Stock Patterns." Carnegy Johnson. (4) 10:37-9, March 1900.

Listings by name of simple border, elaborate border and without border.

3035 "Book-Plate of Robert Shirley, 13th Lord Ferrers." Alfred A. Bethune-Baker. (1) 10:39-41, March 1900.

Considerable family history.

3036 "Book-Plates for Identification." (4) 10:42-3, March 1900.

Two identified.

3037 "Recent Book-Plates." 10:43, March 1900.

Several designed by John Vinycomb.

3038 "Letters." 10:44, March 1900.

William Penn controversy continues.

3039 "Notes of the Month." 10:45-7, April 1900.

"It was urged that the greatest possible economy should be exercised in all matters of expenditure to meet the reduction in the annual income of the Society."

3040 "Book-Plates for Identification." (4) 10:47, 53, April 1900.

Three identified.

3041 "Book-Plates of Brooklyn Book-Lovers." 10:48-50, April 1900.

Maverick designed the earliest plate (1789) for Erasmus Hall Library; article reprinted from *Brooklyn Daily Eagle* (December 17, 1899).

3042 "Our Frontispiece." (1) 10:50, April 1900.

Plate for John Stokes, M.D. designed by Henry Gustave Hiller.

3043 "Book-Plate by Gordon Craig." (1) 10:50, April 1900.

Woodcut for American actor John Drew.

3044 "Book-Plate of King William IV." 10:50, April 1900.

Inquiry seeking verification of plate thought to belong to King William IV.

3045 "Urn Book-Plates." (8) 10:51, 58, April 1900.

Illustrations only.

3046 "First Book-Plate Auction of 1900." 10:52-3, April 1900.

Prices moderate and "persons present never exceeded a dozen."

3047 "Arms of Archdeacon Paley and John Ruskin." 10:54, April 1900.

Several instances of private assumption of arms given which indicate "laxity of the Herald's College between 1630 and 1845."

3048 "Ferrar Book-Plates." (1) 10:54-5, April 1900.

Dated allegorical plate.

3049 "Book-Plate of Ralph Cox." (1) 10:55, 59, April 1900.

Another plate not appearing in Hamilton's *Dated Book-Plates*.

3050 "Book Notice." 10:55-6, April 1900.

J. W. Simpson editor of new quarterly, *Book of Book-Plates*, featuring work of James Guthrie, Gordon Craig, R. Anning Bell.

3051 "Reputed Bewick Book-Plate." (1) 10:56, April 1900.
Actually Bewick woodcut done for members of Typographical Society of Newcastle-upon-Tyne, formed about 1817, and "used as vignettes on title-pages of numerous tracts."

3052 "Letters." 10:56-7, 59-60, April 1900.
More on William Penn plate and Exchange Club.

3053 "Notes of the Month." 10:61-2, May 1900.
Portion of library of late Walter Hamilton auctioned at Sotheby's.

3054 "Book-Plates for Identification." (3) 10:62,66-7, May 1900.
Five identified.

3055 "Badges of Dignity in France." "Fess Checquy." 10:63-6, May 1900.
Dignitaries and high officers of state were entitled to "add to their heraldic achievement certain exterior marks." Knowledge of these would be useful to collectors of French ex libris.

3056 "Alexander Nesbit's *System of Heraldry*." W. Cecil Wade. 10:68-70, May 1900.
Folio, published in Edinburgh in 1722, frequently referred to in Sir Walter Scott's novels.

3057 "Book-Plate of the Marquess of Dufferin and Ava." (1) 10:Frontispiece, 70-1, May 1900.
Held offices of Governor-General of Canada, Viceroy of India, and Vice-Admiral of Ireland.

3058 "Railway Book-Plates." 10:71, May 1900.
F. W. Goudy designed plate used by Chicago and Alton Railroad for their *Alton Limited*.

3059 "Book-Plate Thievery." 10:71, May 1900.
Letter reprinted from *The Nation* in which W. C. Lane warns collectors of theft of covers containing old bookplates from Harvard Library.

3060 "New Book-Plate by Mr. J. Winfred Spenceley." (1) 10:72-3, May 1900.
Proofs sent by artist include plates for Detroit Public Library, Women's Club of Wisconsin, and University of Missouri Library.

3061 "Book-Plate of M. Cyprien Gourand, Jun." (1) 10:73, May 1900.
New member and probably youngest collector (sixteen) has plate designed by Henry Andre.

3062 "William Massey, 1691-1768." (1) 10:74-5, May 1900.
A "miscellaneous writer and translator" some of whose works are in the British Museum.

3063 "Letters." 10:75-6, May 1900.
Argument continues relative to the Exchange Club, including short letter from George C. Peachey.

3064 "Notes of the Month." 10:77-8, June 1900.
Brothers of the Book publishing a subscription monograph, *Some Children's Book-Plates: An Essay in Little,* by Wilbur Macey Stone.

3065 "Criminal Side of Book-Plate Collecting." 10:79-80, June 1900.
Library at Rylands taken to task for harsh suggestion in *Library Association Record* that theft of Harvard bookplates could be prevented if possession of a library's bookplates were a criminal offense.

3066 "White Kennett." W. Bolton. (3) 10:81-4, June 1900.
Three bookplates represent his ascent as "plain Presbyter, then Dean, and lastly as Bishop."

3067 "Book-Plates for Identification." (4) 10:84, June 1900.
Illustrations only.

3068 "Austrian Book-Plates." (2) 10:85-6, June 1900.
Highlights from article by Count zu Leiningen-Westerburg in German journal.

3069 "Letter." 10:86, June 1900.
Details concerning Ralph Cox.

3070 "Urn Plates." 10:87, June 1900.
Additional list.

3071 "Alexander Nisbet." 10:87, June 1900.
Despite spelling in some biographical dictionaries above is indicated as correct spelling.

3072 "Further Notes on Some Non-Conforming Church Libraries and Their Book-Plates." (6) 10:88-9, June 1900.
Plates indicate lending period of one week, one renewal and fines.

3073 "Trial of Warren Hastings." (1) 10:89-90, June 1900.
Though printed on ex libris paper, plate would appear to be admission ticket to Trial of Warren Hastings which began on February 13, 1788 and lasted seven years and three months, with acquittal on April 23, 1795.

3074 "Rhyming Warning for Book-Borrowers." 10:90-2, June 1900.
Warnings in English, Latin, and alternate lines of each.

3075 "Rare Norfolk Book-Plate." (1) 10:92, June 1900.
John Holmes, teacher and author of Latin and Greek grammars, had unusual plate mostly in Greek.

3076 "Notes of the Month." 10:93-6, July 1900.
Brief review of Annual Meeting.

3077 "Book-Plate Identification." (7) 10:96,101,107, July 1900.
Seven identified; 428 submitted thus far.

3078 "Shrewsbury School Library Book-Plates." Rev. F. R. Ellis. (4) 10:97-9, July 1900.
Details of three plates used at school since about 1750.

3079 "Sir Robert Naunton." (1) 10:99-100, July 1900.
Over thirty quarterings detailed for Sir Naunton, who held various offices during reign of James I.

3080 "Treasurer's Financial Statement." 10:102,105-6, July 1900.
Maximum membership of 500 sought.

3081 "President's Address." 10:103-5, July 1900.
Membership at 435 as against 450 during prior year.

3082 "Warren Hastings Trial." E. R. J. Gambier Howe. 10:106-7, July 1900.
Of particular interest to ex libris collectors is that "the ordinary book-plate of 'William Chambers Surveyor General of his Majesties Works' " was printed on card and used to admit bearer to Sir William's own box.

3083 "Some Recent Book-Plates." (4) 10:between 96-7, 108, July 1900.
Excellent examples of half-tone process plates by John Vinycomb.

3084 "Book-Plate of the Manchester Law Library." (1) 10:108, July 1900.
Designed by J. Buch whose plates range in date from 1790 to 1840.

3085 "Notes of the Month." 10:109-10, August 1900.
James Guthrie's *The Elf* and a Gordon Craig brochure both receive critical comment.

3086 "Rylands Book-Plates." (9) 10:111-6, August 1900.
Plates for various family members, several designed by Father Anselm, a heraldic artist credited with doing about two-thirds of the coats of arms in Foster's *Peerage*.

3087 "*Scottish Heraldry*." 10:117-9, August 1900.
Review of Sir James Balfour Paul's book; last chapter deals with arms on bookplates.

3088 "Book-Plates for Identification." (2) 10:119, August 1900.
Two offered for identification.

3089 "Royal Library at Nineveh, B.C. 668-626." (1) 10:120-1, August 1900.
Excerpt from German ex libris journal and letter concerning "mark of possession" on early clay tablets.

3090 "Letter." 10:121, August 1900.
W. Bowley engraved one of the Shrewsbury School bookplates; also noted for brass memorial tablets.

3091 "Book-Plate of B. Bagnall." (1) 10:121, August 1900.
Bernard Bagnall submitted his new plate designed by John Bagnall.

3092 "New Book-Plates." (1) 10:122, August 1900.
Unusual plate designed for Royal Naval and Military Bazaar held in June of 1900 to benefit Princess Christiana homes for disabled soldiers and sailors.

3093 "List of Landscape Book-Plates." J. F. Verster. (4) 10:123-4, between 136-7, August 1900.
Alphabetical by owner with brief description and name of artist.

3094 "Notes of the Month." 10:125-6, September 1900.
J. F. Verster invited additions to his alphabetical list of mottoes, etc. on British and American plates.

3095 "Late H. S. Ashbee." (4) 10:127-9, September 1900.
Eulogy for deceased member; his several plates, of which three were punning, incorporate an ash tree and a bee.

3096 "List of Landscape Book-Plates." J. F. Verster. 10:130-1, September 1900.
Letters B and C.

3097 "Late Andrew W. Tuer and His Book-Plates." (3) 10:132, September 1900.
Tuer "was a man of many book-plates, all eccentric in style."

3098 "Book-Plate Identification." 10:133, September 1900.
Seven identified.

3099 "Plates Wanted." 10:133, September 1900.
W. Bruce Bannerman lists forty-two Sherborn plates he would like to acquire by purchase or exchange.

3100 "Letters." 10:134-5, September 1900.
Lengthy discussion of Book-Plate Exchange Club.

3101 "New Book-Plate." (1) 10:135, September 1900.
Bristol publisher J. W. Arrowsmith has plate with general design by J. Shelton and a "pretty little figure at the anvil" by Walter Crane.

3102 "New Books on Book-Plates." 10:135, September 1900.
Thomas Moring, well-known engraver, has issued two books of his work entitled *Fifty Book-Plates on Copper* and *One Hundred Book-Plates Engraved on Wood.*

3103 "Address of the Honorable Secretary." W. H. K. Wright. 10: 136-40, September 1900.
Ex Libris Journal in part outgrowth of *Book-Plate Collector's Miscellany* which was also edited by Wright.

3104 "Notes of the Month." (1) 10:141-2, October 1900.
Frontispiece is printed from copper of Dr. George C. Peachey's new bookplate.

3105 "List of Landscape Book-Plates." 10:143-7, 150-1, October 1900.
C through H.

3106 "Book-Plates for Identification." (8) 10:148-9, October 1900.
Eight offered for identification.

3107 "Recent Book-Plates." 10:151, October 1900.
Two plates etched by Gwladys Whittaker.

3108 "Wants and Exchanges." 10:151, October 1900.
German count wants seventeen specific Sherborn plates; Buckinghamshire resident wants plates of "distinguished families" from that area.

3109 "Book Notice." 10:152, October 1900.

Review of *The Wade Genealogy* by Captain Wade of New York Public Library.

3110 "Letters." 10:153, October 1900.
George Eyre Evans commends unstinting efforts of *Journal* editor.

3111 "Naunton Book-Plate." 10:154, October 1900.
Additional comments on numerous quarterings of this plate.

3112 "Book-Plate of Mrs. Anne Hunter, Wife of Celebrated Surgeon." John Hunter. (1) 10:154, October 1900.
Author of well-known "My Mother bids me bind my hair"; Haydn set some of her songs to music.

3113 "Sir James Balfour Paul, Lyon on Book-Plates and Book-Stamps." (1) 10:155, October 1900.
"The cult of the book-plate has had a remarkable revival in late years, and threatens to become more of a vehicle for the gratification of the collector than a *bona fide* index to the ownership of books."

3114 "Oldest Book-Plate." 10:156, October 1900.
Author of German *Journal* article states Egyptian bookplate to which he referred is of earlier period.

3115 "Book-Plate of Lord Raymond of Abbots Langley." 10:156, October 1900.
Identification of plate pictured in July issue.

3116 "Urn Plate." (1) 10:156, October 1900.
Addition to supplementary list of June.

3117 "Notes of the Month." 10:157-60, November-December 1900.
Numerous articles in journals and newspapers noted.

3118 " 'Book-Plates' of Babylonia and Assyria." Theophilus G. Pinches. 10:161-5, November-December 1900.
Further interesting details on these early "marks of acquisition."

3119 "Late Mr. H. S. Ashbee." (1) 10:165, November-December 1900.
Portrait of late member who published *Iconography of Don Quixote*.

3120 "Exhibition of Ex Libris at Antwerp." 10:165, November-December 1900.
Sixty page illustrated catalog issued.

3121 "Book-Plates Designed by Mr. C. E. Elred." (2) 10:166,178, November-December 1900.
Amateur artist's own plate shows warships of both 16th and 18th centuries.

3122 "List of Landscape Book-Plates." J. F. Verster. (16) 10:167-74, November-December 1900.
H through M.

3123 "Modern Book-Plate Designers. No. 18—H. J. Fanshawe Bradeley." 10:175-6, November-December 1900.
Twenty-six year old artist originally specialized in ladies' bookplates.

3124 "New Book-Plates by Miss C. Helard." 10:between 166-7, 177, November-December 1900.

"The one pictorial in the lot . . . shows clearly that Miss Helard is capable of good work quite apart from heraldry."

3125 "Modern Designers of Book-Plates." 10:178, November-December 1900.

Complete list of artists written about in series and month and year of Journal in which they appeared.

3126 "*Ex Libris* Album." 10:178, November-December 1900.

Members requested to send copies of their plates for the Society's album.

3127 "Book-Plates for Identification." (4) 10:179,183, November-December 1900.

Ten identified.

3128 "Book Notice." 10:180-1, November-December 1900.

Considerable comment on second edition of Warren's guide, issued under editorship of his sister.

3129 "Book-Plate Exchange Club." 10:181, November-December 1900.

Vacancies exist on membership list.

3130 "Notes on Some Gilpin Plates." (1) 10:182-3, November-December 1900.

William Gilpin plate etched by animal painter S. Gilpin, probably the Reverend's younger brother.

3131 "Letters." 10:183, November-December 1900.

Another Warren Hastings ticket unearthed.

3132 "Messrs. Puttick & Simpson's Eleventh Sale of Book-Plates." 10:184, November-December 1900.

Catalog and actual sale disappointing.

3133 "Notes of the Month." 11:1-2, January 1901.

Several magazine articles mentioned.

3134 "Address by Sir James Balfour Paul." 11:3-8, January 1901.

Thrust directed at "modern young men" editing *Book of Book-Plates*.

3135 "Exchanges." 11:8, January 1901.

Two members seek to exchange their own Sherborn plates for others by same artist.

3136 "Book-Plates for Identification." (7) 11:9,16, January 1901.

Four identified.

3137 "List of Book-Plates of Medical Men, British and American." George C. Peachey. 11:10-12, January 1901.

A and B.

3138 "Landscape Book-Plates." (4) 11:13,16, January 1901.

Owner feels description inaccurate and sent plate.

3139 "American Letter." Charles Dexter Allen. 11:14-16, January 1901.

Notes of auctions, new books, Harvard larceny, taste in bookplates.

3140 "Victoria, Queen and Empress." 11:17, February 1901.
Tribute to Victoria who died January 22, 1901.

3141 "Notes of the Month." 11:18, February 1901.
Considerable details on articles in German *Journal*.

3142 "Letters." 11:18, February 1901.
Members hope *Journal* will not change to quarterly.

3143 "Altered Chippendales." Frederick Cattle. (2) 11:19-21, February 1901.
Additions to lists of April 1899 and February 1900.

3144 "Book-Plate of Finlay of Castle Toward." (1) 11:21, February 1901.
Plate and description by Heraldic Painter of Lyon Office.

3145 "List of Book-Plates of Medical Men, British and American." George C. Peachey. (6) 11:22-6, February 1901.
List continued through S.

3146 "Book-Plates of John Wilkes." (3) 11:26-7, February 1901.
Many-sided character, known by Hogarth's portrait; though a demogogue his armorial bearings appear on all three plates.

3147 "Book-Plates for Identification." (4) 11:28, February 1901.
No text.

3148 "Notes of the Month." 11:29-30, March 1901.
New volume in Messrs. Bell's Ex Libris series announced.

3149 "Book-Plates for Identification." (5) 11:31, between 40-1, 44, March 1901.
Eleven identified.

3150 "Book-Plate Wrongly Described." Julian Marshall. 11:32, March 1901.
Bookseller miscataloged plate as to country and date.

3151 "List of Book-Plates of Medical Men, British and American." George C. Peachey. 11:33-5, March 1901.
List continued.

3152 "Ex Libris Collecting of Count Zu Leiningen-Westerburg of Neupasing, Near Munich." (1) 11:36-7, March 1901.
Translation of article in German *Journal:* includes list of seventeen collectors whose ex libris number from 1,500 to 20,200.

3153 "American Letter." Charles Dexter Allen. (1) 11:38-9, March 1901.
Recounts visit during the winter to Edwin Davis French in the Adirondack Mountain area; Maxfield Parrish in nearby cottage.

3154 "Mr. H. W. Fincham." 11:39, March 1901.
Details his work as churchwarden in restoring St. John's Church which stands on site of ancient Priory Church of the Hospitallers.

3155 "How I Designed the Jobbins' Family Book-Plate." 11:40-1, March 1901.
Imaginary dialogue between artist and member of family in selecting design for bookplate; author probably Miss S. K. Phelps.

3156 "Messrs. Puttick & Simpson's Twelfth Sale of Book-Plates." 11:41, March 1901.

Lots inaccurately described, prices generally low at auction, attendance small.

3157 "List of Landscape Book-Plates." (1) 11:41-3, March 1901.

S and T.

3158 "Notes to Illustrations." (2) 11:Frontispiece, 43-4, March 1901.

Joint plate for Edward and Marianna Heron-Allen designed by Ella F. G. Hallward and engraved by Harry Sloane.

3159 "Letters." 11:44, March 1901.

Correspondent seeks angling plates; another requests information on engraver named Charles Warren.

3160 "Notes of the Month." (1) 11:45-6, April 1901.

Articles in French and German journals mentioned; frontispiece is portrait plate of Charles Dexter Allen.

3161 "Medmenham Friars." W. Bolton. (2) 11:47-51, April 1901.

Unholy brotherhood whose members "all were rakes, gamblers, or debauchees."

3162 "Book-Plates for Identification." (7) 11:between 48-9, 51, April 1901.

Elaborate plate offered for identification.

3163 "Wilkes Book-Plate." (1) 11:51, April 1901.

Plate of Israel Wilkes, rich distiller.

3164 "List of Book-Plates of Medical Men, British and American." George C. Peachey. 11:52-3, April 1901.

C and D.

3165 "Recent Book-Plates." (4) 11:54-6, April 1901.

Several by Louis Rhead described; also E. D. French, Miss Helard, Miss Whittaker, and Miss Phelps.

3166 "Our January Exhibition." 11:56-7, April 1901.

No catalog prepared, but list given indicating plates exhibited by various members.

3167 "American Letter." Charles Dexter Allen. 11:58-9, April 1901.

Bowdoin's *Rise of the Book-Plate* given a close review with particular criticism concerning lack of explanation of many illustrations, which have been enlarged and/or reduced in size without apparent reason.

3168 "Book Notice." 11:60, April 1901.

German Book-Plates is latest addition to Bell series.

3169 "Annual Meeting and Exhibition." 11:61, May 1901.

Tenth annual meeting scheduled for June 28th.

3170 "Notes of the Month." 11:61-2, May 1901.

New Canadian journal has bookplate series.

3171 "Letters." 11:62, May 1901.
Thairlwall seeks perfect copy of plate attributed to John Lambert; name erased on all copies he has seen.

3172 "Modern Book-Plate Designers. No. 19—Mr. Allan Wyon." (21) 11:63-6, 4 supplemental pages, May 1901.
Members of Wyon family have held office of Chief Engraver of His (or Her) Majesty's Seals since 1816.

3173 "*Wilkes and Liberty.*" W. Bolton. (3) 11:67-70, May 1901.
More on disreputable Medmenham group whose members rose to public power in spite of private sins and follies.

3174 "List of Book-Plates of Medical Men, British and American." George C. Peachey. 11:71-2, May 1901.
D through F.

3175 "Recent Book-Plates." (6) 11:73-5, May 1901.
Dr. A. W. Clark, Health Officer of Lawrence, Kansas, has designed nearly twenty bookplates during last three years.

3176 "German Ex Libris Literature." 11:76, May 1901.
Numerous German periodicals mentioned.

3177 "Notes of the Month." 11:77-8, June 1901.
Reminder of meeting and exhibit during the month.

3178 "Book-Plates for Identification." (6) 11:78,89,92, June 1901.
Eight identified.

3179 "Modern Book-Plate Designers. No. 20—Mr. William Phillips Barrett." (8) 11:79-82, between 88-9, June 1901.
Barrett is skillful designer whose work is executed by engraver of J. & E. Bumpus; chronological list includes plates for many titled men and women.

3180 "Royal Tressure of Scotland." "Fess Checquy." (3) 11:83-7, June 1901.
This figure features fleurs-de-lis placed alternately with heads in and out.

3181 "Cowper Book-Plate." W. Bolton. 11:88-9, June 1901.
Additional searching reveals plate discussed previously in *Journal* is indeed that of poet.

3182 "List of Book-Plates of Medical Men, British and American." George C. Peachey. (1) 11:87, 90-1, June 1901
F and G.

3183 "Gleanings from An Old Album." Sir James Balfour Paul. (1) 11:93-9, July-August 1901.
President's address.

3184 "Cowper's Book-Plate." 11:99, July-August 1901.
H. Gough concedes new information appears to confirm plate of the poet.

3185 "Royal Tressure of Scotland." "Fess Checquy." (3) 11:100-102, July-August 1901.

Several color variations described and caution given as to proper proportions between tressure and shield.

3186 "Annual Meeting." 11:103-5, July-August 1901.

"More than seven hundred members had been enrolled since the Society was first formed in February, 1891" and present membership is 420.

3187 "German Book-Plate Artist." (5) 11:106-8, July-August 1901.

Chronological list of plates executed by Alexander; some of his book-plates are "beautiful specimens of colour-printing."

3188 "List of Book-Plates of Medical Men, British and American." George C. Peachey. (2) 11:109-11, July-August 1901.

G and H.

3189 "Book-Plates for Identification." (4) 11:112, July-August 1901.

Total of 477 submitted.

3190 "Our Exhibition." 11:113-4, July-August 1901.

Featured were plates of colleges, libraries and institutions.

3191 "Notes of the Month." 11:115, July-August 1901.

Mentions article in French journal on armorial bindings.

3192 "Notes to Illustrations." (4) 11:between 112-3,115, July-August 1901.

John Vinycomb, a Society Vice President, exhibited his work at Annual Meeting.

3193 "Ex Libris Society." 11:116, July-August 1901.

Statement of accounts for year ending July 27, 1901.

3194 "Notes of the Month." 11:117-8, September 1901.

Numerous articles in foreign journals.

3195 "Royal Tressure: The Metals." "Fess Checquy." (3) 11:119-21, September 1901.

Further detailed descriptions.

3196 "Book Notice." 11:121, September 1901.

Review of *Book-Plates* which contains fifty-five prints direct from the original coppers by W. P. Barrett, published by John and E. Bumpus.

3197 "List of Book-Plates of Medical Men, British and American." George C. Peachey. (2) 11:122-3, 127, September 1901.

Continuation of list.

3198 "American Letter." Charles Dexter Allen. 11:124-6, September 1901.

Quotes from several newspaper clippings without identifying the specific papers.

3199 "Recent Book-Plates." (1) 11:126-7, September 1901.

Pictured is plate designed by Louis Rhead for infant son of *Vogue* editor.

3200 "Our Exhibition." (4) 11:between 120-1, 124-5, 128, September 1901.
Exhibition list concluded.

3201 "Notes of the Month." 11:129, October 1901.
Ashbee collection of 2500 plates brought fifteen pounds at auction.

3202 "Royal Tressure: Various." "Fess Checquy." (4) 11:130-3, October 1901.
Two royal burghs of Scotland entitled to display the tressure: Aberdeen and Perth, formerly St. John's.

3203 "List of Book-Plates of Medical Men, British and American." George C. Peachey. (4) 11:134-8, October 1901.
J through M.

3204 "Recent Book-Plates." (2) 11:139-40, October 1901.
Wilbur Macey Stone quoted: "Everyone who can use India ink in a pen, and, alas, many a one who cannot, is making book-plates."

3205 "Book-Notices." 11:141-2, October 1901.
Review of book by Von Walter von Zur Westen.

3206 "Letter." 11:142-3, October 1901.
New secretary for Book-Plate Exchange Club lists thirteen rules; a few vacancies in membership limited to twenty-five.

3207 "Book-Plate Identification." (1) 11:133, 144, October 1901.
Seven identified.

3208 "Notes of the Month." 11:145-7, November 1901.
Mentioned articles in *Queen, Studio, American Printer* as well as ex libris journals in Germany, Switzerland, and France.

3209 "Book-Plates for Identification." (6) 11:148, 158, November 1901.
Four identified including fifth plate submitted.

3210 "Acadian Book-Plates." (3) 11:149-51, November 1901.
Based upon articles appearing in new Canadian quarterly, *Acadiensis*.

3211 "Hewer." Arthur J. Jewers. 11:152-3, November 1901.
Further details sought on Hewer Edgley Hewer; last will of both Hewer and his wife abstracted.

3212 "List of Book-Plates of Medical Men, British and American." George C. Peachey. 11:154-5, November 1901
Continuation of list.

3213 "Recent American Book-Plates." (5) 11:147, 153, 156, 158, November 1901.
All plates by William Edgar Fisher from collection of George May Elwood.

3214 "An Interesting Book-Plate." (1) 11:157-8, November 1901.
Lengthy quote from medical journal concerning plate of L. M. Griffiths which features medicine, tree of life, "Shakespere," and motto from Ovid.

3215 "Southey Book-Plate." 11:158, November 1901.
Arthur Jewers draws attention to irregularity in list of Landscape Book-Plates.

3216 "Notes to Illustrations." (6) 11:147, 159-60, November 1901.
Variety of plates shown.

3217 "Book Notice." 11:160, November 1901.
Review of Wilbur Macey Stone's *Some Children's Book-Plates*.

3218 "Ex Libris of Queen Victoria of England." (5) 11:161-3, December 1901.
Summary of article appearing in German ex libris journal.

3219 "Hewer." Cecil T. Davis. (1) 11:164-9, December 1901.
Hewer and Pepys about 1690 "appear to have had separate establishments in the same house."

3220 "Some Recent Book-Plates." 11:169, December 1901.
Several designs submitted by John Williams.

3221 "New Harvard Book-Plate." (1) 11:170, December 1901.
Design for James Russell Lowell Memorial Library plate by Bertram Grosvenor Goodhue.

3222 "Book-Plate of Mr. W. N. Patterson." (1) 11:170, 175, December 1901.
Portrait plate in one circular medal from which is suspended smaller medal.

3223 "List of Book-Plates of Medical Men, British and American." George C. Peachey. 11:171-2, December 1901.
O through P.

3224 "American Letter." (3) 11:173-5, December 1901.
News in a conversational style.

3225 "Notes of the Month." 11:175-6, December 1901.
Mention of C. D. Allen's article in recent *Century*.

3226 "Book-Plates for Identification." (4) 11:following 176, December 1901.
Illustrations only.

3227 "Ex Libris for the Empress Frederick." (3) 12:1-2, January 1902.
Brief summary of another article from German journal.

3228 "Letter." 12:2-3, January 1902.
Correspondent commends *Acadiensis* and comments on Hewer and William Edgar Fisher.

3229 "Notes of the Month." 12:3-4, January 1902.
Numerous foreign articles as well as continuing items in new Canadian journal mentioned.

3230 "Book-Plates for Identification." (2) 12:following 4, January 1902.
Illustrations only.

3231 "Book-Plates of Sir Philip Sydenham." Carnegy Johnson. (7) 12:5-8, February 1902.
Sir Philip had eleven plates in twenty-three states.

3232 "Hewer." Alfred A. Bethune-Baker. (1) 12:9-10, February 1902.
Puzzle of coat of arms solved; they belong with paternal name of "Edgley."

3233 "*Gil Ex Libris Italiani.*" J. F. Verster, 12:10-11, February 1902.
Volume on Italian bookplates includes 378 pages of alphabetical listings and a chronological list of dated plates.

3234 "Recent Book-Plates." 12:11, February 1902.
Plate for Elizabeth Le Roy Emmet executed by Mrs. P. Swinnerton Hughes.

3235 "List of Book-Plates of Medical Men, British and American." George C. Peachey. 12:12-3, February 1902.
P through R.

3236 "Sale of Book-Plates by Messrs. Sotheby, Wilkinson, & Hodge." 12:14, February 1902.
First sale in a year; prices much higher than on last two sales.

3237 "Children's Book-Plates." 12:14-5, February 1902.
Further details on Stone's book, limited to 350 copies at one dollar each.

3238 "Notes of the Month." 12:15-8, February 1902.
Passing of Gilbert Ifold Ellis noted.

3239 "Musical Book-Plates." J. F. Verster. 12:19-22, March 1902.
Interesting descriptions with reference to illustrations in prior issues of *Journal.*

3240 "Book-Plates for Identification." (5) 12:22, 25, 31, March 1902.
Seven identified.

3241 "Art in Modern Book-Plates." W. H. K. Wright. (1) 12:23-5, March 1902.
Considerable comment generated by G. R. Dennis' recent article in *Artist* which, in part, said: "It is a fact that the artistic value of Ex Libris is generally ignored by the serious collector."

3242 "Ireland Book-Plates." (3) 12:26-30, March 1902.
Son forged documents for his father who was Shakespeare-mad.

3243 "Notes of the Month." 12:30, March 1902.
French and German journals mentioned.

3244 "Moehsen Book-Plates." (1) 12:Frontispiece, 32, March 1902.
Large library-interior plate of German doctor.

3245 "List of Book-Plates of Medical Men, British and American."George C. Peachey. 12:33-4, March 1902.
Letter S.

3246 "Book-Plate of the Late Cecil John Rhodes." (1) 12:35-6, April 1902.
R. Anning Bell designed plate showing first landing of Dutch at the Cape; though instructed not to place name on plate, owner's initials are entwined in ornamental border.

3247 "Andrew Coltee Ducarel." Cecil T. Davis. (1) 12:37-8, April 1902.
Ducarel proved an "antiquary" can make a good librarian in his post as keeper of the library of the Archbishop of Canterbury at Lambeth.

3248 "Book-Plate of Samuel French." (1) 12:38, April 1902.
Unusual plate for Wisconsin architect.

3249 "Interesting Irish Book-Plate." Robert Day. (1) 12:39, April 1902.
"Consequent upon" the famine in Ireland in 1846 the Parsontown Mechanic's Institute ceased to exist and its bookplate is quite rare.

3250 "Moehsen Book-Plate." 12:40, April 1902.
Plate included in *German Book-Plates;* Moehsen was court physician and a "learned numismatist."

3251 "Recent Book-Plates." 12:40, April 1902.
Four plates designed by P. F. Gethin described.

3252 "Book-Plates for Identification." (4) 12:40,45,46, April 1902.
Illustrations only.

3253 "Ireland Book-Plates." 12:41-2, April 1902.
"Shakesperean *[sic]* forger, who lived on past middle age, rejoicing in his sin and only bewailing the penalties which it brought down on him."

3254 "Book-Plate of 'Dartrey.'" 12:42, April 1902.
Reprint from *Miscellanea Genealogica et Heraldica.*

3255 "Library Interior Book-Plates." (2) 12:41-3, April 1902.
Two plates exhibited by Sir Arthur Vicars.

3256 "Book Notices." 12:43-5, April 1902.
New journal, *The Ancestor,* being published with emphasis on "family history, heraldry, and antiquities."

3257 "Book-Plate of the Right Hon. Arthur J. Balfour." (1) 12:46, April 1902.
Plate designed by Miss Helard for leader of House of Commons and First Lord of Treasury.

3258 "List of Book-Plates of Medical Men, British and American." George C. Peachey. 12:47-8, April 1902.
S and T.

3259 "Notes of the Month." 12:49-50, April 1902.
Activity in Germany, France, and United States.

3260 "Windsor Book-Plates of H. M. King Edward VII." (3) 12:51-3, May 1902.
Special proof set of fifty with remarque to be issued to benefit King Edward's Hospital Fund; price eight pounds and eight shillings.

3261 "Hollander Book-Plate." 12:53, May 1902.
Plate misidentified in previous article as Flemish; actually, owner lived in Riga, Livonia, Russia.

3262 "Exeter Cathedral Library and Its Book-Plates." (3) 12:54-6, May 1902.
Leofric, who came to Exeter in middle of 11th century as first Bishop, may have made earliest known catalog of books in English.

3263 "Some More Acadian Book-Plates." 12:57, May 1902.
Additional details from articles in Canadian journal.

3264 "Lord Nelson's Book-Plates." Frederic Cattle. (1) 12:58-9, May 1902.
Description of two additional Nelson plates.

3265 "Book-Plate of the Rev. Thos. Brooke." (1) 12:59, May 1902.
Bookpile plate used by man born about 1700.

3266 "Notes on the Pictorial Book-Plate." Thomas Wood Stevens. 12:59-61, May 1902.
Article reprinted from *Inland Printer*, April 1902.

3267 "Book-Plate Identification." 12:61, May 1902.
Ten identified.

3268 "Announcements." 12:61, May 1902.
Anticipated articles noted.

3269 "List of Book-Plates of Medical Men, British and American." George C. Peachey. 12:62-4, May 1902.
List concluded.

3270 "Notes of the Month." 12:65-6, May 1902.
Coronation festivities during June make day of Annual Meeting impractical until July.

3271 "Notes of the Month." 12:67-8, June 1902.
Sir Walter Besant "acquired his books for use, and not for sale."

3272 "Book-Plates of New College, Oxford." J. Henderson Smith. (5) 12:69-72, June 1902.
Founded in 1375; earliest plate dated 1702.

3273 "St. Stephens Church, Wandsworth, S.D." Cecil T. Davis. (1) 12:72, June 1902.
"It is not often that one meets with a book-plate specially designed for use in a place of worship."

3274 "Book-Plate of Mansergh." (1) 12:Frontispiece, 72, June 1902.
Plate designed by Miss Helard.

3275 "Sir Horace Mann and the Walpoles." W. Bolton. (5) 12:73-7, June 1902.
Some interesting highlights on fighting within the family.

3276 "Book-Plate of the Barnstaple Clerical Library." (1) 12:77, June 1902.
Established in 1826 and "kept up by subscription, chiefly by clergymen, to the present time."

3277 "Rev. Dr. Thomas Bray and the Parochial Library." (4) 12:78-81, June 1902.
Alphabetical list of numerous libraries he founded.

3278 "Letter." 12:82, June 1902.
Correspondent feels Nelson plate in previous article misidentified.

3279 "Book-Plate of Dr. Samuel W. French." 12:82, June 1902.
Member willing to exchange his plate.

3280 "Note to Illustration." (1) 12:68,82, June 1902.
While not a bookplate, it was designed by John Vinycomb for use of Royal Warrant holders.

3281 "Notes of the Month." (1) 12:83-4, July 1902.
W. Bruce Bannerman new editor of *Miscellanea Genealogica et Heraldica* after death of Dr. Joseph Jackson Howard.

3282 "Modern Book-Plate Designers. No. 21—Mr. Graham Johnson." (8) 12:85-90, July 1902.
"It is safe to say that at the present time no more beautiful register exists in Europe than that of the Lyon office, and it owes this position entirely to the industry and skill of Mr. Johnson."

3283 "Footprints on the Sands of Time." Alfred A. Bethune-Baker. (3) 12:91-5, July 1902.
"The plate of a single famous man will by the mere effect of natural association compel our attention to quite a host of plates of his contemporaries."

3284 "Rough List of Legal Book-Plates." S. A. Grundy-Newman. 12:95-6, July 1902.
Start of alphabetical list by owner which includes inscription, style and date.

3285 "Book-Plates of R. Anning Bell." (2) 12:97, July 1902.
Plates for Marie Clay and Fanny Dove Hamel Lister.

3286 "Letters." 12:98, July 1902.
Count Leiningen-Westerburg will exchange his plate for "engraved or etched examples of such as are not already" in his collection.

3287 "President's Address." 12:99-102, August 1902.
"I wage war against that 'monstrous regiment' of neurotic women who too often peer and gibber at us from book-plates."

3288 "Borlase Book-Plates." Arthur J. Jewers. (6) 12:103-8, August 1902.
Family tree indicating plates for six members.

3289 "Letters." (1) 12:108-10, August 1902.
Correspondent and editor of *The Ancestor* continue their disagreement.

3290 "Book Notice." 12:110-11, August 1902.
Review of *The Ancestor;* knowledge of heraldry helpful with armorial bookplates.

3291 "Gurney Book-Plate." (1) 12:11, August 1902.
Large plate designed by Mrs. Gurney for her husband and etched by W. Monk.

3292 "Annual Meeting." 12:112-6, August 1902.
Active membership at 450. Index prepared for first ten volumes.

3293 "Annual Dinner." 12:116-21, August 1902.
Running account of toasts and after dinner speeches.

3294 "Book-Plates for Identification." (6) 12:111, between 118-9, August 1902.
Six offered for identification.

3295 "Notes of the Month." 12:121-2, August 1902.
Numerous articles in foreign as well as English and Canadian journals.

3296 "Modern Book-Plate Designers. No. 21—E. B. Bird." (4) 12:123-6, September 1902.
"During the recent poster craze, Mr. Bird was one of the foremost designers, his bold style being very convincing."

3297 "Annual Exhibit." 12:127-31, September 1902.
List by exhibitor of plates and association items entered in exhibit of bookplates of royal and titled persons.

3298 "Book-Plate Identification." 12:127-31, September 1902.
Five identified.

3299 "American Letter." (4) 12:132-4, September 1902.
Wide variety of news on American bookplate literature and artists.

3300 "Letters." (1) 12:134-6, September 1902.
Article on silversmith Carden Terry quoted from *Journal of Cork Historical and Archaeological Society*.

3301 "Notes of the Month." (1) 12:137-8, September 1902.
Suggestion made by Dr. Peachey at Annual Dinner that interest in bookplates be fostered by lectures; George Day furnishes lantern slides for such lectures.

3302 "Sir John Hill." George C. Peachey. (1) 12:139-41, October 1902.
Poem on would-be M.D. author: "For physic and farces his equal there scarce is. His farces are physic, his physic a farce is."

3303 "Curious Book-Rhyme." 12:141, October 1902.
Lengthy rhyme exhorting cleanliness while reading borrowed books.

3304 "Annual Exhibition." 12:143-7, October 1902.
Completion of listing giving items exhibited.

3305 "Rough List of Legal Book-Plates." (13) 12:Frontispiece, 142, 144-6, 148-50, October 1902.
A and B.

3306 "Book Notice." 12:151, October 1902.
Review of *Some Feudal Coats of Arms*.

3307 "Exchanges." 12:151, October 1902.
Three individuals in Germany and one in U.S. offer to exchange.

3308 "Letters." 12:152, October 1902.
Discussion continues concerning authenticity of Ann Stuart, Baroness of Castle Stuart, plate.

3309 "Book-Plate Identification." (1) 12:152-4, October 1902.
Seven identified.

3310 "Notes of the Month." 12:153-4, October 1902.
Sale of Gilbert I. Ellis collection at Sotheby's.

3311 "Lord Proprietor of Carolina." Alfred A. Bethune-Baker. (1) 12:155-7, between 166-7, November 1902.
Also one of the "Company of Royal Adventurers into Africa."

3312 "Book-Plate of Mr. S. R. Ginn." (1) 12:Frontispiece, 157, November 1902.
Printed "directly from the copper" of landscape plate engraved by Will Foster.

3313 "Balfour Book-Plate." (1) 12:157, November 1902.
Plate designed by Graham Johnson.

3314 "Book-Plates for Identification." (4) 12:158, November 1902.
Illustrations only.

3315 "Rough List of Legal Book-Plates." 12:159-60, November 1902.
B's completed and C started.

3316 "Book-Plates of the Rev. F. Vyvyan Jago Arundell, M.A., J. P., Sometime Rector of Landulph, Cornwall." Rev. Wickham M. Birch. (3) 12:161-3, November 1902.
"In 1815 he took by royal license the name and arms of Arundell of Tal" from the maternal side of the family.

3317 "Borlase Plates." (2) 12:163, November 1902.
Two additional plates for this family.

3318 "Exchanges." 12:163, November 1902.
Large plate etched by August Stoehr offered for exchange by Count Leiningen-Westerburg.

3319 "Library of Westminster Abbey." 12:164, November 1902.
Quotes from paper read in October 1860 concerning ownership of books in Abbey.

3320 "Letters." (1) 12:164-5, November 1902.
Plate illustrated is believed to be that of Thomas Winckley who was executed for his part in rebellion of 1715.

3321 "Sale of Late Mr. G. Ellis' Collection at Messrs. Sotheby, Wilkinson, & Hodge's Rooms." 12:165-6, November 1902.
Prices given by lot; it was felt that smaller lots would have realized higher prices proportionately.

3322 "Book Notice." 12:167-8, November 1902.
Lengthy review of quarterly, *The Ancestor*.

3323 "New Book-Plates by Miss Gwladys Whittaker." 12:168, November 1902.
Includes plates for a sister, a friend, and a solicitor.

3324 "Notes of the Month." 12:169-70, November 1902.
Death of Sir Juland Danvers noted.

3325 "Book-Plate of Fleming of Rydal." George C. Peachey. (5) 12:172-6, between 182-3, December 1902.

Considerable detail as well as family tree for Daniel Fleming, born in 1633.

3326 "Rough List of Legal Book-Plates." S. A. Grundy-Newman. 12:177-8, December 1902.
Letter C.

3327 "American Letter." (3) 12:179-80, December 1902.
Chronological list of plates designed by Thomas P. Hapgood, Jr.

3328 "Two Sales of Book-Plates." 12:181-2, December 1902.
Description of sale of Dr. J. Jackson Howard's collection and a small unidentified, but good, collection.

3329 "Book-Plate of the Hove Library." (1) 12:182, December 1902.
Article reprinted from *Art Journal*.

3330 "Book-Plate Identification." (1) 12:183, 186, December 1902.
Numerous plates identified.

3331 "Check List of Anonymous Plates." 12:183, December 1902.
Recapitulation of 117 plates thus far not identified, including two duplicates, out of total of 521.

3332 "*Studio* Book-Plates." 12:184, December 1902.
Conflicting attitudes concerning merits of modern design and heraldry in bookplates expressed by reviewer and author of *Studio* article.

3333 "Book-Plate of Mr. John Wilson." (1) 12:Frontispiece, 184, December 1902.
Original copper by Graham Johnston used for frontispiece.

3334 "Notes of the Month." 12:185-6, December 1902.
W. H. K. Wright gave lecture using "over one hundred slides."

3335 "Notes of the Month." 13:1-2, January 1903.
"A very pithy little article" appeared in *Picture Postcard and Collector's Chronicle* for January 1903.

3336 "Rough List of Legal Book-Plates." S. A. Grundy-Newman. (4) 13:3-5, January 1903.
C and D.

3337 "On Topographical Collecting of Book-Plates." Alfred A. Bethune-Baker. 13:6-8, January 1903.
Alphabetical hand-list of Worcestershire bookplates.

3338 "New Book on Book-Plates." 13:9-10, January 1903.
Review of *Book-Plates of Today* edited by Wilbur Macey Stone.

3339 "Book-Plate Identification." (2) 13:8,10, January 1903.
Fifteen identified including five among first dozen submitted.

3340 "American Notes." 13:11, January 1903.
New York publisher announced Book-Plate Zodiac Calendar for 1903.

3341 "Book-Plate of the Speaker." (1) 13:Frontispiece, 11, January 1903.
Plate designed by G. J. F. Badeley for Rt. Hon. W. C. Gully, Speaker of House of Commons.

3342 "Book-Plate of Mr. E. H. Ebsworth." (1) 13:9,11, January 1903.
Designed by Graham Johnston of the Lyon Office, Edinburgh.

3343 "Letter." 13:11, January 1903.
George Potter disclaims a plate being circulated with his name and the year 1902 on it.

3344 "Description of the Book-Plate Designed and Engraved by Mr. C. W. Sherborn for Downside Abbey." 13:12, January 1903.
Details of eighth and latest plate for use in monastery library.

3345 "Notes of the Month." 13:13-4, February 1903.
Several foreign journal articles mentioned.

3346 "Rough List of Legal Book-Plates." (5) 13:15-8,22, February 1903.
D through G.

3347 "Lectures on Book-Plates." 13:19-21, February 1903.
Lectures mentioned given by W. H. K. Wright and G. C. Peachey; slides used by Wright listed.

3348 "To My Books." Honorable Mrs. Caroline Elizabeth Norton nee Sheridan. 13:22, February 1903.
A sonnet "communicated in the form of a leaflet by the Hon. Wm. A. Courtenay, LLD," an Ex Libris member in South Carolina.

3349 "Book-Plates for Identification." (7) 13:23, 28, February 1903.
Illustrations only.

3350 "Book Notice." 13:24-5, February 1903.
Review of *The Ancestor* in detail.

3351 "Library Book-Plates." (2) 13:25-6, February 1903.
Featured are plates for Gosport and Limehouse District Public Library.

3352 "Exchange." 13:26, February 1903.
Mrs. Getting lists six plates she would like to obtain by exchange or purchase.

3353 "Letter." 13:27, February 1903.
Concerning anonymous Gore plate.

3354 "Book-Plate Notes." S. Hollyer. 13:27-8, February 1903.
Quotes article from *Literary Collector* which comments extensively on Truesdell article in *Ex Libris Journal*.

3355 "Special Meeting." 13:29, March 1903.
Lecture and exhibition by EPIDIASCOPE, "an entirely new and wonderful apparatus which displays objects on the screen without the intervention of the ordinary slides as used in the magic lantern. Book-plates may be presented direct from the originals."

3356 "Index Notes." 13:29-30, March 1903.
Task of indexing volumes I to XII completed and printing solicited on subscription basis of 100 copies minimum.

3357 "Notes of the Month." 13:30-1, March 1903.
Sale of Richard H. Winslow collection in Dublin.

3358 "Rough List of Legal Book-Plates." S. A. Grundy-Newman. (4) 13:32-5, March 1903.
G and H.

3359 "Recent Book-Plates." (7) 13:36-40, 42, March 1903.
Discusses plates designed by Arnold A. Greig, G. H. McCall, Graham Johnston, Myra Stachan, and Neish of London.

3360 "Book Notice." 13:40, March 1903.
Smith Family name "not unknown to the ancient Egyptians and to the Romans."

3361 "Letters." 13:41, March 1903.
Suggested that topographical list should include owner's date of birth and death and any general particulars for ease of identification.

3362 "Romance of Book-Plates." Charles Dexter Allen. 13:43, March 1903.
Zero weather kept attendance low at Art Club lecture according to *Providence Journal*.

3363 "Tavistock School Label." (1) 13:44, March 1903.
Present schoolhouse built in 1837.

3364 "Mary Alexander Book-Label." 13:44, March 1903.
Correspondent seeks information concerning owner of small leather plate.

3365 "Lectures on Book-Plates with Stereopticon Illustrations." 13:44, March 1903.
Circular announcing availability of Charles Dexter Allen, "terms given on application."

3366 "Notes of the Month." 13:45-8, April 1903.
Epidiascope used in illustration of Mr. Wright's lecture is property of Carl Zeiss of Optical Works, Jena.

3367 "Annual Meeting and Exhibition." 13:48, April 1903.
Twelfth Annual Meeting scheduled for June at Westminster Palace Hotel.

3368 "Rough List of Legal Book-Plates." S. A. Grundy-Newman. 13:50-3, April 1903.
H to L.

3369 "Letters." (1) 13:54-6, April 1903.
States Welsh male descendants take father's first name as their last name thus creating confusion for those unaware of this custom.

3370 "Recent Book-Plates." (5) 13:47,49,56,60, April 1903.
German admirer of Charles Dickens represents porch and entrance of Gadshill on his bookplate; on another Pickwick is seen fishing.

3371 "Frontispiece." (1) 13: Frontispiece, 56, April 1903.
Plate engraved by Martin Tyroff for Wilhelmi Alexandri Balaus.

3372 "London and Middlesex Book-Plates." 13:56-7, April 1903.
Reviews in detail two articles by Alfred Bethune-Baker appearing in *Home Counties Magazine*, edited by W. J. Hardy.

3373 "Burnham Book-Plate." (1) 13:58, April 1903.
Plate by E. D. French including old mill and landscape as in several other Burnham plates.

3374 "Downside Abbey Plate." 13:58, April 1903.
This may be obtained through exchange for another Sherborn plate or by contributing ten shillings to the Library fund.

3375 "Ulster Arts Club." 13:58-60, April 1903.
John Vinycomb gave address on ex libris.

3376 "First List of Subscribers to General Index." 13:60, April 1903.
Fifty-five to date.

3377 "Worcester Art Museum Plate." (1) 13:59-60, April 1903.
Designed by E. D. French.

3378 "Annual Meeting and Exhibition." 13:61, May 1903.
Chippendale plates will be featured in exhibit.

3379 "Notes of the Month." 13:62-3, May 1903.
Eighty page catalog issued for sale of bookplates in Paris.

3380 "Book-Plates Designed by Bruno Heroux, of Leipzig." (4) 13: Frontispiece, 64-5, 67, May 1903.
His plates are "chiefly symbolic and his works certainly rank with those of M. Klinger and O. Greiner."

3381 "Sale of Book-Plates." 13:65-6, May 1903.
Details of sale by Messrs. Puttick and Simpson of unnamed collection; again attendance low and prices not high.

3382 "Book Notice." 13:66-8, May 1903.
Review of *Ancestor*, now in second year.

3383 "*Downside Review*." 13:68, May 1903.
Contains plate executed by C. W. Sherborn.

3384 "Letters." 13:68, May 1903.
Correspondent seeks information about B. and J. Cole, whose work is dated 1700 and 1720 respectively.

3385 "A Polish Book-Plate." W. Roberts. (1) 13:69, May 1903.
Plate of Paul Ksawery Brzostowski, born 1730 and died 1828.

3386 "Sir Nicholas Bacon's Book-Plate." Kirke Lathrop. 13:69–70, May 1903.
"Gerald Leigh. . . . gives a cut of Sir Nicholas Bacon's arms to illustrate the complete achievement of a knight. This cut is the same in every particular as the Bacon plate in the Bagford Collection in the British Museum."

3387 "List of Subscribers to General Index." 13:70, May 1903.
Revised list totals 97.

3388 "Rough List of Legal Book-Plates." S. A. Grundy-Newman. (8) 13:71-6, May 1903.
List continued.

3389 "Notes of the Month." 13:77-8, June 1903.
Twelfth Annual Meeting scheduled June 22nd and 23rd.

3390 "Book-Plate of Colquhoun Club." (1) 13:Frontispiece, 79-81, June 1903.
Dining Club of Royal Society of Literature named for late President, Sir Patrick de Colquhoun; extremely large plate detailed by artist, Philip H. Newman.

3391 "Letter." 13:81, June 1903.
Member intends exhibiting Sir Tho. Tresame Knight plate; asks others to show their impressions which may be variant states.

3392 "Rough List of Legal Book-Plates." S. A. Grundy-Newman. (4) 13:83-7, June 1903.
O-R.

3393 "Jewish Book-Plates." 13:88, June 1903.
Artists May Sandheim and Celia Levetus both design plates of "distinctly Jewish character."

3394 "Abarom or Abarough Book-Plates." 13:88, June 1903.
James C. Getting seeks plates of the above family.

3395 "New Book-Plates of Miss May Sandheim." 13:89, June 1903.
Those of Herbert Bentwick and Sidney Dark described.

3396 "Stuart Arms." 13:89, June 1903.
James C. Getting also interested in bookplates of this family.

3397 "Boston Public Library Book-Plates." (4) 13:79, 81-2, 89, June 1903.
Plates for special collections illustrated including those formed in names of John Adams, George Ticknor, Longfellow, and Allen A. Brown.

3398 "Regimental Library Book-Plate of the King's Own Borderers." (1) 13:90-1, June 1903.
Regiment originally raised in Edinburgh in 1689.

3399 "Two Plymouth Book-Plates." (2) 13:91, June 1903.
Plymouth Public (Proprietary) Library plate engraved by R. Silvester.

3400 "Book-Plate and Seal of the Somersetshire Archaeological and Natural History Society." (1) 13:90,92, June 1903.
Design combines bookplate and seal.

3401 "List of Subscribers to General Index." 13:92, June 1903.
One hundred minimum exceeded.

3402 "Notes of the Month." 13:93-6, July 1903.
Wide variety of periodical articles mentioned.

3403 "Hapton Family and Their Book-Plates." Rev. Wickham M. Birch. (6) 13: 97-100, July 1903.
Earliest plate dates from 1611 and shows twenty-two quarterings.

3404 "Book-Plate of General Sir Reginald Pole-Carew." Arthur J. Jewers. (1) 13: 101-3, July 1903.
Excellent example of work of George W. Eve.

3405 "Book-Plate of Mr. Alexander Price Haig." (1) 13:103, July 1903.
Designed by Graham Johnston, Heraldic Artist to Lyon Court, Edinburgh.

3406 "Recent Book-Plates." (5) 13:96, 104-5,107, July 1903.
Included at Annual Exhibit were plates designed by Hon. Frances Wolseley, daughter of the "well-known Field Marshall."

3407 "Letter." 13:105, July 1903.
Correspondent feels #485 misidentified.

3408 "Ecclesiastical Seals of Cornwall." W. Iago. 13:105-6, July 1903.
Summary of talk given at Royal Institution of Cornwall.

3409 "Rough List of Legal Book-Plates." S. A. Grundy-Newman. 13:107-10, July 1903.
R through T.

3410 "Twelfth Annual Exhibit." 13:111, July 1903.
Alphabetical list of exhibitors.

3411 "Treasurer's Financial Statement." 13:111-2, July 1903.
In six years Treasurer James T. Armstrong has increased funds from a minus eighteen pounds to a favorable balance in excess of 248 pounds!

3412 "Stuart Arms." 13:112, July 1903.
A. J. Jewers states coat given by Getting is for family of Bayly, not Stuart.

3413 "List of Subscribers to General Index." 13:112, July 1903.
Now totals 118.

3414 "Notes of the Month." 13:113-4, August 1903.
Acadiensis continues to contain bookplate articles.

3415 "Catalogue of the Franks Collection." Carnegy Johnson. 13:115-7, August 1903.
First volume, numbering some 13,182 items, off the press; heraldic information furnished as well as date, signature and style.

3416 "Some Book-Plate Notes." Arthur Schomberg. 13:117, August 1903.
Extract from will of Thomas Gore, dated July 1683.

3417 "Rough List of Legal Book-Plates." S. A. Grundy-Newman. 13:118-20, August 1903.
Conclusion of list.

3418 "Annual Exhibition." 13:121-3, August 1903.
Alphabetical list of exhibitors and items shown.

3419 "Ascent to the Book-Plate." J. Rogers Rees. (3) 13:124-5, August 1903.
"The real booklover, in the spirit of proud ownership, beautifies, and at the same time secures unto himself, his possession by a book-plate of characteristic design and occasionally of masterly workmanship."

3420 "Book-Plates of Mr. F. G. House, of London." (5) 13:125, Unnumbered supplement, August 1903.
Some of these were included in recent exhibit.

3421 "New Book-Plate of the Chelsea Public Library." (1) 13:Frontispiece, 125, August 1903.
Motto from Carlyle used: "The true University of these days is a collection of Books."

3422 "Book Notice." 13:126, August 1903.
Review of brochure on "Herald's College and Coats of Arms, regarded from a legal aspect."

3423 "Book-Plates of Boys." Arthur J. Jewers. (2) 13:127, August 1903.
Plates for William Boys, born 1735.

3424 "Zur 'Ex Libris Bewegung.' " 13:128, August 1903.
Reprint in German from German journal.

3425 "List of Subscribers to General Index." 13:128, August 1903.
Latest list.

3426 "Notes of the Month." (1) 13:129-31, September 1903.
Illustrated plate designed by C. E. Eldred for Mary E. Harvey.

3427 "Franks Book-Plates at the British Museum." Alfred A. Bethune-Baker. 13:133-6, September 1903.
"There seems no conclusive reason why each great central library should not aspire to a fairly representative collection of British plates."

3428 "Book-Plate of William Alton." (1) 13:136, September 1903.
Copy here reproduced has been trimmed thus eliminating name of designer and engraver; however, tentative identification made from Fincham.

3429 "Stanley Book-Plate." 13:136, September 1903.
Additional information sought.

3430 "List of Chippendale Plates." 13:137-8, September 1903.
Alphabetical list of plates in recent exhibit.

3431 "Letter." (1) 13:139, September 1903.
Prices from recent "clearance catalog" given.

3432 "Book Notice." 13:140, September 1903.
The Ancestor for July reviewed.

3433 "New Book-Plates by Graham Johnston." (5) 13:130,132,141, September 1903.
Three plates are for members of one family.

3434 "Jewish Book-Plates." 13:141, September 1903.
Several more plates mentioned.

3435 "Rough List of Legal Book-Plates." 13:142-4, September 1903.
Additions and corrections to A and B.

3436 "Notes of the Month." (1) 13:145-8, October 1903.
G. P. Denham designed plate for Royal Albert Memorial Public Library.

3437 "Jewish Book-Plates." Israel Solomons. 13:149-50, October 1903.
Lists the colors and emblems of the twelve tribes of Israel.

3438 "Letters." (1) 13:150-1, October 1903.
One correspondent added to list of West Indian and Jewish plates.

3439 "Book Notice." 13:152, October 1903.
Another issue of *Ancestor* reviewed.

3440 "Book-Plate of Mr. Elkan Adler." (1) 13:frontispiece, 152, October 1903.
A lawyer and collector of Hebrew manuscripts, his plate was designed by May Sandheim.

3441 "Legal Book-Plates." (5) 13:150, 153, October 1903.
Illustrations only.

3442 "List of Chippendale Plates." 13:154-5, October 1903.
Alphabetical list continues.

3443 "Book-Plate of Mr. Henry Lawrence." (1) 13:156, October 1903.
Designed by Florencia R. Sarg and engraved by Will Foster.

3444 "Herts Book-Plates." 13:156, October 1903.
Mentions article in *Home Counties Magazine*.

3445 "Old Scottish Book-Plates." Andrew Ross. 13:157-60, October 1903.
Reprinted from *Scotsman* identifying the engravers of heraldic plates prepared under supervision of Alexander Nisbet.

3446 "Query." 13:160, October 1903.
What is proper place in a bound volume for the bookplate of a second owner?

3447 "Notes of the Month." 13:161-2, November 1903.
Lengthy review of J. J. Guthrie article in *Magazine of Art*.

3448 "Notes on Two Book-Plates." (2) 13:Frontispiece, 163-4, November 1903.
Interesting details of life of Daniel Parsons, who relinquished his title of clergyman upon becoming a Catholic, and his great-uncle Dr. Robert Lovell.

3449 "Julian Marshall." Carnegy Johnson. 13:165, November 1903.
Death of collector whom the author ranked with Sir Wollaston Franks and the Rev. T. W. Carson.

3450 "Book Notice." 13:165-6, November 1903.
Review of biographical pamphlet by Hugh Walker on Warren, Lord

De Tabley, "it is as a poet that Lord De Tabley will be best known to this and succeeding generations."

3451 "Forthcoming Works on Book-Plates." 13:166, November 1903.

Announces Charles E. Goodspeed's series of twelve brochures to be printed on leading designers; George F. Kelly is preparing work on American designers, and *Literary Book-Plates* to be issued by Scott-Thaw.

3452 "Rough List of Legal Book-Plates." S. A. Grundy-Newman. (7) 13:164,167-70, November 1903.

Further additions and corrections, B and C.

3453 "Ex Libris: A Word on the Designing and Designers of Book-Plates." 13:171-3, November 1903.

Quotes from article by Fred Hotchkiss Miner in October issue of *Literary Collector*.

3454 "Masonic Book-Plate." 13:173, November 1903.

Next issue will contain article by Robert Day.

3455 "Pratt Institute." (1) 13:173, November 1903.

Bookplate of training school in industrial and other arts.

3456 "List of Chippendale Plates." 13:174-5, November 1903.

Plates exhibited at annual meeting listed.

3457 "List of Subscribers to General Index." 13:176, November 1903.

Revised list.

3458 "Notes of the Month." (1) 13:177-8, December 1903.

Graham Johnston's plate for Peter Jeffrey Mackie shown.

3459 "Masonic Ex Libris." Robert Day. (8) 13:179-86, December 1903.

Quotes John Hill Burton speaking of C. K. Sharpe: "He was not a black letter man, or a tall copyist, or an uncut man, or a rough edge man, or an Early English Dramatist, or an Elzevirian, or a broadsider, or a pasquinader, or an old brown calf man, or a Grangerite, or a tawny moroccoite, or a gilt topper, or a marbled insider, or an *editio princeps* man."

3460 "Book-Plate of Robert Udney." George Clulow. (1) 13:187-9, December 1903.

Plate after an engraving by Cosway and not originally suspected of being a bookplate.

3461 "Letter." 13:189, December 1903.

Another exhortation to return borrowed books.

3462 "New Book-Plates." 13:189, December 1903.

Packet of plates from J. B. Vervliet of Antwerp which he uses for bibliography, numismatics, periodical press, folklore (two), and a sixth general plate.

3463 "Rough List of Legal Book-Plates." S. A. Grundy-Newman. (1) 13:190-2, December 1903.

Further additions and corrections, C.

3464 "Additional Notes." 13:192, December 1903.
Article on John Hervey plate in *Miscellanea Genealogica et Heraldica*, a "very high-class periodical."

3465 "Sir Albert Woods, Garter." 14:1-2, January 1904.
Death claims one of original members of Ex Libris Society. "A kindly, genial gentleman, he lived a long and useful life, clouded over by much domestic bereavement."

3466 "Exchanges." 14:2, January 1904.
Members are plagued with exchange requests from abroad; too many are "process plates which we do not and cannot value and which are certainly not a fair offer in exchange for a finely-engraved impression from copper."

3467 "Portrait Book-Plates, British and American." (4) 14:3-9, January 1904.
Editor and Sir Arthur Vicars exhibited portraits at annual meeting and have compiled a narrative list.

3468 "Book-Plates of Captain Von Carlshausen." 14:8, January 1904.
Describes five plates sent by German enthusiast.

3469 "Lord De Tabley." 14:9-10, January 1904.
Mr. Peachey taken to task for harsh assessment made of Lord De Tabley in October *Journal*. Contention over relative merits of his work as poet and bookplate authority.

3470 "Book-Plate of Miss Frances Rodd." (1) 14:10, January 1904.
Plate designed by Mrs. Swinnerton Hughes.

3471 "To Our Members. Greeting!" 14:10-11, January 1904.
Design by Graham Johnston.

3472 "Letter." 14:11, January 1904.
Help sought to identify anonymous plates published in earlier issues.

3473 "Notes of the Month." 14:12, January 1904.
Articles in German and French journals described.

3474 "Notes of the Month." 14:13-4, February 1904.
Commenting on *Book and Book-Plates*, edited by J. J. Guthrie, "they regard the book-plate only as a work of art; we regard it from its many-sided character . . . embracing a period of over four centuries."

3475 "Portrait Book-Plates, British and American." (4) 14:15-8, February 1904.
Thus far beards predominate in the portraits! Among them H. W. Fincham.

3476 "List of Masonic Book-Plates." 14:19-21, February 1904.
Descriptive list concluded.

3477 "Modern Book-Plate." 14:22-4, February 1904.
Article reprinted from *Books and Book-Plates* makes barbed remarks at "quasi-learned society" and says, "The rise of the collector, indeed, may be blamed for many difficulties into which art has been plunged."

3478 "Book-Plates Designed by Miss Marjorie Murray." (6) 14:22-4, February 1904.

"It is evident Miss Murray is *en rapport* with her subject . . . ."

3479 "List of Jewish Book-Plates." Israel Solomons. (4) 14:25-7, February 1904.

Alphabetical list cross referenced with Franks number.

3480 "Letter." (1) 14:27-8, February 1904.

George Peachey replies to the De Tabley letter.

3481 "Rough List of Legal Book-Plates." 14:29-31, February 1904.

Further additions and corrections, C through F.

3482 "Book-Plates Designed by Mr. J. R. Blake." (2) 14:32, February 1904.

Plates for Lord Barrymore and Sir Edmund Thomas Bewley.

3483 "Identification Department." (1) 14:21, 32, February 1904.

New numbering begun; experts are W. Bruce Bannerman and James Roberts Brown.

3484 "Notes of the Month." 14:33-4, March 1904.

Review of set of six volumes on Swedish bookplates limited because printed in Swedish; however, profuse illustrations and excellent index indicate valuable addition to ex libris literature.

3485 "Marryat Book-Plates." Cecil T. Davis. (4) 14:35-9, March 1904.

Earliest is for Captain Marryat, writer of sea-tales, born 1792.

3486 "Book-Plate of Chancellor St. George." (1) 14:39, March 1904.

Further information sought concerning owner who was apparently Chancellor of Clogher in 1717.

3487 "Murfield Book Society." 14:39, March 1904.

Details concerning this Society sought and will be published along with its bookplate.

3488 "Beautiful Portrait Plate." (1) 14:frontispiece, 40, March 1904.

Memorial plate bearing the likeness of J. N. C. Davies-Colley, Surgeon at Guy's Hospital, designed by C. W. Sherborn.

3489 "Portrait Book-Plates, British and American." (4) 14:41-3, March 1904.

List concluded and additions solicited.

3490 "American Letter." 14:43-4, March 1904.

Part of round-robin poem composed by bookplate enthusiasts after evening at Wilbur Macey Stone's:

My house is full of book-plates
They're hung upon the wall,
You'll find them in the attic
And tacked up in the hall.

If there are plenty of them
I care not for their looks,
I paste them round most anywhere
Except within my books!

3491 "Book-Plate by C. E. Eldred." (1) 14:44, March 1904.
Plate for Leon Boutry, member of Society of Norman Authors.

3492 "Rough List of Legal Book-Plates." S. A. Grundy-Newman. (1) 14:45-6, March 1904.
F and G.

3493 "Book Notices." (1) 14:47-8, March 1904.
Review of book on Scottish arms; *The Ancestor; Chippendale Book-Plates, English and American*, by James Dorman.

3494 "Notes of the Month." 14:49-50, April 1904.
Annual meeting scheduled for June 28th and 29th.

3495 "American Letter." Charles Dexter Allen. 14:51-5, April 1904.
Alphabetical list of women bookplate designers, also price list from recent auction with high of $9 for Samuel Mather, dated 1755; Edwin Davis French brought exceedingly high prices for a living artist.

3496 "Book-Plates Designed by Ethel Cassels Gillespy." (3) 14:41-3, 55, April 1904.
In many cases engraving as well as design executed by Miss Gillespy.

3497 "Rough List of Legal Book-Plates." S. A. Grundy-Newman. (6) 14:56-7, 63-4, April 1904.
Letter G.

3498 "List of Jewish Book-Plates." Israel Solomons. (5) 14:54-5,58-9,61, April 1904.
F and G.

3499 "Book-Plate of the Port Elizabeth Public Library, South Africa." (1) 14:60, April 1904.
Fred W. Cooper, pupil of Walter Crane, designed plate.

3500 "Portrait Plates." 14:61, April 1904.
E. D. French identified portrait in Holden plate as that of the owner's favorite author, George William Curtis, and mentions other portrait plates he has engraved.

3501 "Book-Plates by Captain Nevile Wilkinson." (1) 14:60, April 1904.
Artist is Coldstream Guard and student at Royal College of Art Engraving School.

3502 "Book-Plate of Mr. Thomas Wainwright." (1) 14:61, April 1904.
Plate shows Barnstaple Grammar School where Wainwright was headmaster for twenty-one years; poet John Gay was an "old boy" of this school.

3503 "Book Notices." 14:62, April 1904.
Review of *Scottish Armorial Seals.*

3504 "St. George Plate." 14:61, April 1904.
Carnegy Johnson, Robert Day, and William Chamney all submit information.

3505 "Book-Plate Sale, April 18, 1904." George Potter, 14:63, April 1904.
"There was not an item in the Catalogue to draw collectors, or to fetch

such a price as was likely to make the auctioneers satisfied with the total result."

3506 "Book-Plate of Sir Charles Hanbury Williams," (1) 14:Frontispiece, 63, April, 1904.

Born in 1708, he was MP, ambassador to various courts, friend of Horace Walpole.

3507 "*General Index*, vol. I to XII." 14:64, April 1904.

Price to be 7s 6d; complete list printed and more subscribers still hoped for.

3508 "Annual Meeting and Exhibition." 14:65, May 1904.

Meeting will be in Royal Medical Chirurgical Society rooms; pictorial plates will be featured in exhibit.

3509 "Notes of the Month." 14:66-8, May 1904.

Charles Dexter Allen is circulating letter to Americans inviting them to join Ex Libris Society and receive the *Journal*, $8 the first year and $5 thereafter. It is still possible to obtain back issues for a full run.

3510 "Late Mr. John Webb Singer." 14:68, May 1904.

"For years we have relied upon him and his estimable wife for assistance at our annual exhibitions."

3511 "Book-Plates of Swire of Cononley." George C. Peachey. (3) 14:69-70, May 1904.

Earliest plate shown is for Samuel Swire, born 1627, died 1701.

3512 "Modern Book-Plate Designers, L. S. Ipsen." Charles Dexter Allen. (4) 14: Frontispiece, 71-3, May 1904.

Artist a Dane, long resident in United States, also designed bookcovers and posters; chronological list of his plates given.

3513 "Book-Plate of William Angus." (1) 14:73,77, May 1904.

Plate combines symbols of psychical research, the motto "Say what you think, not what you think other people think," and small figure representing Prudentia, since owner is manager of Prudential Assurance Company of Edinburgh.

3514 "Book-Plate of Belfast Library." (1) 14:Frontispiece, 73, May 1904.

Designed by John Vinycomb.

3515 "Henry Flitcroft." George Potter. 14:74, May 1904.

Considerable biographical information given.

3516 "Notes on Jewish Book-Plates." 14:74-6, May 1904.

H through M.

3517 "American Letter." Charles Dexter Allen. 14:77-8, May 1904.

Dodd, Mead exhibiting 400 to 500 plates mostly from collection of Miss Marie Gerard Messenger.

3518 "Book Notices." 14:79-80, May 1904.

Book-Plates by Edward Almack is "merely a short gossip on Ex Libris, and must, therefore, not be taken seriously." While perhaps useful to beginners it offers nothing for old collectors, according to reviewer. Light review of *Stamp-Fiends' Raid* by W. E. Imeson.

3519 "Book-Plate of John Shuckburgh." (1) 14:79-80, May 1904.
Owner born 1744, died 1782.

3520 "Annual Meeting and Exhibition." 14:81, June 1904.
Revised program shows exhibit to be open Tuesday evening; banquet at Florence Restaurant.

3521 "Notes of the Month." 14:81-3, June 1904.
Exhibit of plates during current month sponsored by Swan Electric Engraving Company whose various methods of reproduction are used on some of the plates shown.

3522 "Letter." 14:83, June 1904.
Alfred A. Bethune-Baker rebutts George C. Peachey's reply and still feels his "condemnation of Lord de Tabley, then too only recently dead, was altogether uncalled for . . . ."

3523 "Book-Plate of Sir Charles Hanbury Williams." 14:83, June 1904.
Statement of actual ownership of plate which appeared in April issue made at request of Lt.-Colonel Hanbury-Williams.

3524 "Modern Pictorial Book-Plates." James J. Guthrie. 14:85-6, June 1904.
"Even in this little art of the book-plate, those who have created anything specially worthy of attention have done so in their own peculiar fashion."

3525 "Book-Plate Sale, May 30, 1904." George Potter. 14:87-8, June 1904.
Lots described and priced.

3526 "Book-Plates of Miss Bertha E. Saltmarsh." (6) 14:87-9,91,93, June 1904.
Plates of American artist printed through kindness of Eben N. Hewins.

3527 "On Sale Records." 14:90, June 1904.
"I would contend that the average price of a class of plate is of scarcely more use to a collector than the average size of a lump of chalk would be to a geologist."

3528 "Book-Plate of the Royal Naval Barracks, Devonport." (1) 14:90, June 1904.
Charles E. Eldred designed this new plate for the Officers' Library.

3529 "Book Notice." 14:91, June 1904.
Another volume of *The Ancestor* reviewed.

3530 "List of Jewish Book-Plates." (6) 14:84,92,96, June 1904.
N through R.

3531 "Book-Plate of Lewis Hainsworth." (1) 14:Frontispiece, 93, June 1904.
Proof copy furnished by Messrs. Matthews and Brooke.

3532 "Swire Book-Plate." 14:93, June 1904.
Correspondent believes he has a Swire plate not illustrated.

3533 "Rough List of Legal Book-Plates." S. A. Grundy-Newman. 14:94-5, June 1904.

Letter H.

3534 "Book-Plates of James Ward and S. A. Grundy-Newman." (2) 14:96, June 1904.

Ward plate attractive monogram; other portrait plate designed by Miss Gwladys Whittaker.

3535 "Notes of the Month." (1) 14:97-8, July 1904.

Numerous papers mentioned which had notices of Annual Exhibit.

3536 "Letter." 14:98, July 1904.

Bethune-Baker and Peachey dispute continued. Peachey is "against such playing-to-the-gallery tactics."

3537 "Annual Meeting." 14:99-105, July 1904.

Sir James Balfour Paul sent in resignation as President. Banquet menu printed in French; toasts limited to four: The King and the Royal Family, The Ex Libris Society, Visitors and Ladies, The Chairman (Joseph Knight).

3538 "Annual Exhibition." 14:106, July 1904.

Alphabetical list of exhibitors.

3539 "Book-Plate of the University of California." (7) 14:100-5,107, July 1904.

"It is a matter for regret that the art of the engraver was not called in to the aid of the artist, for the plates are merely process plates, and not the best of their kind."

3540 "Exchanges." 14:107, July 1904.

Count Leiningen-Westerburg and Mr. Behrend willing to exchange.

3541 "Two Royal Book-Plates." 14:108, July 1904.

Reprint from *Daily Telegraph* mentions bookplates of Queen and Princess Victoria; all requests to reproduce her plate denied by the Queen, "not wishing to favor one more than another."

3542 "Identification." (1) 14:108, July 1904.

No. 1 of new series.

3543 "Winifred Ingestre." (1) 14:108-9, July 1904.

Illustration only.

3544 "Letter." 14:109, July 1904.

"An enterprising scoundrel has put into circulation" ten copies of old plates "all newly engraved or reproduced in some ingenious manner." Current plate designed by E. D. French for an institution will not be given away; ten proof sets in three colors will be sold at $25 each. "It is . . . a hint to impecunious owners of libraries, of the manner in which they may possess themselves of artistic book-plates at the expense of a few amateurs."

3545 "Jewish Book-Plate." (1) 14:109, July 1904.

Plate of Albert H. Jessel from May article.

3546 "Rough List of Legal Bookplates." S. A. Grundy-Newman. 14:100-12, July 1904.

Alphabetical list continued.

3547 "Notes of the Month." 14:113-4, August 1904.

A few special copies of *General Index* available printed on one side only, for annotations; cost ten shillings and six pence.

3548 "Book-Plate Identification." (1) 14:114,120, August 1904.

No. 1 identified and No. 3 submitted.

3549 "Book-Plate of City of Westminster Public Libraries." (1) 14:Frontispiece, 114, August 1904.

Designed and etched by Walter W. Burgess.

3550 "Book-Plate of Mr. T. B. Senior." (1) 14:114,119, August 1904.

Cherub-angel is taken from painting known as Frari Triptych by Giovanni Bellini.

3551 "New Book-Plates by Graham Johnston." (2) 14:114-5, August 1904.

Plates for Sir Matthew Arthur Bart and Walter Peel.

3552 "Annual Exhibition." (1) 14:115-23, August 1904.

Full list of exhibited materials.

3553 "Book-Plates and Biography." F. E. Marshall. 14:123-4, August 1904.

Interesting confusion of dates has one man killed in a duel at age 119, another born nineteen years after the death of his father.

3554 "Book Notice." 14:124-5, August 1904.

"To make such a collection [bookplates] brings a good time, without a headache next morning," quoted from preface to Zella Dixson's *Concerning Bookplates*.

3555 "List of Festoon Book-Plates." J. F. Verster. (6) 14:126-8, August 1904.

Alphabetical list with description and corresponding Franks number.

3556 "Notes of the Month." 14:129-30, September 1904.

American member comments on E. D. French proof sets: "No one was under any obligation to purchase them."

3557 "Francis Garden, Engraver." Frank E. Marshall. (3) 14:131-3, September 1904.

Considerable confusion concerning engraver who signed himself variously as "Gardner, F.," "F. Gardner," "F. Garden" and "F. Gardin."

3558 "Rough List of Legal Book-Plates." S. A. Grundy-Newman. 14:134-5, September 1904.

K and L.

3559 "Susanna of Our Elders." Frank E. Marshall. (1) 14:136-7, September 1904.

Interesting attempt to identify to which Susanna Smith plate belonged.

3560 "Dudleius Woodbridge. Anglus Americanus." Carnegy Johnson. (1) 14:137, September 1904.

Mentions other similarly designed plates.

3561 "Book Notices." 14:138-9, September 1904.
Includes one on Spanish bookplates, Scottish heraldry, and *The Ancestor* which does not contain specific bookplate articles.

3562 "Book-Plate Identification." (9) 14:Frontispiece, 139, between 140-1, September 1904.
No. 3 identified.

3563 "Wants and Exchanges." 14:139, September 1904.
Three persons name specific wants including German who desires *en-bloc-exchange* (send fifty of one kind for fifty different plates).

3564 "Letters." 14:140-2, September 1904.
Battle over Lord de Tabley continues; query concerning Strawberry Hill engraving from Gray's Odes used as bookplate.

3565 "List of Festoon Plates." J. F. Verster. (2) 14:141-4, September 1904.
B's.

3566 "Notes of the Month." 14:145-6, October 1904.
Regular edition of *General Index* available to members at seven shillings.

3567 "Rough List of Legal Book-Plates." S. A. Grundy-Newman. (2) 14:146-9, 150, October 1904.
L and N.

3568 "Book-Plates of Graham Johnston." (3) 14:Frontispiece, 150, October 1904.
Frontispiece from original copper lent by owner, Major W. H. R. Saunders.

3569 "Gourlay Book-Plate." Arthur J. Jewers. 14:150, October 1904.
Plea for "law to prevent anyone engraving or drawing heraldry unless fully qualified."

3570 "New Book-Plates by Captain Nevil[e] Wilkinson." (2) 14:150, 153, 156, October 1904.
Plates for Sir Edward Hamilton and Alice Bosville.

3571 "Pescod Book-Plate." Arthur J. Jewers. 14:151, October 1904.
Added biographical and heraldic information.

3572 "Book-Plate of Jasper Farmer." 14:151, October 1904.
Farmer was a First Lieutenant in Royal North British Fusileers; the plate "undoubtedly" by Henry Dawkins.

3573 "Coat Armour in America." 14:152-4, October 1904.
Reprinted from *New York Sun*, August 7, 1904; College of Heralds established in England in 1483.

3574 "Book-Plate of Thomas Hood." (1) 14:154, October 1904.
Described as "mock heraldic" in Franks catalogue; probably plate of son who was founder and editor of *Fun*.

3575 "Book-Plate of Sanders." (1) 14:154-5, October 1904.
Plate by new artist, G. B. Sanders.

3576 "Book-Plate Identification." 14:155, October 1904.
Ill health compels James Roberts Brown to relinquish all active work; department to be handled by F. J. Thairlwall.

3577 "Francis Garden, Engraver." Carnegy Johnson. 14:155, October 1904.
More sleuthing to pin down work of multi-signature engraver.

3578 "Book-Plates Included in *Visitation of England and Wales*." 14:156-7, October 1904.
Bookplates appearing in volumes I to XI listed by year.

3579 "Legal Book-Plates." (3) 14:151, 157, October 1904.
Illustrations only.

3580 "List of Festoon Plates." J. F. Verster. 14:158-60, October 1904.
B and C.

3581 "Notes of the Month." 14:161-3, November 1904.
Concluding volume of Franks Catalogue released.

3582 "*Le Blason De Conleurs En Arms*." 14:165, November 1904.
Plate in this volume "has been printed direct from a copper plate on the *verso* of the fly-leaf before the title-page." It is probably for Sir Henry Brooke (1569-1618) described as "but one degree from a fool." He was condemned to death for plot against the king.

3583 "Notes from Wales." 14:166-7, November 1904.
General Index indicates several articles on Wales, Welsh authors and members.

3584 "Book-Plate of C. J. Phillips, Esq." (1) 14:167, November 1904.
Phillips, managing director of firm dealing in foreign stamps, shows his interest in his bookplate.

3585 "Book-Plates of University of California." (2) 14:168, November 1904.
Robert Belcher plate for book on California history, and Temple Emanu-El for Semitic philology and literature.

3586 "Book Notice." 14:169, November 1904.
Still no actual bookplates in *The Ancestor*.

3587 "Garden Chippendales and Others." Frederick Castle. 14:170, November 1904.
Author sees no reason why all Chippendales attributed to Garden "should not be dated before 1746" when he went to America.

3588 "Letters." 14:171, November 1904.
Armorial plate of Cardinal Gozzadini printed in red, black and yellow and "cannot be earlier than the year 1709."

3589 "Notes of the Month." 14:171, November 1904.
"Unprofitable discussion on Lord de Tabley" which has "degenerated into a mere personal dispute upon literary style" has been closed with approval of Council of Society.

3590 "Book-Plate Identification." (7) 14:162-3, 169-70,172, November 1904.

Numbering system reverting to continuation of original, thus new series #1 becomes 537.

3591 "List of Festoon Plates." (9) 14:Frontispiece, 164,171,173-6, November 1904.

C and D.

3592 "W. K. Burford." (1) 14:Frontispiece, December 1904.

Descriptive note will appear next month.

3593 "Notes of the Month." 14:177-8, December 1904.

Some members still owe "7s. 6d., with 3d. in postage" for copies of the *General Index* they have already received.

3594 "Catalogue of the Franks Collection." Carnegy Johnson. 14:179-80, December 1904.

Further details of the wealth of information offered by the Franks Catalogue.

3595 "Sales of Book-Plates in Paris." 14:181-3, December 1904.

Extract from French report, a little more detail on individual plates than in most reports of English sales.

3596 "Book-Plate of McKie of Borgaly." (1) 14:181, 183, December 1904.

Plate by Graham Johnston for Lt.-Colonel King's Own Scottish Borderers.

3597 "Book-Plates for Identification." (8) 14:184-6, December 1904.

Eight identified.

3598 "Letters." 14:187-8, December 1904.

More on Garden, Cardiganshire and from *Welsh Gazette*.

3599 "Book-Plate of Duchess of Roxburghe." (1) 14:188, December 1904.

Design adapted by Capt. N. R. Wilkinson from printer's mark of Gabriel Giolito (Venice, circa 1547) and printed on paper dated 1690.

3600 "Book-Plate of Edwin H. Halthouse." (1) 14:179,188, December 1904.

Plate designed by Miss E. M. Cooper, daughter of J. D. Cooper, wood engraver.

3601 "Book-Plate in Fiction." 14:188, December 1904.

Quote concerning a bookplate from historical novel by Albert Louis Cotton titled *The Company of Death;* author is member of Ex Libris Society.

3602 "Notes from Amsterdam." J. F. Verster. (1) 14:189, December 1904.

An exhibit including bookbindings and bookplates held at Middleburg.

3603 "List of Festoon Plates." J. F. Verster. (3) 14:178,183,186,190-2, December 1904.

D and E.

3604 "Irish Book-Plates." (1) 15:Frontispiece, January 1905.

Plate for Donegal gives notice of article in next issue.

3605 "Notes of the Month." 15:1-2, January 1905.
Reference to several foreign journals.

3606 "Eighteenth-Century Leicestershire Church Library." J. Paul Rylands. (1) 15:3-5, January 1905.
Library of Thomas Bate left to the church by his will dated October 23, 1727.

3607 "Book-Plate Identification." (9) 15:5,8-9, January 1905.
Seven identified.

3608 "List of Festoon Plates." (1) 15:2,6-7, January 1905.
E and F.

3609 "Rough List of Legal Book-Plates." 15:10-3, January 1905.
N to P.

3610 "Book-Plate of Mr. Charles H. Dymond." (1) 15:14, January 1905.
Plate designed by C. E. Eldred.

3611 "Exchanges." 15:14-6, January 1905.
Member each from France, Austria and Germany and two from England willing to exchange.

3612 "Book-Plate Artist's Impressions." 15:14-5, January 1905.
Lengthy quote from *Harold Nelson: His Book of Book-Plates*.

3613 "Book-Plate of Royal Naval College, Osborne, Isle of Wight." (1) 15:15, January 1905.
Plate for Cadets' Library designed by Charles E. Eldred.

3614 "Notes of the Month." (1) 15:16, January 1905.
Charles A. Massey issued catalog of 2500 bookplate items.

3615 "Notes of the Month." 15:17-8, February-March 1905.
"Some lots of book-plates made remarkable prices" at recent Edinburgh sale.

3616 "Price-Cleveland Book-Plate." A. H. Arkle. (1) 15:19-20, February-March 1905.
Anonymous plate identified, Franks No. 24,137.

3617 "James Pierot—An Interesting Plate." Edwin S. Potter, M.D. (1) 15:20-2, February-March 1905.
Pierot noted as having survived being "walled up" for twenty-one days without food or water; survival due "to a hen who daily laid an egg in the recess of the small window of the cell."

3618 "Book-Plate of Ludwig Saeng." (1) 15:18,22, February-March 1905.
Designed by German artist, Paul Bürck.

3619 "Book-Plates Designed by Mr. F. G. House." (4) 15:22, between 28-9, February-March 1905.
Insert presented by Messrs. Truslove and Hanson for whom artist works.

3620 "Exchanges." 15:22, February-March 1905.
Two members have E. D. French plates for exchange.

3621 "Irish Book-Plates in Order of Counties." William Chamney. (2) 15:23-5, February-March 1905.
Begins with Co. Antrim.

3622 "Book-Plates for Identification." (4) 15:26,29,30, February-March 1905.
Seven identified.

3623 "Rough List of Legal Book-Plates." S. A. Grundy-Newman. 15:27-8, February-March 1905.
Further additions and corrections.

3624 "Book-Plate of James Paine." (1) 15:29, February-March 1905.
Plate of architect who lived from 1725 to 1789; in 1783 was high sheriff for Surrey.

3625 "Letters." 15:30, February-March 1905.
Another plate forged by "Pertinax" is that of "Philip Ludwell of Greenspring in Virginia Esqr."

3626 "List of Festoon Plates." J. F. Verster. 15:31-2, February-March 1905.
F and G.

3627 "Alfred L. Richman." (1) 15:Frontispiece, April-May 1905.
Illustration only.

3628 "Notes of the Month." 15:33-5, April-May 1905.
Pamphlet from Stockholm on plates of Hasse W. Tullbergs by Axel L. Romdahl.

3629 "Death of Mr. James Roberts Brown." George Potter. 15:35, April-May 1905.
One of founders of Ex Libris Society, with W. H. Fincham initiated Identification Page, Exchange Club owes its inception to him. He was heard to say more than once that he found the Franks' Catalogue "as good as a three-volume novel."

3630 "Festoon Book Plates." (4) 15:36, April-May 1905.
Illustrations only.

3631 "Modern Book-Plate Designers, Mr. Harold Nelson." (4) 15:37-40, April-May 1905.
List of thirty-eight plates selected as "worthy of notice" from an artistic point of view.

3632 "New Book-Plate of the Library of the University of California." 15:40, April-May 1905.
Plate designed by Mrs. A. R. Wheelan.

3633 "Letter." 15:40, April-May 1905.
Carnegy Johnson hopes Charles Dexter Allen's "Supplemental List of Early American Book-Plates" will include updated annotations on those already listed.

3634 "Shakespeare's Coat of Arms." J. Vinycomb. (3) 15:41-3, April-May 1905.
College of Arms has two drafts of the intended grants of 1596 and 1599.

3635 "Book-Plate Identification." (6) 15:43,49, April-May 1905.
Five identified.

3636 "Book-Plates of Counties." 15:43, April-May 1905.
Correspondent suggests a number of people "undertake the whole country, county by county" to compile an exhaustive list.

3637 "Irish Book-Plates in Order of Counties." William Chamney. (1) 15:44-6, April-May 1905.
County Armagh.

3638 "Old Plates." 15:47-8, April-May 1905.
Correspondent suggests reproducing interesting old plates, both signed and unsigned.

3639 "Sale of Book-Plates." George Potter. 15:48 April-May 1905.
"[There were] few plates of exceptional interest or value."

3640 "List of Festoon Plates." J. F. Verster. 15:50-1, April-May 1905.
G and H.

3641 "American Book-Plate Designers." (1) 15:52-3, April-May 1905.
Series of twelve monographs issued by Trousdale Press; the "little brochures are charming." Commends Bird for not doing process work which is so often found in America.

3642 "New Library Book-Plate." (1) 15:53, April-May 1905.
Plate for Public Library of District of Columbia.

3643 "Price-Cleveland Plate." 15:53, April-May 1905.
Question about same plate but "without the tinted backgrounds."

3644 "Rough List of Legal Book-Plates." S. A. Grundy-Newman. 15:54-6, April-May 1905.
R and S of additions and corrections.

3645 "Notes of the Month." 15:57-8, June 1905.
Letter to members delinquent in dues stating that "it should not be necessary for the officers of the Society to expend a considerable portion of a Member's subscription in postage-stamps on application for payment."

3646 "Irish Book-Plates, in Order of Counties." William Chamney. (2) 15:58-9, June 1905.
County Carlow.

3647 "Festoon Book-Plates." (4) 15:60,68, June 1905.
Illustrations only.

3648 "J. Winfred Spenceley's Book-Plates." 15:61-3, June 1905.
Review of descriptive checklist issued by Trousdale Press includes 135 plates and "as a frontispiece there is a capital portrait of Mr. Spenceley."

3649 "Book-Plates for Identification." (6) 15:64-5, June 1905.
Four identified.

3650 "Book-Plate of Alfred L. Richman." 15:65, June 1905.
Frontispiece for last issue, plate designed by James J. Guthrie.

3651 "Gift Plate of Thomas, 8th Earl of Pembroke and 5th of Montgomery." Carnegy Johnson. (1) 15:65, June 1905.
Plate engraved by Simon Gribelin about 1708-9 when Lord Pembroke was Lord High Admiral of Great Britain and Ireland.

3652 "Book-Plates of Mr. John Vinycomb." (4) Frontispiece, between 60-1, and 68-9, 66, June 1905.
Vinycomb was for many years "principal artist for Messrs. Marcus Ward & Co., Belfast."

3653 "Book-Plate of Mr. Percy Siddons Hoyte." (1) 15:66, June 1905.
"There is nothing very distinctive about it, but [it] is a fair specimen of Mr. Eldred's nautical and semi-nautical designs."

3654 "*A Little Book of Book-Plates*," 15:66-7, June 1905.
One issue of the *Elf*, "a little publication of a somewhat erratic character," is devoted to bookplates of James J. Guthrie who edits this publication.

3655 "Book-Plate of Louise Gosford." (1) 15:67, June 1905.
Designed by W. P. Barrett who has executed plates for several members of the Royal Family.

3656 "Book-Plate of P. D. Huet, 1630." Arthur J. Jewers. 15:67-8, June 1905.
A classical scholar who took Holy Orders at forty-six; he wrote his memoirs in Latin.

3657 "Book-Plate of Mr. Arthur M. Robinson." (1) 15:68, June 1905.
Plate executed by Gilbert P. Gamon, based on a stained-glass panel designed by the same artist.

3658 "Rough List of Legal Book-Plates." S. A. Grundy-Newman. 15:69-71, June 1905.
Further corrections S to V.

3659 "Ex Libris Society." 15:72, June 1905.
Notice of Annual Meeting and exhibit.

3660 "Notes of the Month." 15:73-4, July-August 1905.
Note on catalog offering library of late James Roberts Brown; his bookplate collection held by family for sale in one lot.

3661 "Selwyn College Library." Cecil T. Davis. (3) 15:75-6,87, July-August 1905.
Named after Bishop of New Zealand, contains 15,000 books.

3662 "Annual General Meeting and Exhibition." 15:77-8, July-August 1905.
Usual reports; Charles Dexter Allen again resigns, perhaps to be replaced by Frank E. Marshall of Philadelphia.

3663 "Ex Libris Exhibition, 1905." (2) 15:Frontispiece, 79-84, July-August 1905.
Items exhibited by each member listed.

3664 "Book-Plate Identification." (8) 15:85,88-9, July-August 1905.
Four identified.

3665 "Book-Plate of Dorothy Allan." (1) 15:85, July-August 1905.
Plate of spinster aunt of "noted antiquary George Allan."

3666 "Book-Plate of Nicholas Robinson, Esq." (1) 15:86, July-August 1905.
Combination heraldic and pictorial plate explained.

3667 "New Book-Plates of Graham Johnston." (4) 15:between 76-7,80-1,82,85, July-August 1905.
All heraldic plates.

3668 "Book-Plates of Mr. and Mrs. W. B. Whall." (2) 15:87, July-August 1905.
Plates executed by Messrs. Barnicott & Pearce from the owner's rough sketches.

3669 "List of Festoon Plates." J. F. Verster. 15:90-1, July-August 1905.
H's.

3670 "Ex Libris Society." 15:92, July-August 1905.
Financial statement.

3671 "Notes of the Month." 15:93-4, September 1905.
Mrs. Rath-Merrill reports sale of remarque and India proofs of Ohio Alcove bookplate for the Manila Memorial Library has resulted in proceeds over $400.

3672 "Some Australian Book-Plates." John Lane Mullins. (6) 15:95-101, September 1905.
Article, reprinted from Sydney publication *Art and Architecture*, quotes Elbert Hubbard: "And so a fad, which gives joy without headache, peace without stupor, and friends who are not rivals, is worth cultivating; its basis is human sympathy, and its excuse for being—book-plates."

3673 "Book-Plates for Identification." (4) 15:102-3, September 1905.
Department now conducted by W. Bruce Bannerman and F. J. Thairlwall.

3674 "Comyn Book-Plate." 15:103, September 1905.
Identity of plate's owner sought.

3675 "Letter." (1) 15:103-4, September 1905.
Delight of discovering the bottom plate when top three peeled off.

3676 "New Book-Plate of Mr. F. G. House." (1) 15:104, September 1905.
Plate for Frederick Lucking who is "evidently interested in the mysticism and lore of ancient Egypt."

3677 "Book-Plate of Sir James Balfour Paul." (1) 15:Frontispiece, 104, September 1905.
Owner is "one of the most erudite and authoritative heralds now living."

3678 "Book-Plate of George Robert Hewlett." (1) 15:94,105, September 1905.
Plate designed and etched by Mrs. M. E. Rath-Merrill.

3679 "Book-Plates by Mr. Ern Hill." (4) 15:between 104-5,105, September 1905.
Plates were in annual exhibit.

3680 "Book-Plate of George Putnam Upton." (1) 15:105, September 1905.
Designed by Mrs. Amy S. Mulligan of Chicago.

3681 "Book-Plate of Katherine Kennedy Erskine." (1) 15:105-6, September 1905.
Designed by May Sandheim.

3682 "Queries." 15:106, September 1905.
Four questions of identification posed by S. A. Grundy-Newman.

3683 "Irish Book-Plates in Order of Counties." William Chamney. (1) 15:107-8, September 1905.
County Cavan.

3684 "Notes of the Month." 15:109-11, October 1905.
Willi Geiger is an artist whose "designs are intensely original, in fact some of them are grotesque."

3685 "Dated Plates." Carnegy Johnson. 15:112-6, October 1905.
Dates range from 1687 to 1709 for "Brighton" plates unrecorded in Hamilton's list.

3686 "Letter." 15:116, October 1905.
Information sought on James Elmy, a tanner at Beccles.

3687 "An Uncommon Book-Plate: Mr. James Arrow, of Clapham." (1) 15:117, October 1905.
Thirteen arrows on which are mottoes from the Bible, Shakespeare and Chaucer, each with the word *arrow*.

3688 "Description of the Book-Plate of Dom Walter Mackey, O.S.B." (1) 15:118, October 1905.
Bookplate collection at Downside Abbey, near Bath, started by Daniel Parsons.

3689 "Book-Plate of Rev. G. R. J. Fletcher." (1) 15:111,118, October 1905.
A bold design by Harold Nelson.

3690 "Rough List of Legal Book-Plates." S. A. Grundy-Newman. 15:119-21, October 1905.
Further corrections and additions.

3691 "List of Festoon Plates." J. F. Verster. 15:122-4, October 1905.
H and J.

3692 "Notes of the Month." 15:125-6, November 1905.
Mostly foreign journals.

3693 "Irish Book-Plates, in Order of Counties." William Chamney. 15:127-30, November 1905.
County Clare.

3694 "Notes on a Medical Book-Plate." George C. Peachey. 15:130, November 1905.

Interesting comments on advantages of "unqualified quack[s]" so long as they do not pose as "registered medical men."

3695 "List of Chippendale Book-plates Not Included in the Catalogue of the Franks Collection." Frederick Cattle. (8) 15:126,131-4, November 1905.
Alphabetical list.

3696 "Interesting Book-Plate for the Brimfield Library, Massachusetts." (1) 15: 135-6, November 1905.
Reprinted from article by M. Anna Tarbell in *Springfield Republican* of May 20, 1903.

3697 "Book-Plate of Miss May Sandheim." (1) 15:133,136, November 1905.
Designed for Winifred Pawling.

3698 "Letter." 15:137, November 1905.
More on the Elmy question.

3699 "Book-Plate of Ernest Hill." (1) 15:137, November 1905.
Designers own plate received award at Royal College of Arts in a national competition.

3700 "Rough List of Legal Book-Plates." S. A. Grundy-Newman. 15:138-40, November 1905.
Corrections W to Y.

3701 "Book Plates for Identification." (1) 15:140, November 1905.
Only one for identification.

3702 "Notes of the Month." (1) 15:141-2, December 1905.
Council passed motion to publish names of members delinquent in dues for 1905 or earlier years.

3703 "Book-Plate of Jesus College, Oxford." J. Henderson Smith. (8) 15:143-7, December 1905.
Many of the plates for Oxford colleges were engraved between 1700 and 1705 and are still in use.

3704 "Book-Plate Identification." (2) 15:147,154, December 1905.
One identified.

3705 "List of Chippendale Book-Plates not Included in the Catalogue of the Franks Collection." Frederic Cattle. (8) 15:148-52, December 1905.
B's.

3706 "Baker Plates Not in the Franks Collection." Alfred A. Bethune-Baker. 15: 153-4, December 1905.
Another twenty-five plates added to fifty-five in Franks collection.

3707 "List of Festoon Plates." J. F. Verster. 15:155-6, December 1905.
J and K.

3708 "Notes of the Month." 16:1-2, January 1906.
Comments on Andrew Lang, who years ago "could not see anything that was good" in the Ex Libris Society.

3709 "Book-Plates." Andrew Lang. 16:3-6, January 1906.
Mr. Lang tempers somewhat his condemnation of bookplate collectors since hearing Sir Augustus Franks, "a man of greatest learning," was the "chief collector of book-plates."

3710 "Notes on an Early Australian Book-Plate." Carnegy Johnson. (1) 16:7-8, January 1906.
Plate for Osmond Gilles who came to "this colony in 1836."

3711 "Noteworthy Sale of Book-Plates." George Potter. 16:8-9, January 1906.
Collection of James Roberts Brown sold for £540 or 16,000 plates at rate of thirty-four pounds per thousand.

3712 "Wallace Book-Plate." (1) 16:Frontispiece, 10, January 1906.
Designed by Graham Johnston.

3713 "Book-Plate of Earl of Durham." (2) 16:8-10, January 1906.
Etching by Captain Nevile R. Wilkinson.

3714 "New Book-Plate by Miss Mary C. Lawson." (1) 16:10, January 1906.
Artist's address furnished for any who might desire her services.

3715 "Book-Plate of Mr. Percy F. Atkin." (1) 16:5,11, January 1906.
Portrait of Thackeray by Eyre Crowe.

3716 "New Book-Plate by Miss E. Cassels Gillespy." (1) 16:3,11, January 1906.
Presentation plate for Botolph Claydon Public Library.

3717 "Exchanges." 16:11, January 1906.
Mrs. Mary E. Rath-Merrill will exchange copies of the Ohio Alcove gift plate she designed.

3718 "List of Chippendale Book-Plates Not Included in the Catalogue of the Franks Collection." (9) 16:12-6, January 1906.
B and C.

3719 "Editorial Notes." 16:17, February 1906.
Special offer to new members will be back volumes of *Journal* (whole set of sixteen) at five guineas. Current members may fill in missing issues at ten shillings per volume.

3720 "Notes of the Month." 16:17-8, February 1906.
Several foreign journals mentioned.

3721 "Book-Plate of Grylls." Archd. C. Glynn. (6) 16:19-22, February 1906.
William Grylls of Tavistock had his arms confirmed to him in 1575.

3722 "Cole Book-Plate." 16:22, February 1906.
In folio volume dated 1611 is "printed from a small wood block his arms and crest on an oval."

3723 "List of Festoon Plates." J. F. Verster. 16:23-4, February 1906.
K and L.

3724 "Official Notices." 16:25, March-April 1906.
Annual exhibition will be May 31 and June 1st.

3725 "Notes of the Month." 16:25-6, March-April 1906.
Official ex libris journal of Spain (Barcelona) "is a capital production."

3726 "Book-Plate of Wadham College, Oxford." J. Henderson Smith. (6) 16:27-30, March-April 1906.
It would appear that engraver of "Brighton" volume in Franks Collection "worked not on commission but on speculation, engraving arms of anyone he thought likely prospect."

3727 "English Royal Heraldry." 16:31-2, March-April 1906.
Reprint from News-Letter of Bibliographical Society.

3728 "Book-Plates for Identification." (8) 16:33,37-8,46, March-April 1906.
F. J. Thairlwall and W. Bruce Bannerman handling this department.

3729 "List of Chippendale Book-Plates Not Included in the Catalogue of Franks Collection." 16:34-6, March-April 1906.
C and D.

3730 "Book-Plate of Mr. H. Plowman, F.S.A." (1) 16:37, March-April 1906.
Designed by Seymour Lucas.

3731 "Book-Plate of Late Mr. Julian Marshall." W. Bolton. 16:39-41, March-April 1906.
60,000 separate bookplates to be sold.

3732 "Correspondence." 16:42, March-April 1906.
London publisher issuing "Panel Books" which will have "a specially designed book-plate affixed to the inside of each cover."

3733 "Book-Plate for the Thomas Greenwood Library for Librarians." (1) 16:43-6, March-April 1906.
Donation of 10,000 volumes which "may be of professional service to librarians."

3734 "Lyon Office, Edinburgh." 16:47-8, March-April 1906.
As early as 1377 there is mention in the records of a Lyon Herald.

3735 "New Book-Plate." (1) 16:48, March-April 1906.
Animal artist, E. Caldwell, designed plate featuring African game for Henry Anderson Bryden, author of books on travel and sport.

3736 "Notes of the Month." 16:49-51, May 1906.
Mrs. Rath-Merrill, who studied under William Morris, is member of Needle Crafters' Society.

3737 "Book-Plates for Identification." (3) 16:52, May 1906.
Three offered for identification.

3738 "Canadian Book-Plates." 16:53-4, May 1906.
Extracts from Canadian journal, *Acadiensis*.

3739 "Exchanges." 16:54, May 1906.
Owners of a Sherborn and an Eve willing to exchange with others having plates by these two artist-engravers.

3740 "Chippendale Book-Plates." (7) 16:55-6,60, May 1906.
Illustrations only.

3741 "Irish Book-Plates, in Order of Counties." William Chamney. (3) 16:57-9, May 1906.
County Cork.

3742 "On General Exchanges." 16:60, May 1906.
Collectors besieged by plates "of little thought, less fitness, and as cheap as a process can make it" are advised to return them "postage unpaid."

3743 "New Book-Plates." (2) 16:60, May 1906.
Pet as well as ancestral home included by artist, Major E. Bengough Ricketts.

3744 "List of Festoon Plates." J. F. Verster. 16:61-2, May 1906.
L and M.

3745 "Suggestions for a Book-Plate." John Vinycomb. 16:63, May 1906.
"We conceive the book-plate should have a direct and personal bearing, and to be of an enduring and not of a temporary character."

3746 "New Book-Plate by Miss Mary C. Lawson." (1) 16:63, May 1906.
Plate for Worcester High School for Girls.

3747 "Ex Libris Society." 16:64, May 1906.
Annual exhibit will feature American bookplates, bookplates by American artists, and ladies' plates.

3748 "Notes of the Month." 16:65, June 1906.
Deaths of Russell Spokes and A. Godwin Fowles lamented.

3749 "Exhibition 1906." 16:66,68, June 1906.
In spite of unfortunate circumstances surrounding date of exhibit being in the "week of the Derby and the Oaks, on the eve of Whitsuntide," plus clashing with the Marshall sale at Sotheby's, nearly 200 signed the visitor's book.

3750 "After the Sale." 16:69, June 1906.
Lively account of Marshall sale.

3751 "Letter." 16:69, June 1906.
Carnegy Johnson seeks scarce examples of bookpile bookplates to include in his updating of Sir Arthur Vicar's 1893 list.

3752 "Mr. Julian Marshall's Book-Plates." (9) 16:67, 70-4, June 1906.
Reprint from June 1902 article in *Connoisseur*.

3753 "New Book-Plates: Book-Plate of Alfred Molony." (1) 16:Frontispiece, 74, June 1906.
Design by Mrs. P. Swinnerton Hughes.

3754 "Book-Plate Identification." 16:74, June 1906.
Three identified.

3755 "Sale of the Book-Plates of the Late Mr. Julian Marshall." George Potter. 16:75-6, June 1906.

"The presence of a prominent American collector doing even more to send the prices up . . . some twenty-five per cent."

3756 "New Book-Plates by Mr. Ernest Hill." (4) 16:76, between 76-7, June 1906.

One features a cricketeer, stanza of music, and emblems of boating, music and tennis.

3757 "New Book-Plates: Sir Richard Tangye, K.T." (1) 16:76, June 1906.

Portrait plate.

3758 "List of Chippendale Book-Plates Not Included in the Catalogue of the Franks Collection." Frederic Cattle. (4) 16:77-9, June 1906.

D and E.

3759 "Book Review." 16:80, June 1906.

John Vinycomb's *Fictitious and Symbolic Creatures in Art* with special reference to their use in British heraldry; "book is certain to become a standard work of reference for student of heraldry."

3760 "Book-Plate of Ernst Paulus." (1) 16:80, June 1906.

Portrait plate of new member of Ex Libris Society.

3761 "Notes of the Month." 16:81-4, July 1906.

References from foreign, American and British journals.

3762 "Exhibition, 1906." (4) 16:85-92, July 1906.

Items exhibited by each member listed.

3763 "New Book-Plates: Dr. T. N. Brushfield, F.S.A." (1) 16:92, July 1906.

"One of best authorities living on the history of Sir Walter Raleigh" features this "Devon worthy" on his bookplates.

3764 "New Book-Plate by Mrs. P. Swinnerton Hughes." (1) 16:93, July 1906.

Designed for Arthur Fitzhenry Townshend.

3765 "Book-Plates Designed by Mrs. Jane E. Cook, Wantage." (3) 16:94-5, July 1906.

Five plates described.

3766 "New Book-Plates by Frank G. House." (4) 16:95-6, July 1906.

Plates described.

3767 "Some Book-Plates Designed, Engraved and Printed by Charles E. Dawson." (15) 16:8 unnumbered pages, July 1906.

One tipped in plate; all printed in green ink.

3768 "Notes of the Month." 16:97-8, August-September 1906.

Deferred Annual Meeting will be held October 30th.

3769 "Joannes Baptista Jacobs Engraving." Willoughby A. Littledale. (1) 16:99-100, August-September 1906.

Question as to whether actually portrait bookplate or tradesman's business card.

3770 "Ex Dono Plate of Richard Baylie, Dean of Salisbury and President of S.

John's College, Oxford." Carnegy Johnson. (1) 16:101, August-September 1906.
Plate bears date 1668.

3771 "Book-Plate of Chetham's Library, Manchester." (1) 16:101, August-September 1906.
Established in 1653, it now has 53,000 volumes.

3772 "Joseph Holland, 1585." George H. Viner. (1) 16:102-5, August-September 1906.
Details on manuscript and bookplate purchased at Marshall sale; plate has "arms filled-in in pencil" and signature of owner.

3773 "New Book-Plate by Mr. Harold Nelson." (1) 16:105, August-September 1906.
Allegorical plate for M. Nelson depicts knight in full armour.

3774 "Irish Book-Plates, in Order of Counties." William Chamney. 16:106-7, August-September 1906.
County Cork continued.

3775 "Book-Plates for Identification." (4) 16:108, August-September 1906.
Four for identification only.

3776 "Wright Book-Plates." Arthur J. Jewers. (7) 16:109-14, August-September 1906.
Plates of 17th and 18th century "set out almost an epitome of biographical data" (place and date as well as full name).

3777 "Book-Plates Designed by Mrs. Pickford Waller." (3) 16:115, August-September 1906.
Illustrations only include plates for Sybil and Maud Waller.

3778 "List of Festoon Plates." J. F. Verster. 16:116-7, August-September 1906.
M's.

3779 "New Book-Plate." (1) 16:118, August-September 1906.
Plate of Bertram L. Dyer, librarian in Kimberley, South Africa; one border is the Welsh national emblem, the leek.

3780 "*Scots Peerage*." 16:118, August-September 1906.
Review of first volume of "definitive Peerage of Scotland."

3781 "Book-Plates." (2) 16:118, August-September 1906.
Plates for Eva M. Spielmann and Mary Caroline Lawson.

3782 "Richard & Nora Ladenburg." (1) 16:Frontispiece, October-November 1906.
Article in July issue, page 95.

3783 "Notes of the Month." 16:119-22, October-November 1906.
Official announcement of death of Count Leiningen-Westerburg reprinted from German Ex Libris journal.

3784 "Book-Plates for Identification." (4) 16:123, October-November 1906.
Illustrations only.

3785 "Wright Book-Plates." (8) 16:124-30, October-November 1906.
Plates presented under arrangement of similarity of arms.

3786 "New Book-Plate of Miss Mary C. Lawson." 16:130, October-November 1906.
Plate illustrated in last issue.

3787 "Irish Book-Plates, In Order of Counties." William Chamney. 16:131-3, October-November 1906.
County Cork, D-H.

3788 "Letter." 16:134, October-November 1906.
Sources and costs given for supplies to mount and house a bookplate collection; stamp hinges suggested or Higgins' Photo-Mounter.

3789 "Notes of the Month." 16:135-7, December 1906.
Death of Edwin Davis French noted.

3790 "Book-Plate Identification." 16:137, December 1906.
Four identified.

3791 "Wright Book-Plates." (4) 16:138-41, 151, December 1906.
Article concluded.

3792 "Letter." (1) 16:Frontispiece, 141, December 1906.
Bookplate (?) with crest and arms of Tittlebat Titmouse used as frontispiece to popular novel, *Ten Thousand A Year* by Samuel Warren.

3793 "Irish Book-Plates, In Order of Counties." William Chamney. 16:142-5, December 1906.
Alphabetical list continued.

3794 "Dobson Book-Plate." (1) 16:146, December 1906.
Plate for Rev. J. Dobson is example of work of J. Skinner of Bath.

3795 "Book-Plate of Honble George Sidney Herbert." 16:146, December 1906.
Executed from pen and ink drawing by Capt. Nevile Wilkinson.

3796 "List of Chippendale Book-Plates Not Included in the Catalogue of the Franks Collection." Frederic Cattle. (5) 16:141,147-9, December 1906.
F.

3797 "Bickham Jr." 16:150, December 1906.
Quote from secondhand book catalog.

3798 "Ex Libris Society." 16:150, December 1906.
Statement of receipts and payments.

3799 "Edwin Davis French." (1) 17:Frontispiece, 3-4, January 1907.
Death came December 8, 1906 to this unexcelled artist. He was a "facile linguist" interested in universal language; secretary of the Volapuk Society and active in Esperanto and Idiom Neutral.

3800 "Notes of the Month." 17:4-6, January 1907.
California Book-Plates, edited by Sheldon Cheney, "is a very unpretentious little periodical . . . ."

3801 "Bookplates from South Africa." (2) 17:6-7, January 1907.
Work of young art student, Julia G. Gordon.

3802 "Bookplates of Miss Violet Hardy." (1) 17:6,8, January 1907.
Designed by A. Hardy and engraved by Wyon.

3803 "Bookplate of the Cosmos Club." (1) 17:6,8, January 1907.
Designed by William Fuller Curtis and engraved by Edwin D. French for Cosmos Club in Washington, D.C.

3804 "Notes on a Collection of Book-Plates by Richard Mountaine and William Haskall (Both of Winchester) and on Some Book-Plates Attributed to William Henshaw." C. Davies Sherborn. 17:9-12, January 1907.
Checklist of eighty-five for Mountaine, twenty-six for Haskall, and nineteen trade cards.

3805 "Notes of the Month." 17:13-5, February 1907.
Lengthy quotes from article in *London Opinion*.

3806 "Book-Plates of Aug. F. Ammann." (7) 17:Frontispiece, 15-8, between 24-5, February 1907.
A large plate was designed by Hasse W. Bullberg of Stockholm.

3807 "Mr. Sherborn's List of Montaine and Haskall Book-Plates." F. J. Thairlwall. 17:16,19, February 1907.
Important classification of plates previously attributed to Wm. Hogarth, Wm. Hibbert, and Wm. Henshaw.

3808 "Bickham." Arthur Schomberg. 17:19-20, February 1907.
More secondhand book catalog entries useful in gathering biographical details on early bookplate engravers and artists.

3809 "New Book-Plate by Mr. E. C. Eldred." (1) 17:18,20, February 1907.
Curious plate for Miss A. M. Minninick pictures a stone in a valley which is the meaning of her name in Celtic.

3810 "Book-Plates by Mr. Wilfred Drake." (4) 17:20-1, February 1907.
Drake of "the well-known firm of Stained Glass Artists," features a skull in three of the four designs illustrated.

3811 "Book-Plate of Strachey." (1) 17:20-2, February 1907.
Plate for Dame Strachey designed by Graham Johnston.

3812 "Exchanges." 17:22, February 1907.
Interesting letter, dated February 21, 1890, from Augustus W. Franks to a correspondent giving him additions for his early dated plates and wishing to exchange duplicates.

3813 "Book-Plate of Lynn, Mass., USA, Public Library." (1) 17:24, February 1907.
Engraved by Sydney Smith.

3814 "List of Festoon Plates." J. F. Verster. 17:25-6, February 1907.
M and N.

3815 "List of Chippendale Book-Plates Not Included in the Catalogue of the Franks Collection." Frederic Cattle. (3) 17:23,27-8, February 1907.
G.

3816 "Announcements." 17:29, March 1907.
Annual meeting scheduled for June 27th and 28th; exhibit to feature Colonial bookplates, heraldic curiosities, erroneous or spurious heraldry, and armorial bindings.

3817 "Notes From All Sources." 17:29-30, March 1907.
Bookplates exhibited by Royal Society of Painters, Etchers and Engravers.

3818 "American Notes." 17:30-1, March 1907.
Title of *California Book-Plates* changed to *Book-Plate Booklet*.

3819 "California Book-Plates—A Survey." 17:34-5, March 1907.
Reprinted from November 1906 issue of *California Book-Plates*.

3820 "Irish Book-Plates." (6) 17:36-7,40, March 1907.
Illustrations only.

3821 "New Book-Plates by Mr. Graham Johnston." 17:32-3,38-9, March 1907.
Plates for Cadell, Tonge, and Talbot.

3822 "New Book-Plates by F. G. House." (3) 17:between 34-5,38, between 38-9, March 1907.
Plates for Miss Astley, Gladys Jameson, and Lady Cavendish.

3823 "Book-Plate for the Devonport Royal Dockyard Orphanage." (1) 17:Frontispiece, 38, March 1907.
Plate used in presentation volumes given to children leaving the orphanage; established in 1849 with Prince of Wales as patron.

3824 "Exchanges." 17:39, March 1907.
List of owners of plates by Henry Andre of Paris who wish to exchange.

3825 "English Heraldic Society." 17:40, March 1907.
Suggests formation of new society.

3826 "List of Festoon Plates." J. F. Verster. 17:41-4, March 1907.
N-P.

3827 "Notes." 17:45-8, April 1907.
Lengthy quote from bookplate article in first issue of *Expert:* an Illustrated Weekly Newspaper for Collectors and Connoisseurs.

3828 "Bickham." 17:49, April 1907.
Conclusion of listing.

3829 "Modern Book-Plate Designers: William Edgar Fisher." (5) 17:49-53, April 1907.
"He works mainly in pen and ink," but hopes soon "to become expert enough at etching to discard the pen and take up the needle."

3830 "New Book-Plates by Mr. Graham Johnston." (3) 17:Frontispiece, between 52-3, 53, April 1907.
Illustrations only.

3831 "Colonial Book-Plates." Helen Frances Brackett. 17:53-6, April 1907.
Author claims earliest American plate is dated 1679 and belonged to Rev. John William.

3832 "British 'Book-Pile' Ex Libris." Carnegy Johnson. (6) 17:53, 56-62, April 1907.
Updating of Sir Arthur Vicars' list of 1893.

3833 "Mr. Bostonian and His Book-Plates." 17:63-5, May 1907.
"The collecting of book-plates has now become a craze that rivals the stamp-collecting fever"; quote reprinted from *Boston Sunday Herald*.

3834 "Notes." 17:65-8, May 1907.
Lengthy quotes from *English Illustrated Magazine* and *Journal of American History*.

3835 "List of British 'Book-Pile' Book-Plates to 1890." Carnegy Johnson. (4) 17: 69-73, May 1907.
C to H.

3836 "List of Festoon Plates." J. F. Verster. (4) 17:74-8, May 1907.
P-R.

3837 "An Appeal." 17:79, June-July 1907.
"More than £150" overdue to the Society for subscriptions, some covering dues for 1906 and prior.

3838 "Late Mr. Joseph Knight, F.S.A." 17:79-80, June-July 1907.
Knowledgeable on stage history, drama critic, editor of *Notes and Queries*, "Sylvanus Urban" of *Gentleman's Magazine*, seventy-eight at death.

3839 "Death of Mr. Hartwell De La Garde Grissell." George Potter. 17:81, June-July 1907.
Mr. Grissell "possessed a very fine bookplate by Sherborn."

3840 "Some New Book-Plates." (2) 17:81,91, June-July 1907.
Will Foster designed plate for R. Gill Monk, and L. S. Ipsen for Francis M. Williams.

3841 "Book-Plates by Miss Bertha Gorst." (4) 17:91, between 86-7,91, June-July 1907.
Artist feels "a book-plate should never be trivial in character, and fitting as a label for books grave and gay."

3842 "Lord Major's Book-Plate." (1) 17:Frontispiece, 81, June-July 1907.
Plate for Sir W. P. Treloar executed by Alfred J. Downey.

3843 "Book-Plates of the Late Mr. Joseph Knight, F. S. A." (3) 17:82-3, June-July 1907.

Early plate (1881) designed by W. Bill Scott, second plate showing a knight in armour was designed by Sebastian Evans, and a third is a design "undoubtedly taken from the title page or frontispiece of some old work."

3844 "Lecture on 'The Cult of Book-Plates.' " Dr. George C. Peachey. 17:84-8, June-July 1907.

"The personal equation in the great majority of book-plates is the feature of special interest."

3845 "Annual Exhibition, 1907." 17:88, June-July 1907.

Some members contribute each year; if a wider response is not made the Council may drop the annual exhibition. Annual banquet abandoned due to lack of response. "Attendance at the Chairman's lecture was fairly good, but the leading members of the Society were prominent by their absence."

3846 "List of Exhibitors and Exhibits." 17:89-93, June-July 1907.

Though Colonial and Early American plates featured, only Sheldon Cheney and William E. Fisher from the United States sent exhibits.

3847 "Belgian Collegiate Book-Plate." (1) 17:93, June-July 1907.

Plate, dated 1748, engraved for Canon and Regius Professor at University of Lowvain.

3848 "Notes." (1) 17:between 88-9, 94, June-July 1907.

Interesting plate for Sidney Mendelssohn's Africa collection, features Rhodes portrait and map of Africa.

3849 "List of British 'Book-Pile' Book-Plates." Carnegy Johnson. (4) 17:95-8, June-July 1907.

H to M.

3850 "Irish Book-Plates." William Chamney. 17:99-100, June-July 1907.

H to L.

3851 "Notes of the Month." 17:101-3, August-September 1907.

Concerning work of Max Klinger: "the usual foreign type—fanciful, figurative, with the usual mixture of mermaids, skulls, naked figures, masks, etc.—and to English eyes look as unlike a book-plate [as] anything could possibly be."

3852 "Stewart Book-Plates." (38) 17:104-8, 8 unnumbered pages after 120, August-September 1907.

Charles Edward Stewart had collected over 200 plates for different branches of the Stewart family.

3853 "New Book-Plate by Mr. Graham Johnston." (1) 17:108, August-September 1907.

Plate for Nora Davidson.

3854 "Book-Plate of Mr. George Grazebrook." (1) 17:Frontispiece, 108, August-September 1907.

"Another of Miss Lawson's most beautiful book-plates."

3855 "On the Lettering of Book-Plates." H. I. Hall. (11) 17:109-11, August-September 1907.

"It will, of course, be understood that one implies no disparagement of modern work," especially "highly distinguished calligraphers, for example, Gill and Grailly Hewitt."

3856 "Wright Book-Plates. Part II." Arthur J. Jewers. 17:112, August-September 1907.
Conclusion of article.

3857 "List of Festoon Plates." J. F. Verster. 17:113-4, August-September 1907.
R-S.

3858 "List of British 'Book-Pile' Book-Plates to 1890." Carnegy Johnson. (3) 17:115-8, August-September 1907.
M-P.

3859 "Irish Book-Plates." William Chamney. 17:119-20, August-September 1907.
L and M.

3860 "Notes." 17:121-3, October 1907.
W. Roffe engraved bookplate for Ruskin; a few proofs were pulled but it was never used.

3861 "Frances Garden, Engraver." Carnegy Johnson. 17:124-5, October 1907.
List of plates signed by this engraver.

3862 "Three New Book-Plates by Mr. Graham Johnston." (3) 17:125-6, October 1907.
Plates for George A. Hobson, Oscar H. Stoehr, the Gray Library.

3863 "Scarce Heraldic Portrait." (1) 17:127-8, October 1907.
Details concerning Frances, Duchess of Richmond and Lennox.

3864 "Book-Plate Identification." (4) 17:Frontispiece, 128, October 1907.
Department revived with plates numbering 615 through 618.

3865 "Book-Plate of Miss Mary Wilson." (1) 17:128, October 1907.
Designed by Miss Gertrude Thomson.

3866 "Old Nottingham Book-Plate." J. Potter Briscoe. (1) 17:129, October 1907.
Large plate used by Nottingham Corporation. "The woodcut . . . may represent an actual ducal or other residence. The other portions of the design are stock pieces." Each is identified from original printed source.

3867 "British Heraldic Association." 17:130-2, October 1907.
Eleven point program outlined for proposed society.

3868 "Letter." Carnegy Johnson. 17:132, October 1907.
Response to "California authority."

3869 "List of British 'Book-Pile' Book-Plates to 1890." Carnegy Johnson. (4) 17:131-6, October 1907.
P-S.

3870 "Notes." (1) 17:137-41, November 1907.
Proposed subscription (200) publication of monograph on Daniel Parsons.

3871 "New Book-Plate by Mr. Graham Johnston." (1) 17:143, November 1907.
Designed for Edith D. Stuart Gray.

3872 "New Book-Plate by Miss Mary C. Lawson." (1) 17:Frontispiece, 142, November 1907.
Plate for Grace Elizabeth Lawson.

3873 "Mr. Claude Bragdon on Book-Plates." 17:142-3, November 1907.
"A book-plate is a symbol of self; being a symbol, it should be simple; being of self, it should be personal."

3874 "Book-Plates by Mr. Thomas Shepard, of Willingborough." (9) 17:143-4, unnumbered between 144-5, November 1907.
Brief sentence about each plate.

3875 "Francis Hoffmann, Engraver." 17:144, November 1907.
Article on this "unknown" in *Walford's Antiquarian*.

3876 "Correspondence." 17:144-5, November 1907.
Suggested again that *Journal* become a quarterly.

3877 "A London Silversmith of the Eighteenth Century." Ed. F. Strange. (12) 17:146-50, November 1907.
Account book (1771-1777) revealed underneath pasted-in prints.

3878 "List of British 'Book-Pile' Book-Plates to 1890." Carnegy Johnson. (2) 17:150-4, November 1907.
List concluded.

3879 "Darcy Lever and Other Lancashire Ex Libris." Carnegy Johnson. (3) 17:Frontispiece, 155-7, December 1907.
Darcy Lever was knighted in 1737.

3880 "Notes on Some Colonial Book-Plates." Frederic Cattle. 17:157-9, December 1907.
Details on several Jamaica families.

3881 "A Manual of Costume." 17:160, December 1907.
A wealth of material on "the opening period of heraldic devices."

3882 "An Old French Dedicatory Book-Plate." James Arrow. (1) 17:160-1, December 1907.
". . . thrusting its presence upon the reader's notice directly under the front cover of a volume and thus forming a book-plate which is not a book-plate."

3883 "Exchanges." 17:161, December 1907.
A. A. Hunter would like to buy duplicates of other Hunter plates, gives Franks' numbers.

3884 "Modern Book-Plate Designers: Miss Dyke." (5) 17:162-3, December 1907.
Young artist has designed fifteen bookplates since 1901.

3885 "Book-Plate by Mr. Ern Hill." (1) 17:164, December 1907.
Plate for Marion G. B. Little.

3886 "Book-Plate of the Rev. Dudley C. Cary-Eleves." (1) 17:164, December 1907.
Another T. Shepard design.

3887 "Notes." 17:165, December 1907.
Only ten subscribers to Daniel Parson's monograph.

3888 "Heraldry for All, A Discursive Paper." William Bolton. (8) 17:166-9, December 1907.
This paper "is meant to illustrate how heraldry, in some form or other, meets the eye in many unexpected places and often affords to the thoughtful mind food for reflection."

3889 "Book-Plate of Aug. F. Ammann." (1) 18:Frontispiece, 1, January 1908.
Work of F. G. House printed directly from the plate.

3890 "Brief Sketch of Ettrick Family." (2) 18:1-4, January 1908.
First of the line recorded was "a Captain of the Horse" when Boulogne surrendered to Henry VIII in 1544.

3891 "Book-Plate of Aikman." (1) 18:4, January 1908.
Designed by Graham Johnston.

3892 "Book-Plate of John Bollinger." (1) 18:5, January 1908.
Plate for Librarian of Cardiff Public Libraries.

3893 "American Book-Plates." 18:6-7, January 1908.
Paul Revere engraved four or five bookplates.

3894 "Notes." (1) 18:7-10, January 1908.
Reviews two bookplate books published by Otto Schultze of Edinburgh.

3895 "Visiting Cards." James Arrow. 18:10-11, January 1908.
In times past visiting cards with pictorial designs were used, similar to the pictorial bookplate.

3896 "Rough List of Legal Book-Plates." S. A. Grundy-Newman. 18:12-6, January 1908.
Second list of addenda.

3897 "Notes." (14) 19:17-9, February 1908.
Treasurer, S. A. Grundy-Newman, again urges members to pay current and back dues. Illustrations are for last month's article on visiting cards.

3898 "Lancashire Ex Libris." (1) 18:20, February 1908.
Correspondent sends in plate for reproduction.

3899 "Notes on Some Modern Book-Plates." T. Cann Hughes. (5) 18:20-3, February 1908.
Memorial bookplates to be used in award books.

3900 "Notes on Some Colonial Book-Plates." Frederick Cattle. (3) 18:23-4, February 1908.
Details on plates for Edward B. Long, Lady Moore, and Sir John Taylor.

3901 "Annual General Meeting." 18:25-6, March-April 1908.
Minor changes noted including addition of word "Honorary" before titles of Treasurer and Secretary.

3902 "Notes." 18:27-9, March-April 1908.
Mostly on German ex libris activity.

3903 "For Identification." (5) 18: unnumbered between 28-9,36, March-April 1908.
Illustrations only.

3904 "American Notes." 18:29, March-April 1908.
Comments on *Book-Plate Booklet*.

3905 "An Anglo-Swiss Book-Plate." Jean Grellet. (1) 18:30-1, March-April 1908.
"This curious book-plate is probably a unique instance of an English sailor appearing, according to the rules of heraldry, to have married a Swiss town."

3906 "Book-Plate of Mr. Henry Newbolt." (1) 18:32, March-April 1908.
Designed by Frank Brangwyn.

3907 "Librarian's Book-Plate." (1) 18:32, March-April 1908.
Plate for Charles F. Newcombe.

3908 "Exchange." 18:32-3, March-April 1908.
Miss Dorth Furman (USA) willing to exchange her Arthur Nelson Macdonald for plates of "equal merit."

3909 "Book-Plate by Will Foster." (1) 18:33, March-April 1908.
Plate for Worcestershire Brine Baths Hotel includes arms of Worcester, town of Droitwich and exterior view of hotel.

3910 "Q's Book-Plate." (1) 18:34, March-April 1908.
Plate of Arthur Thomas Quiller-Couch, who "spends his time chiefly in writing, yachting, and fishing."

3911 "Correspondence." 18:34, March-April 1908.
Arthur Schomberg asked about American work of Robert Hancock.

3912 "Sir Alfred Newton's Book-Plate." (1) 18:35, March-April 1908.
Printed direct from the copper by Alfred J. Downey.

3913 "Dr. Edward Symes-Thompson." 18:35, March-April 1908.
Memoir by widow will include portrait and bookplate designed by John Leighton.

3914 "Book-Plate of Baron Iveagh." (1) 18:between 32-3,35, March-April 1908.
Plate designed and etched by Captain Nevile R. Wilkinson for Edmund Cecil Guinness.

3915 "Rough List of Legal Book-Plates." 18:37-40, March-April 1908.
Second list of addenda continued.

3916 "Notes." 18:41-2, May 1908.
Annual exhibition featuring European plates is scheduled for July 7-10 at Alpine Club, Savile Row.

3917 "*Edwin Davis French, A Memorial. His Life. His Art.*" 18:43, May 1908.
Only 475 copies issued of special memorial book which contains several bookplates by this "little master."

3918 "Lord Iveagh." 18:43, May 1908.
Incorrectly referred to in prior issue as Baron; actually "he was created a Viscount in 1905."

3919 "On Book-Plates." P. Neville Barnett. (1) 18:Frontispiece, 44-5, May 1908.
Reprinted from *Australian Magazine,* April 1908.

3920 "Book-Plates of Georges Hantz." 18:45-6, May 1908.
Twenty-five plates by artist-engraver Georges Hantz of Geneva issued in portfolio-books by Karl W. Hiersemann.

3921 "William Milton, of Bristol, Engraver." Carnegy Johnson. (4) 18:46-8, May 1908.
Fincham listed only nine plates by this artist and additional plates attributed to him are here described.

3922 "Book-Plate Identification." (2) 18:49, May 1908.
Four identified.

3923 "New Book-Plates." (2) 18:between 48-9,50, May 1908.
Plates of Clement Shorter, editor of *Sphere* and *Tatler,* and Francis John Tennant.

3924 "Leigh Book-Plates." (2) 18:between 44-5, 50, May 1908.
Plates from collection of Arthur Schomberg.

3925 "Lancashire." 18:50, May 1908.
Additional facts about plate mentioned in J. Carlton Stitt's article (page 20, February).

3926 "Gwendolen Peck." (1) 18:50, May 1908.
Illustration only (see June 1908).

3927 "List of Festoon Plates." J. F. Verster. (8) 18:51-6, May 1908.
S's.

3928 "Rough List of Legal Book-Plates." 18:57-60, May 1908.
Continuation of addenda.

3929 "Notes." 18:61-2, June 1908.
Insufficient response to Rev. H. Walter Mackey's appeal for subscribers to monograph on Parson's collection; project abandoned after only thirty-forty replies.

3930 "Book-Plates Designed by Arthur DeWitt Brooks, Cleveland, Ohio, U.S.A." 18:62, June 1908.
Seven plates briefly described.

3931 "Grimaldis and Some Grimaldi Book-Plates." Rev. A. B. Grimaldi. (7) 18:62-8, June 1908.
While essentially Italian, there are important family branches in Spain, France and Belgium.

3932 "William Milton of Bristol, Engraver." Carnegy Johnson. (2) 18:68-9, June 1908.
Additional facts.

3933 "Book-Plate of John Harold Greig." (1) 18:between 68-9,69, June 1908.
Designed by Mary C. Lawson.

3934 "Beazley Book-Plate." (1) 18:Frontispiece, 70, June 1908.
Plate from wash drawing by Graham Johnston.

3935 "New Book-Plate by Ern Hill." 18:70, June 1908.
Plate for Gwendolen Peck illustrated last month.

3936 "Book-Plate Identification." 18:70, June 1908.
Two identified.

3937 "Hints on Book-Plate Collecting" by An Old Collector [W. K. K. Wright]. 18:71-6, June 1908.
Walter Hamilton "claims earliest known collector of bookplates John Bagford, the typographical antiquary, who died in 1710." This claim open to question.

3938 "Rough List of Legal Book-Plates." S. A. Grundy-Newman. 18:77-80, June 1908.
C and D.

3939 "Notes." 18:81-3, July 1908.
Names of twelve new members listed.

3940 "Notes on Some Colonial Book-Plates." Frederic Cattle. (6) 18:83-6, July 1908.
Interesting family history given.

3941 "Book-Plates of J. Skinner of Bath." Carnegy Johnson. (7) 18:Frontispiece, 86-9, July 1908.
Details of considerable interest and chart of Skinner plates noted by Hardy, Fincham and others.

3942 "For Identification." (4) 18:between 88-9, July 1908.
Illustrations only.

3943 "Book-Plates of Elisabeth Cecil." J. C. Woods. (1) 18:89-90, July 1908.
Sleuthing indicates this may be Lady Cecil.

3944 "Book-Plate Exhibition at Liverpool." 18:90-1, July 1908.
Ex Libris included in Historical Exhibition of Liverpool Art.

3945 "Sale of Book-Plates." 18:91, July 1908.
Sotheby sale included lots from collections of Sir Arthur Vicars, John Morgan, and Arthur J. Jewers.

3946 "List of Festoon Plates." J. F. Verster. (4) 18:92-6, July 1908.
S-W.

3947 "Annual Exhibition." 18:97-100, August-September 1908.
Despite more vigorous efforts by active members, turnout still disappointing.

3948 "Notes." 18:100-1, August-September 1908.
Mention of article in *Bibliophile*.

3949 "Bohemian Book-Plates—Past and Present." Lad. J. Zivny. (8) 18:101-5, August-September 1908.
Editor notes he "cannot hold himself responsible for any typographical errors . . . or for the spelling of proper names" in this article.

3950 "Some New Book-Plates by Mr. Paul Nash." 18:107, August-September 1908.
Six described.

3951 "Our Souvenir Exhibition Catalogue." 18:107, August-September 1908.
Will be sent post free for one shilling.

3952 "Masonic Book-Plates." 18:107, August-September 1908.
Reprint from *Boston Evening Transcript* re A. Winthrop Pope articles in *New England Craftsman*.

3953 "Book-plate Identification." (7) 18:108-9,111, August-September 1908.
Total of 637 plates submitted to date for identification.

3954 "Will Milton." 18:110, August-September 1908.
Will of English engraver, dated 24th August, 1790, sent in by Arthur Schomberg.

3955 "Book-Plate for Lord Bishop of Truro." (1) 18:Frontispiece, 110, August-September 1908.
Illustration printed directly from the copper.

3956 "Book-Plates Designed by Mr. W. P. Barrett." (5) 18:between 106-7,110, August-September 1908.
These were part of recent Seventeenth Annual Exhibition.

3957 "Book-Plate of Lady Edith Neeld." (1) 18:between 100-1,110, August-September 1908.
Member will exchange her plate for those of "corresponding style and value."

3958 "Book-Plate of Richard Ashmole Cooper, of Ashlyns Hall, Berkhamsted." (1) 18:112, August-September 1908.
Brief description.

3959 "Notes." 18:112, August-September 1908.
Commends Sheldon Cheney, editor of *Book-Plate Booklet*, for article in *Overland Monthly*.

3960 "Irish Book-Plates." William Chamney. 18:113-6, August-September 1908.
N-T.

3961 "Notes." 18:117-9, October 1908.
Joseph Winfred Spenceley died October 18th at age of 45.

3962 "Notes on the Book-Plates of Public Schools." Rev. J. Alfred Ross, M.A. (6) 18:119-21, October 1908.
Kings College, when founded by Henry VI in 1440, consisted of a

Provost, ten fellows, four clerks, six choristers, a schoolmaster, twenty-five poor scholars and "a like number of infirm men," thus combining "characteristics of a college of secular priests, an eleemosynary schools for boys, and an almshouse."

3963 "Matthew Skinner, of Exeter." Carnegy Johnson. (2) 18:121-3, October 1908.

Three plates described.

3964 "In the Clouds." 18:123-4, October 1908.

Numerous plates described with unusual usage of clouds, such as Minerva standing on a cloud, cupids moving through clouds, an angel reposing on a cloud.

3965 "Book-Plates of J. Skinner, of Bath." 18:124, October 1908.

Five more probable Skinner plates described.

3966 "For Identification." (4) 18:125, October 1908.

Illustrations only.

3967 "Sir Jeffry Wyattville." Rev. A. B. Grimaldi, M.A. (1) 18:126-7, October 1908.

Interesting biographical details.

3968 "Masonic Book-Plates." 18:127, 129-30, October 1908.

More from *New England Craftsman* article.

3969 "Bohemian Book-Plates." (3) 18:128, October 1908.

Illustrations for article in last issue.

3970 "Our Frontispiece." (1) 18:Frontispiece, 130, October 1908.

Design by W. P. Barrett printed direct from copper.

3971 "Irish Book-Plates." William Chamney. 18:131-2, October 1908.

T-W.

3972 "Hon. Gerald Ponsonby." Carnegy Johnson. 18:133, November-December 1908.

Mr. Ponsonby will be mourned by collectors and authors who always found him generous in sharing his extensive collection and invaluable information; he died November 30, 1908.

3973 "Notes." 18:134-5, November-December 1908.

Articles mentioned in both foreign and English-language journals as well as several sale catalogs.

3974 "Notes on Public School Book-Plates." Rev. J. Alfred Ross. (5) 18:136-8, November-December 1908.

Four more school plates described.

3975 "Book-Plate Lantern Lectures." 18:138, November-December 1908.

Slides belonging to the Society may be borrowed for use by a member in "his own locality."

3976 "Our Frontispiece." (1) 18:Frontispiece, 138, November-December 1908.

Another W. P. Barrett plate printed directly from copper.

3977 "Phrenological Book-Plate." (1) 18:139, November-December 1908.
John Wilson, Professor of Phrenology, may have used plate as visiting or trade card, as well as possibly as a bookplate.

3978 "Book-Plate Competition." 18:139, November-December 1908.
Suggestion under consideration that prizes should be offered art school students for best bookplate designs.

3979 "Masonic Book-Plates." 18:140, November-December 1908.
Notes on final article in *New England Craftsman*.

3980 "Correspondence." 18:140, November-December 1908.
Suggests various lists of bookplates be printed separately for sale to members; editor notes it is financially impractical.

3981 "Mr. Daniel Phaer as a Book-Plate Designer." Gordon Bottomley. 18:142, November-December 1908.
Artist believes bookplate "must not only be a statement of the fact of ownership, but a thing of beauty, a work of art as significant and harmonious as a cameo or an engraved gem."

3982 "Book-Plates by Mr. C. F. A. Voysey." 18:142, November-December 1908.
Nine listed by name.

3983 "Book-Plate Sale." Carnegy Johnson. 18:142-3, November-December 1908.
Descriptions of lots, buyers, and prices.

3984 "Portrait of Bilibald Pirkheimer as an Ex Libris." 18:143-4, November-December 1908.
English authorities quoted in affirmation; however, not mentioned as bookplate by German specialists nor "classed as such in any of Durer's Iconographies."

3985 "Book-Plate of John William Balfour Paul." 18:144, November-December 1908.
Graham Johnston plate described.

3986 "Thomas Crafton Croker's Book-Plate." (1) 18:144, November-December 1908.
Looks more like entry for *Who's Who* than a bookplate.

3987 "Book-Plate of Mr. W. T. Bednall." (1) 18:145, November-December 1908.
Landscape plate of man from Adelaide, South Australia.

3988 "Book-Plate of the Torquay Public Library." (1) 18:145, November-December 1908.
Designed by student, Miss C. Mary Higgs.

3989 "Book-Plates of Paul Nash." (2) 18:between 140-1, 146, November-December 1908.
Two new designs "which are a marked improvement upon those noticed in a recent number."

3990 "Book-Plate Identification." 18:146, November-December 1908.
Seven identified.

3991 "Special Plates." (2) 18:between 142-3, and 144-5, 146, November-December 1908.

Corrected plate furnished by Messrs. J. and E. Bumpus for Sir David Lionel Goldsmid-Stern-Solomons; the second illustration is a miniature copy of the same plate "engraved by hand under the personal direction of Mr. W. P. Barrett."

3992 "List of Festoon Plates." J. F. Verster. (6) 18:147-50, November-December 1908.

W's.

3993 "Rough List of Legal Book-Plates." S. A. Grundy-Newman. 18:151-2, November-December 1908.

Addenda continued.

JOURNAL OF ROYAL HISTORICAL AND ARCHAEOLOGICAL ASSOCIATION OF IRELAND

3994 "Notice of Book-Plates Engraved by Cork Artists." Robert Day. 7:10-4, January 1885.

Day had copies of forty-eight signed bookplates executed by Green of Cork; mentions other artists who worked prior to 1840.

JOURNAL OF THE SOCIETY FOR ITALIC HANDWRITING

3995 "Italic Booklabels." Philip Beddingham. (3) Issue No. 33:26-8, Winter 1962.

Work of Reynolds Stone and Diana Bloomfield illustrated. Stone "alone must be considered the English master of the incised letter on wood."

K

KERAMIC STUDIO [See also **DESIGN**.]

3996 "Bookplates." (3) 15:156, February 1914.

Plates illustrated by C. W. Browne, Florence Gough and Alice Morse.

3997 "Book Plates by Delia Robinson." (5) 21:96, October 1919.

No text.

KOROTH [Quarterly Journal Devoted to the History of Medicine and Science]

3998 "Physicians' Ex-Libris." Dr. S. I. Plashkes. (1) 1:347, IV, October 1956.

In Jerusalem "Exhibition of book-plates, which reflects the historic and artistic aspects of the Jewish ex-libris, is devoted to book-plates prepared for Jewish physicians." Article states ten percent of all bookplates are for medical men.

L

LADIES' FIELD [See also WOMAN AT HOME and HOME CHAT]

3999 "On Ladies' Book-Plates." Gleeson White. (9) 3:382-3, November 12, 1898.
While some feel "book-plates for ladies are a modern fad . . . yet they have a long pedigree, and go back to respectable ancestry."

4000 "Postal Cards Designed Like Ex Libris." 4:602, March 11, 1899.
Suggested that personalized postal cards for women bear designs similar to *ex libris*.

4001 "On Ladies' Book-Plates." (7) 6:187-8, July 8, 1899.
Exhibit of ladies' bookplates by Ex Libris Society at the Westminster Palace Hotel.

4002 "King's Bookplate." (3) 17:275, April 26, 1902.
George W. Eve designed and etched Royal Windsor bookplate used during reign of Queen Victoria, and has made alterations in initials for use by King Edward VII; reproduced by special permission of His Majesty.

LADY

4003 "Linocuts and Ex Libris." Peter Ratazzi. (2) 875, 877, June 9, 1960. [Volume number unavailable.]
"The *ex-libris*, book label used for indicating ownership of library items, has lately escaped its original purpose, and is nowadays a messenger of friendship between collectors in different countries."

4004 "English Book-plates." P. C. Beddingham. (3) 289-90, February 23, 1961. [Volume number unavailable.]
"Artists like Eric Gill, Sir Frank Brangwyn, Robert Gibbings, Rex Whistler, Reynolds Stone and Joan Hassall have done much to establish the world-wide reputation of book-plates produced" in England.

LANCASTER COUNTY HISTORICAL SOCIETY

4005 "Lancaster Book Plates." Joseph H. Dubbs. 8:29-35, November 6, 1903.
Author doesn't feel "sharp criticism" by Charles Dexter Allen of bookplate of Lancaster physician Dr. George Thomas justified; considerable information on plates of residents of this Pennsylvania county.

LANTERN

4006 "American Book-Plates." (1) 1:182-92, April 15, 1913.
Details on Washington's bookplate and forgery detected by Dr. W. F. Poole, Chicago Public Library, and J. M. Toner at auction in 1863.

4007 "American Book-Plates. Eugene Field's Book Plate and Genealogy." (1) 2: 26-30, n.m. 1913.

Field family traced back to 15th century; Eugene Field used the original coat of arms as his bookplate.

4008 "Troubadours and Book Plates." 2:46-51, July 1913.

"The 'ex libris' is not here to protect the book for the owner. It is like the engraving on the signet ring or the name on a family tomb-stone, which lends individuality to something which anyone else might otherwise procure."

4009 "A Few Chicago Book Plates." (10) 2:51-64, July 1913.

Descriptions and illustrations include Chicago Historical Society, Newberry Library, John Crerar Library, Ruthven Deane, Charles F. Jilson, William Carver Williams, Art Institute, Julius Doerner.

4010 "George Washington's Book Plate." (1) 2:121-3, August 1913.

A collector of curios got possession of Washington's plate after his death, struck a few copies and destroyed the plate. Collectors cautioned against forgeries.

4011 "Notes." (3) 2:124, 130-2, August 1913.

Illustrations include plates of Fritz von Frantzius, Chicago banker and art connoisseur, and Leroy T. Goble, collector of bookplates.

LEIGH HUNT'S LONDON JOURNAL

4012 "Hints for Table Talk." "Bookworm." Issue No. 34: 267, November 19, 1834.

Includes Scottish verse of admonishment which author prefers to "namby-pamby" statement of ownership; also alludes to rhyme of "lower classes" beginning "O ye theif! how daur ye steal!"

LEISURE

4013 "Book Plating As a Hobby." (2) 4:38, March 1937.

Suggests using an individual design for each book—reprints of sketches, etchings, bookcovers and designs which can be snipped from a Sunday book supplement; add "Ex Libris" and your name, and paste in an appropriate book.

LIBRARIES

4014 "Book Plate for Fisk University." (1) 34:431-2, November 1929.

Of twelve designs submitted in competition, the winner was Miss Donzleigh Jefferson whose plate showed a slave ship sailing from Africa to America guided by Jubilee Singers.

THE LIBRARY [Library Record of Bibliography]

4015 "Review." 3:17-19, 1891

Ex libris books by Warneck and Bouchot reviewed.

4016 "Bookplates." W. J. Hardy. 3:47-53, 1891.

4017 3:93-98, 1891.
Interesting facts about both owners and engravers of bookplates.

4018 "Notice." 3:335, 1891.
First issue of *Journal of the Ex Libris Society* mentioned.

4019 "A Bibliography of Book-Plates." 4:262, 1892.
Review of W. H. Fincham and James Roberts Brown privately printed (1892) book on ex libris; contained 158 items; limited to 100 copies.

4020 "Chelsea Public Library." 5:54, 1893.
C. W. Sherborn to execute bookplate for Chelsea Public Library.

4021 "Reviews." 5:61-2, 1893.
Reviews of *English Book-Plates* (Egerton Castle) and *French Book-Plates* (Walter Hamilton). Both are recommended despite errors pointed out by reviewer.

4022 "Review." 5:148-9, 1893.
Book Plates by W. J. Hardy reviewed.

4023 "Bookplate." 5:196, 1893.
St. George, Hanover Square, Library has bookplate designed by C. R. B. Barrett, M.A.

4024 "Review." 6:28-9, 1894.
English Book-Plates, Ancient & Modern by Egerton Castle reviewed.

4025 "Review." 6:156-7, 1894.
The Bookplate Annual and Armorial Yearbook, 1894, a new venture by Leighton, reviewed.

4026 "Chelsea Public Library." 8:216, 1896.
C. W. Sherborn has completed bookplate for Chelsea Public Library. Motto: The true university of these days is a collection of books (Thomas Carlyle).

4027 "Review." 9:26, 1897.
Second edition of Hamilton's *French Book-Plates* reviewed.

4028 "Review." 2nd Series, 1:113, 1899-1900.
Review of *Die Schweizerischen Bibliothekzeichen* which consisted of one sentence: "A very superfluous production."

4029 "Franks Collection of Armorial Book-Stamps." Alfred W. Pollard. (9) 2nd Series, 3:115-34, April 1902.
Over 300 books with 16th, 17th, and 18th century armorial book stamps on bindings.

4030 "Origin and Evolution of the Book-Plate." G. H. Viner. (13) 5th Series, 1:39-44, June 1946.
Comments on dated labels in particular.

LIBRARY ASSOCIATION RECORD

4031 "Criminal Side of Book-Plate Collecting." 2:247-8, May 1900.
"If more libraries would take the precaution exercised by at least one

library within our knowledge of making the possession of a copy of any of its bookplates a criminal offense," there would be fewer "depredations such as those committed at the Harvard Library."

4032 "Ex Libris." Reginald Bioletti. 39:100-4, March 1937.
Historical background, information for cataloging a large collection, details of collection in Liverpool Public Library.

4033 "King's New Bookplates." 4:207, May 1902
"We are sorry to learn that His Majesty has given permission to Mr. Eve to present fifty sets of these plates to King Edward's Hospital Fund, to be sold for eight guineas each set, for by so doing Royal countenance is given . . . to the pernicious craze for collecting what were originally intended to serve as marks of ownership."

LIBRARY JOURNAL

4034 "Bibliography." 18:27, January 1893.
One hundred copies privately printed of W. H. Fincham's bibliography of bookplate literature.

4035 "Ex Libris Society of London." 18:155, May 1893.
Entering third year with over 300 members.

4036 "New Bookplate for Yonkers Library." (1) 59:219, March 1, 1934.
General collection bookplate gift of Sidney Risenberg, resident artist.

4037 "New Bookplate for Children's Room." (1) 59:316, April 1, 1934.
Yonkers artist, Mrs. Helen Lossing Johnson, made gift of plate to Children's Department of Yonkers, New York, Public Library.

4038 "Bookplates Collection." J. F. Smith. 62:227, March 15, 1937.
Ex Libris Collection acquired October, 1934 by Liverpool Public Libraries. Any who are interested are invited to send sample to be included.

4039 "New Bookplate." (1) 62:389, May 1, 1937.
Rockwell Kent made gift of design for bookplate to be used in Library of Congress Rare Book Collection. Believed to be first instance of special bookplate for Library.

4040 "Charm of Bookplates." Helen R. Richards. (5) 63:584-7, August 1938.
Historical background of early French, English and American bookplates.

4041 "Newbery-Caldecott Bookplates." (1) 64:556, July 1939.
Bookplates designed for use in books awarded Newbery or Caldecott Medal. Librarians can order supply from *Publishers' Weekly*.

4042 "Memorial Bookplates." (2) 65:30, January 1, 1940.
Two bookplates designed for Minneapolis Public Library for use with John P. Rossitu gift of 12,000 pieces of band music and Gerald H. Burgess gift of books on stamp collecting.

4043 "It Takes a Master." (1) 69:153, February 15, 1944.
Special bookplate designed by Bruce Rogers and printed by Peter Beilenson for Ingersoll Fund Books, Brooklyn Public Library.

4044 "Lima Public Library Stresses 'Living Memorials.'" Georgie G. McAfee. (8) 71:86-91, January 15, 1946.

Outright gifts, income from investments donated, occasional gifts at Christmas given in name of deceased family members, service men, etc.; library better equipped to make purchases from list which allows donor selection from the needs of the particular library. List of possible selection; special memorial bookplates for such collections.

4045 "Bookplates Pointed a Finger." Mary E. Conron. (2) 76:1503-4, October 1, 1951.

Bookplates designed for hospital library to help keep patients from taking books home; label is 6x8 and "yellow as smallpox sign."

4046 "Bookplates Bring Back Books." (2) 86:2079, June 1, 1961.

Designed by Mary Conron primarily for hospitals in New York; printed in English and Spanish for many Puerto Rican patients who thought books a gift.

4047 "Bookplate Exchange." 92:1778, May 1. 1967.

Flinders University of South Australia presented outstanding bookplate collection by artist, G. D. Perrottet.

4048 "Dunmore Library." George H. Reese. 93:1554, April 15, 1968.

Books from John Murray, Earl of Dunmore, sought; some can be identified by his bookplate.

4049 "Bookplates for All." 93:4630-1, December 15, 1968.

Review of Edward H. Shickell volume, *Bookplates for Libraries*, limited to 400 copies; 75 original designs printed in four colors.

LIBRARY NEWS BULLETIN [Washington State Library]

4050 "Many Bookplates in Library Show." (2) 32:17-8, January-March 1965.

Exhibit at Spokane Public Library sponsored by American Society of Bookplate Collectors and Designers.

LIBRARY OF CONGRESS [See **QUARTERLY JOURNAL OF LIBRARY OF CONGRESS**]

LIBRARY REVIEW

4051 "Ex Libris Society." July 1892. [Unable to locate.]

Source: *Journal of Ex Libris Society* 6:80, August 1892: "The *Library Review* (edited by Mr. Kineton Parks) for July, 1892, has a short paragraph commendatory of our Journal. It says: 'The illustrations with which it is loaded, and the interesting articles it contains, make it one of the most interesting of all the "special" publications of the day.'"

THE LIBRARY WORLD

4052 "*Bookplates for Libraries*." K. C. Harrison. 70:169, December 1968.

"All who are concerned with the art of the book should obtain this volume," says reviewer of Edward H. Shickell and William R. Holman book.

LINCOLN LORE

4053 "Lincolniana Bookplates." (2) No. 1271, August 17, 1953.

H. Alfred Fowler authored volume on Lincoln collectors; plates have been designed by E. D. French; Brady photographs often used as models.

LITERARY COLLECTOR

4054 "Book Plate Vandal." A. J. Bowden. 1:20-1, October 1, 1900.

"We should collect book plates, not for the sake of having more examples than the next man, but for the enlightenment of posterity and the sake of historical research. With proper study much of value and interest may be learned of famous or comparatively obscure people, with the *ex libris* as the starting point."

4055 "A Book-Plate Suggestion." Charles Dexter Allen. (2) 2:55-7, June 1901.

"Really the book-plate should have no commercial value; it should not be possible to buy a book-plate." Allen's "suggestion" is to have a suitable design and motto for the booklover's plate. Becoming necessary to have a plate to give away and one to use.

4056 "The Study of Book-Plates." W. J. Hardy. (5) 3:3-8, October 1901.

Historical summary. ". . . examples of yesterday—the time when book plates were made, not for displaying the eccentricities of owner and designer, but as readily identifiable marks of ownership; to the time when they were made to place in one's books and not to exchange with one's friends."

4057 "Book-Plate Reminiscences." Henry Blackwell. 4:45-8, May-June 1902.

Blackwell started collection in 1877 when book brought to him for binding contained plate worthy of preservation. "There is a big future for book-plates and the time will surely come when they will command high prices. My advice to all collectors is, do not part with your collections." Good review of articles appearing as early as 1822 in *Gentleman's Magazine*.

4058 "Book-Plate Notes." S. Hollyer. 5:80-1, January 1903.

Quotes Ex Libris *Journal* (September 1902) that bookplates designed in U.S. are not highly thought of by English collectors; author thinks otherwise. Surprised that portrait plates are not more popular.

4059 "Ex Libris." Fred Hotchkiss Miner. (4) 6:169-73, October 1903.

Concerned with designing and designers of bookplates. Mention of twelve brochures to be issued by Charles B. Goodspeed, Boston.

4060 "The Franks Book-Plates at the British Museum." Alfred A. Bethune-Baker. 7:178-81, April 1904.

First volume of catalogue issued for Sir A. W. Franks collection of about 40,000 plates. Urges other libraries to establish collections though great labor and expense would be involved to approximate Franks collection.

4061 "Forged Book-Plates." 8:121-2, August 1904.

Warning to collectors reprinted from *Journal of Ex Libris Society*.

4062 "Anthony H. Euwer's Book-Plates." 8:185, October 1904.
Refers to article on this artist in *Craftsman*.

4063 "Notes." 9:38, November-December 1904.
Third and last volume of Catalogue of Franks Collection of Book-Plates in British Museum issued; work of E. R. J. Gambier Howe; 35,098 plates in 58 volumes.

4064 "Notes." 9:75, January-February 1905.
Reference to University Library of Edinburgh bookplate; also Joseph Sattler, German illustrator, who did bookplates.

4065 "Notes." 9:111, March 1905.
Charles Dexter Allen glad to receive data for Supplemental List of Early American Bookplates he is preparing.

4066 "Notes." 10:31, July 1905.
Use of colors in bookplates noted in article from *Books and Book-Plates*. Stewart Dick quoted: "A library marks a man at once as a crank."

4067 "Notes." 10:34, July 1905.
W. P. Truesdell publishing check-list of J. Winfred Spenceley's bookplates, which number 135.

LITERARY DIGEST

4068 "An Artistic Exponent of 'Neo-Judaism.' " (1) 24:801, June 14, 1902.
E. M. Lilien has done designs for bookbinding and bookplates; plate shown is for a German Social-Democratic deputy and represents a woman as Freedom wearing the crown of labor.

LITERARY NEWS

4069 "The Book-Plate's Petition." N.S. 11:246, August 1890.
Poem printed from Austin Dobson's *Poems on Several Occasions*.

4070 "*Bookworm*." N.S. 15:56, February 1894.
Mentions article on English and American bookplates in this magazine.

4071 "*Book-Plate Annual*." N.S. 16:89, March 1895.
Issued by Macmillan at $1.75 net.

LITERARY OBSERVER.

4072 "Bookplate of Bastille." 1:35, June-July 1934.
Illustration of plate for Chateau Royal de La Bastille.

4073 "Bookplate of George Macdonald." 1:112, October-November 1934.
Illustration only.

LITERARY REPOSITORY

4074 "Bookplates." Issue No. 1:1, 1966.

H. L. Hoover, Rector Emeritus of St. Bartholomew's in Hartville, South Carolina, wants to correspond and trade with other bookplate collectors.

4075 "Gerald Manley Hopkins." (1) Issue No. 1:1-2, 1966.

Among items offered from collection of Hopkins' manuscripts and relics was author's bookplate with motto: *Esse quam Vidiri* (to be rather than to seem).

LITERARY REVIEW AND BOOK PLATE COLLECTOR

4076 "Book-Plate of Margarethe Strauss by Franz Stassen." (1) 1:16, November 1902.

Plate represented question "as to who will better find the knowledge of the end of all things, natural sciences or philosophy."

4077 "Ex Libris Notes and News." Winfred Porter Truesdell. (3) 1:17-9, November 1902.

Punning plate of J. W. Arrowship pictured.

4078 "Book-Plate Designers and Their Work: Jay Chambers." (16) 1:20-7, November 1902.

Chambers one of three-man team called the Triptych; pupil of Howard Pyle.

4079 "Book-Plate of Hildebrand Brandenburg (1470)." (1) 1:21, November 1902.

Illustration only.

4080 "Review of Ex Libris of Hermann R. C. Herzel." (1) 1:28, November 1902.

Favorable review of this Swiss exponent of bookplate art; published in Berlin.

LITERARY WORLD [Boston]

4081 "A Library Pest." 12:228, July 2, 1881.

Editorial about book borrowers who do not return books and quotes from Warren.

4082 "Study of Book-Plates." 12:271, August 13, 1881.

Generally favorable review of Warren's book.

4083 "Book Plates." 24:195, June 17, 1893.

"Marks of private pride and ownership are bookplates."

LITERARY WORLD [London]

4084 "Book Auction." 48:310, October 27, 1893.

Comment of surprise that a copy of Pope's *Iliad* containing David Garrick's bookplate only brought six shillings at Puttick and Simpson's auction.

4085 "Coincidence During Hall Caine Play Rehearsal." 50:130, August 24, 1894.
During rehearsal of Hall Caine's *The Manxman*, actor portraying Philip Christian who is made Deemster used stage prop book containing bookplate reading "The Deemster Christian—Isle of Man."

LITERATURE

4086 "Ex Libris." 3:192, August 27, 1898.
Note of article in *Journal of Ex Libris Society* on "Odd Volumes and Their Bookplates"; compares publications of Roxburghe Club which are "exceedingly, not to say painfully, solid" while those of Club of Odd Volumes are "chiefly post prandial."

4087 "Ex Libris." 3:262, September 17, 1898.
George Bell to issue *German Book Plates* by G. R. Dennis.

4088 "Book-Plates." W. G. Bowdoin. (11) 3:Supplement 1-4, November 23, 1898 [bound in November 12, 1898; no issue for November 23rd despite quote by W. G. Bowdoin, *Rise of the Bookplate*, 1901, page 38].
"Aside from other uses, book-plates seem to revive and keep alive such studies as heraldry, blazonry, biography, even history and political science, especially in France."

4089 "Notes." 3:478, November 19, 1898.
Gleeson White "has left his family almost totally unprovided for" with his death at 47; private funds are being raised and a Civil List pension sought for his widow.

4090 "Notes of the Day." 6:305, April [21], 1900.
A plea made to Joseph Simpson, editor of the quarterly *Book of Book-Plates*, to suggest a name less "clumsy and ambiguous" than bookplate and more "grammatical" than ex libris.

4091 "Library Notes." 6:373, May 12, 1900.
Harvard University librarian advises collectors of theft of bookplates. Other librarians blame "system of open access" used at Harvard.

4092 "Book-Plates Old and New." (3) 8:335-6, April 27, 1901.
Illustrations from *German Book Plates* are for the Emperor and Bismarck, and one designed by Goethe.

LIVERPOOL BULLETIN

4093 "English Book-Plate Styles." J. F. Smith. (11) 1:18-29, February 1952.
"First use of the term 'book-plate' is found in John Ireland's *Hogarth Illustrated*, 1791."

LONDON JOURNAL

"[Rhyming Warning to Book Borrowers.]" 1834. [Unable to locate.]
Source: *Journal of Ex. Libris Society* 8:87, June 1898.

LONDON MAGAZINE

4094 "Book Plates, Their Romantic History and Value." (11) 10:464-468, May 1903.

Editor of *Connoisseur* gives interesting historical review, discusses designers and possessors of bookplates.

LONDON MERCURY

4095 "Bookplate in Relation to the Book-Arts." James Guthrie. 12:69-72, May 1925.

Mostly about printing and decoration (etching, engraving, lithography) of the book and only briefly concerns the bookplate as a unit of this decoration.

LONDON OPINION

4096 "On Books and Book-Plates." J. H. Yoxall. (1) 12:377, March 9, 1907.

"Of course, the proper place for such a book-plate is in a book. It is a pity to separate them. Collect the books as well."

4097 "More About Book-Plates." J. H. Yoxall. 12:417, March 16, 1907.

"The value of a plate may depend on the art of it, the rarity of it, or the personality of the original owner of it."

THE LONE HAND

4098 "Dr. Morrison." A. E. Wearne. (3) 472-8, October 1, 1910.

Australian Dr. George Ernest Morrison, Peking correspondent for the London *Times,* has a bookplate featuring the kangaroo.

4099 "On Book-Plates and Some Australian Designs." Bertram Stevens. (14) XXXVI, XXXVIII, XL, XLI, XLIV, XLVI, December 1, 1910.

"A collection of modern plates has all the charm of a miniature picture gallery, and exhibits some characteristics of the owners as well as the designers."

4100 "Some Book-plates." (4) XXVII, XXX, December 2, 1912.

Illustrated are plates with Australian association—Captain Cook, Clement K. Shorter's plate drawn by Phil May, Alex Trumbull's featuring a Maori pah, and Sir Samuel Way, South Australian Chief Justice.

4101 "Australian Bookplates." (4) XXXII, XXXIV, January 1, 1913.

Artist Eirene Mort pictures gum tree rooted in continent of Australia for her own plate; others by Lionel Lindsay, Sydney Ure Smith, and Walter Jardine.

LONGMAN'S MAGAZINE

4102 "At the Sign of the Ship." Andrew Lang. 37:286, January 1901.

It appears that "the amateurs of Book-plates have split into two camps, one cherishing bookplates as things of beauty, while the other set measure a plate by its rarity. Would that there were no book-plate collectors! A book-plate is of next to no interest, except on the book where the owner placed it. . . . plate and book being divorced lose interest."

THE LUDGATE

4103 "Bookplates of Some Notable People." W. H. K. Wright. (14) N.S. 3:387-94, February 1897.

Illustrations include plates for Chief Rabbi Adler, Thomas Carlyle, Charles Dickens, Gladstone, Oliver Wendell Holmes, Henry Irving, Phil May and Alfred Tennyson.

4104 "Bookplates of Illustrious Women." W. H. K. Wright. (20) N.S. 4:200-6, June 1897.

Illustrations mostly of royalty and nobility; compliments Norna Labouchere's book.

M

MADAME

4105 "[Review of *Studio*.]" January 14, 1899. [Unable to locate.]

Source: *Journal of Ex Libris Society* 9:2, January 1899: "*Madame* of Jan. 14 has also an illustrated review of the late Mr. Gleeson White's *Studio* book-plate number."

MAGAZINE OF AMERICAN HISTORY

4106 "Queries." 5:376, November 1880.

Correspondent seeks further information on H. Dawkins who designed bookplate of Benjamin Kissam.

4107 "Washington's Book Plate." (1) 6:88, February 1881.

Illustration only.

4108 "Kissam Book-Plate." 6:224-5, March 1881.

Bookplate engraver Dawkins turned his talents to counterfeiting; was arrested in May, 1776; however, in 1778 he engraved copperplate for military commissions issued by Governor Clinton.

4109 "Kissam Book-Plate." 6:302, April 1881.

A Kissam kin believes Dawkins was a London engraver because a plate he designed is in a book published in London in 1731.

4110 "William Smith." (1) 6:264-74, April 1881.

Arms, not bookplate, illustrated, but listed in Hewins bibliography.

4111 "Original Documents: Sir Henry Clinton's Original Secret Record of Private Daily Intelligence." (1) 12:162-75, August 1884.

Illustration is bookplate for Henry Clinton, grandson of Sir Henry.

MAGAZINE OF ART [See also **ART AND PROGRESS** and **AMERICAN MAGAZINE OF ART**]

4112 "Ex Libris." December 1893.[Unable to locate.]

Source: *American Book-Plates,* Charles Dexter Allen, page 393, item #36; *Rise of the Book-Plate,* W. B. Bowdoin, page 38. Article is review of Castle's book.

4113 "Ex Libris." (7) 17:51-2, 1894.

Reviewer of *English Book-Plates* states the majority of bookplate "designs past and present are too tamely mechanical to be interesting."

4114 "Book Plate by Charles Naish." (1) 23:287-8, [April] 1897.

Engraved plate for Frederick Naish.

4115 "Mr. Harold Nelson, Black and White Artist." Arthur Fish. (7) 25:40-2, November 1900.

Nelson began as engraver of heraldic designs on domestic plate at age of twenty-three in 1894.

4116 "Ephraim Lilien." Solomon J. Solomon. (6) 27:240-2, March 1903.

Plate shown is for Rich Fischer, social democrat.

4117 "Reviews." 27:260, March 1903.

James Guthrie's *The Elf* mentioned.

4118 "Concerning Recent British Book-Plates." James J. Guthrie. (26) 28:87-91, December 1903.

Work shown by J. Walter West, H. Ospovat, Rosie Pitman, Harold Nelson, Bengough Ricketts, C. M. Gere, Gordon Craig, C. Richardson, W. M. Stone, J. W. Simpson, A. Duncan Carse, E. H. New, Paul Woodraffe, D. Y. Cameron, and J. J. Guthrie.

4119 "Illustrated Books." Irvin Haas. (2) 30:524-6, August 1937.

Includes critical review of Pynson Printers' publication of Rockwell Kent's bookplates and marks. "Because the plates are so crisply designed and drawn their triteness of conception is overlooked and the observer remains impressed until he begins to use his mind as well as his eyes."

4120 "Ex Libris." 34:390-1, August-September 1941.

Review of *Year Book* of American Society of Bookplate Collectors and Designers, edited by Carlyle S. Baer.

MANCHESTER PUBLIC FREE LIBRARIES QUARTERLY RECORD [England]

4121 "Thomas Greenwood Library for Librarians." W. E. A. Axon. 9:90-1, July-September 1905.

Gift of ten thousand volumes plus generous endowment for future extension; especially strong in bibliography.

MANCHESTER REVIEW

4122 "Book Labels." Walter Harris. 10:184-5, Winter 1964-65.

Harris feels book labels, usually containing only name and possible date sometimes with a decorative border, should be recorded separately from bookplates which he apparently considers mostly armorial.

MANUSCRIPTS [Australia]

4123 "The Bookplate: Its Interest for Australians." Camden Morrisby. (3) No. 3, 66-9, November 1932.

"The dictionary definition should have an addendum and should read: It is often, too, a sure revelation of character, showing up the owner's attitude in all its variants, and displaying for the gaiety of nations man's little vanities, parades of learning, pride of mind and affections; but also, and just as often, his literary affections, artistic aspirations, and personal ideals."

4124 "The Bookplate. II. Brangwyn As A Designer." John Preece. (3) No. 4, 64-7, February 1933.

"Art critics will discuss their technique, their vigour, and their beauty, but we who have the bookplate in mind wonder whether the artist is aware of a discrepancy between the design which should be in conformity with a bookplate, and that which is only a picture in miniature."

4125 "The Bookplate. III. Eric Thake." H. B. Muir. (3) No. 5, 62-6, May 1933.

Muir states, "With the exception of heraldic, etching is not the ideal medium for the bookplate." Chronological list (1926-1932) of nineteen plates by this Australian artist.

4126 "Lionel Lindsay's Bookplates." Camden Morrisby. (4) No. 6, 60-6, August 1933.

Includes chronological list (1912-1933) of twenty-five plates indicating whether etching, pen and ink, or woodcut.

4127 "The Bookplate. V. Adrian Feint." Frank E. Lane. (5) No. 7, 64-74, November 1933.

Includes chronological checklist of 128 plates created between 1922 and 1933. "His technique and treatment are peculiarly his own, although one may find examples of the influence exerted by his admiration of Rockwell Kent."

4128 "The Bookplate. VI. Gayfield Shaw." John Preece. (2) No. 8, 66-71, February 1934.

Includes two chronological checklists totaling thirty-five plates divided into those etched and those engraved.

4129 "The Bookplate. VII. G. D. Perrottet." H. B. Muir. (3) No. 9, 61-6, May 22, 1934.

Includes chronological list (1929-1934) of sixty plates. Artist known for his "use of multiple blocks printed in two or more colours."

4130 "The Bookplate. VIII. The David Scott Mitchell Collection." Camden Morrisby. (2) No. 10, 44-8, August 30, 1934.

Approximately 6,000 bookplates, mostly Australian and English, bequeathed to State by Mitchell who "succumbed to the charm of the bookplate" when an old man.

4131 "The Bookplate. IX. Bookplates of Jaroslav Dobrovolsky." George D. Perrottet. (1) No. 11, 48-9, November 25, 1934.

Czechoslovakian artist often employs two or more blocks for his plates and uses inks in two tones of the same color to achieve a wide "range of tone values."

MANUSCRIPTS [U.S.]

4132 "Sylvia Beach Collection." Howard C. Rice, Jr. (3) 18:3-8, Summer 1966.

Publisher of James Joyce used bookplate for her Shakespeare and Company lending library in Paris.

MARK HOPKINS INSTITUTE REVIEW OF ART

4133 "[Bookplate Competition Won by Albertine Wheelan.]" [Unable to locate journal.]

Article appeared "about 1900" but source unrecorded.

MARYLAND HISTORICAL MAGAZINE

4134 "Early Maryland Bookplates." Edith R. Bevan. 39:310-4, December 1944.

Thomas Sparrow of Annapolis engraved woodcuts for prominent Marylanders of his day.

THE MASTERKEY

4135 "Ex Libris." Charlotte T. Tufts. (7) 41:cover, 45-6, April-June 1967.

Cover shows famous bookplates used in the Southwest Museum library; another illustration shows branded books.

4136 "Ruskin Art Club Marks Anniversary." (1) 42:132-3, October-December 1968.

Illustration is bookplate for Hector Alliot Memorial Library of Archaeology at Southwest Museum.

MD

4137 "Ex Libris." (4) 3:141, August 1959.

Oldest bookplate known to be owned by a physician was that of Dr. Dietrich Block, University of Wittenberg, Germany; made for him in 1509 by Lucas Cranach.

MEDICAL LIBRARY ASSOCIATION BULLETIN [See **BULLETIN OF MEDICAL LIBRARY ASSOCIATION**]

MEDICAL PICKWICK

4138 "On Medical Book-Plates." Herman T. Radin. (8) 1:315-9, August 1915.
"A most charming by-path of print-collecting is the collection of book-plates."

MENTOR

4139 "The Romance of Bookplates." 16:63, March 1928.
Brief (three paragraphs) historical review.

MERCK REPORT

4140 "Bookplates of Famous Physicians." Walter K. Frankel, M.D. (15) 59:15-8, January 1950.
Author says oldest medical bookplate that made by Lucas Cranach (1472-1553) for Dr. Dietrich Bloch. Alexander Anderson, though a graduate of Columbia medical school, preferred being a wood engraver.

METROPOLITAN MUSEUM OF ART BULLETIN [See **BULLETIN OF METROPOLITAN MUSEUM OF ART**]

MEXICAN ART & LIFE

4141 "Fire Marks & Ex-Libris." Jose Juan Tablada. (22) No. 7, 2 unnumbered pages, July 1939.
"The fire mark dies were made of iron and bronze and were heated to red for stamping them on the top and bottom edges of the book, and even at the risk of damaging it, upon the hide or parchment covers." Ten ex libris illustrated.

MINIATURE BOOK NEWS

4142 "A Milestone." 1:1, June 1966.
This issue completes first year of publication; contemplated future articles include one on miniature bookplates and collectors.

4143 "Letters from our Readers." 1:1, June 1966.
Dr. Samuel Hordes of New York sent a copy of his miniature bookplate.

4144 "Recent Publications." 2:4, March 1967.
Miniature volume on bookplates by Abraham Horodisch published in Amsterdam.

4145 "Miniature Bookplates." (17) 2:7, March 1967.
Contemporary plates including those of Robert Hitchman, Wilbur Macey Stone, Julian Edison, Ruth Adomeit, and one in Japanese; smallest is that of James Henderson, measuring 3 x 2 millimeters.

4146 "Miniature Books About Miniature Books." 4:6-7, June 1969.
Reference again to Horodisch's *Miniatur Ex Libris*, published in 1966, with ninety-five pages of text "plus numerous pages with cuts of varied and unusual miniplates."

MINING AND METALLURGY

4147 "Library Book Plate Based on Agricola." Gilbert L. Campbell. (1) 25:435, September 1944.
Plate for library of School of Mines and Metallurgy at Rolla, Missouri, uses illustrations from the 1561 edition of Agricola outlining mining practices.

MINNEAPOLIS INSTITUTE OF ART BULLETIN [See BULLETIN OF MINNEAPOLIS INSTITUTE OF ART]

MINNESOTA MEDICINE

4148 "What Are Bookplates?" Cleora Wheeler. 40:436-7, June 1957.
A bookplate is "a small work of art in the general sense of the word."

4149 "Bookplate Collecting and Exhibiting." Cleora Wheeler. 40:509-10, July 1957.
Mentions current and past societies of collectors and repeat exhibitors such as the Grolier Club.

4150 "Preservation of Bookplates." Cleora Wheeler. 40:585, 599, August 1957.
"Good collections should be given only to institutions that can adequately care for them," to quote Louis J. Bailey, Chief Librarian, Queen's Borough Public Library.

4151 "Size and Material of Bookplates." Cleora Wheeler. 40:656-7, September 1957.
Discusses design, paper, methods of reproduction, cost of plate and prints.

4152 "Steel Engraved Bookplate." Cleora Wheeler. 40:728-9, October 1957.
Suggests "Non-Wrap Paste" by B. H. Fuller Co. of St. Paul at two dollars a quart to be used to paste bookplate squarely on inside cover.

4153 "Bookplate Lettering and References." Cleora Wheeler. (12) 40:808-10, November 1957.
Suggested references "easily understood" are *Bookplates for Beginners*, Alfred Fowler; *Some American College Bookplates*, Harry Parker Ward; and *Book of Artists' Own Bookplates*, Ruth Saunders.

MISCELLANEA GENEALOGIA ET HERALDICA

4154 "Examples of Armorial Book-plates." (4) 1:284, 1868.
John Hooke, Sergeant at Law, 1733, father of historian Nathaniel Hooke.

4155 "Examples of Armorial Book-plates." (3) 1:299, 1868.
Genealogy and heraldry in some detail for Samuel Billingsley, John Egerton, and Powell Snell.

4156 "Armorial Book-Plates." (4) 2:130, 1876.
James Franklin Fuller and Gordon Willoughby James Gyll.

4157 "Examples of Armorial Book-Plates." (7) 2:253-4, 1876.
Arthur Williams, Richard Mostyn, Vaughn Watkin Williams, Salesbury, and W. W. E. Wynne.

4158 "Armorial Book Plate and Signature of Alan second Viscount Middleton." (1) 2:258, 1876.
The title tells the story.

4159 "Armorial Bookplates." (4) N.S.1:118, 1874.
Illustrations only of plates for Croker and three different Fox families.

4160 "Armorial Bookplates." (1) N.S. 2:87-8, 1877.
Bookplate for Hilliard has motto in Greek, "The half is more than the whole," which is explained by Macaulay in Moore's *Life of Byron* as proverb of old Hesiod, like the Dutch policy in Spice Islands of cutting most precious trees to raise value of the remainder.

4161 "Family of Haselwood." (2) N.S.2:128, 1877.
Motto: Quod me mihi reddit amicum. (That which makes me on good terms with myself, i.e. a good conscience.)

4162 "Pedigree of Family of Furneaux." (1) N.S.2:171-5, 1877.
Bookplate illustrated.

4163 "Grant of Supporters to Sir William Maynard Gomm, G.C.B." (1) N.S.2:184, 1877.
Bookplate illustrated.

4164 "Boddington Pedigree." N.S. 2:244-7, 1877.
Another armorial bookplate.

4165 "Kennett Pedigree." (1) N.S.2:287-8, 1877.
Bookplate illustrated.

4166 "Lorimer Scotland." (1) N.S.2:421-3, 1877.
Bookplate illustrated.

4167 "Armorial Bookplate, Rev. George Thomas Palmer, M.A." (1) N.S.2:487, 1877.
Bookplate illustrated.

4168 "Barker Pedigree." (1) N.S.2:505-10, 1877.
Bookplate illustrated.

4169 "Armorial Bookplates." (3) N.S.2:525, 1877.
Henry Bowdon, John Bruno Bowdon, Col. Butler Bowdon; Colonel's quite attractive.

4170 "Armorial Bookplates." (2) N.S.2:556, 1877.
Valentine Dudley Henry Cary-Eleves.

4171 "Armorial Bookplates." (1) N.S.2:570, 1877.
Potter of Ardview.

4172 "Armorial Bookplates." (1) N.S.2:583, 1877.
William Thomas Waldy.

4173 "Strangeways." (2) N.S.3:22, 1880.
Bookplates illustrated.

4174 "Pedigree of the Longs of Semington." (1) N.S. 47, 1880.
Bookplate illustrated.

4175 "Pedigree of Family of Woodrooffe." (1) N.S.3, 65-70, 1880.
Bookplate illustrated.

4176 "John St. George." (1) N.S.3:82, 1880.
Bookplate illustrated.

4177 "Armorial Bookplates." N.S.3:95, 1880.
Hyett family.

4178 "Genealogical Memoranda Relating to the Mitchell Family." (2) N.S.3:101-2, 143, 1880.
Armorial bookplate illustrated.

4179 "Armorial Bookplates." (2) N.S.3:156, 1880.
Plate designed by John Leighton for Thomas William Carson; also illustrated bookplate of Daniel Burr.

4180 "Notes on the Family of Andrews." (1) N.S.3:169-71, 1880
Mention of armorial bookplate of Robert Andrews.

4181 "Armorial Bookplates." (2) N.S.3:182, 1880.
William Waggett of Cork arms pictured, as well as bookplate of Isaac Saunders Leadam, A.M.

4182 "Pedigree of the Bedfords." (2) N.S.3, 189, 1880.
Bookplate illustrated.

4183 "Family of Harrington." (1) N.S.3, 194-7, 1880.
Bookplate illustrated.

4184 "Armorial Bookplate." (1) N.S.3:206, 1880.
Plate for Edward Arthur White designed by J. H. Le Keux.

4185 "Armorial Bookplate." (1) N.S.3:226, 1880.
Plate for W. M. Walters.

4186 "Pedigree of Nott." (1) N.S.3:233, 1880.
Bookplate illustrated.

4187 "Additions to Walters Pedigree." (1) N.S.3:252, 1880.
This bookplate has squirrels on it, as did the previous Walters plate.

4188 "Pedigree of Tomes." (10) N.S. 3:273-9, 1880.
Illustrations actually appear to be seals and coats of arms rather than bookplates, but article is indexed as "Armorial Bookplates."

4189 "Armorial Bookplate." (1) N.S.3:290, 1880.
Bookplate for Arthur Francis Gregory; almost impossible to determine up side of this circular plate.

4190 "Armorial Bookplate." (1) N.S.3:327, 1880.
Plate of William Courthope who edited Debrett's *Peerage*.

4191 "Armorial Bookplates." (2) N.S.3, 353, 1880.
Plates for Robert and Edward Hoblyn.

4192 "Armorial Bookplate." (1) N.S.3:402, 1880.
Plate incorporates seal of Archdeaconry of Carlisle and Arms of the Venerable William Jackson.

4193 "Family of Dalton." (1) N.S.3:438, 1880.
Armorial bookplate "gives the Dalton arms quartering Norcliffe and Wray."

4194 "Armorial Bookplate." (1) N.S.3:445-7, 1880.
Plate of James Elwin Millard, D.D., born 1823.

4195 "Armorial Bookplate." (1) N.S.4:6, 1884.
Plate for Hon. Rev. Sidney Meade.

4196 "Armorial Bookplate." (1) N.S.4:18, 1884.
Illustration only of plate for Bartholomew C. Gidley.

4197 "Armorial Bookplates." (2) N.S.4:54, 1884.
Brief details of Hayman family and plates for Mathew Hayman and Rev. Samuel Hayman.

4198 "Armorial Bookplate." (1) N.S.4:67, 1884.
Family history of William Wickham; bookplate motto: "Manners makyth man."

4199 "Armorial Bookplate." (1) N.S.4:78, 1884.
Pedigree of Arthur Underhill, LL.D.

4200 "Armorial Bookplate." (1) N.S.4:102, 1884.
Details on Traherne of Coedriglan and St. Hilary, Co. Glamorgan. Motto: "Ofna Dduw a'r Brehin" (Fear God and the King).

4201 "Armorial Bookplate." (1) N.S.4:131, 1884.
Family history and plate for Reginald Pole.

4202 "Armorial Bookplate." (1) N.S.4:154, 1884.
Plate and pedigree of Thomas Carew.

4203 "Armorial Bookplate." (1) N.S.4:166, 1884.
Plate and family history of Littleton of Cornwall.

4204 "Armorial Bookplates." (2) N.S.4:190, 1884.
Pedigree and plate of Pringle of Whytbank.

4205 "Armorial Bookplate." (1) N.S.4:202, 1884.
Plate for Oliver Heywood.

4206 "Pedigree of the Family of Fletcher." (2) N.S.4:214-8, 1884.
Lengthy pedigree and plate illustrated.

4207 "Genealogical Memoranda Relating to the Wilmer Family." (2) N.S. 4:238-9, 1884.
Extracts from the registers, plus two plates.

4208 "Armorial Bookplates." (2) N.S.4:250-1, 1884.
Family history of Symons of Hatt and Soltau of Little Efford.

4209 "Armorial Bookplate." (1) N.S.4:274, 1884.
Paragraph about George Collins of Ham and plate illustrated.

4210 "Armorial Bookplates." (2) N.S.4:287-8, 1884.
Bookplates represent the Arms of the South Devon and North Devon branches of the Wollcombe family which separated in the 16th century.

4211 "Armorial Bookplate." (1) N.S.4:300, 1884.
Plate for Thomas Charlton Clutton.

4212 "Armorial Bookplate." (1) N.S.4:314, 1884.
Plate for Ozias Humphry.

4213 "Grant of Arms to William Heysham of East Greenwich." (1) N.S.4:375, 1884.
Grant printed and plate illustrated.

4214 "Lynch." (1) N.S.4:387, 1884.
Monumental inscription in Latin and bookplate for John Lynch, D.D., Dean of Canterbury.

4215 "Chauncy Book-Plates." (3) Second Series 1:28, 1886.
Illustrations of plates for Charles Chauncy, M.D., Nathaniel Chauncy, and Charles Snell Chauncy.

4216 "Pedigree of Family of Conder." (1) Second Series 1:61, 1886.
Plate for Edward Conder.

4217 "Chetwode Book-plate." (4) Second Series 1:90, 1886.
Four different plates using two different coats of arms.

4218 "Chetwode Bookplates." (2) Second Series 1:122, 1886.
Plate for Lady Mary Booth's library at Oakley; also Knightley Chetwood of Woodbrook in Queen's County in Ireland.

4219 "Armorial Bookplates." (4) Second Series 1:140, 1886.
Plates for Skinner and Smyth families.

4220 "Armorial Bookplates." (4) Second Series. 1:172, 1886.
Foxley, Skinner, Barnard, and Ramsden illustrated (actually says armorial ledger stones, Church of Holy Trinity, Hull).

4221 "Armorial Bookplates." (2) Second Series 1:235, 1886.
Plates for Henry Shank and Shank of Castlerigg.

4222 "Armorial Bookplates." (1) Second Series 1:268, 1886.
Family history and plate of Elizabeth, Countess of Exter (1681-1721).

4223 "Armorial Bookplate." (1) Second Series 1:285-6, 1886.
History of Sir Edward Dering and his bookplate.

4224 "Dade Bookplate." (1) Second Series 1:311, 1886.
Illustration and monumental inscriptions.

4225 "Armorial Bookplates." (2) Second Series 1:347-8, 1886.
Plates for John Murray and Joseph Smith, British Consul at Venice.

4226 "Armorial Bookplates." (2) Second Series 1:364, 1886.
Plates for Canon Walpole and Henry Spencer Walpole.

4227 "Armorial Bookplates." (2) Second Series 2:24, 1888.
Plates for William Draper.

4228 "Bookplates, Tucher and Scheurl." (2) Second Series 2:104-5, 1888.
Facsimilies of armorial bookplates "variously treated by Durer and Cranach, which, whether regarded as associated with those giants of early heraldic design or as being the first known instances of bookplates at all, are of unusual interest."

4229 "Tucher and Scheurl." (1) Second Series 2:120, 1888.
Illustration for article on 104.

4230 "Bisse Bookplates." (2) Second Series 2:152, 1888.
Plates illustrated for Dr. Philip Bisse, Lord Bishop of St. David's, and Thomas Bisse.

4231 "Bookplate and Seal of Bartlett of Marldon, St. Mary Church." (1) Second Series 2:294-6, 1888.
Plate engraved by Mr. Wyon.

4232 "Armorial Bookplate." (1) Second Series 2:368, 1888.
Plate for Owen.

4233 "Darwin Bookplates." (2) Second Series 3:19, 1890.
Two dated plates, 1717 and 1771.

4234 "Dering Bookplates." (3) Second Series 3:56, 1890.
Plates for Sir Edward Dering and Deborah Lady Dering; also illustrated is plate for Rev. Phillips Monypenny.

4235 "Grant of Supporters to Sir Robert Murray Keith, K.C.B., 1772." (2) Second Series 3:88, 1890.
Pictured are plates for Robert Keith and Sir Robert Murray Keith, K.B.

4236 "Armorial Bookplates." (2) Second Series 3:188, 1890.
Plates for John Conduitt and Charles C. Barton.

4237 "Shuckburgh Book Plates." (2) Second Series 3:253, 1890.
Plates for Stewkley Shuckburgh and Sir George Shuckburgh.

4238 "Armorial Bookplates." (2) Second Series 3:260, 1890.
Two plates for the Hopkins family.

4239 "Armorial Bookplate." (1) Second Series 3:276, 1890.
Plate for Rachel, Duchess of Beaufort, 1706.

4240 "Confirmation of Arms and Grant of Crest to Thomas Burfoot of London, 1752." (1) Second Series 3:397, 1890.
Plate for Richard Burfoot illustrated.

4241 "Armorial Bookplates." (4) Second Series 4:25, 1892.
Actually says Arms of Ledger Stones, Eye Church, Suffolk and shows those for Nathaniel D'Eye, 1718; Martha Cullum, 1732; Mary, wife of Francis D'Eye, 1747; and Thomas D'Eye, 1756.

4242 "Armorial Bookplates." (2) Second Series 4:40, 1892.
Plates for Ball and Richard Ball Dodson.

4243 "Armorial Bookplate." (1) Second Series 4:89, 1892.
Plate for Paul Jodrell of Duffield (died 1728 at 82).

4244 "Armorial Bookplate." (1) Second Series 4:120, 1892.
Plate for Sir Spencer Lambert Hunter Vassall has motto: Every bullet has its billet; this expression was used when Col. Vassall was hit and some of his men wished to stop and pick him up; he said, "Push on brave 38th, never mind me; every bullet has its billet."

4245 "John Cooke, Esq., of Swifts in Cranbrook." (1) Second Series 4:136, 1892.
Plate for John Cooke bears the date 1712.

4246 "Armorial Bookplate." (1) Second Series 4:152, 1892.
Plate for Sir George Cooke of the Inner-Temple, London, with date 1727.

4247 "Armorial Bookplate." (1) Second Series 4:168, 1892.
Bookplate for Thomas Harrison bears date of 1698.

4248 "Langley Bookplates." (4) Second Series 4:184-5, 1892.
Four different Langley family bookplates including one for Henry Langley who lost his right hand at seige of Clonmel in 1650 and thereafter wore an iron hand.

"This iron hand he thenceforth wore
His various works to settle;
Thus proving still, just as before,
Himself a man of mettle."

4249 "Armorial Bookplate." (1) Second Series 4:201, 1892.
Plate for William Windham who died at forty-four in 1761.

4250 "Confirmation of Arms of Thomas Augustus Prentice of Armagh, 1890." (1) Second Series 4:216, 1892.
Bookplate for John George Prentice.

4251 "Armorial Bookplate." (1) Second Series 5:232, 1892.
Two Yardley bookplates dated 1721 and 1739.

4252 "Armorial Bookplate." (1) Second Series 5:89, 1894.
Plate for Richard Pritchett.

4253 "Armorial Bookplate." (1) Second Series 5:104, 1894.
John Benson bookplate.

4254 "Phillips Bookplate." (1) Second Series 5:136, 1894.
Plate designed and etched by George W. Eve and "included in this year's Royal Academy Exhibition (No. 1520)."

4255 "Carter and Andrews Pedigree." (1) Second Series 5:168, 1894.
Bookplate for Thomas Carter.

4256 "Armorial Bookplates." (15) Second Series 5:between 192-3, 1894.
Includes plates for Gery Milner-Gibson-Cullum and various members of the family with one or more of these last three names, dated as early as 1760 and as late as 1850.

4257 "Irish Bookplates." (2) Second Series 5:264, 1894.
Bookplates for Thomas Ridgate Maunsel (died 1812) and Disson Darling (will dated 1766).

4258 "Irish Bookplates." (2) Second Series 5:281, 1894.
These two plates (as did the previously noted Irish bookplates) feature the coat of arms framed by stacks of books, with objects of individual interest scattered or laid on top.

4259 "Armorial Bookplates." (3) Third Series 1:16, 1896.
Two plates for William Griffith, one dated 1707.

4260 "Bookplate of Charles O'Brien." (1) Third Series 1:49, 1896.
This plate is from the collection of Sir Wollaston Franks, K.C.B., P.S.A.

4261 "Reviews." Third Series 1:62, 1896.
Comments on *Journal of Ex Libris Society*, volume 4, parts 4, 5, and 6.

4262 "Bookplates of Thomas Windham of Tale, C. Devon." (1) Third Series 1:80, 1896.
One of the family, Christabel Wyndham, was wet-nurse to Charles II.

4263 "Armorial Bookplates." (2) Third Series 1:89, 1896.
Plates of William Donne and Rev. William Sayer Donne.

4264 "Armorial Bookplates." (2) Third Series 1:112, 1896.
Plates for John Godfrey and Henry Gale.

4265 "Review." Third Series 1:128, 1896.
Journal has feature "Bookplates for Identification."

4266 "Bookplate of Sir Robert Clayton." (2) Third Series 1:137, 1896.
Two slightly different versions of armorial bookplate.

4267 "Reviews." Third Series 1:160, 1896.
Work of Mark Lambert of Newcastle similar in style to that of his master, Bewick.

4268 "The Hon. Sir Andrew Hume, 1707." (1) Third Series 1:176, 1896.
Bookplate bears date 1707 and motto: "True to the end."

4269 "*Journal of Ex Libris Society*." Third Series 1:192, 1896.
Publication well worthy of support it is receiving on both sides of ocean.

4270 "Armorial Bookplate." (1) Third Series 1:217, 1896.
Plate for Lancelot Shadwell, Lincoln's Inn.

4271 "Reviews." Third Series 1:256, 1896.
More complimentary comments on Ex Libris publication.

4272 "Reviews." Third Series 2:31, 1898.
"The American touts for plates will be hopefully met with scant notice."

4273 "Bookplate of John Gore of London." (1) Third Series 2:49, 1898.
Plate for John Gore (died in 1765 at 74).

4274 "Reviews." Third Series 2:63, 1898.
Favorable comment on Ex Libris publication.

4275 "Armorial Bookplate." (1) Third Series 2:81, 1898.
Plate for William Priaulx dated 1732.

4276 "Bookplate of James Tobin." (1) Third Series 2:88, 1898.
Publisher of tracts relating to sugar trade in 1792.

4277 "Reviews." Third Series 2:98, 1898.
Journal continues "to keep up the prestige of the work."

4278 "Bookplate of Nathaniel Tucker of London, Face Painter, 1740." (1) Third Series 2:132, 1898.
Some of his portraits, chiefly clergymen, were engraved.

4279 "Frederick." Third Series 2:134, 1898.
Mention of "plain bookplate with ornamental border" in folio bible, 1583.

4280 "Review." Third Series 2:139, 1898.
Work of Hopson included.

4281 "Review." Third Series 2:176, 1898.
Dues raised to a guinea and membership limited to 500 in Ex Libris Society.

4282 "Armorial Bookplate." (1) Third Series 2:185, 1898.
Plate for Thomas Alured Pincke (died 1771).

4283 "Reviews." Third Series 2:212, 1898.
Favorable comment on *Journal*.

4284 "Four Tempest Bookplates and Their Owners." (4) Third Series 2:236-40, 1898.
Included are plates dated 1702 and 1722.

4285 "Reviews." Third Series 2:259, 1898.
Objection "to the American system of sending over here letters asking for days' searching, or an exchange of bookplates, when only a single stamp is placed on their letter, mulcting the English correspondent of three-pence on every lapse."

4286 "Armorial Bookplates." (2) Third Series 2:292, 1898.
Plates for Huguenot refugee family of Teissoniere, known as Dayrolles.

4287 "Reviews." Third Series 2:308, 1898.
Reviews October-December 1897 issues of *Journal of Ex Libris Society.*

4288 "Armorial Bookplate." (1) Third Series 2:301, 1898.
Plate for John Wilson of the Commons House, Sandbach.

4289 "Freeman." (1) Third Series 3:17, 1900.
Plate for Rev. William Freeman, Curate and Lecturer of St. Botolph, Aldersgate.

4290 "Reviews." Third Series 3:30-1, 1900.
In addition to comment on *Journal* reviews *Artists and Engravers of British and American Bookplates*, whose author is given as Henry W. Pincham (Fincham).

4291 "Bookplate of Thomas, Lord Trevor, 1738." (1) Third Series 3:49, 1900.
Plate dated 1738.

4292 "Reviews." Third Series 3:64, 1900.
Plate of scarce coat of arms of "Buchanan of that Ilk." Plates for identification now number over 300 in *Journal.*

4293 "Bookplate of Peter Upcher." (1) Third Series 3:81, 1900.
Upcher was admitted a Burgess of Colchester, 1772.

4294 "Review." Third Series 3:99, 1900.
Comment on *Journal of Ex Libris Society.*

4295 "Harborough. (1) Third Series 3:116, 1900.
Bookplate for Dr. John Harborough (Dr. of Phisick).

4296 "Reviews." Third Series 3:140, 1900.
Comment on *Journal.*

4297 "Armorial Bookplates." (2) Third Series 3:164, 1900.
Plates for two members of the Dury family.

4298 "Reviews." Third Series 3:180, 1900.
Laments loss of Walter Hamilton "in the prime of life."

4299 "Carvick." (1) Third Series 3:197, 1900.
Plate for Thomas Carvick with motto: Be stedfast.

4300 "Reviews." Third Series 3:220, 1900.
Bookplates to identify number 371 in Ex Libris Society publication.

4301 "Reviews." Third Series 3:259-60, 1900.
Comment on *Journal.*

4302 "Armorial Bookplate." (1) Third Series 3:277, 1900.
Plate for Robert Rayne.

4303 "Reviews." Third Series 3:300, 1900
Comment on *Journal.*

4304 "Armorial Bookplate." (1) Third Series 4:1, 1902.
Plate for the Right Noble Thomas Duke of Leeds, dated 1701. Apparently some question of his right to use certain quarterings.

4305 "Reviews." Third Series 4:36, 1902.
Appeal for assistance in preparing articles for *Journal.*

4306 "Reviews." Third Series 4:76, 1902.
Plates to identify now number 421 in *Journal of Ex Libris Society.*

4307 "Bookplate of Lord Raymond of Abbots Langley." (1) Third Series 4:93, 1902.
Probably the plate of the second and last Lord Raymond who held the peerage from 1732 to 1756.

4308 "*Journal of Ex Libris Society.*" Third Series 4:116, 1902.
Review of contents of July and August issues.

4309 "Arms of the Dukes of Gordon." (2) Third Series 4:133, 1902.
Earlier plate for one of five Dukes of Gordon (1684 to 1836); other bookplate for Cosmo George, Duke of Gordon in Scotland, who succeeded to the title in 1728.

4310 "Reviews." Third Series 4:151-2, 1902.
Reviewer suggests making the *Journal* a quarterly.

4311 "Reviews." Third Series 4:186-7, 1902.
November-December 1900 *Journal* a double issue.

4312 "Bookplate of Thomas, Lord Mansel." (1) Third Series 4:205, 1902.
Date of this plate is between 1736 and 1743.

4313 "Reviews." Third Series 4:228, 1902.
Plates to identify total 467 in Ex Libris magazine.

4314 "Bookplates of 'Wilmot, Viscount Lisburne,' and of 'Wilmot, Earl of Lisburne.'" (2) Third Series 4:245, 1902.
Probably these two plates are for Wilmot Vaughn and were made between 1766 and 1800.

4315 "Reviews." Third Series 4:264, 1902.
Current "vacation" issues of *Journal* excellent.

4316 "Reviews." Third Series 4:303-4, 1902.
No. 479 to be identified as "evidently a Bewick plate" in *Journal.*

4317 "Bookplate of 'Dartrey.'" (1) Third Series 5:17, 1904.
Bookplate for Thomas Dawson who was created Baron Dartrey in 1770.

4318 "Reviews." Third Series 5:38, 1904.
Full page of details concerning *Journal.*

4319 "In Memorian: Joseph Jackson Howard, LLD., F.S.A." (1) Third Series 5: 41-3, 1904.
Dr. Howard originated this magazine in 1866; was among first to collect armorial bookplates, and had many valuable, scarce, brilliant specimens.

4320 "Reviews." Third Series 5:79-80, 1904.
Comment on *Journal*.

4321 "Bookplate of Rev. R. E. H. Duke." (1) Third Series 5:96, 1904.
Appears to be George W. Eve plate.

4322 "Reviews." Third Series 5:120, 1904.
There are now 512 plates for identification in *Journal*.

4323 "Bookplate of Lloyd." (1) Third Series 5:137, 1904.
Plate of Humphrey Lloyd of Denbigh, celebrated antiquary; Lloyd arms impale those of his wife Barbara, sister and heir of Lord Lumley.

4324 "Reviews." Third Series 5:160, 1904.
Comment on Ex Libris Society publication.

4325 "Reviews." Third Series 5:199, 1904.
Comment on *Journal*.

4326 "Reviews." Third Series 5:239-40, 1904.
Comment on *Journal*.

4327 "Bookplate of Amelia, Sophia, Countess." (1) Third Series 5:249, 1904.
Presumed mistress of George II; this was the last peerage conferred on a Royal favorite.

4328 "Reviews." Third Series 5:279-80, 1904.
Comment on *Journal*.

4329 "Bookplate of John Hervey, Esq." (1) Third Series 5:296, 1904.
Plate is dated 1698; two other varieties of Hervey's bookplate appear in book by Dr. Howard.

4330 "Reviews." Third Series 5:323, 1904.
British Museum publishes first part of Franks Collection Catalogue.

4331 "Bookplate of Bolle or Bolles, Esq." (1) Fourth Series 1:Frontispiece, 1906.
From collection of W. Bruce Bannerman.

4332 "Reviews." Fourth Series 1:39, 1906.
Brief review of *Journal*.

4333 "Reviews." Fourth Series 1:80, 1906.
Brief review of *Journal*.

4334 "Reviews." Fourth Series 1:120, 1906.
General Index to volumes I to XII issued for Ex Libris publication.

4335 "Reviews." Fourth Series 1:160, 1906.
Brief review of *Journal*.

4336 "Bookplate of P. D. Huet, 1630." (1) Fourth Series 1:177, 1906.
A classical scholar, his bookplate is worded in Latin.

4337 "Cockburn." (1) Fourth Series 1:190, 1906.
William Cockburn's bookplate "bears his arms."

4338 "Reviews." Fourth Series 1:200, 1906.
Ex Libris Society members are not giving Editor help he needs to issue publication on schedule.

4339 "Douglas, Duke of Dover." (1) Fourth Series 1:201 and 277, 1906.
Bookplate engraved between 1708 and 1711.

4340 "Reviews." Fourth Series 1:240, 1906.
Brief review of *Journal*.

4341 "Bookplate of the Rev. B. S. Lombard." (1) Fourth Series 1:257, 1906.
Plate is the work of Mary C. Lawson, about 1905.

4342 "Bookplate of Late Mr. Joseph Foster, Hon. M.A. Oxon." (1) Fourth Series 1:279, 1906.
Joseph Foster was noted genealogist.

4343 "Bookplate of William Bruce Bannerman, F.S.A." (1) Fourth Series 1:297, 1906.
Designed and engraved on copper by C. W. Sherborn for new editor of this magazine.

4344 "Reviews." Fourth Series 1:327, 1906.
Plates for identification number 596 in Ex Libris publication.

4345 "Reviews." Fourth Series 2:47, 1908.
Brief review of *Journal*.

4346 "Reviews." Fourth Series 2:96, 1908.
Index to volume XV of *Journal*.

4347 "Armorial Bookplates." (2) Fourth Series 2:118, 1908.
Plate for Isaac Le Heup, who died 1747, and Thomas Discipline.

4348 "Reviews." Fourth Series 2:144, 1908.
Brief review of *Journal*.

4349 "Armorial Bookplate." (1) Fourth Series 2:157, 1908.
Plate of Lewis Montolieu (d. 1817).

4350 "Reviews." Fourth Series 2:180, 1908.
August and September, 1906 issues reviewed of *Journal of Ex Libris Society*.

4351 "Armorial Bookplate." (1) Fourth Series 2:181, 1908.
Plate for Edmund Poley dated 1707.

4352 "Reviews." Fourth Series 2:220, 1908.
Brief review of *Journal*.

4353 "Reviews." Fourth Series 2:260, 1908.
Brief review of *Journal*.

4354 "Reviews." Fourth Series 2:300, 1908.
Paragraph about Ex Libris Society.

4355 "Reviews." Fourth Series 2:340, 1908.
Brief review of Ex Libris publication.

4356 "Armorial Bookplate of Richard Golightly." (1) Fourth Series 3:1, 1910.
Richard Golightly died 1855.

4357 "Reviews." Fourth Series 3:48, 1910.
Brief review of *Journal*.

4358 "Reviews." Fourth Series 3:96, 1910.
Over six hundred plates to be identified in *Journal*.

4359 "Reviews." Fourth Series 3:144, 1910.
Brief review of Ex Libris publication.

4360 "Reviews." Fourth Series 3:191, 1910.
Brief review of *Journal*.

4361 "Reviews." Fourth Series 3:239, 1910.
Tribute to Gerald Ponsonby who died November 30, 1908.

4362 "Armorial Bookplates." (4) Fourth Series 3:242, 1910.
Plates for various Marryat family members.

4363 "Armorial Bookplate." (1) Fourth Series 3:274, 1910.
Thomas Tyssem Bazely (1808-1894).

4364 "Armorial Bookplate." (1) Fourth Series 3:281, 1910.
Plate for James F. Fuller.

MISCELLANY [See **BOOK-PLATE COLLECTOR'S MISCELLANY,** Supplement to **WESTERN ANTIQUARY**]

MODERN ART

4365 "Report of Competition—A Book Plate." (9) 4: nine unnumbered pages following page 68, April 1, 1896.
"Probably only a designer who is as much of a book lover as he is an artist can make a successful book plate."

MODERN PHARMACY

4366 "Pharmaceutical Bookplates." Louis Ginsberg. (5) Issue No. 3:6-7, 1958.
Marco Birnholz, Austrian pharmacist and bookplate collector, had over 350 plates executed for him by European artists.

MONTHLY CHRONICLE OF NORTH-COUNTRY LORE AND LEGEND

4367 "Joseph Barber, Bookseller and Copper-Plate Printer." 2:158-9, April 1888.
Quotes *Newcastle Curant* of November 29, 1740 in which Joseph Barber advertised as "music and copperplate printer." Considerable biographical data.

MOTIF

4368 "In Pursuit of Ephemera." John N. C. Lewis. (44) Issue No. 7:84-89, Summer 1961.

Illustrations include bookplate of St. Helena Artillery Library; mentions Mrs. Bella C. Landauer who worked on her collection the day of her death and went to a movie where she died.

4369 "Rex Whistler." Issue No. 7:102-3, Summer 1961.

Review of book by Laurence Whistler and Ronald Fuller about artist who created bookplates as well as larger works.

THE MUSES

4370 "Intellectual Recreations for Poets. No. 1 The Study of Ex Libris and Book-Plate Collecting." H. Berkeley Score. (8) 1:17-20, 1893-96.

The Ex Libris Society was started in 1891 "by a few enthusiastic gentlemen . . . now it has members all over the world, especially in America, where clever men are always glad to welcome any new and interesting intellectual recreation."

MUSEUM BULLETIN [See **BULLETIN OF METROPOLITAN MUSEUM OF ART**]

MUSICAL NEWS

4371 "An Ornamental Book-Plate." T. Lea Southgate. (1) 51:234, October 7, 1916.

Title page engraved by J. Collins showing thirty-four old instruments reproduced, omitting title, as proposed musical bookplate.

MUSICAL QUARTERLY

4372 "Book-Plates of Musicians and Music-Lovers." Sheldon Cheney. (17) 3:446-52, July 1917.

"Friendships naturally are formed with people of the same tastes, and business associations may be largely molded by the influences of one's leisure hour hobbies. . . . book-plate . . . was for centuries stiffly heraldic in character. Of recent years . . . pictorial coat-of-arms, a graphic index to the tastes of the owner."

4373 "On Musical Book-Plates." Herman T. Radin. (23) 25:135-41, April 1939.

Composers most frequently pictured are Bach, Beethoven, Mozart, Wagner, Schubert and Brahms.

N

THE NATION

4374 "*Artists and Engravers of British and American Book-Plates.*" 66:114, February 10, 1898.

Scathing remarks about collectors of bookplates in this "review" of Fincham's reference volume "for Book-Plate and Print Collectors."

4375 "Book-Plate Thievery." William C. Lane. 70:260, April 5, 1900.
Librarian of Harvard writes "some one who has had access to the book-stack has cut from a large number of older books the front covers on which the book-plate is pasted."

NATIONAL EDUCATION ASSOCIATION JOURNAL

4376 "School Citizenship Project." (12) 16:253, November 1927.
Bookplates designed by students of Powell Junior High, Washington, D.C., for school library.

NATIONAL LIBRARY OF MEDICINE NEWS—U.S.

4377 "Bookplates." 13:2, December 1958.
Exhibit of bookplates of thirty "eminent American physicians" scheduled during December at National Library of Medicine.

NATIONAL RETIRED TEACHERS ASSOCIATION [See **NRTA**]

NEW COLOPHON

4378 "A Scrapbook of Strays." Paul McPharlin. (7) 1:200, 202, April 1948.
George E. Pettengill collects binders' and bookdealers' labels or trade cards which are usually small and are placed in a corner position in order "not to be covered with bookplates."

4379 "A Scrapbook of Strays." Paul McPharlin. (2) 1:304, July 1948.
Trade coats of arms for Saddler's Society and Society of Chair Makers; indexed as book labels though not actually bookplates.

4380 "A Seventeenth Century Book-Label Problem." Edward Naumburg, Jr. (9) 2:41-53, January 1949.
"I own to this gambler's weakness, and, in my search for old glass—whale-oil lamps or vigil lights—I have found some of my rarest juvenile books."

4381 "Firsts in a Manner of Speaking." Vincent Starrett. 2:68-81, January 1949.
"At least one bookplate may properly be called a first edition." Richard Le Gallienne wrote a poem, for sale of his books at auction in 1905, which was printed as a bookplate and placed in each sale volume.

NEW ENGLAND CRAFTSMAN

"Remarks on Some Masonic Book Plates and Their Owners." A. Winthrop Pope.

4382 (7) 3:403-11, August 1908.
4383 (7) 3:443-51, September 1908.
4384 (11) 4:7-17, October 1908.

4385 (6) 6:52-7, November 1910.

4386 (9) 6:85-93, December 1910.

4387 (9) 6:209-16, April 1911.

Biographical details of individual Masons who had bookplates; many Lodges had libraries of general interest with appropriate plates. Paul Revere was Most Worshipful Grand Master of Grand Lodge of Massachusetts (1795-7); comment that his heraldry was faulty.

NEW ENGLAND HISTORICAL AND GENEALOGICAL REGISTER

4388 "Heraldic Book-Plates of Early New England and New York." Richard C. Lichtenstein. (4) 40:295-9, July 1886.

List of 204 persons and families in New England and New York who used armorial engraved bookplates prior to 1830; two-thirds of plates engraved in America, remaining from England. Nathaniel Hurd at the head of the list both in "execution and fertility of design."

4389 "Early Southern Heraldic Book Plates." Richard C. Lichtenstein. 41:296-7, July 1887.

Together with previously published list of New England and New York plate owners, 375 persons of 288 families represented. Only one female possessor of a plate listed—Elizabeth Graeme.

4390 "Daniel Ravenel of South Carolina." William A. Courteny. 49:297-9, July 1895.

"His collection of book-plates was certainly the largest in number, the most valuable in rarity, and the most captivating, in the south."

NEW ENGLAND JOURNAL OF MEDICINE

Bookplate Collection of Boston Medical Library

4391 1-(1) 252:233, Februrary 10, 1955.

General bookplate for special valuable gifts.

4392 2-(1) 252:324, February 24, 1955.

Solomon H. Hyams Collection.

4393 3-(1) 252:589, April 7, 1955.

Oliver Wendell Holmes.

4394 4-(1) 252:641, April 14, 1955.

William Norton Bullard.

4395 5-(1) 252:1142, June 30, 1955.

James Read Chadwick, M.D.

4396 6-(1) 253:378, September 1, 1955.

John W. Farlow, M.D.

4397 7-(1) 253:469, September 15, 1955.

John C. Warren, M.D.

4398 8-(1) 253:617, October 6, 1955.
George Hayward, editor of *New England Journal of Medicine*.

4399 9-(1) 253:1084, December 15, 1955.
Isaac Foster.

4400 10-254:39, January 5, 1956.
James Jackson.

4401 11-(1) 254:483, March 8, 1956.
Massachusetts Medical Society.

4402 12-(1) 254:579, March 22, 1956.
John Homans, II.

4403 13-254:715, April 12, 1956.
Harvard University Medical College Library.

4404 14-(1) 254:1005, May 24, 1956.
Charles Goddard Weld.

4405 15-(1) 255:504, September 13, 1956.
John Mark Gourgas.

4406 16-(1) 256:322, February 14, 1957.
Portrait plate of George Hoyt Bigelow.

4407 17-(1) 257:1081, November 28, 1957.
Arthur Tracy Cabot.

4408 18-261:607, September 17, 1959.
Alfred Stille, M.D.

4409 "From the Books of —." 252:244, February 10, 1955.
"The personal bookplate, which an irreverent age might facetiously and certainly erroneously characterize as the hallmark of a gentleman who wished to be considered a scholar (or vice versa), is nearly as old as the printed book."

NEW ENGLAND MAGAZINE

4410 "Early American Artists and Mechanics, No. 1 Nathaniel Hurd." (1) 3:1-7, July 1832.
"To a superior mode of execution he added a Hogarthian talent of character and humor."

4411 "Sir William Pepperrell and the Capture of Louisburg." Victoria Reed. (24) 12:413-32, June 1895.
Lengthy article includes illustration of his bookplate.

NEW IDEA WOMAN'S MAGAZINE

4412 "Book-Plates." Julia Darrow Cowles. (10) 17:28-9, January 1908.
A brief, general introduction to bookplates; states a bookplate may be copyrighted.

NEW SOUTH WALES BOOKPLATE CLUB

4413 "Founders Brochure." (12) No. 1, 1932.

Three pages with brief text about the artists (Adrian Feint, George D. Perrottet and Gayfield Shaw) and four bookplates by each artist illustrated.

NEW YORK GENEALOGICAL AND BIOGRAPHICAL RECORD

4414 "Samuel Provoost, First Bishop of New York." General Jas. Grant Wilson. (1) 18:1-13, January 1887.

Samuel Provoost (born 1742) was "perhaps earliest of American bibliophiles." His armorial bookplate originally showed his name engraved Provost; additional letter adopted in 1769.

4415 "Book Notices." 26:96, April 1895.

Review of volume 6 of *Journal of Ex Libris Society*.

NEW YORK HISTORICAL SOCIETY QUARTERLY

4416 "Bookplates: The Oliver Clement Sheean Collection." George A. Zabriskie. (6) 34:58-64, January 1950.

Exhibit of 800 plates; explains differences between woodcuts and steel or copper engravings. Longfellow used visiting card as bookplate.

4417 "Collecting and Recollecting." Bella C. Landauer. (7) 43:334-49, July 1959.

Collection started in 1923 with $100 purchase including bookplates, prints, other graphic art. No bookplates illustrated.

NEW YORK JOURNAL OF DENTISTRY

4418 "New Book Mark." B. W. Weinberger. (1) 2:406-7, November 1932.

Bookplate for the New York Academy of Medicine First District Dental Society includes a portrait of Fauchard and the border design incorporates the names of writers on dentistry from various countries.

NEW YORK PUBLIC LIBRARY BULLETIN [See **BULLETIN OF NEW YORK PUBLIC LIBRARY**]

NEW ZEALAND EX LIBRIS SOCIETY

Brochure No. 1

4419 "Bookplates with Reference to Examples in Alexander Turnbull Library." Johannes C. Andersen. (5) 10-19, 1930.

"I have indeed heard that many plates produced are made by people who have no idea of their going into books at all—who do not themselves possess books. Your harness would not be much good if you had not your horse in mind."

4420 "Launching an Ex Libris Society." Pat Lawlor. (2) 20-3, 1930.

Spurred by enthusiasm generated by P. Neville Barnett, author launched New Zealand Society.

4421 "Our Auckland Branch." (1) 25, 1930.
Under presidency of Dr. E. B. Gunson.

4422 "Art in Bookplates, address by Dr. Gunson." (2) 26-9, 1930.
Slide-illustrated lecture.

4423 "List of N.Z. Plates." (3) 32-7, 1930.
Alphabetical by owner, giving designer when known.

4424 "Announcements." (1) 38-9, 1930.
Secretary will give names of artists to members wishing a plate designed.

4425 "Membership of N.Z. Ex Libris Society." (1) 40-2, 1930.
Five U.S. members listed.

4426 "Constitution and Rules." 43-4, 1930.
Among objectives "to promote and extend use of bookplates."

Brochure No. 2

4427 "New Zealand Book-plate Artists and Their Work." Johannes C. Andersen. (11) 6-30, 1933.
Comments on the numerous current artists and the plates they have created.

4428 "Book-plates for Books." Ronald Halloway. (2) 31-6, 1933.
Many plates today "seem designed as a separate 'collector's item' rather than to perform their rightful function."

4429 "List of New Zealand Book-Plate Artists and Their Plates." 37-43, 1933.
Includes owner of plate, date, and medium.

4430 "Members." 44-5, 1933.
Four members from U.S., including Carlyle S. Baer, Helen Basset, Katherine Burnham, and W. R. A. Hays.

Brochure No. 3

4431 "Book Plates." (8) 94-113, 1936.
Comments on eight tipped-in plates; names of living artists for individuals wishing a plate made; lists of bookplates exhibited by various categories.

[Unable to locate Brochures No. 4 and 5.]

Brochure No. 6

4432 "Art of the Bookplate." P. Watts Rule (7) 1-10, 1951.
Credit for historical information given to P. Neville Barnett, Bertram Stevens and Gleeson White.

4433 "Early French Bookplates." David H. Graham. (4) 11-5, 1951.
French grammarian and lexicographer M. Pierre Larousse was the first to insert the term ex libris in a French dictionary in 1866.

4434 "A Brief History." Pat Lawlor. 16-19, 1951.
New Zealand Society founded in 1930, dormant during World War II, and recently revived; bibliography of five previously printed brochures.

4435 "New Turnbull Library Bookplate." (1) 19, 1951.
New plate deemed advisable because original was "heraldically unorthodox."

4436 "Deciding on a Bookplate." F. W. Reed. 20-2, 1951.
Difficulties of producing a bookplate from the owner's idea through the finished plate and final printing.

4437 "Some Danish Bookplates." Johannes C. Andersen. (2) 23-5, 1951.
Six plates described by Danish artist, Viggo Julius von Holstein-Rathlon, Ph.D. and author.

4438 "Some Early Printed Maori Items in the Hawke's Bay Museum." Alice Woodhouse. 26-8, 1951.
No mention of bookplates.

NEWS-LETTER OF THE LXIVMOS

4439 "*Philobiblon.*" Issue No. 9, 5, July 15, 1928
Editor of new book magazine is publishing series of five volumes, last of which is about Merrymount Press, containing bibliography of Updike's books and many illustrations, including bookplates.

4440 "Bookplates for Miniature Books." Wilbur Macey Stone. (2) Issue No. 9, 7-8, July 15, 1928.
Smallest in his collection measures 5/8" x 1/2", made for William E. Spaulding of New Hampshire. Illustrated is author's plate cut in wood by J. J. Lankes.

4441 "Miniature Bookplates." Winifred Prescott. Issue No. 16, 7-9, March 15, 1929.
Tiny bookplates, at least those mentioned in this essay, range from 7/16" by 8/16" to 2" by 2". Lists numerous specific plates by various artists.

NEWS NOTES [Texas Library Association]

4442 "On Texas Bookplates." Sarah Chokla. (1) 11:cover, 2-3, January 1935.
Mentions plates of Maury Maverick which incorporated brand "MK"; University Club of Dallas; Stanley Marcus, then president of the Texas Book Club.

NEWS NOTES OF CALIFORNIA LIBRARIES

4443 "Book-plates." William A. Brewer. 4:266-72, April 1909.
Historical review, comments on collecting, suggestions for having your own plate made, and much information on bookplate activity in California.

4444 "Reference Department." 4:283, April 1909.
List of reference volumes on bookplates in State Library, similar to list accompanying Brewer article.

NORTHERN ECHO [Darlington, England]

4445 "Ex-Libris." January 25, 1897. [Unable to locate.]
Reprint of article from *Globe*, January 22, 1897; also mentioned in *Journal of Ex Libris Society*, 7:14, February 1897.

NORTHWESTERN UNIVERSITY BULLETIN [See **DENTAL RESEARCH AND GRADUATE STUDY QUARTERLY**]

NORTON'S LITERARY LETTER

4446 "Curiosa Americana." (6) 1:3-4, October 1857.
George Washington's bookplate (Exitus Acta Probab); also shown, his visiting card and seals bearing his initials.

NOTES AND NEWS [Organ of British Bookplate Club]

4447 Issue No. 1:1-3, January 1960.
A. B. Keeves, editor of defunct *Bookplate Collectors News*, attempts to form British Bookplate Club; he will provide club room in his home to house collection and library; club would be used to exchange plates among members on a unit system.

4448 Issue No. 2:4-7, September 1, 1960.
Twenty members resulted from first 100 invitations; progress slow what with editor in Morocco from February through May and then plagued with muscular rheumatism and pneumonia.

4449 Issue No. 3:8-13, November 1960.
List of Founder Members, club exchange system, notes on the library, and an English artist who does "abstracts, nudes & morbid subjects."

4450 Issue No. 4:14-21, April 1961.
Membership now at fifty; dues amounted to £54.12.5 and expenditures left a "carry forward" of £11.7.1. Keeves says "main reason for dropping the B.C.N. [was that] I found it was turning me into a Professional too quickly. . . . The amateur can be as unorthodox as he likes and be forgiven several mistakes but the pro cannot afford even one serious blunder and may only deviate when he is very certain of his ground. This is partly the reason why scientific works and even official bookplate publications make such dull reading on the whole."

NOTES AND QUERIES [Bookplate Exchange Club of England]

Source: *Bibliography of Bookplates Compiled from Various Sources* by P. C. Beddingham, 1962; comment in letter dated August 16, 1969, P. C. Beddingham to A. Arellanes: "*[Notes and Queries]* is a manuscript notebook journal of about 600 pages which was circulated among members of the Bookplate Exchange Club. It covers the period 1943-1963, and contains questions and answers by members of the Club. It is contained in six notebooks and was either written or typed."

[No entry number assigned as this does not qualify as as a periodical; however, its existence should be of interest.]

NOTES AND QUERIES

First Series

4451 "[Bookplates.]" 1:212, February 2, 1850.
Whose was the bookplate with the following device: an eagle or vulture feeding with a snake, another bird nearly as large as herself; a landscape with the sea in the distance "very meanly engraved."

4452 "[Bookplates.]" 3:495, June 21, 1851.
Daniel Parsons inquires about English bookplates dated prior to 1698.

4453 "[Bookplates.]" 4:46, July 19, 1851.
Refer to Parsons' question.

4454 "[Bookplates.]" 4:93, August 2, 1851.
Further note on Parsons.

4455 "[Bookplates.]" 4:354, November 1, 1851.
Early plate for Joseph Holland (1585) offered by T. W. King of College of Arms.

4456 "[Bookplates.]" 6:32, July 10, 1852.
Charles Clark's whimsical bookplate "A Pleader to the Needer When a Reader."

4457 "[Bookplates.]" 7:26, January 1, 1853.
Mentions Durer's early plate for Pirkheimer and bookplate of the former Duke of Mecklenburg pasted in Vesalius' anatomical work (Badil, 1555).

4458 "[Bookplates.]" 11:265, April 7, 1855.
"When did the earliest book-plate appear with the husband and wife's arms? Is it in accordance with heraldry to have it so? Do not some heralds consider it bad heraldry?"

4459 "[Bookplates.]" 11:351, May 5, 1855.
In a 1698 bookplate wife's coat of arms is given with husband's; "marshalling the wife's coat with her husband is the universal practice." Answered by Parsons.

4460 "[Bookplates.]" 11:471, June 16, 1855.
Bookplate dated 1669 for Gilbert Nicholson noted as earlier yet.

4461 "[Bookplates.]" 12:35, July 14, 1855.
Daniel Parsons asks for description of Nicholson plate.

4462 "[Bookplate.]" 12:114, August 11, 1855.
Description of Nicholson plate given briefly.

Second Series:

4463 "[Bookplates.]" 10:409, November 24, 1860.
In order to identify volumes from famous libraries, correspondent

desires to obtain rubbings of bookstamps and eventually publish manual to enable "a connoissuer to detect the stamp of any celebrated library at once."

Third Series:

4464 "Armorial Book-Plates." 6:306, October 15, 1864.
J. J. Howard offers his duplicates for exchange.

4465 "[Bookplates.]" 8:308, October 14, 1865.
Unknown engraver made bookplate 10" x 7 3/4", described in detail, with motto in Hebrew, Latin and Greek: Unto the pure all things are pure.

4466 "[Bookplates.]" 12:117, August 10, 1867
In connection with earlier article on Richard Dean, regicide, there is a footnote mentioning bookplates.

4467 "[Bookplates.]" 12:218, September 14, 1867.
The footnote "book-plates are no authority. They generally mean nothing at the present day" has brought forth indignant inquiry from D.P. to justify such statement.

Fourth Series:

4468 "[Bookplates.]" 4:409, November 13, 1869.
Edward West requests information on armorial plates prior to 1700 and offers exchange of duplicates from his collection.

4469 "[Bookplates.]" 4:518-9, December 11, 1869.
Mentions blank shields prepared to receive arms printed in books.

4470 "[Bookplates.]" 5:65, January 15, 1870.
Describes what is probably bookplate of H. Eckius pasted in volume printed about 1515, though engraving is probably about 1530.

4471 "[Bookplates.]" 5:210, February 19, 1870.
More haggling over minor points.

4472 "[Bookplates.]" 5:286, March 12, 1870.
Mentions John Leighton's article in June 1866 issue of *Gentleman's Magazine*.

4473 "[Bookplates.]" 9:160, February 24, 1872.
Death of George Barclay, designer of heraldic plates, noted; asks if there is a collection of his work.

4474 "[Bookplates.]" 10:519, December 28, 1872.
F. G. Lee will exchange with others interested in heraldic bookplates.

Fifth Series:

4475 "[Bookplates.]" 1:60, January 24, 1874.
Henry Pakitt offers to exchange or buy duplicate plates.

4476 "[Bookplates.]" 1:199, March 7, 1874.
Rev. Dr. Lee, collector of heraldic bookplates, has several hundred duplicates he is willing to exchange.

4477 "[Bookplates.]" 1:386, May 16, 1874.
William Jackson Pigott described arms, crests, and mottos found on bookplates which he cannot find in Burke's *General Armory*.

4478 "[Bookplates.]" 2:159, August 22, 1874.
Dr. Howard has many duplicate armorial bookplates for exchange.

4479 "[Bookplates.]" 4:464, December 11, 1875.
Another reference to Charles Clark's bookplate poem.

4480 "[Bookplates.]" 5:35, January 8, 1876.
Correspondent has copy of Clark's bookplate but with variations in the text and title.

4481 "[Bookplates.]" 6:369, November 4, 1876.
Requests identification of plate engraved by Barnes & Co. and gives the inscription.

4482 "[Bookplates.]" 6:465, December 9, 1876.
With increased interest in bookplates "I should like to ask whether any one . . . is preparing a handbook of bookplates."

4483 "[Bookplates.]" 6:543, December 30, 1876.
Requests description of coat of arms (6:369) to help identify plate.

4484 "Heraldic Book-Plate." 7:28, January 13, 1877.
Description given in hopes of identification.

4485 "Book-Plates." 7:36, January 13, 1877.
Mentions French bookplate volume by Poulet-Malassis which has gone through two editions; states no work in English on subject but refers to article in September 1876 issue of *Art Journal*.

4486 "Book-Plates." 7:76-7, January 27, 1877.
Mention again of John Leighton's article.

4487 "Heraldic." 7:76, January 27, 1877.
Offers possible answer to previous inquiry (7:28).

4488 "Earliest Known Book-Plates." 7:233, March 24, 1877.
Quote from Scott's *Life of Durer* concerning Pirkheimer book label engraved by this famous artist.

4489 "Mottoes on Book-Plates." 7:427, June 2, 1877.
"Videte et cavete ab avaritia" or "The wicked borroweth and payeth not again."

4490 "Heraldic Book-Plates." 7:435, June 2, 1877.
Collector with "large collection of choice and curious book-plates" will make exchange of duplicates or buy old plates.

4491 "Heraldic Book-Plates." 7:515, June 30, 1877.
Purchaser (I.I.H.) of collection assembled by Miss Jenkins of Bath says "A register of collectors' names would be of great value."

4492 "Heraldic Book-Plates." 8:38, July 14, 1877.
J. Wilson is first to offer his name for register of collectors.

4493 "Heraldic Book-Plates." 8:79, July 28, 1877.
S. A. Newman and Gerald Ponsonby add their names.

4494 "Mottoes on Book-Plates." 8:111-12, August 11, 1877.
Contributions by five correspondents, including J. Leicester Warren.

4495 "Heraldic Book-Plates." 8:118, August 11, 1877.
R. R. Lloyd and Thomas W. Carson join list of collectors.

4496 "Heraldic Book-Plates." 8:158, August 25, 1877.
Charles Williams another collector.

4497 "Heraldic Book-Plates." 8:178, September 1, 1877.
A. E. Lawson also collects.

4498 "Book-Plates." 8:200, September 1877.
J. Leicester Warren requests particulars on English bookplates, heraldic, and otherwise, which bear dates prior to 1699; in event his list is published he will acknowledge such assistance and indicate who possesses any "noteworthy book-plate."

4499 "Mottoes on Book-Plates." 8:258, September 29, 1877.
One motto was used by Roger Pepys, cousin to Samuel.

4500 "Book-Plates." 8:298, October 13, 1877.
Two plates described which may date prior to 1679.

4501 "Book-Plates." 8:397, November 17, 1877.
Correspondent lists plates dated between 1703-1746.

4502 "Book-Plates." 8:517, December 29, 1877.
Emily Cole offers duplicates of Sir Francis Fust's plate to "any collector who will kindly say where a letter shall be addressed."

4503 "Arrangement of Collection." 9:20, January 12, 1878.
Mr. Smith has his collection in alphabetical order but wonders if he should "call the collection in order of precedence, from Duke to Esquire, with index at end?"

4504 "Book-Plate." 9:29, January 12, 1878.
Information requested on R. T. Pritchett plate.

4505 "Book-Plate." 9:75, January 26, 1878.
One correspondent says Mr. Pritchett was a gun-maker in Regent Street and "a man of ingenious artistic tastes." Another that the plate was designed by "himself. His studio is at No. 1, Clifford's Inn."

4506 "Book-Plates." 9:198, March 9, 1878.
Notes on Birnie arms and plate of Lord Mayor of London, dated 1679.

4507 "Paper on Book-Plates." 9:360, May 4, 1878.
Paper by Rev. D. Parsons in Third Annual Report of Oxford University, Archeological and Heraldic Society, 1837.

4508 "Book-Plate Query." 10:428, November 30, 1878.
Identity of heraldic plate requested.

4509 "Dated Book-Plate." 11:446, June 7, 1879.
English bookplate dated 1668 in book published in 1657.

4510 "Dated Book-Plates." 12:33, July 12, 1879.
Description of Neville Catelyne's plate dated December 3, 1660.

Sixth Series:

4511 "My Collection of Bookplates." 1:2-4, January 3, 1880.
G.W.D. of Athenaeum Club gives interesting account of his collection which includes plates of Popes, Cardinals, Royalty, and those of lesser rank. Introduction aimed at those who condemn collecting mania because of supposed damage to valuable books in removing plates.

4512 "Book-Plates." 1:128-9, February 28, 1880.
Three replies to G.W.D.; one at length referring to Poulet-Malassis' monograph.

4513 "Book-Plates." 1:197-9, March 6, 1880.
C.I.M.Z. describes his collection; another rendition of Thomas á Kempis motto.

4514 "Book-Plates." 1:266, March 27, 1880.
J. J. Howard offers duplicates from his armorial collection; he acquired foreign bookplates of late Dr. Wellesley, Oxford.

4515 "Book-Plates." 1:336, April 24, 1880.
Request for details concerning plates of Lord Keane, Sir William Pigott, James Grey, Charles Kelly and William Maguire.

4516 "Book-Plates." 1:386, May 8, 1880.
Offers proper identity of plate in G.W.D.'s article.

4517 " 'As' on a Book-Plate." 1:516, June 26, 1880.
Questions use of "as on bookplate: 'As, William Senior, Esq.' "

4518 "Book-Plates." 2:34, July 10, 1880.
Identified individuals from previous inquiry. (1:336).

4519 "Book-Plates." 2:94, July 31, 1880.
Additional information on Sir Pigott.

4520 "Book-Plates." 2:255, September 25, 1880.
Sir Pigott and Lord Keane related by marriage.

4521 "Book-Plates." 2:272, October 2, 1880.
Description of printed plate of "Thomas Bell, 1644."

4522 "Book-Plates." 2:302-3, October 16, 1880.
C.I.M.Z. of Oxford and Cambridge Club describes some unusual plates in his collection.

4523 "Book-Plate." 2:367, November 6, 1880.
Identity of plate requested.

4524 "Book-Plate." 2:397, November 13, 1880.
Symbola Heroica (1736) often helpful in identifying mottoes of nobility and baronets of that period.

4525 "Book-Plate." 2:427, November 27, 1880.
Another call for help in identifying plate.

4526 "Book-Plates." 2:445, December 4, 1880.
"To take a book-plate from the inside of a volume is only just a degree less criminal than to tear out the title-page," says R. R. of Boston, Lincolnshire.

4527 "Removal of Book-Plates." 2:491, December 18, 1880.
Good Friend, for love of books, forbear
To touch the book-plate pasted here;
At those who save it none shall scoff,
But cursed be he who soaks it off.

4528 "Arrangement of Book-Plates." 3:28, January 8, 1881.
Question concerning arrangement and classification.

4529 "Removal of Book-Plates." 3:31, January 8, 1881.
"The Book-Plate's Petition" (by Austin Dobson) printed as by a Gentleman of the Temple, Cheltenham, September 31, 1792.

4530 "Book-Plate." 3:73, January 22, 1881.
Plate identified as that of Francis Haarer.

4531 "Arms on a Book-Plate." 3:126, February 12, 1881.
Another plea to identify a plate by the arms.

4532 "Arrangement of Book-Plates." 3:130-1, February 12, 1881.
Suggests loose sheets of "stout paper" about 18" x 13", with plates hinged for easy removal, in alphabetical order by nationality or subject, kept in a wooden box or one "covered with leather made to look like a book."

4533 "Arrangement of Book-Plates." 3:195, March 5, 1881.
Suggests arrangement by style: Jacobean, Chippendale, and Modern (after 1880).

4534 "Dated Book-Plates." 3:204-5, March 12, 1881.
Beginning of article by C.I.M.Z.

4535 "Arms of a Book-Plate." 3:278-9, April 2, 1881.
Identified as arms of Peshall.

4536 "Accumulated Book-Plates." 3:289, April 9, 1881.
A. H. described dilemma when successive owners have pasted their bookplates one on top of the other and he wants to "get at the hidden history contained in the earliest book-plates."

4537 "Arms of Book-Plate." 3:299, April 9, 1881.
Claims arms of Peshall inaccurately described.

4538 "Dated Book-Plates." 3:302-3, April 16, 1881.
More of C.I.M.Z.'s interesting article.

4539 "Book-Plates." 3:386, May 14, 1881.
Duplicates of Burton bookplate will be sent to first seven or eight "collectors who may like to have one." Signed "Ed. Marshall."

4540 "Shall We Collect Ex-Libris?" John Eliot Hodgkin. 3:402-3, May 21, 1881.
"Enthusiastic collectors have described with all the ardour of a Dibdin the gems of their gatherings, . . . there have not been wanting correspondents who denounced as Vandalesque the removal of a single label from the boards on which they found it."
"To compare great things with small, does the national conscience, of which we often hear, approve or condemn the rape of the Elgin marbles?"
An inquiry to a bookseller elicited the following answer: "We don't *sell* them; if we get any we put them in other books, as we find all books sell better by auction with a bookplate in."
Also asks for translation of a stenographic or cryptographic inscription on a bookplate.

4541 "A Book-plate." Richard Hemming. 3:429-30, May 28, 1881.
Wonders if it is usual to "employ astronomical signs with heraldic in emblazoning arms or bookplates."

4542 "Accumulated Book-Plates." (6thS. 3:289) 3:473, June 11, 1881.
Suggestion for removing successive layers of bookplates: "In about a pint of hot water put nearly half a fluid ounce of pure nitric acid, then with a camel hair brush damp well the book or any other papers required to be removed from their fastening by either paste, dexterine, etc. just to the edge and a trifle over the object to be removed, and a few minutes after any bookplate print, engraving, etc., can easily be removed."

4543 "Something New in Book-Plates." 3:506-7, June 25, 1881.
Photographic portrait bookplate for William J. Thomas discussed from an article in *Athenaeum*, May 28.

4544 "Austro-Hungarian Ecclesiastical Book-Plates and their Owners." H. Astley Williams. 3:508, June 25, 1881.
Requests particulars concerning the dignitaries and English translations of the Latin names.

4545 "Accumulated Book-Plates." (6thS. 3:289, 473) 4:16, July 2, 1881.
Original inquiry misunderstood by respondent.

4546 "Dated Book Plates." Charles A. Federer. 4:206, September 10, 1881.
Right Hon. Basil Fielding, Earl of Denbigh, 1703, and Sir Edmund Anderson, Baronet, 1708.

4547 "Dated Book-Plates." F. Pierrepont Barnard. 4:247, September 24, 1881.
Three plates dated 1700, 1702, and 1714.

4548 "Book-Plates." Ed. Marshall. 4:266, October 1, 1881.
Comments that "A Greek motto must be very uncommon."

4549 "Mounting of Book-Plates and Autograph Letters." T. Martin Wears. 4:305, October 15, 1881.

Suggests a home-made stamp hinge construction using "foreign note paper" and whitest gum arabic.

4550 "Book-Plates with Greek Mottoes." (6th S. 4:266) 4:414, November 19, 1881.

Bookplate for Thomas Ruddiman (1674-1757).

4551 "Dated Book-Plates." 4:466, December 10, 1881.

Two correspondents list plates dated as early as 1702.

4552 "Dated Book-Plates." Richard R. Holmes. 4:486, December 17, 1881.

Royal Library has volume with bookplate dated 1679.

4553 "Book-Plates with Greek Mottoes." (6th S. 4:206, 414) 4:497, December 17, 1881.

Worthington plate, *circa* 1700, has Greek motto.

4554 "Early Dated Book-Plates." F. R. Ellis. 5:9, January 7, 1882.

"William his Booke: 1633."

4555 "Exchange of Heraldic Book-Plates." Arthur J. Jewers. 5:46, January 21, 1882.

Wants to establish exchange list.

4556 "Earliest Dated Book-Plate." G. J. Gray. (6th S. 5:9) 5:78, January 28, 1882.

Claims Francis Frampton's 1631 plate, rather than his 1633 plate mentioned by Ellis, is earliest.

4557 "Earliest Dated English Book-Plate." William John Hardy. 5:151-2, February 25, 1882.

Nicholas Bacon, 1574, and Willielmi Willmer, 1613, entered in the contest.

4558 "A Curious Book-Plate." F. P. Marsh Jackson. 5:226, March 25, 1882.

Full description of bookplate printed May 30, 1754.

4559 "Book-Plates with Greek Mottoes." E. Farrer. (6th S. 4:226, 414, 497) 5:296, April 15, 1882.

The Handbook of Mottoes lists eleven Greek mottoes out of a total of 6,000.

4560 "A Book-Plate." 5:305, April 22, 1882.

Plate in medical volume includes human figure showing muscles.

4561 "Curious Book-plates." 5:324, April 28, 1882.

Apparently misindexed; cannot locate.

4562 "Book-Plates." Robert Day. 5:346, May 6, 1882.

Plate for William FitzGerald (1698) not known to Warren when writing his book.

4563 "Book-Plate Query." Alfred Wallis. 5:407, May 27, 1882.

Seeks information concerning ecclesiastic portrait plate.

4564 "Curious Book-Plate." Ed. Marshall. 5:457, June 10, 1882.

Plate of W. Jones, printer, includes poem of admonition against lending.

4565 "Book-Plate Query." (6th S. 4:407) 6:14, July 1, 1882.
Specific answer to previous question of identity.

4566 "Curious Book-Plate" R. W. Hackwood. (6th S. 5:226, 374, 457) 6:15, July 1, 1882.
Poem quoted by Mr. Marshall "as old as the hills."

4567 "Book-Plate." Cross Fleury. 6:68, July 22, 1882.
Asks identity of Joseph Ignace.

4568 "Curious Book-Plate." 6:76, July 22, 1882.
Volume purchased from Quaritch previously owned two hundred years ago by man with same name as writer of this note.

4569 "Book-Plates with Greek Mottoes." (6th S. 4:266, 414, 497; 5:296) 6:136, August 12, 1882.
Two more correspondents list their plates with such mottoes.

4570 "Book-Plate Query." Alfred Wallis. (6th S. 5:407, 6:14) 6:157, August 19, 1882.
Renders thanks for reference to Warren work.

4571 "Book-plates." Monkbarns. 6:161-2, August 26, 1882.
Detailed descriptions of numerous plates from his small collection.

4572 "Book-Plates with Greek Mottoes." (6th S. 4:266, 414, 497; 5:296; 6:136) 6: 218, September 9, 1882.
Identifies a previous plate by its motto.

4573 "Book-Plate." Gustave Masson. (6th S. 6:38) 6:237, September 16, 1882.
Foresta family belonged to Provence.

4574 "Book-Plates." (6th S. 6:161) 6:298, October 7, 1882.
Asks identity of member of House of Hanover which Monkbarns described.

4575 "Dated Book-Plates." John Woodward. (6th S. 3:204, 302) 6:357, October 28, 1882.
Identifies two plates from previous articles.

4576 "Book-Plates with Greek Mottoes." (6th S. 4:266, 414, 497; 5:296; 6:136, 218). 6:398, November 11, 1882.
Two more entrants.

4577 "Early Dated Ex Libris." J. Eliot Hodgkin. 7:146-7, February 24, 1883.
Two plates with printed dates of June 22, 1650 and March 5, 1684.

4578 "Book-Plates." Edmund Waterton. 7:166, March 3, 1883.
Dated 1623.

4579 "Bookplates with Greek Mottoes." E. Farrer. (6th S. 4:266, 414, 497; 5:296; 6:136, 218, 398) 7:295-6, April 14, 1883.
Thus far eleven such plates mentioned in *Notes and Queries;* of three added in this article, one was engraved by J. Skinner.

4580 "Rev. Adam Clarke's Book-Plate." W. Frazer. 7:304-5, April 21, 1883.
Another Greek motto.

4581 "Book-Plates with Greek Mottoes." John C. Galton. (6th S. 4:266, 414, 497; 5:296; 6:136, 218, 398; 7:295) 7:336, April 28, 1883.
Two more mottoes from the New Testament.

4582 "Foreign Book-Plates." 8:268, October 6, 1883.
Asks name of inexpensive guide to foreign bookplates.

4583 "Book-Plates with Greek Mottoes." Herbert Rix. (6th S. 4:266, 414, 497; 5: 296; 6:136, 218, 398; 7:295, 336) 8:278, October 6, 1883.
Pirckheimer's plate by Durer had Greek motto between a Hebrew and Latin one.

4584 "Foreign Book-Plates." (6th S. 8:268) 8:298, October 13, 1883.
Suggests books by Poulet-Malassis and Stoeber, as well as articles in *Printing Times and Lithographer.*

4585 "Curious Book-Plate or Ex-Libris." W. E. Buckley. 8:308, April 18, 1884.
Seeks information concerning John Collet.

4586 "Curious Book-Plate." W. D. Macray and Constance Russell. (6th S. 9:308) 8:437, May 31, 1884.
Considerable information on Collet family.

4587 "Early Dated 'Ex-Libris.' " 9:486, June 21, 1884.
Arms described.

4588 "Book-Plates." 10:24-5, July 12, 1884.
Several plates described including John Ramsay's containing an American Indian and motto "Drop as rain, distill as dew."

4589 "Boteler Book-Plate." 10:27, July 12, 1884.
Family plate offered for exchange.

4590 "Early Dated Ex-Libris." 10:34, July 12, 1884.
Identifies plate of June 12th and adds key for inscription which is not a single sentence.

4591 "Bookplates." 10:129, August 16, 1884.
Three plates briefly described for identification.

4592 "Date of Book-Plate Required." 10:269, October 4, 1884.
Date of one plate and family name of second sought.

4593 "Date of Book-Plate Required." 10:373, November 8, 1884.
Answer to October 4th inquiry.

4594 "Heraldic Book-Plate." 11:267, April 4, 1885.
Asks "how to describe heraldically a figure suspended beneath the shield."

4595 "Heraldic Book-Plate." 11:410, May 23, 1885.
Answer: "For a compartment a monstrous man chained." "Compartment" is "peculiar to Scottish heraldry."

4596 "Book-Plate." 11:411, May 23, 1885.
Reply to 9:267, Arthur Chevrell, says C.R.M.

4597 "Book-Plate." 11:433, May 30, 1885.
Two different correspondents say answer to 9:267 is Arthur Charlett.

4598 "Book-Plate." 11:451, June 6, 1885.
C.R.M. corrects his reply and votes for Charlett.

4599 "Ancient Book-Plate." 12:8, July 4, 1885.
Identity of Anne Therese Ph.D'YVE [sic] sought.

4600 "Heraldic Book-Plate." 12:10, July 4, 1885.
Meaning of lozenge sought.

4601 "Parochial Book-Plates." 12:69, July 25, 1885.
Wording identical on plates for libraries in different counties or diocese.

4602 "Ancient Book-Plate." 12:78-9, July 25, 1885.
Flemish family of Yve is answer to 12:8.

4603 "Parochial Book-Plates." 12:152, August 22, 1885.
These libraries founded under Act of Parliament implemented by Dr. Bray, passed in seventh year of Queen Ann entitled "An Act for the Better Preservation of Parochial Libraries in that part of Great Britain called England."

4604 "Pair of Curious Book-Plates." 12:288, October 10, 1885.
Typographical plate which states "The Noble Art and Mystery of Printing was first invented and practiced by John Faust . . . in 1451 . . . and brought into England by William Caxton 1471 . . ." and a second version credits John Guttenberg and John Islip with dates of 1440 and 1471.

4605 "Pair of Curious Book-Plates." 12:352, October 31, 1885.
Simon Islip given credit for entry of printing into England.

4606 "Pair of Curious Book-Plates." 12:415-6, November 21, 1885.
So-called bookplates (12:288, etc.) said to be souvenirs printed "on the Thames during the great frost."

4607 "Heraldic Book-Plates." 12:429, May 28, 1885.
Armorial composition described for identification.

4608 "Antiquity of Book-Plates." 12:512, December 26, 1885.
Three early examples given from books in Bodleian Library.

Seventh Series

4609 "Book-Plates." 1:448, June 5, 1886.
Two plates described for identification.

4610 "Book-Plates." 2:16, July 3, 1886.
Answers to 1:448.

4611 "Book-Plate of Graeme." 2:49, July 17, 1886.
Plate for "James Graeme of Buchlyvie, 1715" found beneath a later plate; engraver's name "A Burdon Scu."

4612 "Book-Plates." 2:56, July 17, 1886.

No. 1 again identified as Smith (Smyth); birds in No. 2 are not martlets "but seapies."

4613 "Book-Plate of Graeme." 2:98, July 31, 1886.
Original correspondent referred to Burke's *Landed Gentry* and Anderson's *Scottish Nation.*

4614 "Book-Plate of Graeme." 2:154, August 21, 1886.
Lists offices held by various family members.

4615 "Book-Plate and Inscription." 2:364-5, November 6, 1886.
Cavalier Francesco Vargas Macciucca had monogram bookplate and opposite flyleaf was pasted printed sheet containing fifteen rules for book borrowers.

4616 "Curious Book-Plate." 2:410, November 20, 1886.
Poem with capital letters appearing irregularly throughout.

4617 "Curious Book-Plate." 2:455, December 4, 1886.
Distribution of capital letters in 2:410 spells out owner's name, occupation and adddress: James Crispin Haig Greg, Solicitor de Tilbury.

4618 "Date of Book-Plate." 3:248, March 26, 1887.
Date asked for plate described.

4619 "Owner of Book-Plate Wanted." 4:109, August 6, 1887.
Plate described.

4620 "Book-Plate." 4:148, August 1887.
Seeking owner of plate described as arms of City of London, crest, supporters, motto and two lines of type.

4621 "Book-Plate." 4:212, September 10, 1887.
Description in 4:148 is "an advertisement of the best sort of sealing wax" of Dutch manufacture!

4622 "Book-Plate: Heylbrouck, Engraver." 5:48, January 21, 1888.
Identity of plate's owner sought, as well as information about engraver.

4623 "Book-Plate: Heylbrouck, Engraver." 5:174, March 3, 1888.
Information offered suggests engraver "probably a relative of the better known Michael Heylbrouck."

4624 "Suffolk Book-Plates." 6:508, December 29, 1888.
Fred A. Crisp asks collectors to "favor" him with name of any ancient or modern Suffolk plates to include in list he is about to print.

4625 "Book-Plate." 11:109, February 7, 1891.
Plate described for identification.

4626 "Book-Plate." 11:213, March 14, 1891.
Identification as Nicolai of prior inquiry in Warnecke.

4627 "Book-Plate." 11:333, April 25, 1891.
Interesting note that Nicolai, a Berlin bookseller, may have been troubled by "a spectral illusion."

4628 "Book-Plate." 12:27, July 11, 1891.
Plate described for identification.

Eighth Series

4629 "Bowyer Book-Plate." 1:7, January 2, 1892.
Further identification sought of William Bowyer of Denham.

4630 "Royal Book-Plates." 1:126, February 13, 1892.
Horace Monckton describes three plates and raises questions.

4631 "Royal Book-Plates." 1:175, February 27, 1892.
Arthur Vicars states first two plates "undoubtedly the well-known book-plates of the Duke of Sussex."

4632 "Engravers of Book-Plates." 1:247, March 26, 1892.
Further information sought on R. Mountaine and "Ard. Burden, Sculp."

4633 "Engravers of Book-Plates." 1:324, April 16, 1892.
Arthur Vicars furnishes brief answer and refers to April *Ex Libris Journal* for full details on Mountaine.

4634 "Rabelais Book-Plate." 2:147, August 20, 1892.
Quotes from French publication.

4635 "Book-Plate." 2:188, September 3, 1892.
Plate, probably of a "Naval officer of rank," described for identification.

4636 "Book-Plate." 2:274, October 1, 1892.
Plate "evidently that of William Mathew, Captain-General and Commander-in-Chief of the Leeward Islands, who died in 1752."

4637 "Book-Plate." 2:490, December 17, 1892.
Some of the Mathew quarterings appear in Burke's *Heraldic Illustrations*.

4638 "Portraits as Book-Plates." 3:81, February 4, 1893.
Fredk. Hendriks questions that portraits said to be used by Pepys, Pirckheimer and John Vennitzer were ever actually used as bookplates by these individuals.

4639 "Book-Plate." 3:97, February 4, 1893.
Clarification sought on "Smiths of Barbados."

4640 "Portraits as Book-Plates." 3:129-30, February 18, 1893.
Interesting comments by John Leighton.

4641 "Portraits as Book-Plates." 3:210, March 18, 1893.
Fredk. Hendriks enlightens us further.

4642 "Chevalier D'Eon's Book-Plate." 6:88, August 4, 1894.
John Leighton would like to own "all the houses he [D'Eon] resided in when in London and Westminster."

4643 "Chevalier D'Eon's Book-Plate." 6:151-2, August 25, 1894.
Further reference to his bookplates and other more controversial aspects of his/her life.

4644 "Mrs. Margaret Combridge." 6:469, December 15, 1894.
Walter Hamilton describes a plate measuring 18 1/4" x 11 1/2" "and printed from massive woodcut type."

4645 "Mrs. Margaret Combridge." 7:36, January 2, 1895.
Brief biography of "donor of the book" John Thorpe.

4646 "Book-Plate of Nirgends Priory." 7:143-4, February 23, 1895.
"A Pleader to the Needer When a Reader" reprinted as well as poem "The Prior's Book-Plate."

4647 "Book-Plate of Nirgends Priory." 7:255, March 30, 1895.
Reference to Mr. Gosse's "The Abuse of the Book-Plate" in the January 26th *Athenaeum*.

4648 "Novel Notions of Heraldry." 10:340, October 24, 1896.
Some Americans, whose ancestors were granted arms in England, still rightly use them.

Ninth Series

4649 "Early Belfast Book-Plates." 2:464, December 10, 1898.
Belfast Library plate dated 1765, Rev. James Mackay plate "of an earlier date," and that of fourth Earl of Donegall would pre-date 1757 (his death).

4650 "Book-Plate." 3:287, April 15, 1899.
Identity of plate with coat of arms and initials sought, "infers" name Rice.

4651 "Book-Plate." 3:417-8, May 27, 1899.
"No family of Rice has a crest as described."

Tenth Series

4652 "Tynte Book-Plate." 1:449-50, June 4, 1904.
Believes quarterings on shield wrongly arranged for plate dated 1704.

4653 "Tynte Book-Plate." 2:19, July 2, 1904.
Intricate family relations detailed.

4654 "Foreign Book-Plates." 2:287-8, October 8, 1904.
Five armorial plates described for identification.

4655 "Book-Plate Motto, 'Torcular conculcavi solus.'" 4:109, August 5, 1905.
Requests name of owner, and place and date of sale.

4656 "Book-Plate Verses." 9:167, February 29, 1908.
Verse on plate of James Smith.

4657 "Badges on Book-Plates." 10:289, October 10, 1908.
Arthur Stephens Dyer seeks lists of plates "charged with the badges of their owners."

Eleventh Series

4658 "Buckeridge Book-Plate." 4:150, August 19, 1911.
Seeks identity of two family plates.

4659 "Moyle Book-Plate." 4:210, September 9, 1911.
Are there any armorial plates of this family extant?

4660 "Spurring Book-Plate." 4:289, October 7, 1911.
Again Mr. Dyer asks who is Richard Aeneas Spurring.

4661 "Book-Plate: Owner Wanted." 5:169, March 2, 1912.
Describes woodcut, probably Italian, *circa* 1610.

Twelfth Series

4662 "Heraldic." 4:219, August 1918.
Coat of arms described.

4663 "Pharmaceutical Book-Plates." 6:131, April 17, 1920.
Plea for descriptions of English pharmacists' plates which appear to be very few.

4664 "Pharmaceutical Book-Plates." 6:192, May 8, 1920.
Gives reference to *Chemist and Druggist* articles.

4665 "Armorial Book-Stamp." 6:230, May 22, 1920.
Describes bookstamp for identification.

4666 "Bookplate: Charles Fox." 9:231, September 17, 1921.
Were Charles and Richard Fox related to Whig statesman?

4667 "Bookplate: Charles Fox." 9:296, October 8, 1921.
Apparently no relationship.

4668 "Bookplate of D. Andrews de Swathling." 10:191, March 11, 1922.
What is object held in dexter paw of demi-lion on this plate?

4669 "Book-Plate of De Andrews de Swathling." 10:236, March 25, 1922.
A human heart is held in paw; junior branch of family shows a human head between demi-lion's paws.

Fourteenth Series

4670 "Sussex Book-Plates." 160:116, February 14, 1931.
Wants Sussex plates prior to 1800.

4671 "Sussex Bookplates." 160:177, March 7, 1931.
Four owners listed.

4672 "Sussex Bookplates." 160:249, April 4, 1931.
Richard Bardwell, who died 1804, added to list.

4673 "Book-Plates Designed by Hilaire Belloc." 165:45, July 22, 1933.
Edward Heron-Allen suggests looking through eighteen volumes of the *Ex Libris Journal!*

4674 "Book-Plate Find." 168:241, April 6, 1935.
Plate for William Thompson, dated 1751, found while a contractor was demolishing a home.

Fifteenth Series

4675 "Heraldic Book-Plates: Identification Wanted." 174:299, April 23, 1938.
Gilbert H. Doane describes several plates for identification.

4676 "Heraldic Book-Plates." 174:339, May 7, 1938.
Identification of several offered.

4677 "Identification of Arms on Bookplate." 185:138, August 28, 1943.
Several descriptions given.

4678 "Identification of Arms on Bookplate." 185:267, October 23, 1943.
Identifies one as Daniell.

4679 "Bookplate of Thomas Eyre, 1792." 186:248, May 20, 1944.
Who was Thomas Eyre?

4680 "Bookplate of Thomas Eyre." 187:20, July 1, 1944.
Identified as of Hassop, Bakewell, Derbyshire.

4681 "C.A.D.A." 187:80, August 12, 1944.
Initials appear on wreath-ribbon armorial bookplate of Thomas Eyre.

4682 "Bookplate of Thomas Eyre." 187:83, August 12, 1944.
Detailed family history.

4683 "Book-Plate of Duke of Norfolk." 188:236, June 2, 1945.
Henry Howard and Thomas Eyre listed as executors on bookplate used to identify books bequeathed by will of Duke.

4684 "*Le Blason.*" 193:177, May 1, 1948.
Belgian journal devoted to genealogy, heraldry and sigillography; of "interest to British readers is the book plate of John, Earl of Lauderdale."

4685 "Thomas Gray's Annotations to Pope's Essay on Man." M. Kallich. N.S. 12: 454-5, December 1965.
Concerns annotations or marginalia, but was cross referenced as bookplate item.

NOTICIAS

4686 "Carl Oscar Borg." (11) 11:1-23, Summer 1965.
Better known as a Western painter, Borg also did etchings and bookplates, though none is illustrated or even mentioned in this biographical article.

NOTTS. & DERBYSHIRE NOTES AND QUERIES

4687 "Derbyshire Ex-Libris." F. E. Murray. (1) 2:168-9, December 1894.
Plate for Francis Edwin Murray by W. R. Kean incorporates elements of library interior, emblematic and portrait.

4688 "Notts. Bookplates: Byron and Milbanke. (1) 3:1-3, January 1895.
Quotes from *Journal of Ex Libris Society* concerning controversy about Lord Byron's bookplate.

4689 "Notts. and Derbyshire Book-plates." F. E. Murray. (1) 3:17-8, February 1895.
Plate for Henry Coape of Duffield pictured and discussed.

4690 "Derbyshire Book-plates." F. E. Murray. (1) 3:33-4, March 1895.
Plate discussed is that of Rev. Gray Granville, vicar of Ilam.

4691 "Notts. and Derbyshire Book-plates." F. E. Murray. (1) 3:49-50, April 1895.
"The purists will no doubt condemn the plate . . ." of Rev. John Tinkler.

4692 "Bookplates." 3:53, April 1895.
F. E. Murray has a second bookplate "not for exchange, being intended by the owner solely for insertion in presentation books."

4693 "Notts. and Derbyshire Book-plates." (3) 3:149-2, October 1895.
Plates for Sir Henry Hunloke and John T. Godfrey.

4694 "Notts. and Derbyshire Book-plates." (1) 3:180-1, December 1895.
Illustration is plate for Nottingham Mechanics' Institution Reference Library.

4695 "Notts. and Derbyshire Bookplates." (1) 4:15, January 1896.
Plate of Mrs. Marry E. Allen of Duffield designed by Starr Wood.

4696 "Notts. and Derbyshire Book-plates." Frank Murray. (1) 4:21-2, January 1896.
Plate of archaeologist Llewellynn Jewitt.

4697 "Notts. and Derbyshire Book-plates." (1) 4:42, March 1896.
Plate designed by John Williams for Mrs. Sophia Elizabeth Hall.

4698 "Notts. and Derbyshire Book-plates." (1) 4:84, June 1896.
I. Lees Bilbie designed plate featuring Sherwood Forest, Robin Hood and Nottingham Castle for a collection of books about Nottinghamshire for Percy and Alice Cropper.

4699 "Notts. and Derbyshire Bookplates." (1) 4:110, July 1896.
Another Robin Hood plate designed by J. T. Farnsworth for Percy and Alice Cropper.

4700 "Notts. and Derbyshire Bookplates." (1) 5:167, November 1897.
A third plate designed by J. T. Farnsworth for Percy and Alice Cropper is a library interior.

4701 "Notts. and Derbyshire Bookplates." (1) 6:14, January 1898.
Pictured is plate of Derby Social and Literary Institution.

4702 "Notts. and Derbyshire Bookplates." J. H. Slater. (1) 5:58-9, April 1898.
Pictured is plate of J. Harold Herbert; several others briefly described.

NRTA JOURNAL (National Retired Teachers Association)

4703 "Unique Art of Bookplates." (7) 16:47, September-October 1965.
"A library identified by bookplates will endure through ages to come, a beautiful, treasured and revered heritage to posterity."

O

OBSERVER

Source: *Bibliography of Bookplates Compiled from Various Sources* by P. C. Beddingham, 1962; "Catalogue of an exhibition of bookplates organised by The Observer newspaper in conjunction with The National Book League. London, 1952." Exhibit also mentioned in *Spectator*, 188:43, January 11, 1952. Charming forward to catalog by Sir Francis Meynell.

OHIO STATE JOURNAL

"Needle Crafter's Society and Mrs. Rath-Merrill." [Unable to locate.]
Source: *Journal of Ex Libris Society*, 16:50, May 1906, notes article in "recent issue"; however, questionable if any actual mention of bookplates, though Mrs. Rath-Merrill active in bookplate field.

OLD NORTHWEST GENEALOGICAL QUARTERLY

4704 "Book Plate of the Maine Historical Society." (1) 7:37, January 1904.
Designed by D. McN. Stauffer for Society which was incorporated in 1822.

4705 "Some Historical Book-Plates." Zella Allen Dixson. (4) 7:42-4, January 1904.
Illustration of plate for Society for the Propagation of the Gospel in Foreign Parts; also Chateau Royal de la Bastille. Rev Thomas Bray (1656-1730), Andrew Carnegie of the 17th century, devoted his life and income to founding libraries in isolated places including Annapolis, Maryland.

4706 "Ohio Alcove and Book Plate." (1) 7:45, January 1904.
Ohio D.A.R. voted to establish memorial alcove in American Library, Manila, P.I. and had special bookplate designed for these volumes.

4707 "How Japan Keeps Her Records." Zella Allen Dixson. (4) 8:43-7, January 1905.
Three versions of bookplates for Tokio Library are shown; also Kanazawa Library (Hojo family, 1275 AD) which became public library of that city.

4708 "Book plate." (1) 8:following 435, October 1905.
Plate for Eliza Smart Shepardson designed by Bertha Wilkes.

4709 "Bookplates of the Popes." (2) 12:205, October 1909.
Plates for Popes Gregory XV (1621) and Innocent X (1644) illustrated; designs similar.

OLD TIME NEW ENGLAND

4710 "Notes on Bookplates of Amos Doolittle." Francis W. Allen. (2) 39:38-44, October 1948.
Colonial engraver chiefly known for "Four Views of the Battle of Lexington, Concord, etc." Nineteen plates either signed or attributed to Doolittle.

OPTIMIST [Boone, Iowa]

4711 "Anent Book-Plates, Being a Thumbnail History." Jay Chambers. (10) 1: 272-82, January 1901.
Article lives up to the title.

ORANGE COUNTY MEDICAL ASSOCIATION BULLETIN [See **BULLETIN OF ORANGE COUNTY MEDICAL ASSOCIATION**]

ORIGINAL COLOUR PRINT MAGAZINE

4712 "Value of Colour in Bookplate Heraldry." 1:22, June 1, 1924.
"The engraved heraldic book-plate in black and white, even in its most ambitious moments, is a frank acknowledgment that it is but a substitute for its vanished glory; such is the half articulate language of the conventional lines, horizontal, vertical, or diagonal, to Dexter, or to Sinister, in a copper-plate engraving."
"No one would be so foolish as to suggest that all bookplates should be in colour, for he would be confronted with the question of cost, but in the case of heraldic bookplates they would gain tremendously."

4713 "Value of Design in Bookplates." 1:69, June 1, 1925.
"Design is latent in all good pictorial presentation of nature, though too elusive to be adequately defined."

"Birth and Development of the Bookplate." George H. Viner.

4714 1:31-7, June 1, 1924
4715 (4) 2:84-9, June 1, 1925.
4716 3:138-41, June 1, 1926.
Various styles described.

OUTLOOK

4717 "American Bookplates." E. H. Bierstadt. (3) 50:982-3, December 8, 1894.
Brief summary of bookplate history and review of Charles Dexter Allen's book "written for the advanced collector."

4718 "Children's Book-Plates." Zella Allen Dixson. (6) 72:812-6, December 6, 1902.

Brief historical survey of bookplates; comments on children's plates illustrated including a punning plate, and some rhymes of warning to book borrowers.

OVERLAND MONTHLY

4719 "Regarding Book-plates." K. Porter Garnett. (6) n.s. 24:617-22, December 1894.

General background, a poem, and hints for collectors.

4720 "Book-plates East and West." Sheldon Cheney. (10) n.s. 52:186-90, August 1908.

Background article for beginner from earliest plates to Maxfield Parrish.

OXFORD UNIVERSITY ARCHAEOLOGICAL AND HERALDIC SOCIETY [Third Annual Report of Proceedings]

4721 "Of Book-Plates, A Paper from the Rev. D. Parsons, Read to the Society, Monday, December 5, 1836." 3:17-21, 1837.

"Nothing need be said of the beauty of the book-plates of the present day: they are such as might be expected from a revival of the taste dormant since 1688."

P

PACIFIC BINDERY TALK

4722 "Collecting Bookplates." Della Haverland. 5:165-8, April 1933.

Collection of Katherine F. Ball of Santa Barbara State College discussed, including classification of styles.

4723 "The Dawson Collection." Dorothy M. Drake. 7:87, January 1935.

Collection given to George Washington High School, Los Angeles, by Ernest Dawson, bookseller, so that students might have first hand knowledge of "rare books"; contest held to design bookplate for collection.

4724 "Armorial Plates Shown." 10:116, February 1938.

Exhibit at California State Library.

4725 "Ex Libris." Grace Murray, 12:31-2, October 1939.

Exhibit in Print Room of California State Library. Mention of tri-lingual letter used by bookplate collector in Portugal.

THE PAGE

4726 "Four Bookplates." Gordon Craig. (4) Specimen Copy, 1899.
Illustrations only of plates for Ellen Terry, James Pryde, Oliver Bath and Miss Edith Craig which were designed and engraved by Gordon Craig.

4727 "Four Bookplates." Gordon Craig. (4) Christmas, 1900.
Plates for Charles Dalmon, W. H. Downing, William Winter, Roche, S. B. Brereton.

4728 "Thirteen Bookplates." Gordon Craig. (13) 4:1 & 2, 1901.
More plates designed and engraved by Gordon Craig; most plates seem too dark, not enough white in them.

PAINT POT

4729 "Book-Plates." John Lane Mullins. (3) 1: Issue No. 1, 2 pages, December 1925. [Page numbers unavailable.]
"No child who can read is too young to sport a bookplate."

PALATINE NOTE-BOOK

4730 "Lancashire and Cheshire Heraldic Bookplates." 1:16, January 1881.
"It is proposed to draw up as complete a list of local book-plates as can be obtained, with the view of making an alphabetical arrangement of it in these pages."

4731 "Lancashire and Cheshire Book-Plates." 1:31, February 1881.
Warren's *Guide to the Study of Book-Plates* lists some local plates.

4732 "Towneley Book-Plate." 1:52, March 1881.
The plate for the translator of Hudibras appears to be Chippendale in style, "the ornamental flowers being rather in excess."

4733 "Lancashire and Cheshire Book-Plates." 1:53, March 1881.
Additional "local" plates noted from Warren's book.

4734 "Rev. Joshua Brookes's Book-Plate." 1:69, April 1881.
The plate is "somewhat ornate in character" and is perhaps the work of Bottomley, engraver of Manchester.

4735 "Book-Plate of the Hebbert Family." 1:114, June 1881.
A heraldic plate.

4736 "Book-Plate of William Falconer, Esq., Chester." 1:128, July 1881.
An elaborate plate about four inches square "in an inartistic Chippendale style."

4737 "Chetham Library Book-Plate." (1) 1:195-6, November 1881.
New plate for Chetham's Hospital and Library.

4738 "Note." 1:209, December 1881.
Lord Tabley is "drawing up an account of the historical and artistic relics and associations of his mansion at Tabley."

4739 "Book-Plate of Sir. Thomas Gerard, Bart., 1750." 1:217, December 1881.
This plate is "a neat specimen of engraving in the Chippendale style."

4740 "Book-Plate of the Manchester Literary Club." (1) 2:18, January 1882.
Plate engraved by R. Langton for use in Club library of about 750 volumes.

4741 "Book-Plate of Rd. Rowlinson of Warrington." 3:51, February 1883.
One plate found beneath another in old volume.

4742 "Book-Plate of Richard Rowlinson of Warrington." 3:97, April 1883.
"This gentleman was a respectable solicitor. . . ."

4743 "Richard Towneley." 3:190-1, August 1883.
Richard Towneley spoken of "as an authority on the satellites of Jupiter."

4744 "Local Book-Plate." 3:237, October 1883.

Reader, be thou grave or gay,
Peruse me through, I pray, with care,
My leaves deface not that I may
Be lent again to one as fair,
Children and grease are most my dread,
Return me then as soon as read.

PALL MALL MAGAZINE

"Ex Libris." W. E. Henley.
During 1899 and 1900 book section called "Ex Libris" but not about bookplates; occasional reference made in *Journal of Ex Libris Society* to this misleading title.

PAPER AND PRINTING TRADES JOURNAL

4745 "Ex-Libris." (4) 34:48, March 1881.
"The collecting of bookplates is a harmless pursuit enough when kept within reasonable bounds."

4746 "Ex-Libris." (3) 36:19, September 1881.
"Book plates, though in themselves perhaps but trifling things, have lately received increased attention, both from bibliophiles and artists."

4747 "Curious Book-Plate." (1) 40:45, September 1882.
Mention of item from *Notes and Queries* on plate of Martha Savill bearing legend about John Faust and William Caxton.

PENCIL POINTS

4748 "An Architect's Hobby: The Design of Bookplates." Gerald Lynton Kaufman. (9) 8:731-4, December 1927.
Part of the lure for an architect designing bookplates is the similarity to his regular work, only the process is "reduced to a small scale."

4749 "Bookplates of Elliott L. Chisling." (4) 10:147-58, March 1929.
Considerable article on artist, but only one sentence refers to his bookplates; four are illustrated.

4750 "Competition for a Bookplate Design." (6) 10:358, May 1929.
Competition, restricted to office staff, held by Benjamin Wistar Morris III, New York architect, for bookplate design to be used for personal and architectural libraries.

4751 "Bookplates of Thomas Ewing King." Lawrence S. Bellman. (7) 12:641-56, September 1931.
Seven bookplates among illustrations but no reference to bookplate work in text.

4752 "Drawing for a Bookplate." Matthews M. Simpson. (1) 13:721, October 1932.
Illustration only of a bookplate by and for Matthews Simpson featuring a tree of life with child at the bottom and skeleton at the top.

4753 "Bookplate for Dr. Malcolm Goodridge, Designed and Drawn by Greville Rickard." (1) 16; sup. 13, March 1935.
Illustration only.

4754 "Group of Bookplates by Arthur Stoughton." (6) 19:127-8, February 1938.
Architect Stoughton did pen and ink drawings as hobby; plates depict architectural motifs, landscapes, and symbolism.

4755 "Designs by W. A. Dwiggins." Paul Hollister. (8) 19:145-52, March 1938.
Text makes no comments on Dwiggins bookplates, but eight are illustrated on page 149.

PENNSYLVANIA MAGAZINE OF HISTORY AND BIOGRAPHY

4756 "Sir John St. Clair, Baronet." Charles R. Hildeburn. (2) 9:1-14, 1885.
One illustration is bookplate of Sir John.

PFIZER SPECTRUM

4757 "Ex Libris." (16) 5:14-5, January 1, 1957.
Wide variety of physicians' bookplates are illustrated including "psychosomatic medicine in the 18th century, practiced via bookplate" which read "The Gift of Dr. Nash, to me—In Hopes of my Improvement, 1784."

PHILADELPHIA MEDICINE

4758 "Medical Bookplates and Their Meanings." Samuel X. Radbill. (4) 53:704-5, 707, 709, May 31, 1957.
"While the skull symbolizes death, the butterfly, the Greek word for which is Psyche, meaning also the soul, symbolizes life and immortality."

PHI LAMBDA KAPPA QUARTERLY [Medical Fraternity]

4759 "Bookplates As A Hobby." B. B. Weinstein. 15:23, 1941. [Unable to locate.]
Source: Personal correspondence from Dr. Samuel X. Radbill, June 25, 1966. Dr. Rittenberg, advertising manager of *Phi Lambda Kappa Quarterly*, wrote in August, 1969 that he could "find no article such as you refer to."

PHILOBIBLON [Vienna, 1928-40.]

Source: *News-Letter of the LXIVMOS* #9, 5, July 15, 1928; however, not in English. Some bookplates printed by Merrymount Press appear in volume for 1928. Those with a reading knowledge of German and an interest in books, printing and related subjects should find a wealth of material in this magazine.

PHILOPOLIS

4760 "Design for the New Book Plate." (1) 1:14, October 25, 1906.
Mechanics-Mercantile Library bookplate designed by Arthur F. Mathews, who also designed doorway of building.

PHOTO-ERA MAGAZINE

4761 "Something About Photographic Bookplates." James E. Horning. (4) 49: 171-6, October 1922.
Recipes furnished for making bookplates by photographic processes; special advantage in ease of making same plate in varying sizes.

PHOTOGRAM [See **PROCESS PHOTOGRAM**]

PICTURE POSTCARD AND COLLECTOR'S CHRONICLE

4762 "Book-Plates and Their Meaning." Russell Nadin. (4) 9-10, January 1903.
Bookplates "did not become general until the 18th century, when they succeeded in gaining the fickle favors of fashion, and gave employment to many of the most skilled engravers of the period."

4763 "Designing of Bookplates." Janet S. Robertson. (1) 81, April 1903.
Among mottoes quoted: "I have sought rest everywhere, and nowhere have I found it but in a corner with a book," Thomas a Kempis.

PM [Journal for Production Managers]

4764 "Barnacles from Many Bottoms." (2) 2:15, January 1936.
Typophiles made testimonial book for Bruce Rogers; the illustrations are bookplates, one for BR, other for William Reydel.

POPULAR EDUCATOR

4765 "Concerning Book-plates." Julia W. Wolfe. 43:307 *et seq.*, February 1926.
Edmund Gosse quoted as defining a bookplate as "the outward and visible mark of the citizenship of a booklover."

POPULAR MECHANICS

4766 "Blueprint Your Bookplates by Photography." (4) 57:131, January 1932.
A "do-it-yourself" article.

PORTFOLIO

4767 "Art Chronicle." 24:XXI, 1893.
"The gathering of book-plates has one great advantage over most other forms of collecting, in that the amateur can always, if he likes, add one more to the prizable stock."

POTTER'S AMERICAN HISTORICAL RECORD [See **AMERICAN HISTORICAL RECORD**]

PRATT INSTITUTE MONTHLY

4768 "Concerning Book-Plates or Ex Libris." Louise Both-Hendriksen. (14) 3:46-53, November 1894.
English term, bookplate, "first used in 1791, first admitted to a dictionary in 1888."

4769 "Library." Louise Both-Hendriksen. 3:87, December 1894.
A review of *American Book-Plates* by Charles Dexter Allen. "One charm of the work is, that from beginning to end, we are kept in touch with American history and literature."

PRINCETON UNIVERSITY LIBRARY CHRONICLE

4770 "Sylvia Beach Collection." Howard C. Rice. (1) 26:7-13, Autumn 1964.
Proprietor of Paris bookshop, Shakespeare and Company, and publisher of James Joyce used special bookplate for her lending library.

PRINT

4771 "Dartmouth College Library." (1) 1:65, June 1940.
Illustration of engraving on wood.

4772 "Marks, Bookplates, Monograms and Imprints." Hugo Steiner-Prag. (23) 2: 64-5, October 1941.
Illustrations only, no text.

4773 "Bookplate Year Book." Clare Ryan Talbot. (1) 2:158-9, October 1941.
Illustration is part of cover design for *Year Book* edited by Carlyle Baer, "probably one of the few notable living ex librists."

4774 "Collecting Bookplates." Clare Ryan Talbot. 2:159-60, October 1941.
Review of Gilbert H. Doane's *About Collecting Bookplates*, printed by Black Mack, the Handpress.

4775 "Theodore Brown Hapgood: American Designer, 1871-1938." William A. Kittredge. (40) 3:1-24, Summer 1942.
Six of illustrations are bookplates. Artist's work includes "hand-illuminated memorials, architectural monuments, plaques and inscriptions in wood, bronze, stone and marble, embroidered vestments for the church, and decorative designs and lettering for books, bookplates, and other printing."

PRINT COLLECTORS' CHRONICLE

4776 "Bookplate Notes." (3) 1:13, Winter 1939.
Three plates engraved by Stephen Gooden shown, two for Royal Windsor Library.

4777 "Check-List of Bookplates by Will Simmons." Oliver C. Sheean. (1) 1:13-4, Winter 1939.
Descriptions of twelve plates.

4778 "Bookplate Notes." 1:27-8, May 1939.
Dr. Gilbert H. Doane interested in getting in touch with enthusiasts of early American bookplates; Carlyle S. Baer and Clara T. Evans have compiled census of bookplate collections.

4779 "Check-List of Bookplates of Frank W. Benson." Oliver C. Sheean. (2) 1:27-8, May 1939.
Descriptions of seven plates.

4780 "Check-List of Bookplates by Paul H. Smith." Oliver C. Sheean. (1) 1:28-9, May 1939.
Fifteen plates described briefly.

4781 "Classified." 1:29, May 1939.
Advertisements placed by Dr. Radbill, Dan Burne Jones, Oliver Sheean, Carlyle S. Baer, and Box B 10 who is interested in Gooden's Harold Hartley plate.

4782 "Bookplate Notes." (1) 1:44-5, September 1939.
Bookplates to be used in books given the Newbery and Caldecott awards each year.

4783 "Check-List of Bookplates by Asa Cheffetz." (1) 1:45 *et seq.*, September 1939.
Artist did plates for author S. N. Behrman and film producers Walter Wanger and David O. Selznick.

4784 "Classified." 1:45, September 1939.
Seven out of ten advertisements concern bookplates.

4785 "Check-List of Bookplates by John Buckland Wright." (2) 1:50, September 1939.
Descriptions of thirteen plates.

4786 "Bookplate Notes." (2) 2:28, April 1940.
Arthur N. Macdonald died February 6th; created some five hundred bookplates, mostly line engravings.

4787 "Check-List of Bookplates by Ernest Haskell." Oliver C. Sheean. (1) 2:29, April 1940.
Nine plates described including one for Pierre Lorillard.

PRINT COLLECTORS' CLUB

4788 "Bookplates." J. F. Badeley. (35) No. 6, 1-68, 1927.
"Bookplates can afford exquisite examples of the talent of some of the greatest artists of each epoch." Lecture delivered November 18, 1925.

PRINT-COLLECTORS' QUARTERLY

4789 "Concerning the Woodcuts of Gordon Craig." Haldane Macfall. (1) 9:407-32, December 1922.
Article includes numerous prints; one bookplate illustrated with odd skeletal creature hovering over the initial D.

4790 "Notes: Portrait Bookplate by Count Sigismund von Spreti." (1) 19:182, July 1932.
Etching signed by Francois De Cuvillies, the Younger; von Spreti (1732-1809) was official of Bavarian Academy of Science.

PRINT CONNOISSEUR

4791 "Harry Townsend, Bookplate." (1) 10:39, January 1930.
Bookplate for Althea Noble.

4792 "Jay Chambers, Artist." Wilbur Macy Stone. (1) 10:72-5, January 1930.
Chambers, fledgling from Howard Pyle's class at Drexel Institute, made more than 100 bookplates.

4793 "Wild Life Etchings of Will Simmons." Dorothy Pletcher. (7) 10:98-119, April 1930.
Bookplates included among works of versatile artist.

PRINTER AND BOOKMAKER [See also **AMERICAN PRINTER**]

4794 "The Collecting of Book Plates." 25:209-10, December 1897.
Quotes Edmund Gosse and Andrew Lang, both of whom deplored the collecting of bookplates.

PRINTING & GRAPHIC ARTS [PAGA]

4795 "Akke Kumlien: 1884-1949." Bror Zachrisson. (8) 1:45-56, September 1953.
Swedish artist-calligrapher-typographer demonstrated great skill in executing the mirror monogram as illustrated in the ex libris for Bengt Petri.

4796 "Hawthorne House." Roderick D. Stinehour. (11) 1:65-72, December 1953.
Connecticut book publisher also uses "printer's flowers" and rules to solve small problems such as book labels or ex libris.

4797 "Jimmy Wardrop." Gilbert Highet. (1) 6:19-22, February 1958.
Author's bookplate created by calligrapher Wardrop early in his career.

4798 "Notes on the Gehenna Press." Dorothy King. (10) 7:33-44, June 1959 (?).
"All its (Gehenna Press of Esther and Leonard Baskin) work reflects the care lavished on these matters, whether for broadside, prospectus, keepsake, bookplate, announcement, invitation, letterhead, or the sustained effort required for a book."

4799 "J. J. Lankes." Ray Nash. (15) 8:97-109, 1960.
Wood engraving specialist has 1224 woodblocks "enumerated and annotated in his forty-year record book."

PRINTING ART

4800 "Book-Plate Designs." (26) 19:41-8, March 1912.
Among illustrations are plates designed by Theodore B. Hapgood, Adrian J. Iorio, W. A. Dwiggins, E. B. Bird, and an end paper design with bookplate.

4801 "Ex Libris Designs." (34) 24:41-8, September 1914.
More by W. A. Dwiggins, Louis Rhead, Walt Harris, Charles Rollinson, Robert Sneider, Wilbur Macey Stone.

4802 "Samuel Pepys." (1) 24:108, October 1914.
Pen drawing by Carl S. Junge.

4803 "Lewis Buddy III Book-plate." (1) 24:128, October 1914.
Plate designed and engraved by Gordon Craig.

4804 "A Certain Wood Engraver." (4) 24:177-84, November 1914.
Howard McCormick illustrated books, magazine covers, and designed bookplates.

4805 "Winifred Gable Bookplate." (1) 24:500, February 1915.
Illustration only of plate designed by Carl Junge.

4806 "Some Bookplate Designs." (30) 28:105-12, October 1916.
Quotes Temple Scott: "An artistic bookplate is the expression in decorative illustration of the proprietor's tastes, made by an artist who has sympathetically realized the feeling intended. It should objectify one, and only one, salient characteristic, either of temperament, habit, disposition, or pleasure, of its owner. If it does less, it is not individual; if it does more, it is not satisfying."

4807 "Bookplates by W. D. Teague." (2) 29:46-7, March 1917.
Plates designed for Ernest Elmo Calkins and wife, and Arnold and Theresa Behn.

4808 "Work by Harvey H. Dun." (1) 29:119, April 1917.
Bookplate in typographic arrangement of Elizabethan printers.

4809 "Work of William P. Schoonmaker." (8) 29:194, May 1917.
One of illustrations was artist's 1916 Christmas card.

PRINTING TIMES AND LITHOGRAPHER

4810 "Curiosities of Book-Plates. 1. Object and Origin of the Book-Plate." (5) 8: 265-8, November 15, 1882.
Bookplate for W. J. Thoms, editor of *Notes and Queries*, includes his portrait, arms and autograph.

4811 "Curiosities of Book-Plates. 11. Artistic, Heraldic and Punning Examples." (7) 8:290-2, December 15, 1882.
". . . a good collection of interesting book-plates possesses such artistic beauty, and the collector will be led to study history and heraldry to aid him in his pursuit,—a correlative educational advantage not always appertaining to the pursuit of the 'collector.' "

PRINTING WORLD [See **BRITISH AND COLONIAL PRINTER AND STATIONER**]

PRINTS

4812 "Some Contemporary Makers of Bookplates." Oliver Clement Sheean. (4) 8: 133-8, February 1938.
Comments on American and European bookplate artists.

PRIVATE LIBRARY [Quarterly journal of Private Library Association]

4813 "Bookplates." P. C. Beddingham. (9) 2:6-10, July 1958.
Mentions *Bookplate Collector's News* as only current literature in English on the subject but "such articles as 'Eroticism in Bookplates' can hardly be expected to capture the interest of family historians and antiquarians."

4814 "Collecting Bookplates." Philip Beddingham. 2:53-5, April 1959.
Author has four plates: a wood engraving showing interest in books and ships, a calligraphic name label for paperbacks, and two which were "fancies of the moment" used for exchange only.

4815 "Foreign Bookplates." Philip Beddingham. (3) 2:70-3, August 1959.
Belgians and Dutch seem to be most active both as bookplate collectors and artists.

4816 "Concerning Bookplates." Philip Beddingham. 3:6-7, January 1960.
Bookplate Collector's News suggests *philebrist* for bookplate collector and *philebrism* for the science of collecting them.

4817 "Collecting Andrew Lang." Roger Lancelyn Green. (1) 4:155-60, October 1963.
Illustration is Lang's bookplate designed by Herbert Jones in 1894.

PROCEEDINGS OF THE CHARAKA CLUB

4818 "Aristocratic Bookplates and Their Working Cousins." Robert Latou Dickinson. (20) 8:177-84, 1935.

Welcomes the "abandonment of silly-frilly coat of arms of the pseudo-heraldic era." Suggests use of exterior book label for hymn books or those to be loaned, package or envelope labels, and a symbol label for all one's possessions.

PROCEEDINGS OF THE ROYAL SOCIETY OF MEDICINE

4819 "Book-Plates of Medical Men." George C. Peachey. 23:493-5, February 1930.

"Not once, but on many occasions, in my biographical studies, has a book-plate afforded me the information of a marriage sought for elsewhere in vain."

PROCEEDINGS OF SOCIETY OF ANTIQUARIES OF LONDON

4820 [Note.] 15:47, 1894.

Meeting of January 11, 1894 mentions that among heraldic manuscripts exhibited by A. W. Franks were engravings by Jost Ammon of a bookplate for the Scheurl family.

4821 "Early Heraldic Book-Plates." 15:214-221, 1894.

Sir A. Wollaston Franks, President, at meeting of May 31, 1894 made lengthy remarks on heraldic bookplates. Refering to exhibit said "could have . . . largely increased number . . . but would have been wearisome to all but ex-libris maniacs, of which I regret to say that there are but too many."

4822 [Note.] 15:293, 1895.

Mention of bookplate of Sir Nicholas Bacon.

PROCESS PHOTOGRAM

4823 "Special Subject Competion." J. T. Price. 6:104-7, April 1899.

One category is the bookplate. "Here the idea is to encourage the photography of objects with a purpose—we do not so much want pretty pictures as a book label."

4824 "A Photographic Book-Plate." Ernest W. Jackson. (1) 6:360-2, December 1899.

"If it should ever become the rule for photographers to design (by means of the camera) their own book-plates, it seems not unlikely that the publication and exhibition of the same will add a new source of interest to the already far-reaching art of photography."

PROFESSIONAL ART QUARTERLY

4825 "Designing Bookplates." Dan Burne Jones. (5) 2:17-19,34,46, June 1936.

Artist details his experiences in designing plates; last page is illustration and advertisement placed by artist.

PROGRESS IN AUSTRALIA

4826 "A Note on Pictorial Bookplates." Rex Wood. (2) 2 pages, July 7, 1934. [Volume and page numbers unavailable.]

Artists mentioned are Adrian Feint, Lionel Lindsay, G. D. Perrottet, Eric Thake, Norman Lindsay.

4827 "Australian Bookplates: The Work of Adrian Feint" by "Ex Libris." (3) 16-7, December 7, 1934. [Volume number unavailable.]

"As a student of that doyen of Australian teachers, Julian Ashton, his [Feint's] craftsmanship is excellent."

PUBLICATION OF THE AMERICAN JEWISH HISTORICAL SOCIETY

4828 "American Jewish Bookplates." Philip Goodman. (64) 45:129-216, March 1956.

Scholarly article concerning college bookplates with Hebrew inscriptions, plates for Judaic and Helvetic collections, major Jewish libraries, and plates of American Jews.

PUBLISHERS' CIRCULAR AND BOOKSELLERS' RECORD OF BRITISH AND FOREIGN LITERATURE [British Books]

4829 "Book-Plates." 55:130, August 8, 1891.

"But it is useless complaining, for the mania has laid hold of a large number of collectors, and a strong illustration of the way in which the taste has spread is to be found in the fact that during the last few weeks a special society of book-plate collectors has been formed."

PUBLISHERS' WEEKLY

4830 "Foreign Notes." 43:851, June 3, 1893.

"The collection of bookplates is now a recognized pastime." Comments also on imaginary bookplates of M. L. Joly.

4831 "A Book Plate Magazine." 81:161-2, April 2, 1912.

Notice of first issue of *Ex Libran*, published by H. Alfred Fowler in Kansas City.

4832 "Work of W. F. Hopson, Dean of American Bookplate Artists." Frederick M. Hopkins. 129:630, February 1, 1936.

Sterling Memorial Library at Yale has complete collection of Hopson's work; exhibited at Library of Congress in 1930.

4833 "Newbery & Caldecott Bookplates." (1) 136:10, July 1, 1939.

Drawing by Raymond Lufkin of faces of two medals.

Q

QUAKERIANA

4834 "Marginalia." 5:77, July 1894.

Exhibit at Royal Antiquarian Society included "a great many old book plates."

QUARTERLY JOURNAL OF THE LIBRARY OF CONGRESS

4835 "Early Library of Congress Bookplates." Frederick R. Goff. (17) 26:55-61, January 1969.

"Characteristic of their time, they display both dignity and taste, in spite of the fact that their basic design is undistinguished."

QUARTERLY NEWS-LETTER (Book Club of California)

4836 "The Collecting of California Bookplates." Clare Ryan Talbot. 6:4-9, September 1938.

Probably the first California bookplates were the *marcas del fuego* or convent bands that were used in early Mission libraries.

4837 "Exhibition Notes." 18:41-2, Spring 1953.

Frank Schwabacher suggested exhibit of members' bookplates.

4838 "Exhibition Notes." 18:92-3, Fall 1953.

Members' bookplates exhibited as result of suggestion from fellow member.

4839 "Vallejo Bookplate." 19:18, Winter 1953.

When visiting the General Vallejo home and museum in Sonoma you may see, in glass case, the bookplate "made by him on the Zamorano press which he brought to Sonoma in 1837."

4840 "Morgan A. and Aline D. Gunst Memorial Library." 29:18-9, Winter 1963.

Library devoted to Book Arts and History of the Book, bookplate designed by Grabhorn Press.

4841 "Collecting Book Club Ephemera." Duncan H. Olmsted. 30:81-8, Fall 1965.

Among other items an announcement of an exhibit and a lecture by Rev. W. A. Brewer about bookplates on April 30, 1913.

4842 "Exhibition of Design & Calligraphy by Theo Jung." 34:62-3, Summer 1969.

While not specifically mentioned, this calligrapher-printer has designed bookplates.

QUARTERLY QUERIES OF SOCIETY OF GENEALOGISTS

"Dr. G. C. Peachey's Paper." March 2, 1919.
Reference to this talk in *Bookplate Chronicle* (1:21, January 1920); however, talk not published by the Society of Genealogists (letter dated March 31, 1969 from Society's Secretary to Mrs. Arellanes).

QUARTERLY RECORD [See **MANCHESTER PUBLIC FREE LIBRARIES QUARTERLY RECORD.**]

QUARTO

4843 "Book Plate." Dora Curtis. (1) 1:32, 1896.
Fanciful plate for F. Every-Leggatt.

QUEEN

(Articles not seen by Audrey Arellanes; portion of details for annotations furnished by Dorothy Dockterman, September 1969.)

"[Bookplate of Walter Besant.] January 23, 1892. [Unable to locate article and/or illustration in January 23 or 30, 1892 or January 21, 1893.]
Source: Unknown.

4844 "Library Serials." 91:675, April 23, 1892.
Brief comment on *Journal of Ex Libris Society*.

4845 "Library Serials." 92:366, August 27, 1892.
Comment on *Journal of Ex Libris Society*.

4846 "Library Serials." 93:151, January 28, 1893.
Journal of Ex Libris Society mentioned.

4847 "*English Book-Plates*." 93:152, January 28, 1893.
Review of Egerton Castle's book.

4848 "Ex Libris—The Book-Plates of Cultured Women." 99:909-10, May 23, 1896.
This article was widely reprinted, *New York Recorder, San Francisco Chronicle, Kansas City Star, Hartford Post* according to note in *Journal of Ex Libris Society* 6:100, June 1896.

4849 "History and Origin of Some Peculiar Coats of Arms." Sir Arthur Vicars. 110:807, 810, November 23, 1901.
Heraldry and bookplates.

4850 "Bookplates of Some Celebrated Men." F. R. Ellis. 114:945-6, December 5, 1903.
Source: *Journal Ex Libris Society* 13:178, December 1903.

"[Death of E. D. French.]" [Unable to locate.]
Source: *Journal of Ex Libris Society* 18:7, January 1908, indicates article by Lady Bellingham on American bookplates mentioning W. F. Hopson and note on French's death (December 8, 1907).

R

READER MAGAZINE

4851 "Aubrey Beardsley As A Designer of Book-Plates." Albert E. Gallatin. (3) 1: 126-8, December 1902.

His first plate, executed in 1893, was for Dr. John Lumsden Propert, famous collector of miniatures.

REFORMED CHURCH MESSENGER

4852 "Whitehall Papers." 57:2-3, June 12, 1889.

Comments on bookplate of Reformed minister Peter Miller and mottoes against borrowing which make reference to chapter and verse in scripture.

RELIQUARY AND ILLUSTRATED ARCHAEOLOGIST

4853 "Thomas Barritt." Thomas Gibbons. 4:133, 1897.

Unable to locate this article which was noted in *Journal of Ex Libris Society* (7:16, February 1897) as a "long paper by Thomas Gibbons about Thomas Barritt in *Reliquary* IV p. 133, 1897." Volume and year don't match; III is 1897 and IV is 1898; article doesn't appear to be in either volume.

REVIEW OF MEDICINE [Turgu-Mures]

"First Rumanian Ex Libris." 10:228-30, 1964. [Unable to locate.]

Source: Wellcome Institute of History of Medicine, London. Article in Rumanian with abstract in English.

REVISTA OCCIDENTAL

4854 "Ex Libris Omega Kappa." Lawrence Clark Powell. (1) 19-20, 1936.

Occidental Chapter of Phi Gamma Delta after thirty-five years has bookplate for budding library.

RHODE ISLAND HISTORICAL SOCIETY COLLECTIONS

4855 "Early Providence Book Plates." (6) 30:97-101, October 1937.

Bookplates struck from type and type ornaments in vogue following American Revolution. Some identified as produced by printer Bennett Wheeler (1782-1806).

ROCHESTER UNIVERSITY LIBRARY BULLETIN

4856 "Louis J. Bailey Bookplate Collection." Margaret Butterfield. (1) 15:17-24, Winter 1960.

Rochester graduate of 1905, librarian-book collector, Louis Bailey gave extensive bookplate collection to his alma mater, with plates mounted, annotated, catalogued and classified.

ROCKY MOUNTAIN RAIL REPORT

4857 "Bert Fullman Memorial Collection." (1) Issue No. 93, June 1967.

Memorial fund established in the name of retired Moffat Railroad engineer; Club purchased Howard Fogg painting and Tom Gray, Jr., designed bookplate for volumes which will be presented to Western History section of Denver Public Library.

ROOT AND BRANCH

4858 "Some Thoughts About Book-Plates." James Guthrie. (1) 2:8-11, September 1917.

"Our Book-plate is no more than a mark shut within the privacy of our books and may not be made for other and more public aims."

4859 "Bookplate of Walter Bradley." (1) 2:28, December 1917.

Illustration only.

4860 "Bookplate of Jacob de Graaff." (1) 2:64, March 1918.

Illustration only.

4861 "Bookplate." (1) 2:69, June 1918.

Thistle type flower and leaf with initials HB on ribbon would appear to be a bookplate though not so identified.

4862 "Bookplate of C. F. Shaw." (1) 3:np, August-September 1919.

Illustration only.

4863 "Bookplate." (1) 3: Issue No. 2, np. [1919].

Initials entwined in a heart.

RQ [Reference Services Division of the American Library Association]

4864 "In Review." 8:151-2, Winter 1969.

Reviewer of *Bookplates for Libraries* says "Along with the Maryland manuscript bibliography this takes top honors for the best format, binding, typography and reproduction of any titles examined over the past few months."

S

ST. AIDAN'S MESSENGER [Sydney, Australia]

4865 "Bookplates." Frank E. Lane. April 1930. [Unable to locate.]

As annotated by H. B. Muir: General article with special reference to bookplate mottoes.

ST. LUKE'S SOCIETY JOURNAL

4866 "[Bookplates.]" [Unable to locate.]

Source: *Builder* 69:269, October 19, 1895.

"The St. Luke Society also now publishes a journal, and the knowledge of book-plates has become in these latter days the trade of a band of connoisseurs."

ST. NICHOLAS

4867 "Children's Bookplates." Wilbur Macey Stone. (14) 30:42-6, November 1902.

Basic background article for children; plates by Gelett Burgess, Kate Greenaway. Gordon Craig quoted: "A bookplate is to the book what a collar is to a dog."

4868 "Book-plate of James Whitcomb Riley." Jennie M. Elrod. (2) 50:268-9, January 1923.

Riley was superstitious; someone made him a bookplate showing a Continental lad, arms full of books. At first count he thought there were thirteen books and would not use the plate. Closer count revealed fourteen. Riley sent his plate to the author with this poem:

"Who hath not more/Than he can pack
Hath meagre store/Of lore, Alack."

4869 "Collecting Bookplates." Lavinia Davis. (5) 61:22 *et seq.*, November 1933.

Excellent background article directed at children with suggestions about becoming a collector and how to select your own bookplate.

ST. PAUL'S

4870 "Ex Libris. A Chat About Ladies' Bookplates." (4) 8:410-11, May 30, 1896.

The bookplate is described as "a sort of title-deed to ownership."

SATURDAY NIGHT

4871 "California History as Told in Bookplates." (1) 15:4, July 27, 1935.

Charming interview with Mrs. Clare Ryan Talbot prior to publication of *Historic California in Bookplates*.

SATURDAY REVIEW [London]

4872 "Book Plates." 50:525-6, October 23, 1880.

"A pleasant book on a dry subject is a boon to readers," is the reviewer's opening comment on Warren's *Guide to Study of Book Plates*.

4873 "Book-Plates." 72:120-1, July 25, 1891.

Review of first issue of *Journal of Ex Libris Society* criticizes inclusion of Leighton's article from *Gentleman's Magazine* of 1866 without updating the material.

4874 "Ex-Libris Society." 73:238-9, February 27, 1892.

"Next to an umbrella," said Mr. Warren (now Lord de Tabley), "there is no item of personal property concerning the appropriation of which lax ideas of morality are current as a book. If you neglect to restore a horse, a greatcoat, or a pocket handkerchief, some social stigma will probably attach to you should the depredation become generally known. In the case of a book borrower there is no such nemesis."

4875 "English Book-Plates." 75:77-8, January 21, 1893.

Review of Castle's book and rambling bits of bookplate history.

4876 "*French Book-Plates.*" 75:157-8, February 11, 1893.

Review of Walter Hamilton's book which is a "distinctly valuable addition to the literature" in spite of some quibbling concerning selection of illustrations already in Poulet-Malassis.

4877 "More About Book-Plates." 75:635-6, June 10, 1893.

". . . 'book-platers' to use for once the crushing term of certain humorous critics, the same who see the similarity of book-plate collecting to door-knocker gathering."

4878 "Book-Plates." 79:388, March 23, 1895.

Caustic reviews of Charles Dexter Allen's *American Book-Plates, Art in Book-Plates* introduced by Warnecke, and John Vinycomb's *On the Processes for the Production of Ex Libris.*

4879 "*Book-Plate Annual.*" 84:564, November 20, 1897.

Reviewer of John Leighton's *Book-Plate Annual and Armorial Year Book* states that as "an heraldic work the book is pure drivel" and mentions several specific coats of arms presented "none of which will stand investigation."

SATURDAY REVIEW OF LITERATURE

4880 "Bookplates and Marks." Carl Purington Rollins. 5:1168, July 6, 1929.

Highly complimentary review of *The Bookplates and Marks* by Rockwell Kent; also discusses W. A. Dwiggins book of printers' marks and Clarence P. Hornung's *Bookplates by Harold Nelson.*

4881 "Bowling Green." (1) 10:703, May 19, 1934.

Christopher Morley's column has Sherlock Holmes crossword puzzle, later used as a bookplate, originated by Mycroft Holmes.

4882 "Bowling Green." (1) 10:727, June 2, 1934.

Solution to Holmes puzzle printed; among those with correct solution were Vincent Starrett, who has a Sherlockian plate, and Walter Klinefelter, who wrote a book on such plates.

4883 "Genesis of a Bookplate." A. Ranger Tyler. (1) 11:582, March 30, 1935.

Plate designed on basis of Arabian magic square of four; numbers add vertically, horizontally, and diagonally to thirty-four.

SAVOY

4884 "Two Eighteenth Century Book-Plates." (2) 1:51,53, October 1896.
Plates for Marie Antoinette and the Bastille.

SCHOOL ACTIVITIES

4885 "Book Plates." Dorothy Leggitt. 24:80, October 1952.
Three paragraph item—"Monograms, trade marks, and bookplates are truly ways of saying, 'PERSONALLY YOURS.' "

SCHOOL AND HOME EDUCATION

4886 "Simple Book-Plates for Children's Libraries." Grace Jewett Austin. 29:347-8, June 1910.
"If the children learn to take an interest in book-plate literature, it will give them much biographical and historical knowledge."

SCHOOL ARTS MAGAZINE

4887 "Bookplate Design." Charles Dexter Allen. (11) 8:191-203, November 1908.
"Originality in bookplate design does not call for new objects: it is found in the treatment of old themes, in the feeling expressed, in the way the thing is done."

4888 "Dry Point Bookplates, Home Made Prints with Simple Equipment." Benton Court. (5) 24:10-3, September 1924.
Specific instructions for making a dry point bookplate; one page diagrams part of the process; one page shows four plates made by this method.

4889 "Bookplates Boys Like to Make." Charles F. Pietsch. (6) 24:32-4, September 1924.
Linoleum block prints by students of Woodlawn High School, Birmingham, Alabama.

4890 "Bookplates." Beulah Mary Wadsworth. (10) 26:288-9, January 1927.
Half the illustrated plates are by Art Supervisor Wadsworth, remaining by students.

4891 "Fun of Bookplates." Vernet Johnson. (9) 27:86-8, October 1927.
Linoleum blocks printed by two methods.

4892 "Bookplates as a 'Good Book Week' Project." Lois J. Ware. (8) 30:42-5, September 1930.
Elementary school children designed bookplates as art project.

4893 "Bookplate Design." Orrin F. Stone. (7) 34:207 *et seq.*, December 1934.
Two essentials to keep in mind: does the design fit the person for whom it is intended and will the design be suitable for the method of reproduction to be used.

4894 "Bookplates and Blueprints." (13) 35:425-6, March 1936.
Suggestions for blueprinting bookplates are pictured.

4895 "Book Plates Fifth and Sixth Grades, Fayette, Ohio." (8) 39:180, January 1940.

Do-it-yourself bookplates for elementary grade children.

4896 "Bookplates, Marks of Distinction." Miriam Grace Helms. (22) 46:142-3, December 1946.

Series of pictures shows gradual development of design; fourteen completed plates illustrated, mostly rather crude work.

SCHOOL LIFE

4897 "Library Bookplate." Edith A. Lathrop. (1) 19:123, February 1934.

Bookplate for library of Technical High School, Omaha, Nebraska, features face of Lincoln and quotation: "Without a love of books the richest man is poor."

SCIENTIFIC AMERICAN

4898 "Greetings by Photography." Jacob Deschin. (3) 153:284-5, November 1935.

Greeting cards and bookplates made from photographs and reproduced; should use paper called "insurance bromide"; only one illustration is a bookplate.

SCIENTIFIC AMERICAN SUPPLEMENT

4899 "Book Plates of Celebrated Women." (5) 41:16797, February 22, 1896.

Review of Norna Labouchere's *Ladies' Book Plates*.

SCOTSMAN

4900 "Old Scottish Bookplates." 8, July 28, 1903. [Volume number unavailable.]

"To the exlibris cult the publication [1892] of the Nesbit plates suggested fresh fields for exploration. Might it not be possible, it was suggested, to discover some at least of these fine examples of the work of our early Scots engravers in the form of book plates?"

SCOTTISH HISTORICAL REVIEW

4901 "Lives of Authors." Walter Raleigh. (4) 1:1-18, October 1903.

Bookplate of John Aubrey, "best of Seventeenth Century gossips." Aubrey referred to by contemporary as "a shiftless person, roving, and magotiedheaded. . . ."

4902 "Reviews of Books." 6:408-10, July 1910.

The Scots Peerage, edited by Sir James Balfour Paul, reviewed.

SCOTTISH REVIEW

4903 "Book-plates." Henry Gough. 21:315-29, April 1893.

Description and comments on books by Castle, Warren, Hamilton and two privately printed groups of bookplates. Also reference to *Antiquarian* inquiries by Daniel Parsons.

SCRIBNER'S MAGAZINE

4904 "Art of the Book-Plate." Frank Weitenkampf. (12) 47:765-8, June 1910.
Quoting the author: "Beraldi baldly asserts that 'the worth of a bibliophile is in inverse ratio to the dimension of his ex-libris.' "

SERIF

4905 "Bookplate of Epes Sargent." (1) 1:front cover inside, April 1964.
One of four signed bookplates by Paul Revere.

4906 "Bookplate of Oliver Wendell Holmes." (1) front cover inside, July 1964.
Plate engraved in part by J. W. Spenceley, who was 18 at the time.

4907 "Bibliographical Notes. A Sidelight on the 'Chambered Nautilus' Bookplate." Mary DeVold. 1:29-31, July 1964.
Letter from Holmes to Messrs. John A. Lowell & Co., Boston printers and engravers, concerning alterations to be made in engraving his bookplate.

4908 "Bookplate of John Adams." (1) 1:front cover inside, October 1964.
Design originally offered as basis for United States seal; failing that used as bookplate.

4909 "Bookplate of Francis Hopkinson." (1) 1:front cover inside, December 1964.
Hopkinson, signer of the Declaration of Independence, had plate engraved by Henry Dawkins.

4910 "Bookplate of Robert Dinwiddie." (1) 2:front cover inside, March 1965.
Plate combines traditional English heraldry with personal invention.

4911 "Bookplate of DeWitt Clinton." (1) 2:front cover inside, June 1965.
Ribbon and wreath style plate designed by Peter R. Maverick.

4912 "Bookplate of William Penn." (1) 2:front cover inside, September 1965.
Plate dated 1703, which indicates it was made after Penn returned to England in 1701; motto as shortened and misspelled is meaningless.

4913 "Bookplate of Isaac Norris." (1) 2:front cover inside, December 1965.
One of three known bookplates signed by James Turner.

4914 "Bookplate of Henry D. Gilpin." (1) 3:front cover inside, March 1966.
An American author, lawyer and classical scholar, Gilpin served as Attorney General under Van Buren.

4915 "Bookplate of George Bancroft." (1) 3:front cover inside, June 1966.
The plump cherub of Bancroft's plate has been identified as that in Raphael's painting of the Madonna de Foligno.

4916 "Bookplate of Charles Carroll." (1) 3:front cover inside, September 1966.
Signer of the Declaration of Independence, Carroll lived from 1738 to 1832.

4917 "Bookplate of Horace Walpole." (1) 4:front cover inside, March 1967.
Owner of Strawberry Hill Press had his plate engraved "Mr. Horatio Walpole" although he signed himself Horace.

4918 "Bookplate of Richard Henry Dana." (1) 4:front cover inside, June 1967.
Plate for Francis Dana (1743-1811) engraved by Nathaniel Hurd and used by subsequent generations of family.

4919 "Bookplate of Henry Alfred Fowler." (1) 4:front cover inside, September 1967.
Plate engraved by Charles W. Sherborn "reflects a fault all too common among book-plates after the use of coats of arms became less common, the desire of the owner to include too many details of his life or interests."

4920 "Book-plate of William Byrd." (1) 4:front cover inside, December 1967.
Plate of "founding father" of Byrd "dynasty of Virginia statesmen" was late Jacobean in style and engraved in England.

4921 "Bookplate of Gouverneur Morris." (1) 5:front cover inside, March 1968.
Same plate was used by his father and his half-brother, who was a signer of the Declaration of Independence.

4922 "John Chandler, 1693-1762." (1) 5:front cover inside, June 1968.
"Chandler's plate is Chippendale and one of the finest examples of the work of Nathaniel Hurd."

4923 "Book-plate of James Giles." (1) 5:front cover inside, October 1968.
Typical plate of Revolutionary period used "an armorial frame with most un-heraldic bearings." Signed "R. Montgomery, Sculp."

4924 "Book-plate of Samuel Chase." Mary De Vold. (2) 5:front and back cover inside, December 1968.
"Son of Liberty" and delegate to First Continental Congress had one bookplate "typical of the late Chippendale period" plus another simple typographic label.

4925 "Book-plate of Richard Varick." (1) 6:front cover inside, March 1969.
"Patriotic features have been substituted for the armorial charges and bearers, the whole being assembled in late Chippendale style."

4926 "Book-plate of Daniel Webster." (1) 6:front cover inside, June 1969.
Simple plate "but one of the few which has the facsimile of a signature instead of a printed name."

SEWANEE REVIEW

4927 "Dr. Arthur Wellington Clark's Design for Bookplate." Prior to November, 1907. [Unable to locate.]
Source: Unknown.

SKETCH [London]

4928 "A Chat with Mr. Walter Crane." (7) 2:642-3, July 19, 1893.
Among illustrations are portrait of artist, a bookplate, book illustration and finger plates.

4929 "Small Talk." (1) 9:13, January 30, 1895.

Library of Edmund Yates, journalist, auctioned at Sotheby's; note on exhibit of Ex Libris Society and poem similar to Austin Dobson's "Book-plate's Petition."

4930 "Randolph Churchill's Bookplate." (1) 11:140, August 14, 1895.

Famous bookbinder, Zaehnsdorf, engraved Churchill plate showing interior "view of the Assembly of which he was so distinguished a member."

4931 "Ladies As Book-Collectors." (3) 13:490,, April 8, 1896.

Interesting review of Norna Labouchere's book.

SKETCH BOOK [Chicago]

4932 "Something About Bookplates." V. H. (15) 2:6-16, May 1903.

"Among these [fads] is the use of bookplates, a fashion which has never really been dead, though it may be admitted that it slept soundly while the nineteenth century was in its prime."

4933 "Objects of the Book-Plate." Ralph Fletcher Seymour. (18) 2:17-22, May 1903.

Briefly touches on methods of producing and designs of bookplates.

4934 "Modern Bookplate Collecting." Lutie E. Stearns. (13) 2:23-8, May 1903. (Sterns in Index)

Among collectors "a bookplate is a calling card and letter of introduction in one."

4935 "Collections of Bookplates from the House of the Blue Sky Press." Iva G. Swift. (7) 2:29-31, May 1903.

Plea for art above the quest for the dollar.

4936 "Concerning Book-Plates: An Appreciation." Mae J. Evans. (6) 3:317-20, June 1904.

"The collecting of book-plates brings a good time, without a headache next morning."

4937 "Advance of the Book-Plate." Anne C. Justice. (4) 3:321-3, June 1904.

At London sale during March a Paul Revere plate brought $165.

4938 "Book-Plates." (7) 3:323-7, June 1904.

Illustrations only; several designed by Mrs. Alexander W. Mackenzie.

4939 "Sketch Book Prize Competition for June." (2) 3:343-4, June 1904.

Illustrated are first and second prize winners in bookplate competition.

4940 "Book Plates." (4) 5:43, September 1905.

No text; plates by Ralph Fletcher Seymour for George Barr McCutcheon and Preston A. Perry, and by Charles B. Falls for John A. Williams and Ray Brown.

SOCIÉTÉ GUERNESIAISE REPORTS AND TRANSACTIONS

4941 "Heraldry from Bookplates." E. F. Carey. (10) 10:341-4, plates XIII, XIV, XV, 1928.

"A series of armorial bookplates has been introduced for the purpose of illustrating the later stages of the decline and fall of heraldic design."

SOCIÉTÉ INTERNATIONAL D'HISTOIRE DE LA MEDECINE

4942 "Medical Symbolism on Bookplates." Samuel X. Radbill. (10) 1-3, September 1952.

"Medical legends and stories, fables with medical content or allusion, famous medical men of the past, medical instruments and armamentaria, medical plants, clinical scenes, hospital views, medical society and college seals (themselves replete with medical symbolism), and other ideas without end are pictorially used on medical bookplates."

SOCIETY OF BOOK-PLATE BIBLIOPHILES

4943 "Twenty Book Plates." George Wolfe Plank. (20) 21 unnumbered pages, Publication No. 1, 1917.

Twenty original plates tipped in; artist in England when printed and no text available.

4944 "Norwegian Ex Libris." Gerhard Gade. (21) 28 unnumbered pages, Publication No. 2, 1917.

Brief introduction, biographical paragraph about each of thirteen artists, ten-entry bibliography of articles mostly published in Stockholm, and reproductions of twenty-one plates.

4945 "Masonic Bookplates." Winward Prescott. (13) 1-29, Publication No. 3, 1918.

Monograph including list of over 170 Masonic ex libris.

4946 "A List of Canadian Bookplates." Winward Prescott. (51) 1-156, Publication No. 4, 1919.

Book-length review of Canadian bookplates and alphabetical checklist.

SOCIETY OF MEDICAL HISTORY OF CHICAGO BULLETIN [See **BULLETIN OF THE SOCIETY OF MEDICAL HISTORY OF CHICAGO**]

SOUTH AFRICAN LIBRARIES

4947 "Some Notes on the History of Bookplates." A. Porter. 27:18-23, July 1959.

In particular mentions publication *South African Bookplates* from the Percival J. G. Bishop collection with a preface by R. F. M. Immelman.

SOUTHERN CALIFORNIA PRINTING TEACHERS YEAR BOOK

4948 "Typographical Name Labels and Bookplates of Printers." Edith Emerson Spencer. 2:3 unnumbered pages, 1934.

"The printed book and the bookplate, for some four and a half centuries, have been, like the dog-star Sirius and the starry hunter Orion, close companions."

SOUTHERN WOMAN'S MAGAZINE

"[Bookplates.]" October 1904. [Unable to locate.]
Source: Unknown.

SOUTHGATE MUSICAL NEWS

4949 "Ornamental Musical Book Plates." 234, October 7, 1916. [Unable to locate.]
Source unknown and unable to find journal listed in Union Serials for United States or Great Britain.

SPECIAL LIBRARIES

4950 "Book Reviews." 59:802, December 1968.
Bookplates for Libraries: Contemporary Designs for School, Public, College and University Libraries presents seventy-eight plates printed in four colors by artist and calligrapher Edward Shickell; designs may be used without permission.

SPECTATOR

4951 "*A Guide to the Study of Book-Plates.*" 56:1323, October 13, 1883.
Comment on Warren's book: "It is a solid, trustworthy, and conscientious book, and worthy of all commendation."

4952 "Exhibition of Bookplates." Harold Nicolson. 188:43, January 11, 1952.
Comments on exhibit of National Book League in connection with *Observer;* author dislikes bookplates.

STANFORD ALUMNUS

4953 "Jewel Fund Bookplate." (1) 14:160-3,166, January 1913.
Fund created from sale of Mrs. Jane L. Stanford's jewels to be invested and proceeds used to purchase books. Edwin Howland Blashfield has captured this selfless giving in the bookplate he designed for Stanford University.

STRAND

4954 "Henry Stacy Marks, R. A." Harry How. (13) 2:110-20, August 1891.
"Mr. Marks has been referred to as the light comedian of the brush. He says himself that if he had not been an artist he would have been an actor."

4955 "Handwriting of Mr. Gladstone from March, 1822 to March, 1894." J. Holt Schooling. (33) 8:73-89, July 1894.
Gladstone's handwriting analyzed; one illustration is his bookplate bearing the motto "Fide et virtute."

4956 "Book-Plates." (6) 39:513-4, May 1910.
Illustrations include plates for Thomas Carlyle, Frederic Leighton,

Lord Wolseley, Rider Haggard, Sir L. Alma-Todema, and a gift plate for Gladstone.

"Dickens Testimonial Stamp."

4957 41:75, February 1911.

4958 41:269, March 1911.

4959 41:416, April 1911.

4960 41:685, June 1911.

A special centenary penny stamp honoring Dickens issued; however, no bookplate reference.

STUDIES IN PHILOLOGY

4961 "Owners' Jingles in Early Printed Books." C. F. Bühler. 62:647-53, October 1965.

Inscriptions in English, Latin, Greek and French quoted mostly from volumes in Pierpont Morgan Library, some admonishing possible book thieves.

STUDIO

4962 "Designing for Book-Plates; with Some Recent Examples." G[leeson] W[hite]. (9) 1:24-8, April 1893.

Designs by R. Anning Bell, Herbert P. Horne, Warrington Hogg, Alan Wright. "The book-plate itself, although but a trivial thing, has some relation to scholarship, which dignifies and raises it to a higher place than is usually accorded to mere commercial decoration in black and white."

4963 "Some Recent Book-Plates—With Seven Examples." (7) 1:148-50, July 1893.

Examples by T. Erat Harrison, R. Anning Bell, Leslie Brooke, Warrington Hogg and Aymer Vallance.

4964 "Book-Plates." (3) 1:252-3, September 1893.

Designs by Sidney Heath and R. Anning Bell.

4965 "Design for a Book-Plate." (1) 2:116, January 1894.

R. Anning Bell design for Frederick Brown.

4966 "Some Recent Volumes on the Printed Book and Its Decoration." (9) 2:140-3, January 1894.

Reviewer of *English Bookplates* says "Mr. Castle's crisp and eminently readable text needs no praise, it is not often one gets so much solid fact presented so easily and lightly."

4967 "*The Book-Plate Annual and Armorial Yearbook*, 1894." (1) 2:221, March 1894.

Reviews state it is a "well-produced annual."

4968 "Book-Plate." (1) 2:222, March 1894.

R. Anning Bell designed plate for sheets or volumes of music.

4969 "Book-Plate." (1) 2:224, March 1894.

Plate by Harry Napper for Victor W. Burnand.

4970 "Frederic Leighton." (2) 3:122-3, July 1894.
Two plates designed by R. Anning Bell for Sir Leighton, Bt. P.R.A.

4971 "Book-Plates." (3) 3:159-60, August 1894.
Designs by E. H. New and R. Anning Bell.

4972 "Book-Plates." (2) 3:192, September 1894.
Plates by J. Walter West and Hugh Thomson.

4973 "Awards." Supplement XXV-XXIX. (22) n.d.
Each competitor was to be presented "with a block of his design."

4974 "New Publications." XXV. n.d.
Dated Book-Plates by Walter Hamilton given favorable review.

4975 "Book-Plates." (2) 4:68, November 1894.
Both designed by R. Anning Bell.

4976 "New German Designer: Joseph Sattler." Charles Hiatt. (10) 4:92-7, December 1894.
Seven dynamic plates are ex libris. "It is quite clear that Sattler paid to Durer the complete homage of imitation."

4977 "Notes of Recent Book-Plates." G[leeson] W[hite]. (8) 4:197-200, February 1894.
Designs by C. H. Townsend, W. A. Weyer, Louis Davis, J. E. Southall, W. E. Keene and J. Walter West.

4978 "Editor's Room." IX n.d.
Review of *Ex Libris*, Berlin journal.

4979 "Bookplates." (1) 5:39-40, April 1895.
Plate designed by E. H. New for C. E. Mathews.

4980 "On the Work of J. Walter West." A. Lys Baldry. (8) 6:139-47, December 1895.
No mention of painter's bookplate work.

4981 "Reviews." (2) 6:188-9, December 1895.
Dated Book-Plates by Walter Hamilton and Norna Labouchere's *Ladies' Book-Plates* both given generally favorable review.

4982 "Some Recent Book-Plates." Gleeson White. (11) 7:93-8, March 1896.
A bookplate "should always be a decorated label, not a label arbitrarily placed on a panel of decoration."

4983 "Ex Libris Society Exhibit." (3) 8:42-3, June 1896.
Illustrations of plates by J. Walter West and F. L. Emanuel.

4984 "National Competition. South Kensington 1896." 8:224,226, September 1896.
Plates by T. J. Overnell and H. Nelson illustrated.

4985 "Reviews." 9:72-3, October 1896.
Joseph Sattler's enigmatic *Meine Harmonie* reviewed; mentions his "extraordinarily clever etchings and bookplates."

4986 "Some Recent Book-Plates, Mostly Pictorial." Gleeson White. (18) 10:110-18, March 1897.
A bookplate design should be "one that does not pall by repetition."

4987 "Reviews of Recent Publications." 10:141, March 1897.
Ex Libris essays by Charles D. Allen given "excellent" rating.

4988 "Work of Mr. Byam Shaw." Gleeson White. (12) 10:209-21, May 1897.
Bookplate for Isabella R. Hunter is one illustration among many works of painter.

4989 "Designs for Book-Plates." iii-iv, n.d. (6)
First prize to Ethel Kate Burgess.

4990 "Review." 11:67, June 1897.
Amsterdam publication on musical bookplates reviewed.

4991 "Some Glasgow Designers." (1) 11:98, July 1897.
One bookplate among illustrations.

4992 "Some Glasgow Designers." (3) 11:234-5, September 1897.
Three plates by J. Herbert McNair.

4993 "Reviews." 13:59, February 1898.
Decorative Heraldry by G. W. Eve reviewed.

4994 "Bookplate." (1) 13:180, April 1898.
Designed by A. Rassenfosse.

4995 "Reviews." 14:70, June 1898.
Artists and Engravers of British and American Bookplates given favorable review.

4996 "Design for a 'Pictorial' Book-Plate." 14:216-7, August 1898.
Catherine M. Mann and Edgar G. Perman received first and second prizes.

4997 "British Book-Plates." Gleeson White. (79) 15:2-47, Winter 1898-99.
"Wiser folk know that many 'etchings' are as valueless as the average engraving in a patent medicine pamphlet, and these care no more for a bad book-plate than they do for the 'chromo-prints' enclosed in packets of cheap cigarettes. . . . Rubbish, be it in the form of book-plates or cigar-ends, is merely rubbish, and charms you no more after it has been sorted, classified, collected, and indexed, than when it reposed in a waste-paper basket, or lay unheeded in the gutter."

4998 "French Book-Plates." Octave Uzanne. (17) 15:47-58, Winter 1898-99.
"The mania for acquiring these little works is epidemic and cosmopolitan, and nearly as severe as the postage-stamp craze."

4999 "Some American Book-Plates." (19) 15:58-63, Winter 1898-99.
Illustrations include plates by Louis J. Rhead, W. S. Hadaway, Mary Prendiville, and B. G. Goodhue; text rather disappointing.

5000 "German Book-Plates." Hans W. Singer. (25) 15:63-8, Winter 1898-99.
Illustrations include plates by Joseph Sattler and Max Klinger.

5001 "Some Austrian Book-Plates." Wilhelm Scholermann. (6) 15:68-73, Winter 1898-99.

Author claims there are only three living Austrian bookplate designers: Ernst Krahl, Hugh Strohl, and Emil Orlik.

5002 "Belgian Book-Plates." Fernand Khnopff. (7) 15:73-8, Winter 1898-99.

"A book-plate is a unique thing, umpretentious in point of size, and of definite character; something that must be specially commissioned, and, moreover, cannot decently exist or be displayed without justification—or, in other words, without a library of books for it to be placed in.

5003 "Book-Plate." (1) 15:276, January 1899.

Plate by Miss Sandheim for Michael Adler.

5004 "Mr. Arthur H. Mackmurdo and the Century Guild." Aymer Vallance. (12) 16:183-92, April 1899.

Designs include furniture, bronze mantelpiece, screen, mirror, lamp and a bookplate for Holmes Spicer.

5005 "Bookplates." (11) 19:268-71, May 1900.

Plates illustrated are by Harold Nelson, Alexander Fisher, and Maurice De Lambert.

5006 "Awards." (16) 20:61, 64-7, June 1900.

Winners listed for designing a pictorial bookplate.

5007 "Designs for a Bookplate." (16) 22:61,64-7, February 1901.

Award winners named.

5008 "Some Thoughts on the Art of Gordon Craig with Particular Reference to Stage Craft." Haldane MacFall. (14) 23:246-55, September 1901.

Four illustrations are bookplates. "In his very bookplates there is this dramatic sense—indeed, over his craftsmanship there broods always the mood of the dramatist."

5009 "Bookplate by J. Walter West." (1) 24:276,281, January 1902.

Designed for Howard Wilford Bell.

5010 "King Edward's Bookplate." (3) 26:52,54, June 1902.

Three different plates by George W. Eve; sets being "sold in aid of King Edward's Hospital Fund of London."

5011 "Awards." 26:313, September 1902.

Bookplate design award will be made known in October.

5012 "Designs for Book-Plates, Some Remarks Upon the Results of Competition." Aymer Vallance. (35) 27:120-9, November 1902.

Actual names of artists not given.

5013 "Design for a Book-Plate." 27:151,155, November 1902.

List of winners using actual identity.

5014 "Dr. Hans Przibram." (6) 27:222-3, December 1902.

Bookplates featuring animals—"A touch of quaint humour render[s] his small bookplates very charming."

5015 "Design for a Book-Plate." (15) 30:272-5, December 1903.
Award winners listed.

5016 "Reviews." 32:271, August 1904.
Bookplates by Edward Almack briefly reviewed.

5017 "Bookplate." (1) 34:30, February 1905.
Designed by Hans Volkert for his own use.

5018 "Two Italian Draughtsmen: Alfredo Baruffi and Alberto Martini." Vittorio Pica. (10) 34:137-42, March 1905.
Illustrations include two bookplates by Baruffi which are "worthy of figuring beside those of the English Ricketts, of the German Sattler, and of the Belgian Khnopff and Rassenfosse."

5019 "Reviews." 34:179, March 1905.
Ex Libris is a collection of bookplates by Spanish artist Señor A. de Riquer. "When, say a hundred years hence, the art of the late nineteenth and early twentieth centuries is written upon, the cult of the *Ex-libris* will not be neglected."

5020 "Book-Plate." (1) 34:349, May 1905.
Design by D. Waterson with space for owner's name.

5021 "Studio-Talk." (2) 35:74,78, June 1905.
Plates designed by W. Mellor "full of vigour and decorative quality."

5022 "Book-Plate." (3) 35:327,330, September 1905.
Three designs by Winifred L. Stamp.

5023 "Design for a Book Label." (17) 36:89-90,93, October 1905.
Award winners listed.

5024 "Studio-Talk." (3) 37:158-9, March 1906.
Three bookplates, each featuring a woman, by J. Walter West.

5025 "Imperial Arts and Crafts Schools, Vienna." A. S. Levetus. (28) 39:323-34, January 1907.
Two bookplates among illustrations with overall design like wallpaper or a textile with the name in the middle.

5026 "Studio-Talk." (4) 39:348,351, January 1907.
Four bookplates by Harold Nelson.

5027 "Recent Work of Mr. J. Walter West, RWS." A. L. Baldry. (16) 40:87-100, March 1907.
Three bookplates shown as well as more ambitious works.

5028 "Miss Dewar." (2) 42:316-7, January 1908.
Two bookplates by Lewthwaite Dewar, member of Glasgow Society of Lady Artists.

5029 "Studio-Talk." (2) 46:147-8, March 1909.
Two bookplates by Glasgow artist Jessie M. King.

5030 "Monograms, Marks, and Ex Libris by George Auriol." (39) 47:227, August 1909.

Only one actually labeled as a bookplate.

5031 "Etched Book-Plates." Frank Newbolt. (11) 48:216-23, December 1909.

"Book-plates are the product of democracy, and afford evidence of the spread of education."

"The perfect label suggests at once the owner and the designer. The old heraldic engraving suggested nothing except that the owner claimed the right to bear arms."

5032 "National Competition of Schools of Art, 1910." (1) 50:302, September 1910.

Bookplate by Dorothy M. Payne illustrated.

5033 "Bookplate."(1) 51:74, October 1910.

Design by Marie Stiefel.

5034 "Bookplates." (3) 52:227-8, April 1911.

Designs by R. Anning Bell.

5035 "Studio-Talk." (6) 64:50-1, February 1915.

Bookplates all designed by C. F.A. Voysey.

5036 "Reviews." 65:289, September 1915.

Review of *Ex Libris Engraved on Wood* with twenty plates, preface by Ettore Cozzani, printed in Turin.

5037 "Studio-Talk." (2) 71:38, June 1917.

Bookplates by Toronto artist, F. Stanley Harrod.

5038 "Studio-Talk." (4) 73:67-8, March 1918.

Bookplates designed by Harold Nelson.

5039 "Stephen Gooden, A.R.A., R.E." Campbell Dodgson. (8) 131:10-4, January 1946.

Gooden executed plates for Royal Windsor Library, Liverpool Medical Institute, Lakeside Press.

5040 "Bookplates." Mark Severin. (15) 131:177-80, June 1946.

In designing bookplates, Severin believes each should be personal to the owner and adapts his theme and technique accordingly.

5041 "*Ex Libris Kunde*." 136:127, October 1948.

Review of bibliography by John Schwenke; covers works since 1880, commentary, and 275 reproductions; comprehensive for Holland and Belgium.

5042 "N.E.K. Year Book 1947." 136:200, December 1948.

First year book of Dutch society, paperbound, ninety-two pages; reviews fifteen years of Society's activities.

SUNSET

5043 "Some California Book-Plates." Sheldon Cheney. (15) 18:332-6, February 1907.

Largest California collection (4,000) belonged to W. A. Brewer of Burlingame.

Cheney says, "The California collectors work under a disadvantage, in that books on the subject are not plentiful in the libraries. . . . there is no one place where more than half a dozen of the books are found together." About the bookplate—"Its artistic and antiquarian appeal wins its way to the heart of the book lover and its good sense recommends it to the mere book-owner."

SUSSEX COUNTY MAGAZINE

5044 "Howard Book Plates." J. E. S. King. (2) 3:402, June 1929.

Illustrated are plates of Edward (the 9th) Duke of Norfolk and John Baker Holroyd (Lord Sheffield).

SYDNEY MAIL

5045 "Charm of the Bookplate." P. Neville Barnett. (7) 15, August 29, 1923. [Volume number unavailable.]

Illustrated are plates by W. S. Percy, J. Barclay Godson, Lionel Lindsay, Roy Davies, and E. Warner.

5046 "Vice-Regal Bookplates." P. Neville Barnett. (7) 9, October 8, 1924. [Volume number unavailable.]

Illustrated are plates for Countess Longford, Lord Denman, Matthew Nathan (Governor of Queensland), Admiral Sir Harry Rawson, Lord Onslow, Lady Northcote, and Dame Margaret Davison.

5047 "The Bookplate of Queen Alexandra." P. Neville Barnett. (1) December 1925. [Unable to locate.]

As annotated by H. B. Muir: A description and reproduction of the plate by W. P. Barrett.

5048 "Bookplates." (2) July 17, 1929. [Volume and page numbers unavailable.]

Illustrated are plates of Mr. and Mrs. G. K. Chesterton and Compton Mackenzie.

T

TECHNOLOGY REVIEW [M.I.T.]

5049 "Bookplates by Elisha Brown Bird, '91." (10) 38:81, 104, December 1935.

Five of the bookplates illustrated are related to M.I.T.; the remaining are institutional plates. Short biographical note mentions work as cartoonist on Boston *Herald* and that he was first artist to sketch baseball games in progress.

TIME MAGAZINE

5050 [Maury Maverick] (1) 1929. [Unable to locate.]
Reference is made in NEWS NOTES of the Texas Library Association to an article about Maury Maverick which included an illustration of his bookplate in TIME during 1929 ["On Texas Bookplates," by Sarah Chakla, 11:Issue No. 1, January 1935].

TIMES LITERARY SUPPLEMENT

5051 "Heraldic Tinctures." George H. Viner. 358, July 26, 1917.
Comments on heraldry and bookplates and whether color should be used.

5052 "Bibliography of Book-Plates." 344-55, May 27, 1926.
Refers to Verna B. Grimm bibliography with introduction by George W. Fuller and "random thoughts" by Winward Prescott.

5053 "[Letters.]" 355, May 27, 1926.
Officer of Ex Libris Society states new collectors concerned only with number and scarcity of bookplates.

TIT-BITS

5054 "Who has the finest collection of book-plates (ex libris) in this country?" 25: 42, October 21, 1893.
A. W. Franks probably has the largest; also mentioned are collections of James Roberts Brown of the Ex Libris Society and Dr. Howard of the Heralds' College.

TO-MORROW

5055 "Book-Plates." Norna Labouchere. 3:285-93, May 1897.
"Quaint as a leaf out of an old block book, the simple art of the first book-plates stated the fact required, and adorned the statement with the few, strong, adequate lines of representation which told their tale perhaps more directly than the elaborate designs of later days."

TOWN CRIER

5056 "Washington Bookplates." Frederick Starr. (2) 20:5, October 17, 1925.
Plea for knowledge of bookplates used by Washington state residents or plates designed by artists of that state. George W. Fuller's plate illustrated.

5057 "Washington Bookplates." Frederick Starr. (6) 20:33-4, 48, December 12, 1925.
There are three types of bookplate artists: professional artist who condescends to "do a plate," professional designer who is quite willing and competent, and the non-professional who is skilled with pen, brush, or graver.

5058 "Washington Bookplates." Frederick Starr. (2) 21:9,14, January 16, 1926.
Quotes that bookplate collecting "is on a par with making a button-string."

5059 "Washington Bookplates." Frederick Starr. (2) 21:5, February 27, 1926.
Discussion of Washington state institutional plates which in general are utilitarian rather than artistic.

5060 "Washington Bookplates." Frederick Starr. (2) 21:9,14, March 27, 1926.
Mentions that Fuller bibliography, published by Spokane Public Library, is "just off the press."
"Periodical articles on bookplates, which are immensely numerous and practically inaccessible, are not listed."
Lists 150 Washington bookplates.

5061 "Washington Bookplates." Frederick Starr. (6) 22:39-40, December 10, 1927.
Details given concerning plates illustrated, including Masonic plates on which book is to be published.

TRANSACTIONS & STUDIES OF THE COLLEGE OF PHYSICIANS OF PHILADELPHIA

5062 "S. Weir Mitchell." John H. Talbott. (1) 30:192-207, April 1963.
Illustration is portrait of S. Weir Mitchell used in bookplate of Library of College of Physicians of Philadelphia.

TRANSACTIONS OF AMERICAN COLLEGE OF SURGEONS [See **BULLETIN OF AMERICAN COLLEGE OF SURGEONS**]

TRANSACTIONS OF BIBLIOGRAPHICAL SOCIETY

5063 "Inscriptions in Books." Gilbert R. Redgrove. 4:37-46, November 1896-June 1898.
"It was a bad day for collectors, I venture to think, when book-plates came into fashion . . . for owners no longer wrote their names in books."

5064 "Bagford's Notes on Bookbindings." Cyril Davenport. 6:123-59, October 1902-March 1904.
Small mention of bookplates and that they are among items of collection catalogued in British Museum.

TRANSACTIONS OF CAMBRIDGE BIBLIOGRAPHICAL SOCIETY

5065 "Origin of Sir Nicholas Bacon's Book-plate." E. R. Sandeen. 2:part 5, 373-6, 1958.
In 1574 Sir Nicholas Bacon donated seventy volumes toward rebuilding Cambridge University Library; each had a bookplate showing his coat of arms. Interesting account of actual evolvement of the coat of arms and the resulting bookplate.

TRANSACTIONS OF HISTORICAL SOCIETY OF LANCASHIRE AND CHESHIRE [See **HISTORIC SOCIETY OF LANCASHIRE.**]

TRANSACTIONS OF ROYAL HISTORICAL AND ARCHAEOLOGICAL SOCIETY OF IRELAND [Royal Society of Antiquaries]

5066 "Robert Day—Cork Artists." 4th Series 7:10-4, 1885.
Note from Robert Day listing Cork artists, in particular forty-eight plates by Mr. Green and his father.

TRANSACTIONS OF ROYAL SOCIETY OF LITERATURE

5067 "Poet Cowper and His Surroundings." 2nd S. 22:134-64, 1901.
Page 163 contains picture of William Cowper's bookplate.

TRANSACTIONS SOCIETY GUERNESIAISE [See **SOCIÉTÉ GUERNESIAISE REPORTS AND TRANSACTIONS**]

TYDE WHAT MAY

5068 "A Few Book-Plates." [Mrs. Margaret Haig Stuart]. (3) No. 3, 68-70, Winter 1894.
This privately printed family journal used for a title the motto which appears on their bookplate: "Tyde What May."

TYPE [**TYPE AND TALENT**]

5069 "Book Plates." James Guthrie. Issue No. 5:64-6, 1917.
"The bookplate which is right, suitable for its purpose, interesting, charming, is indeed rare and hard to come at."

U

UCLA LIBRARIAN

5070 "Exhibit of Sonnenschein Gift of Bookplates." (4) 19:85-6, September 1966.
Nearly 4,000 plates and over 100 books given to Department of Special Collections.

5071 "Edward Gordon Craig: An Exhibit." (1) 20:43-4, October 1967.
Craig was "the revolutionist and visionary of the modern theatre." Exhibit included woodcuts and bookplates.

UNESCO BULLETIN FOR LIBRARIES

5072 "Book-Plates for Literacy." (1) 21:220-1, July-August 1967.
Bookplates (ten for one dollar) being sold by National Council of Women to provide funds "to bring literacy to some of the 500 million women in the world who have never had a chance to go to school."

UNITED EMPIRE [Royal Colonial Institute Journal]

5073 "Adrian Feint Plates for Duke & Duchess of York." (2) 18:382, July 1927.
As mementos of their visit to Australia bookplates were executed by Adrian Feint, an etching of Parliament House, Canberra, for the Duke, and a woodcut of Australian flora for the Duchess.

UNIVERSITY OF CALIFORNIA CHRONICLE

5074 "The Bookplate." Beulah Mitchell Clute. (25) 24:147-60, April 1924.
Brief historical survey and details of plates illustrated including some in color.

V

VANITY FAIR

5075 "Bookplate Designs by Rockwell Kent." (6) 32:84, April 1929.
"Already known as an artist, he sets himself up now under the sign of the psychiatrist, endeavouring to interpret in one emblematic figure and design the essential secret of one individual."

VASSAR QUARTERLY

5076 "Bookplates of Timothy Cole." Oliver S. Tonks. (4) 17:9-13, February 1932.
Noted engraver did not make first bookplate until between 1904 and 1906 when he was over fifty; chronological lists totaling twenty-two engraved plates given.

VETERINARY ALUMNI QUARTERLY

5077 "Library of the College of Veterinary Medicine, The Ohio State University, and Its Bookplates." Fritz Volkmar. (3) 21:1-8, December 1933.
University gift plate designed by Thomas E. French and etched by A. N. Macdonald, also the general University bookplate.

VICTORIAN

5078 "What Is Heraldry?" Rev. G. C. Allen. Issue No. 3, September 1897. [Unable to locate.]

Source: *Journal of Ex Libris Society* 7:151, November 1897: " 'What Is Heraldry?'—Such is the ambitious title given by the Rev. G. C. Allen to a short paper which occupies three pages in No. 3 of *The Victorian*, the September issue . . . he devotes most of his attention to the crying abuses in the assumption and bearing of arms by persons who are not entitled to them."

Walter Hamilton drew attention to fact cover of *Victorian* incorrectly shows "golden lion of England, the harp of Erin, and the field of the Scottish standard . . . *argent* when they should be *or*."

VIRGINIA MAGAZINE OF HISTORY AND BIOGRAPHY

5079 "Rootes Family." T. R. Rootes. (1) 4:204-11, October 1896.
Extensive family history and Philip Rootes' plate illustrated.

VISITATION OF ENGLAND AND WALES

5080 "Charles Francis Cole." (1) 1:12, 1893.
Pedigree and plate by Sherborn (1892).

5081 "John Bartlett." (1) 1:65-7, 1893.
Round bookplate.

5082 "John Clay." (1) 1:68-70, 1893.
Bookplate designed by Harry Soane.

5083 "General Sir John St. George." (1) 1:105-8, 1893.
Pedigree and bookplate.

5084 "Joseph Bowstead Wilson." (1) 1:177-9, 1893.
Plate has initials CWS and date 1892.

5085 "John William Ryland." (1) 1:245-8, 1893.
Another Sherborn dated plate.

5086 "William Flory." (1) 1:253, 1893.
G. W. Eve plate dated 1891.

5087 "Gwatkin." (1) 2:1-4, 1894.
Plate with initials of artist JEH.

5088 "Dugdale of Griffin, Blackburn, Co. Lancaster." (1) 2:73-6, 1894.
Pedigree and bookplate.

5089 "Britton of Bristol and Litton House, Engield, Co. Essex." (1) 2:77-9, 1894.
G. W. Eve plate.

5090 "Prideaux-Brune of Prideau Place, Co. Cornwall." (1) 2:97-100, 1894.
Arms and motto only on plate.

5091 "Langley." (1) 2:101-4, 1894.
While listed as a bookplate in the *Journal of Ex Libris Society*, illustration does not appear to be actually a bookplate.

5092 "Lockett of Liverpool." (1) 2:108-12, 1894.
Circular ex libris signed "Gurney, Sculp."

5093 "Price of Glynlleck." (1) 2:159-60, 1894.
Plate by G. W. Eve dated 1894.

5094 "Gwatkin of Potterne, Debizes, Co. Wilts." (2) 2:166-8, 1894.
Engraved plate for Stewart B. Gwatkin.

5095 "Rivington." (1) 3:20-4, 1895.
Plate for Charles Robert Rivington.

5096 "Molesworth." (1) 3:37-9, 1895.
Sir Lewis William Molesworth's plate.

5097 "Weldon." (3) 3:40, 1895.
Two plates, both by G. W. Eve, one circular and printed in red.

5098 "Burke of Auberies, Bulmer, Co. Essex." (1) 3:43-5, 1895.
Harold Burke's plate with motto: Ung roy, ung foy, ung loy.

5099 "Glazebrook of Liverpool." (1) 3:56-60, 1895.
Plate for Thomas Twanbrook Glazebrook with artist's initials CWS, 1892.

5100 "Chance of Birmingham." (1) 3:65-9, 1895.
Plate by G. W. Eve for James Frederick Chance.

5101 "Fletcher of Lawneswood." (1) 3:75-81, 1895.
Coat of arms and motto.

5102 "Macnamara." (1) 3:91-4, 1895.
F. N. Macnamara plate.

5103 "Taylor of Liverpool." (1) 3:95-6, 1895.
William Francis Taylor, D.D., plate.

5104 "Herbert of Llanarth." (1) 3:121-4, 1895.
Circular plate for Edward Herbert done by "Orthner & Honle, 3, St. James St., S.W."

5105 "Chisenhall-Marsh of Gaynes Park, Epping, Co. Essex." (1) 4:6-8, 1896.
William Swaine Chisenhall-Marsh plate.

5106 "Brine of Blandford, Co. Dorset." (1) 4:17-22, 1896.
Plate for James Gram Brine.

5107 "Hall of Llanover and Abercard, Co. Monmouth." (2) 4:27-31, 1896.
Plate for C. R. Hall.

5108 "Green of Spalding, Co. Lincoln." (1) 4:45-7, 1896.
Armorial by Eve, printed in burnt sienna, features a dragon.

5109 "Warde of Squerryes Court, Co. Kent." (2) 4:55-64, 1896.
John Ward and C. A. M. Warde plates.

5110 "Wood of Gwernyfed, Co. Brecon." (2) 4:69-72, 1896.
Two different plates of Thomas Wood.

5111 "Scarsdale." (2) 4:77-82, 1896.
Two plates pictured differ mostly in that female figures on one are less draped than in the other.

5112 "Hill of St. Catherine's Hill, Co. Worcester." (1) 4:107-9, 1896.
Plate for Thomas Romley Hill.

5113 "Molesworth of Pencarrow, Co. Cornwall." (2) 4:110-2, 1896.
Plates for Mary Ford and Sir William Molesworth.

5114 "Marshall of Northfield, The Uplands, Strand." (1) 4:119-20. 1896.
Mark Bell Marshall plate printed in blue.

5115 "Firth." (1) 4:141-4, 1896.
Coat of arms and motto.

5116 "Taunton of Kingswood, Co. Surrey." (1) 4:167-9, 1896.
Plate for William Garnett Taunton with artist's initials of C.E.T.

5117 "Bate of Kelsterton, Co. Flint." (1) 4:173-4, 1896.
Plate for Thomas Bate.

5118 "Pearce-Edgcumbe of Somerleigh Court, Co. Dorset." (1) 5:14-6, 1897.
Plate for Sir Edward Robert Pearce-Edgcumbe.

5119 "Onslow." (1) 5:39-42, 1897.
Arthur Onslow's plate signed by Coles, Sculpt. and W. Kent Delin.

5120 "Greenwood of Swarcliffe Hall, Co. York." (2) 5:129-31, 1897.
Plates for John Greenwood and Hubert John Greenwood.

5121 "Gay of Falmouth, Co. Cornwall." (1) 5:165, 1897.
Two mottoes for W. Gay: "Gwyr yn erbyn y byd" and "toujours gai."

5122 "Cowper-Essex of Yewfield Castle." (1) 6:11-2, 1898.
Plates for Henry Swainson Cowper.

5123 "Langman." (1) 6:24-6, 1898.
Philip Lawrence Langman plate appears to be by G. W. Eve.

5124 "Marten." (1) 6:58-64, 1898.
Plate for Judge Sir Alfred Geare Marten, Inner Temple.

5125 "Longstaff." (1) 6:70-1, 1898.
Coat of arms and motto.

5126 "Lawrence of City of London." (1) 6:78-80, 1898.
William Lawrence, Esq., Alderman.

5127 "Perceval." (4) 6:89-98, 1898.
Henry Perceval bookplate and Spencer Perceval portrait.

5128 "Fanshawe of Parsloes, Co. Essex." (3) 6:113-6, 1898.
Plates for J. G. Fanshawe, John F. Fanshawe, and a monogram.

5129 "Back of Curat's House." (1) 6:124-6, 1898.
Plate measuring 5 by 6 1/2 inches for Major Philip E. Back.

5130 "Master of Bourton Grange, Co. Somerset." (1) 6:139-44, 1898.
Streynsham Master's bookplate.

5131 "Bailey of Co. Kent." (1) 7:46-50, 1899.
Plate for James S. Bailey.

5132 "Newdigate of Kirk." (3) 7:53-60, 1899.
Plates for Sir Edward and Francis W. and Francis A., the latter two having similar design.

5133 "I'Anson of Denton Hall." (2) 7:65-6, 1899.
Plate for William Andrew I'Anson dated 1889.

5134 "Price." (2) 7:87-90, 1899.
Edward U. A. Price had two plates, one measuring about 4 1/2 x 6 inches.

5135 "Chafy, Co. Worcester." (1) 7:110-2, 1899.
Plate with peacock by G. W. Eve for William Kyle Westwood Chafy.

5136 "Dicken." (1) 7:138-44, 1899.
Dicken without any first name has the lion somewhat like that assumed by Charles Dickens.

5137 "Swithinbank." (1) 7:151-2, 1899.
Denham Court Library plate probably of Harold William Swithinbank.

5138 "Partridge of Hockham Hall, Co. Norfolk." (1) 7:161-4, 1899.
Henry Thomas Partridge.

5139 "Webb." (2) 8:9-12, 1900.
Plate for William Wilfrid Webb and one with coat of arms and motto.

5140 "Allanby."(1) 8:17-9, 1900.
Plate for Montgomerie.

5141 "Bolding." (1) 8:73-4, 1900.
Bolding armorial plate.

5142 "Hyett." (1) 8:122-4, 1900.
Plate for F. A. Hyett.

5143 "Colman." (1) 8:142-8, 1900.
Jeremiah Colman.

5144 "Boyd." (1) 8:161-4, 1900.
Plate for Edward Fenwick Boyd.

5145 "Jessel." (2) 9:71-2, 1901.
Plates for Sir Charles Jessel and H. M. Jessel.

5146 "Strickland." (3) 9:97-102, 1901.
Plates for Sir George Strickland, William Strickland and Sir William Strickland (1808).

5147 "Middleton." (1) 9:126-36, 1901.
Plate for Digby, 9th Baron, Middleton.

5148 "Brocklebank." (1) 9:141-4, 1901.
Plate for J. Brocklebank with initials C. W. S. and date 1896.

5149 "Clippingdale." (1) 9:169-74, 1901.
Plate for G. H. Clippingdale.

5150 "Clapton." (1) 10:9-12, 1902.
Plate for Edward Clapton, M.D.

5151 "Sherborne." (1) 10:20-4, 1902.
Plate for Sherborne Library of Baron of Sherborne.

5152 "Earle." (1) 10:105-12, 1902.
Plate for Thomas Earle.

5153 "Blackburne." (1) 10:142-4, 1902.
Plate for Robert Ireland Blackburne.

5154 "Wood." (1) 11:110-2, 1903.
Plate for Henry Wood dated 1896.

5155 "De Mauley." (1) 11:132-6, 1903.
William Ashly Webb, 3rd Baron De Mauley, has plate with artist's initials H. J. F. B., 1903.

5156 "Peel." (1) 12:23-4, 1904.
Plate for Mervyn Lloyd Peel.

5157 "Avebury." (1) 12:64-72, 1904.
Plate for Lord Avebury.

5158 "Howard." (3) 12:125-6, 1904.
Plate by G. W. Eve for Joseph Jackson Howard, co-editor with Frederick Arthur Crisp of *Visitation of England and Wales* until his death in April 1902; also plate of his son Arthur Dashwood Howard, M.D. by Eve.

5159 "Duncan." (1) 12:160-2, 1904.
Plate for William Mac Dougal Duncan.

5160 "Adams." (1) 13:24-8, 1905.
Plate for Percy Walter Lewis Adams.

5161 "Fletcher." (1) 13:57-60, 1905.
Plate for Caleb Fletcher.

5162 "Crisp." (1) 13:155-20, 1905.
Plate of Frederick Arthur Crisp.

5163 "Speeding." (1) 13:153-8, 1905.
Plate for R. Deey Speeding.

5164 "Nelson." (2) 13:184-94, 1905.
Plate for Earl Nelson.

5165 "Barry." (1) 14:1-18, 1906.
Plate for Sir John Wolfe Barry, KCB.

5166 "Brassey." (1) 14:58-68, 1906.
Plate for Thomas, Baron Brassey.

5167 "Talboys." (1) 14:98-102, 1906.
Plate for James Charles Getting by Will Foster shows Doughton Manor [1627-1818] and Doughton Cottage [1903].

5168 "Darrell." (1) 14:134-6, 1906.
Plate for Darrell, Trewornan, Cornwall.

5169 "Crisp."(1) 14:143-4, 1906.
Fred Crisp's plate.

5170 "Harwood." (1) 14:177-8, 1906.
Plate for Henry Harwood Harwood.

5171 "Jalland." (1) 14:189-90, 1906.
Plate for Boswell George Jalland.

5172 "Walker." (1) 15:52-6, 1908.
Samuel Walker's plate.

5173 "Pearson." (1) 15:164-6, 1908.
Plate for William Carter Pearson.

5174 "Bazely." (3) 16:97-102, 1909.
Plate for Thomas Tyfsen Bazely and portraits of an admiral born in 1740 and a rear-admiral born in 1767.

5175 "Lambert." (1) 17:8-14, 1911.
Frederic Lambert's plate.

5176 "Hayter." (2) 17:54-6, 1911.
Bookplate for Angelo Kirby Hayter.

5177 "Moor." (1) 17:104-10, 1911.
Plate for Caroli Moor, S.T.P.

5178 "Parish." (1) 18:89-94, 1914.
Plate for Charles Woodbyne Parish.

5179 "Adamson." (1) 18:143-4, 1914.
Plate for Lt. Colonel J. G. Adamson.

5180 "Pennyman." (1) 18:170-6, 1914.
Plate for James Worsley Pennyman.

5181 "Somers." (1) 18:Addenda, Lxiv, 1914.
Plate for Benjamin Edward Somers, M.A.

5182 "Cazalet." (1) 19:1-4, 1917.
Plate dated 1902 for William Marshall Cazalet.

5183 "Ficklin." (1) 19:148-50, 1917.
Plate for Philip Berney Ficklin.

5184 "Baker." (1) 20:53-4, 1919.
Plate for William Baker, Esq.

5185 "Whitmore." (1) 20:137-40, 1919.
Plate for Francis H. D. C. Whitmore.

5186 "Attwood." (1) 21:54-6, 1921.
Plate for Thomas A. C. Attwood.

5187 "Trower." (1) 21:100-8, 1921.
Plate for Henry Trower.

NOTES [Bound separately; illustrations with caption only; no title or text.]

5188 (3) 1:58-9, 1896.
Bookplates for Henry Goldney, Fra. Bennett Goldney, and Frederick Hastings Goldney.

5189 (2) 1:64-5, 1896.
Plates for James Vivian of Pencalenich and Joseph Richards.

5190 (1) 1:74-5, 1896.
Plate for Sir John Gresham, 6th and last Baronet of Titsey Place, Surrey.

5191 "(2) 1:100-1, 1896.
Plates for John Grubb and John Eustace Grubbe.

5192 (1) 1:115, 1896.
Plate for John Repps.

5193 (1) 2:10-1, 1897.
Plate for John Plumbe Tempest.

5194 (2) 2:28-9, 1897.
Plates for Sir George Tempest and Major John Tempest.

5195 (1) 2:37-8, 1897.
Plate for John Guille.

5196 (1) 2:55, 1897.
Plate for F. A. Blaydes.

5197 (2) 2:93, 1897.
Plates for Ralph Assheton and Thomas Brooke.

5198 (1) 2:96, 1897.
Plate for Everard Barton.

5199 (1) 2:106, 1897.
Plate for Reginald Stanley Faber.

5200 (2) 2:108, 1897.
Plates for Edward Platt-Higgins and Henry Platt-Higgins.

5201 (1) 2:116, 1897.
Plate for B. W. Malineux Hawkley.

5202 (4) 2:120, 1897.
Two plates for Benjamin Boddington, and one each for Thomas Francis Boddington and Reginald Stewart Boddington.

5203 (1) 2:122, 1897.
Plate for Henry Frederick Compon Cavendish.

5204 (1) 3:2, 1898.
Lord John Murray's bookplate.

5205 (2) 3:24, 1898.
Plates for Thomas Tindal Methold and Henry Methold.

5206 (1) 3:36, 1898.
Plate for George Daniell.

5207 (1) 3:36, 1898.
Plate for Rev. Peregrine Curtois.

5208 (4) 3:48, 1898.
Plates for John Benson, Richard Pritchett, Thomas Hext, and Rick Mant.

5209 (1) 3:52, 1898.
Plate for Jeremiah Spark.

5210 (2) 3:62, 1898.
Plates for Arthur J. Schomberg and Isaac Schomberg, M. D.

5211 (1) 3:70, 1898.
Henry L. Byrth.

5212 (2) 3:75, 1898.
Plates for Anthony Littledale and Willoughby Asgon Littledale.

5213 (1) 3:86, 1898.
Plate for John Pilkington.

5214 (1) 3:98, 1898.
Plate for Rev. W. T. Bree, M.A.

VOGUE

5215 "The Book-Plate." Eleanor Boykin. (6) 63:138 *et seq.*, April 1, 1924.
Author quotes H. S. Rowe concerning the bookplate: "Nestling in a book unknown and unseen until the book is opened, whether quaint or commonplace, artistic or otherwise, it speaks with a mute eloquence to all those not absolutely dead to its many charms."

VOLKSWAGON MAGAZINE

"Ex Libris Signe de Propriete." Mark F. Severin. (17) No. 3, March 1963.
Published in Brussels, Belgium; not in English. Variety of plates illustrated including miniature for Max Horn, a musical plate, Prime Minister's library plate of 1925, a Japanese.

VOLTA REVIEW [Alexander Graham Bell Association for the Deaf]

5216 "Meum non tuum." Florence Seville Berryman. (3) 36:221-3, 238, April 1934.
"The deafened person is a trifle more in need of a hobby than the average hearer, since many diversions . . . cannot be counted on to fill our spare time."

"Some enterprising research worker, who studied a large number of miscellaneous suicides . . . discovered that not one of them had a hobby."

W

WALFORD'S ANTIQUARIAN MAGAZINE & BIBLIOGRAPHICAL REVIEW [See **ANTIQUARIAN MAGAZINE & BIBLIOGRAPHICAL REVIEW**]

WALL'S ETCHED MONTHLY

5217 "Bookplate." (1) 1:unnumbered page, March 1921.
Plate for Edwin Markham etched by Bernhardt Wall.

5218 "Bookplate." (1) 2:unnumbered page, August 1921.
Plate for Ruth Athey.

5219 "Book-Plates." Charles Dexter Allen. 2:two unnumbered pages, August 1921.
Brief statement about the bookplate made by C. D. Allen.

WALL'S ETCHED QUARTERLY

5220 "Bookplate." (1) 1:Plate 15, January-February-March 1922.
Plate etched for A. C. Hunter showing oil wells.

5221 "Bookplate." (1) 1:Plate 24, April-May-June 1922.
Elizabeth Richards Otis' etched bookplate.

5222 "Bookplate." (1) 1:Plate 3, July-August-September 1922.
Plate for Ethel T. Drought shows mission.

5223 "Bookplate." (1) 1:Plate 12, October-November-December 1922.
Plate for Jessie Voight etched by Bernhardt Wall.

WEEKLY SCOTSMAN

5224 "Armorial Bearings." April 4, 1896.
Not really about bookplates; defines right to arms which, of course, is of interest in relation to armorial bookplates.

WELSH GAZETTE

5225 "[Letter from John Lane about Robbery.]" [Unable to locate.]
Source: *Journal of Ex Libris Society* 17:30, March 1907: "in a recent issue of THE WELSH GAZETTE there was an amusing letter from Mr. John Lane, describing a burglary of his publishing office, at Vigo Street. We

are glad to learn that 'although there is no evidence that this new and discriminating collector has a book-plate—there is abundant evidence that he has a book-mark, for his thumb and fingerprints have been photographed at Scotland Yard.' Bill Sykes, his mark, apparently."

WESTERN ANTIQUARY [See also **BOOK-PLATE COLLECTOR'S MISCELLANY**]

5226 "Book-Plate of Francis Drake." 1:32, May 1881.
Seeks identity of family relationship.

5227 "Book-Plates." 1:174, February 1882.
Advance notice of Hamilton book; author's address given for those wishing to exchange plates with him.

5228 "Heraldic Book-Plates." 2:197, March 1883.
Editor especially interested in plates connected with Devon and Cornwall.

5229 "Armorial Book-Plates." 2:211-2, March 1883.
Notes on three plates contributed by Arthur J. Jewers from *Miscellanea Genealogica et Heraldica*.

5230 "Glynn Family." (1) 4:Frontispiece, 38, July 1884.
Armorial plate for J. H. Oglander Glynn.

5231 "Bookman's Paradise." (2) 9:Supplement 2, June-July 1890.
Catalog of Caxton and bookshop discussed.

5232 "Book-Plate Collector's Miscellany." (4) 9:Supplement 3-5, June-July 1890.
New supplement to *Western Antiquary* described.

5233 "Book-Plate Bibliography." Rev. T. W. Carson. 9:Supplement 4, June-July 1890.
Foreign and American items.

5234 "Rev. Daniel Parson's Paper." James Roberts Brown. 9:Supplement 5-7, June-July 1890.
Introduction by Brown to complete text of Rev. Parson's 1836 paper.

5235 "Sir Joshua Reynolds in London." James Roberts Brown. 9:Supplement 7, June-July 1890.
Correction to article printed from *Book Buyer*.

5236 "Quaint and Humorous Mottoes on Bookplates." Walter Hamilton. 9:Supplement 7-8, June-July 1890.
Among others "Book-Plate's Petition" is quoted.

WESTERN CAMERA NOTES

5237 "Book Plates." Malcolm Chandler. (2) 6:152, June 1903.
Method for making a photographic bookplate briefly described including proportions for "a developer which will give a great deal of contrast."

WESTERN COLLECTOR

5238 "Bookplates and Bookmen in California." Clare Ryan Talbot. (15) 3:12 *et seq.*, January 1965.

Many aspects of early California history reflected in bookplates; Mrs. Talbot authored *Historic California in Bookplates*.

WESTERN WOMAN

5239 "Bookplate Designer." (7) 13, Issue No. 2-3, 84-5, 1948.

Illustrations are work of Donna F. Davis, "distinguished as a book plate designer and also as a painter in water colors and pastel."

WESTMINSTER BUDGET

5240 "In A Library. A Few Words on Book-Plates." (2) 13:9, 23, January 6, 1899.

"In order to stamp them [books] as your very own you should place at the beginning of each one of your books a book-mark, as you put a ring upon the finger of your betrothed."

WILSON LIBRARY BULLETIN

5241 "Book Rhymes Wanted." 12:388, February 1938.

Librarian seeks short rhyme for private bookplate exhorting return of book if borrowed; unable to recall inscription she had seen.

5242 "Bookplate Mottoes Aimed at Forgetful Book Borrowers." 12:475, March 1938.

Responses to request in February for rhymes.

5243 "Book Rhymes." 12:587-8, May 1938.

Among total of thirty-one responses is one sought:

"They borrow books they will not buy
They have no ethics or religions
I wish some kind Burbankian guy
Could cross my books with homing pigeons."

5244 "Bookplates." Eleanor B. Church. (4) 14:562-4, April 1940.

Libraries should use appropriate bookplates; college libraries often use college seal.

5245 "Some Canting Bookplates." Eleanor Bradford Church. (4) 18:310-1, December 1943.

Canting (playing on owner's name) described and illustrated, including: Jacobi Solis Cohen—Cohen denotes blessing in Jewish faith, plate shows hands upraised and spread; A. Church Lane—lane leading to a church; Ball—cat with a yarn ball; Ryder—man on horseback; Frederick Starr—two stars, one for Congo Free State, other signifying his name.

5246 "Australian Bookplates: Some Makers and Owners." R. H. Croll. (7) 23:53-55, September 1948.

Bookplates are "liaison between literature and pictorial art." Interesting facts on artists Norman and Lionel Lindsay, Adrian Feint. One plate illustrated is for Cross by Lionel Lindsay featuring a "swagman, veteran of the tracks with his tired old dog along and 'Matilda' up." Basically same as article in *Book Handbook* [1:381, 1948].

5247 "Month in Review." 42:875, May 1968.

Roger Beacham of Austin, Texas offering *Bookplates for Libraries, Contemporary Designs for Schools, Public, College and University Libraries* at $12.95.

5248 "An Approach to Contemporary Library Bookplates." William R. Holman. (11) 43:unnumbered insert between 348-353, December 1968.

Multicolor illustrations and well printed text plugging work of artist Edward H. Shichell and his book *Bookplates for Libraries.*

WILTSHIRE ARCHAEOLOGICAL AND NATURAL HISTORY MAGAZINE

5249 "The Last Will of Thomas Gore, The Antiquary." Rev. Canon J. E. Jackson. 14:1-12, September 1873.

Mention of several copperplates on which are "engraven my parental coat with my quarterings" some of which were used in identifying his books.

WILTSHIRE NOTES AND QUERIES

5250 "William Leach." (1) 2:482-4, June 1898.

Trade label illustrated which was designed by F. Milton who is mentioned in Fincham's *Artists and Engravers of British and American Bookplates.*

5251 "Some Wiltshire Book-Plates." (3) 2:494-500, September 1898.

Brief biographical notes on Rev. Daniel Parsons and description and family notes on four Wiltshire plates.

WINDMILL

5252 "Gleeson White. An Appreciation." Wilfred Praeger. (1) 1:87-93, April 1899.

"I sought peace everywhere and found it not, save in nooks with books" is the motto "round the fanciful design of the bookplate drawn" for Gleeson White by Alan Wright.

5253 "Book Plate." T. H. Robinson. (1) 2:109, Winter 1900.

Plate for Leonard Wingate Morley by T. H. Robinson measures almost 5" x 8".

WINTERTHUR PORTFOLIO

5254 "Francis Skinner, Bookbinder of Newport. An Eighteenth-century Craftsman Identified by His Tools." William and Carol M. Spawn. (9) 2:47–61, 1965.

Rubbing from binding owned by John Tanner illustrated and noted that it bears his "printed bookplate dated 1749."

WOMAN AT HOME [See also **LADIES' FIELD** and **HOME MAGAZINE**]

5255 "Right Hon. Arthur James Balfour, M.P." (1) 553, March 1902. [No volume number on bound volume at British Museum.]

Illustration of Balfour's bookplate contained within article about Prime Minister.

WOMAN'S HOME COMPANION

5256 "The Book-Plate as a Gift." Elizabeth Hallowell Saunders. (7) 37:33, December 1910.

Samples illustrated include design featuring old-fashioned cross stitch needlework, a joint bookplate given as a wedding gift, and a child's punning plate showing a flower for Violetta.

5257 "They're Block-Printed." Margaret O. Goldsmith. (5) 48:34 *et seq.*, December 1921.

Instructions for cutting the design, ink and paper to use in making block-printed bookplates and greeting cards. Some problems with their causes and remedies are listed.

WOMAN'S MIRROR [See **AUSTRALIAN WOMAN'S MIRROR**]

WOMEN'S CITY CLUB MAGAZINE [San Francisco]

5258 "Book Plates." Louise E. Winterburn. (1) 12:13,21, February 1938.

"The job of collecting [bookplates] is inexplicable to one who has never indulged in this fascinating 'hobby' of bringing nations and peoples into closer proximity through these little treasures of art."

"If you would escape idle days and know the job of living through silent contact with others, start the 'hobby' today of collecting book plates."

"One beholds in book-plate form a world of interesting personages, whose letters, with autographs and foreign stamps, form a collection within a collection."

THE WORLD

5259 "Modern Bookplates." (26) Book-Lover's Supplement IX-XII, October 30, 1906.

"The bookplate is a very charming subject for study, disquisition, and even dispute among those who have leisure and like to include in their hobbies one which is antiquarian and artistic."

WORLD REVIEW

5260 "Tales A Bookplate Tells." Rita S. Halle. (5) 5:38-9, October 3, 1927.
Comments on plates for modern American Presidents and authors. Prizes of five and three dollars offered high school students to design an imaginary bookplate for a prominent man or woman.

5261 "Heraldry of Business Books." Kendall Banning. (1) 5:61, October 10, 1927.
Business bookplate often features trade mark.

5262 "Here Are the Winning Designs." (2) 6:11, February 6, 1928.
First prize to imagined plate for Benito Mussolini; second featured Charles Lindbergh.

X

XTRA

5263 #9
This issue of C. H. Dexter house organ definitely featured bookplates but unable to locate a copy even from Dexter archives.

5264 #14. (22) Scattered throughout pages 1-27, dated between 1914 and 1917.
A wide variety of designs and methods of production for bookplates.

5265 #21. (20) Scattered throughout pages 4-13, about 1917.
Another potpourri of plates, several postage stamp size.

5266 #28. (11) Pages 2, 4, 6, 11, 13.
Widely varied selection of bookplates.

Y

Y DRYCH

5267 "Blackwell Exhibit of Bookplates at Brentano's, New York." March 21, 1895. [Unable to locate.]
Source: W. G. Bowdoin, *Rise of the Book-Plate*, page 40; this was Welsh newspaper published in Utica, New York.

YALE UNIVERSITY LIBRARY GAZETTE

5268 "Medical Library Plate." 6:88, April 1932.
Plate used for library of original books marked "1742 Library."

5269 "Kohut Memorial Collection." (1) 7:91, April 1933.
Bookplate of Alexander Kohut Memorial Collection; exhibition from this collection shown at Yale April 23 to June, 1933.

5270 "Spech Collection." (1) 7:96, April 1933.
Bookplate pictured for William A. Spech Collection of Goetheana.

5271 "Bookplates of the College and Libraries." (9) 8:77-80, October 1933.
Plates illustrated including that of Carl Purington Rollins, printer to the University in early days.

5272 "Robinson Crusoe at Yale." Henry Clinton Hutchins. (1) 11:37, October 1936.
Bookplate for Robinson Crusoe Collection at Yale in Memory of Erminie Bridgman Hutchins. Sketch by Emerson Tuttle.

5273 "Baskerville Collection." (1) 11:41, January 1937.
Bookplate for John Baskerville Collection in memory of Percy Williams Harvey.

5274 "Notes on Recent Acquisitions." 17:24, July 1942.
Henry Roger Winthrop Collection of 2,000 bookplates including works by Eve, French and Sherborn.

5275 "Notes on Recent Acquisitions." 17:40, October 1942.
Henry Rogers Winthrop gave 500 volumes and 80 bookplates including 60 signed proofs of J. Winfred Spenceley.

5276 "Recent Exhibitions." 29:133, January 1955.
Exhibition illustrating types of bookplates held November 2 to December 31, 1954.

5277 "Pearson-Lowenhaupt Collection of English and American Bookplates." Warren H. Lowenhaupt. (2) 30:49-59, October 1955.
Collection numbers about 100,000 and was assembled via purchase and exchange by Dr. J. Sidney Pearson and the author.

5278 "Recent Exhibitions." 30:128, January 1956.
An exhibition of international bookplate incunables from the collection of Pearson-Lowenhaupt was held November 25, 1955 to January 15, 1956.

5279 "Recent Acquisitions." 31:55, July 1956.
An additional 9,000 Anglo-American bookplates from Warren H. Lowenhaupt, Class of 1914.

5280 "Arvid Berghman Bookplates." Warren H. Lowenhaupt. 35:46-7, July 1960.
Collection of 3,800 armorial plates acquired by Yale from Swedish collector.

5281 "Bruce Rogers and His Work." H. M. Marvin. 36:13-23, July 1961.
Mentions briefly Bruce Rogers' own bookplate and one designed by him for Dr. Marvin.

5282 "Earliest French Bookplate." Warren H. Lowenhaupt. (2) 36:138-9, January 1962.
Jacques Thiboust used woodcut stamped on extra leaf when books were bound in 1520.

5283 "Andrews Memorial Bookplate Collection of Irene D. Andrews Pace." 37:178-81, April 1963.

Mrs. Pace had 300 different styles of bookplates for her own use in exchanging so that exchange could be on a fair basis.

5284 "Collection of Estonian Bookplates." Warren H. Lowenhaupt. 40:197-201, April 1966.

Alexander Kaelas' widow relates how her husband saved his bookplate collection in his flight during WW II from Estonia to Finland; the fact most of his plates were hinged made them easy to remove and light to carry.

YEAR BOOK [American Bookplate Society, Kansas City]

5285 "Winward and Hazel Prescott." (1). 1:Frontispiece, 1915.

Center panel by C. W. Sherborn.

5286 "List of Officers." 1:5, 1915.

William F. Hopson, President; Henry Blackwell, Vice President, H. A. Fowler, Secretary-Treasurer.

5287 "Constitution." 1:7-9, 1915.

Principles of organization outlined.

5288 "Joseph C. Egbert, M.D." (1) 1:10, 1915.

Plate by Sidney L. Smith.

5289 "The First Year Book." 1:11-2, 1915.

Membership of 115.

5290 "A Check-List of Bookplates by Sidney L. Smith." (3) 1:13-25, 1915.

Chronological list and alphabetical index of 142 plates plus 5 which he completed that J. Winfred Spenceley had left unfinished.

5291 "List of Members." 1:27-35, 1915.

Alphabetical list.

5292 "William Edgar Fisher." (1) 2:Frontispiece, 1920.

Artist's own plate.

5293 "List of Officers." 2:3, 1920.

William Edgar Fisher, President; Alfred Fowler, Secretary-Treasurer.

5294 "Cameron Mann Plate." (1) 2:6, 1920.

Designed by W. E. Fisher.

5295 "Constitution." 2:7-9, 1920.

Basis for organization outlined.

5296 "A List of Book-Plates by William Edgar Fisher." (3) 2:11-19, 1920.

Several musical plates, Women's Club of Fargo (S.D.), Bowdoin College.

5297 "List of Members." (1) 2:21-34, 1920.

William Howard Taft listed as honorary member residing at Hotel Taft, New Haven, Conn.

YEAR BOOK [American Society of Bookplate Collectors and Designers]

5298 "F. Charles Blank." (1) 1:Frontispiece, 1923.
Artist's own plate.

5299 "Officers." 1:3, 1923.
Rev. Arthur Howard Noll, President; Elisha Brown Bird, Vice President; Carlyle Salomon Baer, Secretary-Treasurer.

5300 "Report of Secretary." Carlyle S. Baer. 1:4-6, 1923.
Society formed in June, 1922 with twenty-six charter members. Collection of 2,000 plates given to Library of Congress.

5301 "Frederick Charles Blank and His Art." John Roth. (2) 1:6-8, 1923.
Artist carved and engraved historical material for Panama-Pacific Exposition.

5302 "Bookplates of Arthur Howard Noll." Albert Chalmers Sneed. (3) 1:9-15, 1923.
Article written by Director of University Press of Sewanee, Tennessee, where nearly all of Dr. Noll's plates were printed, as well as the *Year Book*.

5303 "Bookplates of Elisha Brown Bird." George N. Sargent. (3) 1:16-21, 1923.
His design for Amherst College engraved at Tiffany. Majority of plates reproduced by photogravure.

5304 "Dr. Joseph Crawford Egbert." 1:22-3, 1923.
Dr. Egbert's collection given by widow to Society.

5305 "Library of Congress Collection." 1:24, 1923.
Letter acknowledging Society's gift.

5306 "List of Active Members." 1:25-7, 1923.
Fifty-one active, two honorary, and twenty libraries.

5307 "Officers." 2:3, 1924.
Elisha B. Bird new President.

5308 "Report of Secretary-Treasurer." Carlyle S. Baer. 2:4-6, 1924.
Traveling loan collection in constant use.

5309 "Work of Sara B. Hill." Rachel Mc M. M. Hunt. (3) 2:Frontispiece, 6-14, 1924.
Plate for naturalist William Beebe illustrates scene from his book *Jungle Peace*. Checklist of thirty-nine plates.

5310 "Bookplates of Margaret Ely Webb." Wilbur Macey Stone. (3) 2:15-22, 1924.
Miss Webb's "are designs one would not tire of encountering in volume after volume; and, after all, that is the final test of a bookplate."

5311 "Cynthia Pugh Littlejohn: Her Bookplates." Elizabeth Goelet Rogers Palfrey. (3) 2:23-8, 1924.
Newcomb College graduate conveyed feeling of campus in Robert Baker plate.

5312 "List of Active Members." 2:29-31, 1924.
In addition to individuals many libraries are members.

5313 "American Society of Bookplate Collectors and Designers." (1) 3:Frontispiece, 1925.
Society's plate designed by F. C. Blank.

5314 "Officers." 3:3, 1925.
Elisha B. Bird and Carlyle S. Baer again President and Secretary-Treasurer.

5315 "Report of Secretary-Treasurer." 3:4-5, 1925.
Twelve new members; four members dropped for non-payment of dues.

5316 "Mrs. George A. Preston." Carlyle S. Baer. 3:6, 1925.
In memory of deceased charter member whose personal plate was designed by French with *remarque* by Macdonald and Spenceley.

5317 "Design and Bookplates." Ralph M. Pearson. (3) 3:7-13, 1925.
"Design is the important matter in bookplates, subject is the means instead of the end."

5318 "Early American Bookplates." Florence Seville Berryman. (50) 3:14-26, 1925.
Portraits and bookplates of twenty-five early Americans including signers of the Declaration of Independence and Colonial gentry.

5319 "Charles Joseph Rider as a Designer of Bookplates." Marion Carmichael. (3) 3:27-34, 1925.
Plate for Ernest Dawson in 1925—"[A] pen drawing. Likeness of owner and family in border of verbena. High Sierra scene. Books."

5320 "Bookplates of Frank Slater Daggett." (1) 3:35-6, 1925.
Scientific plate designed by daughter for father who was director of Los Angeles Museum of History, Science and Art.

5321 "Autobiography of Edwin Davis French Extra-Illustrated by Winward Prescott." (1) 4:Frontispiece, 1926.
Shows how a volume may be extra-illustrated.

5322 "Officers." 4:3, 1926.
Bird and Baer still President and Secretary-Treasurer respectively.

5323 "Report of Secretary-Treasurer." Carlyle S. Baer. 4:4-5, 1926.
Fifteen new members.

5324 "Mrs. Edgar C. Leonard." Cornelia Eames Anthony. 4:6-7, 1926.
Designer as well as collector, her collection given by Colonel Leonard to New York State Library.

5325 "Bookplates." Anthony Euwer. (4) 4:8-19, 1926.
Checklist includes sixty-one plates.

5326 "Bookplate Extra-Illustrating." Winward Prescott. 4:20-7, 1926.
Recommends Higgin's "vegetable glue" for mounting additional

plates on sheets of good paper to be bound in volumes on bookplates. Prescott has 70 such books containing 11,642 plates.

5327 "Canting Bookplates." Hetty Gray Baker. (4) 4:29-35, 1926.
College of Heraldry would not refer to a punning or canting plate but "a rebus alluding to the family name of the owner." Occasionally the color of the paper is the keynote—Brown University.

5328 "Ex Libris Art of Edmund Hart New." Gardner Teall. (5) 5:5-17, 1927.
Illustrator of Izaak Walton's *Compleat Angler* designed nearly a hundred bookplates.

5329 "Modern Trend in Some Continental Ex Libris." Winward Prescott. (12) 5: 18-29, 1927.
Current wood-cut artists "depend for their effect on the use of masses of black."

5330 "Year 1927 in Bookplate Publishing." 5:30, 1927.
Again majority are foreign publications.

5331 "William F. Hopson and His Book Plates." George Dudley Seymour. (6) 6: 5-24, 1928.
Designed over 200 bookplates; checklist.

5332 "Mexican Indian Motifs in Bookplates." Frederick Starr. (9) 6:24-34, 1928.
Aztec, Zapotec and Maya designs, together with mottos in hieroglyphics, make dramatic bookplates.

5333 "Sidney Hunt." Maurice Fort. (3) 6:35-41, 1928.
"He regards the bookplate, not as a minor art, but as an art-form as potentially important among the graphic arts as, let us say, the sonnet among the arts of literature."

5334 "Year 1928 in Bookplate Publishing." 6:42, 1928.
Another year dominated by foreign publications.

5335 "Joseph C. Egbert." (1) 7:Frontispiece, 1929.
Plate engraved by Sidney L. Smith.

5336 "Alfred James Downey—Engraver." Exly Brist. (3) 7:5-13, 1929.
Checklist included plates designed and engraved by this artist. (from 1907 to 1929).

5337 "Sidney L. Smith." 7:14-6, 1929.
This designer and engraver of over 200 bookplates didn't begin his "bookplate period" until after he was fifty (b. June 15, 1845, d. Aug. 31, 1929).

5338 "Bookplates of Ainslie Hewett." Edith Emerson Spencer. (5) 7:17-31, 1929.
Checklist includes 114 plates created from 1907 to 1929.

5339 "The Bookplate in Australia, Its Inspiration and Development." P. Neville Barnett. (7) 7:32-45, 1929.
Traces development from first settlement at end of 18th century through formation of Australian Bookplate Society in 1923, many artists mentioned.

5340 "Regarding Bookplates." Ralph Fletcher Seymour, (7) 7:46-57, 1929.
Includes an extensive checklist of plates created from 1902 to 1929.

5341 "Year 1929 in Bookplate Publishing." Winward Prescott. 7:58-60, 1929.
More foreign publications than those in English.

5342 "Adrian Feint's Book-Plates." John Lane Mullins. (6) 8:4-23, 1930.
This Australian artist designed his first bookplate in 1922; now has one-hundred to his credit. Birds in Barbara Rixson plate particularly delicate.

5343 "Motion Picture Bookplates." Hettie Gray Baker. (21) 8:24-41, 1930.
Motto on Hobart Bosworth's plate from *The Tempest:* "My Library was Dukedom large enough." Some may be surprised at how many film notables of this era had bookplates.

5344 "Decorative Quality in Heraldic Bookplates." Winward Prescott. (4) 8:42-6, 1930.
Two Dutch artists use masses of black and white in these heraldic plates.

5345 "Dr. Arthur Howard Noll." (1) 8:46-8, 1930.
In memoriam for Dr. Noll, minister, civic leader, author, lawyer, artist, co-founder of American Society of Bookplate Collectors and Designers, its first president, and only life member.

5346 "The Year 1930 in Bookplate Publishing." Winward Prescott. 8:49-51, 1930.
Again mostly foreign publications.

5347 "Bookplates of Timothy Cole." Oliver S. Tonks. (7) 9:4-17, 1931.
Twenty-three bookplates engraved by Timothy Cole, the first when he was already fifty-two.

5348 "Bookplates of Dorothy Sturgis Harding." C. Howard Walker. (5) 9:18-26, 1931.
"Bookplates should represent, in decorative miniature, the tastes of the owners of the books marked by them. They can inform, as does heraldry, concerning the preferences and mental background of their owners, but all within so small a compass that expression must be terse and trenchant; and restraint is as essential as clearness of intention."

5349 "Fred Thompson, Designer and Bookplate Engraver, 1851-1930." John Hudson Elwell. 9:27-30, 1931.
Checklist spans years 1881 to 1925, only partial as artist did not sign all his plates.

5350 "Clannfhearghuis of Stra-Chur." (1) 9:31, 1931.
Plate for Chief of an ancient Scots Highland clan engraved by Charles J. Lumb.

5351 "William August Brewer." (1) 9:32-3, 1931.
Rev. Brewer, California bookplate collector, died June 23, 1931.

5352 "Winward Prescott." 9:33, 1931.
This well-known bookplate collector dies as result of accident.

5353 "Bookplates of A. N. Macdonald." Thomas E. French. (3) 10:4-14, 1932.
Macdonald engraved title pages, illustrations, head and tail-pieces, and 360 bookplates for which a checklist accompanies this article.

5354 "Lino-Cut Bookplates." George D. Perrottet. (3) 10:15-21, 1932.
Artist gives considerable detail on how to print multi-colored bookplates from linoleum blocks.

5355 "Bookplates of G. D. Perrottet." Camden Morrisby. (1) 10:22-5, 1932.
Artist respects limitations of lino-block and achieves attractive bookplates with "distinct poster-like effect, their colour-registration so exact and clean . . . and their lettering so clean and harmonious. . . ."

5356 "Oscar T. Blackburn, Engraver." H. E. MacDonald. (4) 10:26-35, 1932.
Checklist, from 1910 to 1933, includes sixty-four plates.

5357 "Bookplate Remarques." Winward Prescott. (1) 11:4-15, 1933.
Thorough discussion of remarques from original purpose to current use on bookplates.

5358 "Edith Emerson's Bookplate Designs." Marian Greene Barney. (3) 11:15-22, 1933.
Primarily a painter, Edith Emerson has also created eight bookplates, including one for Otis Skinner.

5359 "On Behalf of Accuracy." Cleora Clark Wheeler. (3) 11:23-31, 1933.
Artist stresses accuracy, especially in the lettering on bookplates; checklist of twenty-nine plates.

5360 "Some Uses of the Imaginative Bookplate." Margaret Ely Webb. (3) 11:32-8, 1933.
"The chief end of a Bookplate is to please one person and to label his book legibly." Checklist of seventy-one plates by Margaret Ely Webb.

5361 "Bookplates of Frederick Charles Blank." Herbert Edwin Lombard. (3) 12: 6-13, 1934.
Author's miniature plate shown; checklist of forty-seven plates.

5362 "A Collector's Criticism of the Bookplates of Sara B. Hill." Carlyle S. Baer. (2) 12:14-20, 1934.
Artist's work consistently exhibits great skill; continuation of checklist of bookplates through #50.

5363 "My Bookplates." Allen Lewis. (4) 12:21-31, 1934.
Allen Lewis describes problems of printing bookplates as well as designing them; checklist of thirty-nine from 1900 to 1935.

5364 "Biographical Sketch of John William Jameson With Descriptive Check-list of His Bookplates." Jerome K. Wilcox. (3) 13:6-14, 1935.
Artist did many unsigned bookplates for commercial stationers as well as ninety-one signed plates.

5365 "Wilbur Macey Stone and His Bookplates." Margaret Ely Webb. (4) 13:15-29, 1935.

Checklist includes fifty-seven bookplates created by Stone, an engineer; also list of books and articles written.

5366 "Bookplate Designs of Dan Burne Jones, B.A.E." Doris E. Hight and John Baima. (6) 13:30-9, 1935.

Strength and simplicity of line are revealed in his bookplates; checklist of thirty.

5367 "An Interesting Letter." 13:40-3, 1935.

Letter to Edwin Davis French by J. Winfred Spenceley enclosing his essay "A Sunday Morning Walk by the River"; a glimpse of the man behind the artist.

5368 "Bookplates of John W. Evans." Cornelia Eames Neltnor Anthony. (4) 14:6-13, 1936.

After deaths of William Watt and Timothy Cole, Evans considered "last of great wood engravers"; at eighty-two made beautiful plate for Frank Dell Anthony and Cornelia Eames Anthony.

5369 "Editorial Note." 14:13, 1936.

Short letter from Timothy Cole (1928) concerning John Evans.

5370 "A Short Talk on Wood-Engraving." John W. Evans. 14:14-20, 1936.

Talk given on anniversary of Evans' 81st birthday. Quotes Timothy Cole: "Engraving on wood is properly considered a *white line* method . . . the white line is nature's way, for the sun in rising lightens up a darkened world."

5371 "Ideas about the Making and Printing of Bookplates." James Guthrie. (5) 14:21-9, 1936.

Guthrie "discovered that an ordinary zinc block could be made to yield beautiful results when printed by hand on good paper." Checklist.

5372 "Leslie Victor Smith and His Bookplates." Edith Stewart Danvers. (3) 14:30-8, 1936.

Better known for his landscapes and portraits, "his bookplates are not merely a label of possession but a little piece of art." Checklist of forty-nine plates.

5373 "Bookplate of the Army Medical Library of Washington." Lt.-Col. Edgar Erskin Hume. (1) 14:39-43, 1936.

Bookplate made from seal long out of use but typical of that earlier period; it was struck off at the Government Printing Office in partial celebration of the Library's centenary.

5374 "Thomas W. Nason as a Maker of Bookplates." Ann Silbaugh. (4) 15:4-9, 1937.

Essentially a maker of fine prints, Nason created twenty-two bookplates; checklist included.

5375 "Checklist of the Year Books of the Society." 15:10 *et seq.*, 1937.

Bibliographical references for years 1923-1936. Most of early *Year Books* out of print and edition exhausted.

5376 "Introduction for a Checklist of the Bookplates of Dorothy Sturgis Harding." Rockwell Kent. (4) 15:11-2, 1937.

Among plates created by Dorothy Harding is that of Eleanor Roosevelt.

5377 "Census of Bookplate Collections." Clara Therese Evans and Carlyle S. Baer. 15:15-60, 1937.

Replies by state from public, college and university libraries indicating how collection was acquired, if available to public, how collection is arranged, and if it is being increased. Toronto, Magdalene College of Cambridge, and Liverpool, as well as United States responded.

5378 "James Webb with Brush and Needle." Clare Ryan Talbot. (16) 16:4-27, 1938.

Webb created bookplate using native yucca in design for author of *Historic California in Bookplates*. Two checklists totaling eighty-five plates.

5379 "A Personal Recollection of Dorothy Furman." Margaret Ely Webb. 16:28-32, 1938.

Happier days remembered with an avid bookplate collector.

5380 "Adrian Feint." Sydney Ure Smith. (8) 16:33-43, 1938.

"Adrian Feint is so experienced in his work that he knows to a nicety how far he can go towards satisfying his client, without overloading his design." Checklist covers bookplates 101 to 192.

5381 "Bookplates of Pierre Clement De Laussat." Charles Midlo. (2) 16:44-7, 1938.

Fate of nobleman during French Revolution traced through bookplate.

5382 "An Austral Engraver, Gayfield Shaw and His Bookplates." Robert H. Croll. (2) 17:4-8, 1939.

A printer, Shaw did not handle an engraving tool until past middle-age.

5383 "Bookplate Work of Gayfield Shaw." F. Charles Blank. (2) 17:9-14, 1939.

Correspondence between bookplate artists develops into friendship; checklist of fifty-plates.

5384 "William W. Alexander, A Canadian Engraver." Sidney H. Howard. (3) 17:15-22, 1939.

Painter as well as engraver, Alexander executed forty-one plates.

5385 "Japanese Bookplates." Winward Prescott. (4) 17:23-35, 1939.

Prescott relied heavily on prior Starr article. Quotes one bookplate owner concerning exchange: "What, give away my bookplate! I wouldn't think of it; why, it's like my toothbrush."

5386 "A Little Known American Bookplate." Carlyle S. Baer. (2) 17:36-7, 1939.

Prints from woodblock and electrotype of same plate for J. P. C. Winship (1832-1910).

5387 "Carl Stephen Junge, Ninety-two Ex Libris and Other Fancies." Leroy Truman Goble. (7) 18:4-17, 1940/1941. (Published 1942)

Biographical sketch of versatile artist by longtime friend; alphabetical checklist.

5388 "Bookplates of Nathaniel Hurd (1730-1777)." Hollis French. (1) 18:20-62, 1940/1941.

In 1894 Allen listed twenty-eight plates signed by Hurd; forty have now been identified as signed by Hurd; detailed descriptions of the plates in alphabetical order.

5389 "Edith Cleaves Barry." Carlyle S. Baer. (4) 18:62-69, 1940/1941.

Chronological checklist of twenty-nine bookplates.

5390 "Alexander Scott Carter, R.C.A., M.R.A.I.C. An Appreciation." Leslie Victor Smith. (3) 19:6-12, 1942. (Published 1943)

Architect, illuminator, bookplate artist.

5391 "Etched Bookplates of Ella Dwyer." George Perrottet. (3) 19:13-20, 1942.

Australian artist uses etching, "the only medium suitable for the delicacy and charming imagination shown in most of Miss Dwyer's work." Chronological checklist of thirty-five plates.

5392 "George D. Perrottet, Designer and Craftsman." Albert Collins. (3) 19:21-8, 1942.

Checklist (44-162) updates the list from the 1932 *Year Book*.

5393 "Continuation of the Check-list of the Bookplates of Allen Lewis." 19:29, 1942.

Chronological checklist (40-58) updates the list in the *Year Book* for 1934.

5394 "Continuation of the Check-List of the Book-Plates of John W. Evans." (2) 19:30-1, 1942.

Checklist continues from *Year Book* for 1936.

5395 "W. H. W. Bicknell and His Bookplates." Carlyle S. Baer. (5) 20:6-11, 1943/1944. (Published 1947)

Artist's self-appraisal: "The portrait plates are the best I think." Chronological checklist.

5396 "Ruth Thomson Saunders, Bookplate Designer." Irene Dwen Andrews. (8) 20:12-9, 1943/1944.

Artist, designer, and publisher of four books about bookplates; chronological checklist of 103 plates.

5397 "Contemporary Ex Libris." Peter Fingesten. (5) 20:20-31, 1943/1944.

Michel Fingesten created more than 2,000 plates; he died in an internment camp near Cosenza, Italy.

5398 "Allen No. 737 (?)" Carlyle S. Baer. 20:32-6, 1943/1944.

Originally identified by Allen as for Beverly Robinson, who was involved in the Arnold treason plot.

5399 "Continuation of the Check-List of Arthur N. Macdonald." Thomas E. French. 20:37-8, 1943/1944.

Year Book for 1932 had chronological list from 1896 to 1932; current list updates to 1940.

5400 "William Edgar Fisher." Wilma Hall Fowler. (3) 21:6-23, 1945/1946. (Published 1948)

Mrs. Alfred Fowler gives warm personal picture of versatile artist; chronological checklist of 199 bookplates.

5401 "Woodcut Bookplate." Norman Kent. (8) 21:24-32, 1945/1946.

"The truth of the matter is that the tribulations of a bookplate artist are akin to those of a portrait painter." Chronological (but undated) list of twenty-five bookplates.

5402 "Bookplates of Philadelphia Physicians." Samuel X. Radbill, M.D. 21:33-55, 1945/1946.

Autobiographical letter and detailed checklist "from the days of the city's first founding to the present time" which is to be continued.

5403 "Designer Jaroslav Vodrazka About Himself." (3) 22:4-15, 1947/1948. (Published 1950)

"Often I think only an unexpected occurrence will break my 'bookplate possession' and keep collectors from asking for further dozens of graphic bookplate improvisations." Chronological checklist from 1921 through 1948, several hundred bookplates.

5404 "Continuation of the Check-list of the Bookplates of Oscar Taylor Blackburn." (1) 22:16-7, 1947/1948.

Year Book for 1932 had items 1-64; current list 65-98.

5405 "Check-List of Bookplates of Philadelphia Physicians." Samuel X. Radbill, M.D. (3) 22:18-39, 1947/1948.

Interesting details about each doctor and his plate.

5406 "Bookplates of Harry Marvin French." Mary Alice Ercolini. (4) 23:4-14, 1949/1950. (Published 1951)

For many years French engraved bookplates for Shreve & Company, the "Tiffany of the West"; artist called bookplates his "dream work." A partial alphabetical checklist.

5407 "Thomas Sparrow, Early Maryland Engraver and Patriot." Carlyle S. Baer. (7) 23:15-21, 1949/1950.

Much diligent digging to add to sparse facts known about Sparrow, who was wood engraver of bookplates and early Maryland paper money.

5408 "P. Neville Barnett, A Super Bookman." Alan P. Rigby. (3) 23:22-7, 1949/1950.

Details concerning forthcoming *Australian Book-Plates*

5409 "Loring Gary Calkins." Sarah Briggs Latimore. (2) 23:28-31, 1949/1950.

"As an etcher, his work shows great versatility."

5410 "My Bookplates." Loring Gary Calkins. (3) 23:32-8, 1949/1950.

"It [bookplate] must thrill him to see it in his books, or else the artist has failed." Chronological checklist of fourteen.

5411 "Bookplates of Herbert Francis Wauthier." Phyllis King. (6) 24:4-14, 1951. (Published 1953)

A heraldic engraver, Wauthier was an editor of the "English Bookplate Magazine, in association with the late Sidney Hunt."

5412 "Check-List of the Bookplates of Herbert Francis Wauthier." (1) 24:15-7, 1951.

List separated into those of heraldic (copper engraved) style and wood engravings.

5413 "Ernest Haskell." Elmer Johnson Porter. (2) 24:18-24, 1951.

Well-known American graphic artist also did eleven bookplates detailed in checklist.

5414 "Notes on the Bookplates of Amos Doolittle." Francis W. Allen. 24:25-32, 1951.

Reprint of article from *Old-Time New England*, October 1948.

5415 "Dorothy Sturgis Harding—An Appreciation." Joseph W. P. Frost. (4) 25:6-13, 1952/53. (Published 1955)

Continuation of checklist brings total plates designed by this artist to 106. Artist makes interesting use of massive black areas to accentuate fine white line.

5416 "Marco Birnholz—Ex Librist." Philip Goodman. (11) 25:14-25, 1952/53.

A Vienna pharmacist, Marco Birnholz had numerous personal plates, many with Jewish or pharmaceutical themes.

5417 "Checklist of Bookplates by Sara Eugenia Blake." Samuel X. Radbill. (3) 25: 26-37, 1952/53.

Chronological (1941-1955) list of eighty-three plates. "Although she was a copyist in most of her work there is a definite individuality about every one of her bookplates."

5418 "A Descriptive Checklist of the Bookplates of Elisha Brown Bird." Carlyle S. Baer. (7) 26:4-41, 1954/1955 (Published 1956)

Bird, a member of the *New York Times* art department for eighteen years, was president of the American Society of Bookplate Collectors and Designers; the descriptive checklist includes 212 plates in chronological order and is accompanied by an alphabetical index.

5419 "Bookplates of Louis Agassiz Fuertes." Mary Fuertes Boynton. (1) 27:4-11, 1956. (Published 1958)

Chronological descriptive checklist includes twelve plates by this ornithological illustrator.

5420 "My Bookplates." Jeannette Campbell Shirk. (3) 27:12-20, 1956.

Miss Shirk, librarian-artist, relates details of bookplate commissions; one bookplate was used as Christmas card; checklist of some twenty-odd plates.

5421 "Joseph Grinnell, 1877-1939." George S. Swarth. (1) 27:21-4, 1956.

Dr. Grinnel's lifetime interest in natural history of California is shown in his bookplate designed by noted zoologist, Walter Kenrick Fisher.

5422 "Eunice Barnard Haden." (3) 27:26-9, 1956.
Checklist of ten bookplates by this Washington, D.C. artist.

5423 "The Urge for Another Bookplate." Carlyle S. Baer. (2) 27:30-3, 1956.
Bookplate for books on standardbred horse using Alexander Pope painting of Major Delmar, champion trotter, as half-tone printed in color in frame by Carl S. Junge.

5424 "Rudolph Stanley-Brown 1889-1944, Architect—Designer—Etcher." Katherine Oliver Stanley-Brown. (6) 28:4-15, 1957. (Published 1958)
Designer of twenty-five public buildings, five bookplates, and fifty etchings and dry points.

5425 "*Guide to the Study of Book-Plates*, Hon. J. Leicester Warren, M.W." 28: 17-25, 1957.
Reprint of the first few pages of Warren's 1880 book, the first dealing with bookplates in English.

5426 "Description of Bookplate." Violet Oakley. (1) 28:26-8, 1957.
Pictured and described is plate of Cosmopolitan Club, Philadelphia.

5427 "Lincolniana Bookplates." Louis J. Bailey. (3) 29:4-9, 1958. (Published 1960)
Includes checklist of over fifty plates using Lincoln in the illustration, referring to him or those of known Lincoln collectors. Author's plate incorporates four cent Lincoln postage stamp.

5428 "Bookplates of Henry Emerson Tuttle." Gilbert McCoy Troxell. (3) 29:10-8, 1958.
Chronological checklist of thirty plates falls into two sections—1908 to 1919 and 1930 to 1945.

5429 "Bookplate Art of Efraim M. Lilien." Louis Ginsberg. (3) 29:19-26, 1958.
List of forty-nine plates of this artist who is called the Jewish Beardsley.

5430 "Values of Certain Early American Bookplates." Carlyle S. Baer. (42) 30:5-77, 1959/1960. (Published 1962)
Twenty-seven different sources of auction prices between 1896 and 1927 listed, and an alphabetical checklist of bookplates with full description, auction source and price, and whether or not listed in Allen's *American Book-Plates*.

5431 "Bookplates of David Garrick." Carlyle S. Baer. (1) 31:6-9, 1961/1962. (Published 1964)
Discusses question of two copperplates, each engraved by John Wood and so signed on the plate, but with other differences including a dot or period which is on the original or lost copper but not on the engraved one.

5432 "Notes on Doctor Frederick Starr." Robert Hitchman. (4) 31:10-19, 1961/1962.
Professor of anthropology specializing in studies of Mexico, central Africa, and Japan, his bookplates reflected these interests.

5433 "Recent Bookplates of Carl S. Junge." Carlyle S. Baer. (4) 31:20-7, 1961/1962.

Alphabetical checklist of thirty-six additional plates. Artist an innovator in the use of color in bookplates.

5434 "Leo Wyatt and His Bookplates." Leo Wyatt. (3) 31:28-38, 1961/1962.
Autobiographical sketch by this British engraver who spent some time in South Africa. Artist gives personal descriptions of a dozen plates he engraved while in South Africa.

5435 "List of Lincolniana Bookplates." Louis J. Bailey. 31:39-41, 1961/1962.
Additions to list appearing in 1958 *Year Book*.

5436 "Little Known Ornithological Bookplates." (1) 32:4-6, 1963/1964. (Published 1966)
Plate for G. Frean Morcom (born in Wales in 1845) designed by Frieda Lueddemann who did scientific line drawings.

5437 "Mrs. Roy A. Hunt (Rachel McMasters Miller Hunt) 1881-1963." (1) 32:7-11, 1963/1964.
Mrs. Hunt was one of two last surviving founders of ASBC&D, editor of Society's *Year Book* for 1924, and her greatest contributions are in the fields of botany and horticulture.

5438 "Final Check-List of the Bookplates of Adrian Feint." Thelma Clune. (1) 32:12-9, 1963/1964.
Chronological list from 1922 to 1944 of 221 plates giving the name of owner and method of reproduction.

5439 "A Few Examples of Ecclesiastic Bookplates." Rev. Canon Enrico S. Molnar. (10) 33:4-15, 1965/1966. (Published 1969)
Two types of "religious" bookplates—those with religious motifs and those used by clergymen, church institutions and dignitaries. Checklist of forty-one plates designed by Rev. Molnar, of Bloy House Theological School in Pasadena, between 1942 and 1968.

5440 "Master of a Thousand Opuses. Istvan Drahos, 1895/1968." Dr. Nicholas G. Lippoczy. (4) 33:16-27, 1965/1966.
Hungarian artist created over 470 bookplates, mostly woodcuts, from 1937 to 1942 and 1948 to 1968. His comment on the period 1943 to 1947: "War, no tools, no wood, no work."

YELLOW BOOK

5441 "Book Plate for Major-General Gosset by R. Anning Bell." (1) 1:251, April 1894.
No text, illustrations only.

5442 "Book Plate for J. L. Propert, Esq. by A. Beardsley." (1) 1:251, April 1894.
No text, illustration only.

5443 "Bookplate for Georgie Evelyn Cave by A. J. Gaskin." (1) 9:185, April 1896.
No text, illustration only.

5444 "Book Plate for Isobel Verney Cave by Mrs. A. J. Gaskin." (1) 9:235, April 1896.
No text, illustration only.

5445 "Book Plates for Egerton Clairemonte, H. B. Marriott, Watson and S. Carey Curtis." Patten Wilson. (3) 13:199, 201, 203, April 1897.
No text, illustrations only.

INDEX BY SUBJECT AND ARTIST

Note: No entry numbers have been assigned to articles appearing in foreign journals or to certain other articles of doubtful existence. These articles will be referenced in the Index by Subject and Artist and in the Index by Author (p. 463) by the name of the periodical in which they appeared.

INDEX BY AUTHOR

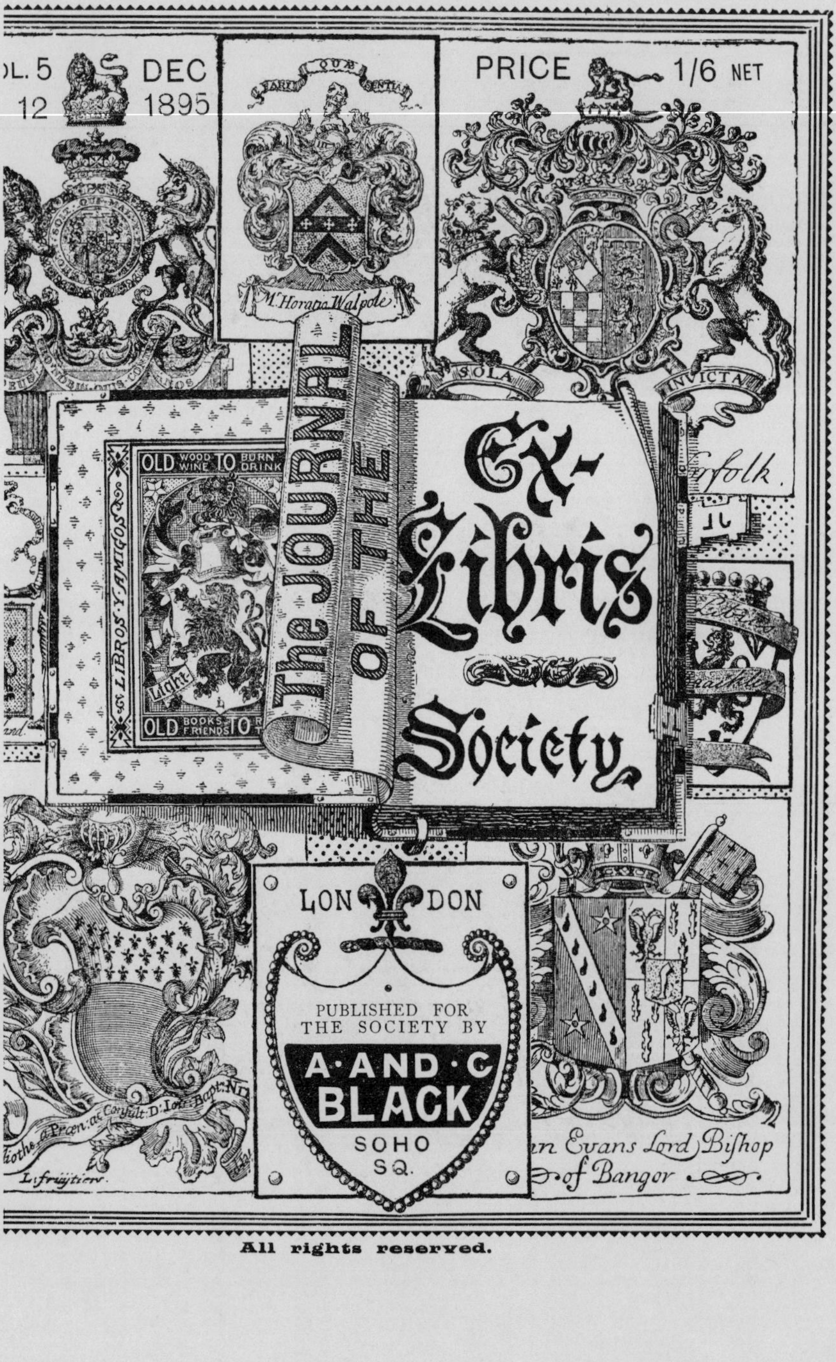
OL. 5 DEC
12 1895
PRICE 1/6 NET
Mr. Horatio Walpole
SOLA INVICTA
The JOURNAL OF THE
EX-Libris Society
OLD WOOD TO BURN
OLD WINE TO DRINK
LIBROS Y AMIGOS
OLD BOOKS TO READ
OLD FRIENDS TO TRUST
LONDON
PUBLISHED FOR THE SOCIETY BY
A·AND·C BLACK
SOHO SQ.
of Bangor